Unconventional Lawmaking in the Law of the Sea

Unconventional Lawmaking in the Law of the Sea

Edited by

NATALIE KLEIN

UNSW Sydney

OXFORD
UNIVERSITY PRESS

OXFORD
UNIVERSITY PRESS

Great Clarendon Street, Oxford, OX2 6DP,
United Kingdom

Oxford University Press is a department of the University of Oxford.
It furthers the University's objective of excellence in research, scholarship,
and education by publishing worldwide. Oxford is a registered trade mark of
Oxford University Press in the UK and in certain other countries

First Edition published in 2022

Impression: 1

Published in the United States of America by Oxford University Press
198 Madison Avenue, New York, NY 10016, United States of America

British Library Cataloguing in Publication Data

Data available

Library of Congress Control Number: 2021951892

ISBN 978–0–19–289782–4

DOI: 10.1093/oso/9780192897824.001.0001

Printed and bound by
CPI Group (UK) Ltd, Croydon, CR0 4YY

Foreword

I

One of the predominant features of contemporary societies is their flexibility to incorporate remarkable changes in people's lives. The international community is no exception.

This book, *Unconventional Lawmaking in the Law of the Sea,* edited by Natalie Klein,[1] is about how the international community is evolving as a result of change, and responding to its challenges and complexities by developing international rules and standards of behaviour that take account of the effects of change.

Although states are the main actors within the international system, different actors other than states operating in the international scene are also contributing to the development of international law.

Technology also plays a significant role in bringing about important changes in the manner in which human activities are conducted in the international field, which may require the adoption of regulations due to the impact of new technologies on the environment.

However, states seem to be a step behind in the process of adapting formal international law to certain new situations that must be acknowledged in order to ensure governance in international society.

Hence, a variety of new forms of 'unconventional' lawmaking are actually posing a real test to traditional legal thinking attached to well-established concepts arising from the sources of international law formally recognized in Article 38 of the Statute of the International Court of Justice.

The possibility of considering 'informal' or 'unconventional' lawmaking as an independent source in the realm of traditional jurisprudence has yet to be seen, even though an important segment of international regulations appears to be considered by many scholars as a tool for the development of international law. Many of those regulations are being classified; some regulations are defined as 'soft law', while other 'informal' rules are considered, if not 'binding' in a formal legal sense, to be effective regulations that transcend the notion of 'soft law'.

Different diagnoses attached to traditional legal thinking in international law have not, so far, been able to convey a suitable theory of how the international legal system actually functions, in order to encompass all the complexities and changes and issues that are transforming the current international scene, and the legal system thereof. Conventional legal thinking, in general terms, tends to be conservative.

The 'formal' ways and means to adapt international law to changes in the international field are solely operated by states. A variety of mechanisms exist, but most important are the rules concerning the interpretation, and the amendments and modification of treaties, as

[1] The editor of this book, Natalie Klein, is well-known as a scholar and author in topics related to the law of the sea, with a trajectory of more than twenty years of unyielding and valuable research.

defined in the Vienna Convention on the Law of Treaties (VCLT), in Articles 31 to 33 and Articles 39 to 41.

Subsequent practice, a process informal in character, is specifically mentioned in the VCLT as relevant for the interpretation of treaties. It is interesting to highlight subsequent practice as a factor for adaptation, since it has been considered a useful tool for interpreting the meaning of international legal instruments. Given its informal character, it is considered to be efficient in facilitating the process of adaptation of treaties.[2]

The common understanding is that subsequent practice is a concept applicable only to state parties, and most rightly so, since states are the actors intervening in the making of formal international law. However, given the fact that informal lawmaking in the international sphere is taking place, one may well wonder if a subsequent practice by actors other than states is indirectly influencing the process of adaptation to change through the adoption of rules, regulations, memoranda of understanding, codes of conduct or standards.

II

The United Nations Convention on the Law of the Sea (LOSC) is an example of the way in which substantial changes have been introduced in the international legal order concerning governance in the seas and oceans, through the adoption of a treaty negotiated in an international conference: the Third United Nations Conference on the Law of the Sea. This is truly conventional lawmaking.

Yet, the main purpose of this book, as its title readily conveys, is to clearly expose the appearance of an important segment of international regulations, the origins of which do not respond to the traditional sources recognized by 'formal' international law, and to beg the questions for which the science of jurisprudence should find answers. As Natalie Klein, the editor of this book, explains in Part I (Introduction), the purpose of the book is to understand this international practice 'within the law of the sea'.

The topic of this book—to determine what informal law is and what it is not—is an important, interesting, and thought-provoking journey into the realm of legal science, as are the profound and thorough analyses, following the introduction, of different examples of how 'unconventional' or 'informal' lawmaking have influenced the law of the sea in different ways.

[2] For example, Irina Buga states that, 'the informal character of subsequent practice can facilitate treaty adaptation even if uncertainty remains as to certain aspects of the process. Subsequent practice is relevant to the LOSC in a number of ways: First, it serves as a tool for treaty interpretation, pursuant to Article 31 of the Vienna Convention on the Law of Treaties (VCLT). Second, and crucially, it can constitute the parties agreement to modify the treaty. This may be the case where subsequent practice diverges from the text to such an extent that it can no longer be said to constitute an act of interpretation, but rather becomes, in effect, an act of modification ... This process of tacit modification by subsequent practice is not incompatible with the rigid mechanisms for formal amendment in the LOSC. Third, subsequent practice can potentially generate new (regional or universal) customary norms that may, as *lex posterior*, impact LOSC obligations. Through its various legal effects, subsequent practice can also serve as a vehicle to regime interaction, adapting the Convention in line with the developments in other fields as environmental law.': Irina Buga, 'Between Stability and Change in the Law of the Sea—Subsequent practice, Treaty Modification, and Regime Interaction' in DR Rothwell and others (eds), *The Oxford Handbook of the Law of the Sea* (OUP 2015) 46, 47–48.

At the outset, an overriding consideration is made with respect to the nature of the LOSC as an international legal system firmly based in a 'treaty',[3] meaning that it is a binding instrument governed by international law. Failure to comply with obligations established in its provisions raises issues concerning state responsibility.

The Convention is considered by some authors as the 'constitution of the oceans'[4]—a treaty entered into by the unusual number of 168 parties, including the European Union—making it one of the most reputable formal agreements in the field of international law (very close to being considered universal), and one of the most important instruments since the adoption of the United Nations Charter.

Having defined the legal nature of the Convention as formal law, the introductory chapter of the book turns to consider an array of international instruments under the heading of 'agreements that are not treaties', noting that 'disagreements may arise as to whether an agreement is formal law or not'. In both cases, variations exist 'with respect to names, form and substance'. However, a common element is highlighted in relation to the term 'agreement', whether formal or informal, since it 'still captures the manifestation of consent to cooperate in a designated way in relation to a particular area'.

The studies that follow the introduction clearly show that informal lawmaking has an important role in the establishment of regulatory instruments and provisions concerning many different aspects of the law of the sea. The quest of the authors of this book is to determine its proper significance. These studies seek to give an answer to the question of why informal lawmaking matters.

That the importance of informal international law is gradually increasing is clearly evident in relation to many different aspects of the law of the sea.

As mentioned in the introduction, many examples may be found, one of which—the Food and Agriculture Organization's regulations to prevent, deter, and eliminate illegal, unreported and unregulated (IUU) fishing (the International Plan of Action on IUU fishing and the Model Scheme on Port State Measures to Combat IUU Fishing)—is esteemed as a significant contribution in defining the expectations of the international community concerning the behaviour of fishing vessels and of flag states in this field of international law.[5]

Another of the examples mentioned is the contribution of the International Maritime Organization (IMO), which, in addition to the international conventions celebrated under its auspices, has provided multiple instruments in the form of circulars, guidelines, and recommendations.

Why are the developments introduced by informal lawmaking significant?

[3] The use of the term 'treaties' in the Introduction is a general way to refer to those international legal instruments included in the concept of 'formal law'.

[4] See, eg Agustín Blanco Bazán, 'Jurisdicción penal y Derecho del Mar. Aspectos jurisdiccionales en la prevención y el castigo de actos criminales en la Convención de las Naciones Unidas sobre el Derecho del Mar y el Convenio para la represión de Actos ilícitos contra la seguridad de la navegación marítima' in Leopoldo MA Godio (ed), *El Sistema de Solución de Controversias de la Convención de Naciones Unidas sobre el Derecho del Mar* (EUDEBA 2019) 581–85.

[5] The International Tribunal for the Law of the Sea, in its advisory opinion on the request submitted by the Sub-Regional Fisheries Commission (SRFC), has noted that, although the definition of IUU fishing contained in paragraph 3 of the IPOA-IUU is voluntary, this definition was subsequently incorporated and reaffirmed in Article 1(e) of the Port State Measures Agreement, and also included in the decisions of some regional fisheries management organizations (RFMOs), the national legislation of a number of states, and the law of the European Union. *Request for Advisory Opinion Submitted by the Sub-Regional Fisheries Commission* (Advisory Opinion) ITLOS Reports 2015, 4, para 92.

Several reasons are suggested:

- The interaction of informal lawmaking with formal international law, and its possible relevance for the interpretation and application of the provisions of the LOSC.
- In the understanding that the Convention is, in some respects, a framework agreement needing further elaboration 'outside the treaty',[6] as is the case with Part XII, in which references to 'generally agreed international rules and standards' are made, meaning that informal lawmaking is further considered relevant for the interpretation and application of the Convention.
- The role of informal lawmaking 'in creating and sharing expectations around state conduct at sea'. As an example, informal agreements may be used to 'benchmark' the content of the 'diligence' required in cases where states can be held responsible for failing to exercise 'due diligence'.
- Given the current challenges affecting the adequate governance of the seas and oceans, informal lawmaking may provide the means for better cooperation among states and other stakeholders.

Since the content of the book refers to a host of different examples of informal international instruments and provisions, the introduction refers to and describes the elements that provide the context in which informality appears to be relevant in lawmaking.

The elements mentioned are: (1) the process of informal lawmaking; (2) the actors intervening in informal lawmaking; and (3) the outcome of the process.

The Process of Informal Lawmaking

Informal international lawmaking, as depicted in the introduction, refers to 'a process of international cooperation to reach agreements other than treaties between public authorities'. In other words, the 'process' refers to the mechanics, substance, and form of the agreements denoted, when reference is made to informal lawmaking.

The participation of private actors or international organizations in this context is not essential, even though 'informal lawmaking as a process allows for relevant non-state actors to assemble and share expertise and information, learn more about an issue, and bargain on what standards of behaviour are acceptable' for addressing a particular issue.

The kind of cooperation involved in the process of international informal lawmaking 'typically entails "norm-setting or public policy-making by public authorities" and on this basis warrants the description of "lawmaking"'. As explained by the author of the introduction, we are dealing here with the kind of agreements the adoption and implementation of which would affect the incentives and behaviour of states.

Different reasons are acknowledged as an encouragement for adopting informal lawmaking, but they are basically summarized in Lipson's description of 'informality', quoted in the introduction, as 'a device for minimizing the impediments to cooperation, at both the international and the domestic levels'.[7] However, as noted by Klein in her

[6] Part XII is an example of needing further elaboration 'outside the treaty', in which direct or implied references are made in sections 2, 4, and 5 to 'generally agreed international rules and standards'.

[7] Charles Lipson, 'Why are some International Agreements Informal?' (1991) 45(5) Intl'l Org 495, 500.

introduction, informal lawmaking is increasing due to several factors, including a reluctance, observed by some scholars, on the part of states to amend the LOSC, as well as a shared feeling of 'treaty stagnation' or 'treaty saturation'. Another factor noted is the appearance, on the international scene, of non-state actors who are increasingly influencing the adoption of more 'inclusive and transparent' informal agreements to properly take into account their needs.

Klein also, correctly, mentions the influence of the current multipolar political dynamics, which have motivated a disinclination, on the part of some states, to commit to global cooperation: a situation that diminishes the probability of achieving binding agreements.

Participants in Informal Lawmaking

Informal agreements—in contrast to formal treaties, which can only be adopted with the consent of the authorities empowered by the constitution of the contracting states, or by their duly appointed representatives—may be adopted by different government officials or agencies, whatever the denomination of the instrument (memorandums of understanding, circulars, 'gentlemen's agreements', codes of conduct, etc.).

The importance of the informal agreement rests in the cooperation constituting its object and purpose, which may be strengthened by specifying the behaviour expected from the contracting parties, thereby enhancing their understanding of the object, scope, and extent of their cooperation.[8]

Also important is the possibility that non-state actors may also be engaged in the development of legal informal instruments establishing cooperative new measures and information sharing. While states remain necessary entities from the point of view of legitimation and control, the engagement of different actors and stakeholders—such as shipping companies, seafaring unions, scientific bodies, and conservation groups—may be necessary for varied reasons, but authors that refer to non-state actors in the context of informal lawmaking mention the need to resort to multiple sources of complex knowledge and networking experience 'beyond what States can shoulder'[9].

In Klein's opinion, a core advantage of these informal agreements is the engagement with non-state actors 'who can positively contribute to information and understandings on which states rely in developing their views on how to deal with a shared matter of concern', since broad participation by stakeholders 'enhances good governance through improved transparency, facilitating information-sharing, distributing responsibilities and accountabilities, and enhancing cooperation'.

[8] Klein gives several examples of informal agreements adopted by state authorities not empowered to enter into formal agreements, who have signed instruments to enhance cooperation in different areas of mutual concern: for example, the two legally non-binding memoranda of understanding signed by the United States Defense Department and the Chinese Ministry of National Defense, 'to follow in the event of air or maritime encounters, as well as establishing a notification mechanism'. She also mentions the 'arrangement' of the Australian Border Force with the Indonesian Maritime Security Agency 'to improve cooperation in addressing shared maritime security concerns'.

[9] Klein quotes Joost Pauwelyn Ramses A. Wessel and Jan Wouters, 'When Structures become Shackles: Stagnation and Dynamics in International Lawmaking' (2014) 25(3) European JIL 733, 742 (citations omitted): 'This diverse network society has given rise to new actors and new forms or processes of cooperation, other than those traditionally recognized by international law. The State remains a pivotal entity of interest aggregation, legitimation and control. Yet, it is supplemented, assisted, corrected, and continuously challenged by a variety of other actors ... Problem solving in a complex knowledge/network society will require action beyond what States can shoulder. It needs pragmatic deliberation involving multiple sources of knowledge, experience and control.'

Outputs of Informal Lawmaking and their Normative Value

The third element conveying significance to legal instruments adopted by informal lawmaking is the output, or end result, of the normative process. Informal agreements may be very diverse in content and form, but experts have observed that they are used more frequently in some areas than others, including in international economic law or environmental law, as well as throughout the law of the sea.

As described by Klein, the differing types of informal agreements will depend on the goals the parties wish to achieve. These goals may be aspirational, functional and tailored for responding to a specific international concern, or aimed at establishing standards of conduct.

This author further refers to different shades of normative significance of the process of informal lawmaking, establishing a distinction between 'normative intent' and 'normative effect'.

Normative intent, in Klein's words, 'could simply be understood as a question of whether the actors developing standards or modes of conduct intend for them to be legally binding or not'.

Normative effect reflects on the actual result the agreement produced, derived from the process of informal lawmaking, assessing whether behaviour has altered to align with what was agreed, has had some kind of impact on state conduct, or has resulted in no behavioural change at all.

In the assessment of the impact on behaviour, there is a temporal element, since the normative intent refers to the initial purpose of the agreement, while the normative effect considers what the result of the process was.

A further consideration is made by Klein to clarify the distinction between the two aspects of the normative significance of the output. An agreement may be made with no normative intent, since the intervening actors did not intend to create formally binding law, but it may end up producing a normative effect, whether by conforming to the basis of a treaty, by contributing to the development of customary international law, or by informing domestic law. Another possible situation may arise when a normative intent exists between actors in a given process but ultimately no normative effect is achieved.

The author notes that a classical distinction is made between formal and informal law. Formal law is typically binding, and entails state responsibility, whereas informal law does not. However, Klein argues that 'this dichotomy is not as inexorable as [it] may first appear'. Legal principles such as 'estoppel' and 'acquiescence' appear to be functional in explaining why, in certain cases, there is no clear dividing line between formal and informal law.

In addition, the connections between informal agreements and the LOSC may have consequences for state responsibility. These implications derive from the 'due diligence' requirements in the Convention, as observed in both advisory opinions given by the International Tribunal for the Law of the Sea: one by the Tribunal as a whole,[10] and the other by its Seabed Disputes Chamber.[11]

[10] *Request for Advisory Opinion Submitted by the Sub-Regional Fisheries Commission* (Advisory Opinion) ITLOS Reports 2015, 4, para 129 (citing Seabed Advisory Opinion).

[11] *Responsibilities and Obligations of States with Respect to Activities in the Area* (Advisory Opinion) ITLOS Reports 2011, 10, para 242.

The significance of informal lawmaking in the law of the sea can be best ascertained when considering the interrelationship of a new agreement with the LOSC.

As provided for in Article 311, paragraph 3 of the Convention, state parties may agree to modify or suspend the operation of a provision solely between themselves under certain conditions, namely that such agreements do not relate to a provision, derogation from which is incompatible with the effective execution of the object and purpose of the Convention; provided, further, that such agreements shall not affect the application of the basic principles embodied in the Convention; and that such agreements do not affect the enjoyment by other state parties of their rights, or the fulfilment of their obligations under the Convention.

In other words, as Klein points out, 'treaties that are "expressly permitted or preserved by other articles" in the LOSC are permissible and intended to ensure the integrity of the Convention and underline its constitutional importance'. In contrast, 'informal agreements would not be captured by Article 311 of the LOSC'.

However, informal agreements may have several potential consequences for the LOSC. As suggested by Klein, they may be relevant as guidance for the interpretation or application of the provisions of the Convention, or may reflect evidence of obligations prescribed in the Convention. They may also reflect, or be considered as evidence of, the 'subsequent practice' mentioned in the VCLT, relevant for the interpretation of the LOSC.

Article 293 of the Convention allows international courts or tribunals within the dispute settlement system of the LOSC to apply 'other rules of international law not incompatible with [the] Convention'. The author of the introduction here puts a question mark regarding whether or not informal agreements are included in the aforementioned provision of the Convention. One possibility is that informal agreements might not be a considered as applicable law, precisely because they are not formally binding, but the question remains inconclusive, since 'the issue has not been addressed in a case to date'.[12]

III

This book is a very significant contribution to international law and, in particular, to the law of the sea, for several reasons. First, it raises questions of fundamental importance in order to understand how international law is developing in an atmosphere of constant change, creating different challenges and issues that impact on the international community, and still awaits a proper answer from the point of view of contemporary jurisprudence. Second, it reflects on several important topics and issues concerning the law of the sea and its current development. Third, it focuses on the ways of approaching modern lawmaking, with an emphasis on 'informal' or 'unconventional' lawmaking.

[12] The author refers to the ICJ as having contemplated the possibility that recommendations adopted by consensus by the International Whaling Commission may be relevant to the interpretation of the International Convention for the Regulation of Whaling (*Whaling in the Antarctic (Australia v Japan: New Zealand intervening)* (Judgment) [2014] ICJ Rep 226, para 46): 'Article VI of the Convention states that "[t]he Commission may from time to time make recommendations to any or all Contracting Governments on any matters which relate to whales or whaling and to the objectives and purposes of this Convention." These recommendations, which take the form of resolutions, are not binding. However, when they are adopted by consensus or by a unanimous vote, they may be relevant for the interpretation of the Convention or its Schedule.'

While a particular framework, set out in the introduction, confers an overall consistency to the book, the studies contained in each of its chapters enrich the content of the whole by providing a better understanding of a range of topics and issues relating to the law of the sea, all of which purport to provide an answer to the key themes: why does informal lawmaking matter? And what are the consequences of informal lawmaking for the law of the sea?

This book has been organized in six parts: Part I contains the introduction, and each of the following four parts refers to a particular area of the law of the sea (maritime security, shipping, marine resources, and marine environment), and the last, Part VI, contains the concluding chapter.

Parts II to V contain several studies that refer to different topics, encompassing issues that challenge and affect normal human activities in the sea, but which do not find adequate solutions in the LOSC or other rules of international law. Therefore, these studies refer to different ways in which state agencies, international organizations, and other non-state stakeholders are in the process of enhancing cooperation by creating non-binding instruments in which such cooperation is expected to be carried out as a way of finding responses that may pave the way to proper solutions of those issues.

Reading these chapters may lead to a deeper comprehension of the current law of the sea, as well as to a better understanding of the need to give adequate attention to the broad segment of informal regulations that are part of the current governance of the seas and oceans of the world. It will also lead to comprehension of why unconventional lawmaking and its normative outcomes matter!

Elsa Kelly

Preface

In essence, the purpose of this book is to explore the current ways actors operating at the international level are developing standards of behaviour to regulate varied maritime activitiesbeyond traditional top-down lawmaking. As illustrated in this book, there are a variety of international lawmaking actors, other than states, who are influencing the process and content of ocean governance decisions on matters traditionally limited to states, including in relation to maritime security and the management of ocean resources. This 'soft law' or 'informal law' is now prolific in ocean governance, and so it is timely to consider its significance for the law of the sea. In considering its significance, there is also scope to consider future applications of this type of lawmaking, and its potential to influence international law more generally, as well as the law of the sea, in the years ahead.

The law of the sea is, typically, traced back to the 'battle of the books' between Hugo Grotius and John Selden, and, in some respects, this contest reflected a form of informal lawmaking. This centuries-old debate still influences current discourse on the law of the sea, but that discourse now encompasses many more laws and agreements. The modern precepts of the law of the sea are drawn from the United Nations Convention on the Law of the Sea (LOSC), and this important instrument maintains a constitutive force in the legal order of the oceans. In the Preamble of the LOSC, states agreed that the LOSC was created 'to settle ... all issues relating to the law of the sea', but also acknowledged 'that matters not regulated by this Convention continue to be governed by the rules and principles of general international law'. There are many different international agreements regulating diverse aspects of ocean use, varying in their geographical coverage. It must be acknowledged that treaty and customary international law have dominated the field of the law of the sea.

Yet, with the notable exception of the current negotiations relating to a new treaty for protection of areas beyond national jurisdiction, an increasingly common phenomenon has been the growth of informal lawmaking as part of ocean governance. This practice has emerged in response to deficiencies and gaps in the formal law, coupled with difficulties in amending or modifying existing treaties and customary international law. Instead, diverse actors have turned to informal lawmaking. In discussing 'informal law' and 'informal lawmaking', this book draws on the excellent work of Joost Pauwelyn, Ramses Wessel, and Jan Wouters (eds), *Informal International Lawmaking* (OUP 2013). They describe informal lawmaking as involving (to paraphrase) international cooperation to reach agreements (other than treaties) between public authorities, with or without the participation of private actors or international organizations, in varied institutions and networks. Given these changes in how rules are being made, it is timely to assess the different gap-filling techniques and new forms of cooperation that are increasingly emerging in the regulation of the oceans. These developments may influence our interpretation and application of existing law, as well as contribute to the development of new law.

This book's title refers to 'unconventional lawmaking', following a suggestion from Seline Trevisanut. There is a deliberate double meaning at work here, as the book discusses agreements and lawmaking processes that do not count as 'conventions' or treaties. The focus is, instead, on less usual forms of lawmaking, and a key avenue of exploration throughout the book is concerned with the different ways that non-binding agreements are being used. Primarily, the authors refer to 'informal law' and 'informal lawmaking'.

A further motivation for this project is reflected in the participants assembled to contribute to this work. They are all women scholars in the law of the sea, drawn from across the globe. The initial planning did not involve a focus on gender, but was ultimately shaped as such, even though the substantive content of the book is not specifically gender-related. One reason for this approach is because the editor attended a workshop some years ago, prior to the appointment of Judge Elsa Kelly to the International Tribunal for the Law of the Sea (ITLOS), where she discussed, with another workshop participant, the fact that ITLOS remained, at that time, an all-male international court. The other participant had asked one of the ITLOS judges about this, and that judge had asked 'but who are the women in the law of the sea?'. This book answers that question. In fact, there are many more women in the law of the sea than there are contributors to this book, but we remain a distinct minority, especially in the area of maritime security. But here we are. A second reason for the gender balance in this book is because there are many women students and early-career researchers in this area, and it has been a delight to meet with many of them at different conferences and workshops, and hear about their work. This book provides a small opportunity to showcase how many of us are undertaking important work in this field, in the hope that other women interested in the law of the sea can be encouraged to do so too. The contributors include early-career researchers and more senior researchers, which is appropriate for a book that not only looks at contemporary practice, but also to the future of the law of the sea.

Natalie Klein

Acknowledgements

Thanks are due, foremost, to the fabulous group of women who have worked with me on this book. It has been both a pleasure and a privilege to have had the opportunity to engage with their ideas, and to benefit from their collective wisdom. The project started pre-Covid, in the midst of the Australian bushfires, and has since proceeded during a global pandemic. Given the many difficulties faced over the last two years, I am all the more grateful that we have been able to bring this work to fruition. Thank you to all the contributors for sticking with it despite everything else you have had to deal with!

The initial stages of this book were supported through a workshop, which included the participation of Aline Jaeckel, Youna Lyons, and Robin Warner, and subsequently grew from there. I have very much appreciated the enthusiasm and encouragement of a wider group of scholars who heard about this project, and who contributed thoughts during different presentations.

I am grateful for the funding to support the work on this book, and for the initial workshop, that was provided through an Australian Research Council Future Fellowship. Thanks, also, to UNSW Sydney's Faculty of Law for providing funding support for the workshop.

This book would not have made it to the finish line without the extraordinary efforts of Millicent McCreath and Priscilla Rivas, who are undertaking their doctorates at UNSW Sydney. They were probably more distracted than I should have allowed addressing all the references and formatting issues, but I very much appreciate all that they have done for this book.

And huge thanks, as always, to Matthew, Tessa, Dulcie, and Joshua for their love, support, and forbearance.

Table of Contents

List of Treaties and International Instruments xxv
List of Abbreviations xxxix
Notes on Contributors xlv

PART I INTRODUCTION

1. Meaning, Scope, and Significance of Informal Lawmaking in the Law of the Sea 3
   Natalie Klein
   1.1 Introduction 3
   1.2 What is Informal Law? 6
   1.3 Process of Informal Lawmaking 8
   1.4 Participants in Informal Lawmaking 10
   1.5 Outputs of Informal Lawmaking and their Normative Value 12
   1.6 Significance of Informal Lawmaking for the Law of the Sea 13
   1.7 Concluding Remarks 18

PART II MARITIME SECURITY

2. The San Remo Manual on the Law of Naval Warfare—from Restatement to Development? 21
   Liesbeth Lijnzaad
   2.1 Introduction 21
   2.2 The San Remo Manual 22
      2.2.1 The Traditional Laws of Naval Warfare: The Hague Conventions (1899 and 1907) and Beyond 22
      2.2.2 The Changing Context for the Law of Naval Warfare 24
      2.2.3 Incorporating the LOSC into the San Remo Manual 25
      2.2.4 Drafting the San Remo Manual 27
   2.3 The Many Faces of Informality 28
      2.3.1 The Manual as a Collection of Non-binding Norms 29
      2.3.2 The Availability of Norms and their Acceptance 30
      2.3.3 The Interests of States 33
   2.4 The Trend towards Informality in the Law of Armed Conflict 35
   2.5 San Remo Manual 2.0: Preparing a Sequel? 37
   2.6 Conclusions 41

3. Piracy off the Coast of Somalia and the Role of Informal Lawmaking 44
   Marie Jacobsson and Natalie Klein
   3.1 Introduction 44
   3.2 Existing Legal Framework on Piracy 46
   3.3 Security Council Responses and the Work of the Contact Group on Piracy off the Coast of Somalia 47

3.3.1 Security Council Resolutions 48
3.3.2 Contact Group on Piracy off the Coast of Somalia 49
3.4 The IMO and the Djibouti Code of Conduct, Jeddah Amendment, and Yaoundé Code 51
3.4.1 IMO Actions Responding to Piracy 51
3.4.2 Djibouti Code of Conduct 52
3.4.3 Yaoundé Code and Jeddah Amendment 54
3.5 Other Informal Agreements and Arrangements Responding to Somali Piracy 56
3.5.1 Transfer Agreements 57
3.5.2 Privately Contracted Armed Security Personnel 58
3.5.3 Naval Arrangements 59
3.6 Lessons Learned and Concluding Remarks 60

4. Informal Lawmaking in Maritime Migration 62
Irini Papanicolopulu
4.1 The Informality of Maritime Migration Law 62
4.2 A Perspective on Informal Lawmaking 64
4.3 Informal Lawmaking in Formal Settings 66
4.4 Informal Lawmaking by Informal Actors 69
4.4.1 Non-state Actors and the Development of Informal Instruments 70
4.4.2 Non-state Actors' Practice and its Role in the Creation of Law 72
4.5 Informal Lawmaking: An Easy Way Out or an Easy Way In? 73

5. Unconventional Lawmaking and International Cooperation on Illegal Bunkering at Sea 76
Yurika Ishii
5.1 The Problem: Illegal Bunkering and the Limits of Formal Law 76
5.1.1 Illegal Bunkering and its Social Harms 77
5.1.2 Jurisdictional Limits under the Law of the Sea 78
5.1.3 The Significance of Informal Lawmaking 81
5.2 Regulations within the Jurisdiction Allocated under the LOSC 81
5.2.1 Fisheries Management 81
5.2.2 Environmental Protection 83
5.3 Regulation by Non-flag States 85
5.3.1 General Overview and State Practice 85
5.3.2 The Roles of Informal Instruments 86
5.4 Concluding Remarks 89

PART III SHIPPING

6. Unconventional Lawmaking in the Compliance Mechanism for the International Regulation of Shipping 93
Zhen Sun
6.1 Introduction 93
6.2 Lawmaking at the IMO 94
6.2.1 Structure and Membership of the IMO 94
6.2.2 Elements of the Lawmaking Process at the IMO 95
6.2.3 Instruments Adopted under the Auspices of the IMO 98
6.3 Compliance Mechanisms under the IMO Regulatory Regime 100
6.3.1 Compliance and Control 101
6.3.2 Member State Audit Scheme 104

6.4 The Interaction between Unconventional Lawmaking and Formal Treaty Law 107
6.4.1 The Role of Non-state Actors 107
6.4.2 The Role of Non-mandatory Instruments 109
6.5 Conclusion 111

7. Unconventional Law for Unconventional Ships? The Role of Informal Law in the International Maritime Organization's Quest to Regulate Maritime Autonomous Surface Ships 112
Anna Petrig
7.1 Introduction 112
7.2 MASS Posing Exceptional Regulatory Challenges 113
7.3 The IMO's Efforts to Integrate MASS in its Regulatory Framework 116
7.4 IMO and Informal Law 118
7.5 Informal Law and MASS 124
7.5.1 Post-law Function of Informal Law: Informing the Interpretation of Treaties 124
7.5.2 Pre- and Para-law Function of Informal Law: Paving the Way for, or even Replacing, Treaties 131
7.6 Conclusion 136

8. The Use of Informal Agreements to Enhance Navigational Safety 137
Natalie Klein
8.1 Introduction 137
8.2 Formal Law Regulating Navigational Safety 140
8.2.1 The LOSC and Customary International Law 140
8.2.2 COLREGS and other International Treaties 142
8.3 Informal Agreements on Navigational Safety and their Intersection with Existing Legal Principles 143
8.3.1 Declaration of Conduct and Code of Conduct 144
8.3.2 Code for Unplanned Encounters at Sea 147
8.3.3 China–US MoUs 150
8.3.3.1 Behavior MoU 151
8.3.3.2 Notification MoU 153
8.4 Alternative Explanatory Paradigms for Informal Agreements on Navigational Safety 154
8.4.1 Confidence-building Measures 155
8.4.2 Experimentalist Governance 156
8.5 Concluding Remarks 159

PART IV MARINE RESOURCES, RESEARCH, AND TECHNOLOGY

9. Unconventional Lawmaking in the Offshore Energy Sector: Flexibilities and Weaknesses of the International Legal Framework 163
Seline Trevisanut
9.1 Introduction 163
9.2 The Fragmented Legal Framework 164
9.2.1 The *Ratione Materiae* Fragmentation at the Global Level 165
9.2.2 The Geographical Fragmentation at the Regional Level 169
9.3 Unconventional Lawmaking in Conventional Fora 172

9.3.1 Unconventional Lawmaking by the International Maritime Organization and Global Treaty Bodies 172
9.3.2 Unconventional Lawmaking by Regional Seas Treaties Bodies 175
9.4 Unconventional Lawmaking by Unconventional Actors 177
9.5 Concluding Remarks: Unconventional Law or Conventional Means of Interpretation 180

10. Formal and Informal Lawmaking by the International Seabed Authority: An Artificial Distinction? 183
Tara Davenport
10.1 Introduction 183
10.2 Formal Lawmaking by the ISA 186
10.2.1 Source of Authority 186
10.2.1.1 Regulations 186
10.2.1.2 Standards 187
10.2.2 Process of Adoption 188
10.2.2.1 Regulations 188
10.2.2.2 Standards 190
10.2.3 Participants 191
10.2.3.1 Regulations 191
10.2.3.2 Standards 193
10.2.4 Normative Intent 193
10.2.4.1 Regulations 193
10.2.4.2 Standards 195
10.2.5 Normative Effect 195
10.3 Informal Lawmaking by the ISA 197
10.3.1 Formal Processes Leading to Informal Outputs: Regional Environmental Management Plans 197
10.3.1.1 Source of Authority 198
10.3.1.2 Process of Adoption 198
10.3.1.3 Participants 199
10.3.1.4 Normative Intent 200
10.3.1.5 Normative Effect 201
10.3.2 Semi-formal Processes Leading to Informal Outputs: Recommendations and Guidelines 202
10.3.2.1 Source of Authority 202
10.3.2.2 Process of Adoption 202
10.3.2.3 Participants 203
10.3.2.4 Normative Intent 203
10.3.2.5 Normative Effect 204
10.3.3 Informal Processes Leading to Informal Outputs 205
10.4 Conclusions 207

11. The Significance of Informal Lawmaking in International Fisheries Law 210
Zoe Scanlon
11.1 Introduction 210
11.2 The Formal Legal Framework in International Fisheries Law 210
11.3 Informal Instruments in the International Fisheries Sphere 213
11.3.1 FAO Code of Conduct and Technical Guidelines for Responsible Fisheries 213

11.3.2 IPOA–IUU 213
11.3.3 Other IPOAs 214
11.3.4 FAO Guidelines 215
11.3.5 UN General Assembly Resolutions 215
11.4 The Contribution of Informal Fisheries Instruments to International Fisheries Law 216
11.4.1 The Incorporation of Modern Approaches into International Fisheries Law 216
11.4.2 The Incorporation of Global Standards into Law, and a Catalyst for Legal Action 220
11.4.3 Detailed Guidance on Implementation 224
11.4.4 Informal Instruments as Interpretive Guidance 226
11.4.5 The Development of Customary International Law? 227
11.5 The Capacity of Informal Instruments to Influence International Fisheries Law 228
11.5.1 The Non-binding Nature of Informal Instruments 229
11.5.2 Influence Derived from Development Process and Quality 229
11.6 Conclusion 231

12. Marine Scientific Research and Informal Lawmaking 233
Chie Kojima
12.1 Introduction 233
12.2 The LOSC Framework on Marine Scientific Research 235
12.2.1 Definition of Marine Scientific Research 237
12.2.2 Definition of 'Competent International Organizations' 238
12.2.3 Relationship with Part XII of the LOSC on the Protection and Preservation of the Marine Environment 239
12.3 Examples of Informal Lawmaking in Marine Scientific Research 241
12.3.1 Informal Lawmaking on Marine Scientific Research by International Organizations 241
12.3.1.1 Division for Ocean Affairs and the Law of the Sea of the United Nations 241
12.3.1.2 Intergovernmental Oceanographic Commission of the United Nations Educational, Scientific and Cultural Organization 243
12.3.1.3 International Seabed Authority 245
12.3.2 Extending Formal Law for the Participation of Non-state Actors in Marine Scientific Research 245
12.3.3 Influence of Voluntary Standard-setting by Non-state Actors on Informal Lawmaking 247
12.4 Conclusions 248

13. The Role of Informal Lawmaking in Facilitating Marine Technology Transfer and Data Sharing 250
Erika Techera
13.1 Introduction 250
13.2 The Marine Technology Landscape 251
13.3 The Use of Marine Technologies for Fishing 254
13.3.1 The LOSC Framework 254
13.3.2 Informal Law and the Use of Marine Technology 256
13.4 Development and Transfer of Marine Technologies 259

13.4.1 The LOSC Framework 259
13.4.2 Informal Law Supporting the Development and Transfer of Technology 261
13.5 Exchange and Sharing of Data 264
13.5.1 The LOSC Framework 264
13.5.2 Informal Law on Data Collection and Sharing 264
13.6 Analysing the Significance of Informal Law Relating to Fishing Technologies 265
13.7 Concluding Remarks 268

PART V MARINE ENVIRONMENT

14. The Sustainable Development Goals and Informal Lawmaking Processes: How a Voluntary Initiative Sets International Standards for Governments and the Private Sector 271
Anastasia Telesetsky
14.1 Introduction 271
14.2 Sustainable Development Goals and Goal 14 272
14.2.1 History of Goal 14 274
14.2.2 Targets under Goal 14 274
14.3 SDGs Operating as Standards for Implementing the Law of the Sea 276
14.3.1 Target 14.5 (Increase Waters under Marine Protection) 278
14.3.2 Target 14.c 281
14.4 Role of Private Sector in Implementing SDG14 and Informal Lawmaking by Private Business Sector 282
14.4.1 Fisheries Commitment towards MSC Certification 285
14.4.2 Marine Plastic Pollution 286
14.5 Concluding Thoughts about SDGs as an Informal Lawmaking Process 287

15. Informal International Lawmaking as a Panacea in the Absence of Regime Focus? Marine Debris, Plastics, and Microplastics 290
Rosemary Rayfuse
15.1 Introduction 290
15.2 International Recognition of the Problem of Marine Plastic Debris 292
15.3 Defining 'Informal International Lawmaking' 296
15.4 Informal Lawmaking and Ship-source Marine Plastic Debris 298
15.5 Informal Lawmaking and Land-based Sources of Marine Plastic Debris 302
15.6 Conclusion 308

16. Unconventional Lawmaking in the Law of the Sea and Area-based Conservation Measures 309
Karen N Scott
16.1 Introduction 309
16.2 'Unconventional' or 'Informal' Lawmaking and the Law of the Sea 309
16.3 Defining Area-based Conservation Measures 313
16.4 'Conventional' Sources of Area-based Conservation Measures 314
16.5 'Unconventional' Sources of Area-based Conservation Measures 315
16.5.1 Binding Area-based Conservation Measures Adopted by RFMOs and Regional Seas Organizations 316
16.5.1.1 OSPAR 316
16.5.1.2 CCAMLR 317

16.5.2 Binding Area-based Conservation Measures Adopted by the IMO 320
16.5.3 Binding Area-based Conservation Measures Adopted by the ISA 321
16.5.4 Non-binding 'Pledges' to Establish MPAs and other Area-based Conservation Measures 322
16.5.4.1 UN and CBD Targets to Protect 10 % of the Oceans by 2020 323
16.5.4.2 2014 Hamilton Declaration for the Conservation of the Sargasso Sea 325
16.5.5 Non-binding Guidelines and other Measures Adopted by International Organizations and Institutions 326
16.5.5.1 The CBD, Area-based Protection, and Ecologically or Biologically Significant Marine Areas (EBSAs) 326
16.5.5.2 FAO and VMEs 327
16.5.6 Non-binding Guidelines and other Measures Adopted by the IUCN 328
16.5.6.1 IUCN Protected Area Guidelines 328
16.5.6.2 Important Marine Mammal Areas (IMMAs) and the IUCN Global Standards for the Identification of Key Biodiversity Areas (KBAs) 329
16.6 'Unconventional' Area-based Conservation Measures and the International Legally Binding Instrument for the Conservation and Sustainable Use of Biodiversity beyond National Jurisdiction (ILBI) 329
16.7 Concluding Remarks 332

17. Sea Level Rise and the Law of the Sea: Filling the Legal Gaps through Informal Lawmaking 334
Nilüfer Oral and Tutku Bektaş
17.1 Introduction 334
17.2 Gaps in the Legal Regime in Relation to Sea Level Rise 335
17.2.1 Legal Uncertainty Surrounding the Effects of Sea Level Rise on Baselines and the Outer Limits of the Maritime Spaces Measured from the Baselines 336
17.2.2 Legal Uncertainty Surrounding the Effects of Sea Level Rise on Islands 338
17.3 Current Processes for Informal Lawmaking for Sea Level Rise 339
17.3.1 Processes and Mechanisms under the UNFCCC and the Paris Agreement 339
17.3.1.1 Cancun Adaptation Framework and National Adaptation Plans 340
17.3.1.2 Warsaw International Mechanism for Loss and Damage 341
17.3.1.3 Nationally Determined Contributions 342
17.3.1.4 Subsidiary Body for Scientific and Technological Advice and Oceans Dialogue 343
17.3.1.5 Nairobi Work Programme on Impacts, Vulnerability, and Adaptation to Climate Change 345
17.3.2 Efforts under the Existing LOSC Regime 345
17.3.3 Informal Lawmaking Efforts as Subsequent Agreements and Subsequent Practice 346
17.3.4 Regional Informal Lawmaking Processes for Sea Level Rise 349
17.3.4.1 Work Undertaken by the Pacific Islands Forum 349
17.3.4.2 Efforts by Small Island Developing States and CARICOM 350
17.3.5 International Courts and Tribunals 351
17.4 Conclusion 354

PART VI CONCLUSION

18. Informal Lawmaking and the Future of the Law of the Sea: Developing Legal Infrastructure and Regulating Human Activity 359
Ellen Hey
18.1 Introduction 359
18.2 Developing Legal Infrastructure 360
18.2.1 Relations between the Global South and the Global North 360
18.2.1.1 Decision-making at UNCLOS III 361
18.2.1.2 Developing the Deep Seabed Mining Regime 362
18.2.1.3 Transferring Marine Technology 363
18.2.2 Informal Instruments in the Relationship between the Global South and Global North 364
18.2.3 The Exercise of Jurisdiction at Sea 365
18.2.3.1 Early Examples 365
18.2.3.2 Stabilizing Baselines 366
18.2.3.3 The BBNJ Negotiations 368
18.2.3.4 Combating Armed Robbery and other Illicit Activities in the Territorial Sea of Somalia and the Gulf of Aden 371
18.2.3.5 Legal Effect 372
18.3 Regulating Human Activity 373
18.3.1 Regulating Human Activity Based on Inter-state Cooperation 374
18.3.2 Private Standard Setting 376
18.3.3 Administration 378
18.4 Concluding Remarks 378

Bibliography 381
Index 397

List of Treaties and International Instruments

1. TREATIES (IN CHRONOLOGICAL ORDER)

1907

Hague Convention (IV) respecting the Laws and Customs of War on Land (adopted 18 October 1907, entered into force 26 January 1910) *reprinted in* Natalino Ronzitti (ed), *The Law of Naval Warfare: A Collection of Agreements and Documents with Commentaries* (Martinus Nijhoff 1988). 41

Hague Convention (VI) relating to the Status of Enemy Merchant Ships at the Outbreak of Hostilities (adopted 18 October 1907, entered into force 26 January 1910) *reprinted in* Natalino Ronzitti (ed), *The Law of Naval Warfare: A Collection of Agreements and Documents with Commentaries* (Martinus Nijhoff 1988) 21, 23

Hague Convention (VII) relating to the Conversion of Merchant Ships into War-Ships (adopted 18 October 1907, entered into force 26 January 1910) *reprinted in* Natalino Ronzitti (ed), *The Law of Naval Warfare: A Collection of Agreements and Documents with Commentaries* (Martinus Nijhoff 1988). 21, 23

Hague Convention (VIII) relative to the Laying of Automatic Submarine Contact Mines (adopted 18 October 1907, entered into force 26 January 1910) *reprinted in* Natalino Ronzitti (ed), *The Law of Naval Warfare: A Collection of Agreements and Documents with Commentaries* (Martinus Nijhoff 1988) 21, 23

Hague Convention (IX) concerning Bombardment by Naval Forces in Time of War (adopted 18 October 1907, entered into force 26 January 1910) *reprinted in* Natalino Ronzitti (ed), *The Law of Naval Warfare: A Collection of Agreements and Documents with Commentaries* (Martinus Nijhoff 1988). 23

Hague Convention (X) for the Adaptation to Maritime Warfare of the Principles of the Geneva Convention (adopted 18 October 1907, entered into force 26 January 1910) *reprinted in* Natalino Ronzitti (ed), *The Law of Naval Warfare: A Collection of Agreements and Documents with Commentaries* (Martinus Nijhoff 1988) 23

Hague Convention (XI) relative to certain Restrictions with regard to the Exercise of the Right of Capture in Naval War (adopted 18 October 1907, entered into force 26 January 1910) *reprinted in* Natalino Ronzitti (ed), *The Law of Naval Warfare: A Collection of Agreements and Documents with Commentaries* (Martinus Nijhoff 1988) 21, 23

Hague Convention (XII) relative to the Creation of an International Prize Court (adopted 18 October 1907) (not in force) *reprinted in* Natalino Ronzitti (ed), *The Law of Naval Warfare: A Collection of Agreements and Documents with Commentaries* (Martinus Nijhoff 1988). 23

Hague Convention (XIII) concerning the Rights and Duties of Neutral Powers in Naval War (adopted 18 October 1907, entered into force 26 January 1910) *reprinted in* Natalino Ronzitti (ed), *The Law of Naval Warfare: A Collection of Agreements and Documents with Commentaries* (Martinus Nijhoff 1988). 21, 23

1910

Additional Protocol to the Convention relative to the Establishment of an International Prize Court (adopted 19 September 1910) (not in force) *reprinted in* D Schindler and J Toman, *The Laws of Armed Conflicts* (Martinus Nijhoff 1988) 839 23

1944

Convention on International Civil Aviation (adopted 7 December 1944, entered into force 4 April 1947) 15 UNTS 295. 194

1945

Charter of the United Nations 25, 27, 28, 37, 45, 47, 48, 350
Statute of the International Court of Justice 5, 6, 30, 31, 123, 227, 307, 310, 330, 331, 349, 350

1946

Constitution of the World Health Organization (adopted 22 July 1946, entered into force 7 April 1948) 14 UNTS 185 194
International Convention for the Regulation of Whaling (adopted 2 December 1946, entered into force 10 November 1948) 161 UNTS 72 .... 11, 14, 204, 226, 234, 312, 345

1948

Convention on the International Maritime Organization (adopted 6 March 1948, entered into force 17 March 1958) 289 UNTS 3 .... 93, 112, 173, 296

1949

Geneva Convention (II) for the Amelioration of the Condition of Wounded, Sick and Shipwrecked Members of Armed Forces at Sea (adopted 12 August 1949, entered into force 21 October 1950) 75 UNTS 85 21

1957

Agreement relating to Refugee Seamen (adopted 23 November 1957, entered into force 27 December 1961) 506 UNTS 126 63

1958

Convention on Fishing and Conservation of the Living Resources of the High Seas (adopted 29 April 1958, entered into force 26 September 1968) 559 UNTS 285 4
Convention on the Continental Shelf (adopted 19 April 1958, entered into force 10 June 1964) 499 UNTS 311 .... 4, 364
Convention on the High Seas (adopted 29 April 1958, entered into force 30 September 1962) 450 UNTS 1 .... 4, 45
Convention on the Territorial Sea and the Contiguous Zone (adopted 29 April 1958, entered into force 10 September 1964) 516 UNTS 205 .... 4, 137

1959

The Antarctic Treaty (adopted 1 December 1959, entered into force 23 June 1961) 402 UNTS 71 .... 239, 313, 316

1966

International Convention on Load Lines (adopted 5 April 1966, entered into force 21 July 1968) 640 UNTS 133 142

1969

International Convention on Civil Liability for Oil Pollution Damage (opened for signature 29 November 1969, entered into force 27 June 1975) 973 UNTS 319 167
Vienna Convention on the Law of Treaties (adopted 23 May 1969, entered into force 27 January 1980) 1155 UNTS 331 .... 6, 64, 128, 150, 174, 194, 226, 333, 344, 345, 351

1971

Convention on Wetlands of International Importance especially as Waterfowl Habitat (adopted 2 February 1971, entered into force 21 December 1975) 96 UNTS 245 312

International Convention on the Establishment of an International Fund for Compensation for Oil Pollution Damage (opened for signature 18 December 1971, entered into force 16 October 1978) 11 ILM 284 167

1972

Agreement between the Government of the United States of America and the Government of the Union of Soviet Socialist Republics on the Prevention of Incidents on and over the High Seas (adopted 25 May 1972, entered into force 25 May 1972) 852 UNTS 151 150

Convention for the Protection of the World Cultural and Natural Heritage (adopted 16 November 1972, entered into force 17 December 1975) 1037 UNTS 151 312

Convention on the International Regulations for Preventing Collisions at Sea (adopted 20 October 1972, entered into force 15 July 1977) 1050 UNTS 16 . . . . 142, 143, 147, 148, 149, 150, 152, 153

Convention on the Prevention of Marine Pollution by Dumping of Waste and Other Matter (opened for signature 29 December 1972, entered into force 30 August 1975) 1046 UNTS 120 (London Convention) 166, 167, 173, 290, 296

1973

International Convention for the Prevention of Pollution from Ships (as Modified by the Protocol of 1978 Relating Thereto) (adopted 2 November 1973, entered into force 2 October 1983) 1340 UNTS 184 . . . . 83, 84, 90, 100, 102, 103, 105, 109, 167, 291, 292, 296, 297, 298, 312, 318, 319

1974

International Convention for the Safety of Life at Sea (adopted 1 November 1974, entered into force 25 May 1980) 1184 UNTS 1 . . . . 68, 83, 95, 96, 97, 99, 100–103, 105, 109, 122, 124, 125, 135, 142, 319, 358, 372, 375

1976

Convention for the Protection of the Mediterranean Sea Against Pollution (adopted 16 February 1976, entered into force 12 February 1978) 1102 UNTS 27 (Barcelona Convention) 176, 300

Protocol for the Protection of the Mediterranean Sea against Pollution from Land-Based Sources and Activities (LBS Protocol) (as amended 7 March 1996) (signed 17 May 1976, entered into force 11 May 2008) to the Convention for the Protection of the Mediterranean Sea Against Pollution (adopted 16 February 1976, entered into force 12 February 1978) 1102 UNTS 27 (Barcelona Convention) <https://www.unep.org/unepmap/who-we-are/barcelona-convention-and-protocols> 300

Treaty of Amity and Cooperation in Southeast Asia (adopted 24 February 1976, entered into force 15 July 1976) 1025 UNTS 297 146

1977

Protocol Additional to the Geneva Conventions of 12 August 1949, and relating to the Protection of Victims of International Armed Conflicts (Protocol 1) (adopted 8 June 1977, entered into force 7 December 1978) 1125 UNTS 3 21

Protocol Additional to the Geneva Conventions of 12 August 1949, and relating to the Protection of Victims of Non-International Armed Conflicts (Protocol II) (adopted 8 June 1977, entered into force 7 December 1978) 1125 UNTS 609 21

1978

Convention on Cooperation in the Northwest Atlantic Fisheries (adopted 24 October 1978, entered into force 1 January 1979, amendments in force 18 May 2017) 1135 UNTS 369 . . . . 82, 212

International Convention on Standards of Training, Certification and Watchkeeping for Seafarers (adopted 7 July 1978, entered into force 28 April 1984) 1361 UNTS 2. . . . . 95, 142, 296
Kuwait Regional Convention for Co-operation on the Protection of the Marine Environment from Pollution (opened for signature 24 April 1978, entered into force 1 July 1979) 1140 UNTS 133 . . . . . 171, 175

1979

Convention on the Conservation of Migratory Species of Wild Animals (adopted 23 June 1979, entered into force 1 November 1983) 1651 UNTS 333 . . . . . 10, 11, 174
International Convention against the Taking of Hostages (adopted 17 December 1979, entered into force 3 June 1983) 1316 UNTS 205. 47
International Convention on Maritime Search and Rescue (adopted 27 April 1979, entered into force 22 June 1985, as amended) 1184 UNTS 278 . . . . . 5, 68

1980

Convention on Future Multilateral Cooperation in North-East Atlantic Fisheries (adopted 18 November 1980, entered into force 17 March 1982) 1285 UNTS 129 . . . . . 218, 368
Convention on the Conservation of Antarctic Marine Living Resources (adopted 20 May 1980, entered into force 7 April 1982) 1329 UNTS 47 . . . . . 218, 314

1982

Agreement Concerning Interim Arrangements Relating to Polymetallic Nodules of the Deep Sea Bed (adopted 2 September 1982, entered into force 2 September 1982) (1982) 21 ILM 950 360
United Nations Convention on the Law of the Sea (adopted 10 December 1982, entered into force 16 November 1994) 1833 UNTS 397

1984

Provisional Understanding Regarding Deep Seabed Matters (adopted 3 August 1984, entered into force 2 September 1984) (1987) 26 ILM 1502. 360

1986

Vienna Convention on the Law of Treaties between States and International Organizations or between International Organizations (adopted 21 March 1986) (not in force) UN Doc A/CONF.129/15 369

1988

Convention for the Suppression of Unlawful Acts against the Safety of Maritime Navigation (adopted 10 March 1988, entered into force 1 March 1992) 1678 UNTS 221. . . . . 47, 80, 125, 143
United Nations Convention against Illicit Traffic in Narcotic Drugs and Psychotropic Substances (adopted 20 December 1988, entered into force 11 November 1990) 1582 UNTS 95 . . . . . 80, 143

1989

Agreement and Joint Statement on Uniform Interpretation of the Rules of International Law Governing Innocent Passage (USA-USSR) (23 September 1989) 28 ILM 1444. 150
Basel Convention on the Control of Transboundary Movements of Hazardous Wastes and Their Disposal (adopted 22 March 1989, entered into force 5 May 1992) 1673 UNTS 57. . . . . 373, 374
Convention for the Prohibition of Fishing with Long Driftnets in the South Pacific (adopted 29 November 1989, in force 17 May 1991) 29 ILM 1449. 254
Protocol to the Kuwait Regional Convention for Co-operation on the Protection of the Marine Environment from Pollution, Concerning Regional Co-operation in Combatting

Pollution by Oil and Other Harmful Substances in Cases of Emergency (opened for signature 29 March 1989, entered into force 17 February 1990) 2056 UNTS 68. 171

1991

Convention on Environmental Impact Assessment in a Transboundary Context (opened for signature 25 February 1991, entered into force 10 September 1997) 1989 UNTS 310 (Espoo Convention) 167, 168, 169, 175, 177

Protocol on Environmental Protection to the Antarctic Treaty (adopted 4 October 1991, entered into force 14 January 1998) 2941 UNTS 3 . . . . . 313, 316

1992

Convention for the Protection of the Marine Environment of the North-East Atlantic (opened for signature 22 September 1992, entered into force 25 March 1998) 2354 UNTS 67 (OSPAR Convention) 368, 170, 314, 315

Convention on Biological Diversity (adopted 5 June 1992, entered into force 29 December 1993) 1760 UNTS 79 . . . . . 167, 173, 174, 181, 200, 239, 270, 276, 309, 311, 312, 321, 323–326, 329, 330, 342, 360, 366, 367

Convention on the Protection of the Marine Environment of the Baltic Sea Area (opened for signature 9 April 1992, entered into force 17 January 2000) 2099 UNTS 195 (Helsinki Convention) 170

United Nations Framework Convention on Climate Change (adopted 9 May 1992, entered into force 21 March 1994) 1771 UNTS 107. . . . . 167, 270, 332, 333, 337–343, 345, 346, 348–353, 360

1993

Agreement to Promote Compliance with International Conservation and Management Measures by Fishing Vessels on the High Seas (adopted 24 November 1993, entered into force on 24 April 2003) 2221 UNTS 91 . . . . . 212, 214, 254, 256

1994

Agreement on Trade-Related Aspects of Intellectual Property Rights (adopted 14 April 1994, entered into force 1 January 1995) 1869 UNTS 299. 362

Agreement relating to the Implementation of Part XI of the United Nations Convention on the Law of the Sea of 10 December 1982 (adopted 28 July 1994, entered into force 16 November 1994) 1836 UNTS 3 . . . . . 4, 25, 184, 188–190, 201, 203, 205, 236, 361

Protocol for the Protection of the Mediterranean Sea against Pollution Resulting from Exploration and Exploitation of the Continental Shelf and the Seabed and its Subsoil (opened for signature 14 October 1994, entered into force 29 March 2013). 170

1995

Agreement for the Implementation of the Provisions of the United Nations Convention on the Law of the Sea of 10 December 1982 relating to the Conservation and Management of Straddling Fish Stocks and Highly Migratory Fish Stocks (adopted 4 August 1995, entered into force 11 December 2001) 2167 UNTS 3. . . . . 4, 81, 82, 211, 212, 214, 217–220, 223, 225, 226, 228, 253, 256, 261, 364

Convention for the Protection of the Marine Environment and the Coastal Region of the Mediterranean (adopted 10 June 1995, entered into force 9 July 2004), amending Convention for the Protection of the Mediterranean Sea Against Pollution (adopted 16 February 1976, entered into force 12 February 1978) 1102 UNTS 27 (Barcelona Convention) 300, 313

Protocol Concerning Specially Protected Areas and Biological Diversity in the Mediterranean (adopted 10 June 1995, entered into force 12 December 1999) 313

1996

Protocol to the Convention on the Prevention of Marine Pollution by Dumping of Wastes and Other Matter (opened for signature 7 November 1996, entered into force 24 March 2006) 36 ILM 1 (London Protocol) 239, 247, 290, 296

1997

Kyoto Protocol to the United Nations Framework Convention on Climate Change (adopted 11 December 1997, entered into force 16 February 2005) 2303 UNTS 162 266

1998

Agreement between the Department of Defense of the United States of America and the Ministry of National Defense of the People's Republic of China on Establishing a Consultation Mechanism to Strengthen Military Maritime Safety (adopted 19 January 1998, entered into force 19 January 1998) 37 ILM 530 151
Convention on Access to Information, Public Participation in Decision-Making and Access to Justice in Environmental Matters (opened for signature 25 June 1998, entered force 30 October 2001) 2161 UNTS 450 (Aarhus Convention) 169, 177, 191, 192

1999

International Convention for the Suppression of the Financing of Terrorism (adopted 9 December 1999, entered into force 10 April 2002) 2178 UNTS 197 80

2000

Convention on the Conservation and Management of Highly Migratory Fish Stocks in the Western and Central Pacific Ocean (adopted 5 September 2000, entered into force 18 June 2004) 2275 UNTS 43 217
Protocol against the Smuggling of Migrants by Land, Sea and Air, supplementing the United Nations Convention Against Transnational Organized Crime (adopted 15 November 2000, entered into force 28 January 2004) 2241 UNTS 507 . . . . . 62, 143
United Nations Convention against Transnational Organized Crime (adopted 15 November 2000, entered into force 29 September 2003) 2225 UNTS 209 80

2003

Agreement Concerning Co-Operation in Suppressing Illicit Maritime and Air Trafficking in Narcotic Drugs and Psychotropic Substances in the Caribbean Area (adopted 10 April 2003, entered into force 18 September 2008) 2005 Digest 147, TRB 2010 No 253 (Treaty No 010467) 24
Convention for the Strengthening of the Inter-American Tropical Tuna Commission established by the 1949 Convention between the United States of America and the Republic of Costa Rica (adopted 27 June 2003, entered into force 27 August 2010) <https://www.iattc.org/IATTCdocumentationENG.htm> 217
Protocol on Strategic Environmental Assessment to the Convention on Environmental Impact Assessment in a Transboundary Context (opened for signature 21 May 2003, entered into force 11 July 2010) 2685 UNTS 140 169
United Nations Convention against Corruption (adopted 31 October 2003, entered into force 14 December 2005) 2349 UNTS 41 80

2004

International Convention for the Control and Management of Ships' Ballast Water and Sediments (adopted 13 February 2004, entered into force 8 September 2017) IMO Doc BWM/CONF/36 . . . . . 100, 265
Regional Cooperation Agreement on Combating Piracy and Armed Robbery against ships in Asia (adopted 11 November 2004, entered into force 4 September 2006) 2398 UNTS 199 . . . . . 52, 54

2005

Protocol of 2005 to the Convention for the Suppression of Unlawful Acts against the Safety of Maritime Navigation (adopted 14 October 2005, entered into force 28 July 2010) IMO Doc LEG/CONF.15/21 . . . . 47, 80, 143

2006

Maritime Labour Convention (adopted 23 February 2006, entered into force 20 August 2013) 2952 UNTS 3 51
Southern Indian Ocean Fisheries Agreement (adopted 7 July 2006, entered into force 21 June 2012) 2835 UNTS 409 . . . . 218, 221

2009

Agreement on Port State Measures to Prevent, Deter and Eliminate Illegal, Unreported and Unregulated Fishing (adopted 22 November 2009, entered into force 5 June 2016) [2016] ATS 21 . . . . 7, 17, 212, 256
Convention on the Conservation and Management of High Seas Fishery Resources in the South Pacific Ocean (adopted 14 November 2009, entered into force 24 August 2012) 2899 UNTS 211 . . . . 212, 217

2015

Paris Agreement to the United Nations Framework Convention on Climate Change (adopted 12 December 2015, entered into force 4 November 2016) (2016) 55(4) ILM 740. . . . . 321, 333, 337–341, 345, 346, 348–350, 352, 360, 372

2017

Agreement on Enhancing International Arctic Scientific Cooperation (adopted 11 May 2017, entered into force 23 May 2018) <https://oaarchive.arctic-council.org/handle/11374/1916>. 224, 245

2. SELECTED INTERNATIONAL INSTRUMENTS (IN ALPHABETICAL ORDER)

'Copenhagen Declaration on Anti-Doping in Sport' (2 January 2003) <https://www.wada-ama.org/en/resources/world-anti-doping-program/copenhagen-declaration> 119
'Declaration of Principles Governing the Sea-Bed and Ocean Floor, and the Subsoil Thereof, beyond the Limits of National Jurisdiction', UNGA Res XXV/2749 (17 December 1970) UN Doc A/RES/XXV/2749 363
'Declaration on the Establishment of a New International Economic Order' UNGA Res S-6/3201 (1 May 1974) UN Doc A/RES/S-6/3201. 358
'Development of an international legally binding instrument under the United Nations Convention on the Law of the Sea on the conservation and sustainable use of marine biological diversity of areas beyond national jurisdiction' UNGA Res 69/292 (19 June 2015) A/RES/69/292 328
'EU-Turkey statement, 18 March 2016' (18 March 2016) <https://www.consilium.europa.eu/en/press/press-releases/2016/03/18/eu-turkey-statement/> 66–67
'Global Compact for Safe, Orderly and Regular Migration' UNGA Res 73/195 (19 December 2018) UN Doc A/RES/73/195. 63
'Honolulu Strategy: A Global Framework for Prevention and Management of Marine Debris' (25 March 2011) <https://wedocs.unep.org/bitstream/handle/20.500.11822/10670/Honolulu%20strategy.pdf?sequence=1&isAllowed=y> 303, 304
'International legally binding instrument under the United Nations Convention on the Law of the Sea on the conservation and sustainable use of marine biological diversity of areas beyond national jurisdiction' UNGA Res 72/249 (24 December 2017) A/RES/72/249. . . . . 4, 62, 328, 360

'Large-scale Pelagic Drift-net Fishing and Its Impact on the Living Marine Resources of the World's Oceans and Seas' UNGA Res 46/215 (20 December 1991) UN Doc A/Res/46/215. . . . . 215, 222, 254, 255, 295

'Our Ocean, Our Future: Call for Action' UNGA Res 71/312 (6 July 2017) UN Doc A/RES/71/312 . . . . 293, 321, 322

'SIDS Accelerated Modalities of Action (SAMOA) Pathway' UNGA Res 69/15 (15 December 2014) UN Doc A/RES/69/15 348

'Technical Guidelines for the Identification and Environmentally Sound Management of Plastic Wastes and for the Disposal' (23 August 2002) UN Doc UNEP/CHW.6/21. 374

'The Future We Want', UNGA Res 66/288 (27 July 2012) UN Doc A/RES/66/288. . . . . 270, 292

'Transforming Our World: The 2030 Agenda for Sustainable Development', UNGA Res 70/1 (25 September 2015) UN Doc A/Res/70/1 . . . . 86, 243, 292, 308, 321, 339, 361

2011 Guidelines for the Implementation of the Declaration of Conduct on the South China Sea (20 July 2011) <https://cil.nus.edu.sg/wp-content/uploads/2019/10/2011-DOC-Guidelines.pdf>. 146

2012 Guidelines for the Implementation of MARPOL Annex V (02 March 2012) MEPC.219(63) <https://wwwcdn.imo.org/localresources/en/KnowledgeCentre/IndexofIMOResolutions/MEPCDocuments/MEPC.219(63).pdf>. 298

African Union, 'African Charter on Maritime Security and Safety Development in Africa (Lomé Charter)' (15 October 2016) <https://au.int/en/treaties/african-charter-maritime-security-and-safety-and-development-africa-lome-charter> 55

Agreement on Basic Principles Guiding the Settlement of Sea-Related Issues between Vietnam and China (11 October 2011) <http://vietnamembassy-usa.org/news/2011/10/vn-china-basic-principles-settlement-sea-issues> 144

ASEAN's Six-Point Principles on the South China Sea (20 July 2012) <https://www.asean.org/storage/images/AFMs%20Statement%20on%206%20Principles%20on%20SCS.pdf> 146

Barcelona Convention, 'Report of the 19th Ordinary Meeting of the Contracting Parties to the Convention for the Protection of the Marine Environment and the Coastal Region of the Mediterranean and its Protocols' (9-12 February 2016) UNEP(DEPI)/MED IG.22, Decision IG.22/3: Mediterranean Offshore Action Plan in the Framework of the Protocol for the Protection of the Mediterranean Sea against Pollution resulting from Exploration and Exploitation of the Continental Shelf and the Seabed and its Subsoil 171

CARICOM, 'CARICOM Declaration for Climate Action' (Thirty-Sixth Regular Meeting of the Conference of the Heads of Government of the Caribbean Community (CARICOM), Barbados, 2-4 July 2015) <https://caricom.org/caricom-declaration-for-climate-action/>. 349

CBD Executive Secretary, 'Voluntary Guidelines on Biodiversity-Inclusive Impact Assessment' (2006) UN Doc UNEP/CBD/COP/8/27/Add.2, Annex II 174

CBD, 'Decision IX/20: Marine and Coastal Biodiversity' (9 October 2008) UN Doc UNEP/CBD/Cop/DEC/IX/20, Annex I: Scientific Criteria for Identifying Ecologically or Biologically Significant Marine Areas in Need of Protection in Open-Ocean Waters and Deep-Sea Habitats 200, 324

CBD, 'Decision VIII/28: Voluntary Guidelines on Biodiversity-Inclusive Impact Assessment' (15 June 2006) UN Doc UNEP/CBD/COP/DEC/VIII/28 174

CBD, 'Decision X/2: The Strategic Plan for Biodiversity 2011-2020 and the Aichi Biodiversity Targets' (29 October 2010) UN Doc UNEP/CBD/COP/DEC/X/2 . . . . 276, 321

CDI/ICS/OCIMF/SIGTTO, 'Ship-to-Ship Transfer Guide for Petroleum, Chemicals and Liquefied Gases' (Witherby Seamanship 2013) <https://www.witherbyseamanship.com/ship-to-ship-transfer-guide-for-petroleum-chemicals-and-liquefied-gases.html> 87

CMS, 'Memorandum of Understanding on the Conservation of Migratory Sharks' (12 February 2010) <http://www.cms.int/sharks/en/page/sharks- -text> 11

Codice di Condotta per le ONG Impegnate nelle Operazioni di Salvataggio dei Migranti in Mare (Italian Code of Conduct) (2017) <https://www.interno.gov.it/sites/default/files/allegati/codice_condotta_ong.pdf>. 63

Copenhagen Process on the Handling of Detainees in International Military Operations, 'Copenhagen Process: Principles and Guidelines' (2012) < https://iihl.org/wp-content/uploads/2018/04/Copenhagen-Process-Principles-and-Guidelines.pdf> 36

Declaration on the Conduct of Parties in the South China Sea (4 November 2002) <https://asean.org/?static_post=declaration-on-the-conduct-of-parties-in-the-south-china-sea-2> . . . 138, 139, 143–147, 156–159

Declaration on the Establishment of the Arctic Council (19 September 1996) <https://oaarchive.arctic-council.org/bitstream/handle/11374/85/EDOCS-1752-v2-ACMMCA00_Ottawa_1996_Founding_Declaration.PDF?sequence=5&isAllowed=y> . . . 372

Delap Commitment on Securing our Common Wealth of Oceans (Parties to the Nauru Agreement, 2 March 2018) <https://www.pnatuna.com/sites/default/files/Delap%20Commitment_2nd%20PNA%20Leaders%20Summit.pdf> . . . 11, 365

Espoo Convention, 'Report of the Third Meeting of the Parties to the Convention on Environmental Impact Assessment in a Transboundary Context' (13 September 2004) ECE/MP.EA/6, Decision III/8: Guidance on Public Participation in Environmental Impact Assessment in a Transboundary Context . . . 168

FAO, 'Code of Conduct for Responsible Fisheries' (31 October 1995) <http://www.fao.org/tempref/docrep/fao/005/v9878e/v9878e00.pdf> . . . 5, 213, 251, 254

FAO, 'International Guidelines for the Management of Deep-sea Fisheries in the High Seas' (Rome 1999) <http://www.fao.org/3/i0816t/i0816t00.htm> . . . 15, 200, 215, 217, 221, 222, 325

FAO, 'International Plan of Action for Reducing Incidental Catch of Seabirds in Longline Fisheries' (Rome 1999) <http://www.fao.org/tempref/docrep/fao/006/x3170e/X3170E00.pdf> . . . 214, 223, 230

FAO, 'International Plan of Action for the Conservation and Management of Sharks' (Rome 1999) <http://www.fao.org/tempref/docrep/fao/006/x3170e/X3170E00.pdf> . . . 4, 214, 217, 218, 223, 230

FAO, 'International Plan of Action for the Management of Fishing Capacity' (Rome 1999) <<http://www.fao.org/tempref/docrep/fao/006/x3170e/X3170E00.pdf> . . . 214

FAO, 'International Plan of Action to Prevent, Deter and Eliminate Illegal, Unreported and Unregulated Fishing' (Rome 2001) <http://www.fao.org/3/y1224e/Y1224E.pdf> . . . 17, 214, 256

FAO, 'Model Scheme on Port State Measures to Combat Illegal, Unreported and Unregulated fishing' (Rome 2007) <http://www.fao.org/3/a0985t/A0985T.pdf> . . . 17, 219, 256

FAO, 'Reykjavik Declaration on Responsible Fisheries in the Marine Ecosystem' (Rome 2001) <http://www.fao.org/tempref/FI/DOCUMENT/reykjavik/y2198t00_dec.pdf> . . . 218

FAO, 'The Rome Declaration on the Implementation of the Code of Conduct for Responsible Fisheries' (Rome 1999) < http://www.fao.org/3/X2220e/X2220e00.htm> . . . 223

FAO, 'Voluntary Guidelines for Catch Documentation Schemes' (Rome 2017) <http://www.fao.org/3/a-i8076e.pdf> . . . 264

FAO, 'Voluntary Guidelines for Flag State Performance' (Rome 2015) <http://www.fao.org/3/a-i4577t.pdf> . . . 15, 215, 224, 225, 230

FAO, 'Voluntary Guidelines on the Marking of Fishing Gear' (Rome 2019) <http://www.fao.org/3/ca3546t/ca3546t.pdf> . . . 215, 225, 230, 299

HELCOM, 'Recommendation 18/2 on Offshore Activities' (12 March 1997) HELCOM Recommendation 18/2 . . . 175

Human Rights at Sea, 'Voluntary Code of Conduct for Search and Rescue Operations Undertaken by Civil Society Non-Governmental Organisations in the Mediterranean Sea' (2017) <https://www.humanrightsatsea.org/wp-content/uploads/2017/03/20170302-NGO-Code-of-Conduct-FINAL-SECURED.pdf> . . . 64, 375

ICRC, 'Guidelines on the Protection of the Natural Environment in Armed Conflict' (2020) <https://shop.icrc.org/guidelines-on-the-protection-of-the-natural-environment-in-armed-conflict-rules-and-recommendations-relating-to-the-protection-of-the-natural-environment-under-international-humanitarian-law-with-commentary> . . . 36

ICRC, 'The Montreux Document on Pertinent International Legal Obligations and Good Practices for States related to Operations of Private Military and Security Companies during Armed Conflict' (2008) <https://www.eda.admin.ch/dam/eda/en/documents/aussenpolitik/voelkerrecht/20192511-montreux-document_EN.pdf> . . . 36, 59

ILA, 'Baselines Under the International Law of the Sea', ILA Resolution 1/2012 <http://ilareporter.org.au/wp-content/uploads/2015/07/Source-2-Baselines-Resolution.pdf> . . . 335

ILA, 'Committee on International Law and Sea Level Rise', ILA Resolution 5/2018 <https://www.ila-hq.org/images/ILA/Resolutions/ILAResolution_5_2018_SeaLevelRise.pdf> 335, 365

ILC, 'Draft Conclusions on Subsequent Agreements and Subsequent Practice in Relation to the Interpretation of Treaties, with Commentaries' (2018) <https://legal.un.org/ilc/texts/instruments/english/draft_articles/1_11_2018.pdf> 14, 127, 226, 344

IMO, 'Code for Recognized Organizations' (RO Code) (17 May 2013) IMO Res MEPC.237(65) 102, 109

IMO, 'Code for the Implementation of Mandatory IMO Instruments' (19 December 2005) IMO Res A.973(24) 104

IMO, 'Code of Conduct concerning the Repression of Piracy and Armed Robbery against Ships in the Western Indian Ocean and the Gulf of Aden' (Djibouti Code of Conduct) (29 January 2009) IMO Doc C.102/14. . . . . 4, 45, 51–57, 59, 87, 370

IMO, 'Code of Conduct concerning the Repression of Piracy, Armed Robbery against Ships, and Illicit Maritime Activity in West and Central Africa' (Yaoundé Code of Conduct) (25 June 2013) <https://wwwcdn.imo.org/localresources/en/OurWork/Security/Documents/code_of_conduct%20signed%20from%20ECOWAS%20site.pdf>. 45, 51, 54–56, 87–89

IMO, 'Code of Practice for the Investigation of the Crimes of Piracy and Armed Robbery Against Ships' (29 November 2001) IMO Res A.922(22) 54

IMO, 'Enhancement of Safety of Life at Sea by the Prevention and Suppression of Unsafe Practices Associated with Alien Smuggling by Ships' (4 November 1993) IMO Res A.773(18) 68

IMO, 'Framework and Procedures for the Voluntary IMO Member State Audit Scheme' (21 December 2005) IMO Res A.974(24) 104

IMO, 'Generic Guidelines for Developing IMO Goal-Based Standards' (14 June 2011) IMO Doc MSC.1/Circ.1394 . . . . . 109, 122

IMO, 'Guidance for Company Security Officers (CSOs) – Preparation of a Company and Crew for the Contingency of Hijack of Pirates in the Western Indian Ocean and the Gulf of Aden' (9 December 2010) IMO Doc MSC.1/Circ.1390. 52

IMO, 'Guidance to Shipowners and Ship Operators, Shipmasters and Crews on Preventing and Suppressing Acts of Piracy and Armed Robbery Against Ships' (29 May 2002) IMO Doc MSC/Circ.623/Rev.3 54

IMO, 'Guidance to Shipowners and Ship Operators, Shipmasters and Crews on Preventing and Suppressing Acts of Piracy and Armed Robbery against Ships' (23 June 2009) IMO Doc MSC.1/Circ.1334 58

IMO, 'Guidelines and Standards for the Removal of Offshore Installations and Structures on the Continental Shelf and the Exclusive Economic Zone' (19 October 1989) IMO Res A.672(16). 172, 173

IMO, 'Guidelines for Safety Zones and the Safety of Navigation around Offshore Installations and Structures' (7 December 2010) IMO Doc SN.1/Circ.295 172

IMO, 'Guidelines for the Authorization of Organizations Acting on Behalf of the Administration' (4 November 1993) IMO Res A.739(18). 102

IMO, 'Guidelines for the Designation of Special Areas and the Identification of Particularly Sensitive Sea Areas' (6 November 1991) IMO Res A.720(17). 319

IMO, 'Guidelines for the Designation of Special Areas under MARPOL 73/78 and Guidelines for the Designation of Particularly Sensitive Sea Areas' (29 November 2001) IMO Res A.927(22). 319

IMO, 'Guidelines for the Identification and Designation of Particularly Sensitive Sea Areas' (1 December 2005) IMO Res A.982(24) 319

IMO, 'Guidelines for the Use of Electronic Certificates' (20 April 2016) IMO Doc FAL.5/Circ.39/Rev.2. 127

IMO, 'Guidelines on Implementation of the International Safety Management Code by Administrations' (23 November 1995) IMO Res A.788(19). 102, 135

IMO, 'Guidelines on Management for the Safe Operation of Ships and for Pollution Prevention' (19 October 1989) IMO Res A.647(16). 102

IMO, 'Guidelines on Methods for Making Reference to IMO and Other Instruments in IMO Conventions and Other Mandatory Instruments'(29 November 2001) IMO Res A.911(22) 119, 121, 122
IMO, 'Guidelines on the Treatment of Persons Rescued at Sea' (20 May 2004) IMO Res MSC.167(78) 5, 63, 68
IMO, 'Guidelines to assist Flag States in the Implementation of IMO Instruments' (27 November 1997) IMO Res A.847(20) 104
IMO, 'Instruments Implementation Code' (III Code) (4 December 2013) IMO Res A.1070(28) 105, 109, 110, 135
IMO, 'Interim Measures for Combating Unsafe Practices Associated with the Traffic or Transport of Migrants by Sea' (16 December 1998) IMO Doc MSC/Circ.896 68
IMO, 'Interim Recommendations for Port and Coastal States Regarding the Use of Privately Contracted Armed Security Personnel on Board Ships in the High Risk Area' (16 September 2011) IMO Doc MSC.1/Circ.1408 . . . . . 58, 59
IMO, 'International Code for Ships Operating in Polar Waters' (01 January 2017) IMO Doc MEPC 68/21/Add.1 . . . . . 98, 110, 296
IMO, 'International Management Code for the Safe Operation of Ships and for Pollution Prevention' (ISM Code) (4 November 1993) IMO Res A.741(18) 102
IMO, 'Measures to Prevent Acts of Piracy and Armed Robbery Against Ships' (17 November 1983) IMO Res A.545(13) 51
IMO, 'Piracy and Armed Robbery against Ships in Waters off the Coast of Somalia' (23 November 2005) IMO Res A.979(24) 51
IMO, 'Piracy and Armed Robbery against Ships in Waters off the Coast of Somalia' (15 June 2007) IMO Doc MSC.1/Circ.1233 51
IMO, 'Procedures for the Identification of Particularly Sensitive Sea Areas and the Adoption of Associated Protective Measures and Amendments to the Guidelines contained in Resolution A.720(17)' (25 November 1989) IMO Res A.885(21) 319
IMO, 'Promulgation of Rules for the Design and Construction of Bulk Carriers and Oil Tankers Confirmed by the Maritime Safety Committee to be in Conformity with the Goal-based Ship Construction Standards for Bulk Carriers and Oil Tankers' (4 December 2018) IMO Doc MSC.1/Circ.1518/Rev.1 123
IMO, 'Recommendations to Governments for Preventing and Suppressing Piracy and Armed Robbery Against Ships' (16 Jun 1999) IMO Doc MSC/Circ.622/Rev.1 54
IMO, 'Revised Code of Conduct Concerning the Repression of Piracy, Armed Robbery against Ships and Illicit Maritime Activity in the Western Indian Ocean and the Gulf of Aden Area' (Jeddah Amendment) (12 January 2017) <https://wwwcdn.imo.org/localresources/en/OurWork/Security/Documents/A2%20Revised%20Code%20Of%20Conduct%20Concerning%20The%20Repression%20Of%20Piracy%20Armed%20Robbery%20Against%20Ships%20Secretariat.pdf> 4, 45, 51, 54–56, 59, 370
IMO, 'Revised Guidelines for Verification of Conformity with Goal-Based Ship Construction Standards for Bulk Carriers and Oil Tankers' (7 December 2018) IMO Res MSC.454(100) 123
IMO, 'Revised Interim Guidelines to Shipowners, Ship Operators, and Shipmasters on the Use of Privately Contracted Armed Security Personnel on Board Ships in the High Risk Area' (25 May 2012) IMO Doc MSC.1/Circ.1405/Rev.2 59
IMO, 'Revised Interim Recommendations for Flag States Regarding the Use of Privately Contracted Armed Security Personnel on Board Ships in the High Risk Area' (25 May 2012) IMO Doc MSC.1/Circ.1406/Rev.2 59
IMO, 'Revised Interim Recommendations for Port and Coastal States Regarding the Use of Privately Contracted Armed Security Personnel on Board Ships in the High Risk Area' (25 May 2012) IMO Doc MSC.1/Circ.1408/Rev.1 . . . . . 58, 59
IMO, 'Specifications on the Survey and Certification Functions of Recognized Organizations Acting on Behalf of the Administration' (23 November 1995) IMO Res A.798(19) 102
IMO, 'Unified Interpretations of the IGC Code (as Amended by Resolution MSC.370(93))' (28 November 2016) IMO Doc MSC.1/Circ.1559 130
IMO, 'Voluntary IMO Member State Audit Scheme' (27 November 2003) IMO Res A.946(23) . . . 104
Institut de Droit International, 'Manual of the Laws of Naval War' (9 August 1913) <https://ihl-databases.icrc.org/ihl/INTRO/265?OpenDocument> 23, 27

International Code of Conduct Association, 'International Code of Conduct for Private Security Service Providers' (9 November 2010) <https://icoca.ch/the-code/> 59

International Institute of Humanitarian Law, 'San Remo Manual on International Law Applicable to Armed Conflicts at Sea' (1994) < https://ihl-databases.icrc.org/applic/ihl/ihl.nsf/385ec082b509e76c41256739003e636d/7694fe2016f347e1c125641f002d49ce?openDocument>.. 21–41

International Institute of Humanitarian Law, 'The Manual on the Law of Non-International Armed Conflict, With Commentary' (2006) < https://www.legal-tools.org/doc/ccf497/pdf/>.. 35

Inter-Parliamentary Union, 'Hanoi Declaration: The Sustainable Development Goals: Turning Words into Action' (1 April 2015) <http://archive.ipu.org/conf-e/132/rpt-gendebate.htm> 275

InterRidge, 'Statement of Commitment to Responsible Research Practices at Deep-Sea Hydrothermal Vents' (17 February 2006) < http://www.interridge.org/IRStatement>....... 246

IOC, 'Criteria and Guidelines on the Transfer of Marine Technology' (2005) <https://unesdoc.unesco.org/ark:/48223/pf0000139193.locale=en> 242, 249, 259–261, 264, 265, 362

IOC, 'Procedure for the Application of Article 247 of UNCLOS by the Intergovernmental Oceanographic Commission of UNESCO – Marine Scientific Research: A Guide to the Implementation of the Relevant Provisions of UNCLOS (UNESCO 2007) <https://unesdoc.unesco.org/ark:/48223/pf0000157009>...................................... 242

IRSO, 'Code of Conduct for Marine Scientific Research Vessels' (17-20 October 2007) <https://irso.info/wp-content/uploads/International_RV_Code_final.pdf> 246

ISA, 'Regulations on Prospecting and Exploration for Polymetallic Nodules in the Area' (13 July 2000) ISBA/6/A/18.. 184, 193, 195, 196, 198, 200–203, 205

ISA, 'Regulations on Prospecting and Exploration for Polymetallic Sulphides in the Area' (7 May 2010) ISBA/16/A/12/Rev.1... 184, 198

ISA, 'Regulations on Prospecting for Cobalt-rich Ferromanganese Crusts in the Area' (22 July 2013) ISBA/19/C/17.. 184, 198

ISO, 'Ships and Marine Technology – Guidelines for Private Maritime Security Companies (PMSC) providing Privately Contracted Armed Security Personnel (PCASP) on Board Ships (and pro forma contract)' ISO 28007-1:2015 <https://www.iso.org/standard/63166.html>.. 59

ISO, 'Specification for Security Management Systems for the Supply Chain' ISO 28000:2007 <https://www.iso.org/standard/44641.html> 59

IUCN, 'A Global Standard for the Identification of Key Biodiversity Areas: Version 1.0' (2016) <https://portals.iucn.org/library/node/46259>............................ 309, 327

Joint Statement on the Application of the Code for Unplanned Encounters at Sea in the South China Sea (7 September 2016) <https://asean.org/wp-content/uploads/2016/09/Joint-Statement-on-the-Application-of-CUES-in-the-SCS-Final.pdf> 138–139, 147

Memorandum di intesa sulla cooperazione nel campo dello sviluppo, del contrasto all'immigrazione illegale, al traffico di esseri umani, al contrabbando e sul rafforzamento della sicurezza delle frontiere tra lo Stato della Libia e la Repubblica Italiana (2017 Memorandum of Understanding between Italy and Libya) (2 February 2017) <http://www.governo.it/sites/governo.it/files/Libia.pdf>................................ 67

Memorandum of Understanding between the Department of Defense of the United States of America and the Ministry of National Defense of the People's Republic of China Regarding the Rules of Behavior for Safety of Air and Maritime Encounters (9 and 10 November 2014) <https://archive.defense.gov/pubs/141112_MemorandumOfUnderstandingRegardingRules.pdf>..139, 151–153, 159

Memorandum of Understanding between the United States of America Department of Defense and the People's Republic of China Ministry of National Defense on Notification of Major Military Activities Confidence-Building Measures Mechanism (31 October and 4 November 2014) <https://archive.defense.gov/pubs/141112_MemorandumOfUnderstandingOnNotification.pdf> 139, 151, 153, 155, 158

Montevideo Declaration on the Law of the Sea (8 May 1970) (1970) 9(5) ILM 1081............. 364

MSC, 'The MSC Fisheries Standard' <https://www.msc.org/standards-and-certification/fisheries-standard> 281

Naval Conference of London, 'Declaration concerning the Laws of Naval War' (26 February 1909) <https://ihl-databases.icrc.org/ihl/INTRO/255> 23

NEAFC, 'Scheme of Control and Enforcement' (amendments in force from 7 February 2020) <https://www.neafc.org/book/export/html/15254> 82

OCIMF, 'International Safety Guide for Tankers and Terminals (ISGOTT 6)' (6th edn, 2020) <https://www.ocimf.org/publications/books/international-safety-guide-for-tankers-and-terminals-(isgott-6)> 86

OECD, 'Guidelines for Multinational Enterprises' (2011 edn) <http://www.oecd.org/daf/inv/mne/48004323.pdf> 174–175

OSPAR Commission, 'Guidance on Environmental Considerations for Offshore Wind Farm Development' Reference Number 2008-3 (2008) <http://www.ospar.org/documents?d=32631> 175

OSPAR Commission, 'Guidelines for the Identification and Selection of Marine Protected Areas in the OSPAR Maritime Area' (2003) OSPAR Agreement 2003-17 315

OSPAR Commission, 'OSPAR Code of Conduct for Responsible Marine Scientific Research in the Deep Seas and High Seas of the OSPAR Maritime Area' Reference Number 2008-01 (2008) <https://www.ospar.org/documents?d=32633> 246

OSPAR Commission, 'Recommendation 2003/03 on a Network of Marine Protected Areas' (23-27 June 2003) OSPAR Doc 03/17/1, Annex 9, amended by OSPAR Recommendation 2010/2 (OSPAR Doc 10/23/1, Annex 7) 314

OSPAR Commission/NEAFC, 'Collective Arrangement between Competent International Organizations on Cooperation and Coordination Regarding Selected Areas in Areas beyond National Jurisdiction in the North-East Atlantic' (2014) OSPAR Agreement 2014-09, updated 2018 . . . . . 315, 368

Pacific Islands Forum, 'Forum Communiqué' (Fiftieth Pacific Islands Forum, Funafuti, Tuvalu, 13-16 August 2019) < https://www.forumsec.org/wp-content/uploads/2019/08/50th-Pacific-Islands-Forum-Communique.pdf> 347, 350

Pacific Islands Forum, Kainaki II Declaration for Urgent Climate Change Action Now <https://www.forumsec.org/wp-content/uploads/2019/08/50th-Pacific-Islands-Forum-Communique.pdf> 347

Pacific Islands Forum, Palau Declaration on 'The Ocean: Life and Future' <http://www.forumsec.org/wp-content/uploads/2017/11/2014-Forum-Communique_-Koror_-Palau_-29-31-July.pdf> 347

Plan of Action to Implement the Joint Declaration on ASEAN-China Strategic Partnership for Peace and Prosperity (29 November 2004) <https://asean.org/?static_post=plan-of-action-to-implement-the-joint-declaration-on-asean-china-strategic-partnership-for-peace-putaand-prosperity> 147

Program on Humanitarian Policy and Conflict Research at Harvard University (HCPR), 'Manual on International Law Applicable to Air and Missile Warfare' (Bern 2009) <https://reliefweb.int/sites/reliefweb.int/files/resources/8B2E79FC145BFB3D492576E00021ED34-HPCR-may2009.pdf> 35

Sargasso Sea Commission, 'Hamilton Declaration on Collaboration for the Conservation of the Sargasso Sea' (2018) <http://www.sargassoseacommission.org/storage/Hamilton_Declaration_with_signatures_April_2018.pdf> 323–324

Taputapuātea Declaration on Climate Change (Polynesian Leaders Group, 16 July 2015) <https://www.state.gov/wp-content/uploads/2019/03/248-Deep-Sea-Bed.pdf> . . . 11, 365

UN Global Compact, 'Blueprint for Business Leadership on the SDGs' (2017) <https://blueprint.unglobalcompact.org> 280–282

UN Global Compact, 'Sustainable Ocean Principles' <https://d306pr3pise04h.cloudfront.net/docs/publications%2FSustainable+Ocean+Principles.pdf> 282, 283

UN, 'Guiding Principles on Business and Human Rights' (2011) UN Doc HR/PUB/11/04 <https://www.ohchr.org/documents/publications/guidingprinciplesbusinesshr_en.pdf> 174

UN, 'Report of the Global Conference on the Sustainable Development of Small Island Developing States' (Bridgetown, Barbados, 26 April – 6 May 1994) UN Doc A/CONF.167/9,

Annex II: Programme of Action for the Sustainable Development of Small Island Developing States 348

UN, 'Report of the International Meeting to Review the Implementation of the Programme of Action for the Sustainable Development of Small Island Developing States' (Port Louis, Mauritius, 10-14 January 2005) UN Doc A/CONF.207/11, Resolution 1, Annex II: Mauritius Strategy for the Further Implementation of the Programme of Action for the Sustainable Development of Small Island Developing States 348

UN, 'Report of the United Nations Conference on Environment and Development' (3-14 June 1992), UN Doc A/CONF.151/26 (Vol. I), Annex I: Rio Declaration on Environment and Development. . . . 191, 375

UN, 'Report of the World Summit on Sustainable Development' (26 August to 4 September 2002) UN Doc A/CONF.199/20, Annex: Plan of Implementation of the World Summit on Sustainable Development (Johannesburg Plan of Implementation) 218, 271, 321

UNDRR, 'Sendai Framework for Disaster Risk Reduction 2015-2030' (18 March 2015) <https://www.preventionweb.net/files/43291_sendaiframeworkfordrren.pdf> 339, 343

UNEP, 'Global Programme of Action for the Protection of the Marine Environment from Land-based Activities' (1995) < https://www.unep.org/explore-topics/oceans-seas/what-we-do/addressing-land-based-pollution/governing-global-programme> 12, 290, 292, 301–306

UNEP, 'Guidelines on the Survey and Monitoring of Marine Litter' (2009) <https://wedocs.unep.org/xmlui/handle/20.500.11822/13604> 302

UNEP, 'Guidelines on the Use of Market-based Instruments to Address the Problem of Marine Litter' (2009) <https://wedocs.unep.org/handle/20.500.11822/2435> 303

UNEP, 'Montreal Guidelines for the Protection of the Marine Environment against Pollution from Land-based Sources' (1985) UNEP(092)/E5. . . . 301

UNFCCC, 'Report of the Conference of the Parties on its Nineteenth Session, held in Warsaw from 11 to 23 November 2013' (31 January 2014) UN Doc FCCC/CP/2013/10/Add.1, Decision 2/CP.19: Warsaw International Mechanism for Loss and Damage Associated with Climate Change Impacts. . . . 338–340

United Nations Convention on the Law of the Sea: Understanding of the Preparatory Commission for the International Sea-Bed Authority and for the International Tribunal for the Law of the Sea for Proceeding with Deep Sea-Bed Mining Applications and Resolving Disputes of Overlapping Claims of Mine Sites (11 September 1986) reproduced in (1986) 25(5) ILM 1326 361

Western Pacific Naval Symposium, 'Code for Unalerted Encounters at Sea' (June 2003) reproduced in (2012) 4 Australian Journal of Maritime and Ocean Affairs 126 147

Western Pacific Naval Symposium, 'Code for Unplanned Encounters at Sea: Version 1.0' (22 April 2014) <http://www.ions.global/sites/default/files/CUES-10-Approvedat-the-14th-WPNS-2014422.pdf>. . . . 4, 138, 139, 143, 147–152, 158, 159

List of Abbreviations

ABNJ	Areas Beyond National Jurisdiction
AIS	Automatic Identification System
AJIL	American Journal of International Law
ALDFG	Abandoned, Lost, or Discarded Fishing Gear
ANCORS	Australian National Centre for Ocean Resources and Security
AP I	Protocol Additional to the Geneva Convention of 12 August 1949, relating to the Protection of Victims of International Armed Conflict
AP II	Protocol Additional to the Geneva Conventions of 12 August 1949, and relating to the Protection of Victims of Non-International Armed Conflict
APEI	Area of Particular Environmental Interest
API	American Petroleum Institute
ASMA	Antarctic Specially Managed Area
ASPA	Antarctic Specially Protected Area
AU	African Union
AUNJ	Areas Under National Jurisdiction
BARCO OFOG	Barcelona Convention Offshore Oil and Gas Group
BBNJ	Biodiversity Beyond National Jurisdiction
CAFF	Conservation of Arctic Flora and Fauna
CBD	Convention on Biological Diversity
CBM	Confidence Building Measure
CCAMLR	Commission for the Conservation of Antarctic Marine Living Resources
CCDCOE	Cyber Defence Centre of Excellence
CCSBT	Commission for the Conservation of Southern Bluefin Tuna
CCZ REMP	Regional Environment Management Plan for the Clarion-Clipperton Zone
CDS	Catch Documentation Scheme
CGPCS	Contact Group on Piracy off the Coast of Somalia
CHH	Common Heritage of Humankind
CMI	Comité Maritime International
CMM	Conservation and Management Measure
CMS	Convention on Migratory Species
COBSEA	Coordinating Body of the Seas of East Asia
COFI	Committee on Fisheries
COP	Conference of Parties
COR	Corporate Ocean Responsibility
CPAN	Circumpolar Protected Areas Network
CSR	Corporate Social Responsibility
CUES	Code for Unplanned Encounters at Sea
DER	Draft Regulations on Exploitation of Mineral Resources in the Area
DOALOS	Division for Ocean Affairs and the Law of the Sea
DOC	Declaration on the Conduct of Parties in the South China Sea
DSFG	Deep-Sea Fisheries Guidelines
ECCAS	Economic Community of Central African States
ECJ	European Court of Justice

ECOSOC	Economic and Social Council
ECOWAS	Economic Community of West African States
EEZ	Exclusive Economic Zone
EIA	Environmental Impact Assessment
EMMP	Environmental Management and Monitoring Plans
ESM	Environmentally Sound Management
EU	European Union
FAL	Facilitation Committee (IMO)
FAO	Food and Agriculture Organization
FRA	Japan Fisheries Research and Education Agency
FSA	Fish Stocks Agreement
FSC	Forest Stewardship Council
FSI	Sub-Committee on Flag State Implementation (IMO)
G20	Group of Twenty
GAIRS	Generally Accepted International Rules and Standards
GBSs	Goal-Based Standards
GCOS	Global Climate Observing System
GGC	Gulf of Guinea Commission
GPA	Global Program of Action for the Protection of the Marine Environment from Land-based Activities
GPML	Global Partnership on Marine Litter
HELCOM	Baltic Marine Environment Protection Commission—Helsinki Commission
IACS	International Association of Classification Societies
IAPH	International Association of Ports and Harbors
ICCAT	International Commission for the Conservation of Atlantic Tunas
ICES	International Council for the Exploration of the Sea
ICJ	International Court of Justice
ICLQ	International and Comparative Law Quarterly
ICPC	International Cable Protection Industry
ICRC	International Committee of the Red Cross
ICS	International Chamber of Shipping
ICZM	Integrated Coastal Zone Management
IEC	International Electrotechnical Commission
IFC	International Finance Corporation
IGO	Intergovernmental Organisation
IGR	Intergovernmental Review
ILA	International Law Association
ILBI	International Legally Binding Instrument
ILC	International Law Commission
ILO	International Labour Organization
IMMA	Important Marine Mammal Areas
IMO	International Maritime Organization
INCSEA	Agreement on the Prevention of Incidents on and over the High Seas
IO	Intergovernmental Organization
IOC	Intergovernmental Oceanographic Commission
IOGP	International Association of Oil and Gas Producers
IOM	International Organization for Migration
IPCC	Intergovernmental Panel on Climate Change
IPOA	International Plan of Action
IPOA-Capacity	International Plan of Action for the Management of Fishing Capacity

IPOA–IUU	International Plan of Action to Prevent, Deter and Eliminate Illegal, Unreported and Unregulated Fishing
IPOA–Seabirds	International Plan of Action for Reducing Incidental Catch of Seabirds in Longline Fisheries
IPOA–Sharks	International Plan of Action for the Conservation and Management of Sharks
IPU	Inter-Parliamentary Union
IRENA	International Renewable Energy Agency
IRF	International Regulators' Forum
IRRC	International Review of the Red Cross
ISA	International Seabed Authority
ISGOTT 6	International Safety Guide for Tankers and Terminals, 6th edn
ISO	International Organization for Standardization
ITLOS	International Tribunal for the Law of the Sea
IUU	Illegal, Unreported and Unregulated
KBA	Key Biodiversity Area
LEG	Legal Committee (IMO)
LOSC	United Nations Convention on the Law of the Sea
LRIT	Long-range Identification and Tracking
LTC	Legal and Technical Commission
MARPOL	International Convention for the Prevention of Pollution from Ships
MASS	Maritime Autonomous Surface Ship
MCS	Monitoring, Control and Surveillance
MDGs	Millennium Development Goals
MEA	Multilateral Environmental Agreement
MEPC	Marine Environment Protection Committee (IMO)
MMCA	Agreement on Establishing a Consultation Mechanism to Strengthen Military Maritime Safety
MMPATF	Marine Mammal Protected Areas Task Force
MOP	Meeting of Parties
MOU	Memorandum of Understanding
MPA	Marine Protected Area
MSC	Marine Stewardship Council
MSC	Maritime Safety Committee (IMO)
MSP	Marine Spatial Planning
MSY	Maximum Sustainable Yield
NAFO	Northwest Atlantic Fisheries Organization
NAP	National Adaptation Plan
NDC	Nationally Determined Contribution
NEAFC	North-east Atlantic Fisheries Commission
NGO	Non-governmental Organization
NIEO	New International Economic Order
nm	nautical miles
NOWPAP	Northwest Pacific Action Plan
NWP	Nairobi Work Programme on Impacts, Vulnerability, and Adaptation to Climate Change
OCIMF	Oil Companies International Marine Forum
OECM	Other Effective Area-Based Conservation Measure
OPAGAC	Organization of Associated Producers of Large Tuna Freezers
OPOL	Offshore Pollution Liability Association

OPRC	International Convention on Oil Pollution Preparedness, Response and Co-operation
OSPAR	Convention for the Protection of the Marine Environment of the North-East Atlantic
PCASP	Privately Contracted Armed Security Personnel
PCBs	polychlorinated biphenyls
PET	polyethylene terephthalate
PIF	Pacific Islands Forum
PSMA	Port State Measures Agreement
ReCAAP	Regional Cooperation Agreement on Combating Piracy and Armed Robbery against Ships in Asia
REMP	Regional Environment Management Plan
RFMO	Regional Fisheries Management Organization
RMP	Research and Monitoring Plan
RO	Recognized Organization
ROPME	Regional Organization of the Protection of the Marine Environment
RSCAPs	Regional Seas Conventions and Action Plans
RSE	Regulatory Scoping Exercise
RSRMPA	Ross Sea Region Marine Protected Area
SAMOA	SIDS Accelerated Modalities of Action
SAR	Search and Rescue
SBSTA	Subsidiary Body for Scientific and Technological Advice
SDC	Seabed Disputes Chamber
SDGs	Sustainable Development Goals
SEA	Strategic Environmental Assessment
SIDS	Small Island Developing States
SOISS	South Orkney Islands Southern Shelf
SOLAS	International Convention for the Safety of Life at Sea
SPAMI	Specially Protected Areas of Mediterranean Importance
SPLOS	States Parties to the United Nations Convention on the Law of the Sea
SRFC	Sub-regional Fisheries Commission
SRM	The 1994 San Remo Manual on International Law Applicable to Armed Conflicts at Sea
STS	Ship-to-Ship
SUA	Suppression of Unlawful Acts against the Safety of Maritime Navigation (Convention)
TCC	Technical Cooperation Committee (IMO)
TED	Turtle Excluder Device
TRIPS	Trade-related Aspects of Intellectual Property Rights (Agreement)
UDHR	Universal Declaration of Human Rights
UI	Unified Interpretation
UMS	Unmanned Marine Ships
UN	United Nations
UNEA	United Nations Environment Assembly
UNEP	United Nations Environment Programme
UNESCO	United Nations Educational, Scientific and Cultural Organization
UNFCC	United Nations Framework Convention on Climate Change
UNGA	United Nations General Assembly
UNHCR	United Nations High Commissioner for Refugees
UNICPOLOS	UN Informal Consultative Process on Oceans and the Law of the Sea

UNODC	United Nations Office on Drugs and Crime
VCLT	Vienna Convention on the Law of Treaties
VCLTIO	Vienna Convention on the Law of Treaties between States and International Organizations or between International Organizations
VGCDS	Voluntary Guidelines for Catch Documentation Scheme
VGFSP	Voluntary Guidelines for Flag State Performance
VGMFG	Voluntary Guidelines for the Marking of Fishing Gear
VME	Vulnerable Marine Ecosystem
VMS	Vessel Monitoring System
WCPFC	Western and Central Pacific Fisheries Commission
WIM	Warsaw International Mechanism for Loss and Damage Associated with Climate Change Impacts

Notes on Contributors

Editor

Dr Natalie Klein is a Professor at UNSW Sydney's Faculty of Law and Justice, Australia, and an Australian Research Council Future Fellow. Natalie is also currently President of the Australian Branch of the International Law Association. She was previously at Macquarie University where she served as Dean of Macquarie Law School (2011–17), as well as Acting Head of the Department for Policing, Intelligence and Counter-Terrorism at Macquarie (2013–14). Natalie has been a visiting fellow at the Lauterpacht Centre for International Law at Cambridge University, a non-resident Fellow at the Lakshman Kadirgamar Institute in Sri Lanka and MacCormick Fellow at the University of Edinburgh. Prior to joining Macquarie, Natalie worked in the international litigation and arbitration practice of Debevoise & Plimpton LLP, served as counsel to the Government of Eritrea (1998–2002) and was a consultant in the Office of Legal Affairs at the United Nations. Her masters and doctorate in law were earned at Yale Law School and she is a Fellow of the Australian Academy of Law.

Contributors

Tutku Bektaş holds a Bachelor of Arts (Jurisprudence) from the University of Oxford as an Ahmet Ertegun Scholar, and a Master of Laws (International Legal Studies) from New York University School of Law. She is called to the Bar of England and Wales as an Astbury Scholar of the Honourable Society of Middle Temple, and is a member of the New York State Bar. Upon being appointed to an NYU International Law and Human Rights Fellowship, Tutku Bektaş assisted Dr Nilufer Oral during the 70th session of the International Law Commission. She also worked at the international arbitration department of an international law firm in Paris, the United Nations Office of Legal Affairs and the Centre for International Law (CIL) in the National University of Singapore.

Dr Tara Davenport holds a Bachelor of Laws from the London School of Economics, a Master of Laws (Maritime Law) from the National University of Singapore (NUS), and a Master of Laws and Doctor of Juridical Science from Yale Law School. She is a recipient of a Fulbright scholarship, as well as an NUS Overseas Graduate Scholarship. She is currently an Assistant Professor at NUS, where she teaches Principles of Property Law, Law of the Sea, and International Regulation of Shipping. She is also a Senior Research Fellow at the Centre for International Law (CIL) at NUS, Deputy Director of the Asia-Pacific Centre for Environmental Law (APCEL), member of the Executive Council of the Asian Society of International Law, and a member of the editorial boards of the *Asian Journal of International Law* and *Ocean Development and International Law*. She is co-rapporteur for the International Law Association's Committee on Submarine Cables and Pipelines, and was a member of the Legal Working Group on Deep Seabed Mining Liability. Her research interests are in public international law, law of the sea, marine environmental law, and international dispute settlement.

Ellen Hey is Professor of Public International Law at Erasmus School of Law, Erasmus University Rotterdam; Adjunct Professor at the Norwegian Centre for the Law of the Sea (NCLOS), at the School of Law of UiT–The Arctic University of Norway; and Advisor to the Centre for Environmental Law and Policy (CELP) at the University of Colombo, Sri Lanka.

Yurika Ishii is Associate Professor at the National Defense Academy of Japan. Her areas of interest include general public international law, the law of the sea, and international and transnational criminal law. She has participated in projects of the United Nations Office on Drugs and Crime, Global Maritime Crime Programme since 2018. Her recent writings include 'Relevant Coasts and Relevant Area in the Maritime Delimitation of the EEZ and Continental Shelf' (2020) 51(4) *Ocean Development & International Law* and *Japanese Maritime Security and Law of The Sea* (Brill 2022). She achieved an LLB from the University of Tokyo, Faculty of Law, an LLM from Cornell Law School, and a PhD from the University of Tokyo, Graduate Schools for Laws and Politics, with a thesis on international regulation of economic crimes, which was published in Japanese as *International Regulation of Transnational Crimes* (Yuhikaku 2017).

Ambassador Marie Jacobsson is the Principal Legal Adviser on International Law at the Ministry for Foreign Affairs, Stockholm. She holds a doctoral degree in international law from Lund University, Sweden. She was a member of the United Nations International Law Commission from 2007 to 2016, and ILC's Special Rapporteur for the protection of the environment in relation to armed conflicts from 2013 to 2016. Her reports are available at http://legal.un.org/ilc/. The focus of her work at the Ministry for Foreign Affairs is on international peace and security matters, including the law of the sea. She has extensive experience of high-level multilateral and bilateral negotiations. In 2016, she was appointed Special Representative for Inclusive Peace Process. Her present assignments include designation as arbitrator under Permanent Court of Arbitration, United Nations Convention on the Law of the Sea, the Protocol on Environmental Protection to the Antarctic Treaty, and as alternate arbitrator at the Court of Conciliation and Arbitration within the OSCE.

Elsa Kelly is a former judge at the International Tribunal for the Law of the Sea (from 2011 to 2020). She was the first woman to be appointed to the tribunal. Judge Elsa Kelly previously worked as a career diplomat in the Argentine Foreign Service, and held several positions, including Member and Deputy Head of Delegation to the Third United Nations Conference on the Law of the Sea, Legal Advisor at the Ministry for Foreign Affairs of Argentina, Member of the Higher Council of Ambassadors, Director of Cultural Relations, Director General of Environmental Affairs, Deputy Minister for Foreign Affairs, Ambassador to UNESCO, to Italy, and to Austria. Judge Kelly is the author of articles on public international law, the law of the sea, nuclear non-proliferation, and other related issues, and has been Professor of Jurisprudence and Full Professor of Public International Law at the University of Buenos Aires, and at Argentina's Instituto del Servicio Exterior de la Nación. She has been awarded decorations from Mexico, Ecuador, and the Palmes Académiques from France.

Chie Kojima is a Professor of International Law at the Faculty of Law, Chuo University, Tokyo. She holds bachelor's and master's degrees, and a PhD, in law from Chuo University, and an LLM and a JSD from Yale University. She previously served as a Professor of International Law at Musashino University in Tokyo, an Assistant Professor of Maritime Law and Policy at World Maritime University in Malmö, and a Senior Research Fellow at the Max Planck Institute for Comparative Public Law and International Law in Heidelberg. Her recent publications focus on the protection of the marine environment, maritime security, and human rights at sea. She is a member of the editorial boards of *Ocean Development and International Law* (ODIL), the *Asia-Pacific Journal of Ocean Law and Policy* (APJOLP), and *The Law & Practice of International Courts and Tribunals* (LPICT).

Dr **Liesbeth Lijnzaad** is a judge at the International Tribunal for the Law of the Sea (ITLOS, Hamburg), elected in 2017. She is a member of the Permanent Court of Arbitration, and of the San Remo Institute of International Humanitarian Law. Professor Dr Lijnzaad is also endowed professor in Practice of International Law at Maastricht University in the Netherlands. She is a former Legal Adviser of the Netherlands Ministry of Foreign Affairs and head of its international law department (2006–2017).

Nilüfer Oral is Director of the Centre of International Law at the National University of Singapore. She is a member of the UN International Law Commission, and co-chair of the Study Group on sea level rise in relation to international law. She served as climate change negotiator for the Turkish Foreign Ministry. She has also appeared before the International Tribunal for the Law of the Sea. Dr Oral served on the IUCN Council, was co-chair of the IUCN-WCEL Oceans Specialist Groups and currently serves as a member of the WCEL Steering Committee. She is a Distinguished Fellow of the Law of the Sea Institute at UC Berkeley Law. Dr Oral is on the editorial board of several international law journals, and has published numerous articles, edited several books, and spoken at many international conferences.

Professor **Irini Papanicolopulu** (PhD, University of Milan) is Associate Professor of International Law at the University of Milano-Bicocca (Italy). She has previously held academic positions in the UK—at the University of Glasgow, and the University of Oxford—and has worked as a lawyer for the Italian Ministry of the Environment, and a multinational company. Professor Papanicolopulu conducts research and has published widely in international law, including, among others, the law of the sea, delimitation of maritime boundaries, environmental law, international humanitarian law, human rights law, and the protection of cultural heritage. She has published widely in international journals, is the author of two monographs, including *International Law and the Protection of People at Sea* (OUP 2018), and has co-edited several volumes, including *Gender and the Law of the Sea* (Brill 2019).

Anna Petrig holds the Chair of International Law and Public Law at the University of Basel in Switzerland. She has a PhD in the field of the law of the sea and human rights law, and an LLM from Harvard Law School. Anna is a member of the Bar of the Canton of Berne (Switzerland) and the New York State Bar (USA). Her broad legal experience includes work in private practice, the courts, and the Legal Division of the International Committee of the Red Cross (ICRC). She has provided expert advice and legal counsel on maritime-related matters to the Swiss Government, NGOs, and international organizations, and was involved in the International Maritime Organization's efforts to regulate autonomous ships. Since 2019, Anna has served as judge ad hoc for Switzerland on the International Tribunal for the Law of the Sea (ITLOS), in cases 27 and 29.

Rosemary Rayfuse is Emeritus Scientia Professor in the Faculty of Law and Justice at UNSW Sydney. Her research focuses on the law of the sea, protection of the marine environment in areas beyond national jurisdiction, and the normative effects of climate change on international law. She has special expertise in high seas fisheries, climate change and the oceans, and polar oceans governance, areas in which she has published widely. She is a Fellow of the Academy of Social Sciences in Australia, a member of the IUCN Commission on Environmental Law, and Chair's Nominee on the International Law Association's Committee on International Law and Sea Level Rise.

Zoe Scanlon has advised on public international law, including the law of the sea, for a number of years, in the Office of International Law at the Australian Attorney-General's Department. Zoe has also worked as a legal consultant at the United Nations Food and Agriculture Organization, based in Rome, advising states on the implementation of various fisheries treaties. Prior to this, she worked as a research associate at the Centre for International Law at the National University of Singapore, where her research and teaching focused on law of the sea and environmental law. Zoe has also taught public international law at the Australian National University, and worked as legal adviser to the chairperson of a regional fisheries management organization. Zoe holds an LLM (specializing in public international law) from the University of Sydney, for which she was awarded the Nancy Gordon-Smith Postgraduate Prize for Most Proficient Candidate. Zoe also holds Bachelor of Arts and Bachelor of Laws degrees from the University of Melbourne, and is a graduate of the Rhodes Academy of Oceans Law and Policy.

Karen N Scott is a Professor of Law at the University of Canterbury in New Zealand, President of the Australian and New Zealand Society of International Law (ANZSIL), and editor-in-chief of *Ocean Development and International Law* (ODIL). Karen is on the board of seven journals, including the *Brill Research Perspectives on the Law of the Sea* and the *Australian Yearbook of International Law*. She researches and teaches in the areas of public international law, law of the sea, and international environmental law. Karen has published over seventy edited books, journal articles, and book chapters in these areas. Karen is a university proctor, and was Head of the School of Law at the University of Canterbury between 2015 and 2018. She previously taught at the University of Nottingham, in the UK.

Dr **Zhen Sun** is a Research Officer at the WMU-Sasakawa Global Ocean Institute, World Maritime University, in Malmö, Sweden. She is the co-principal investigator on multiple research and capacity-building programmes. Her main research interests include the law of the sea, regulation of international shipping, gender equality and the law of the sea, ocean governance, and the protection of the marine environment. Prior to joining WMU, Zhen was a Research Fellow at the Centre for International Law (CIL), National University of Singapore. Zhen has lectured for undergraduate and postgraduate students, as well as government officials and practitioners. She has contributed to the editorial work of several book projects, and published journal articles, book chapters, and reports on various topics. Zhen received her law degrees from Hainan University, China University of Political Science and Law, the University of Edinburgh, and the University of Cambridge.

Erika Techera is a professor at The University of Western Australia Law School, and a member of the UWA Oceans Institute. She specializes in international and comparative environmental law, with a particular focus on Indo-Pacific oceans governance. Her research explores marine pollution law, fisheries regulation, marine-protected areas, ocean conservation frameworks, maritime heritage, and marine-based tourism law. Erika's current projects include ongoing work on shark conservation, legal frameworks for mangrove and kelp protection and restoration, and compliance and enforcement of heritage law. Erika is the lead co-editor of the *Routledge Handbook of International Environmental Law* (2021) and *Marine Extremes: Ocean Safety, Marine Health and the Blue Economy* (Routledge 2019). She is a Fellow of the Australian Academy of Law, and is Australia's national focal point on the Indian Ocean Rim Association (IORA) Academic Group.

Anastasia Telesetsky is a professor at California State University-San Luis Opisbo (Cal Poly), where she teaches environmental law in the Department of Natural Resources and Environmental Science. She previously taught at University of Idaho College of Law and University of Auckland. She is a member of the IUCN's World Commission on Environmental Law, and is an editorial board member on the *Asia Pacific Journal of Ocean Law and Policy*. She has contributed chapters to, and co-edited, several books, including *Comparative and Global Environmental Law and Policy* (Aspen Publishers, 2019), the *Routledge Handbook on International Environmental Law* (2021), and *Ecological Restoration and International Environmental Law* (Routledge, 2016).

Seline Trevisanut has been Professor of International Law and Sustainability at Utrecht University School of Law since 2018. Before joining Utrecht in 2012, as Marie Skłodowska-Curie Fellow, she taught and conducted research in various institutions, including Columbia University, the European University Institute, and UC Berkeley. Her publications include a monograph on *Irregular Migration by Sea in International and EU Law* (Jovene 2012, in Italian), and edited volumes, inter alia, on *Migration in the Mediterranean: Mechanism of International Cooperation* (CUP 2015) and *Regime Interaction in Ocean Governance: Problems, Theories and Methods* (Brill 2020).

Editorial Assistants

Millicent McCreath is a Scientia PhD candidate and Teaching Fellow at the UNSW Sydney Faculty of Law and Justice. She was previously a research associate with the Oceans Law and Policy programme at the National University of Singapore Centre for International Law. In 2016, Millicent was Tipstaff (judicial clerk) at the Land and Environment Court of New South Wales. Millicent has a BA (Environmental Studies)/LLB (Hons) from UNSW and LLM (Law of the Sea) from UiT–The Arctic University of Norway.

Priscilla Rivas is a PhD candidate at the UNSW Sydney Faculty of Law and Justice. In 2018, she was an intern in the Fisheries Policy, Economics and Institutions Branch at the Food and Agriculture Organization. Priscilla holds a master's degree in Marine Affairs from the University of Washington, where she conducted a research project with the National Oceanic and Atmospheric Administration, and a BA (Marine Affairs/Environmental Science and Policy) from the University of Miami.

PART I
INTRODUCTION

1

Meaning, Scope, and Significance of Informal Lawmaking in the Law of the Sea

Natalie Klein

1.1 Introduction

Accounts of international law properly focus on formal sources of law, particularly treaties and customary international law, and the formation and operation of these laws. Yet, we must also acknowledge that the conduct of actors in the international sphere is influenced, to differing degrees, by what are variously described as 'gentleman's agreements',[1] soft law,[2] or informal agreements.[3] Studies of what law is, and from whence it comes, are vast in number and perspective. Some of these studies have assessed the perennial question of whether international law is law, and how it is formed. Within these analyses, attention has been brought to bear on different types of agreements that are concluded to set the expectations of those participants as to how certain issues will be addressed. If one sits within a school of thought that there is no international 'law', then there is no need to parse the question of what is and is not 'law' or a 'legal agreement' in the international system. The studies in this book assume that international law exists, but also acknowledge that the forms of international agreements that modulate state conduct are not all the same. It is possible to distinguish between legal/non-legal, hard/soft, binding/non-binding, formal/informal in seeking to describe different agreements, although these distinctions are not always completely binary. Some differentiation is necessary to account for what can readily be observed across many areas of international law.[4] Our purpose is to understand this practice within the law of the sea. For reasons to be explained in this chapter, we refer to such practice as informal lawmaking in the law of the sea.

Both formal and informal sources of law exist within the law of the sea. The modern law of the sea is based firmly in a treaty commonly referred to as 'a constitution of the oceans':[5]

[1] Eg, Michael Bothe, 'Legal and Non-legal Norms—A Meaningful Distinction in International Relations' (1980) 11 NYIL 65, 68; Oscar Schachter, 'The Twilight Existence of Nonbinding International Agreements' (1977) 71(2) AJIL 296, 299. In 2010, Shaffer and Pollack referred to a 'gentleman's club—or epistemic community': Gregory C Shaffer and Mark A Pollack, 'Hard vs. Soft Law: Alternatives, Complements, and Antagonists in International Governance' (2010) 94(3) Minn L Rev 706, 757.

[2] Eg, Christine M Chinkin, 'The Challenge of Soft Law: Development and Change in International Law' (1989) 38(4) ICLQ 850; Pierre-Marie Dupuy, 'Soft Law and the International Law of the Environment' (1991) 12(1) Mich J Intl L 420; Alan Boyle, 'Some Reflections on the Relationship of Treaties and Soft Law' (1999) 48(4) ICLQ 901.

[3] Eg, Anthony Aust, 'The Theory and Practice of Informal International Instruments' (1986) 35(4) ICLQ 787; Charles Lipson, 'Why are some International Agreements Informal?' (1991) 45(5) Intl'l Org 495.

[4] Boyle, 'Some Reflections' (n 2) 901.

[5] Elisabeth Mann Borgese, 'A Constitution for the Oceans' in Elisabeth Mann Borgese and David Krieger (eds), *The Tides of Change: Peace, Pollution and the Potential of the Oceans* (Mason/Charter 1975) 340. See also Alan Boyle, 'Further Development of the Law of the Sea Convention: Mechanisms for Change' (2005) 54(3) ICLQ 563, 566.

Natalie Klein, *Meaning, Scope, and Significance of Informal Lawmaking in the Law of the Sea* In: *Unconventional Lawmaking in the Law of the Sea*. Edited by: Natalie Klein, Oxford University Press. © Natalie Klein 2022. DOI: 10.1093/oso/9780192897824.003.0001

the UN Convention on the Law of the Sea (LOSC or Convention).[6] It was preceded by four earlier treaties,[7] and has been complemented by two additional treaties,[8] with a third potentially on the way.[9] In addition, there is a vast array of multilateral, regional, and bilateral treaties that regulate different aspects of ocean use. While the LOSC has attracted approximately 170 parties, states also argue that the Convention largely reflects customary international law.[10] This book, therefore, starts from a place that the law of the sea is a highly legalized area where these formal sources of law significantly influence state decision-making for activities occurring over 70% of the Earth's surface.

Yet, it is also readily evident, as this book demonstrates, that informal lawmaking is occurring in relation to many different aspects of the law of the sea. Examples of these informal agreements include the Djibouti Code of Conduct on the repression of piracy and armed robbery,[11] the Food and Agriculture Organization's suite of International Plans of Action to enhance management of living marine resources,[12] and the Code for Unplanned Encounters at Sea, which is intended to improve the navigational safety of military vessels and aircraft.[13] Within the International Maritime Organization (IMO), a variety of instruments have been adopted beyond international conventions, and may include circulars, guidelines, or recommendations. For example, the IMO adopted Guidelines on the Treatment of Persons Rescued at Sea that elaborate on obligations found in the International Convention for the Safety of Life at Sea, and the International Convention on Maritime

[6] United Nations Convention on the Law of the Sea (adopted 10 December 1982, entered into force 16 November 1994) 1833 UNTS 3 (hereafter 'LOSC').

[7] Convention on the Territorial Sea and the Contiguous Zone (adopted 29 April 1958, entered into force 10 September 1964) 516 UNTS 205; Convention on the High Seas (adopted 29 April 1958, entered into force 30 September 1962) 450 UNTS 11; Convention on the Continental Shelf (adopted 29 April 1958, entered into force 10 June 1964) 499 UNTS 311; Convention on Fishing and Conservation of the Living Resources of the High Seas (adopted 29 April 1958, entered into force 26 September 1968) 559 UNTS 285.

[8] Agreement relating to the Implementation of Part XI of the United Nations Convention on the Law of the Sea of 10 December 1982 (adopted 28 July 1994, entered into force 28 July 1996) 1836 UNTS 3; Agreement for the Implementation of the Provisions of the United Nations Convention on the Law of the Sea of 10 December 1982 Relating to the Conservation and Management of Straddling Fish Stocks and Highly Migratory Fish Stocks (adopted 4 August 1995, entered into force 11 December 2001) 2167 UNTS 3.

[9] UNGA Res 72/249, 'International legally binding instrument under the United Nations Convention on the Law of the Sea on the conservation and sustainable use of marine biological diversity of areas beyond national jurisdiction' (24 December 2017) UN Doc A/RES/72/249.

[10] The United States has taken this position: 'United States Ocean Policy', Statement by the President (10 March 1983) <https://www.gc.noaa.gov/documents/031083-reagan_ocean_policy.pdf> accessed 12 July 2021.

[11] IMO, 'Code of Conduct concerning the Repression of Piracy and Armed Robbery against Ships in the Western Indian Ocean and the Gulf of Aden' (29 January 2009) IMO Doc C.102/14 (hereafter 'Djibouti Code of Conduct'). For the text of the Djibouti Code of Conduct see <https://au.int/sites/default/files/documents/30848-doc-djibouti_code_of_conduct_0.pdf> accessed 18 July 2021. The Djibouti Code of Conduct was subsequently updated by the 'Jeddah Amendment': IMO, 'Revised Code of Conduct Concerning the Repression of Piracy, Armed Robbery against Ships and Illicit Maritime Activity in the Western Indian Ocean and the Gulf of Aden Area' (12 January 2017) <https://wwwcdn.imo.org/localresources/en/OurWork/Security/Documents/A2%20Revised%20Code%20Of%20Conduct%20Concerning%20The%20Repression%20Of%20Piracy%20Armed%20Robbery%20Against%20Ships%20Secretariat.pdf> accessed 19 July 2021 (hereafter 'Jeddah Amendment'). See, further, Jacobsson and Klein, in Chapter 3 of this volume.

[12] See, eg FAO, 'International Plan of Action for Conservation and Management of Sharks' (Rome, 1999) <www.fao.org/docrep/006/x3170e/x3170e03.htm> accessed 19 July 2021; FAO, 'International Plan of Action to Prevent, Deter, and Eliminate Illegal, Unreported and Unregulated Fishing' (Rome, 2001) <www.fao.org/fishery/ipoa-iuu/en> accessed 19 July 2021. Boyle has noted, in relation to the Code of Conduct on Responsible Fishing and the International Plan of Action on Illegal, Unreported and Unregulated Fishing, that 'in part they reiterate, interpret and amplify relevant provisions of UNCLOS and the 1995 Fish Stocks Agreement': Boyle, 'Further Development' (n 5) 572. See, further, Scanlon, in Chapter 11 of this volume.

[13] Western Pacific Naval Symposium, 'Code for Unplanned Encounters at Sea: Version 1.0' (22 April 2014) <http://www.ions.global/sites/default/files/CUES-10-Approvedat-the-14th-WPNS-2014422.pdf> accessed 20 July 2021. See, further, Klein, in Chapter 8 of this volume.

Search and Rescue.[14] The International Court of Justice (ICJ) has, arguably, utilized informal law in cases concerning the law of the sea.[15] This practice might be drawn from reference to 'elementary considerations of humanity' in the *Corfu Channel* case,[16] reliance on 'evolving law during LOSC negotiations' in *Libya /Tunisia Continental Shelf*,[17] or reference to 'equitable principles' in other maritime delimitation cases.[18]

It can, further, be observed that, while states remain key actors in the law of the sea, there are diverse organizations, groups, companies, and individuals who are also seeking to shape the standards that regulate actions at sea. The International Renewable Energy Agency, for example, collaborates with relevant professional associations to develop standards of operation for offshore renewable energy devices.[19] Expert scientific advice is used to establish Ecologically or Biologically Sensitive Areas at the regional level, pursuant to the framework in the Convention on Biological Diversity.[20] The Marine Stewardship Council's certification incentivizes changes to fishing practices to align with the Food and Agriculture Organization's (FAO) Code of Conduct for Responsible Fishing.[21] Informal lawmaking is considered as a primary mechanism for non-state actors to influence the development of international agreements,[22] especially when compared to the secondary roles accorded to such actors during treaty negotiations.[23]

These developments have significance for the law of the sea for several reasons. First, one of the interesting dimensions of informal lawmaking is its interaction with formal international law.[24] It is necessary to ask whether these efforts at informal lawmaking have relevance for the interpretation and application of the LOSC. Second, the Convention is deliberately drafted as a framework agreement, in some respects, notably Part XII dealing with the marine environment, with the intention that elaboration would occur outside the treaty. References to 'generally agreed international rules and standards' further underline the relevance of informal lawmaking for the interpretation and application of the LOSC. Third, informal lawmaking has an important role in creating and sharing expectations around state conduct at sea. For example, as states are to be held responsible for failing

[14] IMO, 'Guidelines on the Treatment of Persons Rescued at Sea' (20 May 2004) IMO Res MSC.167(78). See, further, Papanicolopulu, in Chapter 4 of this volume.

[15] Eg, Günther F Handl and others, 'A Hard Look at Soft Law' (1988) 82 ASILPROC 371, 374 (comments of Reisman); Bothe (n 1) 87; Francesco Francioni, 'International "Soft Law": a Contemporary Assessment' in Vaughan Lowe and Malgosia Fitzmaurice (eds), *Fifty Years of the International Court of Justice: Essays in Honour of Sir Robert Jennings* (CUP 1996) 167, 169.

[16] *Corfu Channel Case (UK v Albania)* (Merits) [1949] ICJ Rep 4, 22.

[17] *Case Concerning the Continental Shelf (Tunisia/Libyan Arab Jamahiriya)* (Judgment) [1982] ICJ Rep 18, para 46.

[18] It is arguable that the ICJ uses informal law because it may, instead, be posited that the ICJ is relying on general principles of law, as permitted under Article 38(1)(c) of the ICJ's Statute. It should also be noted that the Court was expressly authorized to refer to the LOSC negotiations in the Special Agreement between Libya and Tunisia. See Bothe (n 1) 87.

[19] See Trevisanut, in Chapter 9 of this volume.

[20] See Scott, in Chapter 16 of this volume.

[21] See Telesetsky, in Chapter 14 of this volume.

[22] See Sanderijn Duquet and others, 'Upholding the Rule of Law in Informal International Lawmaking Processes' (2014) 6(1) HJRL 75.

[23] Non-state actors may be able to participate in treaty negotiations as members of state delegations, or may be granted observer status. This level of engagement is dependent on the discretion of states. See Sun, in Chapter 6 of this volume.

[24] Note that Shaffer and Pollack consider that the relationship between these two forms of law can be 'antagonistic', depending on the motivations of the actors in relying on each sort of agreement, and the regime complex in which they are operating. See, generally, Shaffer and Pollack (n 1) 737.

to exercise due diligence, in some instances,[25] it must be considered whether informal agreements may be used to benchmark what diligence is required. Fourth, with increasing pressures on ocean governance in relation to sustainable development, maritime security concerns, 'blue justice', and ocean health, can informal lawmaking provide a (better) means for cooperation to address these pressing matters?

This chapter elaborates on the above issues, and aims to situate the specific studies that follow in this book. Sections 1.2 and 1.3 explore the meaning of informal law and informal lawmaking, respectively, particularly in distinction to what is commonly known as formal international law. Section 1.4 highlights the participants involved in informal lawmaking, and their relevance to this process. Section 1.5 considers the output or form that informal lawmaking may take and, hence, the possible normative value of this activity in the law of the sea. Section 1.6 draws out the possible significance of informal lawmaking for the law of the sea. It is this last dimension—why, or to what extent, informal lawmaking in the law of the sea matters—that is a core question that the authors seek to answer throughout this book.

1.2 What is Informal Law?

Within international law, including the law of the sea, formal law is primarily derived from the sources set out in Article 38 of the ICJ's Statute: treaties, customary international law, and general principles of law. A treaty is defined in the Vienna Convention on the Law of Treaties as 'an international agreement concluded between states in written form and governed by international law, whether embodied in a single instrument or in two or more related instruments and whatever its particular designation'.[26] As a treaty is 'governed by international law', this criterion reflects that the treaty is to be considered as binding as a matter of international law.[27] The LOSC clearly falls within this definition, as do a plethora of other international agreements relevant to ocean governance.

Agreements that are not treaties have been variously labelled as soft law, non-binding agreements, non-legal agreements, informal law, and informal agreements. Debate has arisen as to the content, meaning, and utility of 'soft law'.[28] Reisman has observed that '[t]he adjective "soft", when used to modify the word "law", brings to mind the adverb "slightly", when used to modify the word "pregnant"'.[29] Nonetheless, in the international system, informal agreements create shared expectations as to the standard of conduct in relation to specific international issues. The characteristics of informal agreements include that they augment international cooperation, are not binding as law, and lack any formal mechanisms to review or monitor conduct under the agreement; they may reflect long-term programmes or visions, and their substance may be vague or aspirational, and they may include ready options to amend, change, or exit the arrangement in the future. Informal agreements

[25] See, eg *South China Sea Arbitration (Philippines v China)* (Award of 12 July 2016) PCA Case No 2013-19, paras 962–66.

[26] Vienna Convention on the Law of Treaties (adopted 23 May 1969, entered into force 27 January 1980) 1155 UNTS 331, art 2(1)(a) (hereafter 'VCLT').

[27] Aust (n 3) 795 (referring to ILC commentary in the preparatory texts for the Vienna Convention).

[28] These views are summarized in Francioni (n 15) 168, and in Shaffer and Pollack (n 1) 717–27. See also Handl and others (n 15) 371 (comments of Handl).

[29] W Michael Reisman, 'Soft Law and Law Jobs' (2011) 2(1) JIDS 25, 26.

will vary across these characteristics:[30] for example, some may be precise and create monitoring systems, but remain clear that the agreement is not to be legally binding.

The advantages of informal law have been usefully summarized by Shaffer and Pollack as follows:

- Soft-law instruments are easier and less costly to negotiate.
- Soft-law instruments impose lower 'sovereignty costs' on states in sensitive areas.
- Soft-law instruments provide greater flexibility for states to cope with uncertainty and learn over time.
- Soft-law instruments allow states to be more ambitious and engage in 'deeper' cooperation than they would if they had to worry about enforcement.
- Soft-law instruments cope better with diversity.
- Soft-law instruments are directly available to non-state actors, including international secretariats, state administrative agencies, sub-state public officials, and business associations and non-governmental organizations.[31]

Disagreement may arise as to whether an agreement is formal law or not. In both categories, there are many variations with respect to names, form, and substance. Memoranda of Understanding (MoU), for example, vary in practice as to whether they are legally binding agreements or not. The distinction may not be Manichean, as between formal and informal, or treaty and not a treaty, as some commentators suggest that there is a continuum of informal agreements.[32] The term 'agreement' still captures the manifestation of consent to cooperate in a designated way in relation to a particular area.[33] As will be manifest in the studies in this book, the legal nature and relevance of agreements will vary.

A treaty may be more likely to set out the rights and duties of states with precision,[34] offering the parties clear requirements on what steps must be taken to comply with the terms of the agreement. Treaties do, though, also contain hortatory provisions, where the language may be less precise or less prescriptive, and merely indicate what the aspirations of the parties are in relation to a specific issue. The LOSC contains such provisions, as may be seen in Part XIV on development and transfer of marine technology.[35] Aspirational provisions in treaties are sometimes termed as 'soft law'.[36] However, Raustiala persuasively argues that such provisions should, instead, be viewed as shallow commitments that might render

[30] Chinkin observes there will be 'many variables in form, language, subject matter, participants, addressees, purposes, follow-up and monitoring procedures': Chinkin, 'The Challenge of Soft Law' (n 2) 850. See also Kal Raustiala, 'Form and Substance in International Agreements' (2005) 99(3) AJIL 581, 592–93; Christine Chinkin, 'Normative Development in the International Legal System' in Dinah Shelton (ed), *Commitment and Compliance: The Role of Non-binding Norms in the International Legal System* (OUP 2000) 21, 28.

[31] Shaffer and Pollack (n 1) 719. See also Kenneth W Abbott and Duncan Snidal, 'Hard and Soft Law in International Governance' (2000) 54(3) Intl'l Org 421, 423; Lipson (n 3) 514–17; Boyle, 'Some Reflections' (n 2) 903.

[32] Abbott and Snidal (n 31) 422. See also, Davenport, in Chapter 10 of this volume.

[33] Guzman writes: 'International agreements are, at root, an exchange of promises among States. This is true whether they are full-blown treaties or merely statements of intent; whether they require wholesale changes to domestic practices or merely reflect existing behaviour; and whether or not they include provisions for enforcement.': Andrew T Guzman, 'The Design of International Agreements' (2005) 16(4) EJIL 579, 585.

[34] Abbott and Snidal (n 31) 422.

[35] States are to 'promote', or to 'endeavour' to meet, objectives associated with marine technology. See, eg LOSC (n 6), Arts 266(2), 266(3), 269, and 271. See Techera, in Chapter 13 of this volume.

[36] Boyle, 'Some Reflections' (n 2) 906–07.

the agreement less effective in its operation, but are still binding as treaty commitments.[37] These sorts of treaty provisions are considered as formal law for the purposes of this study; the study's focus is, instead, on informal law, that is agreements that reflect the parties' intent for, or expectation of, cooperation or alignment of behaviour in a designated way in relation to a specific issue, but which are legally non-binding.

1.3 Process of Informal Lawmaking

Informal lawmaking in international law involves the process of international cooperation to reach agreements (other than treaties) between public authorities, with or without the participation of private actors or international organizations, in varied institutions and networks.[38] This cooperation typically entails 'norm-setting or public policy making by public authorities', and, on this basis, warrants the description of 'lawmaking'.[39] What we are seeking to capture is the adoption and implementation of international agreements that affect the incentives and behaviour of states.[40] In line with the views of Lipson, '[i]nformality is best understood as a device for minimizing the impediments to cooperation, at both the domestic and international levels'.[41] As such, formalities traditionally expected in international lawmaking as to the type of agreement, the process by which it is produced, and who may be involved in reaching the agreement, or as targets of the agreement, may be dispensed with in the context of informal lawmaking.[42]

Informal lawmaking, as a process, allows for relevant actors to assemble and share expertise and information, learn more about an issue, and bargain on what standards of behaviour are acceptable, going forward, to address that issue. Without binding obligations, there may be greater scope to smooth over differences in legal traditions and accommodate more readily the nuances of domestic legal doctrine and legislative processes. This process may be undertaken in formal institutions, such as at the meetings of intergovernmental organizations, or may be organized on an ad hoc basis among concerned actors. Discussions on the LOSC could occur during the Meetings of the State Parties (SPLOS), which are organized pursuant to Article 319 of the Convention, but these meetings tend

[37] Raustiala (n 30) 589.

[38] 'Cross-border cooperation between public authorities, with or without the participation of private actors and/or international organizations, in a forum other than a traditional international organization (process informality), and/or as between actors other than traditional diplomatic actors (such as regulators or agencies) (actor informality) and/or which does not result in a formal treaty or other traditional source of international law (output informality).': Joost Pauwelyn, 'Informal International Lawmaking: Framing the Concept and Research Questions' in Joost Pauwelyn, Ramses Wessel, and Jan Wouters (eds), *Informal International Lawmaking* (OUP 2012) 22.

[39] Duquet and others (n 22) 83. Boyle has commented: 'There is at least an element of good faith commitment, and in many cases, a desire to influence State practice and an element of law-making intention and progressive development.' (Boyle, 'Some Reflections' (n 2) 902).

[40] See Guzman (n 33) 610. Guzman goes on to note that treaties and soft law should 'both be considered legal commitments with the potential to affect behaviour' (ibid 611). By contrast, Raustiala argues as follows: '[t]hat many nonbinding commitments ultimately influence State behavior illustrates the complexity of world politics, not the legal character of those commitments': Raustiala (n 30) 590.

[41] Lipson (n 3) 500.

[42] Joost Pauwelyn, Ramses Wessel, and Jan Wouters, 'Informal International Lawmaking: An Assessment and Template to Keep It Both Effective and Accountable' in Pauwelyn and others (eds), 'Informal International Lawmaking' (n 38) 500, 500.

to focus on administrative and budgetary matters rather than substantive issues.[43] The United Nations Open-ended Informal Consultative Process on Oceans and the Law of the Sea (UNICPOLOS) may, instead, consider substantive issues that emerge from the UN Secretary-General's annual report on ocean affairs and the law of the sea.

While the appeal of informal agreements is clear, difficulties do emerge with their development and use. These challenges include the lack of need to implement these agreements through domestic legislative processes, which may reduce the strength of commitment and adherence across a state's government, if various agencies are needed to conform to all aspects of the agreement.[44] There may be a lack of funding or public support for the commitments in informal agreements, domestically, without full implementation.[45] If the provisions within an informal agreement set nebulous standards, the parties involved may not be able to discern readily whether each party is acting consistently. This concern may be compounded in informal arrangements that lack a monitoring or verification mechanism, or have no form of sanctions for deviating from shared expectations. There must be willingness on the part of the relevant actors to engage in informal lawmaking, and to adhere to the standards agreed, when the outcome is not otherwise a set of binding obligations backed by sanctions.[46] Of course, these issues are not necessarily unique in all respects to informal agreements, but may be associated with international law more generally.

Despite these drawbacks, the emergence of increased informal lawmaking in the law of the sea may be explained by several factors. First, there is a strong disinclination among states to consider amending or renegotiating the LOSC. Instead, it remains the cornerstone of the law of the sea. Second, while states are not entirely averse to concluding new treaties addressing ocean issues, Pauwelyn and others have observed phenomena of treaty stagnation and treaty saturation.[47] More treaties and more international institutions are no longer the preferred responses to international concerns. Third, the increasing visibility and influence of non-state actors in international settings necessitates agreements that are more inclusive and transparent in their formation and operation.[48] Finally, the current multipolar political dynamics, and a diminished commitment to global cooperation by some powerful actors (notably the United States) in recent years reduces the probability of widespread agreement on a binding instrument being achieved.[49] Yet, complex problems still require multilateral solutions and informal lawmaking provides a viable option for setting out shared expectations on how to respond.

[43] UN DOALOS, 'Meetings of States Parties to the 1982 United Nations Convention on the Law of the Sea' <https://www.un.org/depts/los/meeting_states_parties/meeting_states_parties.htm> accessed 15 July 2021. See also Oral and Bektaş, in Chapter 17 of this volume.

[44] Abbott and Snidal (n 31) 446.

[45] Boyle, 'Some Reflections' (n 2) 903.

[46] Duquet and others (n 22) 83.

[47] Joost Pauwelyn, Ramses Wessel, and Jan Wouters, 'When Structures Become Shackles: Stagnation and Dynamics in International Lawmaking' (2014) 25 EJIL 738–40.

[48] ibid 741.

[49] The current negotiations for an international legally binding instrument on the conservation and sustainable use of marine biological diversity of areas beyond national jurisdiction remain a test case in this regard.

1.4 Participants in Informal Lawmaking

Informal lawmaking concerns not only the mechanics, substance, and form of the agreements, but also the actors involved in the process of reaching those agreements. Whereas treaties require the consent of a head of state or the executive government of a state,[50] informal agreements may allow for instruments to be adopted by different government officials and agencies. For example, the US Department of Defence and the Chinese Ministry of National Defense have concluded two legally non-binding MoUs that set standards to follow, in the event of air and maritime encounters, as well as establishing a notification mechanism.[51] The Australian Border Force also entered into an arrangement with the Indonesian Maritime Security Agency to improve cooperation in addressing shared maritime security concerns.[52]

The development of new cooperative measures and facilitation of information sharing may necessitate engagement of diverse actors, including shipping companies, seafarer unions, fishing vessels, scientific bodies, and conservation groups. This engagement with diverse stakeholders has been described as follows by Pauwelyn and others:

> This diverse network society has given rise to new actors and new forms or processes of co-operation, other than those traditionally recognized by international law. The State remains a pivotal entity of interest aggregation, legitimation, and control. Yet, it is supplemented, assisted, corrected, and continuously challenged by a variety of other actors ... Problem-solving in a complex knowledge/network society will require action beyond what States can shoulder. It needs pragmatic deliberation involving multiple sources of knowledge, experience, and control.[53]

A core advantage to an informal agreement is, thus, engagement with non-state actors who can contribute positively to information and understandings on which states rely in developing their views on how to deal with shared matters of concern.[54] Broad stakeholder participation enhances good governance through improved transparency, facilitation of

[50] VCLT (n 26) art 7 (listing the representatives with authority to represent and bind a state). See also Duquet and others (n 22) 81.

[51] Memorandum of Understanding between the Department of Defense of the United States of America and the Ministry of National Defense of the People's Republic of China Regarding the Rules of Behavior for Safety of Air and Maritime Encounters (9 and 10 November 2014) <https://archive.defense.gov/pubs/141112_MemorandumOfUnderstandingRegardingRules.pdf> accessed 15 July 2021; Memorandum of Understanding between the United States of America Department of Defense and the People's Republic of China Ministry of National Defense on Notification of Major Military Activities Confidence-building Measures Mechanism (31 October and 4 November 2014) <https://archive.defense.gov/pubs/141112_MemorandumOfUnderstandingOnNotification.pdf> accessed 15 July 2021. See Klein, in Chapter 8 of this volume.

[52] Arrangement between Badan Keamanan Laut Republik Indonesia (the Maritime Security Agency of the Republic of Indonesia) and the Department of Immigration and Border Protection as represented by the Australian Border Force on Maritime Security Cooperation (17 November 2017) cited in the Plan of Action for the Indonesia–Australia Comprehensive Strategic Partnership (2020–2024), 10 February 2020 <https://www.dfat.gov.au/geo/indonesia/Pages/plan-of-action-for-the-indonesia-australia-comprehensive-strategic-partnership-2020-2024> accessed 15 July 2021.

[53] Pauwelyn and others, 'When Structures Become Shackles' (n 47) 742 (citations omitted).

[54] Eg, the governance structure of the MoU on Sharks, adopted under the Convention on Migratory Species, which allows for the involvement of Cooperating Partners, including non-governmental organizations, an Advisory Committee for expert advice, and a Conservation Working Group comprised of shark advocates and marine biologists. See Erika J Techera and Natalie Klein, *The International Law of Sharks* (Brill 2017) 164.

information-sharing, distribution of responsibilities and accountabilities, and enhancement of cooperation.

Trevisanut has observed this shift in participation in relation to industry engagement in the offshore energy sector.[55] Both industry operators and professional associations have contributed to some standard setting, along with information sharing, and collaboration.[56] She further argues that any future global regulation will necessitate involvement of these stakeholders to facilitate implementation and compliance monitoring.[57] Nonetheless, in a setting where environmental concerns and worker safety must be balanced against economic imperatives, the need for states to have regulatory authority, and to set policy priorities, also remains important.[58]

An informal instrument might meet the demands of some actors for action but still preserve a certain amount of freedom for political elites in determining how they might respond to any process or new instrument.[59] In one such instance, states parties to the Convention on Migratory Species (CMS)[60] opted to adopt a non-binding Sharks MoU[61] among varied options available to implement the protection required under Article II of the CMS.[62] Although the non-governmental organizations involved in the discussions predominantly preferred a binding instrument, the vast majority of states in attendance favoured a non-binding instrument.[63] Ultimately, the advantages of a non-binding instrument were that it allowed for a more detailed set of conservation measures to be developed, conflict with existing binding instruments was reduced, and there was a greater expectation of developing broader acceptance among states over time.[64]

Informal agreements may not just be a salve for international civil society actors, but may also have this role in relation to less powerful states. The scope of informal lawmaking may, therefore, accommodate and satisfy diverse interests in formulating expectations around resolving concerns related to the oceans. In this regard, Pacific island states have adopted several non-binding instruments that purport to fix their baselines as a response to the problems posed by climate change and sea-level rise.[65] These developments reflect a collective and collaborative effort in the face of stalled action more broadly on climate change,

[55] Seline Trevisanut, 'The Role of Private Actors in Offshore Energy: Shifting Models of Participation' (2014) 29(4) IJMCL 645.

[56] ibid 657–60.

[57] ibid 662.

[58] ibid 663.

[59] Chinkin, 'Normative Development' (n 30) 41.

[60] Convention on the Conservation of Migratory Species of Wild Animals (adopted 23 June 1979, entered into force 1 November 1983) 1651 UNTS 333.

[61] CMS, 'Memorandum of Understanding on the Conservation of Migratory Sharks' (12 February 2010) <http://www.cms.int/sharks/en/page/sharks- -text> accessed 15 July 2021.

[62] See CMS, 'Meeting to Identify and Elaborate an Option for International Cooperation on Migratory Sharks Under the Convention on Migratory Species' (11–13 December 2007) UN Doc UNEP/CMS/MS1/Report, 2 <http://sharksmou.org/mahé-2007> accessed 20 July 2021.

[63] ibid para 105.

[64] For discussion, see generally Laura Muir and Natalie Klein, 'From IPOA Sharks to Sharks MoU under the Convention on Migratory Species: Progress or Clutter in International Environmental Law?' (2018) 21 JIWLP 190.

[65] Cristelle Pratt and Hugh Govan, 'Our Sea of Islands, Our Livelihoods, Our Oceania: Framework for a Pacific Oceanscape: A Catalyst for Implementation of Ocean Policy' (November 2010) <https://www.forumsec.org/wp-content/uploads/2018/03/Framework-for-a-Pacific-Oceanscape-2010.pdf> accessed 15 July 2021; Taputapuātea Declaration on Climate Change (Polynesian Leaders Group, 16 July 2015) <https://www.state.gov/wp-content/uploads/2019/03/248-Deep-Sea-Bed.pdf> accessed 15 July 2021; Delap Commitment on Securing our Common Wealth of Oceans (Parties to the Nauru Agreement, 2 March 2018) <https://www.pnatuna.com/sites/default/files/Delap%20Commitment_2nd%20PNA%20Leaders%20Summit.pdf> accessed 15 July 2021. See also Oral and Bektaş, in Chapter 17 of this volume.

but the question of whether regional customary law has developed based on this practice remains open.[66] As Chinkin observes, '[w]eaker States might promote a soft law instrument on matters of concern to themselves [and] realistically accept it as the best they can politically achieve and in the hope that it might gain greater force over time'.[67]

1.5 Outputs of Informal Lawmaking and their Normative Value

As noted above, the types and content of informal agreements produced may be highly varied. There are no specific issue areas that prohibit the use of informal lawmaking as a form of international cooperation, but commentators have observed that its use is more widespread in some areas compared to others.[68] The use of informal agreements has particularly been studied in relation to international economic law, arms control, and international environmental law.[69] While the law of the sea is heavily based on treaty and customary international law, informal agreements, as this book demonstrates, are also pervasive throughout the law of the sea.

The types of informal agreements reached between participants will depend on the goals sought to be achieved. In some instances, a broad statement of principles as to how an issue should be addressed, or the creation of aspirational goals, are important first steps in regulating an international concern. UN General Assembly resolutions calling for a global moratorium on large-scale pelagic drift net fishing may be seen through this lens.[70] In other instances, an informal agreement will seek to develop a consistency of approach across national policies or domestic implementation. An informal agreement may be very functional and focused on establishing a mechanism or other practical tools to respond to a matter of international concern, rather than necessarily creating standards against which any actor's behaviour should be measured.[71] In the creation of standards, the significance of the informal agreement may rest more in its practical value than in its normative impact. With some informal agreements, they may reflect all these purposes, given their scale and design. The Global Programme of Action for the Protection of the Marine Environment from Land-Based Activities may be considered to fall within this latter category.[72] The chapters in this volume reflect on the varied significance of informal lawmaking, when taking into account its many characteristics in any specific situation.

Cutting across the process of informal lawmaking, the different actors, and the variety of outputs, it is possible to discern within informal lawmaking what may be described as 'normative intent' and 'normative effect'. Normative intent could simply be understood as a

[66] See Karen N Scott, 'Climate Change and the Law of the Sea in the Asia Pacific' in Donald R Rothwell and David Letts (eds), *Law of the Sea in South East Asia: Environmental, Navigational and Security Challenges* (Routledge 2020) 94, 114–16. See, further, Oral and Bektaş, in Chapter 17 of this volume.

[67] Chinkin, 'Normative Development' (n 30) 34.

[68] Raustiala has observed that informal agreements ('pledges') tend to 'cluster' in certain areas: Raustiala (n 30) 595.

[69] See, eg Chinkin, 'The Challenge of Soft Law' (n 2); Dupuy (n 2); Bothe (n 1) 79–84.

[70] See Scanlon, in Chapter 11 of this volume.

[71] Techera suggests, in her chapter, that programs and projects focused on implementation and capacity building involve the application and use of law and, as such, are not informal lawmaking. See Techera, in Chapter 13 of this volume. Rayfuse also considers programmatic, rather than normative, activity. See Rayfuse, in Chapter 15 of this volume.

[72] See, further, Rayfuse, in Chapter 15 of this volume.

question of whether the actors developing standards or modes of conduct intend for them to be legally binding or not. A more nuanced assessment may be possible whereby normative intent reflects an intention or purpose to develop standards that will alter behaviour and/or an expectation that conduct will adhere to the standards set out in an agreement, without having to reach any specific determination on the legal nature of the commitment.

Normative effect refers to the actual result from the process of lawmaking, or of reaching agreement. It is concerned with assessing whether behaviour has altered to align with what was agreed. There may not be an absolute result, but a variable impact on state conduct.[73] As such, these dimensions have a temporal element, given that normative intent looks at what actors were contemplating at the start of the process, and normative effect considers what the result of the process has been.

For example, a process may not have normative intent (that is, the actors involved may not want to create formally binding law), but it may ultimately produce normative effect (the standards agreed may form the basis of a treaty or contribute to the development of customary international law or may inform domestic laws); or there may be normative intent among the actors concerned in developing a particular output (the intention being to contribute to the development of customary international law) but ultimately (or to date) no normative effect achieved (the hallmarks of formal law are absent, or behaviour has not shifted to align with what was agreed). The normative value that may be ascribed to any informal agreement may, then, influence the significance of that agreement, as discussed in the following section.

1.6 Significance of Informal Lawmaking for the Law of the Sea

With any new agreement on the law of the sea, that instrument's interrelationship with the LOSC has immediate relevance. For new treaties, that relationship is governed by Article 311 of the Convention. While state parties may modify or suspend the operation of certain provisions of the LOSC as between themselves, a number of conditions must be satisfied, as laid out under Article 311(3):

> [P]rovided that such agreements do not relate to a provision derogation from which is incompatible with the effective execution of the object and purpose of this Convention, and provided further that such agreements shall not affect the application of the basic principles embodied herein, and that the provisions of such agreements do not affect the enjoyment by other States Parties of their rights or the performance of their obligations under this Convention.

Further, pursuant to Article 311(4), 'States Parties intending to conclude an agreement referred to in paragraph 3 shall notify the other States Parties through the depositary of this Convention of their intention to conclude the agreement and of the modification or suspension for which it provides.' It might well be anticipated that any intention to modify or suspend the LOSC provisions may provoke unfavourable reactions from other parties

[73] Davenport refers to a sliding scale, in her chapter of this volume (Chapter 10). See also Scott, in Chapter 16 of this volume.

depending on what is proposed, and how it is perceived. Treaties that are 'expressly permitted or preserved by other articles' of the LOSC are permissible.[74] These design features of the LOSC are intended to ensure the integrity of the instrument,[75] and arguably underline its constitutional importance. Informal agreements would not be captured by Article 311 of the LOSC.

Instead, in the context of informal agreements, there are still potentially diverse consequences for the LOSC. Chinkin, in discussing soft law more generally, envisages that informal agreements may 'provide guidance to the interpretation, elaboration, or application' of the Convention, or reflect evidence of Convention obligations.[76] Informal agreements may hold relevance in the interpretation of the LOSC, if the agreement in question is considered as a 'subsequent agreement between the parties regarding the interpretation of the treaty or the application of its provisions'.[77] Further, informal agreements may also be relevant for treaty interpretation if they count as '[a]ny subsequent practice in the application of a treaty which establishes the agreement of the parties regarding its interpretation',[78] or '[a]ny relevant rules of international law applicable in the relations between the parties'.[79] A query might be raised that an informal agreement is not 'applicable' precisely because it is not formally binding between the parties concerned. The International Law Commission has allowed for the possibility that an informal agreement may be taken into account in the interpretation of a treaty if that agreement reflects 'a common understanding ... [that] the parties are aware of and accept'.[80]

When a treaty is adopted, one consequence is that the treaty may be interpreted and applied by international courts or tribunals in assessing the legality of a state's conduct.[81] Informal agreements might not be considered as applicable law in resolving a case in a comparable way, precisely because they are not formally binding. Article 293 of the LOSC allows a court or tribunal constituted under the dispute settlement regime of the Convention to consider 'other rules of international law not incompatible with this Convention'. Informal law may be perceived as falling outside 'rules of international law' because of its non-binding status, but this issue has not been addressed in any case to date. Yet, the ICJ contemplated the possibility that recommendations adopted by consensus within the International Whaling Commission may be relevant to the interpretation of the International Convention for the Regulation of Whaling.[82] Achieving consensus among all state parties to the LOSC in any forum may be possible, albeit not frequent.

A further consequence of formal law is that a violation of that law entails state responsibility. For international relations scholars, the adoption of a treaty is seen as signalling

[74] LOSC (n 6) art 311(5).
[75] Boyle, 'Further Development' (n 5) 577.
[76] Chinkin, 'Normative Development' (n 30) 30–31.
[77] VCLT (n 26) art 31(3)(a).
[78] ibid, art 31(3)(b).
[79] ibid, art 31(3)(c).
[80] International Law Commission, 'Draft Conclusions on Subsequent Agreements and Subsequent Practice in relation to the Interpretation of Treaties' (2018) *Yearbook of the International Law Commission*, vol II, pt 2, Conclusion 10(3).
[81] This dimension may depend on the applicable law of any international court or tribunal.
[82] *Whaling in the Antarctic* (*Australia and New Zealand (intervening) v Japan*), Judgment, 31 March 2014, (2014) ICJ Reports 226, para 46.

commitment to the bargain that has been struck.[83] A treaty requires implementation into domestic law, and ensures that all domestic actors, as well as future governments, are more likely to conform to the agreed requirements.[84] Such consequences are not as immediately apparent for informal agreements.

While there is typically a distinction drawn between formal and informal agreements whereby the former entail state responsibility whereas the latter do not,[85] that dichotomy is not as inexorable as may first appear. An informal agreement may emerge where one state evinces an intention to act in a particular way, and consistently adopts that position. Where another state relies on that expressed intention to its detriment, a claim of estoppel may arise.[86] This argument was pursued by Mauritius in the *Chagos Marine Protected Area* arbitration under the LOSC, in relation to an informal agreement called the 'Lancaster House Undertakings'.[87] The Annex VII Tribunal constituted under the LOSC found that the United Kingdom was estopped from denying Mauritius its fishing rights.[88] What the United Kingdom perceived to be a political commitment to Mauritius ultimately became a binding obligation. The express words of the Undertaking reflected that the United Kingdom had to 'ensure' that fishing rights 'would remain available' to Mauritius, but subject to 'the overarching defence needs of the United States and the United Kingdom's discretion in the routine management of the fishery'.[89] Alternatively to estoppel, a claim of acquiescence may emerge as a result of conduct pursuant to an informal agreement, even if this outcome is contrary to the original intention.[90]

The connections of informal agreements to the LOSC may, further, have implications for state responsibility in the context of determinations as to whether states have met due diligence requirements.[91] In the context of flag states responding to illegal, unreported, or unregulated (IUU) fishing in the exclusive economic zone (EEZ) of another state, the International Tribunal for the Law of the Sea has observed that there is a requirement for flag states ' "to deploy adequate means, to exercise best possible efforts, to do the utmost" to prevent IUU fishing by ships flying its flag'.[92] Flag states are, thus, required to take the necessary measures to ensure compliance of their vessels with the coastal state's laws and regulations applying in its EEZ.[93] What those necessary measures might be could be informed by informal instruments, such as the FAO Voluntary Guidelines for Flag State Performance.[94]

[83] Abbott and Snidal note that, 'By using hard law to order their relations, international actors reduce transactions costs, strengthen the credibility of their commitments, expand their available political strategies, and resolve problems of incomplete contracting.' (Abbott and Snidal (n 31) 422).

[84] ibid 428.

[85] See, eg Schachter (n 1) 300.

[86] See Chinkin, 'Normative Development' (n 30) 30–31; Aust (n 3) 810; Bothe (n 1) 87. See also Hey, in Chapter 18 of this volume.

[87] *Chagos Marine Protected Area Arbitration (Mauritius v United Kingdom)* (Award of 18 March 2015) PCA Case No 2011-03, para 397.

[88] 'Where, as here, the United Kingdom has repeatedly committed to a future course of action with knowledge that another State is acting in reliance upon that commitment, both Mauritius and the Tribunal are entitled to presume that the United Kingdom did not consider such commitments freely revocable' (ibid para 447).

[89] ibid para 455.

[90] Chinkin, 'Normative Development' (n 30) 30–31.

[91] See Dupuy (n 2) 434.

[92] *Request for Advisory Opinion Submitted by the Sub-regional Fisheries Commission* (Advisory Opinion) ITLOS Reports 2015, 4, para 129 (citing Seabed Advisory Opinion).

[93] Consistent with Arts 58(3) and 62(4) of the LOSC (ibid para 134).

[94] FAO, 'Voluntary Guidelines for Flag State Performance' (Rome, 2015) <http://www.fao.org/3/a-i4577t.pdf> accessed 15 July 2021. See Victor Alencar Mayer Feitosa Ventura, 'Tackling Illegal, Unregulated and Unreported Fishing: the ITLOS Advisory Opinion on Flag State Responsibility for IUU Fishing and the Principle of Due Diligence' (2015) 12 Braz J Int'l L 50, 58.

Korseberg has further suggested that the FAO Deep-Sea Fisheries Guidelines could be used in due diligence assessments in relation to high seas fisheries.[95]

Informal lawmaking has further consequences for the LOSC because it is expressly anticipated, within that agreement, that regard will be had to 'generally accepted rules and standards established through the competent international organization or general diplomatic conference',[96] as well as to other legal regimes. A result of this technique is that the LOSC requires adherence, for example, to IMO recommendations and guidelines, as well as treaties adopted under the auspices of the IMO, through such an implied reference.[97] Korseberg has described the relevance of generally accepted international rules and standards (GAIRS) as follows:

> GAIRS can also have a stronger role, namely to inform the content of a specific rule of law set out in a treaty. In such cases, 'their importance derives principally from the influence they may exert on the interpretation, application and development of other rules of law'. In other words, GAIRS not only assist in the interpretation of a rule, they also specify what States must do in order to fulfil the obligation set out in that rule. By coupling GAIRS with obligations found in UNCLOS, the standards set out in the former inform the substantive content of the latter. GAIRS 'then applies to the UNCLOS States Parties concerned by virtue of UNCLOS itself', not the soft-law instrument in question. This is important because it allows the substantive requirements of an obligation to be expanded without the need for another binding legal instrument to be negotiated and agreed to by the parties.[98]

The result of this relationship between GAIRS and the LOSC is that the informal instruments that fit within the category of GAIRS hold an especially important normative role for the law of the sea. These informal agreements may be relevant for questions of interpretation, application, and state responsibility that may arise in inter-state relations under the LOSC.

The practical and policy significance for informal lawmaking in the law of the sea must also be acknowledged. The flexibility and speed that are typically associated with informal lawmaking are especially important when there are pressing issues of ocean governance to address. In some instances, new threats to ocean use and/or resources may not be fully understood, which makes it difficult to anticipate the consequences of legally binding obligations.[99] Informal agreements are more adaptable to uncertainty, but at least start a process of defining key standards and expectations of state conduct in relation to particular issues. Indeed, an informal agreement may provide a testing ground for new rules without immediately establishing legal consequences should those rules have results that are perceived as undesirable by the parties.[100]

Contemporary issues relating to the oceans may be addressed within different institutions or networks. Informal lawmaking may be a strategy adopted in one organization when

[95] See Lene Korseberg, 'The Law-making Effects of the FAO Deep-sea Fisheries Guidelines' (2018) 67(4) ICLQ 801, 809–11 and 830.

[96] Eg, LOSC (n 6) Arts 207–12.

[97] Boyle, 'Some Reflections' (n 2) 906.

[98] Korseberg (n 95) 805–06 (citations omitted).

[99] Abbott and Snidal (n 31) 441.

[100] See ibid 442.

members wish to adopt a position on an issue, but also to defer to the competence of another organization. This approach may be contemplated within the UN Office of Drugs and Crime to deal with fisheries crime, while cooperating with the FAO in view of the latter's competence over fisheries more generally. At times, informal agreements may be preferred to emphasize a state's political position within one organization, or as a strategy to prevent a more coordinated approach or the adoption of a treaty, in relation to an ocean issue.

Where one may need to be wary of the use of informal lawmaking in the law of the sea is in situations where the foundational principles of the LOSC are challenged. Shaffer and Pollack have studied the interaction of 'hard' and 'soft' law, arguing that 'far from "filling in" the details of hard law, a growing body of soft law is promulgated in the hope of undermining the foundations of existing hard law'.[101] This possibility would be problematic to those advocates who insist on maintaining the 'package deal' from the time of the LOSC negotiations, along with the balance of interests on different issue areas that was enshrined in the Convention. Yet, the reality is that these fundamental tenets of the law of the sea are being challenged and, in some instances, for good reason.[102] Shaffer and Pollack proceed to observe that this use of soft law is not necessarily lamentable, but that such conflicts 'reflect a maturation of international law in a pluralistic world in which multiple and overlapping regimes can signal to decision makers to take account of developments in other spheres of international law and politics'.[103]

Finally, it should be observed that informal lawmaking may ultimately lead to the negotiation of a treaty or, in some instances, contribute to the development of customary international law.[104] Dupuy has commented that, in any transition from soft to hard law, factors to consider would include 'the source and origin of the text (governmental or not); the conditions, both formal and political, of its adoption; its intrinsic aptitude to become a norm of international law; and the practical reaction of States to its Statement'.[105] An accretion of binding treaties and additional informal agreements may provide the impetus for the formation of a new treaty, as occurred with the 2009 Port State Measures Agreement.[106] This Agreement drew significantly on the 2005 FAO Model Scheme on Port State Measures to Combat Illegal, Unreported and Unregulated Fishing,[107] as well as the International Plan of Action to Prevent, Deter and Eliminate Illegal, Unreported and Unregulated Fishing.[108]

101 Shaffer and Pollack (n 1) 712.

102 Eg, the Convention's use of a maximum sustainable yield for the management of living marine resources has been criticized, in favour of an ecosystem-based management approach. See, generally, Abdullah Al Arif, 'Exploring the Legal Status and Key Features of Ecosystem-based Fisheries Management in International Fisheries Law' (2018) 27 RECIEL 320. See, further, Scanlon, in Chapter 11 of this volume.

103 Shaffer and Pollack (n 1) 712.

104 Chinkin, 'Normative Development' (n 30) 30–31, although there may be limitations on what informal agreements may contribute in this regard. See Chinkin, 'The Challenge of Soft Law' (n 2) 857. Chinkin has observed that, as soft law is not binding, it is not likely to count as *opinio juris*, and if the actions required are directed at non-state actors, then the ensuing practice is not 'state' practice (ibid 858).

105 Dupuy (n 2) 431. See also Pauwelyn and others, 'When Structures Become Shackles' (n 47) 757 (referring to similar criteria).

106 Agreement on Port State Measures to Prevent, Deter and Eliminate Illegal, Unreported and Unregulated Fishing (adopted 22 November 2009, entered into force 5 June 2016) [2016] ATS 21.

107 FAO, 'Model Scheme on Port State Measures to Combat Illegal, Unreported and Unregulated Fishing' (Rome, 2007) <http://www.fao.org/3/a0985t/A0985T.pdf> accessed 20 July 2021.

108 FAO, 'International Plan of Action to Prevent, Deter and Eliminate Illegal, Unreported and Unregulated Fishing' (Rome, 2001) <http://www.fao.org/3/y1224e/Y1224E.pdf> accessed 20 July 2021. For discussion, see David J Doulman and Judith Swan, 'A Guide to the Background and Implementation of the 2009 FAO Agreement on Port State Measures to Prevent, Deter and Eliminate Illegal, Unreported and Unregulated Fishing' (2012) FAO Fisheries and Aquaculture Circular No 1074 FIPI/C1074, 27 <http://www.fao.org/3/i2590e/i2590e00.pdf> accessed 20 July 2021.

1.7 Concluding Remarks

The chapters following in this volume not only examine topics of notable contemporary significance for the law of the sea, but also bring to the fore an emphasis on modern approaches to lawmaking in an increasingly multipolar world that is both globalized and nationalistic in approaches to international cooperation. While the analysis above has sought to draw out some meanings as to informal law and informal lawmaking, and to provide a frame for the chapters that follow, each author has brought to bear their own considerations and perspectives on what informal law and informal lawmaking mean, and how they operate in international law. Many of the common characteristics, advantages, and disadvantages to informal law and informal lawmaking that are highlighted in the general literature may be discerned within the various issue areas of the law of the sea under examination in this book. Yet, a focus on 'unconventional lawmaking' in the law of the sea is worthwhile not only because of the fundamental importance of ocean governance in international affairs, but because the strong formal legal framework in place is being increasingly, inter alia, tested, thickened, clarified, expanded, undermined, and enhanced by informal agreements.

Consequently, the authors seek to answer the following questions: why does informal lawmaking matter? And what are the consequences for the law of the sea? Potential answers include that the lawmaking effort matters because it gives us practical results we would not have otherwise had, it catalyses timely action, or because it 'thickens' a treaty, fills gaps in a legal regime, or creates standards for determining state responsibility. There is not one single answer across all areas relating to the law of the sea, but close consideration of the differences and details is warranted, to understand the implications for the law of the sea. Is the law of the sea changing for the better or for the worse with this activity? The answers considered in this book will be relevant for current and future understandings of the LOSC, as well as other important treaties, such as those developed under the auspices of the IMO. The experiences from the law of the sea may inform other areas of international law where informal law and informal lawmaking continue as the preferred form of international cooperation. Ultimately, what may seem unconventional now may not be so in the future.

PART II

MARITIME SECURITY

2

The San Remo Manual on the Law of Naval Warfare—from Restatement to Development?

Liesbeth Lijnzaad

2.1 Introduction

The 1994 San Remo Manual on International Law Applicable to Armed Conflicts at Sea[1] (SRM or Manual) fills a gap that has arisen as a consequence of the absence of an update of the various Hague Conventions of 1907 on naval warfare,[2] apart from those aspects of the law that found their way into the Second Geneva Convention for the Amelioration of the Condition of Wounded, Sick and Shipwrecked Members of the Armed Forces (1949) (Second Geneva Convention),[3] and the 1977 Protocols Additional to the Geneva Conventions of 12 August 1949 (Additional Protocol I and Additional Protocol II).[4] The 183 paragraphs of the Manual describe contemporary rules of naval warfare, and are accompanied by an article-by-article commentary (Explanation). This Explanation clarifies the sources of the rules, and provides cross references to other relevant fields of international law.

The Manual is the result of an informal project under the umbrella of the San Remo Institute for International Humanitarian Law (San Remo Institute) in which experts from government, the military, and academia have participated in their personal capacities. It is an informal and non-binding document suggestive of a restatement of existing law, yet in the twenty-five years since its launch in 1994, the Manual seems to have taken on a life of

[1] Louise Doswald-Beck (ed), *San Remo Manual on International Law Applicable to Armed Conflicts at Sea* (CUP 1995) (hereafter 'SRM' or 'Manual').

[2] Hague Convention (VI) relating to the Status of Enemy Merchant Ships at the Outbreak of Hostilities (adopted 18 October 1907, entered into force 26 January 1910); Hague Convention (VII) relating to the Conversion of Merchant Ships into War-Ships (adopted 18 October 1907, entered into force 26 January 1910); Hague Convention (VIII) relative to the Laying of Automatic Submarine Contact Mines (adopted 18 October 1907, entered into force 26 January 1910); Hague Convention (IX) concerning Bombardment by Naval Forces in Tie of War (adopted 18 October 1907, entered into force 26 January 1910); Hague Convention (XI) relative to certain Restrictions with regard to the Exercise of the Right of Capture in Naval War (adopted 18 October 1907, entered into force 26 January 1910); Hague Convention (XIII) concerning the Rights and Duties of Neutral Powers in Naval War (adopted 18 October 1907, entered into force 26 January 1910). These treaties are compiled in: Dotation Carnegie pour la Paix Internationale, *Les Conventions et Déclarations de La Haye de 1899 et 1907* (OUP 1918) and in Natalino Ronzitti (ed), *The Law of Naval Warfare: A Collection of Agreements and Documents with Commentaries* (Martinus Nijhoff 1988).

[3] Geneva Convention (II) for the Amelioration of the Condition of Wounded, Sick and Shipwrecked Members of Armed Forces at Sea (adopted 12 August 1949, entered into force 21 October 1950) 75 UNTS 85 (hereafter 'Second Geneva Convention', or 'GC II').

[4] Protocol Additional to the Geneva Conventions of 12 August 1949, and relating to the Protection of Victims of International Armed Conflicts (Protocol 1) (adopted 8 June 1977, entered into force 7 December 1978) 1125 UNTS 3 (hereafter 'Protocol I', or 'AP I'); Protocol Additional to the Geneva Conventions of 12 August 1949, and relating to the Protection of Victims of Non-International Armed Conflicts (Protocol II) (adopted 8 June 1977, entered into force 7 December 1978) 1125 UNTS 609 (hereafter 'Protocol II', or 'AP II').

Liesbeth Lijnzaad, *The San Remo Manual on the Law of Naval Warfare—from Restatement to Development?* In: *Unconventional Lawmaking in the Law of the Sea.* Edited by: Natalie Klein, Oxford University Press.
DOI: 10.1093/oso/9780192897824.003.0002

its own. Rather than referring to any of the Hague Conventions, authors these days tend to refer to the Manual as a summary of the law.

The intention of the drafters of the Manual was not to create new legal rules, but, rather, to reformulate existing rules from a contemporary perspective. Yet, a critical look at the informal setting in which the Manual was developed is useful, particularly so when a revision is currently being contemplated. In the following discussion, an overview of the development of the Manual will be given, and various aspects of its informality will be explored. This chapter will not discuss the normative content of the Manual in great detail, but it will be addressed in passing to illustrate the sometimes problematic character of the Manual.

2.2 The San Remo Manual

There are few areas more prone to the impact of technology than the laws of war, and maritime law. Maritime technology changes continuously, new weapons are developed, and legal rules that refer specifically to particular technological standards become outdated over time. The Hague Conventions rely on naval know-how as it was at the time of their drafting, predictably leading to the redundancy of some of these rules today, or their inadequacy in light of the development of new means of warfare. While military and naval technology has developed since 1907 (before the First World War), the formal legal rules have not been adapted, nor has there been any explicit call from states for the revision of the written law of naval warfare. Sensible drafting today would imply the inclusion of a mechanism for the updating of technical standards, similar to those commonly seen in instruments adopted at the International Maritime Organization (IMO), where, through a simplified procedure, secondary rules and regulations provide a mechanism for the adaptation of technical norms.[5] That, of course, does not imply that fundamental changes (such as the development of autonomous marine vessels) can necessarily be addressed in such a manner.[6]

2.2.1 The Traditional Laws of Naval Warfare: The Hague Conventions (1899 and 1907) and Beyond

In the nineteenth century, the law of naval warfare had a more prominent role than it has today. At the time, there was a greater awareness of the law of naval warfare amongst those relying on the (peacetime) law of the sea, because if a naval conflict arose, it would have direct consequences for the rules concerning navigation applicable to third states seeking to protect their neutrality. Naval warfare could have a serious impact on the cargo of the merchant fleet, and thus the law of naval warfare was relevant for those with an interest in maritime trade, and particularly for neutral states wishing to continue trading during armed conflict. In the early twentieth century, the law of naval warfare consisted of a set of Hague Conventions, negotiated in 1899 and 1907, as well as some other more or less informal

[5] This process is discussed in more detail in James Harrison, *Making the Law of the Sea: A Study in the Development of International Law* (CUP 2011) 160–64.

[6] Some of the changes under contemplation for maritime autonomous vessels are discussed by Petrig, in Chapter 7 of this volume.

instruments of a similar age, such as the 1909 London Declaration concerning the Laws of Naval Warfare,[7] and the 1913 Oxford Manual on the Laws of Naval Warfare Governing the Relations between Belligerents, produced by the Institut de Droit International.[8] The latter documents provide overviews of the customary law of naval warfare, as it stood at the time.

Amongst the Hague Conventions are agreements dealing with the status of enemy merchant ships at the start of hostilities (VI), the conversion of merchant ships into warships (VII), the laying of automatic submarine contact mines (VIII), bombardment by naval forces in time of war (IX),[9] adaptation to marine warfare of the principles of the Geneva Convention (of 1864) (X),[10] certain restrictions with regard to the right of capture in naval war (XI), the establishment of an international prize court (XII), which did not enter into force, and the rights and duties of neutral powers during naval war (XIII).[11] In 1910, a further Protocol on an International Prize Court was agreed, but this protocol did not enter into force either.[12] At the heart of this so-called 'Law of the Hague' is the conduct of warfare, as opposed to the 'Law of Geneva', which focuses on the protection of people who become victims of armed conflict.

There have been some developments in the law of naval warfare, but these changes are mostly related to the protection of the victims of armed conflict, as opposed to the conduct of hostilities. The Second Geneva Convention focuses specifically on humanitarian law applicable at sea, and incorporates experiences from the Second World War. The recently revised International Committee of the Red Cross (ICRC) Commentary to the Second Geneva Convention presents a contemporary analysis and current interpretation of its content, including the interpretation of provisions that appear to be dated.[13]

The Second Geneva Convention was, in part, updated through Additional Protocol I, and the matter of updating the law of naval warfare was, apparently, discussed at the diplomatic conference in 1974 to 1977. However, it was decided not to undertake this task, given the significant amount of work already involved in addressing land warfare.[14] The only step that was taken was the addition of provisions on the wounded, sick, and shipwrecked, in both Additional Protocols.[15] The need for reaffirmation and clarification of the law of naval warfare was later also mentioned in a resolution at the twenty-fifth Red Cross Conference

[7] Naval Conference of London, 'Declaration concerning the Laws of Naval War' (26 February 1909) (not in force) <https://ihl-databases.icrc.org/ihl/INTRO/255> accessed 16 June 2021, in Dietrich Schindler and Jiří Toman, *The Laws of Armed Conflicts: A Collection of Conventions, Resolutions, and Other Documents* (Martinus Nijhoff 1988) 845–56.

[8] Institut de Droit International, 'Manual of the Laws of Naval War' (9 August 1913) <https://ihl-databases.icrc.org/ihl/INTRO/265?OpenDocument> accessed 16 June 2021, in Schindler and Toman (n 7) 858–75.

[9] Currently covered by the provisions on attacks in AP I (n 4).

[10] Currently covered by GC II (n 3).

[11] For full details, see above (n 2). For a detailed discussion, see Liesbeth Lijnzaad, 'Het Haagsche Zeeoorlogsrecht van 1907 Vandaag (The 1907 Hague Law of Naval Warfare Today)' in Oude Verdragen in een Nieuwe Tijd, Honderd Jaar Haagse Vredesconferentie van 1907 (Old Treaties in a New Era, One Hundred Years since the Hague Peace Conference of 1907), Mededelingen van de Nederlandse Vereniging voor Internationaal Recht, deel 135 (2007) 99; and J Ashley Roach, 'The Law of Naval Warfare at the Turn of Two Centuries' (2000) 94 AJIL 64.

[12] Additional Protocol to the Convention relative to the Establishment of an International Prize Court (adopted 19 September 1910) (not in force).

[13] ICRC, *Commentary on the Second Geneva Convention: Convention (II) for the Amelioration of the Condition of Wounded, Sick and Shipwrecked Members of Armed Forces at Sea* (CUP 2017). See, in particular, the Introduction at 19–27 for the origins of GC II. GC II (n 3) focuses specifically on the humanitarian law applicable at sea.

[14] See AP I (n 4), art 49(3); Roach (n 11) 76–77, and sources mentioned in fn 117 of that publication.

[15] In particular, AP I (n 4), arts 8–20, and AP II (n 4) arts 7–12.

in 1986, but nothing eventuated.[16] The international community has, thus, long been aware of the desirability of (formally) updating the law of naval warfare. While there has been recognition of the need to update relevant texts, no state has taken the initiative for a formal revision of the law of naval warfare. Apparently, the revision of the law of naval warfare has not been of such importance to states as to start a process towards formal amendment or revision of existing treaties.

No formal initiatives have, thus, been taken, although the idea has appeared in academic writing from time to time.[17] Doswald-Beck reports that the experts at San Remo considered that it was 'premature to embark on diplomatic negotiations to draft a treaty'.[18] Yet, there seemed to be agreement between military lawyers and academics that the law of naval warfare needed updating, and this recognition eventually provided the basis to embark on the SRM process.

2.2.2 The Changing Context for the Law of Naval Warfare

There have not been many naval conflicts since the Second World War, with the exception of the Falklands/Malvinas conflict in 1982, as well as situations in which some naval warfare took place, such as during the Iran–Iraq War (1980–88), the Gulf War (Iraq–Kuwait, 1990–91), or the Sri Lankan Civil War (1983–2009), which included hostilities at sea in the course of non-international armed conflict. Instead, military activity at sea seems to have moved to the law enforcement spectrum rather than typical situations of naval conflict. Navies have become charged with the enforcement of UN Security Council Chapter VII resolutions, with activities as diverse as enforcing trade sanctions during the conflict in the former Yugoslavia in the Adriatic Sea,[19] and piracy prevention and interdiction off the coast of Somalia.[20] Navies have also become engaged in drug enforcement and interdiction,[21] or the interception of weapons of mass destruction and related precursors (through arrangements like the Proliferation Security Initiative). While such activities may imply a certain use of force, both for personal self-defence, or to ensure the success of the enforcement

[16] Louise Doswald-Beck, 'San Remo Manual on International Law Applicable to Armed Conflict at Sea' (1995) 309 IRRC 583, 583 referring to 'Work on International Humanitarian Law in Armed Conflicts at Sea and on Land', Resolution VII, 25th International Conference of the Red Cross (1986) in (1986) 255 IRRC 348. Operational paragraph 1 in section A of the Resolution '*notes* that ... some areas of international humanitarian law relating to sea warfare are in need of reaffirmation and clarification on the basis of existing fundamental principles of international humanitarian law'. It appealed to governments to 'co-ordinate their efforts in appropriate fora in order to review the necessity and possibility of updating the relevant texts of international humanitarian law relating to sea warfare'.

[17] See, eg Doswald-Beck, IRRC (n 16) 583–86; Dieter Fleck, 'Topical Approaches Towards Developing the Law of Armed Conflict at Sea' in Astrid JM Delissen and Gerard J Tanja (eds), *Humanitarian Law of Armed Conflict: Challenges Ahead: Essays in Honour of Frits Kalshoven* (Martinus Nijhoff 1991) 407, 412–13; Natalino Ronzitti, 'The Crisis of the Traditional Law Regulating International Armed Conflict at Sea and the Need for its Revision' in Ronzitti (n 2) 50, which states that '[i]t is only worth pointing out that the traditional law of naval warfare cannot be updated by way of interpretation and adaptation of treaties to new realities or by relying on the process which generates customary international law.'

[18] Doswald-Beck, IRRC (n 16) 587.

[19] UNSC Res 787 (16 November 1992) UN Doc S/RES/787; UNSC Res 820 (17 April 1993) UN Doc S/RES/820 and follow-up.

[20] UNSC Res 1816 (2 June 2008) UN Doc S/RES/1816 and follow-up.

[21] See, eg Agreement Concerning Co-Operation in Suppressing Illicit Maritime and Air Trafficking in Narcotic Drugs and Psychotropic Substances in the Caribbean Area (adopted 10 April 2003, entered into force 18 September 2008) <https://2009-2017.state.gov/s/l/2005/87198.htm> accessed 29 June 2021.

operation, they will remain below the threshold of armed conflict and, consequently, do not imply the applicability of the law of naval warfare.

Since the Second World War, the law of the sea has also changed profoundly. Most recently, the 1982 UN Convention on the Law of the Sea (LOSC) brought some changes that have had an impact on the law of naval warfare. The Third UN Conference on the Law of the Sea lasted from 1973 to 1982, and the Convention had already been adopted when the Manual was developed in the period between 1988 and 1994 (although the LOSC would only enter into force in 1994).[22] This timing meant that the contemporary law of the sea was something to be taken into account during the drafting of the SRM.

The Manual does address developments in the LOSC by, inter alia, referring to the various maritime zones that were established by that Convention.[23] This new set of maritime zones created fairly fundamental questions as to the geographical scope of applicability of the law of naval warfare. Traditional law distinguished between neutral states and belligerents, and only the territorial sea of neutral states had been off limits for parties to the conflict, otherwise the conflict could take place anywhere on the high seas, or in the territorial seas of the belligerents. Not only had the territorial sea grown in size in the LOSC, to a maximum of 12 nautical miles (nm), but the contiguous zone and, specifically, the exclusive economic zone (EEZ) had extended certain sovereign rights and jurisdiction of coastal states well into the ocean, to a maximum of 200 nm, or even a possible 350 nm for the continental shelf. This change seemed to substantially limit the space for naval warfare. Additionally, the notion of neutrality was in flux as a consequence of the prohibition of the use of force in the UN Charter.[24] While, before the UN Charter existed, neutrality had to be claimed, the presumption was now reversed, and it could be assumed that states were not participating in the conflict unless proven otherwise.

2.2.3 Incorporating the LOSC into the San Remo Manual

These examples of changes in international law created a need to consider their consequences for the law of naval warfare. Thus, the Manual addresses, in paragraph 10, matters of neutrality law, as well as the position of coastal states, and their rights within zones adjacent to the territorial sea. The LOSC is particularly relevant with respect to neutrality, and the position of states that are not party to the naval conflict. The Manual identifies three geographical situations in which hostile actions may take place, subject to other applicable rules of the law of armed conflict: all of the maritime zones and territory of belligerent states, the high seas, and, subject to paragraphs 34 and 35, the EEZ and continental shelf of neutral states. Paragraphs 34 and 35 address the obligation for belligerent states to have due regard for the rights and duties of the neutral coastal state, both with respect to the economic exploitation of the zones and the protection and preservation of the marine environment. In particular, those paragraphs note that belligerents must have due regard for artificial islands

[22] United Nations Convention on the Law of the Sea (adopted 10 December 1982, entered into force 16 November 1994) 1833 UNTS 397 (hereafter 'LOSC'). Agreement relating to the Implementation of Part XI of the United Nations Convention on the Law of the Sea of 10 December 1982 (adopted 28 July 1994, entered into force 16 November 1994) 1836 UNTS 3 is not very relevant to the SRM.

[23] SRM (n 1) pt I, s IV, Areas of naval warfare, paras 10–12; Pt II, Regions of Operations, paras 14–37.

[24] Charter of the United Nations, Arts 2(4), 51.

and installations established in these zones. With respect to minelaying, there is an obligation to notify the coastal state, the mines should not endanger artificial islands and installations, and, as far as practicable, interference with economic exploitation must be avoided. Finally, there is an obligation to give due regard to the protection and preservation of the marine environment. With respect to paragraph 34, the Explanation observes that 'it is obvious that the terms used come from that Convention [LOSC] and should be interpreted in the light of that Convention'.[25]

Paragraph 36 about hostile actions on the high seas stipulates that these be conducted with due regard for the rights of neutral states with respect to the exploitation and exploration of the natural resources of the seabed and the ocean floor. The Explanation clarifies that the provision deals with activities beyond the EEZ or continental shelf (thus including the Area), and that it had been considered useful to point out that such activities were entitled to protection. The zones for which such concessions were given were not, however, exclusion zones in a military sense.

The notion of due regard does not appear in paragraph 11, which is a precursor to paragraphs 34 and 35 in referring to environmental concerns. The Explanation to paragraph 11 refers to Article 192 of the LOSC as a starting point and describes that, although there was agreement about addressing this matter in the Manual, there was no consensus on creating a legal obligation. Hence, the text of paragraph 11 is hortatory, as opposed to mandatory, and reflects Article 194(5) of the LOSC. The Explanation mentions that paragraph 11 is not an obligation but rather an encouragement: '[T]his soft-law guideline, in time of armed conflict at sea, reflects the general rules of peacetime international environmental law'.[26] This paragraph on rare and fragile ecosystems, and depleted, threatened, or endangered species only speaks of parties to the conflict being '*encouraged to agree* that no hostile actions will be conducted', which would seem to be a lower threshold than that required under the due regard obligation in paragraphs 34 and 35, as stated in the Explanation. It is unclear how the drafters understood these provisions to work together.

Paragraph 12, which deals with areas where neutral states enjoy rights, obliges belligerents to have due regard to the legitimate rights of neutral states.[27] This paragraph is generally considered to be redundant, yet the Explanation describes the debate that took place between the proponents of 'due regard' (as accepted in the law of the sea, and reflecting a balance between the rights of belligerents and the rights of neutrals) and the supporters of the inclusion of the stricter norm of 'respect', which would place a higher burden on the belligerents. In the discussion, 'due regard' became the accepted standard, as it was 'tied so closely to the law of the sea as well as the law of naval warfare', and 'respect' conveyed a sense of an absolute and affirmative duty.[28]

Although these are examples, they demonstrate that efforts were made to refer to rules from the LOSC in the Manual.

[25] SRM (n 1) para 34.2.
[26] ibid 83, para 11.6.
[27] 'Areas' appears to refer directly to maritime zones: see SRM (n 1) 83, para 12.1.
[28] ibid 84, para 12.2.

2.2.4 Drafting the San Remo Manual

Currently, the Manual is taken to be the general standard for the law of naval warfare, with the usual caveat that the SRM is not binding as such, but is, rather, a collection compiled by experts.[29] Several governments have used the Manual when revising their military manuals for their navies, whether as a source of contemporary rules, or as the starting point of a reflection on what their view on the law is.[30] When the SRM is referred to, this tends to be matter-of-factly, without further introduction, as though it is a given that the contemporary law of naval warfare is contained in the Manual, and the Manual is the authoritative source, or at any rate the contemporary standard. From the perspective of lawmaking, this treatment of the SRM suggests that an investigation into its origins and its authority may be interesting.

How did the San Remo Manual come about? The introduction(s) to the SRM itself,[31] in the 1995 edition, mention that it is a contemporary restatement, together 'with some progressive development', of the law applicable to armed conflicts at sea,[32] taking into account recent state practice, technological developments, and the effect of related areas of the law, in particular the UN Charter, the LOSC, air law, and environmental law. This suggests the Manual being a follow-up or a modern equivalent to the 'last such restatement ... undertaken by the Institute of International Law in 1913' leading to the 1913 Oxford Manual on the Laws of Naval Warfare.[33] As mentioned above, that manual was generally considered to give an overview of the customary law of naval warfare at that time.

The Manual describes the drafting process that took place from 1988 to 1994, which included eight round-table meetings. Though the aim was to draft a restatement of the law of naval warfare, as this stood at the end of the 1980s and in the first half of the 1990s, a number of new matters were included, with some choices beyond the scope of the law on naval warfare proper, such as issues related to the *ius ad bellum*.[34] The Summary of the Manual is unusually bold, stating that 'the document will be of major contemporary, future and historical importance, and will help shape generally accepted international law regulating armed conflicts at sea. *There is no other book like it.*'[35]

The introduction to the Explanation, by editor Louise Doswald-Beck, both provides an overview of the preparatory work leading to the Manual, and presents a number of choices that were made along the way.[36] It mentions four 'interconnected reasons' for drafting the

[29] See, egWolff Heintschel von Heinegg, 'Maritime Warfare' in Andrew Clapham and Paola Gaeta (eds), *The Oxford Handbook of International Law in Armed Conflict* (OUP 2014),and references to the Manual in Tiia Lohela and Valentin Schatz (eds), 'Handbook on Maritime Hybrid Threats—10 Scenarios and Legal Scans' (2019) Hybrid CoE Working Paper 5, 29, 30 <https://www.hybridcoe.fi/wp-content/uploads/2020/07/NEW_Handbook-on-maritime-threats_RGB.pdf> accessed 12 June 2021.

[30] See Doswald-Beck, IRRC (n 16) 586, 593; for the UK, see Steven Haines, 'The United Kingdom's Manual of the Law of Armed Conflict and the San Remo Manual: Maritime Rules Compared' (2006) 36 Isr YB Hum Rts 89; for the US, see Jane Gilliland Dalton, 'A Comparison between the San Remo Manual and the US Navy's Commander's Handbook' (2006) 36 Isr YB Hum Rts 71. Undoubtedly, the Manual has been used by many more navies in internal legal debates.

[31] There is a Summary at i; a Foreword by Héctor Gros Espiell at ix; an Introductory Note to the Manual at 5; and an Introduction to the Explanation at 61.

[32] The very first sentence of the Summary at i, and mentioned in the Foreword at ix, Introductory Note at 5, and Introduction to the Explanation at 62.

[33] Institut de Droit International (n 8).

[34] See SRM (n 1), arts 3–9.

[35] ibid, Summary, i (emphasis added).

[36] ibid, Introduction to the Explanation, 61–69.

Manual: first, the need to provide an assessment of the continuing validity of the rules in the 1907 Hague Conventions, and, second, the consequences of new technology and modern methods and means of warfare. Third was the fact that, although the Additional Protocols were meant to update the 1949 Geneva Conventions, they focused mostly on rules applicable to warfare on land. Finally, it had been important to look at developments in other parts of international law, including the UN Charter and the law of the sea. All of these developments had introduced a sense of uncertainty with respect to the law of naval warfare, and it was important to address these issues.

Doswald-Beck also wrote an introduction to the Manual for the Current Developments section of the 1995 American Journal of International Law, providing a more detailed explanation of the reasons for developing the Manual, and describing its content.[37] She stated that 'the value of this document is that it has helped clarify the present state of customary law and, in the case of controversial issues such as exclusion zones, proposes a legal regime that is *as consistent as possible* with both recent state practice and related areas of law'.[38] This piece also refers to the four reasons for drafting the Manual mentioned above. In a further piece in the International Review of the Red Cross, she pays more attention to specific norms of the law of armed conflict that were addressed in the Manual, such as the principle of distinction, and refers to the difficulties experienced in taking into account the LOSC. It had proven difficult to combine the concept of military necessity with respecting the LOSC. Controversies had arisen with respect to protection of the environment, freedom of navigation, exploration and exploitation rights in the EEZs of neutral states, and the lawfulness of so-called exclusion zones.[39]

Quite remarkably, the SRM does not seem to have drawn much attention at the time of its appearance: other than the aforementioned journal contributions by Doswald-Beck, very few publications appeared that drew attention to the Manual.[40] If the Manual was discussed, attention was given to the substantive rules, and not to its origins, or the manner in which it had been drafted.

2.3 The Many Faces of Informality

The Manual is an informal document in a variety of ways.[41] Not only is it the work of an informally organized group of experts (government lawyers, military lawyers, and academics), it is also an informal attempt at stating what, at that point in time, was considered

[37] Louise Doswald-Beck, 'The San Remo Manual on International Law Applicable to Armed Conflicts at Sea' (1995) 89 AJIL 192. See also Doswald-Beck, IRRC (n 16) 595–637.

[38] Doswald-Beck, AJIL (n 37) 193 (emphasis added).

[39] Doswald-Beck, IRRC (n 16) 592.

[40] It is equally difficult to find contemporaneous book reviews: in a summary book review in ICLQ, MJ Dixon spoke favourably of the publication, praising 'the diversity of its contributors, geographically and occupationally, the depth of their scholarship and the sheer breadth of their understanding of this branch of international law': MJ Dixon, 'Book Review: San Remo Manual on International Law Applicable to Armed Conflicts at Sea. Edited by Louise Doswald-Beck' (1997) 46 ICLQ 723.

[41] About informality, see Liesbeth Lijnzaad, 'Pandora's Box, Presumptions about the Development of International Law—Inaugural Address' (Maastricht University, 14 October 2011); see also Michael Bothe, 'Private Normunternehmer im Völkerrecht: Gedanken zur Fortentwicklung des Völkerrechts durch nicht-staatliche Institutionen' in Holger P Hestermeyer and others (eds), *Coexistence, Cooperation and Solidarity: Liber Amicorum Rüdiger Wolfrum, Vol II* (Brill 2012) 1399.

to be the applicable law of naval warfare. It was drafted by these experts in their personal capacities and, apparently, as was stressed many times, without any intention of developing the law of naval warfare. The recurring emphasis on informality and the way in which the work has been described seems almost to downplay the importance of the Manual.

The Foreword to the Manual tells us that the project started in 1987 with an initiative of three professors, which led to a series of meetings with legal and naval experts, eventually resulting in the 1994 Manual. The image is one of informal get-togethers of experts participating on a personal basis, leading to an important, yet informal, document. The Manual, on the front page of its printed edition, identifies itself as having been 'prepared by international lawyers and naval experts convened by the International Institute of Humanitarian Law [the San Remo Institute]'. This description suggests the imprimatur of the Institute, and the convening power that it apparently had to organize the project that led to the SRM. In spite of the role of the San Remo Institute, it would appear that coordination and editing of the Manual were in the capable hands of the ICRC, and, in particular, those of Doswald-Beck. The convening power of the ICRC is better understood than that of the San Remo Institute, but perhaps the participants were on a mission to revisit the laws of naval warfare anyway, and would have participated irrespective of the position of the organizer.

The Manual was brought together by a seemingly informally organized group of experts who considered this endeavour to be an important project on which to spend their time.[42] This group of experts consisted of a majority of persons who were government employees or military lawyers, although all participated in their personal capacities.[43] The expertise and personal authority of the participants have lent credence to the norms that were formulated in the Manual.

2.3.1 The Manual as a Collection of Non-binding Norms

The Manual is a revisiting of the Hague Conventions, and some informal documents relating to naval warfare that had become outdated. In that sense, the Manual stands out amidst informal documents: it did not start from scratch, but essentially relied on pre-existing formal law in the 1907 Hague Conventions. Not everything had become irrelevant, and the Manual was intended to distil the core rules of the law of naval warfare, as perceived to remain relevant in the 1980s and early 1990s. The Foreword stated that the SRM was a 'contemporary restatement of the law, together with some progressive development, which takes into account recent State practice, technological developments, and the effect of related areas of the law'. The emphasis on informality seems to take the shape of modesty here: there is nothing to worry about—this is a very limited effort. It is mostly a restatement.

The Manual is informal in the sense of *not* having the pretence to be the law; it aims to reiterate the existing law, and to include some aspects of development. At the same time,

[42] SRM (n 1) Summary at i, Foreword at ix, Introductory Note at 5.

[43] A list of participants, as well as the composition of the team that authored the Explanation are provided in the publication of the Manual. The rapporteurs and authors consisted of six people with government/military connections, four from academia and one from an NGO. The group of participants consisted of thirty people with government/military connections, twenty-one from academia and five from NGOs; the group of associated experts and observers consisted of fifty-one people with government/military connections, twenty-nine from academia and eleven from NGOs. Amongst them were nine women. See SRM (n 1) Annex, at 46–55.

it was acknowledged that some new rules had been formulated as a consequence of the changes (in warfare, in technology, and in law) that had taken place since 1907. It is, thus, a collection of legally-binding (old) rules, and new rules formulated and proposed by experts. The latter are not binding in a legal sense, and indeed cannot be so, as has been forcefully underlined by Dalton, who points to the absence of customary law, and, worse, a less rigorous approach to what constitutes customary international law.[44]

The Manual is explicitly and frequently qualified as informal and non-binding.[45] However it is, as Doswald-Beck says, 'believed to be present law',[46] while Kraska calls it an 'authoritative restatement of law'.[47] Greenwood considers the Manual to be a 'guide to conduct' existing within customary law.[48] The Manual is further described as being 'very helpful for dissemination purposes' and it is suggested that it 'would encourage the drafting of more national manuals'.[49] It would 'help consolidate contemporary international customary law, promote its coherent development and thereby provide a much firmer foundation for possible future treaty developments than could otherwise have been the case'.[50] The general view appeared to be that the Manual was a good reflection of the law, and that it would be a useful and practical tool for future use. That, in itself, was a functional analysis, not an evaluation in terms of the sources of international law, as set out in Article 38 of the Statute of the International Court of Justice (ICJ Statute).

A possible alternative view is that the work of the San Remo group could be understood as preparatory work for a future treaty on naval warfare. Experts had, however, considered that it was premature to embark on diplomatic negotiations to draft a treaty on this subject, and it would appear that the existence of the Manual itself took away any sense of urgency in that respect: no steps to embark on a formal codification of the law of naval warfare have been taken since, because the Manual seemed to suffice.

2.3.2 The Availability of Norms and their Acceptance

The Manual brought together a compilation of the law of naval warfare in a field where little had been happening for a long time. As noted above, little attention seems to have been paid to the Manual at the time of its publication. It appears that the Manual was received tacitly but positively by its intended audience: specialists of the law of naval warfare, who were likely satisfied that the Manual did not contain any rules that were out of the ordinary. It filled a void perceived by those most interested in the field of the law of naval warfare.

A manual drafted by a group of experts in their private capacities, and under the umbrella of a private institution (the San Remo Institute, assisted by the ICRC) would perhaps

[44] Dalton (n 30) 72–76.

[45] Doswald-Beck, IRRC (n 16) 583–94; James Kraska, 'Military Operations' in Donald R Rothwell and others (eds), *The Oxford Handbook of the Law of the Sea* (OUP 2015) 866, 877.

[46] Doswald-Beck, IRRC (n 16) 587; Doswald-Beck, AJIL (n 37) 195.

[47] Kraska (n 45) 877.

[48] Christopher Greenwood, 'International Humanitarian Law and the Laws of War: Preliminary Report for the Centennial Commemoration of the First Hague Peace Conference 1899' (Centennial of the First International Peace Conference 1999) 54, para 126.

[49] See Doswald-Beck, IRRC (n 16) 587 and Steven Haines, 'War at Sea: Nineteenth-Century Laws for Twenty-First-Century Wars?' (2016) 98(2) IRRC 419, 434. See also the comparison between the Manual and the US Navy's Commander's Handbook by Dalton (n 30) *passim*.

[50] Doswald-Beck, IRRC (n 16) 594.

not, in itself, call for a reaction by states: this exercise had been purely private and informal. There were some signs of acceptance of the Manual, which, although drafted by experts in their personal capacities, formulated obligations of states.[51] It could also be suggested that silence proved the timeliness of the Manual, and implied that the result was generally supported: it was work well done. Alternatively, the absence of a reaction might point to the law of naval warfare having become a limited domain in itself, which did not attract broad attention from either the community of military lawyers or indeed those interested in the law of the sea. In that line of reasoning, the Manual was of interest to what had become a 'niche market' of naval lawyers, and the occasional law of the sea specialist. And, as Doswald-Beck had written, the work on the Manual had been '*intentionally undertaken with a view to arriving at a non-binding document*. In view of the extent of uncertainty in the law, the participants decided that it was premature to think in terms of a draft treaty'.[52] Consequently, there was no reason for states to worry, or to get involved: even the authors of the Manual had said that a treaty would be premature, and they had no intention of developing the law of naval warfare. There was no reason for comments or reactions.

Since its publication, the Manual appears to have become accepted as authoritative, if not binding, without necessarily explicitly stating that it is *legally* binding. There had been no normative intent, as is stated throughout. What the Manual brought together was a set of well-organized rules, seen as a proper reflection of the relevant legal norms as they stood at that time. In a field where rules are difficult to find, or appear to be old-fashioned, it is particularly practical if rules are collected, re-edited, and brushed-up to look like contemporary rules.

If done well, such a revised collection of rules will bring practical benefits: practitioners will start to operate on the understanding that these rules are a relevant and helpful tool and, gradually, the rules will become authoritative. This new (revised) version of old rules will, thus, develop a certain 'predictive' effect in day-to-day reality, which is reinforced by the quality and clarity of the formulation of these norms, as well as the personal authority of the drafters.

Such informal rules are useful in a practical sense: they are available, accessible, and make sense for contemporary military operations. The availability of organized norms makes them operationally attractive, and, over time, these norms will gain a status that would not otherwise be achievable for norms formulated by a self-appointed informal group of experts. Rules formulated in an informal process may gradually become accepted as authoritative norms *because* of their availability and perceived utility. From there, it may no longer be necessary to explain exactly why these norms are, somehow, binding: norms will be followed for a long time without anyone questioning their legal character when the relevant community adheres to these norms. Thus, the informal rules exist, the document gradually obtains authority as states rely on it, and normative effect may develop.

Alternatively, customary law may develop: it is not difficult to see how practice on the basis of informal norms, once it is sufficiently uniform, could become relevant in a legal

[51] Kingdom of the Netherlands and Russian Federation, 'Outcome of the Celebrations of the Centennial of the First International Peace Conference: Report on the Conclusions of the Expert Discussions on the three "Centennial Themes", Peace Palace, The Hague, 17–18 May 1999 and Smolny Institute, St Petersburg, 22–25 June 1999' 16, para 73 <https://www.un.org/law/cod/sixth/54/english/hague.htm> accessed 12 June 2021; see also Roach (n 11) 77; and Haines, 'War at Sea' (n 49) 434–35, about Israel's reliance on the Manual with respect to the Gaza blockade in 2010.

[52] Doswald-Beck, AJIL (n 37) 207 (emphasis added).

sense, as referred to in Article 38(1)(b) of the ICJ Statute. A fundamental caveat, however, is that, with an absence of naval warfare, relevant practice for the development of customary law based on the Manual is not really available. However, a further question would be how to weigh the fact that the Manual appears to have played a role in the formulation of various military handbooks. It raises the question of whether, or how, reliance on informal norms at national level, for example the reception of the Manual by inclusion of its norms in national military handbooks, contributes to their legal effect.

This process of revision and reformulation of old rules, and the formulation of new rules through the interpretation of old principles, helps their acceptance as relevant norms, and, in the end, as rules of law. The fact that the newly formulated rules were based on the old Hague Conventions and their general principles suggests that there is agreement between experts on a consistent, contemporary interpretation and, thus, these rules come with a cloak of obligation *because* they are an agreed contemporary reinterpretation of what had already been binding. There is some kind of instant authority here, related to their pedigree in being drawn from the 1907 Hague Conventions.

It may, however, be difficult to accept that the newly formulated rules are (still) based on pre-existing norms (dating back to 1907), and do not change the original rules in any way. Reinterpreting existing rules to clarify their applicability to modern technology suggests an objective activity of an explanatory nature, but is this necessarily always the case?

In the meantime, this informal process of adopting norms looks inconspicuous because it appears to be based on the practicality of using clear and concrete rules for contemporary situations. The origin of these norms may not have been with states, yet the acceptance of these norms by states, in their practice, may lead to them becoming authoritative. The mere fact that its authors stated that they did not to have the intention of creating law does not necessarily imply that the Manual did not have normative effect. As mentioned before, it could be argued that once it had appeared, the very existence of the Manual made the idea of a formal process of lawmaking through the negotiation of a treaty on naval warfare redundant.

There is a need for caution with respect to the quality of such an informal process, and how it considers substantive norms and state practice, as well as the representativeness of, and participation in, such discussions. The quality and working methods in such a process deserve attention, and a description of working methods and analysis going beyond merely stating that 'the experts discussed , is necessary. Explicit accountability is particularly important: the analytical process used to evaluate norms and their contemporary role should be described, and this articulation should clarify how views have been developed with respect to the existence (or not) of customary law, and the ways in which the existence of acceptance of a practice and the *opinio juris* have been evaluated. Outsiders ought to be able to trace this analysis, and to understand how choices were made in formulating norms. It is not the attraction of the rules formulated that should determine their success but, rather, the thorough methodology used, that provides accountability for the rules developed.[53] The Manual does so, and, in its introduction, gives an overview of how the work was undertaken.[54]

[53] cf the description of the analytical process in Jean-Marie Henckaerts and Louise Doswald-Beck (eds), *Customary International Humanitarian Law* (CUP 2005), Introduction, Assessment of International Customary Law, xxxi–xlv; and ICRC, *Commentary on the Second Geneva Convention* (n 13) 5–14.

[54] SRM (n 1) Introduction at 61–69; Haines, 'War at Sea' (n 49) speaks of a rigorous methodology, 434, fn 56.

2.3.3 The Interests of States

Informal processes take place in various formats, ranging from semi-official (originating in a decision from a formal intergovernmental body such as the International Conference of the Red Cross and the Red Cross movement, or the invitation of a state), to processes that are completely self-organized by experts or institutes with a specific interest. Semi-official processes tend to be more focused on providing accountability for the development of the work by providing reports or elaborate introductions, and also tend to be more balanced in the selection of the participating experts.[55]

It is not uncommon in informal processes to use a somewhat opaque process of selecting participants: it is not necessarily clear who gets to be invited (or who has *not* been invited) and, particularly in privately led processes, these choices would not be explicit. Organizers will stress the importance of participation by practitioners and experts with 'real' experience in the field. They will say something like '[W]e are all friends of the law of naval warfare', and there is a common understanding that 'we' as friends will be torchbearers for the project. The large number of experts with a government or military background is noticeable, and it would seem that a good geographical or gender balance amongst the participating experts is not a top priority in privately led processes. Invitations are not geared towards diversity, but rather expertise and experience, if not like-mindedness. The impact of these processes, in whichever form, will, to a certain extent, depend on the participants and their positions in government, or within the armed forces. As participants, they will not only transmit the views developed by the group, but are also understood to carry these views forward.

To a certain extent, such informal expert meetings mirror diplomatic practices, with participation by invitation and confidential discussions. Selection also happens at governmental expert meetings, particularly when governmental experts meet with a view to considering (or reconsidering) the law in a particularly sensitive field. Confidential meetings of 'high-level officials' are rarely referred to, and will go unnoticed. They will work under so-called Chatham House Rules, and views expressed during such meetings may not be attributed to the speaker or her state, as this would endanger the free flow of discussions, and the willingness to share the more in-depth (political) considerations behind legal opinions. In such a setting, it is clear—at least to those with an understanding of the work of diplomats and government lawyers—that participants are carefully selected: one cannot participate by one's own volition. While outsiders may attack such confidentiality (and the lack of a possibility to scrutinize discussions, or to present their own views), it is normally considered necessary by the organizers and participants. Without the privilege of closed doors, discussions are likely to be less frank and, indeed, more superficial. This would take away the interest in holding such meetings: if everything is discussed before the eyes of the world, more difficult or sensitive questions would not be addressed.

Clearly, the hesitations about the selectivity of such groups come from outsiders, including academic observers. The outside audience may raise questions about the composition, as well as questions focusing on what will be perceived as the work of a selective group

[55] Reports and special papers prepared for the Round Tables and the comments thereon have been published in Wolff Heintschel von Heinegg (ed), *Bochumer Schriften zur Friedenssicherung und zum Humanitäres Völkerrechts*, Vol 7 (Bochum session, 1989), Vol 8 (Toulon session, 1990), Vol 24 (Bergen session, 1992) and Vol 25 (Ottawa session, 1992). For the 1987 San Remo session, see 'General Report of the San Remo Roundtable of Experts, 17 June 1987' (1987) 14(4) Syracuse J Intl'l L & Com 563–64.

with the pretence of having the final view on the matter, while having a specific (governmental) interest. Although the group may have undertaken an important task, the method of its composition (by invitation—a true 'old boys' network?) may cause problems for the acceptance of the results. There is a relationship between the informality of a project and the ownership of its results. Ownership by a limited and exclusive group may hamper broader acceptance once the project is concluded.

If the establishment of new and improved norms is of importance to states, a treaty is clearly the best way forward: written law will likely have the advantage of clarity and transparency. Even if drafting may be sloppy at times (and sometimes on purpose) a treaty will bring clarity about norms, and about which states are bound. Reality tells us, however, that a formal diplomatic process may not always be possible, for a variety of political reasons.

Understanding the functioning of informal lawmaking as a process, and its potential to influence the substantive content of international law, implies that this method may also be used with the (implicit) intention of steering the development of law. If this process is how informal lawmaking functions, there is no need to wait for treaty negotiations that may never happen, and setting up a well-organized informal process may suffice to initiate a process of changing the law. Taking the trouble of formulating the rules on naval warfare as they stood in the first half of the 1990s was an activity with a purpose: there is a reason why such projects are undertaken.[56]

Informality has its benefits for states. Rules formulated by a group of experts will, on the face of it, be no more than rules drafted by a private group with no governmental authority. Governments can ignore, support, or criticize these rules without claiming any ownership. It will be possible to downplay the role of the group of experts for lack of formal authority, when the results of their work are not acceptable. Or, alternatively, states may praise the result as a proper reflection of the law when the text is to one's liking, and the work carries the authority of the best experts working in the field. Apart from the content, there is, of course, the possibility for states to question the group's composition (particularly when one was not invited to participate), or even the very idea of addressing specific subject at particular time, and in manner. States have many ways of either rejecting or embracing the result.

When, for whatever reason, states do not wish to embark on drafting a treaty, an informal instrument provides a viable alternative for formulating norms. Informality creates flexibility for governments with respect to the outcome. It would seem that informal normative projects provide a possibility of giving norms a kind of 'trial run': the newly formulated norms will become accessible, and will provide clarity for practitioners.[57] Their operational utility in military operations can be tested, and the position of allies with regard to these norms evaluated. More generally, governments will want to weigh their reaction to these rules: is this effort merely academic and a non-binding private project of no consequence, or are these norms a well-considered guide for practice and, indeed, a fair reflection of the state of the law? With informal rules, there is no immediate need for states to show their hand, which provides an opportunity for testing the rules.

[56] As is documented in the publication of the Manual, a number of governments and publicly funded institutions provided financial support or meeting space, and a great many military officers and civil servants participated in the work. See SRM (n 1) Introduction, The Process, 64–66 *passim*.

[57] The new norms will be easily available; they will be like prêt-à-porter fashion that can be picked up in a shop.

Also, the newly formulated rules will, presumably, not come as a surprise to the states whose experts have participated. Acceptable rules are likely to have been formulated together with experts from other states. Support for these rules may be anticipated from the other participating states. Jointly, a clarification of the law as it stands will have been achieved, together with some development in new areas for which consensus will have been found during the work.

Informality has a further advantage for those national systems where a government is under an obligation to announce its intention to negotiate a particular treaty or, indeed, to obtain prior parliamentary approval. Starting out with an informal project is clearly no more than an informal project, and so will not require any specific parliamentary oversight.

In sum, it may be concluded that informality has a certain number of advantages for states (or at least for those states whose governmental experts participated) when working on the restatement of the law of naval warfare or, indeed, its development. States ultimately give meaning to informal lawmaking in the operation of international law.

2.4 The Trend towards Informality in the Law of Armed Conflict

In a little-known article, Michael Bothe has addressed the informal meetings creating normative documents that have started to appear over the past twenty years, particularly in the field of the law of armed conflict, addressing contemporary issues of law and the development of law.[58] Bothe discusses, in particular, the 'privatization' of the development of the laws of war through a series of informal processes that address specific fields and concrete issues for which there appears to be no formal or explicit governmental wish for lawmaking. This work leaves space for, as he calls them, 'private normative entrepreneurs' ('Private Normunternehmer') to embark on a discussion process about the adequacy and possible improvement, clarification, or refinement of existing norms. The organizers set the agenda, frame the project, and will be largely responsible for its outcome, and participants will participate in their private capacities.

The San Remo Manual is not the only informal collection of rules of the law of armed conflict, and it will not be the last. Other rules developed in informal or semi-informal settings appeared in the years that followed the publication of the Manual, all dealing with distinct chapters of the law of armed conflict. To name but a few: the 2006 San Remo Manual on the Law of Non-International Armed Conflict,[59] the 2009 Harvard Manual on Air and Missile Warfare,[60] the 2012 Copenhagen Principles and Guidelines on Detention in Military Operations,[61] the Tallinn Manuals 1.0[62] and 2.0,[63] as well as the ongoing development of

[58] See Bothe (n 41).

[59] International Institute of Humanitarian Law, 'The Manual on the Law of Non-International Armed Conflict, With Commentary' (2006) <https://www.legal-tools.org/doc/ccf497/pdf/> accessed 29 June 2021.

[60] Program on Humanitarian Policy and Conflict Research at Harvard University (HCPR), 'Manual on International Law Applicable to Air and Missile Warfare' (Bern, 2009) <https://reliefweb.int/sites/reliefweb.int/files/resources/8B2E79FC145BFB3D492576E00021ED34-HPCR-may2009.pdf> accessed 14 June 2021.

[61] Copenhagen Process on the Handling of Detainees in International Military Operations, 'Copenhagen Process: Principles and Guidelines' (2012) <https://iihl.org/wp-content/uploads/2018/04/Copenhagen-Process-Principles-and-Guidelines.pdf> accessed 29 June 2021.

[62] Under the auspices of the NATO CCOECD in Tallinn: Michael N Schmitt (ed), *Tallinn Manual on the International Law Applicable to Cyber Warfare* (CUP 2013) (hereafter 'Tallinn Manual 1.0').

[63] Under the auspices of the NATO CCOECD in Tallinn: Michael N Schmitt (ed), *Tallinn Manual 2.0 on the International Law Applicable to Cyber Operations* (2nd edn, CUP 2017). Technically, this does not deal with the law

the Woomera Manual on International Law of Military Space Operations.[64] On the more formal side of the scale, the ICRC has produced its customary law study,[65] and guidance on direct participation in hostilities,[66] as well as documents on the law of occupation,[67] and on international humanitarian law and the environment.[68] The 2008 Montreux Manual on Private Military Companies was produced in a state-led process, with the support of the Swiss government.[69]

There seems to be a growing number of informal documents addressing parts of the laws of war, and in each of them the recurring question is whether its content is a restatement—a (re)interpretation of existing (but dated or imprecise) law and its underlying principles, in the light of current developments—or, alternatively, the development of new norms on the basis of these underlying principles as new problems arise. It is most likely that all of these aspects are at stake in every case: sometimes existing norms may suggest subsequent rules for new situations, and at other times even the underlying principles may not suffice, and will require additional creativity to suggest what future norms could be. In the latter case, the question of normative intent and lawmaking will arise. This aspect of creating 'one's own law' is what is most worrying about informal lawmaking in the law of armed conflict: what starts out as a reflection about a restatement may turn into the development of rules that, perhaps without the intention of lawmaking, may still have a very similar normative effect. This phenomenon is why the mention of the SRM including 'some progressive development'[70] leads to some nagging questions, not about the need for additional contemporary rules, but about the way in which these are developed, and with what authority.

This overview, which likely is incomplete, suggests that this process of informal rules slipping into international law is stronger in fields where the common understanding is that any attempt formally to develop the law would be ill-advised. It leads to a number of follow-up questions to be addressed in future: are the laws of armed conflict perhaps more prone to informal lawmaking than other fields of international law and, if so, why? The present book, however, draws our attention to similar developments in the law of the sea, and developments towards informal norm-setting are visible in other fields as well. While there may be good reasons for the reticence to embark on formal lawmaking, the determination *not* to move to the formal development of law leaves a space for the 'private normative

of armed conflict, but with attacks below the threshold of armed conflict. It is currently being redeveloped (Tallinn 3.0 process): see CCDCOE, 'CCDCOE to Host the Tallinn Manual 3.0 Process' <https://ccdcoe.org/news/2020/ccdcoe-to-host-the-tallinn-manual-3-0-process/> accessed 29 June 2021.

64 Under the auspices of Adelaide Law School (Australia): see The University of Adelaide, 'The Woomera Manual' <https://law.adelaide.edu.au/woomera/> accessed 29 June 2021.

65 Henckaerts and Doswald-Beck (n 53).

66 Nils Melzer, 'Interpretive Guidance on the Notion of Direct Participation in Hostilities under International Humanitarian Law' (ICRC 2009) <https://www.icrc.org/en/doc/assets/files/other/icrc-002-0990.pdf> accessed 17 June 2021.

67 Tristan Ferraro (ed), 'Expert Meeting: Occupation and Other Forms of Administration of Foreign Territory' (ICRC 2012) <https://www.icrc.org/en/doc/assets/files/publications/icrc-002-4094.pdf> accessed 29 June 2021; ICRC, *Guidelines on the Protection of the Natural Environment in Armed Conflict* (ICRC 2020).

68 A project somewhat coinciding with the ILC work on the protection of the environment in relation to armed conflicts: see International Law Commission, 'Analytical Guide to the Work of the International Law Commission' <https://legal.un.org/ilc/guide/8_7.shtml> accessed 29 June 2021.

69 ICRC, 'The Montreux Document on Pertinent International Legal Obligations and Good Practices for States related to Operations of Private Military and Security Companies during Armed Conflict' (2008) <https://www.eda.admin.ch/dam/eda/en/documents/aussenpolitik/voelkerrecht/20192511-montreux-document_EN.pdf> accessed 29 June 2021.

70 SRM (n 1) Foreword by Héctor Gros Espiell, ix.

entrepreneurs' who wish to address specific chapters of the law from their own perspectives. Private groups have more flexibility in setting their research agenda than states. Or perhaps this long list of informal restatements that have become documents accepted as authoritative just demonstrates that manuals and informality are in fashion these days.

2.5 San Remo Manual 2.0: Preparing a Sequel?

By the middle of the 2000s, some experts on the law of naval warfare began to comment on the Manual as being outdated. It became clear that the mood started to change with a publication by Heintschel von Heinegg in 2006.[71] The Manual had been discussed at an annual Round Table of the San Remo Institute, and the title of von Heinegg's article ('*How* to update ... ') seemed to take for granted that the Manual concluded in 1994 was already in need of revision some twelve years later, and that it was just a matter of determining the way to do this.

In his view, some aspects of maritime operations were insufficiently covered by the Manual, and the article provides a list of areas that ought to be reconsidered. First of all, some definitions no longer reflected contemporary state practice.[72] Most of the definitions in paragraph 13 are taken from, or at least based on, definitions used elsewhere, as is clear from the Explanation, and is a useful way of cross-referencing the Manual with other parts of international law.[73] One of the problems is the absence of a definition of 'maritime autonomous vehicles' in paragraph 13 of the SRM. At the time of writing the original Manual, this technology was in its infancy, and the phenomenon has very much developed since: it is a clear example of questions that arise in the law of armed conflict as a direct consequence of technological development.

Also, there was a need to reflect again on the 'due regard' principle and the rights of the coastal state or third states, and to provide further guidance as to what this principle entails.[74] This issue appears to be directly connected to the notion of 'hostile actions' in neutral waters, which required more clarity.[75] Other matters mentioned were the references to military aircraft and aerial combat, mine warfare, the lack of a definition of 'blockade', and the methods and means of naval warfare. Moreover, there is, of course, the matter of maritime neutrality, which needed to be considered more generally, including whether or not this doctrine is still of relevance in the law of naval warfare in the era of the UN Charter.

More recently, von Heinegg mentioned that 'a couple of new developments, such as Unmanned Marine Ships (UMS), need to be incorporated. The rules on submarine cables are insufficient because they do not account of their importance for cyberspace, i.e. they are no longer bi-polar connecting merely two countries. There are ... open questions such as the standard of feasibility in light of Article 57(4) AP I[76] and the applicability of the concept

[71] Wolff Heintschel von Heinegg, 'How to Update the San Remo Manual on International Law Applicable to Armed Conflict at Sea' (2006) 36 Isr YB Hum Rts 119.

[72] This is an unusual comment in terms of the law of treaties: surely changing definitions will have an impact on substantive norms. A lack of definitions will not necessarily prevent the development of relevant norms as deduced from general principles of law (such as the law of naval warfare, or indeed the law of the sea).

[73] SRM (n 1) 84–92.

[74] ibid, paras 34–35.

[75] ibid, paras 15–16.

[76] AP I (n 4) art 57(4) reads '[i]n the conduct of military operations at sea or in the air, each Party to the conflict shall, in conformity with its rights and duties under the rules of international law applicable in armed conflict, take all reasonable precautions to avoid losses of civilian lives and damage to civilian objects.'

of direct participation in hostilities.'[77] These views are somewhat different in their emphases from those expressed in the earlier article, but then thirteen years had passed since that article.

Von Heinegg's article had a clear message: it was time to consider revising the Manual. Rapid technological development had made it imperative to reconvene and work on an informal declaration to amend or clarify the Manual, to prevent it becoming marginalized. Yet, also in 2006, Haines considered that 'suggestions that the San Remo process ... should now be repeated and a second revised edition of the resultant manual produced, are assessed as being unlikely to meet with official enthusiasm'.[78] This observation was made at the same time that von Heinegg started to promote a review, reflecting that views at the time apparently differed.

Considering a revision or a reinterpretation of a document that is, itself, already a reinterpretation is an intriguing plan: how often can the law on naval warfare be reinterpreted? In more general terms: can this process of reinterpretation be repeated time and again, or is there an end to it, in light of the declared aim of merely restating, as opposed to developing, the law of naval warfare?

While it has been suggested that there is a need to update the Manual as it 'no longer properly reflect[s] contemporary State practice or meet[s] the realities of modern maritime and naval operations', and would 'ultimately render obsolete the great progress achieved by the San Remo Manual', one may wonder what the effect would be on the Manual's authoritative status. This could also be argued the other way: a revision could put its status into question and reduce its normative effect.

It is unclear, at this stage, whether the aim is to reinterpret the *Paragraphs* of the Manual (the rules themselves) and/or the text of the *Explanation* in the Manual, or perhaps to start from scratch and begin with a contemporary reinterpretation of the original 1907 Hague Conventions. It may well be that all of these approaches will be used. By comparison, the ICRC chose to update the Commentaries to the Geneva Conventions, rather than attempting to update the Conventions.

By putting a revision on the agenda, the project appeared to have moved well away from its origins in the 1907 Hague Conventions. For want of a better expression, the question becomes one about the 'elasticity' of (re)interpretation: for how long, or how often, is it possible to reinterpret old treaties, particularly when actual practice has been mostly absent, and little customary law has developed in the meantime? How far can reinterpretation of written law stretch before it breaks its anchors in the original treaties and becomes creative construction rather than interpretation? Is such interpretation guided by the need for new authoritative norms, where the connection with the old norms is a construction rather than the result of straightforward interpretation? And, if so, does this 'repetition of reinterpretation' not, in fact, demonstrate that what is needed is lawmaking in the traditional sense, in a field where all will agree the norms are in need of an update?

[77] In an email to the author, April 2019. It should be noted that, in the meantime, the ICRC's Interpretive Guidance on the Notion of Direct Participation in Hostilities had appeared, in 2009, and this had received some substantial criticism.

[78] Haines, 'The United Kingdom's Manual of the Law of Armed Conflict and the San Remo Manual: Maritime Rules Compared' (n 30) 111. The reference to 'official enthusiasm' hints at the close connections between participants and government. By 2016, Haines seemed to have changed his mind: Haines, 'War at Sea' (n 49) 447.

Is it possible, or acceptable, to reinterpret the 1907 Hague Conventions without visible state participation? The possibility may not be such a problem, and well-formulated rules tend to tacitly become adopted as authoritative. Acceptability is a different question: where would those new rules come from? Reinterpreting old rules drafted for conflicts and weapons that no longer exist, to create rules appropriate for the use of contemporary military technology, implies interpretation of the old law and its underlying principles, as well as imagination and creativity. Such work is also likely to be influenced by the social connections and backgrounds of the participants or, indeed, their experience in the military. This effort may take the drafters away from the revision of the old treaties, or from their interpretation in line with the underlying principles, presumably with consequences for their normative value. It is not a given that old treaties or the underlying principles necessarily present clear suggestions for contemporary issues.

The 'due regard' standard in the Manual, with respect to the marine environment, and also with respect to cables and pipelines, proved to be a major point of contention.[79] While noting that due regard obligations appear in the LOSC,[80] particularly in terms of obligations to respect the rights of coastal states, Dalton considered that there had not been demonstrations of state practice or *opinio juris* supporting the inclusion of the due regard norms in the Manual. In her comparison between the Manual and the US Navy Commander's Handbook,[81] she strongly disagreed with references to due regard as not pertaining to the law of naval warfare. Haines, writing about the UK's Manual of the Law of Armed Conflict, similarly notes that the rule on due respect for rare and fragile ecosystems or depleted, threatened, or endangered species is 'neither customary law nor worded in a way that suggests any form of obligation whatever'.[82] He continues to state that it was important to 'avoid absolute suggestions that coastal States' activities within their zones of jurisdiction beyond territorial limits have necessary priority over traditional high seas freedoms *protected under the current law of the sea*'.[83]

Even though the San Remo group had earlier dropped 'respect' in favour of 'due regard', these authors suggested that the standard ought to be even less constraining.[84] A late case of having second thoughts, if anything. It is straightforward pushback: the view ought to remain that warfare could take place anywhere but the territorial sea of a neutral or non-participating state, and there was no legal basis for obligations of due regard that might follow from the LOSC. This debate is a struggle about maritime zones and the possibility of naval warfare, or, more precisely, the geographic location of naval conflict.

These comments also demonstrate two other things. First, the view that, as the extended maritime zones are not under full sovereignty of the coastal state, and otherwise essentially remain high seas (where naval warfare can take place), limitations on military action due to the rights established in the LOSC need to be proven to be customary law in order to exist.

[79] References to 'due regard' appear in paras 12, 34–36, 44, 88, and 106.

[80] See LOSC (n 22) arts 58(3), 87(2).

[81] Dalton (n 30) 78–84.

[82] Haines, 'The United Kingdom's Manual of the Law of Armed Conflict and the San Remo Manual: Maritime Rules Compared' (n 30) 99–100.

[83] ibid (emphasis added). The latter part of this sentence seems open for debate: there is no explicit authorization for military activities in the EEZ or on the continental shelf in either Arts 58 or 87 of LOSC. Art87(2) contains a due regard obligation, and the discussion of the high seas freedoms tends to be about peacetime uses, including naval exercises, but never explicitly about naval warfare. Note, though, that Haines relies on an argument from the initial San Remo discussion to choose between 'due regard' and 'respect'.

[84] SRM (n 1) 84, para 12.2.

The inclusion of limitations to high seas rights in the LOSC, following from coastal states' interests in the EEZ—embodied in due regard obligations—in the law of naval warfare, cannot be presumed to form part of the law on naval warfare, as this understanding would first require the development of specific customary law.[85] Second, by implication, the view appears to be that only rules established as customary law ought to appear in the San Remo Manual, which ties in with the idea of the Manual being a restatement.

These comments on due regard differ from the idea of 'some progressive development', as mentioned by Gros Espiell in his foreword to the Manual.[86] If a future revision of the SRM would be stepping away from the due regard standard (particularly as referred to in paragraphs 12, 34, and 35, as well as 36, of the Manual), it would be backtracking from what was progressive development in 1994, more than twenty-five years ago. The wisdom of such an approach would, particularly, need to be considered with respect to paragraphs where the due regard norm refers to the marine environment. Any revision would, presumably, need to take into account the ICRC's 2020 Guidelines on the Protection of the Natural Environment in Armed Conflict, as well as the International Law Commission (ILC)'s Work on Guidelines on Protection of the Natural Environment in Armed Conflict.[87]

Another aspect of the SRM that has been mentioned as needing an update is the standard of protection afforded to cables and pipelines.[88] Cables and pipelines appear twice in the Manual, in paragraphs 37 and 60(a).[89] Paragraph 37 is the most contentious provision, and refers to the obligation to take care to avoid damage to cables and pipelines that do not exclusively serve the belligerents, on the high seas and seabed beyond national jurisdiction. The Explanation is relatively brief, and recognizes that cables or pipelines exclusively serving one or more belligerents might be legitimate military objectives.[90] Dalton comments that the Manual does not provide reasons for abandoning the traditional definition of a military objective (the use of 'might'), which differs from the traditional targeting analysis.[91] Furthermore, she notes that such submarine communications cables, exclusively used by belligerents, do not exist anymore, and thus the rule is not supported by state practice.[92]

This issue is at the heart of the suggestion to reconsider the position of cables and pipelines in the Manual, in view of developments with respect to cyberwarfare. It is not a given that potentially belligerent cyber activity will necessarily take place through cables exclusively serving the belligerent(s), but it is more the case that cables are used by various states and the public at large, and that this use will raise questions of targeting. Moreover, it is perhaps not the individual cable that matters today but, rather, its role within a digital network.

Drawing attention to cables in naval warfare, as related to their role in the cyber domain, brings the Tallinn Manual 1.0 into the discussion.[93] This manual does not explicitly provide rules with respect to cables, but its commentary discusses cables with respect to its Rules 1

[85] This discussion about the applicability of the (peacetime) LOSC in times of naval warfare resembles discussions about the *lex specialis* relationship between human rights law and international humanitarian law and, more generally, questions about priority and applicable law during armed conflict that do require further reflection.

[86] SRM (n 1) ix.

[87] See International Law Commission (n 68) and ICRC (n 67).

[88] For cables and pipelines relevant to naval warfare, see LOSC, Arts 51(2), 58(1), 79, 87, and 112.

[89] Para 60(a) is about the targetability of enemy merchant ships and identifies 'cutting undersea cables and pipelines' as an activity that turns an enemy merchant vessel into a military objective.

[90] SRM (n 1) 111, para 37.1.

[91] Dalton (n 30) 84.

[92] ibid 75, 84.

[93] Schmitt, Tallinn Manual 1.0 (n 62)

(sovereignty over cyber infrastructure)[94] and 3 (jurisdiction over cables on the continental shelf).[95] While it seems reasonable to suggest that a reflection on the connection between the law of naval warfare and the law on cyberwarfare is necessary, this recognition would, in effect, imply a discussion based on two sets of informal rules formulated by self-selected groups of experts.

The issues discussed above are examples of the intricacies of updating the Manual in which it may appear that updating is a simple matter, but it is clearly not. Whether one may want to 'correct' earlier texts (the 'due regard' issue), or address new(er) technologies (the cables issue), the expanding network of informal norms in the law of armed conflict is relevant, and must also be taken into account.

It took some years after von Heinegg's initial article to organize the update process, and apparently the Council of the San Remo Institute decided in 2018 to facilitate activities of the San Remo Manual update process.[96] A first meeting eventually took place in Copenhagen in October 2019.[97] How and whether this process will develop is for the future to see.[98]

2.6 Conclusions

The San Remo Manual has been an important achievement: it made the law of naval warfare accessible again when it appeared in 1994. It is fair to say that the Manual has, by now, become broadly accepted by states,[99] but what is meant by such a statement? Does this mean that it is accepted as a description of the current state of the customary law of naval warfare: a contemporary reinterpretation? Or does it mean nothing more than acceptance as a practical and authoritative tool that provides an organized overview of where the law stands in a field where little formal development has taken place while the technological development of naval warfare has run ahead?

Accepting informal rules as being 'relevant' is a non-legal qualification, and states may not want to be explicit about their opinions on a particular document: there is often no need for an explicit determination. Informality and informal lawmaking exist because states accept informal rules and have an interest in informality. The Manual may be called descriptive

[94] ibid 26, para 1.1.

[95] ibid 30, para 7, mentioning the relevance of LOSC Arts 86 and 87(1)(c), as well as Hague Convention (IV) respecting the Laws and Customs of War on Land (adopted 18 October 1907, entered into force 26 January 1910), Annex: Regulations concerning the Laws and Customs of War on Land, art 54.

[96] See David Letts, 'International Law and Armed Conflicts at Sea: The San Remo Manual—now is the time for a LOTE!' (2020) 63(1) Aust Naval Rev 57 <https://navalinstitute.com.au/international-law-and-armed-conflicts-at-sea/> accessed 29 June 2021.

[97] See International Institute of Humanitarian Law, 'Newsletter N. 81' (Oct–Dec 2019) <https://iihl.org/wp-content/uploads/2020/01/nl.81-1.pdf> accessed 14 June 2021. Further meetings were to take place in Australia, Norway, and the United States. The initial invitation (a list seen by the author, August 2019) showed the participation of twenty-two experts from the Western European and Other Group, one Eastern European, one African, four Asians, two experts from the Latin American and Caribbean Group, and two representatives of the ICRC. Of these thirty-two participants, six were women. The participants included nineteen people with a governmental or military background and ten academics.

[98] It appears that the project got into trouble after the Copenhagen meeting with participants holding divergent views as to the future scope of the project, and whether the aim was a mere update of the 1994 Manual, or whether new issues should be included as well. At the time of writing it is not clear how this would develop.

[99] von Heinegg (n 71) uses this argument for a renewed debate about the Manual and its possible revision (ibid 147).

and non-binding, as the norms, although their formulation may be dated, ultimately reside in the 1907 Hague Conventions, and only required contemporary reinterpretation.

States create international law, including the law of naval warfare, and will be aware of such norms no longer being satisfactory for contemporary combat. Not providing legal rules, and not embarking on the drafting of contemporary legal rules for naval warfare, are implicit decisions of states. Starting negotiations may be difficult, but inaction when it is clear that the law ought to be updated leaves space for others to step forward. Whatever the merits of the informal process that produced the San Remo Manual, the point remains that states failing to formally update the law when it becomes necessary to do so leaves room for private groups of experts to start formulating or reformulating rules as they see fit. This situation is as true now, with a renewed 'San Remo-type process', as it was prior to 1994: it is not a process triggered by states but, rather, by a group of experts.

In an informal process, the timing, the agenda-setting, and the invitations of participants are private undertakings. These characteristics marked the original process, and arise again in relation to the recently started 'update' process. At the helm is a group of experts ('private normative entrepreneurs') who are organizing a discussion about a specific field of law, with the intention of producing rules and norms that are relevant to state conduct. This forum is not created by states to discuss a subject matter that states considered relevant enough to trigger lawmaking. That, in itself, is striking: the law of armed conflict, and the restrictions and limitations it brings for governmental authority, is normally a field very close to the state's sovereign authority. Yet, here we see influential rules that have a bearing on state conduct in naval warfare being formulated by an informal expert group, where we would normally expect to see decision-making by states themselves. However, given the connections of the people involved, this effort will go a long way towards reaching governmental desks, without formal governmental decision-making.

As an informal document, the Manual stands out as being based on a set of old treaties, rather than starting from scratch with new rules for new developments. This foundation means that—hiding in the background—there are formal legally binding agreements, as well as customary laws that have not only been a basis for the development of rules, but also, somewhat, a source of legitimacy. While the rules formulated in an informal process may start out as a revision or reinterpretation of 'old law', their contemporary formulation will make them attractive for reference today. Frequent use of such clearly formulated rules may facilitate them slipping into state practice, like mud ending up on the shore of a river as an alluvial deposit. The quality and clarity of such rules will result in them gaining legal effect, at some point in time.

This new process of revising the 1994 Manual draws attention to another unusual question of whether old and outdated law can be reinterpreted time and again, which, in this chapter, has been referred to as the 'elasticity' of the law. It is a somewhat philosophical question as to how often it is possible to reinterpret the Manual, knowing that the 1994 Manual itself is already a reinterpretation of the 1907 Hague Conventions. On each revision, the new content may be drifting further away from the normative content of the Hague Conventions. Yet, by maintaining a link to the Hague Conventions, the suggestion is made not only that nothing is fundamentally changing, but also that the newly formulated rules will be binding because of their origins in old treaties. This kind of pedigree and authority may be seen as strengthening future legal effect.

The very idea of updating the San Remo Manual highlights another series of puzzles and interrogations that need to be addressed. The questions that follow from the growth of informal lawmaking, specifically in the field of the laws of war, are particularly complex. Issues that seem to require priority attention are matters such as the position of cables and pipelines, in view of the normative developments for cyberspace, as well as the 'due regard' notion with respect to marine environmental concerns. With the revision of the Manual, and the likely reconsideration of the impact of the norms of the LOSC on the customary law of naval warfare, one may also wonder whether the scope of application of such norms is only a discussion within the law of naval warfare or should, instead, be the subject of a broader law of the sea discussion.

Informal and authoritative norms have been, or are being, developed that seem to raise a general question of systemic coherence between informal norms. Thus, when discussing the protection of cables and pipelines during naval conflict, how much attention should be paid to the Tallinn Manual 1.0 with respect to cyberwarfare? Other than the Tallinn manual, not much written law seems to be available. And when debating the idea of limiting references to the due regard norm, or even striking it altogether, how should the guidance provided by the ICRC, or the state of play in the ILC discussions about the environment, be weighed? It also seems that, with informal lawmaking, there will be problems of coherence in terms of the development of rules, and the need to take into account related rules that very much resemble traditional formal lawmaking.

It would be unrealistic to say that the Manual, and the substantive norms of the law of naval warfare it contains, *are* the law, contrary to the frequent reiterations by those most concerned that it is a non-binding document based on the 1907 Hague Conventions. At the same time, the persuasive effect of clearly formulated rules must not be underestimated. Their availability and clarity, in contrast to the 1907 Hague Conventions when read today, makes them attractive for operational purposes and, with that, state practice grows. The contemporary law of naval warfare, thus, seems to have an origin based on state consent as expressed in the 1907 Hague Conventions and the following development of customary law, with an additional layer of private updates and improvements in the form of the Manual. With the current project to update the Manual, a new layer of updates may be added. As to the question of whether the Manual and its potential successor are a restatement or a development of the law of naval warfare, there is no easy answer. At any rate, it would seem that development is inevitable if states do not take the initiative to update the law.

3

Piracy off the Coast of Somalia and the Role of Informal Lawmaking

Marie Jacobsson and Natalie Klein[*]

3.1 Introduction

From 2004, there was an increase in piratical attacks on shipping off the coast of Somalia, which extends from the Gulf of Aden through to the Indian Ocean. A sharp escalation occurred in 2008, causing considerable concern for the seafarers attacked and held hostage during these incidents, as well as interrupting the supply of critical humanitarian aid to Somalia, and threatening international shipping and trade.[1] Due to the initial success of these attacks, the piracy operations, and those involved, became increasingly organized and better resourced.[2]

The overall response from the international community was, ultimately, very complex, entailing engagement among international organizations, regional organizations, and individual states, as well as diverse private stakeholders within the shipping industry. For example, the International Maritime Bureau, a private organization within the International Chamber of Commerce, kept track of the number and nature of the attacks, playing a crucial role in bringing this issue to the attention of the international community.[3] The International Maritime Organization's World Maritime University[4] also worked hard, early in the new century, to bring pertinent issues of maritime security to the attention of the international community, including through a series of symposia on maritime security.[5] The focus in this chapter is on the key stakeholders involved in the legal aspects of responding to the threats posed by the surge in piratical attacks.

The legal responses to this increase in piracy involved various sources of law, as well as varied actors and processes. Existing laws were set out in the UN Convention on the Law

* Thanks to Jack McNally for excellent research assistance in the preparation of this chapter.

1 See, eg Marie Jacobsson, 'International Legal Cooperation to Combat Piracy in the Horn of Africa' in Robert C Beckman and J Ashley Roach (eds), *Piracy and International Maritime Crimes in ASEAN: Prospects for Co-operation* (Edward Elgar 2012) 95–116; J Ashley Roach, 'IMO Policies and Actions Regarding Piracy' in David D Caron and Nilüfer Oral (eds), *Navigating Straits: Challenges for International Law* (Brill Nijhoff 2014) 241, 253.

2 See Anna Petrig and Robin Geiß, *Piracy and Armed Robbery at Sea: The Legal Framework for Counter-Piracy Operations in Somalia and the Gulf of Aden* (OUP 2011) 9–10.

3 Eg, the International Maritime Bureau warned all vessels to avoid sailing within fifty nautical miles of the Somali coast in 2004. See UNODC, 'The Globalization of Crime—A Transnational Organized Crime Threat Assessment' (2010) 196 <https://www.unodc.org/documents/data-and-analysis/tocta/9.Maritime_piracy.pdf> accessed 21 June 2021 .

4 World Maritime University <https://www.wmu.se> accessed 1 July 2021.

5 See, eg Maximo Q Meija Jr and Jingjing Xu (eds), *Coastal Zone Piracy and Other Unlawful Acts at Sea: A Selection of Papers and Presentations from the International Symposium on the New Regime for the Suppression of Unlawful Acts at Sea, 21–23 November 2005, and the International Symposium on Coastal Zone Piracy, 13–15 November 2006* (WMU Publications 2007).

Marie Jacobsson and Natalie Klein, *Piracy off the Coast of Somalia and the Role of Informal Lawmaking* In: *Unconventional Lawmaking in the Law of the Sea*. Edited by: Natalie Klein, Oxford University Press.
DOI: 10.1093/oso/9780192897824.003.0003

of the Sea (LOSC),[6] which reflected provisions from the 1958 High Seas Convention,[7] and additional authority was granted to states in binding Security Council resolutions adopted under Chapter VII of the UN Charter.[8] While the Security Council was able to fill in some perceived gaps in the legal framework, for example by allowing states to undertake law enforcement in the territorial sea of Somalia,[9] the operational reality prompted deeper consideration of a range of legal questions. A key body focusing on these questions was the Contact Group on Piracy off the Coast of Somalia (CGPCS or Contact Group), which sought to coordinate and cooperate with states, regional organizations, intergovernmental organizations, and private industry groups and individuals. A prominent informal instrument developed was the Djibouti Code of Conduct, adopted in 2009,[10] which was subsequently expanded by the 2017 Jeddah Amendment.[11] Extensions to these initiatives are now manifest in additional informal agreements, such as the Yaoundé Code.[12] Coordination among national navies, leading to different regional arrangements, has also contributed to the overall governance, including the ongoing and expanded mandate for the European Union's Operation Atalanta.[13] The overall framework governing responses to piracy off the Somali coast has, thus, entailed a rich complex of binding law, diverse stakeholders, and informal agreements, arrangements, and processes.

This chapter highlights the interaction of informal agreements and processes with the existing hard law as it evolved during the increase of piratical acts off the coast of Somalia. Following this introduction, section 3.2 briefly outlines the existing legal framework in the LOSC to counter piracy, highlighting various difficulties with this regime that were encountered in responding to piracy off the Somali coast. Section 3.3 then describes the Security Council responses, indicating how these binding decisions prompted diverse informal

[6] United Nations Convention on the Law of the Sea (adopted 10 December 1982, entered into force 16 November 1994) 1833 UNTS 397 (hereafter 'LOSC'), arts 100–107, 110–11, and 58.

[7] Convention on the High Seas (adopted 29 April 1958, entered into force 30 September 1962) 450 UNTS 11 (hereafter 'High Seas Convention'), arts 14–23.

[8] UNSC Res 1772 (20 August 2007) UN Doc S/RES/1772; UNSC Res 1801 (20 February 2008) UN Doc S/RES/1801; UNSC Res 1814 (15 May 2008) UN Doc S/RES/1814; UNSC Res 1816 (2 June 2008) UN Doc S/RES/1816; UNSC Res 1846 (2 December 2008) UN Doc S/RES/1846; UNSC Res 1851 (16 December 2008) UN Doc S/RES/1851; UNSC Res 1897 (30 November 2009) UN Doc S/RES/1897; UNSC Res 1918 (27 April 2010) UN Doc S/RES/1918; UNSC Res 1950 (23 November 2010) UN Doc S/RES/1950; UNSC Res 1976 (11 April 2011) UN Doc S/RES/1976; UNSC Res 2015 (24 October 2011) UN Doc S/RES/2015; UNSC Res 2020 (22 November 2011) UN Doc S/RES/2020; UNSC Res 2077 (21 November 2012) UN Doc S/RES/2077; UNSC Res 2125 (18 November 2013) UN Doc S/RES/2125; UNSC Res 2383 (7 November 2017) UN Doc S/RES/2383; UNSC Res 2500 (4 December 2019) UN Doc S/RES/2500; UNSC Res 2554 (4 December 2020) UN Doc S/RES/2554.

[9] UNSC Res 1816 (n 8) para 7.

[10] IMO, 'Code of Conduct concerning the Repression of Piracy and Armed Robbery against Ships in the Western Indian Ocean and the Gulf of Aden' (Djibouti Code of Conduct) (29 January 2009) IMO Doc C.102/14. See, further, IMO, 'The Djibouti Code of Conduct' <https://www.imo.org/en/OurWork/Security/Pages/Content-and-Evolution-of-the-Djibouti-Code-of-Conduct.aspx> accessed 25 June 2021.

[11] 'Revised Code of Conduct Concerning the Repression of Piracy, Armed Robbery against Ships, and Illicit Maritime Activity in the Western Indian Ocean and the Gulf of Aden Area' (12 January 2017) (hereafter 'Jeddah Amendment') <https://wwwcdn.imo.org/localresources/en/OurWork/Security/Documents/A2%20Revised%20Code%20Of%20Conduct%20Concerning%20The%20Repression%20Of%20Piracy%20Armed%20Robbery%20Against%20Ships%20Secretariat.pdf> accessed 19 July 2021.

[12] IMO, 'Code of Conduct concerning the Repression of Piracy, Armed Robbery against Ships, and Illicit Maritime Activity in West and Central Africa' (Yaoundé Code of Conduct) (25 June 2013) <https://wwwcdn.imo.org/localresources/en/OurWork/Security/Documents/code_of_conduct%20signed%20from%20ECOWAS%20site.pdf> accessed 25 July 2021.

[13] European Union, CFSP 2020/2188 of 22 December 2020 Amending Joint Action 2008/851/CFSP on a European Union Military Operation to Contribute to the Deterrence, Prevention and Repression of Acts of Piracy and Armed Robbery off the Somali Coast.

agreements and other initiatives, and highlights the role of the Contact Group. Section 3.4 examines the role of the International Maritime Organization (IMO), especially in leading to the development of Codes of Conduct. Section 3.5 explores further informal agreements and arrangements that were developed in response to piracy off the coast of Somalia. Section 3.6 concludes the chapter with reflections on the lessons learned from the interaction of informal lawmaking with the existing laws on piracy, and considers the potential influence these experiences will have in responding to piracy and other maritime security threats in the future.

3.2 Existing Legal Framework on Piracy

The right to combat piracy rests on a firm foundation in customary international law, with piracy laws found in centuries-old national laws,[14] and addressed in codification efforts from the early twentieth century.[15] It was reflected in the first major multilateral treaty on the law of the sea, namely the 1958 Convention on the High Seas.[16] The provisions in the High Seas Convention were transported to the LOSC almost verbatim.[17] The LOSC is concerned with piratical acts occurring on the high seas and, by virtue of Article 58(2) thereof, in the exclusive economic zone (EEZ) of coastal states, whereas comparable acts occurring in the territorial sea of a coastal state are usually referred to as 'armed robbery', and are subject to the criminal jurisdiction of that coastal state.[18]

The LOSC provides a definition of piracy in Article 101, reflecting the earlier definition from the High Seas Convention,[19] and its shortcomings have been well discussed.[20] In the context of Somali piracy, the criteria in the piracy definition of illegal acts of violence being committed for private ends against another ship, or those on board another ship, were typically satisfied. However, most relevant for present purposes is Article 105 of the LOSC, which provides where and by whom the measures against piracy may be taken:

> [O]n the high seas, or in any other place outside the jurisdiction of any State, every State may seize a pirate ship or aircraft, or a ship or aircraft taken by piracy and under the control of pirates, and arrest the persons and seize the property on board. The courts of the State which carried out the seizure may decide upon the penalties to be imposed, and may also determine the action to be taken with regard to the ships, aircraft or property, subject to the rights of third parties acting in good faith.

[14] Marie Jacobsson, 'Maritime Security: An Individual or Collective Responsibility?' in Jarna Petman and Jan Klabbers (eds), *Nordic Cosmopolitanism: Essays in International Law for Martti Koskenniemi* (Brill 2003) 396 (referring to sixteenth-century Danish law).

[15] See Harvard Draft Convention and Commentary, reprinted in ASIL, 'Codification of International Law: Part IV—Piracy' (1932) 26 AJIL Suppl 739, 743.

[16] High Seas Convention (n 7) art 15.

[17] LOSC (n 6) arts 100–07.

[18] ibid, art 27. See Roach (n 1) 242.

[19] High Seas Convention (n 7) art 15.

[20] See, eg Robert Beckman, 'The Piracy Regime under UNCLOS: Problems and Prospects for Cooperation' in RobertC Beckman and J Ashley Roach (eds), *Piracy and International Maritime Crimes in ASEAN: Prospects for Cooperation* (Edward Elgar 2012) 17. Needless to say, the definition of piracy was subject to lengthy debates, both in the International Law Commission (ILC) in the 1950s and during the negotiations for the adoption of the High Seas Convention.

This provision is relatively permissive, reflecting the old customary rule. In the context of piracy off the Somali coast, when the international community had to face piracy as a threat to international peace and security, it became obvious that Article 105 did not meet contemporary legal requirements, in particular the legal standards of the rule of law and human rights.[21] There was simply no comprehensive legal 'infrastructure' that states could rely on when taking anti-piracy measures.

Hence, additional challenges remained for those states that had decided to fight not only *acts of piracy*, but also *impunity for piratical acts*. States needed to pose the question of whether there was an obligation to act, but also whether there was an obligation to conclude an initial measure taken (such as bringing the suspected pirates of a seized vessel to court), or whether there was a duty to cooperate with other states in this regard. The LOSC contains a broad duty to cooperate, requiring states to 'cooperate to the fullest possible extent in the repression of piracy',[22] but the precise parameters of cooperating in prosecution are not articulated.

Also relevant to the legal framework to respond to piracy off the coast of Somalia were counterterrorism treaties that criminalized both hostage-taking[23] and different forms of maritime violence. Most relevant for the latter is the 1988 Convention for the Suppression of Unlawful Acts against the Safety of Maritime Navigation (SUA Convention),[24] which was updated in 2005 to expand the range of criminal offences and enhance law enforcement opportunities.[25] The SUA Convention is thus likely to encompass maritime violence against ships and those on board ships that would otherwise fall outside the traditional definition of piracy, provided the relevant states concerned are parties to this treaty and have properly implemented it into their national laws.

3.3 Security Council Responses and the Work of the Contact Group on Piracy off the Coast of Somalia

Since the first resolution in 2007 that referred to piracy off the coast of Somalia, the Security Council has adopted a series of resolutions of direct relevance to the issue of piracy in this area.[26] These resolutions have been adopted under Chapter VII of the UN Charter and, thus, the decisions set out therein are binding on all UN member states, in accordance with Article 25 of the UN Charter. In addition to these decisions, the Security Council has called on, encouraged, or urged member states and other organizations to take different actions to improve the international community's responses to piracy off the coast of Somalia.[27] Some of these actions were undertaken within the framework of the Contact Group, and its operations are discussed in this part.

[21] See, eg Petrig and Geiß (n 2) 93–94 and 207 et seq.

[22] LOSC (n 6) art 100.

[23] International Convention against the Taking of Hostages (adopted 17 December 1979, entered into force 3 June 1983) 1316 UNTS 205.

[24] Convention for the Suppression of Unlawful Acts against the Safety of Maritime Navigation (adopted 10 March 1988, entered into force 1 March 1992) 1678 UNTS 221 (hereafter 'SUA Convention').

[25] Protocol of 2005 to the Convention for the Suppression of Unlawful Acts against the Safety of Maritime Navigation (1 November 2005) IMO Doc LEG/CONF.15/21, art 3 *bis*.

[26] See n 8.

[27] Generally, stakeholders have held the view that the most important way to solve the Somali piracy issue is to address the root causes on the ground in Somalia: Jacobsson, 'International Legal Cooperation' (n 1) 102.

3.3.1 Security Council Resolutions

The first major step the Security Council took to address piracy off the coast of Somalia was Resolution 1816, which was adopted in 2008.[28] The resolution was notable for deciding that states were allowed to enter the territorial sea of Somalia, and to use all necessary means to repress both acts of piracy and armed robbery at sea.[29] The Security Council resolutions, thus, sought to overcome the geographical limitations inherent in the LOSC definition of piracy, which applies to the high seas and EEZ,[30] and also to address similar acts that occurred in the territorial sea. The Council's approach, thus, reflected experiences encountered by states in their efforts to repress Somali piracy,[31] and allowed for a more holistic response. The Security Council obtained the cooperation and consent of the Somali government, which underlined the exceptional nature of mandating law enforcement by foreign warships against armed robbery within the territorial sea of a coastal state.[32]

As noted previously, this resolution was binding on all UN member states under Chapter VII of the UN Charter.[33] Piracy, as a whole, was not treated as a threat to international peace and security, as some Security Council members were concerned about the wider implications of such a determination for other piracy hotspots,[34] but, rather, the 'situation in Somalia' was considered the threat.[35] The legal status of the resolution was deliberately limited to the specific situation being addressed, given the affirmation that it was not to 'affect the rights or obligations or responsibilities of member states under international law, including any rights or obligations under the Convention, with respect to any other situation, and ... in particular ... it shall not be considered as establishing customary international law'.[36] This affirmation was repeated in later resolutions.[37] Each resolution, nonetheless, became stronger, as the resolutions progressed the prior decisions of the Council to reflect the realities of the situation.[38]

Once the Security Council had acted,[39] an avalanche of cooperative measures was taken by the international community. Such measures included steps to address the problems that arose in connection with arresting, prosecuting, and punishing persons who attacked ships off the Horn of Africa. Resolution 1851, for example, focused on law enforcement, with 'emphasis on investigation and prosecution and the strengthening of criminal justice mechanisms ... readily apparent'.[40] Notably, the UN Secretary-General reported to the Security

28 UNSC Res 1816 (n 8).

29 ibid, para 7.

30 See above (n 18).

31 France and the United States had pursued pirates into areas of Somali sovereignty prior to the adoption of this resolution. See Matthew C Houghton, 'Walking the Plank: How United Nations Security Council Resolution 1816, while Progressive, Fails to Provide a Comprehensive Solution to Somali Piracy' (2009) 16 Tulsa J Comp & Int'l L 253, 278.

32 Jacobsson, 'International Legal Cooperation' (n 1) 100.

33 UN Charter, art 25.

34 See UNSC 5902nd meeting (2 June 2008) UN Doc S/PV.5902 (especially the intervention of Indonesia).

35 UNSC Res 1816 (n 8) preambular para 12.

36 ibid, para 9.

37 See, eg UNSC Res 2500 (n 8) para 15; UNSC Res 2554 (n 8) para 15.

38 Jacobsson, 'International Legal Cooperation' (n 1) 101.

39 The engagement of the Security Council in this way was not procedurally difficult since the Somalia question had been on the agenda of the Security Council, at the request of Somalia, since 1992, when the weapons embargo was imposed: UNSC Res 733 (23 January 1992) UN Doc S/RES/733.

40 Douglas Guilfoyle, 'Somali Pirates as Agents of Change in International Law-making and Organisation' (2012) 1(3) CJCL 81, 96.

Council that 'commanders of the European and NATO naval forces off the coast of Somalia estimate that around 700 suspects apprehended by the ships under their command have been released between January and June 2010'.[41] The Security Council resolutions called upon states to cooperate in the investigation and prosecution of all persons responsible for, or associated with, acts of piracy or armed robbery at sea, and further acknowledged the work of different organizations, such as the UN Office of Drugs and Crime (UNODC) and Interpol, in assisting state efforts in this regard.[42] The role of the CGPCS in assisting such efforts was also encouraged by the Security Council.

3.3.2 Contact Group on Piracy off the Coast of Somalia

A crucial step in the fight against piracy was the establishment, in January 2009, of the CGPCS, subsequent to the adoption of UNSC Resolution 1851.[43] The CGPCS is often described as an international forum for states, organizations, private companies, and other interest groups that share the aim of combating piracy. This description is accurate, since about eighty states and several international organizations participate in the Contact Group. It serves as an international cooperation mechanism among the varied participants, which include the African Union, the Arab League, the EU, the IMO, and NATO, as well as various departments and agencies of the United Nations, and industry groups. Former chairpersons have described it variously as:

> a 'diplomatic initiative' that grew into an 'expansive, elastic, multi-faceted mechanism' that 'has acted as a lynchpin in a loosely structured counter-piracy coalition', but that has 'no formal institutional existence' [and] as 'an inclusive forum for debate without binding conclusions' without 'any real structural formality'.[44]

The Contact Group has consistently operated on a flexible and inclusive basis, and has not held any status as a formal UN organ. Much of the work is done in the Contact Group's working groups, which were initially entrusted, variously, with capacity building, legal issues, relations with the shipping industry, public diplomacy, and disruption of financial networks. These working groups were reformed, in 2014, to each focus on, respectively, capacity building, legal issues, counter-piracy and mitigation operations, and disrupting pirate networks ashore.[45]

[41] UN Secretary-General, 'Report of the Secretary-General on Possible Options to Further the Aim of Prosecuting and Imprisoning Persons Responsible for Acts of Piracy and Armed Robbery at Sea off the Coast of Somalia, including, in particular, Options for Creating Special Domestic Chambers Possibly with International Components, a Regional Tribunal or an International Tribunal and Corresponding Imprisonment Arrangements, Taking into Account the Work of the Contact Group on Piracy off the Coast of Somalia, the Existing Practice in Establishing International and Mixed Tribunals, and the Time and Resources Necessary to Achieve and Sustain Substantive Results' (26 July 2010) UN Doc S/2010/394, para 20.

[42] See, eg UNSC Res 2500 (n 8) paras 18, 19, 21–22; UNSC Res 2554 (n 8) paras 18, 19, 21–22.

[43] See UNSC Res 1851 (n 8) para 4.

[44] Christian Bueger, Timothy Edmunds, and Robert McCabe, 'Into the Sea: Capacity-Building Innovations and the Maritime Security Challenge' (2020) 41(2) TWQ 228, 236, citing Henk Swarttouw and Donna L Hopkins, 'The Contact Group on Piracy off the Coast of Somalia: Genesis, Rationale and Objectives' in Thierry Tardy (ed), *Fighting Piracy off the Coast of Somalia: Lessons Learned from the Contact Group* (EU Institute for Security Studies 2014) 11–17.

[45] Thierry Tardy, 'Introduction' in Thierry Tardy (ed), *Fighting Piracy off the Coast of Somalia: Lessons Learned from the Contact Group* (EU Institute for Security Studies 2014) 7. See, further, Petrig and Geiß (n 2) 26–27.

Working Group 2 on Legal Issues (the Legal Working Group) rapidly developed as the most important body for the facilitation of coordination, cooperation, and development of legal tools to combat piracy and impunity. Crucial in its activities was providing a forum for information sharing between those involved in fighting against, or most affected by, piracy and armed robbery off Somalia. The Legal Working Group was transformed into the Piracy Legal Forum of the CGPCS in 2014.[46] As a whole, the cooperation had a clear legal dimension, even in the absence of formal decision-making authority.

One initiative of the CGPCS and its Working Group 3 (addressing counter-piracy and mitigation operations) was to develop, with the full collaboration of the shipping industry, a Best Management Practice guidance document providing specific advice to masters of ships operating off the Somali coast.[47] Data as to the number, nature, and location of attacks, as compiled through the International Maritime Bureau, was important in informing these efforts. The IMO endorsed this guidance, and circulated it to member states.[48] In addition, this document led to ten states adopting a New York Declaration, wherein they committed to promulgate the Best Management Practice guidance, and to ensure the adoption of the guidance by their vessels.[49] The Legal Working Group also produced guidelines on best practice for evidence-gathering, which supported the prosecution requirements before Kenyan courts.[50]

Another key legal activity undertaken within the Contact Group and its Legal Working Group was discussion as to the preferred fora or mechanisms for prosecuting and incarcerating captured pirates.[51] Discussions within the Legal Working Group contemplated the benefits and disadvantages of creating a new international court, establishing a new regional court, establishing a hybrid international/national court, or pursuing prosecution before national courts.[52] These discussions further engaged the Contact Group as a whole, as well as work undertaken by the UN Secretary-General and the Secretary-General's Special Adviser on piracy.[53] In addition, the post-trial transfer system developed by the Legal Working Group has been described as one of its main achievements.[54] This work, ultimately, informed the Security Council's support of national prosecutions, and aligned with the UNODC efforts (discussed further below) at capacity-building in the region.[55]

Guilfoyle has noted that the CGPCS falls within a model of new governance that 'eschews top down "command and control" regulation and instead favours experimentation and sharing of best practice, the informal alignment of expectations, and loose horizontal

[46] CGPCS, 'CGPCS—Piracy Legal Forum' <http://www.piracylegalforum.org> accessed 1 July 2021; CGPCS, 'Background' <http://www.piracylegalforum.org/about/background-2/> accessed 1 July 2021.

[47] Huh Chul, 'Working with the Private Sector' in Thierry Tardy (ed), Fighting Piracy off the Coast of Somalia: Lessons Learned from the Contact Group (EU Institute for Security Studies 2014) 41–42.

[48] Tejal Khanna, 'The Normative Role of the International Maritime Organisation in Countering Somali-based Piracy' (2019) 15(1) Mar Aff 51, 57.

[49] Peter Chalk, 'Assessing the Utility of Current Counterpiracy Initiatives off the Horn of Africa' (2012) 35 Stud in Conf and Terr 553, 555.

[50] Douglas Guilfoyle, 'Prosecuting Pirates: The Contact Group on Piracy off the Coast of Somali, Governance and International Law' (2013) 4(1) Glob Pol'y 73, 74.

[51] See ibid 73–79.

[52] ibid 75.

[53] ibid 75–76.

[54] Jonas Bering Liisberg, 'The Legal Aspects of Counter-Piracy' in Thierry Tardy (ed), *Fighting Piracy off the Coast of Somalia: Lessons Learned from the Contact Group* (EU Institute for Security Studies 2014) 36–37.

[55] The UNODC worked closely with the Legal Working Group. See ibid 38–39.

co-operation'.[56] Cooperation can be more easily facilitated in this frame, to share information and respond rapidly to changing situations.[57]

3.4 The IMO and the Djibouti Code of Conduct, Jeddah Amendment, and Yaoundé Code

Until the Security Council took action, the security situation off the coast of Somalia had largely been neglected by the international community, with the sole exception of the IMO, which had voiced concern at an early stage about the situation, and has been the most important legal player in the fight against piracy. As discussed in other chapters in this volume, the IMO plays a key role in developing standards for the safety and security of international shipping.[58] The question of piracy was first placed on its agenda in the early 1980s,[59] but with the rise of piracy and armed robbery at sea in South-East Asia, and off the coast of Somalia, its role became much more prominent.[60] From a lawmaking perspective, it is particularly relevant that the IMO has a regulatory role, since some of its functions are to facilitate the adoption of conventions and other formal treaty instruments, as well as to adopt recommendations (codes, guidelines, and recommended practices) to ensure safety and security at sea. It may, further, be observed that the International Labour Organization has also had a regulatory function in seeking to protect seafarers who have been impacted by acts of piracy or armed robbery against their ships, with a key response being amendments to the Maritime Labour Convention.[61] The IMO, however, remains the focus for this section, given its use of a variety of formal and informal agreements in responding to different aspects of piracy, including piracy and armed robbery off the coast of Somalia.

3.4.1 IMO Actions Responding to Piracy

The IMO Assembly first adopted a resolution on piracy off the Somali coast in 2005, and sought to make strong recommendations to states, as well as requesting the IMO Secretary-General to bring the issue to the attention of the UN Security Council.[62] The IMO's Maritime Safety Committee also adopted circulars[63] urging implementation of an IMO guidance document, including implementation of a guidance document that was developed by the International Chamber of Shipping in 2009.[64] As noted above, the IMO supported the work

[56] Guilfoyle, 'Somali Pirates as Agents of Change' (n 40) 100.

[57] ibid.

[58] See Sun, in Chapter 6 of this volume and Petrig, in Chapter 7 of this volume.

[59] IMO, 'Measures to Prevent Acts of Piracy and Armed Robbery Against Ships' (17 November 1983) IMO Res A.545(13).

[60] See, generally, Roach (n 1) 241.

[61] Maritime Labour Convention (adopted 23 February 2006, entered into force 20 August 2013) 2952 UNTS 3 (amended in 2018). See ILO, 'Enhanced Protection for Seafarers affected by Acts of Piracy and Armed Robbery against Ships' (15 January 2021) <https://www.ilo.org/global/standards/maritime-labour-convention/WCMS_766383/lang--en/index.htm> accessed 21 June 2021.

[62] IMO, 'Piracy and Armed Robbery against Ships in Waters off the Coast of Somalia' (23 November 2005) IMO Res A.979(24).

[63] IMO, 'Piracy and Armed Robbery against Ships in Waters off the Coast of Somalia' (15 June 2007) IMO Doc MSC.1/Circ.1233; IMO, 'Piracy and Armed Robbery against Ships in Waters off the Coast of Somalia' (16 April 2009) IMO Doc MSC.1/Circ.1302.

[64] Roach (n 1) 255–56.

undertaken through the Contact Group, including in the development of Best Management Practices. The fifth version of the Best Management Practices to deter Piracy and Enhance Maritime Security in the Red Sea, Gulf of Aden, Indian Ocean, and the Arabian Sea was released in June 2018. The Maritime Safety Committee also supported an industry-led guidance document addressing company security officers preparing hijacking contingencies for shipping companies and crews.[65] Instruments setting out recommendations and guidance that addressed the use of private security personnel on ships to provide protection in what was referred to as a 'High-Risk Area' off the Somali coast were also adopted, under the auspices of the Maritime Safety Committee,[66] and these are discussed further below. In each instance, the development of these instruments was instigated, or strongly influenced, by key industry stakeholder groups.

Another key role for the IMO was initiating a high-level meeting of stakeholders that led to the adoption of the Djibouti Code of Conduct in 2009.[67] The IMO was motivated to support regional cooperation to respond to piracy off the Somali coast, in light of its experience in the development of the Regional Cooperation Agreement on Combating Piracy and Armed Robbery against Ships in Asia (ReCAAP).[68] This regional treaty is centred on the creation of an Information Sharing Centre based in Singapore, and facilitates cooperation and capacity-building for the prevention and repression of piracy and armed robbery. ReCAAP was an important legal response to an increase in piracy and armed robbery in the Malacca and Singapore Straits.[69] However, the acceptance of a binding agreement was elusive in the context of legal responses to piracy off the coast of Somalia. Nonetheless, the adoption of the Djibouti Code of Conduct, although non-legally binding, had a significant effect in galvanising state and regional action to fight both acts of piracy and impunity for piratical acts.

3.4.2 Djibouti Code of Conduct

The Djibouti Code of Conduct, concerning the 'Repression of Piracy and Armed Robbery against Ships in the Western Indian Ocean and the Gulf of Aden', was adopted in 2009 by representatives of concerned states in the region.[70] The lawmaking process for the Djibouti Code of Conduct extended over several years,[71] and began life with a far broader scope in addressing illicit maritime activities.[72] Menzel notes that, as more lawyers and politicians

[65] IMO, 'Guidance for Company Security Officers (CSOs)—Preparation of a Company and Crew for the Contingency of Hijack of Pirates in the Western Indian Ocean and the Gulf of Aden' (9 December 2010) IMO Doc MSC.1/Circ.1390.

[66] See Roach (n 1) 257.

[67] Djibouti Code of Conduct (n 10).

[68] Regional Cooperation Agreement on Combating Piracy and Armed Robbery against Ships in Asia (adopted 11 November 2004, entered into force 4 September 2006) 2398 UNTS 199 (hereafter 'ReCAAP').

[69] For discussion, see Tara Davenport, 'Legal Measures to Combat Piracy and Armed Robbery in the Horn of Africa and in Southeast Asia: A Comparison' (2012) 35(7–8) Stud Confl Terr 570.

[70] Djibouti, Ethiopia, Kenya, Madagascar, Maldives, Seychelles, Somalia, the United Republic of Tanzania, and Yemen, and, later, Comoros, Egypt, Eritrea, Jordan, Mauritius, Mozambique, Oman, Saudi Arabia, South Africa, Sudan, and the United Arab Emirates have since signed, bringing the total to twenty countries out of the twenty-one eligible to sign.

[71] Negotiations commenced in 2005. Khanna (n 48) 56.

[72] Anja Menzel, 'Institutional Adoption and Maritime Crime Governance: The Djibouti Code of Conduct' (2018) 14(2) J Ind Ocean Reg 152, 158.

became increasingly involved, the provisions were 'watered down' and narrowed to address only piracy and armed robbery.[73] The participants involved in negotiations ranged from the littoral states to IMO representatives, and states from outside the region that were interested in supporting capacity-building and the responses to Somali piracy. Ultimately, only littoral states could become participants in the Djibouti Code of Conduct,[74] and this limitation was included because non-littoral states were already parties to other comparable agreements or mechanisms, and there were concerns that it would become unwieldy and less effective with open membership.[75]

The Djibouti Code of Conduct is a non-binding instrument. An informal agreement was, apparently, preferred because 'of the limited capacity of the countries involved' and the preference for expecting cooperation only so far as resources and national laws of each state would allow.[76] Some of the negotiators considered that a binding instrument would take much longer to negotiate, reduce participation among the littoral states, and complicate implementation because of the internal legal processes that would be needed in the adoption and implementation of a treaty.[77] However, it was still anticipated that all states in the region would become signatories (described as 'participants'). The Djibouti Code of Conduct was said to 'become effective from the date it was signed', and was to be open to other regional states to sign at IMO headquarters.[78] In addition, it explicitly urged the signatories to consider the adoption of a binding agreement two years after the Djibouti Code of Conduct was adopted.[79] This eventuality did not occur.

The Djibouti Code of Conduct provided a framework for capacity-building in the Gulf of Aden and Western Indian Ocean to counter the threat of piracy. Participants in the Djibouti Code of Conduct agreed to cooperate 'in a manner consistent with international law' in the following:

(a) the investigation, arrest and prosecution of persons, who are reasonably suspected of having committed acts of piracy and armed robbery against ships, including those inciting or intentionally facilitating such acts;
(b) the interdiction and seizure of suspect ships and property on board such ships;
(c) the rescue of ships, persons and property subject to piracy and armed robbery and the facilitation of proper care, treatment and repatriation of seafarers, fishermen, other shipboard personnel and passengers subject to such acts, particularly those who have been subjected to violence; and
(d) the conduct of shared operations—both among signatory States and with navies from countries outside the region—such as nominating law enforcement or other authorized officials to embark on patrol ships or aircraft of another signatory.[80]

[73] ibid.
[74] Twenty out of a possible twenty-one states did so.
[75] Menzel (n 72) 161.
[76] James Kraska and Raul Pedrozo, *International Maritime Security Law* (Brill 2013) 719.
[77] Menzel (n 72) 161.
[78] Djibouti Code of Conduct (n 10) art 16(2). See also IMO, 'Protection of Vital Shipping Lanes: Note by the Secretary-General' (3 April 2009) IMO Doc C/102/14, paras 7–8.
[79] IMO, 'Protection of Vital Shipping Lanes' (n 78) Annex, Attachment 1, Resolution 1, para 2.2; Djibouti Code of Conduct (n 10) art 13.
[80] IMO, 'Protection of Vital Shipping Lanes' (n 78) para 9.

Another important element of the Djibouti Code of Conduct is the undertaking of signatories to review their national legislation to ensure that their domestic laws both criminalize piracy and allow for investigation, prosecution, and punishment of piracy, so as to avoid situations of impunity.

The Djibouti Code of Conduct contains general references to acting consistently with international law, and also has a safeguards provision designed to ensure that there is no prejudice to existing international law rights and duties.[81] There is obvious reliance on the LOSC, as the Djibouti Code of Conduct utilizes the LOSC definition of piracy,[82] as well as replicating similar law enforcement provisions from the LOSC.[83] The Djibouti Code of Conduct also draws on different provisions of ReCAAP, especially those relating to information sharing, incident reporting, and general assistance among participants.[84] It is, further, notable that the Djibouti Code of Conduct incorporates IMO recommendations and guidance through the use of footnotes referencing these documents.[85] Reliance on both formal and informal sources of law has added to the normative content of the Djibouti Code of Conduct, facilitating its normative effect, even though it was explicitly designated as a non-binding instrument.

A strong infrastructure was put in place to support the implementation of the Djibouti Code of Conduct, given its emphasis on reporting and sharing information.[86] The elements of this infrastructure included advisory services on implementation within the IMO,[87] a regional training centre in Djibouti,[88] and information-sharing centres.[89] Three information-sharing centres were to be created in the region, and these centres were to establish 'a set of standard operating procedures for communicating and exchanging piracy-related information'.[90] The existence of the Djibouti Code of Conduct thus facilitated warnings being sent to international shipping, as well as cross-regional collaboration in responding to piracy attacks.

3.4.3 Yaoundé Code and Jeddah Amendment

The increasing threat to shipping off the coast of West Africa led to the adoption of a Code of Conduct concerning the repression of piracy, armed robbery against ships, and illicit

[81] Djibouti Code of Conduct (n 10) art 15.

[82] ibid, art 1(1).

[83] ibid, art 4. The Djibouti Code of Conduct does allow for the possibility of ship riders, however, in Article 7, which is a law enforcement technique that has been prevalent in US law enforcement efforts against drug smuggling in the Caribbean.

[84] ibid, arts 8, 9, and 10. See also ReCAAP (n 68) arts 9 and 10. Menzel notes that five out of twenty-two provisions of ReCAAP were replicated in the Djibouti Code of Conduct: Menzel (n 72) 160.

[85] See, eg Djibouti Code of Conduct (n 10) art 3, referring to IMO, 'Recommendations to Governments for Preventing and Suppressing Piracy and Armed Robbery Against Ships' (16 Jun 1999) IMO Doc MSC/Circ.622/Rev.1 'as it may be revised' and IMO, 'Guidance to Shipowners and Ship Operators, Shipmasters and Crews on Preventing and Suppressing Acts of Piracy and Armed Robbery Against Ships' (29 May 2002) IMO Doc MSC/Circ.623/Rev.3 'as it may be revised'. In anticipating the revision of these instruments, there was, thus, scope to allow for the evolution of these documents, and incorporation by reference through this drafting technique. See also Djibouti Code of Conduct (n 10) art 6(3), which incorporates IMO Res A.922(22) on the 'Code of Practice for the Investigation of the Crimes of Piracy and Armed Robbery against Ships' (29 November 2001), as it may be revised.

[86] See Menzel (n 72) 158.

[87] IMO 'Protection of Vital Shipping Lanes' (n 78), Annex, Attachment 1, Resolution 2, para 2.

[88] ibid, Annex, Attachment 1, Resolution 3.

[89] Djibouti Code of Conduct (n 10) art 8.

[90] Roach (n 1) 260.

maritime activity in West and Central Africa, adopted in 2013 in Yaoundé (Cameroon). The Yaoundé Code drew on the experience of states implementing the Djibouti Code of Conduct. In addition, the Djibouti Code of Conduct was updated through a revised Code of Conduct, known as the Jeddah Amendment to the Djibouti Code of Conduct 2017.[91] Both the Jeddah Amendment and the Yaoundé Code contain provisions according to which the signatories state their intention of consulting in order to consider eventually transforming the Codes of Conduct into a binding multilateral agreement.[92]

The Yaoundé Code initially involved a collaboration between the IMO, the Economic Community of West African States (ECOWAS), the Gulf of Guinea Commission, and the Economic Community of Central African States (ECCAS), which were concerned about the increase in armed robberies, as well as piracy and kidnapping, occurring in the Gulf of Guinea. The Code was developed by the ECOWAS and ECCAS pursuant to Security Council Resolutions 2018 (2011) and 2039 (2012).[93] It was adopted in 2013 by twenty-five eligible West and Central African states.

There are similarities between the Yaoundé Code and the Djibouti Code of Conduct in that the Yaoundé Code is also a non-binding agreement that anticipates the possibility of a future formal agreement, and is also limited in its membership to specific states of the region. The Yaoundé Code addresses a broader set of maritime crimes compared to the Djibouti Code of Conduct.[94] The list of maritime crimes in the Yaoundé Code instead draws from the African Union's '2050 Africa's Integrated Maritime Strategy'.[95] Nonetheless, Menzel has noted that fourteen out of seventeen provisions from the Djibouti Code of Conduct were included within the Yaoundé Code.[96]

States participating in the Jeddah Meeting,[97] which led to the Jeddah Amendment to the Djibouti Code, drew on the scope of maritime threats warranting cooperation in the Yaoundé Code. The preamble to the Jeddah Amendment notes that participating states wanted to 'build on the experience and success of the Djibouti Code of Conduct' by widening its scope.[98] The Jeddah Amendment, thus, addresses human smuggling and trafficking as well as illegal, unreported, and unregulated fishing. Its scope is not as broad as the Yaoundé Code, but it does adopt eight of the provisions from the latter code, either in part or entirely.[99] There is, however, a stronger emphasis on the blue economy and

[91] Jeddah Amendment (n 11).
[92] Art 17 in the Jeddah Amendment, and art 17(a) in the Yaoundé Code of Conduct.
[93] UNSC Res 2018 (31 October 2011) UN Doc S/RES/2018 and UNSC Res 2039 (29 February 2012) UN Doc S/RES/2039. See, further, Roach (n 1) 263.
[94] See Yaoundé Code of Conduct (n 12) arts 1(5), 2, and 8.
[95] African Union, '2050 Africa's Integrated Maritime Strategy (2050 AIM Strategy)' (6 December 2012) <https://au.int/sites/default/files/documents/30929-doc-2050_aim_strategy_eng_0.pdf> accessed 1 July 2021. 'The African Charter on Maritime Security Safety and Development' was adopted unanimously by African Union leaders in Lomé, Togo in 2016 as another non-binding instrument against piracy: African Union, 'African Charter on Maritime Security and Safety Development in Africa (Lomé Charter)' (15 October 2016) <https://au.int/en/treaties/african-charter-maritime-security-and-safety-and-development-africa-lome-charter> accessed 23 July 2021. For discussion, see Siraja Zamfara Ibrahim, 'Strengths and Weaknesses of the Legal Strategies to Combat Sea Piracy in Nigeria' (MSc Thesis, World Maritime University 2019) 39–40.
[96] Menzel (n 72) 162.
[97] Jordan, Egypt, and Sudan did not participate. The drafters of the Jeddah Amendment included France (Réunion) and four observer states (Japan, Norway, the United Kingdom, and the United States), as well as observers from the UNODC, EU, Interpol, and the East African Standby Force: IMO, 'Djibouti Code of Conduct' <https://www.imo.org/en/OurWork/Security/Pages/DCoC.aspx> accessed 1 July 2021.
[98] Jeddah Amendment (n 11) preambular para 6.
[99] Menzel (n 72) 164.

protection of the marine environment in the Jeddah Amendment, compared with the Yaoundé Code.[100]

Similar to the Djibouti Code of Conduct, the cooperation to be undertaken by states pursuant to the Jeddah Amendment in response to maritime security concerns must be 'consistent with ... available resources and related priorities, their respective national laws and regulations, and applicable rules of international law'.[101] Another similarity to the Djibouti Code of Conduct is the inclusion of a series of 'without prejudice' clauses to preserve existing rights and duties under international law, including in relation to navigational rights and law enforcement.[102]

Like the informal lawmaking processes that emerged from the Contact Group and its various working groups, cooperation to deliver tangible solutions was also evident in the efforts of the IMO to work with affected states and regional organizations to develop the codes of conduct. Both informal lawmaking efforts sought to resolve legal questions emerging from practical responses to piratical attacks and armed robbery off Somalia. The intention was to engage both public and private stakeholders and provide prompt, workable standards for those operating in the waters off Somalia. The Djibouti Code of Conduct, the Jeddah Amendment, and the Yaoundé Code reflect an evolutionary development of informal agreements, with the ongoing engagement of the IMO contributing to normative consistency, and are notable for clearly laying out a path to formal law. While the final step to a treaty has not occurred, at the time of writing, the potential exists and, in the meantime, the contribution of this informal lawmaking effort to standard setting and capacity-building in these regions has been valuable.

3.5 Other Informal Agreements and Arrangements Responding to Somali Piracy

The multifaceted issues emerging from the increased piracy and armed robbery attacks off the coast of Somalia necessitated many specific legal responses. In some instances, more details were needed to elaborate on existing legal principles. For example, while it is well-accepted that there is universal jurisdiction to prosecute pirates, exactly how an offender is moved between jurisdictions, taking into account due process and other human rights, had to be articulated. The use of transfer agreements is discussed in section 3.5.1 below. In other instances, the novelty of the response required the development of new standards, which could still draw on international law and practice from different contexts. The use of privately contracted security personnel could be considered in the latter category, and this practice is addressed in section 3.5.2. Finally, the practical arrangements initiated by joint navy operations are noted in section 3.5.3, which highlights, again, the interaction of formal legal authority with less formal cooperative arrangements.

[100] ibid.
[101] Jeddah Amendment (n 11) art 2(1).
[102] ibid, art 19.

3.5.1 Transfer Agreements

Another use of informal lawmaking occurred through the adoption of transfer agreements so that captured pirates could be prosecuted within the East African region. States that were participating in anti-piracy operations, such as the EU-led Operation Atalanta, the NATO-led Operation Allied Provider and Operation Ocean Shield, and the US-initiated Command Task Force 151 (CTF 151), entered into Memoranda of Understanding with Kenya, the Seychelles, and Mauritius.[103] Ensuring prosecution within the region was dependent on these states establishing the relevant national legal frameworks for investigation, prosecution, and punishment.[104] The practical appeal for such agreements was evident in benefits such as easier access to evidence and witnesses when prosecution occurs more locally, as well as the developed countries' preference that any alleged or actual pirate did not seek asylum in their countries.[105] Thus, criminal prosecution in a state other than the one that arrested the pirates emerged as common practice.[106]

The UNODC played a critical role in capacity-building for states in the region.[107] It has supported states in developing their policing, prosecutorial, and judicial sectors, as well as improving and building prisons.[108] Part of the UNODC's counter-piracy programme has been a piracy prisoner transfer programme, which has enabled the repatriation of pirates to Mogadishu and Somaliland, to prisons refurbished through the Counter-Piracy Trust Fund.[109] An important dimension of the UNODC's efforts has been ensuring that law enforcement efforts, prosecution, and imprisonment align with international human rights standards.[110]

The use of transfer agreements has not only served practical advantages, but has also provided legal benefits. From a legal perspective, these agreements filled gaps in the law enforcement regime under the LOSC in operationalizing the exercise of universal jurisdiction. However, a difficulty with these agreements, which emerges from their informal nature, is that the rights of those accused of piracy are more difficult to guarantee. Due process protections and rights guarantees are commonly included in extradition treaties and formal prisoner transfer agreements. Less certainty, accountability, and transparency all potentially arise with the use of informal transfer agreements.

[103] See Chalk (n 49) 554. See, eg European Union, 'Exchange of Letters between the European Union and the Government of Kenya on the Conditions and Modalities for the Transfer of Persons Suspected of having Committed Acts of Piracy and Detained by the European Union-Led Naval Force (EUNAVFOR), and Seized Property in the Possession of EUNAVFOR, from EUNAVFOR to Kenya and for their Treatment after such Transfer' 2009 OJ (L 79) 49–59 (EU); European Union, 'Exchange of Letters between the European Union and the Republic of Seychelles on the Conditions and Modalities for the Transfer of Suspected Pirates and Armed Robbers from EUNAVFOR to the Republic of Seychelles and for their Treatment after such Transfer' 2009 OJ (L 315) 37–43 (EU); United Kingdom Foreign and Commonwealth Office, 'Prisoner Transfer Agreements' <www.fco.gov.uk/en/global-issues/conflict-prevention/piracy/prisoners> accessed 1 July 2021. See also 'Report of the Secretary-General' (n 41) para 23.

[104] An effort that was highlighted in the Djibouti Code of Conduct. See above (n 10).

[105] Chalk (n 49) 554

[106] See Petrig and Geiß (n 2) 32–35.

[107] Bueger, Edmunds, and McCabe (n 44) 233.

[108] Jacobsson, 'International Legal Cooperation' (n 1) 103.

[109] See UNODC, 'Counter Piracy Programme: Support to the Trial and Related Treatment of Piracy Suspects' (2012), 6 and 14 <https://www.unodc.org/documents/easternafrica/piracy/UNODC_Brochure_Issue_9_Final_webversion.pdf> accessed 22 June 2021.

[110] Bueger, Edmunds, and McCabe (n 44) 233.

3.5.2 Privately Contracted Armed Security Personnel

Private actors were critical in developing standards for the use of Privately Contracted Armed Security Personnel (PCASP), as an additional counter-piracy measure to protect international shipping. It has been claimed that the use of these personnel has been the greatest contribution to reducing the incidence of piracy off the coast of Somalia.[111] The traditional IMO position had been that ship crews should not be armed, in order to avoid the escalation of violence, accidental shootings, and the complicated jurisdictional questions arising in the aftermath of any shooting on board a vessel.[112] The types of legal issues emerging from the deployment of PCASP included rules for embarkation and disembarkation, particularly when arms were also being transported across national boundaries; the deployment of PCASP when traversing the territorial sea of a coastal state and on the high seas; and the use of force by PCASP to repel a piratical attack and/or in self-defence.[113] Nonetheless, there was strong support for a shift in position from the International Transport Workers' Federation, the International Chamber of Shipping, and the shipping insurance companies.[114] The Security Council also supported the use of PCASP.[115] In response, the IMO issued interim guidance, with an emphasis on leaving decisions to individual ships and flag states.[116] While mooted, the development of a treaty on the topic could not obtain consensus.[117]

The legal basis for the role and activities of PCASP, thus, has some ambiguity. A general argument could be made that it falls within the broad obligation to cooperate under Article 100 of the LOSC.[118] Commentators have also explored what legal requirements and obligations could adhere in relation to PCASP under different multilateral treaties, and from customary international law principles relating to the exercise of flag state jurisdiction.[119] Ultimately, informal agreements have, instead, played a key role in regulating the use of PCASP, and have been endorsed through the IMO, and elaborated on in national laws.[120]

[111] Yaron Gottlieb, 'The Security Council's Maritime Piracy Resolutions: A Critical Assessment' (2015) 24(1) Minn J Intl'l L 1, 55.

[112] See Khanna (n 48) 58. See also Commission of the European Union, 'Best Management Practices to Deter Piracy in the Gulf of Aden and off the Coast of Somalia' (2010), annexed to Commission Recommendation of 11 March 2010 on Measures for Self-protection and the Prevention of Piracy and Armed Robbery at Sea [2010] OJ L67/13, art 2(b)(vii), which did not recommend the use of PCASPs, although acknowledged that the matter was to be left to the discretion of the shipowner. These views were also evident in IMO publications. See IMO, 'Guidance to Shipowners and Ship Operators, Shipmasters and Crews on Preventing and Suppressing Acts of Piracy and Armed Robbery Against Ships' (23 June 2009) IMO Doc MSC.1/Circ.1334, para 61; IMO, 'Report of the Maritime Safety Committee on its Ninetieth Session' (31 May 2012) IMO Doc MSC 90/28, para 20.11.5.

[113] For discussion of these legal issues, see eg Anna Petrig, 'The Use of Force and Firearms by Private Maritime Security Companies against Suspected Pirates' (2013) 62(3) ICLQ 667.

[114] See Helge Staff, 'The Emergence of Private Security Governance. Assessing Facilitating Conditions in the Case of Somali Piracy' (2017) 29(1) Glob Change Peace & Sec 21–37.

[115] See, eg UNSC Res 2020 (n 8) and UNSC Res 2077 (n 8).

[116] IMO, 'Interim Recommendations for Port and Coastal States Regarding the Use of Privately Contracted Armed Security Personnel on Board Ships in the High Risk Area' (16 September 2011) IMO Doc MSC.1/Circ.1408. More detailed guidance was issued in 2018: IMO, 'Private Armed Security' <https://www.imo.org/en/OurWork/Security/Pages/Private-Armed-Security.aspx> accessed 23 July 2021.

[117] Khanna (n 48) 58–59.

[118] Michael J Struett, Mark T Nance, and Diane Armstrong, 'Navigating the Maritime Piracy Regime Complex' (2013) 19(1) Glob Gov 93, 96.

[119] See Katinka Svanberg, 'The Use of Private Maritime Guards as an Innovative Means to Fulfil States Duty to Cooperate in the Repression of Maritime Piracy: Part 1' (2020) 1(2) Int J Mar Crime & Sec 31, 40–41. See also Petrig (n 113) 676–79.

[120] Svanberg (n 119) 42.

Informal agreements addressing the use of PCASP to counter piracy off the coast of Somalia were able to draw on documents that had earlier been developed to deal with the use of private military contractors during armed conflict on land.[121] The IMO developed circulars, directed initially to shipowners, as well as governments.[122] As noted previously, more detailed guidance was issued in 2012,[123] which impacted on subsequent industry guidelines.[124] A key driver for developing standards came from the shipping industry, which adopted its own guidelines, which have continued to be updated, as well as a standard contract.[125] The International Organization for Standardization (ISO) has also played a normative role, initially in relation to risk-based quality management,[126] and then more broadly.[127] The enforcement of these ISO standards depends on a voluntary auditing and certification scheme.[128] In some instances, such as regulating the use of force by PCASP, the international standards will refer to the applicability of domestic criminal law.[129]

Lawmaking efforts in this area remain a work in progress. In its 2020 resolution, the Security Council welcomed and encouraged that flag states and port states consider developing 'regulations for the use of [PCASP] on board ships . . . through a consultative process, including through the IMO and ISO'.[130] Whether any formal law eventuates remains to be seen, but, as with the Djibouti Code of Conduct and Jeddah Amendment, the normative effect of these agreements is palpable.

3.5.3 Naval Arrangements

The existing legal framework has been central to the operation of naval contingencies operating off the Somali coast. For example, the EU-led Operation Atalanta draws its legal authority from Chapter VII Security Council resolutions,[131] and binding decisions of the

[121] See, eg ICRC, 'The Montreux Document on Pertinent International Legal Obligations and Good Practices for States related to Operations of Private Military and Security Companies during Armed Conflict' (2008) <https://www.eda.admin.ch/dam/eda/en/documents/aussenpolitik/voelkerrecht/20192511-montreux-document_EN.pdf> accessed 23 July 2021; International Code of Conduct Association, 'International Code of Conduct for Private Security Service Providers' (9 November 2010) <https://icoca.ch/the-code/> accessed 23 July 2021.

[122] IMO Doc MSC.1/Circ.1334 (n 112); IMO, 'Recommendations for Preventing and Suppressing Piracy and Armed Robbery Against Ships' (12 June 2015) IMO Doc MSC.1/Circ.1333/Rev.1 Annex.

[123] IMO, 'Revised Interim Recommendations for Flag States regarding the Use of Privately Contracted Armed Security Personnel On Board Ships in the High Risk Area' (25 May 2012) IMO Doc MSC.1/Circ.1406/Rev.2, Annex; IMO, 'Revised Interim Recommendations for Port and Coastal States regarding the Use of Privately Contracted Armed Security Personnel On Board Ships in the High Risk Area' (25 May 2012) IMO Doc MSC.1/Circ.1408/Rev.1, Annex; IMO, 'Revised Interim Guidance to Shipowners, Ship Operators, and Shipmasters on the Use of Privately Contracted Armed Security Personnel On Board Ships in the High Risk Area' (25 May 2012) IMO Doc MSC.1/Circ.1405/Rev.2, Annex.

[124] Svanberg (n 119) 44.

[125] Known as GUARDCON, which was developed by BIMCO, one of the largest associations representing shipowners. Svanberg (n 119) 45.

[126] ISO, 'Specification for Security Management Systems for the Supply Chain' ISO 28000: 2007 <https://www.iso.org/standard/44641.html> accessed 1 July 2021.

[127] ISO, 'Ships and Marine Technology—Guidelines for Private Maritime Security Companies (PMSC) providing Privately Contracted Armed Security Personnel (PCASP) On Board Ships (and Pro Forma Contract)' ISO 28007-1:2015 <https://www.iso.org/standard/63166.html> accessed 1 July 2021.

[128] Svanberg (n 119) 45.

[129] Petrig (n 113) 689.

[130] UNSC Res 2554 (n 8) para 26.

[131] The Security Council did not mandate Operation Atalanta specifically, but welcomed and commended the operation. See UNSC Res 1897 (n 8) on Acts of Piracy and Armed Robbery against Vessels in the Waters off the Coast of Somalia. One commentator has described this reference as an 'indirect delegation of the activity of naval peacekeeping by the UN to other actors': Khanna (n 48) 54.

European Union. Since its initial focus on piracy and armed robbery, Operation Atalanta has now progressed to addressing fishing activities off the Somali coast, as well as contributing to the monitoring of weapons and drug trafficking, and the illicit charcoal trade.[132] These activities are responses to concerns identified in Security Council Resolution 2551 of 2020. The EU, thus, anticipates that greater maritime policing powers will be exercised on its behalf, as well as that Operation Atalanta's maritime domain awareness will be improved:

> resulting in a more efficient counterpiracy mission and reinforcing EU NAVFOR's role as a maritime security provider in line with the objectives of the EU Maritime Security Strategy. They will also reassure the Shipping Industry in supporting freedom of navigation and trade.[133]

A range of practical measures within this operation builds the structure of cooperation, and has extended to cooperation with non-European states, including Djibouti and Japan.[134] Operation Atalanta has been just one of many European Union initiatives in Somalia, and has consistently sought to operationalize existing international law rights and duties in responding to the challenges presented by activities off Somalia's coast.[135]

The EU's Operation Atalanta worked in combination with NATO's Operation Shield (2009–2016), which was preceded by Operation Allied Provider and Allied Protector.[136] It is also noteworthy that cooperation among states goes beyond formal treaty-based cooperation. The most prominent example, in this regard, is the cooperation reflected in the Combined Maritime Forces, which, as one of its task forces, has established CTF 151 on counter-piracy. The Combined Maritime Forces has thirty-four participating member states, representing five continents.

These naval arrangements are a clear indication of an ambition to deal with an urgent maritime security challenge to the order of the oceans, and to protect freedom of navigation, world trade, the marine environment and its resources, and coastal security. Since it is not realistic for states to expect a separate comprehensive regulation, states have to build on existing international law and also fill in the gaps by means of practical arrangements.

3.6 Lessons Learned and Concluding Remarks

Guilfoyle has commented on the range of cooperative mechanisms that developed relatively rapidly from 2008 onwards to respond to piracy off the Somali coast, observing that 'almost all of [these] have been informal, decentralised and located outside the major international

[132] EU, CFSP 2020/2188 (n 13).

[133] EU Naval Force—Somalia, 'Operation ATALANTA's New Mandate Enters into Force on 1st of January 2021. New Tasks will Reinforce the EU NAVFOR's Counter-piracy Core Responsibilities' (30 December 2020) <https://eunavfor.eu/operation-atalantas-new-mandate-enters-into-force-on-1st-of-january-2021-new-tasks-will-reinforce-the-eu-navfors-counter-piracy-core-responsibilities/> accessed 1 July 2021.

[134] EU Naval Force—Somalia, 'EU Naval Force Somalia Operation ATALANTA Conducts First Trilateral Exercise with Japanese and Djiboutian Forces' (10 May 2021) <https://eunavfor.eu/eu-naval-force-somalia-operation-atalanta-conducts-first-trilateral-exercise-with-the-japanese-and-djiboutian-forces/> accessed 1 July 2021.

[135] Jacobsson, 'International Legal Cooperation' (n 1) 106–10.

[136] NATO, 'Counter-Piracy Operations: Archived' (19 December 2016) <https://www.nato.int/cps/en/natohq/topics_48815.htm> accessed 1 July 2021.

institutions such as the IMO and UN'.[137] However, the discussion in this chapter has reflected the fact that the overarching roles of the UN Security Council and the IMO have provided some consistencies and influences in the formal and informal instruments used and developed to respond to piracy, both off the coast of Somalia and elsewhere. Through endorsement of private actor initiatives in counter-piracy arrangements and agreements, the IMO has facilitated 'private schemes in international rule making'.[138]

All of these instances of cooperation, codes of conduct, and bilateral and regional agreements have taken place without any new comprehensive multilateral convention. It may be claimed that this development lay within the framework of the LOSC, specifically that states are encouraged to cooperate to promote the object and purposes of the Convention and their duty to repress piracy. Or are the regional solutions a gap-filling technique that goes beyond the object and purposes of the LOSC?

The informal lawmaking to combat piracy off the coast of Somalia takes place within the realm of international law. It clearly strengthens the international law of cooperation, including the sometimes-nebulous principle of a duty to cooperate, by establishing new veins of cooperation in incident reporting, information-sharing, best practices, and cooperation in criminal matters. It has also widened the cooperation to include cooperation on environmental matters and sustainable use of natural resources, thereby recognizing cooperation as part of a much-needed holistic approach. It also expands the circle of actors beyond states and international organizations, and shows the need to embrace non-state actors, including private stakeholders.

It has been clear from the combined efforts of the UN Security Council and the international community, that decision making by the Security Council alone could not be relied upon in order to combat piracy off the coast of Somalia.[139] Actors other than states needed to be involved, and the articles in the LOSC addressing piracy were not sufficient. From a purely legal perspective, states had to rely on the wider circle of international law, as provided for in the LOSC, and in particular Articles 301 and 311. The law of state responsibility, international liability, human rights, and regional and bilateral agreements all became a part of the jigsaw puzzle. The cooperation that is needed in order to come to grips with an international problem is really the backbone of informal lawmaking.

[137] Guilfoyle, 'Somali Pirates as Agents of Change' (n 40) 90.

[138] Khanna (n 48) 58, citing Kenneth Abbott and Duncan Snidal, 'Strengthening International Regulation through Transnational New Governance' (2009) 42 Vand J Transnat'l L 501.

[139] The role of the Security Council is likely to be curtailed in the future with Somalia's recent advocacy to cease the renewal of the Security Council authorizations initiated in Resolution 1816 of 2008. See 'Somalia: Anti-Piracy Resolution', *Security Council Report*, 3 December 2021 <https://www.securitycouncilreport.org/whatsinblue/2021/12/somalia-anti-piracy-resolution-3.php> accessed 13 December 2021. Somalia's efforts led to a three-month renewal in Security Council resolution 2608 on 3 December 2021.

4

Informal Lawmaking in Maritime Migration

Irini Papanicolopulu

4.1 The Informality of Maritime Migration Law

We live in an age of informality. We prefer Airbnb to hotels, car sharing to owning our own cars, loosely conceived affective relationships to marriages, polo shirts to suits, and stand-up buffets to formal dining.[1] It should, therefore, come as no surprise that international law has followed suit. While the only current formal multilateral negotiation at the United Nations (UN) level for a new treaty seems to be the Intergovernmental Conference on an international legally binding instrument under the United Nations Convention on the Law of the Sea (LOSC) on the conservation and sustainable use of marine biological diversity of areas beyond national jurisdiction,[2] there are countless initiatives involving informal instruments. After all, '[t]here are obviously many advantages to memoranda of understanding ... over formal treaties and to "results oriented partnerships" over formal international organizations'.[3]

The informality that is typical of current international law is reflected in the legal regulation of irregular migration by sea. This situation may also be seen as a natural consequence of the informality that characterizes irregular migration, which can be defined as 'a migratory movement that takes place outside the regulatory frameworks of the origin, transit and destination countries'.[4] International lawyers have struggled to curb this informality and create a body of law to regulate irregular migration by sea.[5] Notwithstanding these efforts, however, the most recent multilateral treaty that regulates (aspects of) irregular migration by sea is the 2000 Smuggling Protocol.[6] Otherwise, the plethora of acts that have been adopted with respect to irregular migration by sea present one or more characteristics of informality.[7]

[1] This chapter was written in a pre-Covid time. It remains to be seen, once 'normality' returns, whether or not formalism will re-emerge to take the place of informality.

[2] Launched by UNGA Res 72/249 (24 December 2017) UN Doc A/Res/72/249. Information can be found at <https://www.un.org/bbnj/> accessed 12 July 2021.

[3] Eyal Benvenisti, 'Towards a Typology of Informal International Lawmaking Mechanisms and their Distinct Accountability Gaps' in Joost Pauwelyn, Ramses A Wessel, and Jan Wouters (eds), *Informal International Lawmaking* (OUP 2012) 297.

[4] UNODC, 'Migrant smuggling v irregular migration' <https://www.unodc.org/e4j/en/tip-and-som/module-1/key-issues/migrant-smuggling-v-irregular-migration.html> accessed 12 July 2021.

[5] See, eg Patricia Mallia, *Migrant Smuggling by Sea: Combating a Current Threat to Maritime Security through the Creation of a Cooperative Framework* (Martinus Nijhoff 2010); Violeta Moreno-Lax and Efthymios Papastavridis (eds), *'"Boat Refugees"' and Migrants at Sea: A Comprehensive Approach* (Brill 2017); Violeta Moreno-Lax, Daniel Ghezelbash, and Natalie Klein, 'Between Life, Security and Rights: Framing the Interdiction of 'Boat Migrants' in the Central Mediterranean and Australia' (2019) 32(4) LJIL 715.

[6] Protocol against the Smuggling of Migrants by Land, Sea and Air Supplementing the United Nations Convention against Transnational Organized Crime (adopted 15 November 2000, entered into force 28 January 2004) 2241 UNTS 480.

[7] Informal lawmaking, indeed, characterizes the entire field of migration law, as discussed by Vincent Chetail, *International Migration Law* (OUP 2019) 300.

Irini Papanicolopulu, *Informal Lawmaking in Maritime Migration* In: *Unconventional Lawmaking in the Law of the Sea*. Edited by: Natalie Klein, Oxford University Press. © Irini Papanicolopulu 2022. DOI: 10.1093/oso/9780192897824.003.0004

Legal regulation of maritime migration defies traditional understandings of international law in a number of ways. First, it is not addressed by any of the main formal instruments that apply to maritime spaces or human rights protection, except in a cursory way. For example, the few provisions that address migration by sea in the LOSC[8] are either accessory to other provisions dealing with different topics, as in the case of Article 19(2)(g) wherein the loading or unloading of migrants in the territorial sea is just one of the activities that render passage 'non-innocent', or are mixed with different issues, as in the case of the regime applicable within the contiguous zone, described in Article 33 of the LOSC. The same is true for human rights instruments, which are notorious for their lack of acknowledgment of maritime spaces and activities, with a few exceptions, such as the 1961 Agreement Relating to Refugee Seamen.[9]

Second, there is no established international body charged with consideration of migration by sea. Rather, there are some organizations that are charged with all sorts of issues and have in common only the fact that the mandate of each has a bearing on some aspects of maritime migration. The ones that have been discussed most in recent times include the International Organization for Migration (IOM), the United Nations High Commissioner for Refugees (UNHCR), the International Maritime Organization (IMO), and the United Nations Office on Drugs and Crime (UNODC).

Third, the need to address the issues raised by maritime migration, and the lack of dedicated instruments and institutions, has led not only states, but also other actors, including non-governmental organizations (NGOs) and the maritime industry, to become significantly involved. These non-state actors are engaged in the drafting of rules that try to address this phenomenon, as well as in the application of these rules.

In light of the above considerations, this chapter proposes to analyse informal lawmaking concerning maritime migration from a dual perspective. First, it will consider informal lawmaking in formal settings, that is formally constituted international organizations or conferences formally convened by states or intergovernmental organizations. Maritime migration is, in fact, one of the fields where states, even when they act as the main subjects of international law, shy away from formal law and, instead, adopt unconventional solutions at all levels: the global (for example, the Global Compact for Migration[10] and the IMO Guidelines[11]), regional (for example, the September 2019 Malta Declaration by some European states[12]), or national levels (for example, the Italian Code of Conduct for NGOs,[13] and the internal strife between the executive and the judiciary in Italy and other states, which affects the perception of this practice as a basis for the development of customary

[8] United Nations Convention on the Law of the Sea (adopted 10 December 1982, entered into force 16 November 1994) 1833 UNTS 397 (hereafter 'LOSC').

[9] Agreement Relating to Refugee Seamen (adopted 23 November 1957, entered into force 27 December 1961) 506 UNTS 126.

[10] UN General Assembly, 'Global Compact for Safe, Orderly and Regular Migration' UNGA Res 73/195 (19 December 2018) UN Doc A/RES/73/195.

[11] IMO, 'Guidelines on the Treatment of Persons Rescued at Sea' (20 May 2004) IMO Res MSC.167(78) (hereafter 'IMO Guidelines').

[12] Joint Declaration of Intent on a Controlled Emergency Procedure—Voluntary Commitments by Member States for a Predictable Temporary Solidarity Mechanism (adopted on 23 September 2019) <https://www.statewatch.org/media/documents/news/2019/sep/eu-temporary-voluntary-relocation-mechanism-declaration.pdf> accessed 23 July 2021.

[13] Codice di condotta per le ONG impegnate nelle operazioni di salvataggio dei migranti in mare (2017). <http://www.interno.gov.it/sites/default/files/allegati/codice_condotta_ong.pdf> accessed 12 July 2021 (hereafter 'Italian Code of Conduct').

international law). Second, the chapter will address informal lawmaking by 'informal' actors, in particular NGOs (for example, the NGO code of conduct for search and rescue (SAR) operations[14]) and the maritime industry (for example, the International Chamber of Shipping guidelines[15]), as well as the role that these informal actors play in the development of international practice. To do so, it will first discuss what makes this regime informal (section 4.2). It will then analyse acts making up the regime through a binary taxonomy that distinguishes between informal acts in formal settings (section 4.3) and informal acts by informal actors (section 4.4), before offering some concluding thoughts on the dual nature of informal lawmaking, which may provide an easier way out of the system of international law (for states), but also an easier way into the system (for non-state actors) (section 4.5).

4.2 A Perspective on Informal Lawmaking

The binary taxonomy used in this chapter derives from an understanding of informal lawmaking, which partly differs from that used in other works and is, therefore, worth setting out, albeit briefly. These differences relate mostly to the lack of relevance of the process for the purposes of determining whether lawmaking is formal or informal, as well as to the fact that action by non-state actors may assume relevance in the lawmaking process.

It has been argued that informality has to do with 'output, process or the actors involved'.[16] While it is certainly true that lawmaking is informal when 'it dispenses with certain formalities traditionally linked to international law',[17] it is argued here that these formalities relate to the output and the actors involved in the process, rather than the process itself. In fact, traditional international law regulates the output (the sources of international law) and the actors (the subjects of international law) while remaining generally silent on the process. Although it is commonly the case that, in the course of the twentieth century, treaties have been adopted either in intergovernmental conferences or within formally established intergovernmental organizations, these arrangements are by no means a prerequisite for their existence and validity. As the Vienna Convention on the Law of Treaties (VCLT)[18] makes clear, states may choose the forms through which they wish to be legally bound.[19]

As a consequence, lawmaking is informal when it involves outputs or actors different from those identified by existing rules of international law. As far as outputs are concerned, formal outputs are acts that may be considered as treaties. The official denomination of the

[14] Human Rights at Sea, 'Voluntary Code of Conduct for Search and Rescue Operations Undertaken by Civil Society Non-Governmental Organisations in the Mediterranean Sea' (2017) <https://www.humanrightsatsea.org/wp-content/uploads/2017/03/20170302-NGO-Code-of-Conduct-FINAL-SECURED.pdf> accessed 12 July 2021 (hereafter 'NGO Code of Conduct').

[15] ICS, 'Guidance on Large Scale Rescue Operations at Sea' (2nd edn, 2015) <https://www.ics-shipping.org/wp-content/uploads/2015/01/large-scale-rescue-at-sea-min.pdf> accessed 12 July 2021.

[16] Joost Pauwelyn, 'Informal International Lawmaking: Framing the Concept and Research Questions' in Joost Pauwelyn, Ramses A Wessel, and Jan Wouters (eds), *Informal International Lawmaking* (OUP 2012) 13, 15.

[17] ibid.

[18] Vienna Convention on the Law of Treaties (adopted 23 May 1969, entered into force 27 January 1980) 1155 UNTS 331 (hereafter 'VCLT').

[19] Thus, full powers are not necessary if 'it appears from the practice of the States concerned or from other circumstances that their intention was to consider that person as representing the State ... for the purpose of adopting or authenticating the text of a treaty or for the purpose of expressing the consent of the State to be bound by a treaty' (ibid, art 7(1)(b)). Further, states may choose any means to express their intent to be bound by a treaty, as long as they are agreed upon (ibid, art 11).

act does not matter:[20] therefore, Memoranda of Understanding (MoU) may well be treaties or informal outputs, depending on their actual content and purpose, and this issue will be considered further when discussing the role of MoUs in maritime migration. Customary international law should be treated separately, as the term 'lawmaking' seems hardly appropriate in relation to a source of international law that has been conceived of as 'spontaneous'.[21] States, in fact, cannot 'make' custom, although they can certainly contribute to the creation (or, more accurately, emergence) of custom.

Turning to actors, formal actors consist of states and international organizations. These actors are, in fact, the subjects of international law that have traditionally been considered as having the capacity to create rules. In relation to states, there is unanimity in considering that their lawmaking is formal, as far as the actor is concerned. However, it seems too reductive to consider that lawmaking is informal when it engages 'other ministries [apart from the foreign ministers], domestic regulators, independent or semi-independent agencies, ... sub-federal entities, ... or the legislative or judicial branch'.[22] It is *the state* as an abstract entity that is a subject of international law, and has the power to enter into legally binding treaties, not the ministry of foreign affairs or the head of government. It is, therefore, for the state to choose by whom it wants to be represented. The VCLT makes this clear by not setting any limitations or conditions concerning the persons who have full powers to represent the state,[23] or who can be considered to represent the state on the basis of other grounds.[24] In some fields, negotiations led by ministries other than those of foreign affairs have been the rule for decades, and nobody would seriously consider treaties such as the Kyoto Protocol as exercises in informal lawmaking just because they have been negotiated, on behalf of some states, by representatives of the ministry of the environment. Therefore, instances in which the persons taking part in a negotiation are authorized by their state to represent it, and the outcome is a formal one, will not be treated as informal lawmaking.

Similarly to states, intergovernmental organizations are recognised as holding the right to enter into treaties, as a matter of international law.[25] As a consequence, their lawmaking activities are generally formal ones, as far as the actors are concerned, although they may be informal as to the output, for example when they adopt acts that are not legally binding, such as guidelines or best practices.

Finally, actors other than states and international organizations are, by default, informal ones. Other actors, who include subjects as diverse as transnational corporations, insurgents, NGOs, and individuals, have only recently entered international law, and there is great discussion as to their capacity to participate in the making of international law. It is submitted here that their lawmaking activities may, indeed, be relevant for international law, and may consist of informal lawmaking. As has been convincingly argued, the use of private bodies is 'an old trick of governments that seek to evade constitutional constraints and public accountability' and, in any case, governments may be responsible for omissions when they do not control the activities of private actors that have a bearing on others.[26]

[20] VCLT (n 18) art 2(1)(a).

[21] On 'instant' custom, see Bin Cheng, 'United Nations Resolutions on Outer Space: "Instant" International Customary Law' (1965) 5 Indian JIL 23.

[22] Pauwelyn (n 16) 19.

[23] VCLT (n 18) art 7(1)(a).

[24] ibid, art 7(1)(b).

[25] VCLT (n 18).

[26] Benvenisti (n 3) 302.

Other actors may engage in informal lawmaking in two separate ways, which reflect the two main categories of international law norms. In the first place, they may develop, or contribute to the development of, legal instruments, which are informal. In the second place, they may contribute, through their actions, to the crystallization of customary international law, either by bringing cases in front of national and international judges who will eventually adopt statements as to the content of existing law, or by acting in ways that confirm or challenge existing rules, and that trigger positive or negative reactions by states, thus eventually confirming or denying the existence of a certain rule.

In sum, informality may characterize either the output (when it is not a treaty), or the actors (when they are not states or international organizations), or both (when other actors undertake non-treaty actions). On the basis of these considerations, this chapter will, next, focus on lawmaking that is informal because it leads to informal outputs, that is acts that are not treaties under international law, despite the fact that these are negotiated and adopted by formal actors, such as states and international organizations. It will then turn to informal lawmaking by informal actors, identifying instances in which actors other than state and international organizations engage in lawmaking, as defined above.

4.3 Informal Lawmaking in Formal Settings

For the last two decades at least, migration, including irregular migration by sea, has featured prominently in international fora.[27] Global, regional, and subregional organizations have tried to address the multiple aspects of this human activity, and to adopt regulations thereon. One might add that this exercise has led to little success, not only in light of the current numbers of irregular migrants voyaging by sea and the shocking number of deaths,[28] but also because it has not resulted in any formal instrument. However, such an assessment might disregard the multiple acts that have been adopted at the international level by states and international organizations.

A first category of informal acts includes agreements between states that cannot be considered as fully fledged treaties, according to the VCLT. These agreements, which also involve the European Union (EU), are mostly concluded in an effort to prevent the arrival of irregular migrants by sea in destination countries, by controlling departures from countries of origin or transit countries. The most (in)famous example is probably the 2016 EU–Turkey agreement. From a formal point of view, this agreement took the form of a joint statement published in an EU press release.[29] As scholars have highlighted, the 2016 EU–Turkey agreement is informal, both from an international law and an EU law perspective.[30]

[27] Chetail (n 7) 300–39.

[28] In 2016, the deadliest year, so far, in the Mediterranean, at least 5,143 persons lost their lives at sea while trying to cross the Mediterranean Sea into Europe. For updated information, see the website maintained by the International Organization for Migration (IOM) <https://missingmigrants.iom.int/> accessed 12 July 2021.

[29] European Council Press Release, 'EU–Turkey statement, 18 March 2016' <https://www.consilium.europa.eu/en/press/press-releases/2016/03/18/eu-turkey-statement/> accessed 12 July 2021.

[30] Maarten den Heijer and Thomas Spijkerboer, 'Is the EU–Turkey Refugee and Migration Deal a Treaty?' (EU Law Analysis, 7 April 2016) <http://eulawanalysis.blogspot.com/2016/04/is-eu-turkey-refugee-and-migration-deal.html> accessed 12 July 2021; Steven Peers, 'The Final EU/Turkey Refugee Deal: A Legal Assessment' (EU Law Analysis, 18 March 2016) <http://eulawanalysis.blogspot.com/2016/03/the-final-euturkey-refugee-deal-legal.html> accessed 12 July 2021; Carmelo Danisi, 'Taking the "Union" out of "EU": The EU–Turkey Statement on the Syrian Refugee Crisis as an Agreement between States under International Law' (EJILTalk!, 20 April 2017) <https://www.ejiltalk.org/taking-the-union-out-of-eu-the-eu-turkey-statement-on-the-syrian-refu

In the first place, there is some uncertainty concerning the actual parties to this agreement. The title of the instrument and its content refer regularly to the EU and Turkey, however, in a much-discussed pronouncement, the European Court of Justice (ECJ) considered that the agreement had been concluded by the member states and not by the EU itself.[31] In the second place, the exact legal nature of the act is contested. While the EU institutions have claimed that the act is a 'political' rather than 'legal' act, scholars have argued that it is, in fact, an international treaty concluded in a simplified form. It is clear from the text of the agreement that the parties wanted to establish binding commitments, as evidenced from words such as 'decided' and 'agreed', and the constant use of the verb 'will'. However, whether these commitments are legally binding is another issue. The legal nature of the EU–Turkey agreement is, thus, highly debatable.

The 2017 Memorandum of Understanding between Italy and Libya is another example of an act adopted by states to address migration, including migration by sea.[32] The act can be considered 'informal' on two grounds: its form and its parties. In the first place, it was concluded in the simplified form of a MoU, linked to a previous Treaty on Friendship, Partnership, and Cooperation, entered into between Italy and Libya in 2008.[33] A number of elements suggest that this MoU is actually an international treaty, concluded in a simplified form. In the first place, the structure of the act reflects that of international treaties. It contains, apart from the preamble and the substantive provisions, articles on the settlement of disputes (Article 6), on the procedure for its modification (Article 7), and on entry into force and renewal (Article 8), as well as a reference to the official languages, Arabic and Italian, both of which are authentic. Furthermore, the MoU has been published by the Italian

gee-crisis-as-an-agreement-between-states-under-international-law/> accessed 12 July 2021; Mauro Gatti, 'The EU–Turkey Statement: A Treaty that Violates Democracy (Part 1 of 2)' (EJILTalk!, 18 April 2016) <https://www.ejiltalk.org/the-eu-turkey-statement-a-treaty-that-violates-democracy-part-1-of-2/> accessed 12 July 2021; Gloria Fernández Arribas, 'The EU–Turkey Agreement: A Controversial Attempt at Patching up a Major Problem' (2016) 1(3) EurPapers 1097; Mauro Gatti, 'La dichiarazione UE–Turchia sulla migrazione: un trattato concluso in violazione delle prerogative del Parlamento?' (Eurojus.it, 11 April 2016) <http://rivista.eurojus.it/la-dichiarazione-ue-turchia-sulla-migrazione-un-trattato-concluso-in-violazione-delle-prerogative-del-parlamento/> accessed 12 July 2021.

[31] '[T]he Court finds that the expression 'Members of the European Council' and the term 'EU', contained in the EU–Turkey statement as published by means of Press Release No 144/16, must be understood as references to the Heads of State or Government of the European Union who, as during the first and second meetings of the Heads of State or Government on 29 November 2015 and 7 March 2016, met with their Turkish counterpart and agreed on operational measures ... It is clear from that overall context preceding the online publication on the Council's website of Press Release No 144/16 setting out the EU–Turkey statement that, concerning the management of the migration crisis, the European Council, as an institution, did not adopt a decision to conclude an agreement with the Turkish Government in the name of the European Union and that it also did not commit the European Union within the meaning of Article 218 TFEU.... It follows from all of the foregoing considerations that, independently of whether it constitutes, as maintained by the European Council, the Council and the Commission, a political statement or, on the contrary, as the applicant submits, a measure capable of producing binding legal effects, the EU–Turkey statement, as published by means of Press Release No 144/16, cannot be regarded as a measure adopted by the European Council, or, moreover, by any other institution, body, office or agency of the European Union, or as revealing the existence of such a measure that corresponds to the contested measure.': Case T-192/16 *NF v European Council*, Order of the General Court (First Chamber, Extended Composition), 28 February 2017, para 69.

[32] Memorandum di intesa sulla cooperazione nel campo dello sviluppo, del contrasto all'immigrazione illegale, al traffico di esseri umani, al contrabbando e sul rafforzamento della sicurezza delle frontiere tra lo Stato della Libia e la Repubblica Italiana (2017 Memorandum of Understanding between Italy and Libya) (2 February 2017) <http://www.governo.it/sites/governo.it/files/Libia.pdf> accessed 25 July 2021.

[33] Trattato di Amicizia, Partenariato e Cooperazione (Treaty on Friendship, Partnership and Cooperation between Italy and Libya) (30 August 2008), ratified by Italy with Law No. 2009/7 (TFPC).

Ministry of Foreign Affairs in its database of international treaties concluded by Italy.[34] In light of these elements, it is concluded that this agreement is an international treaty, albeit concluded in a simplified form, rather than an informal act. In the second place, the MoU could be considered as 'informal' because of one of its parties, namely that it was concluded with only one of the entities that currently control parts of Libya.

A second category of informal acts involving formal actors includes those acts that have been adopted by international organizations in a form other than that of a formally binding act of the organization. The best-known acts of this type in the field of migration by sea are probably the resolutions and guidelines adopted by the IMO. Starting from 1993, the IMO has adopted a series of acts addressing migration by sea with particular attention to the safety of human life, including the 1993 resolution on safety and migrant smuggling,[35] the 1998 circular on interim measures,[36] and the 2004 Guidelines on the Treatment of Persons Rescued at Sea.[37] The first two instruments were linked to the process that eventually led to the adoption of the 2000 Smuggling Protocol, and, as such, can be seen as a provisional way of addressing issues of concern while waiting for the conclusion of the formal process of negotiation and entry into force of an international treaty.

The 2004 IMO Guidelines would, however, appear to be qualitatively different, as they were adopted not so much in the expectation of a future formal instrument, but, rather, in order to fill gaps caused by the impossibility of states reaching agreement on a further formal instrument. The IMO Guidelines were, in fact, adopted as part of a revision process that led to the amendment of the two treaties that are of fundamental importance for the safety of life at sea, that is the SOLAS[38] and SAR Conventions,[39] and addressed some issues upon which states were unable to agree, including the definition of a 'place of safety'.[40] The IMO Guidelines were adopted by the IMO's Maritime Safety Committee (MSC), 'the highest technical body of the Organization',[41] composed of representatives of all member states. Being guidelines, they are not legally binding in their own right, although their purpose is 'to provide guidance to Governments and to shipmasters with regard to humanitarian obligations and obligations under the relevant international law relating to treatment of persons rescued at sea'.[42] They could, therefore, be seen as a document that partly embodies existing legal obligations, already binding on states as a matter of customary or treaty law, and which partly reproduces moral or social norms ('humanitarian obligations'). The IMO Guidelines, of course, do not specify which content is codification of existing legal obligations, and which is not, and it is up to the interpreter to establish the distinction between the two types of obligations: a distinction that is not always easy to make. They are, however, a

[34] The database can be accessed at <http://itra.esteri.it/Ricerca_Documenti/wfrmRicerca_Documenti.aspx> accessed 17 September 2020.

[35] IMO, 'Enhancement of Safety of Life at Sea by the Prevention and Suppression of Unsafe Practices Associated with Alien Smuggling by Ships' (4 November 1993) IMO Res. A.773(18).

[36] IMO, 'Interim Measures for Combating Unsafe Practices Associated with the Traffic or Transport of Migrants by Sea' (16 December 1998) IMO Doc MSC/Circ.896.

[37] IMO Guidelines (n 11).

[38] International Convention for the Safety of Life at Sea (adopted 1 November 1974, entered into force 25 May 1980, as amended) 1184 UNTS 278.

[39] International Convention on Maritime Search and Rescue (adopted 27 April 1979, entered into force 22 June 1985, as amended) 1405 UNTS 97.

[40] Mallia (n 5) 136–37.

[41] IMO, 'Structure of IMO' <http://www.imo.org/en/About/Pages/Structure.aspx> accessed 12 July 2021.

[42] IMO Guidelines (n 11) para 1.1.

good example of an act of informal lawmaking with normative effect, and possibly one with normative intent,[43] and are certainly useful in assessing the extent to which states are complying with their due diligence obligations under Articles 94 and 98 of the LOSC.[44]

As the examples in this section show, both states and international organizations have had recourse to informal acts in their efforts to regulate different aspects of migration by sea. In particular, states use informal acts to pursue policies of migration control, especially by preventing departures from countries of origin or transit countries, and for ensuring quick repatriation of migrants who have managed to reach destination countries. In this context, informal acts are less onerous, from both a political and a legal perspective. Politically, they allow states to downgrade their commitments into non-legal ones (as in the case of the EU–Turkey agreement) or technical ones (as in the case of the Italy–Libya MoU), to avoid parliamentary scrutiny. In extreme cases, informal acts may even provide an easy way out of binding obligations by creating confusion about basic facts, such as who exactly are the authors of the act and, thus, who must act consistently with the standards set out in these agreements.

International organizations also make ample use of informal lawmaking in their efforts to regulate migration by sea, in particular in order to ensure protection for migrants in danger, as in the case of the IMO instruments. Differently from states, however, international organizations choose informal acts when they are unable to secure agreement on formal acts, such as new treaties or amendments to existing treaties. Informal acts, therefore, seem to be a fallback option to ensure some sort of regulation when otherwise faced with the unwillingness of states to accept formally binding commitments.

Therefore, while both states and international organizations have the power to adopt formal, legally binding acts—treaties and binding decisions—they generally opt for informal acts, albeit for different, and rather opposite, reasons. States prefer informal acts to evade accountability and legal responsibility arising from treaties, while international organizations opt for informal acts to provide adherence by states to previously assumed obligations, and the acceptance by states of new duties. In other words, states adopt informal acts to reduce their duties while international organizations adopt informal acts to increase states' duties.

4.4 Informal Lawmaking by Informal Actors

Apart from formal lawmakers, other international actors are involved in informal international lawmaking. Non-state actors, in particular NGOs and civil society, have had, and continue to have, a prominent role in addressing irregular migration, including migration by sea, and in developing the complex web of instruments that characterizes the field today. Action by non-state actors affects lawmaking in two separate ways, first, they may adopt, or participate in the adoption of, informal acts that purport to regulate aspects of migration by sea. Acts that are informal because they do not fall within the traditional sources of international law are, in fact, the only possibility allowed to non-state actors, who cannot, as such, enter into treaties, either between themselves or with states.

[43] See Klein, in Chapter 1 of this volume.
[44] ibid.

Second, and more subtly, non-state actors may affect formal sources of international law through their actions and advocacy. What probably comes to mind in this context is the lobbying activities of informal actors, and the pressure exercised on states to adopt, or not to adopt, a specific treaty or other formal legally binding instrument.[45] However, there is also another way of affecting international law, which is through actions that influence international custom. This role is independent from theoretical debates as to whether custom may arise out of actions by subjects of international law other than states. Even if one agrees with the International Law Commission that only state action leads to the emergence, modification, and termination of custom,[46] it is still the case that pointed action by some non-state actors will trigger responses by states that then implicate international custom, confirming the existence of a rule or, alternatively, leading to its abandonment. Two types of action have assumed a prominent place in the context of maritime migration—strategic litigation and concrete actions—as will be illustrated in the next subsections.

4.4.1 Non-state Actors and the Development of Informal Instruments

The traditional conception according to which only states and international organizations may enter into treaties remains unchallenged to this day. As a consequence, non-state actors other than international organizations must use informal instruments whenever they want to, or have to, assume international rights and duties. This process may, or may not, involve a state.[47]

On the one hand, informal instruments have been used by states in an attempt to impose duties on non-state actors involved in the rescue of irregular migrants by sea. For example, in 2017, Italy adopted a 'Code of Conduct for NGOs Active in Operations for the Rescue of Migrants at Sea' (the Italian Code of Conduct),[48] and invited all NGOs active in the rescue of migrants in the Mediterranean Sea to sign the code. However, not all NGOs agreed to sign the code.

The code contains a series of obligations that NGOs may voluntarily accept by signature. While signature is not binding, and although the code does not contain any sanction for non-signature, it does provide that 'lack of subscription to this Code of Conduct or failure to comply with the duties provided therein may entail the adoption of measures against vessels involved by the Italian Authorities'. The Italian government, therefore, threatened to close its ports to vessels of NGOs that had not signed the code: a measure contrary to existing international law, as discussed in the next section.[49]

[45] Anne T Gallagher and Fiona David, *The International Law of Migrant Smuggling* (CUP 2014) 37–38.

[46] International Law Commission, 'Draft Conclusions on Identification of Customary International Law', UN Doc A/73/10, in particular 'Conclusion 4', 13.

[47] In this respect, informal lawmaking as understood in this chapter goes beyond what is commonly claimed to be informal lawmaking, ie lawmaking involving at least one state or state authority. See Pauwelyn (n 16).

[48] Italian Code of Conduct (n 13). For a critical comment on the code, see ASGI, 'Posizione sulla bozza di "Codice di condotta per le ONG coinvolte nel salvataggio di migranti in mare"' <https://www.asgi.it/wp-content/uploads/2017/07/Draft-ASGI-Position-Paper_Final_IT.pdf> accessed 12 July 2021.

[49] Pasquale De Sena and Francesca De Vittor, 'La "minaccia" italiana di "bloccare" gli sbarchi di migranti e il diritto internazionale' (SIDIBlog, 1 July 2017) <http://www.sidiblog.org/2017/07/01/la-minaccia-italiana-di-bloccare-gli-sbarchi-di-migranti-e-il-diritto-internazionale> accessed 12 July 2021.

From a substantive point of view, the alleged objective of the Italian Code of Conduct, as expressed in the code itself, is to 'also safeguard the safety of migrants and operators',[50] while further objectives are not mentioned. Some of the duties required of NGOs reflect those contained in international law, such as the use of an Automatic Identification System (AIS) and Long Range Identification and Tracking (LRIT).[51] Other duties seem to recognise the 'quasi-public' functions that NGOs providing search and rescue services in the Mediterranean Sea actually carry out, by asking them to comply with certain duties, such as equipping themselves with means appropriate for mass rescue operations,[52] or to collect the boats and other craft used for the smuggling of migrants,[53] which come quite close to those of state enforcement agencies. Yet, other duties contained in the Italian Code of Conduct seem less in conformity with international law, as they either try to attribute to Italy powers that the law of the sea attributes to flag states,[54] such as control over the funding of NGOs, or because they seem to violate existing rules, such as the right of innocent passage in the territorial sea of any state,[55] or even the duty to save life at sea and other human rights obligations.[56] In short, the code seems to have been adopted with a view to intimidating NGOs carrying out rescue operations in the Mediterranean Sea.[57]

From a formal point of view, the Italian Code of Conduct is an informal act under both international and Italian law.[58] It is certainly not a treaty, because it lacks two fundamental characteristics, that is the actors signing it are neither states nor international organizations (they are NGOs), and it is not reciprocal. The Italian Code of Conduct is, in fact, open to signature by one type of party only—civil society organizations—and has not been signed by the Italian Government, or by any other public authority of the state of Italy. Furthermore, it contains obligations for one type of party only—again, civil society organizations—and does not provide for any duties to be performed by Italy itself. In light of these characteristics, it could be seen as a sort of 'externally imposed' unilateral act by the NGOs who have signed it, which entails for the signatories the 'duty' to comply with its provisions, but does not grant them any 'right(s)', and does not provide for any duty on the party that proposed it: Italy.

50 Here, and in the following analysis, the translation of the Italian text has been conducted by the author of this chapter.

51 The Italian Code of Conduct, thus, requires NGOs not to switch off or delay the regular transmittal of Automatic Identification System (AIS) and Long-range Identification and Tracking (LRIT) signals, as well as to keep the relevant Maritime Rescue Coordination Centre (MRCC) informed of all activities.

52 The Italian Code of Conduct requires NGOs to equip themselves with means and personnel adequately trained to carry out search and rescue and rescue operations, including mass rescue operations in any type of conditions, a requirement that international treaties do not contain.

53 The Italian Code of Conduct requires NGOs to recover the boats and outboard motors used to smuggle migrants by sea, and to inform the International Coordination Centre of Operation TRITON accordingly.

54 The Italian Code of Conduct requires NGOs to declare to their flag state authorities all sources of financing of rescue operations at sea, and to communicate such information to the Italian authorities.

55 The Italian Code of Conduct contains the obligation for NGOs 'not to enter the Libyan territorial waters, except in situations of serious and imminent danger which require immediate assistance', and the obligation 'not to transfer people rescued to other vessels'.

56 The Italian Code of Conduct, arguably, would require NGOs to cooperate with the Libyan Maritime Rescue Coordination Centre in order to return saved migrants back to Libya, where they could be subjected to torture and other forms of inhuman and degrading treatment, or be killed.

57 Irini Papanicolopulu and Giulia Baj, 'Controllo delle frontiere statali e respingimenti nel diritto internazionale e nel diritto del mare' (2020) 1/2020 Diritto, Immigrazione e Cittadinanza 24.

58 Its status under Italian law is equally informal, as it does not fall within any of the acts that the government may adopt, according to Italian law.

Informal instruments are, however, also developed by non-state actors themselves, as in the case of the Code of Conduct for Search and Rescue Operations undertaken by Civil Society Non-Governmental Organisations in the Mediterranean Sea (NGO Code of Conduct).[59] The NGO Code of Conduct was adopted, in 2017, by a group of NGOs active in the protection of human rights at sea, and especially in the provision of search and rescue operations for saving the lives of irregular migrants at sea. The purpose of the code is to 'define and subsequently agree upon a common standard of ethics and operational conduct for the undertaking of efficient, effective and lawful [search and rescue] operations'.[60] It is, therefore, a document that combines legal and practical concerns, and, to a significant extent, reiterates and builds upon existing rules of international law. The fact that NGOs have decided to adopt an informal instrument to set out their practices seems, however, to go beyond the need to have commonly agreed standards of conduct, and points at the necessity of justifying their operations in terms of international law rights and duties, on one hand, and confirming the binding nature of these rules, on the other. From a formal point of view, the NGO Code of Conduct is certainly not legally binding under international law per se, although it could create some kind of legal obligation if considered to be the expression of the unilateral commitment of NGOs, as will be discussed next.

4.4.2 Non-state Actors' Practice and its Role in the Creation of Law

The most visible contribution of non-state actors to informal lawmaking is probably achieved through their actions that challenge states' inaction, and which oblige states to face their international responsibilities, and to take precise stances as to the existence and binding nature of some fundamental principles and rules of international law. In this respect, the rescue operations carried out by NGOs in the Mediterranean Sea are certainly relevant. In more than one case, in fact, actions by NGOs have triggered responses by states that have confirmed existing rules of treaty and customary international law, in the face of state efforts to downplay or bypass those obligations.

The events surrounding a rescue operation carried out by the NGO vessel *Sea Watch 3* in the summer of 2019 illustrate this role of non-state actors. After having rescued some sixty persons off the coast of Libya, and having been contacted by the Libyan Maritime Rescue Coordination Centre (MRCC), *Sea Watch 3* refused to disembark the rescued persons in Libya, claiming that this action would violate human rights and other obligations. It kept sailing, waiting for a different place of disembarkation to be indicated, until eventually, after seventeen days of navigation at sea, the captain decided to enter into the Italian port of Lampedusa without authorization from the Italian authorities, claiming a state of distress.[61] As soon as the vessel was docked, the migrants were allowed to disembark, and the captain and vessel were arrested. They were later released following the decision by Italian judges that the captain and vessel had not breached Italian and international law as the acts of entering into port without authorization were justified on the grounds of the state of distress.[62]

[59] NGO Code of Conduct (n 14).

[60] ibid 7–8.

[61] The events are described in Tribunale di Agrigento, GIP Order of 2 July 2019.

[62] ibid; Corte di Cassazione Cass., sez. III pen., n. 06626/2020. Pierfrancesco Rossi, 'Politica dei "porti chiusi" e diritto internazionale: il caso Sea Watch 3' (5 November 2019) 6/2019 Osservatorio Costituzionale 48; Stefano Calabria, 'I respingimenti in mare dopo il cd. decreto sicurezza-bis (ed in particolare alla luce del comma 1-ter

The activities of *Sea Watch 3* and the decisions of its captain, Carola Rackete, triggered multiple responses by Italian state organs. On the one hand, the Italian government adopted a decree,[63] the purpose of which was to prevent the entry into port of NGO vessels that had rescued irregular migrants in the Mediterranean Sea. On the other hand, the decree, which was considered as hardly compatible with domestic and international law rules by the President of the Italian Republic, as well as scholars,[64] was subsequently challenged in front of the Italian judges, who confirmed the basic rules of international law concerning rescue of persons at sea and the prohibition of refoulement.[65]

As this example illustrates, acts by non-state actors may prompt states to take a position vis-à-vis contested norms of international law, and may trigger international practice that counts towards the creation of customary international law. The unauthorized entry into port by *Sea Watch 3* on the grounds of distress, thus, challenged readings of international law that would exclude the possibility for a vessel in distress to enter into port. The response of Italy was, initially, ambiguous, as the decree adopted seemed to point towards a restriction, if not a complete eradication, of this possibility. However, the successive decisions of judicial authorities, including the Italian supreme courts, confirmed the basic rules of international law in this field, and can certainly be considered as state practice for the purposes of confirming the existence of the possibility for a vessel in distress to enter into a port even without the authorization of the coastal state.

To sum up, non-state actors are often involved in informal lawmaking. First, they may be involved by states in informal acts, which is the only way open to both groups to adopt a joint act, since non-state actors other than international organizations may not enter into treaties. Second, they may also have recourse to informal acts themselves, so as to regulate their conduct and make the principles on which they operate known to the general public. Third, the practice of non-state actors may be quite relevant in the shaping of international custom, and in its recognition, since it may drive unwilling states to act, or to voice their beliefs, in connection with the existence or non-existence of an international customary rule.

4.5 Informal Lawmaking: An Easy Way Out or an Easy Way In?

Informal lawmaking is widespread and transversal in the regulation of migration by sea. It concerns different aspects of this phenomenon, including control of migration by sea, interdiction of irregular migrants, safety concerns, and rescue of irregular migrants in a

dell'art. 11 del d.lgs n. 286/1998)' (Questione Giustizia, 29 July 2019) <https://www.questionegiustizia.it/articolo/i-respingimenti-in-mare-dopo-il-cd-decreto-sicurez_29-07-2019.php> accessed 23 July 2021; Paolo Oddi, 'Soccorrere è un dovere. Commento e riflessioni sull'ordinanza del Giudice per le indagini preliminari di Agrigento sul caso Sea Watch 3 (Carola Rackete)' (2019) 2–8/2019 Diritto Penale e Uomo 31; Carol Ruggiero, 'Dalla criminalizzazione alla giustificazione delle attività di ricerca e soccorso in mare. Le tendenze interpretative più recenti alla luce dei casi Vos Thalassa e Rackete' (2020) 1/2020 Diritto Immigrazione e Cittadinanza 185.

[63] Decreto-legge recante disposizioni urgenti in materia di ordine e sicurezza pubblica, confirmed by Law 8 August 2019, n. 77.

[64] See, eg the critical comments of the (Italian) President of the Republic when agreeing to sign Law 77/2019 <https://www.quirinale.it/elementi/32100> accessed 12 July 2021; Andrea Maria Pelliconi and Marco Goldoni, 'La banalità dei porti chiusi per decreto. Osservazioni sui profili di legittimità del decreto interministeriale 150/2020' (2020) 2/2020 Diritto Immigrazione e Cittadinanza.

[65] Tribunale di Agrigento (n 61); Corte di Cassazione (n 62).

situation of distress. Furthermore, it involves different international actors, not only as recipients of the rights and duties that are thus created, but also as active 'informal lawmakers'. States, international organizations, NGOs, and other private organizations all have recourse to informal lawmaking to pursue their aims.

For states, informal lawmaking is almost the exclusive way that agreements are adopted concerning control of migration by sea and the interdiction of irregular migrants, including cooperation between states of departure—be they states of origin or transit states—and destination states. In this context, informal lawmaking seems to be preferred both for its expediency, which allows states and the EU to create international instruments within a very short time frame, and for its apparent convenience. The often secret, or at least secretive, nature of these acts, which elude parliamentary scrutiny and may also avoid publication, may be convenient for the purposes of keeping operational details hidden and thus facilitating cooperation.

However, it also raises serious doubts as to their legitimacy, both in terms of national and international obligations. At the national level, avoiding scrutiny by parliament, or even—in the case of secret agreements—of civil society, seems to point to some doubts as to the compatibility of these agreements with important principles of the domestic legal order, including fundamental constitutional principles. At the international level, the unwillingness of states to divulge the content of such agreements and, in some cases their coyness in even acknowledging that a particular agreement exists, can be construed as an implicit acceptance of the fact that these agreements may run contrary to other international obligations, including those provided by norms of *jus cogens*, such as the prohibition of torture.[66]

In addition, the informal nature of these acts presents significant challenges for those wishing to hold states accountable by initiating judicial action. As the EU–Turkey agreement has shown, the informal nature of these acts, which escapes traditional classifications of acts according to the international or EU legal frameworks, may provide an easy way out for reluctant courts, which can claim their lack of jurisdiction for acts that do not ordinarily belong to the legal system in which they operate.

If informal lawmaking may provide states an easy way out from the complex legal framework that provides for rights and freedoms of individuals, the same cannot be argued for international organizations. The latter, instead, have increasing recourse to informal lawmaking in response to states' unwillingness to adopt formally binding legal rules. In this context, informal lawmaking allows international organizations to reaffirm existing duties of states, and to elaborate tentative new rules, in the hope that they may eventually find their way into a formal legally binding international instrument, or into customary international law. There is actually some irony in the fact that, after all, intergovernmental organizations are composed of states, and yet they may adopt rules that states are unwilling to adopt themselves. There may be many reasons for this phenomenon. The fact that international organizations are formally distinct subjects of international law certainly has a role to play, combined with the fact that they have their own staff and managers, who may be particularly motivated to reach a certain result, and may invest more time and effort on this aim than any state would. Furthermore, it should be noted that state representatives acting

[66] Reflecting the possibility of informal laws being 'antagonistic' to existing legal principles. Gregory C Shaffer and Mark A Pollack, 'Hard vs. Soft Law: Alternatives, Complements, and Antagonists in International Governance' (2010) 94(3) Minn L Rev 706, 737.

within international organizations may be subject to dynamics that depart from those within their own state administrations.

Finally, for non-state actors other than international organizations, informal lawmaking plays a paramount role in giving them international standing and involving them, although indirectly, in the making of international law. Even when informal lawmaking is imposed upon them by states, as in the case of the Italian Code of Conduct, the ultimate effect of this exercise is to give non-state actors (some) international legal standing, which they would not otherwise have. It is for this purpose that non-state actors have also had recourse to informal lawmaking themselves, as a means of enhancing their legitimacy, since they show that such actors do comply with the core principles and rules of international law as drafted by states. Moreover, they strengthen their international standing in showing themselves capable of mastering the modern art of (informal) lawmaking. In this light, informal lawmaking provides an easy—probably the easiest— way into the international legal system, which would otherwise have been precluded on the basis of the traditional categories of international lawmaking.

5

Unconventional Lawmaking and International Cooperation on Illegal Bunkering at Sea

*Yurika Ishii**

5.1 The Problem: Illegal Bunkering and the Limits of Formal Law

This chapter addresses the functions of informal lawmaking in establishing international cooperation on illegal bunkering at sea. The working definition of 'illegal bunkering' is the ship-to-ship (STS) transfer of oil or fuel at sea in contravention of a state's domestic law where that state has legitimate jurisdiction over the conduct.[1] Such a law would typically require prior notification or authorization of an operation, an officer's attendance at the bunkering site, and a penalty against ships that have conducted unauthorized bunkering.[2] While the operation could occur in any maritime zone—internal water, territorial sea, archipelagic water, exclusive economic zone (EEZ), or high seas, this chapter will focus on the area beyond the state territory.

The United Nations Convention on Law of the Sea (LOSC or the Convention) is based on a 'zonal approach', where the treaty allocates jurisdiction based on the maritime columns. A coastal state has sovereignty over the territorial sea[3] and sovereign rights over the EEZ.[4] The regulation of foreign vessels beyond the EEZ is subject to the flag state's exclusive jurisdiction.[5] However, if the flag state is willing to collaborate with a law-enforcing state, they can overcome these jurisdictional limits on an ad hoc basis. As section 5.3 will explore, unconventional lawmaking—'the process of international cooperation to reach agreements (other than treaties) between public authorities, with or without the participation of private actors or international organizations, in varied institutions and networks'[6]—is an effective means to realize certain policies. Most instruments that 'encourage' states to combat illegal

* This work was supported by JSPS KAKENHI Grant Number JP18K01290.

1 United Nations Office on Drug and Crimes (UNODC)'s Global Maritime Crime Programme (GMCP) manual defines 'illegal bunkering' as '[t]he illegal sale of crude or refined oil, without paying any tax, levies or duties, particularly when that product has been stolen or smuggled': UNODC, *Maritime Crime: A Manual for Criminal Justice Practitioners* (3rd edn, UNODC 2020) 169, <https://www.unodc.org/documents/Maritime_crime/GMCP_Maritime_3rd_edition_Ebook.pdf> accessed 23 June 2021. This chapter adopts wider definition as described in the main text.

2 See section 5.3.1. See also David Testa, 'Coastal State Regulation of Bunkering and Ship-to-Ship (STS) Oil Transfer Operations in the EEZ: An Analysis of State Practice and of Coastal State Jurisdiction Under the LOSC' (2019) 50 ODIL 363.

3 United Nations Convention on Law of the Sea (adopted 10 December 1982, entered into force 16 November 1994) 1833 UNTS 397 (hereafter 'LOSC'), art 2(1).

4 ibid, art 56.

5 ibid, art 92(1).

6 Natalie Klein, 'Meaning, Scope, and Significance of Informal Lawmaking in the Law of the Sea,' in Chapter 1, at 8, this volume. For the conceptualization of the informal lawmaking, see also Joost Pauwelyn, 'Informal International Lawmaking: Framing the Concept and Research Questions' in Joost Pauwelyn, Ramses Wessel, and Jan Wouters (eds), *Informal International Lawmaking* (OUP 2012) 13, 21–22.

Yurika Ishii, *Unconventional Lawmaking and International Cooperation on Illegal Bunkering at Sea* In: *Unconventional Lawmaking in the Law of the Sea*. Edited by: Natalie Klein, Oxford University Press. © Yurika Ishii 2022. DOI: 10.1093/oso/9780192897824.003.0005

bunkering are informal because they are neither a treaty nor a norm reflected in customary international law. Yet, this lawmaking process is important if it pushes the flag state to give the law-enforcing state formal consent to take necessary measures. In the words of Hugh Thirlway, such non-binding instruments could be 'a system of international commitments or obligations that are not regarded ... as binding in the sense that [they] can be enforced in the same way as those imposed by international law proper, but yet are considered as something more than mere political gestures, so that there is an expectation of compliance even if there is no legal duty'.[7] Surveying the impact of such informal lawmaking on illegal bunkering is a worthy endeavour because non-binding agreements, standard setting by non-governmental entities, and international organizations' resolutions have changed international discourse on this topic.

5.1.1 Illegal Bunkering and its Social Harms

Bunkering at sea has been a common practice for a number of reasons. It is more expensive to sell bulk oil on land than at sea because a buyer may have to pay customs tax and a transportation fee. Ports allowing such an operation are limited to those with appropriate equipment. In addition, it is physically challenging for a large oil bunkering vessel to provide oil to smaller fishing vessels or oil rigs. If a collision and subsequent marine pollution occur, the owner of the tanker could be liable for large amounts of damages under the International Maritime Organization (IMO) conventions.[8] As a result, such tanker transfers typically involve transferring fuel to a smaller ship first, and that ship selling the oil to a fishing vessel or transporting it to an oil rig.

The main reasons that international cooperation among flag states of the bunkering vessels and states other than flag states ('non-flag states') is required may be summarized as follows. First, there is an increasingly high number of cases in which the oil delivered in a bunkering operation is of an illegal origin.[9] In some cases, oil has been stolen from pipelines or mixed with impurities, and sold to gain unlawful benefits. This crime is of serious concern, especially in West African countries.[10] The offenders transport the stolen oil to neighbouring countries, where they can readily obtain forged documents. They then transfer the fuel, at sea, to small vessels operating in the Gulf of Guinea. Such transactions not only involve theft but also misrepresentations to buyers and forgery of documents. They may further involve other organized crimes, such as forced labour and bribery of local officials. Such offences often have transnational and global dimensions. The oil stolen in West Africa may be illegally smuggled into South Asian countries.[11] The United Nations Office on

[7] Hugh Thirlway, *The Sources of International Law* (OUP 2014) 188.

[8] For the latest comprehensive review of vessel-source oil pollution under international law, see UNCTAD, *Liability and Compensation for Ship-Source Oil Pollution* (2012).

[9] Ian Ralby, *Downstream Oil Theft: Global Modalities, Trends, and Remedies* (Atlantic Council 2017) 3; Ian Ralby and David Soud, *Oil on the Water: Illicit Hydrocarbons Activity in the Maritime Domain* (Atlantic Council 2018) 6.

[10] UNODC, *Transnational Trafficking and the Rule of Law in West Africa: A Threat Assessment* (2009) 19; Francois Vreÿ, 'Maritime Aspects of Illegal Oil-Bunkering in the Niger Delta' (2012) 4 AJMOA 109. For instance, in Nigeria, the largest oil-producing country in Africa, which is also known for its political instability, offenders systematically steal oil from pipelines and plants. It is reported that Nigeria lost as much as 22 million barrels of oil to theft in the first half of 2019: 'Oil Theft Cost Nigeria 22 Million Barrels in first Half—NNPC', *Reuters* (30 August 2019), <https://www.reuters.com/article/ozatp-uk-nigeria-oil-theft-idAFKCN1VK1NT-OZATP> accessed 23 June 2021..

[11] Ralby (n 9) 52–58; UNODC (n 10) 19.

Drugs and Crimes (UNODC) has signalled alarm at the increase of such 'oil-related crimes' since the end of the 2000s.[12]

Second, bunkering may fuel a vessel engaged in other illegal activities such as piracy, armed robbery, and/or illegal, unregulated, and unreported (IUU) fishing. Furthermore, the bunkering may contribute to offences such as corruption, money laundering, terrorist financing, and other organized crimes, including smuggling and human trafficking.[13] Third, bunkering may cause pollution and environmental hazards if oil is spilled in the ocean. Operations conducted by substandard ships are more vulnerable to such a risk. Furthermore, a vessel with fuel tanks enlarged for smuggling fuel is known to be more dangerous. It may explode, killing those on board, spilling the fuel, and creating hazards to navigation.[14]

Finally, in some cases, oil bunkering involves the transfer of oil to a vessel of a state against which the United Nations imposes sanctions. The flag state of the transferring ship is in breach of its obligations as a member state of the organization. It affects the security of other member states and the international community.

Against the background of an increasing number of vessels registered to flags of convenience, it has become impossible for a single state to solve the problems posed by bunkering vessels. All of these social harms call for international cooperation, not only among flag states and non-flag states, including coastal states, but also international organizations such as the IMO and UNODC, and private sector actors, such as shipping industries.

5.1.2 Jurisdictional Limits under the Law of the Sea

International cooperation is important not only because coastal states and other non-flag states have incentives to monitor and regulate bunkering activities, even when conducted beyond the territorial sea. In addition, their individual actions must not exceed the jurisdictional limits of the LOSC. Whether a state has jurisdiction over bunkering activities is decided based on the vessel's nationality and the place of the conduct. When the bunkering takes place within territorial seas or archipelagic waters, there is no dispute that the coastal state has the authority to regulate it.[15] Notably, the number of arrests and detentions of vessels and individuals engaged in illegal bunkering within a state's territory is rising.[16] On the high seas, bunkering activities are among the freedoms that every state enjoys,[17]

[12] For an overview of the oil-related crimes, see UNODC, 'Maritime Crime' (n 1) 170.

[13] For a non-exhaustive list of wrongdoings, see ibid 171.

[14] See Section 5.2.2 for relevant treaty rules. See also UNODC, 'Maritime Crime' (n 1) 172 (it is reported that fishing vessels with modified fuel tanks that were being used to smuggle extremely low-priced Venezuelan fuel into the Dutch Caribbean island of Aruba exploded in Aruba's harbour in the autumn of 2017, on account of the poor workmanship of the fuel tank modification process).

[15] LOSC (n 3) arts 2(1) and 49(1).

[16] For instance, the *M/V Duzgit Integrity* case concerned São Tomé and Príncipe arresting a vessel registered to Malta and operating within its archipelagic waters: *The Duzgit Integrity Arbitration* (*The Republic of Malta v The Democratic Republic of Sao Tome and Principe*), Award, PCA Case N. 2014-7, 5 September 2016. Recent news reports document similar incidents. For example, on 30 October 2019, Singapore's Police Coast Guard arrested eleven men for their suspected involvement in an illegal transaction of marine gas oil at sea off Northern Tuas, and on 11 October 2018, Malaysian authorities detained an oil tanker over suspicions of committing illegal STS fuel transfer at the Tanjung Pelepas Port near Gelang Patah. See Safety4Sea <https://safety4sea.com/tag/illegal-bunkering/> accessed 23 June 2021.

[17] In *M/V Norstar*, the International Tribunal for the Law of the Sea (ITLOS) denied Italy's authority to prosecute individuals who were engaged in bunkering activities beyond the territorial sea, in contravention of its tax

and a bunkering vessel is subject to the exclusive jurisdiction of the flag state.[18] Whether a state may enforce its law against a vessel when it enters the law-enforcing state's territory is disputed.[19]

Whether a coastal state's law enforcement against a bunkering ship is lawful when that conduct occurs within its EEZ depends on a case-by-case analysis.[20] In general, the coastal state must establish a jurisdictional connection as justified under Article 56(1) of the LOSC.[21] The law enforced must be within the ambit of a coastal state's authority provided in the LOSC.

In *M/V Saiga*, the International Tribunal for the Law of the Sea (ITLOS) held that Guinea's arrest of a vessel under its Customs Code was incompatible with the LOSC.[22] The domestic law was applicable to control and suppress gasoline sales to fishing vessels in the customs radius (*rayon des douanes*), up to 250 kilometres from the coast. Guinea claimed that it was entitled to protect itself against unwarranted economic activities in its EEZ that considerably affected its public interest because there had been substantial fiscal losses caused by illegal offshore bunkering.[23] However, the Tribunal rejected the argument, stating that such recourse to the principle of 'public interest' would 'entitle a coastal State to prohibit any activities in the [EEZ] which it decides to characterize as activities which affect its economic "public interest" or entail "fiscal losses" for it.'[24] It held that this approach would curtail the rights of other states in the EEZ, and would be incompatible with Articles 56 and 58 of the LOSC.[25]

In contrast, if bunkering is directly connected with activities subject to coastal state jurisdiction under Article 56(1) of the LOSC, a coastal state's law enforcement will be justified. In *M/V Virginia G*, ITLOS held that such a connection between fishing and the bunkering of foreign vessels fishing in the EEZ exists, 'since this enables [fishing vessels] to continue their activities without interruption at sea.'[26] The Tribunal noted that 'fishing-related' activities are subject to regulation in several international agreements, and it established a close connection between fishing and various support activities, including bunkering.[27] According to this case, a coastal state may, thus, claim jurisdiction if bunkering is done in direct connection with activities listed in Article 56(1).

law: *M/V Norstar (Panama v Italy)*, Judgment, ITLOS Reports 2018–19, 10, para 219. However, this decision has been criticized as an excessive interpretation of the exclusive flag state jurisdiction principle, as seven judges indicated in their dissenting opinion (ibid, Dissenting Opinion of Judges Cot, Pawlak, Yanai, Hoffmann, Kolodkin, Lijnzaad, and Judge ad hoc Treves, paras 13–15).

[18] LOSC (n 3) art 92(1).

[19] See *M/V Norstar*, Dissenting Opinion of Judges Cot, Pawlak, Yanai, Hoffmann, Kolodkin, Lijnzaad, and Judge ad hoc Treves (n 17) paras 17–19. See also Douglas Guilfolye, 'Article 92,' Alexander Proelss (ed), *United Nations Convention on the Law of the Sea: A Commentary* (Hart Publishing 2017) 700, 702–03.

[20] Rainer Lagoni, 'Offshore Bunkering in the Exclusive Economic Zone' in Ndiaye Tafsir and Rudiger Wolfrum (eds), *Law of the Sea, Environmental Law and Settlement of Disputes* (Martinus Nijhoff 2007) 613.

[21] *M/V Saiga (No. 2) (Saint Vincent and the Grenadines v Guinea)*, Judgment, ITLOS Reports 1999, 10, para 100.

[22] Law 94/007/CTRN of 15 March 1994, Arts 1 and 8; Code des Douanes, Arts 316 and 317; Penal Code, Arts 361 and 363.

[23] *M/V Saiga* (n 21) paras 128 and 130.

[24] ibid, para 131.

[25] ibid.

[26] *M/V Virginia G (Panama/Guinea-Bissau)*, Judgment, ITLOS Reports 2014, 4 [M/V *Virginia G*], para 215.

[27] ibid, para 216.

In *M/T San Padre Pio*, a vessel registered to Switzerland was arrested by Nigeria for conducting unauthorized bunkering of an oil rig within Nigeria's EEZ. Switzerland claimed that Nigeria's arrest of the vessel was excessive and infringed its freedoms. At the provisional measures stage, ITLOS admitted Switzerland's plausible right in this regard, and ordered Nigeria to release the vessel and the crew.[28] However, this decision does not prejudice the merits. The merits of the case have not been decided at the time of writing, and the judgment will be an important precedent concerning this issue.

In summary, the flag state's consent is generally required when a non-flag state seeks to regulate bunkering activities beyond its territorial sea. In the EEZ, coastal states may exercise jurisdiction when those activities are subject to its sovereign rights or jurisdiction, as provided under Article 56(1). It is noted that there is a view that Article 59 applies to the regulation of oil bunkering.[29] However, the provision applies only '[i]n cases where this Convention does not attribute rights or jurisdiction to the coastal state or other states within the [EEZ]'.[30] It would not apply in the present case because the jurisdictional allocation may be based on Articles 56 and 58.

Lastly, in some cases, states are obliged to adopt domestic laws to prosecute certain crimes. For instance, in the case of corruption and money laundering, the Convention against Corruption and the Convention against Transnational Organized Crimes oblige member states to enact a law to criminalize this conduct, and prosecute alleged offenders when the offence took place in their territories or the offender is one of their nationals.[31] Similarly, in the case of terrorist financing, state parties to the Convention against Terrorist Financing must prosecute the offender or extradite the individual to other state parties with jurisdiction.[32] In the maritime domain, law enforcement—for instance, search and visit of the vessel—is allowed only in accordance with the law of the sea as explained above. Furthermore, the Convention Against Illicit Traffic in Narcotic Drugs and Psychotropic Substances,[33] the Protocol against the Smuggling of Migrants,[34] and the Protocol to the Convention for the Suppression of Unlawful Acts against the Safety of Maritime Navigation[35] oblige flag states to respond in instances where another contracting state issues a request to board. However, the coastal state is not entitled to exercise its enforcement jurisdiction beyond its territorial sea without the consent of the flag state, notwithstanding these instruments.[36]

[28] ITLOS, Case No. 27, *M/T San Padre Pio (Switzerland v Nigeria)*, Provisional Measures, Order of 6 July 2019.

[29] Testa (n 2) 363. See also ibid, Declaration of Judge Kittichaisaree, para 2.

[30] LOSC (n 3) art 59.

[31] United Nations Convention against Corruption (adopted 31 October 2003, entered into force 14 December 2005) 2349 UNTS 41, art 42; United Nations Convention against Transnational Organized Crime (adopted 15 November 2000, entered into force 29 September 2003) 2225 UNTS 209, art 11.

[32] International Convention for the Suppression of the Financing of Terrorism (adopted 9 December 1999, entered into force 10 April 2002) 2178 UNTS 197, art 9.

[33] United Nations Convention against Illicit Traffic in Narcotic Drugs and Psychotropic Substances 1988, 1582 UNTS 95, art 17(4).

[34] Protocol against the Smuggling of Migrants by Land, Sea and Air, supplementing the United Nations Convention against Transnational Organized Crime 2000, 40 ILM 384, art 8.

[35] Protocol of 2005 to the Convention for the Suppression of Unlawful Acts Against the Safety of Maritime Navigation 2005, 1678 UNTS 304, art 8*bis* (5).

[36] For a general overview, see Douglas Guilfoyle, *Shipping Interdiction and the Law of the Sea* (CUP 2009).

5.1.3 The Significance of Informal Lawmaking

This brief analysis shows that the jurisdictional hurdles for law enforcement authorities of non-flag states are quite high in the maritime domain beyond the territorial sea. Non-flag states may, instead, utilize informal lawmaking to enhance cooperation with flag states in combating illegal bunkering. Provided that any regulation is consistent with the allocation of jurisdiction set out in the LOSC, informal lawmaking can play a particular role in establishing rules and standards compatible with formal treaties, in order to promote international cooperation in regulating bunkering activities. As Section 2 will explore, Regional Fisheries Management Organizations (RFMO) offer the fora for such collaboration concerning fisheries, and the IMO provides a similar role with regard to protecting the marine environment and safety of navigation.

5.2 Regulations within the Jurisdiction Allocated under the LOSC

The LOSC provides that a coastal state has sovereign rights for exploring and exploiting, conserving, and managing living resources, and jurisdiction concerning the protection and preservation of the marine environment in the EEZ.[37] However, there is the risk that the coastal state may circumvent the limits under the LOSC by imposing excessive restrictions under the label of fisheries management or environmental protection. To this end, states may: (1) conclude either a formal or informal regional agreement; or (2) generate generally accepted international rules and standards (GAIRS), which may involve an informal lawmaking process.

5.2.1 Fisheries Management

The coastal state's exercise of jurisdiction against bunkering vessels may be permissible as long as the STS transfer is directly connected with the fisheries activities carried out in the EEZ, as the analysis above demonstrated. The LOSC provides that a coastal state may enforce its law concerning the living resources in the EEZ, and take measures including boarding, inspection, arrest, and judicial proceedings as may be necessary to ensure compliance with the laws and regulations adopted by it in conformity with the Convention.[38] However, the arrested vessels are subject to the prompt release procedure.[39] Furthermore, the coastal state penalties may not include imprisonment, in the absence of agreements to the contrary by the states concerned, or any other form of corporal punishment.[40]

Bunkering regulation may take place, under the auspices of an RFMO, to overcome the limits of the LOSC. As the Convention provides in Articles 117 and 118, states are obliged to cooperate with other states to conserve marine living resources on the high seas, and to develop appropriate management measures where nationals exploit similar resources or

[37] LOSC (n 3) art 56(1)(a)(b).
[38] ibid, art 73(1).
[39] ibid, art 73(2).
[40] ibid, art 73(4).

different resources in the same area. The LOSC requires member states to set up regional fisheries organizations where appropriate.[41] Furthermore, if both the flag state and the law-enforcing state are parties to the United Nations Fish Stocks Agreement (UNFSA), then a state party that is a member of an RFMO or a participant in its arrangement may, through its duly authorized inspectors, board and inspect fishing vessels flying the flag of another state party to the UNFSA. This provision applies even when the flag state is not a member of the organization or a participant in the arrangement.[42]

RFMOs have started to ensure that their vessels will not conduct bunkering of vessels engaged in IUU fishing. Such a restriction may be imposed under a legally binding treaty. For instance, the North Atlantic Fisheries Organization (NAFO) Agreement[43] provides that each party shall prohibit any vessel entitled to fly its flag from offering fuel to an IUU-listed ship. However, the regulations can be imposed indirectly and informally, too. For instance, the North East Atlantic Fisheries Commission (NEAFC) Scheme of Control and Enforcement, which provides that the regulated fishing activities include refuelling, is updated at the NEAFC annual meeting without a formal treaty-making process.[44]

It is not that the non-flag states are now entitled to board and inspect the bunkering vessels in these cases. Instead, an important framework for international cooperation is provided by the joint inspection schemes.[45] These are reciprocal boarding and inspection schemes between the state parties, and are conducted by RFMOs to promote compliance, and to facilitate enforcement in deterring IUU fishing activities. NAFO, NEAFC, and the Western and Central Pacific Fisheries Commission (WCPFC) have created such programmes. Under these programmes, inspectors are subject to the sole jurisdiction of the inspecting state. Furthermore, only such designated authorities are permitted to inspect fishing vessels flying a foreign flag on the high seas. Each year, the state parties must communicate the inspectors' list to the secretariat of the RFMO, and all contracting parties. Such frameworks are counted as informal lawmaking processes.

Furthermore, there are practices whereby the RFMO's conventions authorize non-flag states to monitor and inspect bunkering activities without the consent of the flag state being required in each case. One example is the Nauru Agreement concerning Cooperation in the Management of Fisheries of Common Interest, concluded among island countries in the South Pacific.[46] At the state parties' meeting, the parties adopt implementing arrangements, which are formal treaties providing for practical matters concerning implementation, that are subordinate to, and governed by, the Nauru Agreement. The third implementing

[41] ibid, arts 117 and 118.

[42] Agreement for the Implementation of the Provisions of the United Nations Convention on the Law of the Sea relating to the Conservation and Management of Straddling Fish Stocks and Highly Migratory Fish Stocks (adopted 4 August 1995, entered into force 11 December 2001) 2167 UNTS 3, art 22(1).

[43] Convention on Future Multilateral Cooperation in the Northwest Atlantic Fisheries (signed 24 October 1978, entered into force 1 January 1979) 1135 UNTS 369, amended 18 May 2017, art 54 <https://www.nafo.int/Portals/0/PDFs/key-publications/NAFOConvention-2017.pdf> accessed 23 June 2021.

[44] NEAFC Scheme of Control and Enforcement, art 1(e) <https://www.neafc.org/mcs/scheme> accessed 23 June 2021. Changes to the NEAFC Scheme are made on the basis of decisions adopted in the annual meeting, which are binding on the contracting parties.

[45] EU IUU Coalition, *Achieving Transparency and Combating IUU Fishing in RFMOs: Reinforcing the EU's Multilateral Actions to Promote Best Practices* (2019) 10, <https://europe.oceana.org/sites/default/files/combating_iuu_fishing_in_rfmos.pdf> accessed 23 June 2021.

[46] Nauru Agreement concerning Cooperation in the Management of Fisheries of Common Interest (signed 11 February 1982, entered into force 4 December 1982, amended April 2010) <https://www.pnatuna.com/content/nauru-agreement> accessed 23 June 2021.

arrangement adopted in May 2019 provides that no purse seine vessel shall, during the validity of a party's licence, conduct any bunkering activities in the high seas of the WCPFC Convention Area east of 130 degrees east.[47] It is quite a broad regulation, because the regulation applies to the bunkering activities even when the vessel is not listed, and its geographical application extends to the high seas. It is also provided that the parties shall review the implementation of these measures at the annual meeting of the parties, and decide on the future application of these measures, taking into account the effectiveness of the measures in reducing fishing mortality, and the extent to which compatible measures are being applied on the high seas and in the waters of other members of the WCPFC. All of the members are parties to the Nauru Agreement (the parent treaty), so that they have less reason not to cooperate, although they are entitled to withdraw from the arrangement.

In summary, the informal lawmaking process enhances international cooperation by sharing awareness of the situation and providing necessary assistance among states. This process has been relevant both in implementing a formal treaty, and in promoting cooperation between the flag states and other contracting states of RFMOs on a less formal basis.

5.2.2 Environmental Protection

Coastal states have jurisdiction to require foreign bunkering vessels within their EEZ to obtain prior authorization for environmental protection, as long as it is compatible with international regulations and standards.[48] Articles 208 and 214 of the LOSC provide for coastal states to enact and enforce laws and regulations to prevent, mitigate, and control pollution of the marine environment arising from activities within their jurisdiction. Further, Article 220, paragraphs (3) to (6) provides the basis for judicial procedures against a vessel navigating in the EEZ that has violated either 'applicable international rules and standards' for the prevention, reduction, and control of pollution from vessels, or the coastal state's laws to the same effect. Therefore, the coastal state must comply with those international rules and standards, which may be reflected in informal law.[49]

One of these international regulations, the International Convention for the Prevention of Pollution from Ships in 1978 and Annex 1 to the 1973 Protocol (MARPOL 73/78) (Oil Pollution Control Rules) was amended in 2009 to require that vessels carrying out the transfer of petroleum cargoes between oil tankers of 150 gross tonnage or more in the EEZ meet the prescribed vessel standard. As a general rule regarding safety and environmental protection, this convention requires that any oil tanker involved in STS operations shall carry on board a plan, which shall be approved by the coastal states' administration.[50] The plan shall be developed, taking into account the information in the best practice guidelines

[47] A Third Arrangement Implementing the Nauru Agreement Setting Forth Additional Terms and Conditions of Access to the Fisheries Zones of the Parties (amended 1 May 2019) <https://www.ffa.int/system/files/3rd%20Arrangement%20PNA.pdf> accessed 23 June 2021, art 6(1). As an exception, this provision 'shall not apply to Kiribati flag purse seine vessels conducting bunkering and provisioning activities with another Kiribati flag vessel in the areas of high seas between the groups of islands in the Kiribati EEZ south of a latitude of 5 degrees 30 minutes North': ibid, art 6(2).

[48] LOSC (n 3) art 56(1)(b).

[49] Lene Korseberg, 'The Law-making Effects of the FAO Deep-sea Fisheries Guidelines' (2018) 67 ICLQ 801, 805.

[50] Protocol of 1978 relating to the International Convention for the Prevention of Pollution from Ships (signed 17 February 1978, entered into force 2 October 1983) 1340 UNTS 61, reg 41(1).

for STS operations identified by the IMO, and incorporated into an existing safety management system as required by the SOLAS Convention.[51] For this purpose, the IMO adopted the Manual on Oil Pollution in 2011.[52] The Manual provides practical guidance related to the prevention of pollution from ships, and describes procedures for handling bunkering and STS operations.

State practice that requires prior permission, as opposed to notification, for STS transfers may, thus, be excessive. Nonetheless, some states impose such a requirement. For instance, Belgium requires vessels to obtain prior permission for STS operations in its EEZ, under its environmental protection regime.[53] Its Ministerial Order of 2001 defined 'activities of offshore bunkering' as 'the transfer of hydrocarbons from one ship to another carried out for a commercial purpose'.[54] The Ministerial Order further provided that offshore bunkering activities would require preauthorization in accordance with a relatively detailed consultation procedure defined under Belgian law. The order was issued as an implementation of the Belgian Environmental Law of 1999, which regulates the commercial undertakings in Belgian maritime areas.[55] This act requires the vessels to operate in Belgian EEZ to obtain prior authorization to meet marine environment protection needs. It provides that navigational activities are not subject to any requirement of prior authorization. Thus, analysis shows that Belgium's subsequent decision to subject bunkering in its EEZ to prior authorization indicates that it does not consider bunkering to be a navigational activity. A request for the authorization of bunkering activities submitted under the relevant consultation procedure must be accompanied by an environmental impact assessment (EIA). The risk of marine pollution from the operation has to be covered by insurance. Before giving authorization, the Belgian authority must consider the prevention and precautionary principles. This regulation is deemed excessive in the light of the MARPOL 73/78, which only requires prior notification.

The United Arab Emirates also has a policy on bunkering within its EEZ for environmental protection purposes. To deal with 'safety, security, and environmental issues' contained in its 2011 regulation concerning an anchorage area, Dubai requires prior authorization by the city authority forty-eight hours before the operation, and only authorized sellers may engage in bunkering. Any violation of these regulations will result in arrest and criminal prosecution.[56] Finally, Sri Lanka's environmental protection regulation also requires a licence to conduct bunkering activities within Sri Lanka's maritime zone.[57] However, to the author's knowledge, these practices have not caused any serious international dispute.

In summary, the basis for any law enforcement is found in formal instruments such as the LOSC and other treaties. However, the informal lawmaking process, mainly through the adoption of standards and guidelines, both by IMO and industrial associations, plays a

[51] ibid.

[52] International Maritime Organization, *Manual on Oil Pollution: Section 1* (IMO 2011).

[53] Ministère des affaires sociales, de la santé publique et de l'environnement, F. 2001-1147, art 1.

[54] ibid.

[55] Loi visant la protection du milieu marin [et l'organisation de l'aménagement des] espaces marins sous juridiction de la Belgique, 20 January 1999, art 20(3).

[56] Dubai Maritime City Authority, Dubai Anchorages Regulations (Maritime Bulletin of 29 May 2011, DMCAMB0111).

[57] Bunkering (Marine Environmental Protection) Regulations No. 02 of 2011, *The Gazette of the Democratic Society of Sri Lanka*, No. 1741/19, 19 January 2012 <http://extwprlegs1.fao.org/docs/pdf/srl133808.pdf> accessed 23 June 2021.

supplemental role in enhancing fisheries management and environmental protection. The contents of the regulations in these areas may vary from one region to another, depending on the actual situations. These areas are easier to regulate because they are within the ambit of the coastal states' jurisdictions under LOSC. The next section will explore the situations where there is no such formal legal basis.

5.3 Regulation by Non-flag States

5.3.1 General Overview and State Practice

When there is no legal basis for states to regulate foreign-flagged vessels' bunkering activities under the LOSC, the flag state has exclusive jurisdiction to regulate bunkering activities. However, a difficulty in preventing illegal bunkering lies in the fact that state officials may not learn the origin of the oil before an STS transfer. The coastal state may seek to implement a comprehensive regime requiring the vessel to obtain prior permission, inspect the oil quality at the bunkering site, and impose sanctions when the vessel is non-compliant.

Some West African countries are following this approach. For instance, Nigeria requires prior authorization for the operation of bunkering vessels within its EEZ. The motivation behind the legislation is the need to combat oil theft. Article 44(3) of its constitution explicitly states that oil and natural gas within its EEZ must belong to the federal government and be managed in a manner prescribed by the National Assembly.[58] The Miscellaneous Offences Act provides for life imprisonment for managing and storing oil 'in Nigeria', without permission or licence, and forfeiture by the federal government of any vehicle, vessel, aircraft, or other means of transport used.[59] As amended in 1998, the Petroleum Law stipulates that the term 'in Nigeria' shall include its EEZ.[60] The bunker needs a certificate from the Nigerian law enforcement agency to prove its legitimacy, and a naval officer will attend the bunker to check the quality of the oil. The bunker will be required to obtain approval from the Ministry of Petroleum and Natural Resources and a certificate from the Maritime Administration and Safety Agency. The navy has the power to arrest and prosecute ships that violate these conditions.

In addition to systemic oil theft, Nigeria has been suffering from piracy and armed robberies at sea, and ships are easily attacked by pirates when they moor to conduct bunkering.[61] For this reason, the Nigerian navy is monitoring the Gulf of Guinea, with the cooperation of other countries, including the United States. Ships that remove their automatic identification system (AIS) device, or that move to a location known for the conduct of illegal activity, will be placed on a watch list, and monitored with special attention.[62] The M/V *San Padre Pio* incident mentioned above occurred in this context.

[58] Constitution of the Federal Republic of Nigeria, 1999, art 44(3) <https://www.wipo.int/edocs/lexdocs/laws/en/ng/ng014en.pdf> accessed 23 June 2021.

[59] Miscellaneous Offences Act, 2004, art 1(17) <https://lawsofnigeria.placng.org/view2.php?sn = 256> accessed 23 June 2021.

[60] Petroleum Act, 1969, as amended in 1998 No. 22 <http://extwprlegs1.fao.org/docs/pdf/nig92407.pdf> accessed 23 June 2021.

[61] UNODC, 'Maritime Crime' (n 1).

[62] IMO, *Guidelines for Owners, Operators and Masters for Protection against Piracy in the Gulf of Guinea Region* (IMO 2018).

The Nigerian Miscellaneous Offences Act is broad enough that it was used to prosecute piracy offences against the M/T *Maximus* in 2016.[63] Pirates took the vessel in the EEZ of Côte d'Ivoire, and Côte d'Ivoire, Ghana, Togo, Benin, Nigeria, and São Tomé and Príncipe cooperated to track the vessel. In the end, the Nigerian navy interdicted the vessel in the EEZ of São Tomé and Príncipe, conducted an opposed boarding, killed one of the pirates, arrested the remaining pirates, and freed the hostages.[64] As Nigeria had not completed an update to its piracy legislation, trying the alleged offenders for piracy was not possible. Instead, Nigeria charged them with offences relating to conspiracy, dealing in petroleum products without authority, and transferring these to another vessel, contrary to Articles 1(17) and 3(6) of the Miscellaneous Offences Act of 2004.[65] In this case, no other states protested against Nigeria's law enforcement.

The practice of Angola also deserves close examination. Although Angola's security situation has not been stable since independence, oil production has increased in recent years, due to China's capital investment. Angola adopted rules by ministerial ordinance in May 2017. Only companies registered in Angola are allowed to bunker ships anchored in the country's EEZ, or other ships on platforms or offshore rigs. Companies are, further, required to hold valid licences issued by Angola's Ministry of Petroleum. They must notify authorities three days before the operation, and Angolan officials will attend the bunkering and inspect the oil samples. Failure to comply with these rules will result in fines, and the vessel could be seized and detained. This regulation is comparable to those imposed against foreign vessels engaged in resource exploration and exploitation within the EEZ and continental shelf.

5.3.2 The Roles of Informal Instruments

As highlighted in the introductory section, it is challenging to justify coastal states' comprehensive regulation against bunkering, because it may exceed the jurisdiction allocated under the LOSC. However, in order to overcome such hurdles, there have been two notable developments.

First, actors in the private sector are setting standards and guidelines for safe bunkering activities. For instance, the International Organization for Standardization (ISO) has been updating procedures and requirements for bunkering. Its first version, which came out in 1998, specified practical procedures for the transfer of bunker fuels to ships. It set standards for measurement of petroleum and related products.[66] It was updated in 2010,[67] and the latest version was adopted in 2020.[68] It provided rules for the transfer of bunkers to vessels, involving bunker tankers, road tankers, and shore pipelines to ensure environmental safety. The latest version was tied to the United Nations Sustainable Development Goals (SDGs),

[63] UNODC, 'Maritime Crime' (n 1) 167.

[64] ibid.

[65] Miscellaneous Offences Act of 2004 (n 67) arts 1(17) and 3(6). The offenders were also prosecuted for the violation of the Money-Laundering (Prohibition) Act of 2011, art 15, and Firearms Act of 2004, arts 3 and 8.

[66] ISO/TR 13739:1998.

[67] ISO 13739:2010.

[68] ISO 13739:2020.

particularly those of ensuring responsible consumption and production, and achieving clean water and sanitation.[69]

To take other examples, the International Chamber of Shipping (ICS) and Oil Companies International Marine Forum (OCIMF), together with the International Association of Ports and Harbors (IAPH), revised their International Safety Guide for Tankers and Terminals (ISGOTT 6) in 2020.[70] This instrument was intended, among other reasons, to enhance the safety of bunkering operations, including the use of alternative fuels such as liquefied natural gas (LNG). Another association among CDI, ICS, OCIMF, and SIGTTO adopted a ship to ship transfer guide for petroleum, chemicals, and liquefied gases in 2013.[71] This agreement provided recommendations on safety, minimum equipment levels, and good operating practices. These two sets of guidelines reflect the thinking of the shipping industries. The adoption of such best practices would count as a part of informal lawmaking.

Second, because oil-related crimes may have a global impact, there has been an effort to ensure flag state cooperation in combating this illegal act. A notable development can be seen in the Yaoundé Code of Conduct adopted in 2013, a non-binding instrument signed by twenty-six state parties.[72] Its list of 'transnational organized crime in the maritime domain' includes 'illegal oil bunkering'[73] and 'crude oil theft'.[74] This 'transnational organized crime in the maritime domain' reflects acts that are not established as maritime crimes in other conventions such as the LOSC, the Drug Control Convention, or SUA Protocol. It was developed by the Economic Community of Central African States (ECCAS), the Economic Community of West African States (ECOWAS), and the Gulf of Guinea Commission (GGC), with the assistance of the IMO. The effort was undertaken according to United Nations Security Council resolutions 2018[75] and 2039.[76] These resolutions encouraged regional organizations to develop a comprehensive regional strategy and framework to counter illicit maritime activities through information sharing and strategic coordination mechanisms, under the auspices of international bodies such as the IMO.[77] Another such instrument is the Djibouti Code of Conduct of 2009, which deals with piracy and armed robbery at sea.[78] The Yaoundé Code of Conduct is intended to establish a comprehensive regional maritime security framework to counter 'transnational maritime crimes'.

The purpose of the Yaoundé Code of Conduct is to cooperate, to the fullest extent possible, in the repression of transnational organized crime in the maritime domain, with a view towards: (a) sharing and reporting relevant information; (b) interdicting ships or

[69] ibid. For SDGs, see UNGA, 'Transforming our World: The 2030 Agenda for Sustainable Development', 21 October 2015, UN Doc A/RES/70/1.

[70] The fourth edition, in 2005, already included a guideline on STS operation. The latest version was adopted in 2020: OCIMF/ICS/IAPH, *International Safety Guide for Tankers and Terminals (ISGOTT 6)* (Witherby Seamanship 2020).

[71] CDI/ICS/OCIMF/SIGTTO, *Ship to Ship Transfer Guide for Petroleum, Chemicals and Liquefied Gases* (Witherby Seamanship 2013).

[72] The Code of Conduct concerning the Repression of Piracy, Armed Robbery against Ships, and Illicit Maritime Activity in West and Central Africa, June 2013 (hereafter 'Yaoundé Code of Conduct') <https://wwwcdn.imo.org/localresources/en/OurWork/Security/Documents/code_of_conduct%20signed%20from%20ECOWAS%20site.pdf> accessed 23 June 2021.

[73] ibid, art 1(5)(d).

[74] ibid, art 1(5)(e).

[75] UN Security Council resolution S/RES/2018, 31 October 2011.

[76] UN Security Council resolution S/RES/2039, 29 February 2012.

[77] Anja Menzel, 'Institutional Adoption and Maritime Crime Governance: The Djibouti Code of Conduct' (2018) 14(2) J Ind Ocean Reg 152, 161–63.

[78] See Jacobsson and Klein, in Chapter 3 of this volume.

aircraft suspected of engaging in transnational organized crime in the maritime domain; (c) ensuring that persons committing, or attempting to commit, the offences are apprehended and prosecuted; and (d) facilitating proper care, treatment, and repatriation of seafarers, fishers, and other shipboard personnel and passengers who have been subjected to crime, particularly those who have been subjected to violence. The cooperation should be made within the ambit of existing domestic and international laws. The Yaoundé Code of Conduct itself does not intend to oblige states to criminalize illegal bunkering. In particular, there is a savings clause that the state parties 'should carry out their obligations and responsibilities under this Code in a manner consistent with the principles of sovereign equality and territorial integrity of states and that of non-intervention in the domestic affairs of other states'[79], and the instrument specifies that 'operations to suppress transnational organized crime in the maritime domain ... are the responsibility of, and subject to the sovereign authority of that Signatory'.[80]

The signatories recognize that multiple states, including the flag state, the state of suspected origin of the perpetrators, the state of nationality of persons on board the ship, and the state of ownership of cargo, may have legitimate interests in certain cases.[81] The first is where the state parties 'intend to cooperate to the fullest possible extent in medical and decedent affairs arising from operations in furtherance of the repression'[82] of the crimes. The second is where the state parties 'intend to ensure that, in seeking the fulfilment of the above objectives, a balance is maintained between the need to enhance maritime security and facilitation of maritime traffic and avoid any unnecessary delays to international maritime trade in West and Central Africa'.[83] Therefore, the signatories intend to liaise and cooperate with such states and other stakeholders, and to coordinate such activities to facilitate rescue, interdiction, investigation, and prosecution.[84] Such conduct, and the support of the conduct of the inquiry, should take into account the relevant international standards and practice, and, in particular, recommendations adopted by the IMO.[85] National legislation is not obligatory under the Yaoundé Code of Conduct, but, rather, it is provided that the state parties 'intend' to establish necessary measures for law enforcement.[86] The measures set out in Article 4 of the Yaoundé Code of Conduct include: (a) appropriate national maritime security policies to safeguard maritime trade from all forms of unlawful acts; (b) national legislation, practices, and procedures, which together provide the security necessary for the safe and secure operation of port facilities and ships at all security levels; and (c) national legislation that ensures adequate protection of the marine environment.

This development sits within a broader effort by countries in the region to combat oil-related crimes. The African Union (AU) adopted Africa's Integrated Maritime Strategy (2050 AIM Strategy) in 2012, which identified threats and vulnerabilities that could fuel violence and insecurity on the African continent.[87] It is a broad policy statement, but demonstrates

79 Yaoundé Code of Conduct (n 72) art 1(3).
80 ibid, art 1(4).
81 ibid, art 3(2).
82 ibid, art 3(4).
83 ibid, art 3(5).
84 ibid, art 3(2).
85 ibid, art 3(3).
86 ibid, art 4.
87 2050 Africa's Integrated Maritime Strategy (2012) (hereafter 'AIM Strategy'), paras 61–62) <https://au.int/en/documents-38> accessed 23 June 2021.

the member states' will to create a coordinated and collaborative partnership that will foster wealth creation in a safe and secure African maritime domain, thereby contributing to its socio-economic development.[88] Yet, the document encourages the member states to 'develop and expand coastal surveillance systems and information sharing mechanisms with relevant parties'.[89] It also adds that '[r]elatively cheap and unsophisticated surveillance equipment such as remote sensors and UAVs can be deployed to monitor vandalism of pipelines and track movement of suspicious cargo'.[90]

The roles for informal lawmaking in this context are as follows: first, an informal instrument informs states and non-state actors, and participants of international organizations, of current situations, best practices, and desirable policies to combat illegal bunkering. It does not oblige the members of the forum to take concrete action, but it will push the actors towards regulation. The commitment captures the manifestation of consent to cooperate. Moreover, such instruments do not include provisions in relation to enforcement and contravention actions, and violations of the instruments do not give rise to state responsibility.[91]

Second, it allows states to agree upon the need to combat illegal bunkering without imposing 'sovereignty costs'.[92] States may not reach a formal agreement on any reallocation of jurisdiction that would allow non-flag states to board and inspect the bunkering vessel easily. The fact that ITLOS has dealt with four cases involving bunkering,[93] and, in each case, the flag state has claimed an excessive exercise of jurisdiction by the law-enforcing state, shows that the hurdles for the non-flag state in implementing its laws remain relatively high. On the other hand, because the informal instruments provide greater flexibility, flag states may agree to the general need for eradicating illegal bunkering. They may potentially agree on law enforcement, even on an ad hoc basis.

5.4 Concluding Remarks

This chapter's analysis shows that informal lawmaking plays a supplemental part in the processes to combat illegal bunkering. It is used to: (1) complement the formal instruments such as the LOSC, in order to provide rules and standards: and (2) establish cooperative frameworks between flag states. If there were not such efforts at informal rulemaking or standard setting, states may not have been able to cope with the increasing threats of oil-related crimes.

The regulation of maritime crimes poses a danger of infringing on the legitimate freedom of the seas, if it is done in a unilateral matter. To accommodate two opposing interests—the

[88] SA: Ambassador Mxolisi Nkosi, 'Address by Ambassador Nkosi, During the UN Security Council Debate on "Transnational Organized Crime at Sea as a Threat to International Peace and Security"', 5 February 2019 <https://www.polity.org.za/print-version/sa-ambassador-mxolisi-nkosi-address-by-ambassador-nkosi-during-the-un-security-council-debate-on-transnational-organized-crime-at-sea-as-a-threat-to-international-peace-and-security-05022019-2019-02-06> accessed 23 June 2021.

[89] AIM Strategy (n 87) para 62.

[90] ibid.

[91] Andrew Guzman, 'A Compliance-based Theory of International Law' (2002) 90 CLR 1826; Andrew Guzman, 'The Design of International Agreements' (2005) 16 EJIL 579, 585.

[92] For the concept of 'sovereignty costs', see Kenneth W Abbott and Duncan Snidal, 'Hard and Soft Law in International Governance' in Judith L Goldstein, Miles Kahler, Robert O Keohane, and Anne-Marie Slaughter (eds), *Legalization and World Politics* (MIT Press 2001).

[93] *M/V Saiga* (n 21), *M/V Virginia G* (n 26), *M/V Norstar* (n 17), and *M/T San Padre Pio* (n 28).

need to suppress illicit acts, and securing the legitimate use of the seas— states have negotiated, and coordinated their activities, through informal instruments and settings. Some of these efforts, such as treaty negotiation, may be conventional. Other measures, such as non-binding agreements like the Yaoundé Code of Conduct, let the interested participants coordinate in combating illicit activities, and may be characterized as unconventional.

In such negotiations, the core framework remains the LOSC. When jurisdiction is allocated under the Convention (see section 5.2 above), the actors wanting to promote bunkering regulation have sought to include bunkering into the activities subject to the coastal state's jurisdiction, such as fisheries, and protection of the marine environment. These steps have, primarily, been achieved through formal treaties such as RFMO conventions and MARPOL, rather than informal instruments such as recommendations, guidelines, and non-binding agreements. However, in the negotiation process, and at the implementation stage, informal cooperation through joint inspection schemes has made law enforcement more effective. The oil and shipping industries, which have high stakes in relation to refuelling regulation, have had opportunities to participate in this process by establishing informal standards and guidelines for their specific operations.

When jurisdiction is not allocated under the LOSC (see section 5.3 above), an informal lawmaking process raises awareness of the problem. It may facilitate agreement on the efforts towards cooperation to combat illegal bunkering. It also encourages states to take steps to address the illicit acts. States may not have reason to oppose the general notion of tackling transnational crimes associated with fuelling, such as oil-related crimes and other organized crimes. Thus, the informal lawmaking process enables states to collaborate, notwithstanding the existing limits of jurisdiction allocated under the LOSC.

Maritime cooperation on oil-related crimes is found in patchworks of frameworks rather than a comprehensive systematic mechanism. It is, therefore, necessary, and useful to continue the efforts of informal lawmaking, in order to let the normative value attributed to these informal agreements potentially enhance global efforts to improve illegal bunkering regulations.

PART III
SHIPPING

6

Unconventional Lawmaking in the Compliance Mechanism for the International Regulation of Shipping

Zhen Sun

6.1 Introduction

International shipping remains the backbone of the world economy, whereby over 80% by volume of world merchandise trade is carried by ships between continents.[1] Shipping is, by nature, an international business that demands uniform global regulation to be fair and efficient. The legal framework under the 1982 United Nations Convention on the Law of the Sea (LOSC) establishes a zonal management approach, whereby states have rights and obligations with regard to international shipping, according to their roles as flag, coastal, and port states.[2] The LOSC is well known for being an umbrella framework convention where detailed rules and regulations related to shipping are developed by competent international organizations, or through general diplomatic conferences. With respect to international shipping, the competent international organization, when used in the singular, refers to the International Maritime Organization (IMO), which is mandated to create a regulatory framework for the shipping industry that is fair and effective, and universally adopted and implemented.[3]

Since its establishment in 1948, the IMO has developed its competence to cover all aspects of international shipping under three comprehensive pillars of maritime safety and security, environment and prevention of marine pollution, and liability and compensation.[4] As of 2021, there are over fifty binding agreements and over a thousand non-mandatory codes, guidelines, recommendations, unified interpretations, and other instruments adopted under the auspices of the IMO.[5] The lawmaking process within the IMO is undertaken by

[1] United Nations Conference on Trade and Development (UNCTAD), 'Review of Maritime Transport 2020', UNCTAD/RMT/2020 (United Nations 2020) <https://unctad.org/webflyer/review-maritime-transport-2020> accessed 19 February 2021, 20.

[2] United Nations Convention on the Law of the Sea (adopted 10 December 1982, entered into force 16 November 1994) 1833 UNTS 397 (hereafter 'LOSC').

[3] IMO, 'Implications of the United Nations Convention on the Law of the Sea for the International Maritime Organization' (30 January 2014) IMO Doc LEG/MISC.8 7; DOALOS, '"Competent or Relevant International Organizations" under the United Nations Convention on the Law of the Sea' (1996) 31 L of the Sea Bull 79–95.

[4] Convention on the International Maritime Organization (adopted 6 March 1948, entered into force 17 March 1958) 289 UNTS 3 (hereafter 'IMO Convention'), art 1.

[5] IMO, '2020 Publications Catalogue' <http://www.imo.org/en/Publications/Pages/Home.aspx> accessed 5 March 2021; Global Integrated Shipping Information System (GISIS), 'Non-mandatory Instruments' <https://gisis.imo.org/Public/INSTR/Default.aspx> accessed 5 March 2021.

Zhen Sun, *Unconventional Lawmaking in the Compliance Mechanism for the International Regulation of Shipping*
In: *Unconventional Lawmaking in the Law of the Sea*. Edited by: Natalie Klein, Oxford University Press.
DOI: 10.1093/oso/9780192897824.003.0006

member states, with the technical and expert assistance of national and international organizations, civil societies, and shipping industries.

The book in which this chapter is included constitutes an ambitious attempt to evaluate the contributions of unconventional lawmaking in the law of the sea in various fields. This chapter focuses on the practice of developing the compliance mechanism in the international regulations of shipping. It argues that, under the auspices of the IMO, the shipping industry and other non-state actors have, in addition to IMO member states, traditionally influenced the development and content of shipping regulations and their implementation, and that non-mandatory instruments are an integral part of the compliance mechanism. The significance of the participation of non-state actors, and the application of non-mandatory instruments, can be observed from two aspects: they have contributed to the design and implementation of a practical and efficient regulatory regime, and have enhanced adherence to international regulations of shipping by all relevant stakeholders.

This chapter is divided into three sections. Section 6.2 discusses the lawmaking process at the IMO, in general, and identifies the unconventional elements. Section 6.3 reviews the process and components of the compliance mechanism developed under the auspices of the IMO (both mandatory and non-mandatory instruments), and discusses the role of different stakeholders at play in the lawmaking process. Section 6.4 explores the rationale and advantages of the unconventional elements in the context of the compliance mechanism for international shipping regulations, and analyses the interaction between unconventional lawmaking and formal treaty law developed under the auspices of the IMO. The two unconventional elements of lawmaking applied in the IMO compliance mechanisms demonstrate another example of the evolution of lawmaking in the law of the sea.

6.2 Lawmaking at the IMO

6.2.1 Structure and Membership of the IMO

The IMO Convention was adopted in 1948, and came into force ten years later.[6] The IMO was originally designed to be an organization providing essentially consultative and technical knowledge and support to governments on international shipping, without binding standard-setting powers.[7] The functions of the IMO have gradually expanded to 'provide for the drafting of conventions, agreements, or other suitable instruments, and recommend these to Governments and to intergovernmental organizations, and convene such conferences as may be necessary'.[8]

The IMO consists of a number of organs. First, an Assembly that is responsible for the overall work programme and general policy and budgetary decisions of the IMO, and which meets once every two years, in regular sessions.[9] The Assembly elects the Council for two-year terms beginning after each regular session, which functions as the executive

[6] IMO, 'Convention on the International Maritime Organization' <https://www.imo.org/en/About/Conventions/Pages/Convention-on-the-International-Maritime-Organization.aspx> accessed 5 March 2021.

[7] Aldo Chircop, 'The International Maritime Organization' in Donald R Rothwell, Alex Oude Elferink, Karen Scott, and Tim Stephens(eds), *The Oxford Handbook of the Law of the Sea* (OUP 2015) 420.

[8] IMO Convention (n 4) art 2(b).

[9] ibid, arts 13 and 15.

organ of the IMO between sessions of the Assembly.[10] The Council is the only IMO organ composed of a limited number of elected members, with the number amended and increased over the years to its current forty members.[11] Much of the substantial work of the IMO is undertaken by five specialized committees: the Maritime Safety Committee (MSC), Marine Environment Protection Committee (MEPC), Legal Committee (LEG), Technical Cooperation Committee (TCC), and the Facilitation Committee (FAL), and supported by a secretariat based at the headquarters in London.[12] The negotiation and drafting of new instruments, including amendments to relevant international conventions, are conducted at the committee level. The work of the committees is supported by subcommittees, working or drafting groups, and corresponding groups, and approved by the Assembly.

The membership of the IMO is open to all states that choose to become parties to the IMO Convention.[13] Currently, the IMO has 175 member states, and 3 associate members, 63 intergovernmental organizations (IGOs) with observer status, and 80 non-governmental organizations (NGOs) with consultative status.[14] Where an international convention assigns the IMO a registration role and confers functions on the committees, state parties to that convention can participate at the committees' meetings, according to the provisions of the convention, even if they are not members of the IMO.[15] Meetings of the IMO are open to all eligible participants, but only member states, and state parties to the relevant international conventions, have the right to vote.[16]

6.2.2 Elements of the Lawmaking Process at the IMO

The IMO essentially operates as a forum that facilitates the creation and development, by states, of regulations concerned with international shipping. This function is consistent with the rules of reference adopted in provisions of the LOSC for states to '[act] through the competent international organization or general diplomatic conference' to establish such international rules and standards.[17]

The general steps that lead to the creation of international conventions under the auspices of the IMO can be summarized as follows: states first need to agree politically to proceed with consideration of a particular subject; the subject needs to generate sufficient support from member states at a committee level to become an agenda item; at the committee meeting, states will decide on the appropriate structure of a new instrument (such as whether to have a new convention, or a protocol to an existing convention); the decision

[10] ibid, arts 16 and 26.
[11] ibid, arts 16 and 17.
[12] Ibid, art 11; IMO, 'Structure of IMO' <http://www.imo.org/en/About/Pages/Structure.aspx> accessed 5 March 2021. The MSC and MEPC are assisted in their work by a number of subcommittees: Sub-committee on Human Element, Training and Watchkeeping (HTW); Sub-committee on Implementation of IMO Instruments (III); Sub-committee on Navigation, Communications and Search and Rescue (NCSR); Sub-committee on Pollution Prevention and Response (PPR); Sub-committee on Ship Design and Construction (SDC); Sub-committee on Ship Systems and Equipment (SSE); and Sub-committee on Carriage of Cargoes and Containers (CCC).
[13] IMO Convention (n 4) arts 4–7.
[14] ibid, arts 8 and 65–67. IMO, 'Member States, IGOs and NGOs' <http://www.imo.org/en/About/Membership/Pages/Default.aspx> accessed 5 March 2021.
[15] International Convention for the Safety of Life at Sea (adopted 1 November 1974, entered into force 25 May 1980) 1184 UNTS 1 (hereafter 'SOLAS'), arts III and VIII.
[16] IMO Convention (n 4) arts 9 and 62.
[17] LOSC (n 2) art 211(1).

to convene any international conference for the adoption of international conventions will be submitted to the Assembly for approval; and, finally, states who participate in the international conference shall decide the procedures of the conference.[18]

The international conventions are open to all states, including those that are not parties to the IMO Convention.[19] Once adopted, the international conventions often assign the IMO Secretariat as the registration authority, and designate a committee to perform certain functions, including developing amendments of the conventions.[20] The international conventions may allow all state parties to participate in the committee meetings and vote on amendments to the convention.[21] The procedure and quorum to convene meetings and vote on amendments relating to the conventions are decided by the provisions of the respective conventions.

In addition to the functions conferred upon them by, or under, international conventions, the five IMO committees consider items that fall within their respective mandates, as requested by the Assembly, the Council, the Secretary-General, a member, any other subsidiary body of the IMO, or a relevant body within the United Nations system.[22] In order to cope with the workload and technical matters, all five committees may establish subsidiary bodies as they consider necessary, assign technical work to relevant subcommittees, and establish working groups on specific matters.

All levels of meeting proceedings are open to all members of the IMO, invited observers of IGOs and NGOs, and invited experts whose expertise may be considered useful to the subject matter.[23] Only member states, individually and jointly, may propose a new agenda item for the committees' meetings. However, all observers and invited experts have access to non-confidential documents, may submit proposals on items for the agendas of the committees, comment on other proposals, and participate in the proceedings without a vote.[24] On matters of concern, the observers may submit joint proposals with a member state to further influence the debate and decision-making process.[25]

All five IMO committees require the presence of a minimum of 25% of the membership of the IMO for a meeting to proceed, and any decision to be taken.[26] The committees'

[18] IMO Convention (n 4) arts 15(l), 29, 34, and 39; Nicholas Gaskell, 'Decision Making and the Legal Committee of the International Maritime Organization' (2003) 18(2) IJMCL 162.

[19] SOLAS (n 15) art IX.

[20] ibid, arts III and VIII; IMO, 'Rules of Procedure of the Maritime Safety Committee' (Basic Documents, vol I, 2018 edn), r 14(4).

[21] Rules of Procedure of the Maritime Safety Committee (n 20) rr 1 and 26(3).

[22] Rules of Procedure of the Maritime Safety Committee (n 20) r 14; IMO, 'Rules of Procedure of the Legal Committee' (Basic Documents vol I, 2018 edn), r 14; IMO, 'Rules of Procedure of the Marine Environment Protection Committee' (Basic Documents vol I, 2018 edn), r 14; IMO, 'Rules of Procedure of the Technical Cooperation Committee' (Basic Documents vol I, 2018 edn), r 14; IMO, 'Rules of Procedure of the Facilitation Committee' (Basic Documents vol I, 2018 edn), r 14.

[23] Rules of Procedure of the Maritime Safety Committee (n 20) rr 5 and 47; Rules of Procedure of the Legal Committee (n 22) rr 5 and 47; Rules of Procedure of the Marine Environment Protection Committee (n 22) rr 5 and 47; Rules of Procedure of the Technical Cooperation Committee (n 22) rr 5 and 47; Rules of Procedure of the Facilitation Committee (n 22) rr 5 and 47.

[24] IMO, 'Rules and Guidelines for Consultative Status of Non-governmental International Organizations with the International Maritime Organization' (Basic Documents vol I, 2018 edn) r 6.

[25] 'Work Programme, Proposal for a New Output for the Fire Protection on Containerships regarding the Review of Relevant Parts of SOLAS Chapter II-2 with regard to Fire Protection in the Cargo Area on and Under Deck' (11 February 2020) MSC Doc.102/21/7, submitted by the Bahamas, Germany, IUMI, BIMCO, and CESA.

[26] Rules of Procedure of the Maritime Safety Committee (n 20) r 34; Rules of Procedure of the Legal Committee (n 22) r 34; Rules of Procedure of the Marine Environment Protection Committee (n 22) r 34; Rules of Procedure of the Technical Cooperation Committee (n 22) r 34; Rules of Procedure of the Facilitation Committee (n 22) r 34.

meetings produce debate by all participants, but votes are rare, as the general IMO approach is to proceed by consensus.[27] The chairperson normally sums up the general debate, and records what has been considered, the prevailing mood, and other positions. When there is a clear or overwhelming majority in favour of a proposal, the proposal will be incorporated into the next working draft of the proposal, but the chairperson will not take any action with regard to any proposals that have not obtained consensus.[28] Whenever possible, the amendments to conventions and other instruments are normally adopted unanimously, without a formal vote.[29]

All member states of the IMO have an equal vote or position to be taken into consideration. However, in reality some are more equal than others, in ways that are not often articulated, largely because of the obvious political sensitivities. It is undeniable that states have different capacities and priorities in the shipping sector, and will, logically, allocate more resources to issues that are of greater importance to them. States with limited resources—especially developing countries—may participate in a less influential manner, or not send delegations for a particular proceeding.[30] Hence, in certain contexts, there is often a key member state, or key group of member states, that has more influence on the negotiations and development of certain subject matters.

Non-state actors play an important role, albeit without a vote, in the work of the IMO. Their general influence can be observed in two ways. First, each member state may appoint its own national delegations, which commonly include industry representatives, especially when the industry representatives can provide expert knowledge on technical matters.[31] There is the possibility that the industry representatives might affect the government's position.[32] Secondly, NGOs that are able to make a substantial contribution to the work of the IMO may apply for consultative status, which is subject to a two-year periodic review.[33] The consultative status provides the external stakeholders with access to documents and meetings at every level of decision-making at the IMO, as well as opportunities to submit documents and invitations to speak on approved agenda items.[34] For example, the industry groups made up 57% of all consultative members at the committee level and 67% at subcommittee level, according to a 2020 report published by Transparency International.[35]

[27] Gaskell (n 18) 186.

[28] IMO, 'Report of the Maritime Safety Committee on its 101st Session' (12 July 2019) IMO Doc MSC 101/24. Example of approving proposed amendments: '3.5 Having noted that no pertinent comments had been submitted, the Committee confirmed the contents of the proposed amendments to the appendix to the annex to the 1974 SOLAS Convention, as set out in annex 1 to document MSC 101/WP.5, subject to editorial improvements, if any.' Example of refraining from taking actions: '3.37 In considering the proposals in document MSC 101/12/3/Rev.1, the Committee noted the following views ... 3.38 In view of the above, the Committee agreed not to take any action with regard to the proposals contained in document MSC 101/12/3/Rev.1.'

[29] Jean Claude Sainlos, 'The International Maritime Organization and the Protection of the Marine Environment' in Davor Vidas and Peter Johan Schei (eds), *The World Ocean in Globalisation: Climate Change, Sustainable Fisheries, Biodiversity, Shipping, Regional Issues* (Brill 2011) 324.

[30] Harilaos N Psaraftis and Christos A Kontovas, 'Influence and Transparency at the IMO: The Name of the Game' (2020) 22 Mar Econ and Logist 151, 157–61.

[31] See, eg Rules of Procedure of the Maritime Safety Committee (n 20) r 7; IMO 'List of Participants' (8 July 2019) IMO Doc III 6/INF.1.

[32] Transparency International, 'Governance at the International Maritime Organization: The Case for Reform' (Transparency International's Climate Governance Integrity Programme), 14 <https://www.transparency.org/en/publications/governance-international-maritime-organisation#> accessed 5 March 2021.

[33] Rules and Guidelines for Consultative Status of Non-governmental International Organizations with the International Maritime Organization (n 24) rr 1 and 10.

[34] ibid, rr 6–7.

[35] Transparency International (n 32) 14.

Since the IMO is an intergovernmental organization, member states maintain the power to vote at all levels of decision-making, but their decisions have been heavily influenced by industries and other non-state actors.[36] There are numerous reasons, both historic and contemporary, why the industries play an important role in the creation, development, and enforcement of international shipping regulations. Despite the fact that ships have been sailing between continents for centuries, a permanent forum for the discussion of shipping issues and the adoption of international shipping regulations was only achieved when the IMO was established. The shipping industries had, traditionally, resisted interference from government regulations. Shipping is a highly technical field, with many government delegations requiring expert knowledge from the shipping industries in order to design regulations that can operate in practice. The shipping industries have acquired strong economic power and technical expertise that give them a firm stand to lobby government positions.[37] Additionally, the shipping industries have, over time, developed industry-specific guidelines and practices on management, operation, and technology that have made their way into the regulations developed by the IMO.[38] Furthermore, the compliance of the shipping industries is the key to ensure the implementation of all shipping regulations. This compliance concern gives governments even more incentive to obtain industries' support before committing themselves to regulations that will not, otherwise, be implemented in practice.

6.2.3 Instruments Adopted under the Auspices of the IMO

Through the IMO, states have developed an extremely comprehensive regulatory regime covering nearly every aspect of ships and their operation. The instruments adopted under the auspices of the IMO can be placed in two categories—mandatory and non-mandatory—according to their legal implications. The mandatory instruments include the nearly fifty main conventions and associated protocols, and the regulatory codes that are made mandatory through conventions.[39] The non-mandatory instruments are made up of over 1,000 guidelines, information documents, recommendations, and unified interpretations to assist in implementation.[40]

[36] James Harrison, *Making the Law of the Sea: A Study in the Development of International Law* (CUP 2011) 157–58; InfluenceMap, 'Corporate Capture of the UN IMO: How Shipping Lobbies to Stay Out of the Paris Agreement on Climate' (October 2017) <https://influencemap.org/site/data/000/302/Shipping_Report_October_2017.pdf> accessed 5 March 2021.

[37] InfluenceMap (n 36).

[38] Eg, the Unified Requirements for Polar Class Ships developed by the International Association of Classification Societies (IACS) was incorporated into the IMO 'International Code for Ships Operating in Polar Waters (Polar Code)' (15 May 2015) IMO Res MEPC.264(68) pt I-A, ch 1, 1.2.10 (hereafter 'Polar Code').

[39] IMO, 'List of IMO Conventions' <http://www.imo.org/en/About/Conventions/ListOfConventions/Pages/Default.aspx> accessed 5 March 2021.

[40] IMO, 'Publications' <http://www.imo.org/en/Publications/Pages/Home.aspx> accessed 5 March 2021; IMO, 'Implementation of Instruments and Related Matters, List of Codes, Recommendations, Guidelines and other Safety- and Security-related Non-mandatory Instruments, Note by the Secretariat' (10 August 2016) IMO Doc MSC 93/INF.2; IMO, 'Any Other Business, List of Codes, Recommendations, Guidelines and other Environment-related Non-mandatory Instruments, Note by the Secretariat' (10 August 2016) IMO Doc MEPC 70/INF7; IMO, 'Another Business, List of Codes, Recommendations, Guidelines and other Non-mandatory Instruments related to the Work of the Facilitation Committee, Note by the Secretariat' (2 January 2017) IMO Doc FAL 41/16/1; IMO, 'Any Other Business, List of Codes, Recommendations, Guidelines and other Non-mandatory Instruments related to the Work of the Legal Committee, Note by the Secretariat' (5 April 2016) IMO Doc LEG 103/13.

This lawmaking practice is exemplified by the International Convention for the Safety of Life at Sea (SOLAS).[41] SOLAS was adopted at an ad hoc conference, according to the rules and procedures agreed upon by participating states, and the adopted convention conferred a registration role on the IMO Secretariat, and designated the IMO to develop and adopt subsequent amendments, both through meetings at the MSC and a conference.[42] There have been nearly 170 amendments since SOLAS was adopted in 1974, leading to substantial changes to the original provisions, as well as updating and expanding the original eight chapters to the current fourteen.[43] In addition, there are over 140 non-mandatory instruments directly related to SOLAS, dealing with unified interpretation of certain phrases, provisions, and requirements, and guidance on better practice and implementation, as well as recommendations for early application and implementation of upcoming mandatory amendments.[44]

The non-mandatory instruments adopted under the auspices of the IMO have different legal implications. Strictly speaking, these instruments belong to a non-binding category that should not be labelled as law, mainly because states will not breach legal obligations if they do not follow or comply with these instruments.[45] However, following the analysis adopted in this book, these instruments are part of informal law, since they 'reflect the parties' intent for, or expectation of, cooperation or alignment of behaviour in a designated way in relation to a specific issue'.[46] The IMO non-mandatory instruments were also debated by all participants, and adopted by various committees and subcommittees by consensus, and, thus, represent the collective decisions of states. More importantly, these instruments are closely followed by the maritime authorities of states, and by shipping industries, especially when the instrument is linked with a mandatory instrument. There are also examples where a non-mandatory instrument has later been developed into a mandatory instrument.[47]

The general practice of lawmaking at the IMO has clearly revealed two elements that make this process unconventional. First, while member states remain the lawmakers, their decisions have been heavily influenced by various non-state actors in the shipping sector. Secondly, the mandatory instruments developed under the auspices of the IMO are supported by a large number of non-mandatory instruments that are closely followed by member states and other stakeholders. The following section will take a close look at the instruments that have made up the compliance mechanism developed under the auspices of the IMO, and discuss the relationship between these mandatory and non-mandatory instruments.

[41] IMO, 'International Convention for the Safety of Life at Sea' (SOLAS), 1974 <https://www.imo.org/en/About/Conventions/Pages/International-Convention-for-the-Safety-of-Life-at-Sea-(SOLAS),-1974.aspx> accessed 5 March 2021.

[42] ibid; SOLAS (n 15) arts III and VIII.

[43] The latest amendment was adopted in IMO, 'Amendments to the International Code for the Construction and Equipment of Ships Carrying Dangerous Chemicals in Bulk (IBC Code)' (13 June 2019) IMO Res MSC.460(101). The latest added chapter was Chapter XIV—'Safety Measures for Ships Operating in Polar Waters'.

[44] IMO, 'Implementation of Instruments and Related Matters, List of Codes, Recommendations, Guidelines and other Safety- and Security-related Non-mandatory Instruments, Note by the Secretariat' (6 February 2014) IMO Doc MSC 93/INF.2 (n 40).

[45] Gunther F Handl and others, 'A Hard Look at Soft Law' (1988) 82 ASILPROC 373, 373–74.

[46] Klein, in Chapter 1 of this volume.

[47] The 1993 'Guidelines on the Enhanced Programme of Inspections during Surveys of Bulk Carriers and Oil Tankers' (4 September 1993) IMO Res A.744(18) were made mandatory under amendments to SOLAS Chapter XI, 'Special Measures to Enhance Maritime Safety, International Code on the Enhanced Programme of Inspections during Surveys of Bulk Carriers and Oil Tankers' 2011 (2011 ESP Code), IMO Res A.1049(27), 20 December 2011.

6.3 Compliance Mechanisms under the IMO Regulatory Regime

While states have developed the regulatory regime of international shipping through the IMO, the IMO has no direct power to enforce this regime. As mentioned above, instruments developed under the auspices of the IMO follow the attribution of jurisdiction among flag, coastal, and port states as laid down in provisions of the LOSC.[48] It is quite common for the mandatory instruments developed under the auspices of the IMO not to include dispute settlement mechanisms concerning the interpretation or application of those conventions.[49] The only such instrument that contains a mandatory dispute settlement procedure is the International Convention for the Prevention of Pollution from Ships (MARPOL), whereby state parties may submit their dispute to arbitration, failing negotiation.[50] It can be argued that disputes concerning the interpretation and application of IMO instruments are, through the rules of reference, subject to the compulsory dispute settlement procedure under Part XV of the LOSC.[51] Another main argument for the lack of mandatory dispute settlement procedures is that the IMO regulatory regime places more emphasis on compliance and control, as enforcement measures are against ships, and are rarely elevated to disputes between member states.

The IMO regulatory regime relies on member states to uphold the standards equally, in order to eliminate substandard shipping. However, the IMO conventions left a notable gap with regard to the lack of enforcement provisions for states that have failed to fulfil their obligations. This gap has contributed to the result that the system has not worked perfectly, and the problem of substandard shipping continues to plague the world's oceans. In response, the compliance mechanism within the IMO regulatory regime has been developed to improve member states' performance.[52]

The initiatives to improve accountability for the various actors in the IMO regulatory regime began in the 1990s, with the establishment of a subcommittee to examine flag state implementation, and the strengthening of port state control regimes, which developed into a mandatory audit scheme in the 2010s.[53] The central pillar is to identify and assist states, mainly as flag states, to meet their obligations under the IMO instruments. Many IMO conventions included provisions for port states to inspect the conditions and compliance of ships calling at their ports, and, thereby, to inspect, indirectly, the level of performance of flag states. The mandatory audit scheme followed a series of IMO measures to improve the performance of states in the discharge of their responsibilities assumed under the IMO

[48] LOSC (n 2) arts 94, 211 and 217–20.

[49] SOLAS, for example, does not have provisions on settlement of disputes. A standard dispute settlement provision is as follows: 'Parties shall settle any dispute between them concerning the interpretation or application of this Convention by negotiation, enquiry, mediation, conciliation, arbitration, judicial settlement, resort to regional agencies or arrangements or other peaceful means of their own choice' (International Convention for the Control and Management of Ships' Ballast Water and Sediments (adopted 13 February 2004, entered into force 8 September 2017) IMO Doc BWM/CONF/36, art 15).

[50] International Convention for the Prevention of Pollution from Ships (as Modified by the Protocol of 1978 Relating Thereto) (adopted 2 November 1973, entered into force 2 October 1983) 1340 UNTS 184 (hereafter 'MARPOL'), art 10.

[51] LOSC (n 2) art 288(2); Annex VIII, art 5.

[52] Efthimios E Mitropoulos, 'IMO: 60 Years in the Service of Shipping' in Norman A Martínez Gutiérrez (eds), *Serving the Rule of International Maritime Law: Essays in Honour of Professor David Joseph Attard* (Routledge 2009) 20–21.

[53] Lawrence D Barchue, 'The Voluntary IMO Member State Audit Scheme: An Accountability Regime for States on Maritime Affairs' (2009) 8 WMU J M Aff 61.

instruments. The audit scheme involves reviewing and assessing states' performance according to a mandatory code.

The mandatory audit scheme and the code heralded a new era for the IMO, in which a mechanism was established to achieve the harmonized and consistent global implementation of IMO standards. The audit reports have generated, and will continue to provide, good practice, and will identify needs for capacity-building and other cooperative activities that can further improve states' performance. These compliance mechanisms are essential to realizing the IMO objectives of safe, secure, and efficient shipping on clean oceans. The following two sections set out how the IMO progressed its rules relating to compliance and control, and the subsequent development of the mandatory audit scheme.

6.3.1 Compliance and Control

When states ratify an international convention, they are expected to implement that treaty, and comply with its obligations. However, in practice, some states lack the expertise, experience, and resources necessary to fulfil their obligations immediately. In addition, many of the international conventions entail vague compliance requirements, such as referring 'to the satisfaction of the Administration', that have led to arbitrary interpretations by some states, and different levels of compliance.[54] In light of this issue, the IMO has developed a procedure for monitoring states' implementation and enforcement, with the aim of achieving uniform compliance by all states, regardless of their maritime traditions.[55] This IMO monitoring procedure of compliance and control is made up of both mandatory and non-mandatory instruments. States (mainly flag states) are the main subject of the IMO compliance and control mechanisms, supplemented by the regulations and standards of other non-state actors who assist the performance of states.

In relation to flag states, a new Sub-committee on Flag State Implementation (FSI) was initially established in December 1992, by a joint decision of the MSC and MEPC, to probe flag state implementation of international conventions on safety and pollution prevention.[56] Responding to an increased demand from states, the FSI was renamed the Sub-committee on Implementation of IMO Instruments (III Sub-committee) in 2013 to address the effective and consistent global implementation and enforcement of IMO instruments, including both mandatory and non-mandatory instruments.[57] The III Sub-committee has become the default body within the IMO for addressing all issues relating to compliance with IMO instruments by member states and other relevant non-state stakeholders, and for further supporting the IMO lawmaking process.[58]

[54] Eg, SOLAS (n 15) ch II, reg 2.3: 'The construction and materials of all means of access and their attachment to the ship's structure shall be to the satisfaction of the Administration.'

[55] Kiriaki Mitroussi, 'Quality in Shipping: IMO's Role and Problems of Implementation' (2004) 13(1) Dis Prev Mngmt 53.

[56] 'International Developments – Other Development: —IMO: Sub-committee on Flag State Implementation' (1993) 19(2) CLB 728.

[57] IMO, 'Review and Reform of the Organization, including Application of the Committee's Guidelines, Restructuring of the Sub-committees, Note by the Secretary-General, Annex 6, Sub-committee on Implementation of IMO Instruments (III)' (8 February 2013) MSC Doc 92/22, art 1.

[58] ibid.

Due to the highly technical nature of the shipping regulations, flag state administrations may entrust certain implementation functions, particularly inspections and surveys, either to surveyors nominated for the purpose, or to recognized organizations (ROs).[59] The administrations shall communicate information regarding ROs to the IMO on the ROs authorizations to carry out surveys and issue certificates on the administrations' behalf.[60] In 1993 and 1995, the FSI developed two guidelines for the authorization of organizations acting on behalf of the administration, and for specifications on the survey and certification functions of ROs, which were adopted by the Assembly, and later made mandatory as Resolution 1 of a new Chapter XI included in SOLAS.[61] In 2013, through resolutions by both the MSC and MEPC, the Code for Recognized Organizations (RO Code) was adopted to address all the applicable requirements for ROs, in an effort to achieve harmonized and consistent global implementation of the requirements established by IMO instruments.[62] Through amendments to SOLAS, MARPOL, and the 1988 Load Line Protocol, parts 1 and 2 of the RO Code were made mandatory from 2015, while part 3 is recommendatory, providing a consolidated instrument containing criteria against which ROs are assessed and authorized/recognized, and giving guidance for subsequent monitoring of ROs by administrations.[63] Through these processes, the IMO indirectly regulates the performance of ROs, as non-state actors, in assisting the implementation of state obligations under IMO instruments.

Another notable group of non-state actors in the international shipping regime is the shipping industry, including the shipowners, companies, and ship managers, all of whom play a preeminent role in complying with IMO regulations. The IMO began work to introduce standards for the safe management and operation of ships by the shipping industry in the 1980s.[64] After introducing non-mandatory guidelines in 1989, a mandatory International Management Code for the Safe Operation of Ships and for Pollution Prevention (ISM Code) was adopted, through amendment to SOLAS, in 1993.[65] To further facilitate the uniform implementation of the ISM Code, the IMO also adopted non-mandatory guidelines on implementation for both member states and relevant industries.[66]

[59] Eg, SOLAS (n 15) ch I, reg 6; MARPOL (n 50) Annex I, reg 6; Annex II, reg 8; annex IV, reg 4; Annex V, reg 5.

[60] IMO, 'Communication of Information on the Authorization of Recognized Organizations (ROs)' (10 July 2001) MSC/Circ.1010-MEPC/Circ.382.

[61] IMO, 'Guidelines for the Authorization of Organizations Acting on Behalf of the Administration' (4 November 1993) IMO Res A.739(18); IMO, 'Specifications on the Survey and Certification Functions of Recognized Organizations Acting on Behalf of the Administration' (23 November 1995) IMO Res A.789(19).

[62] IMO, 'Code for Recognized Organizations (RO Code)' (17 May 2013) IMO Res MEPC.237(65); IMO, 'Code for Recognized Organizations (RO Code)' (21 June 2013) IMO Res MSC.349(92).

[63] IMO, 'Recognized Organizations' <http://www.imo.org/en/OurWork/MSAS/Pages/RecognizedOrganizations.aspx> accessed 5 March 2021.

[64] IMO, 'Safety of Passenger Ro-ro Ferries' IMO Res A.596(15); IMO, 'Guidelines on Management for the Safe Operation of Ships and for Pollution Prevention' (19 October 1989) IMO Res A.647(16). The trigger for the IMO action was the 1987 *Herald of Free Enterprise* disaster, where nearly 200 lives were lost when a ro-ro ferry crossing the English Channel capsized.

[65] IMO, 'International Management Code for the Safe Operation of Ships and for Pollution Prevention' (4 November 1993) IMO Res A.741(18) (hereafter 'ISM Code').

[66] IMO, 'Guidelines on Implementation of the International Safety Management (ISM) Code by Administrations' (23 November 1995) IMO Res A.788(19); IMO, 'Guidance on the Qualifications, Training and Experience Necessary for Undertaking the Role of the Designated Person under the Provisions of the ISM Code' (19 October 2007) IMO Doc MSC-MEPC.7/Circ.6; IMO, 'Revised Guidelines for the Operational Implementation of the International Safety Management (ISM) Code by Companies' (28 June 2013) IMO Doc MSC-MEPC.7/Circ.8.

Another remedy contained in IMO instruments for insufficient flag state implementation is port state inspection, to ensure that ships meet relevant requirements, and to eliminate substandard ships from navigating further.[67] In addition, the major IMO conventions, such as MARPOL and SOLAS, provide that no more favourable treatment is to be given to ships of non-state parties than ships of state parties.[68] The IMO facilitates two aspects of the implementation of port state control . First, it seeks to develop guidance on the Procedures for Port State Control, which are kept under review and updated by taking account of the amendments to IMO instruments, and the experience gained from implementation.[69] Second, the IMO promotes regional cooperation to encourage harmonization and co-ordination of port state control activities, and to develop practical recommendations.[70] To date, there are nine regional port state control agreements, reflected in memoranda of understanding (MoUs), which have been established by government authorities across the world.[71] The secretaries of these regional MoUs have been working closely with the IMO, particularly at the III Sub-committee meetings, to share good practices, and to further develop guidance on port state control activities. Among the thirty-five substantive documents submitted to the Sixth Session of the III Sub-committee meeting in 2019, twenty were submitted by the regional MoUs.[72]

Since 2000, the IMO has further developed guidance for member states to self-assess their performance as flag states under IMO regulations, including through a detailed list of criteria and performance indicators to guide flag states through the assessment process.[73] This mechanism, developed through a non-mandatory instrument, helped to pave the way for a model assessment, or audit, of member state enforcement under IMO regulations.

This IMO monitoring procedure of compliance and control was developed to ensure international oversight of states' implementation of IMO regulations. It has contributed to filling the gap left by the lack of enforcement provisions in IMO instruments. After a few decades of practice, developed through both mandatory and non-mandatory instruments to provide implementation guidance to all relevant stakeholders, the IMO elevated this monitoring procedure by introducing a mandatory audit scheme to assess the overall enforcement of all relevant stakeholders under the IMO regulatory regime.

[67] IMO, 'Port State Control' <http://www.imo.org/en/OurWork/MSAS/Pages/PortStateControl.aspx> accessed 5 March 2021.

[68] SOLAS (n 15) art I(3); MARPOL (n 50) art 5(4).

[69] The first procedure for port state control was developed in 1975, and the latest version was adopted in 2019: IMO, 'Procedures for the Control of Ships' (12 November 1975) IMO Res A.321(IX); IMO, 'Procedures for Port State Control' (4 December 2019) IMO Res A.1138(31).

[70] IMO, 'Regional Co-operation in the Control of Ships and Discharges' (6 November 1991) IMO Res A.682(17).

[71] The nine regional agreements are: Europe and the North Atlantic (Paris MoU); Asia and the Pacific (Tokyo MoU); Latin America (Acuerdo de Viña del Mar); Caribbean (Caribbean MoU); West and Central Africa (Abuja MoU); the Black Sea region (Black Sea MoU); the Mediterranean (Mediterranean MoU); the Indian Ocean (Indian Ocean MoU); and the Riyadh MoU. The United States Coast Guard maintains the tenth port state control regime.

[72] IMO, 'Report to the Maritime Safety Committee and the Maritime Environment Protection Committee' (15 July 2019) IMO Doc III 6/15.

[73] IMO, 'Self-Assessment of Flag State Performance' (29 November 2001) IMO Res A.912(22).

6.3.2 Member State Audit Scheme

The proposal to introduce a model IMO audit scheme came in the early 2000s, through a joint submission of nineteen members of the IMO, as an additional effort to promote states' performance under IMO instruments.[74] The concept of an IMO model audit scheme was approved by the IMO Council and Assembly, to be implemented, initially, on a voluntary basis, due to the lack of consensus; the MSC and MEPC were tasked with developing details of the proposed scheme, and the TCC with considering the issue from a capacity-building perspective.[75]

Following this request, an ad hoc joint MSC/MEPC/TCC working group was established to develop the framework, procedures, and other aspects of the proposed audit scheme. It was agreed by states that the work of this joint working group was to be linked with the FSI and the ongoing development of a draft 'code for the implementation of [mandatory] IMO instruments', with the view that the scope of the audit scheme should be consistent with the draft code.[76] The work of developing the code can be traced to 1997 non-mandatory guidelines to assist flag states with a means of establishing and maintaining measures for the effective application and enforcement of the relevant IMO instruments.[77] When it was proposed that the code be compatible with the proposed audit scheme, it was agreed by the FSI that the code should cover all three stakeholders, namely flag states, coastal states, and port states.[78]

These two items were negotiated intensively for over two years at the committee and sub-committee levels. During this process, a large number of non-state actors made considerable contributions by submitting proposals and participating in discussions.[79] In 2005, the IMO Assembly adopted the Framework and Procedures for the Voluntary IMO Member State Audit Scheme, and the Code for the Implementation of Mandatory IMO Instruments, whereby the code formed the basis of the audit scheme.[80] The voluntary audit scheme was intended to provide an audited member state with a comprehensive and objective assessment of how effectively it was administering and implementing those mandatory IMO instruments that were covered by the scheme. The voluntary audit scheme began in 2006, and

[74] 'Consideration of the Strategy and Policy of the Organization, including the Establishment of an Ad Hoc Council Working Group for the Preparation of the Organization's Strategic Plan, Proposal for the Introduction of an IMO Model Audit Scheme' (15 May 2002) IMO Doc C/88/13/1/Add.1, submitted by Australia, Canada, Cyprus, Denmark, Finland, Germany, Hong Kong China, Indonesia, Italy, Japan, the Netherlands, Norway, the Republic of Korea, Marshall Islands, Singapore, Spain, Sweden, the United Kingdom, and the United States.

[75] IMO, 'Summary of Decisions' (27 June 2002) IMO Doc C 88/D, paras 13.5 and 13.8; IMO, 'Voluntary IMO Member State Audit Scheme' (27 November 2003) IMO Res A.946(23), paras 1–2.

[76] IMO Council, C 90/15/Add.1, 9 June 2003; IMO, 'IMO Model Audit Scheme, Developments concerning the Proposed Voluntary IMO Model Audit Scheme, Note by the Secretary-General' (9 June 2003) IMO Doc C 90/15/Add.1, annex 1: Proposed IMO Model Audit Scheme, Report of the Joint MSC/MEPC/TC Working Group on the Voluntary IMO Model Audit Scheme; IMO, 'Flag State Implementation, Outcome of the Meeting of the Joint MSC/MEPC/TCC Working Group on the Voluntary IMO Member State Audit Scheme (JWGMSA), Note by the Secretariat' (30 March 2004) IMO Doc MSC 78/10/3.

[77] IMO, 'Guidelines to Assist Flag States in the Implementation of IMO Instruments' (27 November 1997) IMO Res A.847(20).

[78] IMO, 'Flag State Implementation, Urgent Matters Emanating from the Eleventh Session of the Sub-committee, Note by the Secretariat' (6 May 2003) IMO Doc MSC 77/15, para 9.

[79] Eg 'Proposed IMO Model Audit Scheme, Industry Guidance' (8 April 2003) IMO Doc MSC 77/INF.18, submitted by the International Chamber of Shipping (ICS), BIMCO, INTERCARGO, and INTERTANKO.

[80] IMO, 'Code for the Implementation of Mandatory IMO Instruments' (19 December 2005) IMO Res A.973(24); IMO, 'Framework and Procedures for the Voluntary IMO Member State Audit Scheme' (21 December 2005) IMO Res A.974(24).

member states were encouraged to volunteer to be audited. Throughout the ten-year period leading to the mandatory audit scheme, sixty-six member states and associate members participated in the voluntary audit.[81]

States, through debates and negotiations at all levels of the IMO, along with participation by non-state actors, then worked towards the introduction of an institutionalized IMO member state audit scheme.[82] A four-year work plan was drawn up in 2010 for a transition towards a mandatory IMO member state audit scheme, as illustrated in Table 6.1. The work was completed in 2013, with the adoption by the IMO Assembly of two resolutions establishing the Framework and Procedures for the IMO Member State Audit Scheme according to an updated audit standard included in the IMO Instruments Implementation Code (III Code).[83] These resolutions are rendered obligatory through amendments to several mandatory IMO instruments, in order to assess the extent to which a member state is complying with the obligations contained in these instruments.[84] The amendments to the mandatory IMO instruments were developed by the MSC for safety-related instruments such as SOLAS, and by the MEPC in relation to MARPOL.[85] A non-exhaustive list of obligations under instruments relevant to the III Code was developed by the MSC and MEPC, and this has been constantly updated to take into account amendments to these instruments.[86] With the entry into force of these amendments to the IMO mandatory instruments, the auditing of member states became mandatory from 1 January 2016. All member states to the IMO are to be audited at periodic intervals not exceeding seven years. The reports are confidential to the audit state, which has the sole right to authorize the release of reports, and the IMO Secretary-General, who can prepare an anonymous consolidated summary report containing lessons learned from the audits.[87]

A key component of the audit scheme, and, in general, all IMO efforts to improve compliance of member states with IMO regulations, is the technical cooperation programme that provides capacity-building activities to member states. IMO's technical cooperation activities began in the 1960s, and are conceived and developed through partnerships between recipient countries, resource providers, and the IMO.[88] Member states have been receiving maritime assistance in all the IMO's fields of competence, based on their needs. The results of the audit scheme have been used to identify the specific needs of individual

[81] GISIS, 'Member State Audits, Reports Overview' <https://gisis.imo.org/Public/MSA/ReportsOverview.aspx> accessed 5 March 2021.

[82] IMO, 'Further Development of the Voluntary IMO Member State Audit Scheme' (25 November 2009) IMO Res A.1018(26), para 1.

[83] IMO, 'Framework and Procedures for the IMO Member State Audit Scheme' (4 December 2013) IMO Res A.1067(28); IMO, 'IMO Instruments Implementation Code (III Code)' (4 December 2013) IMO Res A.1070(28).

[84] IMO, 'Transition from the Voluntary IMO Member State Audit Scheme to the IMO Member State Audit Scheme' (4 December 2013) IMO Res A.1058(28).

[85] IMO, 'Amendments to the International Convention for the Safety of Life at Sea, 1974, as Amended, Chapter XIII Verification of Compliance' (22 May 2014) IMO Res MSC.366(93); IMO, 'Amendments to the Annex of the Protocol of 1978 relating to the International Convention for the Prevention of Pollution from Ships, 1973, Amendments to MARPOL Annexes I, II, III, IV and V to Make the Use of the III Code Mandatory' (4 April 2014) IMO Res MEPC.246(66).

[86] IMO, '2019 Non-exhaustive List of Obligations under Instruments Relevant to the IMO Instruments Implementation Code (III Code)' (4 December 2019) IMO Res A.1141(31).

[87] IMO, 'Framework and Procedures for the IMO Member State Audit Scheme' (4 December 2013) IMO Res A.1067(28), arts 4.1.1., 7.1.2, 7.3.1, and 7.4.3.

[88] IMO, 'Integrated Technical Cooperation Programme (ITCP)' <http://www.imo.org/en/OurWork/Technical Cooperation/Pages/ITCP.aspx> accessed 5 March 2021.

Table 6.1 Time Frame and Schedule of Activities to Institutionalize the IMO Member State Audit Scheme*

IMO Body	Timing	Actions
MSC and MEPC	First half of 2010	Consider how to make the Code for the implementation of mandatory IMO instruments mandatory, including provisions for auditing
MSC and MEPC	Second half of 2010	Identify mandatory IMO instruments through which the Code and auditing should be made mandatory
Council	End of 2010	Establish Joint Working Group (JWG) of MSC, MEPC, FAL, and TCC to review the Framework and Procedures for the Scheme
MSC and MEPC	2011 and 2012	Develop provisions to make the Code mandatory through the identified mandatory IMO instruments
Council	Second half of 2011	Approve a progress report for submission to A 27
Assembly 27	November 2011	Receive a progress report and decide as appropriate
JWG	2011 and 2012	Review the Framework and Procedures for the Scheme
JWG	2013	Finalize the Framework and Procedures, taking into account the finished product of the Code and the related amendments to mandatory IMO instruments
Council	First half of 2013	Approve the Framework and Procedures for the Scheme, for submission to A 28 for adoption
Committees	2013	Adopt amendments to the mandatory IMO instruments concerned for entry into force on 1 January 2015
Assembly 28	November 2013	Adopt resolution on the Framework and Procedures for the Scheme and amendments to those mandatory instruments under the purview of the Assembly
Council, Committees, and Secretariat	2014	Preparatory work for the commencement of an institutionalized audit scheme
States	1 January 2016	Audits under the Scheme became mandatory on 1 January 2016, when the majority of amendments to IMO instruments, adopted for the institutionalization of the Scheme, entered into force.**

*IMO, 'Further Development of the Voluntary IMO Member State Audit Scheme' (25 November 2009) IMO Res A.1018(26), Annex.

**For the list of amendments, refer to IMO, 'Member State Audit Scheme' <https://www.imo.org/en/OurWork/MSAS/Pages/Default.aspx> accessed 5 March 2021.

member states, which can be addressed through targeted technical assistance.[89] The generic lessons learnt from audits could be systematically used as inputs to the programming of the technical assistance, to address the real needs of its recipient member states.

In sum, the effectiveness of the IMO regulatory regime depends upon member states implementing and complying fully with these rules and regulations. However, there are no penalties or remedies for lack of flag state oversight, or for lapses of port state control. To fill the gap left by the lack of enforcement provisions in the IMO instruments, states developed comprehensive compliance mechanisms through the IMO, aimed at promoting states' implementation of IMO obligations. If one uses the establishment of the FSI in 1992 to mark the official beginning of IMO's institutionalized effort to assist states' performance, it took three decades, and hundreds of both mandatory and non-mandatory instruments, to result in a mandatory mechanism on compliance of member states.

6.4 The Interaction between Unconventional Lawmaking and Formal Treaty Law

The international regulation of shipping, as primarily developed under the auspices of the IMO, is a distinct branch of international law. As noted previously, when developing this body of law, states act through IMO committees, Council and Assembly meetings, and ad hoc diplomatic conferences. Despite the fact that the IMO has a formal voting process in its working procedures, votes are rarely taken in its meetings and conferences, and the participants try to reach compromises, in order to adopt instruments by consensus.[90] The lawmaking in this body of law is marked by two unconventional elements, which were both notable in the development of the compliance mechanism: non-state actors playing an important role in the lawmaking process, and the non-mandatory instruments complementing the implementation of, and compliance with, the mandatory instruments, and also being closely followed by member states.[91]

6.4.1 The Role of Non-state Actors

Since its establishment, the IMO has established a practice of encouraging industry participation in the elaboration of decisions and instruments at all levels of its meetings.[92] As states remain the primary actors in developing rules and regulations in the shipping sector, their voting power has not shifted. The non-state actors, on the other hand, have been contributing to the lawmaking process through their interactions with states.

[89] IMO, 'Report to the Maritime Safety Committee and the Marine Environment Protection Committee' (8 September 2021), IMO Doc III 7/17, 718.

[90] Harrison (n 36) 161.

[91] For conceptual discussion on informal international lawmaking, see Joost Pauwelyn, 'Informal International Lawmaking: Framing the Concept and Research Questions' in Joost Pauwelyn, Ramses A Wessel, and Jan Wouters, *Informal International Lawmaking* (OUP 2012) 13–34.

[92] Alfred Popp, 'The Treaty-making Work of the Legal Committee of the IMO' in Aldo Chircop, Norman Letalik, Ted L McDorman, and Susan J Rolston (eds), *The Regulation of International Shipping: International and Comparative Perspectives: Essays in Honor of Edgar Gold* (Brill 2012) 222–23.

The non-state actors that play a role in the development of IMO instruments, including the compliance mechanisms, can be divided into three groups. The first group is the ROs that have been conferred with statutory tasks by flag states' administrations. There are currently nearly 100 ROs registered with the IMO, with duties relating to ship registration, issuance of certifications, and survey and inspection, on behalf of the flag state.[93] The second group is the shipowners or shipping companies that are responsible for the consistent application of the same standards to individual ships. The third group is the seafarers, often in organized unions, who have the task of putting into operation the various safety, security, and anti-pollution measures applicable to the ships. As discussed in the previous sections of this chapter, these non-state actors are represented at the lawmaking process through national delegations of member states, and as accepted observers, or invited independent experts.

In addition to engagement in the lawmaking process, the activities of these non-state actors have also been regulated by the IMO through both mandatory and non-mandatory instruments. However, their accountability is largely limited to commercial consequences, and liabilities towards other non-state actors.[94] Flag states remain responsible for ensuring that any entities acting on their behalf comply with IMO regulations. The flag state should remove ROs that fail to comply with IMO regulations from their recognized list, and may initiate domestic procedures to hold them liable for inaction or wrongdoing, according to the agreement between the flag state and the respective RO.[95]

The non-state actors' contributions to lawmaking at the IMO are frequently informal, indirect, and unacknowledged in the final instruments and, hence, it is difficult to assess the precise role that they have played. A general observation is that the support of non-state actors improves the effectiveness of the compliance mechanisms under the IMO regulatory regime. The participation of these non-state actors in the negotiations often ensures transparency and accountability of states for their positions, as well as bringing in expert knowledge and, sometimes, alternative positions to those of the states.[96] Moreover, the views expressed by the non-state actors offer a bottom-up approach, to ensure that the potential regulations are operational in practice.[97] This contribution is particularly welcomed in the international shipping sector because it improves implementation and compliance.

The litany of non-state actors' participations reviewed above points to the fact that instruments developed under the auspices of the IMO are formed by a much more complex process than traditional state-to-state multilateralism. The hierarchical or vertical structures at the IMO allow non-state actors to contribute to the debate and formulation of agreed-upon rules.[98] The IMO's practice supports the argument that non-state actors can play a complementary and legitimate role in the international lawmaking process.[99]

[93] GISIS, 'Recognized Organizations' <https://gisis.imo.org/Public/RO/Default.aspx> accessed 5 March 2021.

[94] Eg, after the 2002 *Prestige* oil spill incident, (attempted) legal actions were brought against the American Bureau of Shipping and London Steam-Ship Owners' Mutual Insurance Association (London Club) under relevant national jurisdiction.

[95] IMO Res MEPC.237(65) (n 62) app 3: Elements to be Included in an Agreement.

[96] Robert McCorquodale, 'The Individual and the International Legal System' in Malcolm D Evans (ed), *International Law* (5th edn, OUP 2018) 275–77.

[97] Ngwatung Akamangwa, 'Regulatory Influences on Environmental Protection: Why Shipping Companies Comply and when they Don't' (2017) 48(2) ODIL 160, 160–65.

[98] Joseph E Vorbach, 'The Vital Role of Non-flag State Actors in the Pursuit of Safer Shipping' (2001) 32(1) ODIL 34.

[99] Samantha Besson and José Luis Martí, 'Legitimate Actors of International Law-making: Towards A Theory of International Democratic Representation' (2018) 9(3) Juris 504, 504–40; Cecilia M Bailliet, 'Introduction' in Cecilia M Bailliet (ed), *Non-State Actors, Soft Law and Protective Regimes: From the Margins* (CUP 2012) 6–7;

6.4.2 The Role of Non-mandatory Instruments

As discussed in this chapter, international shipping regulations, including the compliance mechanisms, are a combination of both mandatory and non-mandatory instruments. There are many reasons for the existence of a large number of non-mandatory instruments within the IMO regulatory regime. These reasons are also the basis for discussing the value of these non-mandatory instruments.[100]

As noted previously, the IMO regulatory regime is developed through consensus, and voting is rare, particularly at the committee level. Similarly to other international fora, states at the IMO have diverse positions and priorities, so political trade-offs are common. When it is difficult to reach agreement on a wide range of controversial options, one option is for states to modify the content of the agreement in order to reach consensus on less controversial issues. The other option is to choose non-mandatory instruments, but maintain a more comprehensive content. The non-mandatory instrument works as a compromise between those who wanted a perfect, comprehensive binding instrument and those who did not want any instrument. Without the legal implications of a mandatory instrument, the non-mandatory instrument could also contain more precisely worded regulations than a weak or ambiguous provision in a mandatory instrument. Moreover, comparing the potential time spent negotiating, and the lapse of time between the adoption date of a convention and its entering into force, the non-mandatory instruments are easier to develop, and can be implemented immediately. For example, the proposed IMO model audit scheme was implemented on a voluntary basis before states were ready to proceed to a periodical mandatory audit. The voluntary implementation of the audit scheme also provided a testing ground where states further developed the framework and procedures.

Moreover, there are a large number of non-mandatory technical standards and recommendations that play a complementary and mutually reinforcing role to the mandatory instruments. Many IMO instruments address highly technical issues, often setting out goal-based standards whereby the states and operators have the option to choose the specific technology or management that suits them while still meeting the regulation requirements.[101] This flexibility in standards avoids a static instrument that may be overtaken by technological development. Many non-mandatory instruments are developed to provide guidance and recommendations on how to meet these goal-based standards. For example, recognizing that the provision of port reception facilities is crucial for effective MARPOL implementation, the IMO developed guidance on good practice for port reception facility providers and users.[102] There are also numerous non-mandatory instruments that were

Barbara K Woodward, 'International Lawmaking and Civil Society' in Catherine Brölmann and Yannick Radi (eds), *Research Handbook on the Theory and Practice of International Lawmaking* (Edward Elgar 2016) 286–304.

[100] See Alan E Boyle, 'Some Reflections on the Relationship of Treaties and Soft Law' (1999) 48(4) ICLQ 901, 901–13; Mark A Pollack and Gregory C Shaffer, 'The Interaction of Formal and Informal International Lawmaking' in Joost Pauwelyn, Ramses A Wessel, and Jan Wouters (eds), *Informal International Lawmaking* (OUP 2012) 241–70; Alan Boyle, 'Soft Law in International Law-Making' in Malcolm D Evans (ed), *International Law* (5th edn, OUP 2018) 119–35.

[101] IMO, 'Generic Guidelines for Developing IMO Goal-based Standards' (14 June 2011) IMO Doc MSC.1/Circ.1394.

[102] IMO, 'Consolidated Guidance for Port Reception Facility Providers and Users' (1 March 2018) IMO Doc MEPC.1/Circ.834/Rev.1.

developed to facilitate other aspects of the implementation of mandatory instruments, such as guidelines on early implementation of amendments to mandatory instruments.[103]

There have been many examples of IMO non-mandatory instruments that have later formed the basis of mandatory instruments, such as the current RO Code and III Code. This transition usually takes place under one of two circumstances. First, when states are not ready to commit to a legally binding instrument, and opt for a non-mandatory one with the aim of testing the proposed legal standards, and then proceed to adopt a binding instrument when the circumstances have matured. Secondly, when states developed the non-mandatory instrument without the aim of making it legally binding, but later agreed that a mandatory instrument was more suitable for the subject matter. As an example of the second circumstance, states were recommended to follow the polar classes developed by the International Association of Classification Societies (IACS) under the IMO Guidelines for Ships Operating in Arctic Ice-covered Waters, which was later incorporated into the mandatory Polar Code.[104]

The legal implications of each non-mandatory instrument must be assessed in light of all the circumstances, particularly states' opinions on the point or points at issue. What is determinative as to the legal status, in such situations, is often not the title given to the instrument in question, but whether the states intended to create binding legal relationships between themselves on the subject matter. It has been argued that IMO resolutions, which are normally adopted by consensus and, accordingly, reflect global agreement by IMO members, carry such expectations that they will be followed by member states under certain circumstances.[105] A particular case can be made when states request IMO committees to issue unified interpretations of certain provisions or phrases contained in a mandatory instrument. Such unified interpretation, as adopted by the same group of states that developed the mandatory instrument, form a legitimate treaty interpretation. The interaction between such unified interpretation, in the form of a non-mandatory instrument, with the mandatory instrument may transform the former's legal status by creating a 'normative effect', as described in the opening chapter of this book.

International shipping has generated many non-mandatory instruments that play a critical role in supplementing, thickening, and filling gaps in the mandatory framework, and, to a certain degree, broadening stakeholders to include non-state actors. The use of such non-mandatory instruments, whether titled as recommendations, guidelines, codes, standards, or unified interpretations, is significant in signalling the evolution and establishment of standards of behaviour. These non-mandatory instruments are exercising an influence on state practice and industry performance as they stand, with many of them ultimately being converted into legally binding rules.[106]

[103] IMO, 'Guidelines on the Voluntary Early Implementation of Amendments to the 1974 SOLAS Convention and Related Mandatory Instruments' (15 June 2017) IMO Doc MSC.1/Circ.1565.

[104] IMO, 'Guidelines for Ships Operating in Arctic Ice-covered Waters' (23 December 2002) IMO Doc MSC/Circ.399/MEPC/Circ.399, ch 1, 1.1.3; Polar Code (n 38) pt I-A, ch 1, 1.2.10.

[105] IMO, 'Implications of the United Nations Convention on the Law of Sea for International Maritime Organization' (30 January 2014) IMO Doc LEG/MISC.8, 10 (n 3).

[106] Malcolm N Shaw, *International Law* (8th edn, CUP 2017) 87–88.

6.5 Conclusion

The compliance mechanism developed under the IMO regulatory regime is a dual system of non-mandatory codes and guidelines, on the one hand, and the mandatory audit system and III Code, on the other. These instruments were developed through debates and negotiations among member states and non-state actors wherein the former retain voting power for the development of IMO instruments. The large number of non-mandatory instruments within the work of the IMO reflect the many purposes attributed to informal instruments in international lawmaking: filling gaps where there are no mandatory regulations, providing the detailed rules and technical standards required for the implementation of mandatory instruments, and paving the way for the development of legally binding rules.

The IMO's approach offers another example of promoting compliance and implementation of the LOSC, especially as it provides an alternative to the use of the compulsory dispute settlement procedures under that convention. By engaging all stakeholders in the process of lawmaking, and adopting a consensus approach, IMO instruments have secured the widest support from both member states and non-state actors and have, thereby, increased the level of compliance. By focusing on improving member states' capacities and competence, the IMO intends to address the root cause of unsatisfactory performance of states in regulating international shipping.

It is significant that the IMO provides a standing forum dedicated to the discussion and resolution of compliance issues. The IMO has continually adjusted its regulatory regime not only to technical developments within the shipping industry, but also to the evolving demands and expectations of the member states and other stakeholders. IMO mandatory and non-mandatory instruments are both under continuous review by the relevant IMO committees, which amend them or develop new instruments as necessary. The widespread participation of states and non-state actors in the work of the IMO, the consensus approach it employs in decision-making procedures, and the mixed legal instruments that it has produced, all contribute to its success as a key institution in the evolution of lawmaking in the law of the sea.

7

Unconventional Law for Unconventional Ships? The Role of Informal Law in the International Maritime Organization's Quest to Regulate Maritime Autonomous Surface Ships

Anna Petrig

7.1 Introduction

New technologies have regularly been triggers for the creation of new rules, or the amendment of existing rules, by the International Maritime Organization (IMO or the Organization),[1] which is the UN specialized agency in the field of shipping.[2] Maritime Autonomous Surface Ships (MASS)—the term used by the Organization to denote ships 'which, to a varying degree, can operate independent of human interaction'[3]—are not novel in this respect. All the same, MASS stand out from previous technological inventions in various respects, notably because their construction and operation involves not one but several emerging technologies, each of which is, in itself, complex, inchoate, and developing at an unprecedented pace. As a result, their regulation poses exceptional challenges, not only in terms of the content of rules, but also as regards the regulatory techniques to be deployed to achieve 'the safe, secure and environmentally sound operation'[4] of this new type of vessel.

The IMO's interest in autonomous ships and their regulation is relatively recent, but has experienced exponential growth of late. In the span of only half a decade, 'autonomous ships have turned from a non-issue to one of the main regulatory topics' dealt with by the IMO.[5] So far, the main focus of the debate has been on substantive law, while the question of which regulatory techniques are most suitable for integrating MASS into the IMO's legal framework has only been considered at the fringes. The academic debate accompanying the Organization's efforts to regulate MASS in a proactive fashion has, thus far, equally centred around the content of rules, while possible modes of governance have only been discussed

[*] Developments up until 31 March 2021 have been taken into account.

[1] Aldo Chircop, 'Testing International Legal Regimes: The Advent of Automated Commercial Vessels' (2017) 60 Germ Yrbk Intl L 1, 1.

[2] Convention on the International Maritime Organization (adopted 6 March 1948, entered into force 17 March 1958) 289 UNTS 3 (hereafter 'IMO Convention'), art 64.

[3] IMO, 'Report of the LEG Working Group on MASS' (29 March 2019) IMO Doc LEG 106/WP.5, Annex, para 3.

[4] IMO, 'Report of the Maritime Safety Committee on its Ninety-Eight Session' (28 June 2017) IMO Doc MSC 98/23, para 20.1

[5] Henrik Ringbom, Erik Røsæg, and Trond Solvang, 'Introduction' in Henrik Ringbom, Erik Røsæg, and Trond Solvang (eds), *Autonomous Ships and the Law* (Routledge 2021) 3.

Anna Petrig, *Unconventional Law for Unconventional Ships? The Role of Informal Law in the International Maritime Organization's Quest to Regulate Maritime Autonomous Surface Ships* In: *Unconventional Lawmaking in the Law of the Sea*. Edited by: Natalie Klein, Oxford University Press. © Anna Petrig 2022. DOI: 10.1093/oso/9780192897824.003.0007

tangentially.[6] Yet, as '[i]n an age of constant, complex and disruptive technological innovation, knowing what, when, and how to structure regulatory interventions has become more difficult',[7] the question of how to regulate MASS deserves more attention.[8] This is where the present chapter comes in. It probes the normative techniques that seem suitable in the context of MASS by concentrating on the role informal law could play in the IMO's quest to regulate this novel type of vessel—or, in more sloganesque words, and in allusion to the title of this book, it explores the (potential) role of unconventional law for unconventional ships.

First, section 7.2 provides a brief overview as to why MASS differ, as a regulatory object, from previous technologies that have been the drivers for the adoption of new rules under the auspices of the IMO. This discussion is followed by an account, in section 7.3, of the steps undertaken by the IMO so far to bring MASS within its regulatory framework. Section 7.4 demonstrates that the IMO's engagement with informal law is far from novel; rather, informal law has played 'an extremely important part in the functioning of the organization and in the regulation of international shipping' since its inception.[9] The core of this chapter, section 7.5, enquires into the role that informal law could play in the interpretation of existing treaties, with a view to their application to MASS, and in the amendment or creation of new rules governing MASS. The IMO's engagement with informal law, considered alongside the advantages ascribed to informal law in the regulation of emerging technologies,[10] and the fact that the 'age of treaties'[11] is said to be over,[12] suggests that informal law could take centre stage in the IMO's efforts to bring MASS within its normative framework. Of course, as the process of regulating MASS is still in its infancy, nothing more than a forecast is possible at the current juncture.

7.2 MASS Posing Exceptional Regulatory Challenges

The world of shipping has experienced tremendous change since the IMO became operational in 1958.[13] According to its self-perception, 'the Organization was kept busy from the start developing new conventions and ensuring that existing instruments kept pace with changes in shipping technology'.[14] As such, the fact that new technologies function as

[6] Scholarship discussing regulatory techniques for emerging technologies in general, or with regard to specific technologies other than MASS, is abundant: see, eg Gary E Marchant, Braden R Allenby, and Joseph R Herkert (eds), *The Growing Gap between Emerging Technologies and Legal-ethical Oversight: The Pacing Problem* (Springer 2011); Gary E Marchant, Kenneth W Abbott, and Braden Allenby (eds), *Innovative Governance Models for Emerging Technologies* (Edward Elgar 2013).

[7] Mark Fenwick, Wulf A Kaal, and Erik P M Vermeulen, 'Regulation Tomorrow: What Happens When Technology Is Faster Than the Law?' (2016) 6(3) AUBLR 561, 561.

[8] Admittedly, a discussion of suitable regulatory techniques presupposes a certain understanding of the nature and scope of the substantive issues to be regulated.

[9] Frederic L Kirgis, 'Shipping' in Oscar Schachter and Christopher C Joyner (eds), *United Nations Legal Order*, vol 2 (CUP 1995) 732.

[10] See, eg Ryan Hagemann, Jennifer Huddleston Skees, and Adam Thierer, 'Soft Law for Hard Problems: The Governance of Emerging Technologies in an Uncertain Future' (2018) 17(1) CTLJ 37.

[11] An allusion to the (then apposite) opening sentence of Ulf Linderfalk, *On the Interpretation of Treaties* (Springer 2007) 1: 'We live in the age of treaties.'

[12] On the prevailing 'treaty fatigue', see Joost Pauwelyn, Ramses A Wessel, and Jan Wouters, 'When Structures Become Shackles: Stagnation and Dynamics in International Lawmaking' (2014) 25(3) EJIL 733, 739.

[13] Dorota Lost-Sieminska, 'The International Maritime Organization' in Michael Bowman and Dino Kritsiotis (eds), *Conceptual and Contextual Perspectives on the Modern Law of Treaties* (CUP 2018) 909.

[14] IMO, 'Conventions' <www.imo.org/en/About/Conventions/Pages/Default.aspx> accessed 1 April 2021.

an incubator for the amendment of existing rules, or the adoption of entirely new rules, is not novel. As Chircop notes, '[t]he history of international maritime law is punctuated by game-changing technological milestones',[15] and '[t]he technology of shipping has driven much of the *opus* of the ... [IMO]'[16]. Yet, MASS, when looked at from a regulator's perspective, arguably differ from past technological innovations, and even those deemed 'revolutionary' at the time of their introduction, such as containers.

First of all, the advent of MASS amounts to a foundational change for the more than fifty treaties for which the IMO is responsible,[17] as it challenges a basic assumption on which they rest: that ships have an onboard crew responsible for the ship's operation and mission.[18] Ship automation technology, which heralds a shift towards ships with a reduced crew or, in the more distant future, no onboard crew, thus strikes at the heart of these rules.[19] In quantitative terms, this shift implies that the introduction of MASS affects almost every IMO treaty in one way or another.[20] In qualitative terms, the legal issues to be addressed due to the advent of MASS are extremely diverse, given the IMO's regulatory reach, which ranges from maritime safety and security, and the prevention of marine pollution, to liability and compensation arising from shipping operations.[21] On top of this, autonomous ships will raise entirely new legal issues that the Organization has not regulated before.[22] Overall, the normative challenges arising from the introduction of MASS are 'expected to be wide-ranging and far-reaching'.[23]

Second, MASS, as a technology, seem to differ from previous maritime technological inventions. To begin with, MASS are considered a technology that will have a transformative impact on shipping.[24] The view is held that the 'Fourth Industrial Revolution' will 'change the maritime industry as a whole',[25] and that MASS specifically 'require a fundamental "rethink" of shipping in all its aspects', including its regulation.[26] It is true that, throughout the existence of the IMO, new technologies, hailed as 'revolutionary' at the time of their introduction, have surfaced in the maritime world. Think of the introduction in the 1950s and

15 Chircop, 'Testing International Legal Regimes' (n 1) 3.

16 ibid 3–4.

17 IMO, 'Conventions' (n 14).

18 See, eg IMO, 'Summary of Results of the LEG Regulatory Scoping Exercise for the International Convention on Liability and Compensation for Damage in Connection with the Carriage of Hazardous and Noxious Substances by Sea, 2010' (10 January 2020) IMO Doc LEG 107/8/15, para 17.

19 See, eg IMO, 'Summary of Results of the Second Step and Conclusion of the RSE for the International Regulations for Preventing Collisions at Sea 1972' (6 February 2020) IMO Doc MSC 102/5/3, para 31.

20 Henrik Ringbom, 'Developments, Challenges, and Prospects at the IMO' in Henrik Ringbom, Erik Røsæg, and Trond Solvang (eds), *Autonomous Ships and the Law* (Routledge 2021) 63.

21 For the IMO's mandate, see IMO Convention (n 2), art 2.

22 Måns Jacobsson, 'What Challenges Lie Ahead for Maritime Law?' in Proshanto K Mukherjee, Maximo Q Mejia, and Jingjing Xu (eds), *Maritime Law in Motion* (Springer 2020) 281. For concrete examples, see IMO, 'Summary of Results of Analysis of IMO Instruments Under the Purview of the Legal Committee' (13 December 2019) IMO Doc LEG 107/8, para 30.

23 Cleopatra Doumbia-Henry (President, World Maritime University (WMU)), 'Maritime Trade and Transport—An Outlook on the Issues and a Reflection on the Implications for Education and Research' in UNCTAD, *50 Years of Review of Maritime Transport, 1968–2018: Reflecting on the Past, Exploring the Future* (United Nations, 2018) 52.

24 Donald Liu, 'Autonomous Vessel Technology, Safety, and Ocean Impact' in Dirk Werle and others (eds), *The Future of Ocean Governance and Capacity Development: Essays in Honor of Elisabeth Mann Borgese (1918–2002)* (Brill Nijhoff 2018) 490.

25 Doumbia-Henry (n 23) 52.

26 Frank Smeele, 'Switching Off Regulatory Requirements: Flag State Exemptions as a Tool to Facilitate Experiments with Highly Automated Vessels and their Operational Implementation' in Henrik Ringbom, Erik Røsæg, and Trond Solvang (eds), *Autonomous Ships and the Law* (Routledge 2021) 69.

1960s of radar to avoid collisions, automatic identification systems, refrigeration on board vessels and, most importantly, containers.[27] Yet, MASS differ in several respects when compared with, say, containerization, which was certainly the technological invention of the twentieth century that yielded the biggest transformative effect on shipping (and beyond).[28]

One hallmark of MASS is that their construction and operation does not involve one single, relatively simple technology, but several. Artificial intelligence, robotics, and information technology are just three tech buzzwords commonly associated with MASS, each of which covers a myriad of technologies.[29] Furthermore, these technologies are more complex than earlier innovations. While everyone can imagine what a container is (essentially a standardized metal box),[30] the concept of 'autonomy' and the various 'levels of autonomy' remain elusive, against the backdrop of differing interpretations and understandings proposed by doctrine and practice at the current juncture, even when solely considering *maritime* systems.[31] Grasping how MASS will ultimately be designed and operated is further complicated by the fact that various applications allowing for increased ship automation are still in the development phase.[32] MASS, thus, involve technologies that may be qualified as 'inchoate': that is, belonging to those that 'are far from completely developed', which 'differentiates them from more stable ones'.[33] In this regard, MASS differ decisively from containers, which have not significantly changed since their introduction in the 1950s, and for which the current prediction is that '[b]ox sizes will be stable at today's standard' for the next twenty-five years[34] (this is barely surprising as the very concept of containerization is based on standardization).

A further difference to past innovations is that today's emerging technologies 'are racing forward at a pace of technology development that has never before been experienced in human history'.[35] Indeed, when addressing the significant transformation expected in maritime transport, the acting IMO Secretary-General stated that '[t]he next 10 or 20 years will see as much change as we have experienced in the past 100 years'.[36] These ever-shorter

[27] Aldo Chircop and Desai Shan, 'Governance of International Shipping in the Era of Decarbonisation: New Challenges for the IMO?' in Proshanto K Mukherjee, Maximo Q Mejia, and Jingjing Xu (eds), *Maritime Law in Motion* (Springer 2020) 101.

[28] On how containerization upended the maritime world, see Michael B Miller, *Europe and the Maritime World: A Twentieth-Century History* (CUP 2012) 320 (overview), and ch 9, entitled 'Transformation'.

[29] For anecdotal evidence on the number of technologies involved in MASS, see Kevin Heffner and Ørnulf Jan Rødseth, 'Enabling Technologies for Maritime Autonomous Surface Ships' (2019) 1357 J Phys Conf Ser 1, 1.

[30] Despite being 'so simple a concept', containers triggered tremendous change, as 'every other facet of the transport chain was systematically calibrated to handle them': Miller (n 28) 333.

[31] For an overview of various definitions, see, eg Bradley Martin and others, *Advancing Autonomous Systems: An Analysis of Current and Future Technology for Unmanned Maritime Vehicles* (Rand Corporation 2019) 5–7.

[32] Carmen Kooij, Alina P Colling, and Christopher L Benson, 'When Will Autonomous Ships Arrive? A Technology Forecasting Perspective' (Proceedings of the 14th International Naval Engineering Conference & Exhibition, October 2018) 1.

[33] Daniel Gervais, 'The Regulation of Inchoate Technologies' (2010) 47(3) Hous L R 665, 671: inchoate technologies are generally new ones; yet there are indicators next to time, notably that their future use is unpredictable, that social norms in relation to them are in flux and rapidly evolving, that they are not developed by existing firms as part of existing product lines, and that their regulation bears certain risks (ibid 672–74).

[34] Charles Fenton and others, *Brave New World? Container Transport in 2043* (Report by TT Club and McKinsey & Company 2018) 13 and 32.

[35] Gary E Marchant, 'Addressing the Pacing Problem' in Gary E Marchant, Braden R Allenby, and Joseph R Herkert (eds), *The Growing Gap between Emerging Technologies and Legal-ethical Oversight: The Pacing Problem* (Springer 2011) 199; see also IMO, 'Strategic Plan for the Organization for the Six-year Period 2018 to 2023' (8 December 2017) IMO Doc A 30/Res. 1110, para 17.

[36] Kitack Lim (Secretary-General, International Maritime Organization (IMO)), 'Future Developments in Maritime Transport' in UNCTAD (n 23) 37.

innovation cycles,[37] in turn, accelerate the 'pacing problem',[38] which denotes the phenomenon that law usually trails behind technological development.[39] The statement that 'autonomous technology for ships will mature much faster than the development of sufficient . . . regulations'[40] is to be viewed against this background.

All things considered, despite the fact that delegations to the IMO are generally composed of persons with advanced technical knowledge, and that non-governmental organizations (NGOs) and intergovernmental organizations (IOs) add expertise,[41] it seems more challenging to identify the technology to be regulated, and to discern the regulatory object, in the context of MASS than has been the case for previous technological innovations.[42]

7.3 The IMO's Efforts to Integrate MASS in its Regulatory Framework

While, today, the IMO invests significant resources in analysing how MASS could be integrated into its legal framework, the idea that this new type of vessel is a regulatory object to be dealt with by the Organization is a rather recent one. Ringbom identifies as the 'first trace' of such understanding an information paper on 'The IMO Regulatory Framework and its Application to Marine Autonomous Systems', which was submitted by the United Kingdom and two NGOs in 2015—a démarche that, however, 'passed largely unnoticed'.[43] Just a year later, the idea was already gaining more traction when various states suggested the inclusion of autonomous ships in the 'Trends, Developments and Challenges' paper.[44] This document, in turn, informed the IMO's strategic plan for the 2018 to 2023 period, which was adopted in 2017, and which included a strategic direction to '[i]ntegrate new and advancing technologies in the regulatory framework'.[45] At present, this strategic direction is mainly implemented through a so-called regulatory scoping exercise (RSE).

The RSE goes back to a proposal submitted by nine states to the Maritime Safety Committee (MSC), in 2017, to 'undertake a regulatory scoping exercise to establish the extent of the need to amend the regulatory framework to enable the safe, secure and environmental operation' of MASS.[46] This proposal was adopted the same year.[47] The Legal Committee (LEG) followed suit in 2018, as did the Facilitation Committee (FAL) in 2019, when they included in their respective agendas a similar output for the treaties coming

[37] Fenwick, Kaal, and Vermeulen (n 7) 562.

[38] Hagemann, Huddleston Skees, and Thierer (n 10) 58.

[39] Wendell Wallach, *A Dangerous Master: How to Keep Technology from Slipping beyond our Control* (Basic Books 2015) 251.

[40] Liu (n 24) 493.

[41] Rosalie P Balkin, 'The IMO and Global Ocean Governance: Past, Present, and Future' in David J Attard, Rosalie P Balkin, and Donald W Greig (eds), *The IMLI Treatise on Global Ocean Governance, Volume III: The IMO and Global Ocean Governance* (OUP 2018) 24.

[42] See Fenwick, Kaal, and Vermeulen (n 7) 571.

[43] Ringbom, 'Developments, Challenges, and Prospects at the IMO' (n 20) 57–58.

[44] IMO, 'Inputs from Member States, IGOs and NGOs to the Development of the Trends, Developments and Challenges' (8 April 2016) IMO Doc SF-WG 2/INF.2.

[45] IMO Doc A 30/Res 1110 (n 35), paras 17–19.

[46] IMO, 'Maritime Autonomous Surface Ships: Proposal for a Regulatory Scoping Exercise' (27 February 2017) IMO Doc MSC 98/20/2, para 1.

[47] IMO Doc MSC 98/23 (n 4), para 20.2.

under their purview.[48] The objective of the exercise, which today extends to more than forty conventions and protocols,[49] is to better understand whether existing law can accommodate MASS.[50] It is purely 'exploratory' in nature and does not include any drafting exercises.[51] At the time of writing, the RSE is ongoing. As the outbreak of the COVID-19 pandemic brought the work to an abrupt halt, the (ambitious) target completion date of 2020 for the RSE conducted within the MSC and FAL[52] could not be realized.[53] The same is likely to be the case for the 2022 target date set by the LEG,[54] given that it adjusts its timetable to the work of the MSC.[55]

All three committees follow a very similar methodology when conducting the RSE,[56] and this methodology foresees a two-step approach. The first phase involves a provision-by-provision review of each of the selected treaties. The goal is to assess, for each provision, whether it prevents the operation of MASS, and, if not, whether it can be applied without further ado to MASS, or whether it needs to be clarified, amended, or complemented.[57] Thereby, a distinction is drawn between four degrees of autonomy: ships with automated processes and decision support having a crew on board, remotely controlled ships having seafarers on board, remotely controlled ships without onboard crew, and fully autonomous ships.[58] While the focus of this first step is on the substance of the individual rules, the second step considers the instruments as a whole, and pertains to the question of how to address the regulatory needs identified during the first phase. Thereby, the choice is limited to four options: (1) the development of interpretations; (2) the amendment of existing instruments; (3) the creation of new instruments; or (4) none of these options.[59] To keep the exercise manageable, the two-step analysis is undertaken by volunteering member states, acting either individually or as a group. Yet, all IMO member states, NGOs with consultative status, and IOs with observer status are able to comment upon their findings.[60] Since the current chapter focuses on possible regulatory techniques to integrate MASS into the IMO's legal framework, the second step of the RSE is of primary interest. The chapter will, therefore, turn to this issue after an analysis of the role that informal law has played in the IMO so far.

48 IMO, 'Report of the Legal Committee on the Work of its 105th Session' (1 May 2018) IMO Doc LEG 105/14, para 11.8; IMO, 'Report of the Facilitation Committee on its Forty-third Session' (23 April 2019) IMO Doc FAL 43/20, para 19.9.

49 Ringbom, 'Developments, Challenges, and Prospects at the IMO' (n 20) 58–59.

50 See, eg IMO Doc LEG 106/WP.5 (n 3), Annex, para 2.

51 Bureau Veritas, *Guidelines for Autonomous Shipping* (October 2019), s 3.3.1.

52 IMO Doc MSC 98/23 (n 4), para 20.2.11; IMO Doc FAL 43/20 (n 48), para 19.9.1.

53 IMO, 'Report of the Maritime Safety Committee on its 102nd Session' (30 November 2020) IMO Doc MSC 102/24, para 5.1.

54 IMO Doc LEG 105/14 (n 48), para 11.11.

55 IMO, 'Draft Report of the Legal Committee on the Work of its 107th Session' (1 December 2020) IMO Doc LEG 107/WP.1, para 8.7.

56 See IMO, 'Report of the Legal Committee on the Work of its 106th Session' (13 May 2019) IMO Doc LEG 106/16, para 8.5, and IMO Doc FAL 43/20 (n 48), para 19.9.2, reporting the decisions to apply the methodology developed by the MSC. For the sake of brevity, only the LEG methodology is referenced in the following text.

57 IMO Doc LEG 106/WP.5 (n 3), Annex, para 8.

58 ibid, para 4.

59 ibid, para 10.

60 ibid, app 3.

7.4 IMO and Informal Law

Absent a hard and fast definition of 'informal law', and in light of differing understandings of what the concept—often inadequately referred to as 'soft law'[61]—covers,[62] it is necessary to briefly outline how the term is used in the present chapter. Informal law denotes instruments that fulfil four criteria. First, from the qualifier 'informal' (or 'soft'), it follows that the instrument does not belong to a recognized source of international law[63] from which 'formal' (or 'hard') norms emanate. Second, as the word 'law' indicates, only 'normatively worded instruments'[64]—those having a regulatory character—amount to informal law as defined here:[65] that is, instruments governing persons, facts, or situations in a general and abstract way ('general-abstract').[66] Excluded from this definition are, thus, instruments resulting from, or involving, an application of norms to a specific case.[67] Third, despite being informal, these general-abstract norms possess, to varying degrees, normative implications—also termed 'normative effect',[68] 'normative value',[69] 'normative force',[70] 'quasi-legal effect',[71] or 'law-like consequences'[72]—as they 'channel the conduct'[73] or curtail the freedom of the respective addressees. Fourth, states or IOs are either the creators of the instruments, or they 'endorse' instruments elaborated by private actors[74] without public authority involvement.[75] The term 'endorsement' is used here to denote acts of states or IOs that express their approval of a given set of norms resulting from exclusively private cooperation, and by which the public instrument becomes clothed with a certain degree of public authority. Such 'endorsement' can take various forms—it can, for instance, consist of the issuance of a (non-binding) resolution underlying a commitment to implement a private

[61] What follows underlines the finding in Joost Pauwelyn, Ramses A Wessel, and Jan Wouters, 'Informal International Lawmaking: An Assessment and Template to Keep It Both Effective and Accountable' in Joost Pauwelyn, Ramses A Wessel, and Jan Wouters (eds), *Informal International Lawmaking* (OUP 2012) 534 that there is nothing 'soft' in many norms belonging to informal law.

[62] Alan Boyle, 'Soft Law in International Law-making' in Malcolm D Evans (ed), *International Law* (5th edn, OUP 2018) 121.

[63] See, eg Anthea Roberts and Sandesh Sivakumaran, 'The Theory and Reality of the Sources of International Law' in Malcolm D Evans (ed), *International Law* (5th edn, OUP 2018) 89–118.

[64] Term borrowed from Boyle, 'Soft Law in International Law-making' (n 62) 121.

[65] This second criterion is necessary since the first one—that 'informal law' must not belong to a source of international law—is insufficient, because treaties may govern a specific situation resulting from the application of the law (eg a border treaty).

[66] For an incisive description of the elements 'general' and 'abstract', see Edward Yemin, *Legislative Powers in the United Nations and Specialized Agencies* (AW Sijthoff 1996) 5–6.

[67] Dinah Shelton, 'Soft Law' in David Armstrong (ed), *Routledge Handbook of International Law* (Routledge 2009) 70 denotes this type of informal instruments as 'secondary soft law'.

[68] Klein, in Chapter 1 of this volume.

[69] *Legality of the Threat or Use of Nuclear Weapons* (Advisory Opinion) [1996] ICJ Rep 254, para 70.

[70] Thomas Gammeltoft-Hansen, 'The Normative Impact of the Global Compact on Refugees' (2018) 30(4) IJRL 605, 607.

[71] Frederic L Kirgis, 'Specialized Law-making Processes' in Oscar Schachter and Christopher C Joyner (eds), *United Nations Legal Order*, vol 1 (CUP 1995) 159.

[72] Shelton (n 67) 68.

[73] Kirgis, 'Specialized Law-Making Processes' (n 71) 109.

[74] In international law, the divide between 'public' and 'private' is less clear than in the domestic sphere. Here, the term 'private actors' is used to refer to actors other than states and Ios.

[75] The definition is, thus, broader than the one by Joost Pauwelyn, 'Informal International Lawmaking: Framing the Concept and Research Questions' in Joost Pauwelyn, Ramses A Wessel, and Jan Wouters (eds), *Informal International Lawmaking* (OUP 2012) 19, which requires 'public authority involvement'.

standard[76]—and some endorsements considerably enhance the normative effects of these instruments.[77]

The IMO, which is, at times, dubbed a 'standard-setting organization',[78] definitely engages in 'informal lawmaking' as just defined. As regards the first criterion, Henry writes that the 'IMO's legislative instruments can be classified into two broad categories: those of a formal nature and those which are less formal ... [t]he former category includes treaties, the latter recommendations.'[79] She continues by stating that, actually, the only kind of instruments that can be issued by the IMO itself are recommendations.[80] Indeed, even though treaties are facilitated by the Organization, they are ultimately adopted by the member states and are, thus, not attributable to the IMO.[81] By contrast, as per its founding treaty, the IMO is competent to issue recommendations.[82] In theory, a clear dividing line can, thus, be drawn between formal instruments (in IMO parlance, 'mandatory') and informal instruments[83] (in IMO argot, 'recommendatory' or 'not ... mandatory instruments for treaty purposes'[84]). Yet, in practice, which of these two 'boxes' a given instrument falls into—and thus its legal status—has not always been readily determinable.[85]

The term 'recommendations' in Article 2 of the IMO Convention does not refer to a specific type of unilateral act adopted by an organ of the IMO, but, rather, delineates the Organization's powers.[86] Indeed, recommendations—which come under a variety of names,[87] such as guidelines, guidance, regulations, or codes, to name but a few—are issued through different types of unilateral acts, most notably resolutions and circulars.[88] Generally, recommendations are included as an annex to the respective unilateral act.[89] In terms of content, not every recommendatory unilateral act of the IMO possesses the 'lawmaking' characteristics necessary to fulfil the second criterion of our 'informal law'

[76] Eg, the (informal) 'Copenhagen Declaration on Anti-doping in Sport', by which the 193 signatory states 'signalled their intention to formally recognize and implement the World Anti-doping Code' elaborated by private actors: WADA, 'Governments' <www.wada-ama.org/en/who-we-are/anti-doping-community/governments#CopenhagenDeclaration> accessed 1 April 2021.

[77] See text below, accompanying nn 128–3.

[78] See, eg Balkin (n 41) 10.

[79] Cleopatra Elmira Henry, *The Carriage of Dangerous Goods by Sea: The Role of the International Maritime Organization in International Legislation* (Frances Pinter 1985) 58.

[80] ibid.

[81] See IMO Convention (n 2), art 2(b). Various IMO treaties foresee an accelerated amendment procedure (the so-called 'tacit acceptance procedure'), whereby the amendments are adopted by the competent IMO organ, and are deemed to be accepted after the expiry of a certain period of time, unless a predefined number of states parties objected. States, thus, accept the amendments through tacit consent (that is, by not opting out): see Doris König, 'Tacit Consent/Opting Out Procedure' (last updated January 2013) in Anne Peters (ed), *Max Planck Encyclopaedia of Public International Law*, online edition <https://opil.ouplaw.com/home/mpil>, paras 1 and 9–10.

[82] IMO Convention (n 2), art 2(a).

[83] But see Wilhelm H Lampe, 'The "New" International Maritime Organization and its Place in Development of International Maritime Law' (1983) 14(3) J Mar L & Com 305, 318, questioning the binary approach by arguing that IMO Codes 'rank somewhere in between' binding and advisory; similarly, Hélène Lefebvre-Chalain, *La stratégie normative de l'Organisation maritime nternational (OMI)* (Presses universitaires d'Aix-Marseille 2012) 174.

[84] IMO, 'Uniform Wording for Referencing IMO Instruments' (22 January 2002) IMO Doc A 22/Res.911, preambular paras 1–2.

[85] Such difficulty arises, for instance, when informal law is referenced in IMO treaties. To clarify the effect of such references on the legal status of informal law (whether they become part of the treaty or not), the IMO adopted the 'Guidelines on Methods for Making Reference to IMO and Other Instruments in IMO Conventions and Other Mandatory Instruments' IMO Doc A 22/Res.911 (n 84) Annex.

[86] Lefebvre-Chalain (n 83) 171.

[87] Henry (n 79) 73.

[88] Thomas A Mensah and Christoph H Zimmerli, 'L'activité réglementaire de l'OMCI' in Société Française pour le Droit International (ed), *L'élaboration du droit international public* (Éditions A Pedone 1975) 45.

[89] See, eg IMO, 'Interim Guidelines for MASS Trials' (14 June 2019) IMO Doc MSC.1/Circ.1604.

definition. Rather, unilateral acts may serve other purposes, such as coordinating state action, supporting the implementation of treaties, or governing a specific situation.[90]

As regards the third criterion, it would be an exaggeration to state that all IMO recommendations have normative effect.[91] Still, many feature 'more than hortatory design and effect',[92] and some may even possess 'normative significance bordering on authoritative command',[93] with an impact 'virtually equal to ... that of treaty obligations'.[94] At times, even draft recommendations feature normative effects.[95] Explanations provided in doctrine for the (sometimes high) degree of normative force of IMO recommendations can be categorized, roughly, as those relating to the issuer, the process of their adoption, or their content.

In terms of the issuer, it is argued that recommendations of the IMO carry 'great weight since no other organization has authority in this field',[96] and that their legal force is due to the '*autorité morale de son auteur*'.[97] It is further held that they 'command respect' because UN specialized agencies, such as the IMO, are 'recognized as legitimate by the members'.[98] As will be seen later, norms elaborated by private actors—notably by classification societies—play an (increasingly) important role in the IMO's ocean governance model.[99] It is through various 'endorsement' techniques deployed by the Organization—to which this chapter will turn later[100]—that norms issued through purely private cooperation become clothed with the authority of the IMO, which is essential for their normative effects.

The effectiveness of IMO recommendations is further explained by the characteristics of the process through which they are adopted.[101] Indeed, various commentators stress the 'inclusive approach to regulation-making' pursued by the IMO:[102] that is, that norms are issued in a procedure that provides members with 'a meaningful opportunity to participate'.[103] It is highlighted that IMO organs participating in informal lawmaking meet at regular intervals, and follow well-structured work programmes and agendas published in due time, which enable states to make written submissions and prepare their delegations.[104] Moreover, emphasis is put on the fact that IMO organs competent to adopt recommendations are open to all member states.[105] Indeed, membership of the IMO is almost universal, in the sense that the 174 member states,[106] which include all major maritime

[90] Henry (n 79) 5.

[91] Henrik Ringbom, *The EU Maritime Safety Policy and International Law* (Martinus Nijhoff 2008) 24.

[92] Kirgis, 'Specialized Law-making Processes' (n 71) 157; see also ibid 146, where Kirgis terms those informal instruments 'super-recommendations', and provides, as an example, the IDG Code.

[93] Kirgis, 'Shipping' (n 9) 732.

[94] Kirgis, 'Specialized Law-making Processes' (n 71) 154.

[95] ibid 158 (providing the example of draft recommendations for the removal of disused offshore platforms).

[96] Patricia Birnie, 'The Status of Environmental "Soft Law": Trends and Examples with Special Focus on IMO Norms' in Henrik Ringbom (ed), *Competing Norms in the Law of Marine Environmental Protection—Focus on Ship Safety and Pollution Prevention* (Kluwer Law International 1997) 48.

[97] Lefebvre-Chalain (n 83) 174 ('moral authority of its author').

[98] Kirgis, 'Specialized Law-making Processes' (n 71) 109.

[99] See text accompanying n 132.

[100] See text accompanying nn 128-34.

[101] See Obinna Okere, 'The Technique of International Maritime Legislation' (1981) 30 ICLQ 513, 531.

[102] Balkin (n 41) 25.

[103] Kirgis, 'Specialized Law-making Processes' (n 71) 159.

[104] Balkin (n 41) 25–26.

[105] Gaetano Librando, 'The International Maritime Organization and the Law of the Sea' in David J Attard, Malgosia Fitzmaurice, and Norman A Martínez Gutiérrez (eds), *The IMLI Manual on International Maritime Law, Volume I: The Law of the Sea* (OUP 2014) 582.

[106] IMO, 'Status of Conventions' <https://wwwcdn.imo.org/localresources/en/About/Conventions/StatusOfConventions/StatusOfTreaties.pdf> accessed 1 April 2021.

nations,[107] represent 97.36 % of the world merchant shipping tonnage.[108] Furthermore, recommendations are, as a general rule, adopted by consensus, and thus reflect broad agreement between the member states.[109] The fact that IOs and NGOs—notably representing the shipping sector and environmental interests—actively and successfully[110] participate in the lawmaking process[111] is further said to lead to 'regulations that are balanced, pragmatic, and affordable, making member states in turn more inclined to accept and to implement them'.[112] Overall, this approach echoes the view that the key 'to effective norm-promulgation by codes and guidelines [is] the care with which they are prepared'.[113]

Lastly, the effectiveness of informal law is considered to be higher if it relates to subject matters in which some type of international regulation is largely considered important.[114] As regards IMO recommendations, they have been perceived as 'necessary',[115] or even 'indispensable',[116] by the international community, for ensuring safe, secure, and environmentally sound shipping operations. In light of the international dimension of shipping, 'the need for conformity and unity in standards' was recognized early on by the industry,[117] not only to 'maintain a sound image' and 'create a level playing field',[118] but also because of a potential 'sanction of non-participation', such as insurers denying coverage to non-compliant vessels or increasing premiums.[119] More broadly, it is argued that non-mandatory IMO instruments are adopted for their 'practical utility',[120] and that conformity with them is 'motivated not by compulsion but by the idea of mutual benefit'.[121]

In addition to these explanations, it seems possible to argue that effectiveness is enhanced in cases where a link between informal and formal law is established, for example through references to informal law in treaties. Such references do not include incorporation by reference: that is, references in IMO treaties to informal law through which the latter becomes part of the treaty.[122] Rather, certain types of references to informal law in IMO treaties—for instance, in footnotes—do not alter the legal status of the informal instrument. They are generally included with the aim of substantiating a treaty obligation in a specific way. Hence, such references have an impact on the treaty, but also a ripple effect on the informal instrument, as its normative force is increased through the linkage with formal law. This effect is described well in the following quotation stemming from IMO guidelines on methods of referencing recommendatory instruments in IMO treaties:

[107] Harilaos N Psaraftis and Christos A Kontovas, 'Influence and Transparency at the IMO: The Name of the Game' (2020) 22 Mar Econ Logist 151, 154.

[108] See IMO, 'Status of Conventions' (n 106).

[109] Ringbom, The EU Maritime Safety Policy and International Law (n 91) 23; similarly, Librando (n 105) 582.

[110] Especially NGOs representing business interests: see Aldo Chircop, 'The International Maritime Organization' in Donald R Rothwell, Alex G Oude Elferink, Karen N Scott, and Tim Stephens (eds), *The Oxford Handbook of the Law of the Sea* (OUP 2015) 426–27.

[111] For an overview of participating Ios and NGOs, see Psaraftis and Kontovas (n 107) 154–55.

[112] Balkin (n 41) 26.

[113] Kirgis, 'Specialized Law-making Processes' (n 71) 154.

[114] ibid 159.

[115] Balkin (n 41) 26.

[116] Kirgis, 'Shipping' (n 9) 732.

[117] Lost-Sieminska (n 13) 907.

[118] Birnie (n 96) 48.

[119] Wolfgang Graf Vitzthum, 'Schiffsicherheit: Die EG als potentieller Durchsetzungsdegen der IMO' (2002) 62 Heidelberg JIL 163, 166.

[120] Okere (n 101) 530.

[121] David J Padwa, 'The Curriculum of IMCO' (1960) 14(4) Int Org 524, 534.

[122] This type of reference is described in IMO Doc A 22/Res.911 (n 84), Annex, paras 2–5.

> Such standards and specifications [IMO recommendations] referred to in the footnotes [of IMO treaties] are *not regarded as mandatory instruments for treaty purposes*, since they do not appear in the authentic text of the parent convention and can be updated by the Secretariat as necessary; hence, they do not constitute an integral part of the parent convention. *Nevertheless*, Contracting Governments or Parties to the parent conventions are *obliged to* establish national standards not inferior, or at least equivalent, to those developed by the Organization.[123]

References of this type may also relate to external informal law, that is instruments developed outside the IMO by private actors, such as the International Organization for Standardization, the International Electrotechnical Commission, and, most importantly, the International Association of Classification Societies (IACS).[124]

This brings us to the last element of the informal law definition, which pertains to the actors issuing the instruments in question. While some commentators exclude norms adopted without public authority involvement from informal law,[125] the definition proposed in this chapter includes them, provided that states or IOs 'endorse' them. To disregard norms elaborated by private actors would provide an incomplete picture of the normative framework governing the world of shipping. Historically speaking, the improvement of safety at sea was long considered to be a private matter, and it was only during the mid-nineteenth century that governments, progressively, became involved.[126] This legacy still resonates in the IMO, where private normative instruments continue to form an important complement to regulations elaborated by the Organization itself.[127]

Within the IMO, various types of 'endorsement' of private instruments can be observed. References in treaties to informal law that do not change the legal status of the latter have already been mentioned. Another type of endorsement is the verification of conformity process, in the context of the so-called goal-based standards (GBS). As the name indicates, GBS do not set out detailed prescriptive rules at the level of the treaty, but only the goal to be attained and the criteria (so-called 'functional requirements') to be satisfied in order to achieve it.[128] The detailed regulations necessary to implement the GBS, in turn, are developed outside the treaty and, to a certain extent, even outside the IMO, notably through private actors such as classification societies or the industry (for instance, shipbuilders).[129] Yet, in a verification of conformity process, the IMO assesses whether these private rule sets are in line with the goals and functional requirements defined at the level of the treaty.[130]

[123] IMO Doc A 22/Res.911 (n 84), Annex, para 6 (emphasis added).

[124] ibid, para 18.

[125] See Pauwelyn (n 75).

[126] Philippe Boisson, 'Law of Maritime Safety' in David J Attard, Malgosia Fitzmaurice, Norman A Martínez Gutiérrez, and Elda Belja (eds), *The IMLI Manual on International Maritime Law, Volume II: Shipping Law* (OUP 2016) 180.

[127] ibid 184.

[128] The first GBS were adopted in the SOLAS Convention: see Chapter II-1, reg 3–10, which sets the goal regarding the design and construction of bulk carriers and oil tankers (IMO, 'Report of the Maritime Safety Committee on its Eighty-seventh Session' (30 June 2010) IMO Doc MSC 87/26/Add.1, Annex 4). The functional requirements were defined in a resolution of the MSC (see ibid, Annex 1), which became mandatory through a reference in the aforementioned SOLAS regulation.

[129] See IMO, 'Generic Guidelines for Developing IMO Goal-based Standards' (14 June 2011) IMO Doc MSC.1/Circ.1394, Annex, paras 17–18.

[130] ibid, paras 13–16.

Those deemed to be in conformity are published by the IMO,[131] and therewith become an indispensable part of the GBS framework. It is, arguably, no exaggeration to state that those private informal law instruments that get the 'IMO seal' feature normative effects similar to those of formal law.[132] Yet another type of 'endorsement' is the adoption of unified interpretations (UIs) by the competent IMO organ,[133] which are based on interpretations previously developed by the IACS.[134]

The analysis above has defined the concept of 'informal law', and applied it to instruments issued or 'endorsed' by the IMO. An analysis of informal law*making* focusing solely on the output would, however, be incomplete, as informality can also sit with the actors and/or the process.[135] As far as IMO recommendations are concerned, there is little informality with regard to either. Indeed, actors and processes are the same for recommendations and treaties, in terms of the submission of a proposal, assessment of the need for a respective outcome, assignment of the task to a body, and elaboration of the text. Only in the final phase—where a decision must be taken whether the text is submitted to a diplomatic conference (treaty) or the competent IMO organ (recommendation) for adoption—does the process start to bifurcate.[136] Private instruments, by contrast, may have been elaborated by actors and in processes featuring a high degree of informality. However, the various 'endorsement' techniques applied by the IMO are standardized to a great extent through non-mandatory IMO instruments, such as the guidelines on referencing informal law in IMO treaties[137] or the verification of GBS.[138] Overall, actor and process informality are not at all pronounced in IMO informal lawmaking, thus distinguishing this form of informal lawmaking from endeavours where actors and processes are (deliberately) not predefined, and are only specified as the project unfolds ('wait-and-see approach').[139]

To date, the IMO has adopted over 1,000 recommendations covering the entire spectrum of the Organization's mandate.[140] It is, thus, certainly apposite to argue that the IMO has exploited its recommendatory competence to its maximum,[141] and that it participates in the broader trend of international organizations increasingly relying on informal rather than

[131] See, eg IMO, 'Promulgation of Rules for the Design and Construction of Bulk Carriers and Oil Tankers Confirmed by the Maritime Safety Committee to be in Conformity with the Goal-based Ship Construction Standards for Bulk Carriers and Oil Tankers' (4 December 2018) IMO Doc MSC.1/Circ.1518/Rev.1, Annex.

[132] As the IACS is a prime norm-submitter, it will 'play an even more significant role' in IMO lawmaking: Ismael Cobos Delgado, 'The Role of the Classification Societies in Promoting Global Ocean Governance' in David J Attard, Rosalie P Balkin, and Donald W Greig (eds), *The IMLI Treatise on Global Ocean Governance, Volume III: The IMO and Global Ocean Governance* (OUP 2018) 274.

[133] On Uis, see text accompanying n 169 ff.

[134] For a recent example, see DNV, 'IMO Maritime Safety Committee' (11 November 2020) <www.dnv.com/news/imo-maritime-safety-committee-189482> accessed 1 April 2021, as per which the Uis adopted by the IMO were based on unified interpretations elaborated by IACS.

[135] See, eg definition by Pauwelyn (n 75) 22.

[136] Henry (n 79) 84; for an overview on the procedure, see ibid 59–60.

[137] See n 85.

[138] See IMO, 'Revised Guidelines for Verification of Conformity with Goal-based Ship Construction Standards for Bulk Carriers and Oil Tankers', Annex 3 to IMO, 'Report of the Maritime Safety Committee on its One-hundredth Session' (12 December 2018) IMO Doc MSC 100/20/Add.1.

[139] Anna Petrig, 'Democratic Participation in International Lawmaking in Switzerland after the "Age of Treaties"' in Helmut P Aust and Thomas Kleinlein (eds), *Encounters between Foreign Relations Law and International Law: Bridges and Boundaries* (CUP 2021) 209.

[140] IMO, 'IMO–What It Is, OMI–Ce qu'elle est, OMI–Qué es', 4 <www.imo.org/en/About/Pages/Default.aspx> accessed 15 February 2021.

[141] Lefebvre-Chalain (n 83) 173.

formal law.[142] This begs the question of what role informal law could play in the context of regulating MASS, to which we now turn.

7.5 Informal Law and MASS

The RSE, which is, currently, the IMO's main effort in assessing the need to amend the regulatory framework in order to enable the safe, secure, and environmentally responsible operation of MASS, takes as a starting point the treaties for which the Organization is responsible.[143] Against this backdrop, it seems fitting to discuss the potential role of informal law alongside its various functions in relation to treaties. As Boyle stresses, the relationship of informal law to treaties is 'both subtle and diverse'.[144] Indeed, a distinction can be drawn between its post-law, pre-law, and para-law functions,[145] depending on whether the informal instrument in question is intended to complement, prepare, or replace formal law.[146]

First, this section explores the post-law function of informal law, that is its potential role and value in the process of interpreting existing treaties in light of MASS. Second, the section sketches how informal law may pave the way for the enactment of new treaty rules (pre-law function), and to what extent it may replace them altogether (para-law function). In doing so, reference is made to views that have been expressed by states and other entities in the course of the RSE. Yet, these must only be understood as exemplary and preliminary, as the RSE is ongoing. Moreover, at times, views on the appropriate path forward diverge,[147] or making a choice is deemed either premature[148] or requiring a preceding policy decision.[149]

7.5.1 Post-law Function of Informal Law: Informing the Interpretation of Treaties

The interim results of the RSE indicate that the integration of MASS into the existing legal framework raises a significant number of legal issues. Some relate to concepts that appear in specific conventions only,[150] while others pertain to terms or elements featuring in several IMO treaties.[151] In the latter category, the concept of the 'master' figures prominently,[152] in relation to which, simply put, clarification is needed as to who performs this role, and its

142 ibid 236.
143 See section 7.3 above.
144 Alan E Boyle, 'Some Reflections on the Relationship of Treaties and Soft Law' (1999) 48 ICLQ 901, 913.
145 Linda Senden, *Soft Law in European Community Law* (Hart 2004) 120.
146 ibid 31.
147 See, eg IMO Doc MSC 102/5/3 (n 19), paras 16–17 (charts providing overview on chosen options).
148 See, eg IMO, 'Summary of Results of the Second Step of the RSE for SOLAS Chapter II-2 and Associated Codes' (17 February 2020) IMO Doc MSC 102/5/19, para 5.
149 See, eg IMO, 'Summary of Results of the LEG Regulatory Scoping Exercise for the International Convention on Civil Liability for Oil Pollution Damage, 1992 (1992 CLC)' (8 January 2020) IMO Doc LEG 107/8/2, para 11.
150 See list in IMO Doc LEG 107/8 (n 22), paras 13–26.
151 ibid, para 5.
152 See, eg IMO, 'Summary of Results of the First and Second Steps of the RSE for the Nairobi International Convention on the Removal of Wrecks, 2007' (20 December 2019) IMO Doc LEG 107/8/1, para 8; IMO Doc MSC 102/5/3 (n 19), Annex 4, 1; IMO, 'Summary of Results of the Second Step of the RSE for SAR 1979 Convention' (11 February 2020) IMO Doc MSC 102/5/13, paras 20.

functions, if the vessel is without on-board crew.[153] Another cross-cutting issue pertains to the certificates that ships must carry, according to various IMO instruments: notably, how these could be requested and produced, absent seafarers aboard vessels, and what format they could take.[154] Horizontal issues also appear in provisions governing liability: for example, it is unclear what provisions referring to the mental states of human beings who engage in specific conduct (such as 'negligence' or 'intention') imply, if a machine rather than a person is acting.[155]

Deliberations by the competent IMO committees on the most appropriate way forward to address these and further issues have yet to take place.[156] Nevertheless, some lines of convergence and divergence can already be discerned at this stage. First of all, interpretation is considered a suitable approach for a great deal of issues,[157] and is generally deemed a 'lighter' response than amendments[158] 'to accommodate newly developed technologies and increasing automation' in IMO treaties.[159] An exception to this approach can, however, be found in the (seemingly rare) instances where existing provisions prevent the operation of MASS altogether. Solving such hard conflicts appears to require amendment of rules, or the creation of new ones.[160] Even where tensions are less pronounced, some participants have expressed a preference for amendment over interpretation, for the sake of legal certainty,[161] especially where such provisions 'impose obligations on a person'.[162] Views also differ on how to proceed in relation to horizontal issues. Some have cautiously suggested that the IMO could pursue an 'overriding' approach to interpretation or amendment,[163] while others have expressed reluctance to do so, as the same term may carry different meanings and functions in different treaties, or even in the distinctive provisions of the same treaty.[164]

The RSE methodology does not provide any further specification regarding the option of 'developing interpretations'.[165] From the interim results of the RSE, the option is understood to entail only interpretations undertaken at the international level, and not interpretations at the domestic level by individual (flag) states.[166] Yet, so far, it has not crystallized from

[153] IMO Doc LEG 107/8 (n 22), para 7.

[154] See, eg ibid para 12; IMO, 'Summary of Results of the LEG Regulatory Scoping Exercise for the Athens Convention Relating to the Carriage of Passengers and their Luggage by Sea, 2002' (10 January 2020) IMO Doc LEG 107/8/13, para 9.5.

[155] IMO Doc LEG 107/8 (n 22), para 8.1.

[156] On the schedule of the RSE, see text accompanying nn 52–55.

[157] See, eg IMO Doc MSC 102/5/3 (n 19), para 21; IMO, 'Summary of Results of the LEG Regulatory Scoping Exercise of the International Convention on Salvage, 1989' (10 January 2020) IMO Doc LEG 107/8/11, paras 7.4–7.5; IMO, 'Summary of Results of the LEG Regulatory Scoping Exercise for the Athens Convention Relating to the Carriage of Passengers and their Luggage by Sea, 1974' (10 January 2020) IMO Doc LEG 107/8/12, para 7; IMO, 'Summary of Results of the Second Step of the Regulatory Scoping Exercise for the International Convention on Tonnage Measurement of Ships, 1969 (TONNAGE 1969)' (10 February 2020) IMO Doc MSC 102/5/8, para 8.

[158] IMO Doc LEG 107/8 (n 22), para 28.

[159] IMO Doc MSC 102/5/3 (n 19), para 21.

[160] See, eg IMO Doc LEG 107/8 (n 22), para 27.

[161] See, eg IMO Doc LEG 107/8/1 (n 152), para 7.4.

[162] See, eg IMO Doc MSC 102/5/19 (n 148), para 10.

[163] See, eg IMO Doc LEG 107/8 (n 22), para 5; see IMO Doc LEG 107/8/13 (n 154), para 9.5.

[164] See, eg IMO, 'Summary of the Results of the Second Step of the RSE for SOLAS Chapter VI and Associated Codes' (17 February 2020) IMO Doc MSC 102/5/20, para 8.

[165] See IMO Doc LEG 106/WP.5 (n 3), Annex, para 8.

[166] See, eg IMO, 'Summary of Results of the LEG Regulatory Scoping Exercise for the Convention for the Suppression of Unlawful Acts Against the Safety of Maritime Navigation, 1988' (9 January 2020) IMO Doc LEG 107/8/5, para 9, where the suggestion 'that any issues requiring legal interpretation can be made in *domestic* legal systems' (emphasis added) was not made under option one ('developing interpretations') but, rather, option four ('none of the above as a result of the analysis') of the RSE methodology.

the RSE whether interpretations will be provided by IMO organs[167] or, rather, by the states parties to the respective treaties.[168] In terms of tools deployed to achieve a uniform interpretation, reference was made, in the course of the RSE, to means applied by the IMO in the past, and which could apply in the context of MASS too, notably to UIs[169] and guidelines issued by the competent IMO committees.[170] As regards interpretations adopted by the IMO, two questions are of particular interest in the present context: first, whether these amount to informal law, as defined earlier; and, second, what their potential interpretative function and value could be.

As regards the informal law definition,[171] the first criterion—that the instrument must not belong to a formal source of international law—is clearly fulfilled, as IMO organs only possess recommendatory powers.[172] For UIs specifically, their non-mandatory character is underlined in a note by the secretariat, according to which the circulars containing them are 'inviting Member Governments to apply the UIs as appropriate or to use them as guidance and to bring them to the attention of all Parties concerned'.[173] True, consolidated versions of IMO treaties published by the Organization may comprise relevant UIs, but they clearly do not form part of the treaties.[174] Despite being informal, commentators attest that interpretations have certain normative force, as required by the third criterion of our informal law definition. Kirgis, for instance, states that IMO members 'treat committee interpretations as authoritative', and, in cases of disagreement, members would generally request their modification rather than simply flout them.[175] Explanations for the normative effects of IMO interpretative acts echo those provided for IMO recommendations in general. It is, for instance, argued that UIs 'contain valuable explanatory elaborations of the highly technical regulations' and are, therefore, of 'great practical utility for professional users' such as inspectors.[176] Further, with respect to MASS specifically, it is deemed possible to achieve 'a fairly high degree of uniformity as regards the application of a large number of provisions' through interpretative Assembly resolutions, because these are adopted by consensus.[177] Finally, the fourth criterion of the informal law definition—the need for public authority involvement—is undoubtedly also met, as IMO organs either issue the interpretations or 'endorse' private interpretations, for example by recasting unified interpretations developed by the IACS into UIs of the IMO.[178]

The least evident criterion of our definition is the second one: that the instrument contains 'law' or, in other words, governs persons, facts, or situations in a general and abstract

[167] Suggested in, eg IMO, 'Summary of Results of the LEG Regulatory Scoping Exercise for the Convention relating to Civil Liability in the Field of Maritime Carriage of Nuclear Material, 1971' submitted by Australia (9 January 2020) IMO Doc LEG 107/8/3, para 6.1; and IMO Doc LEG 107/8/11 (n 157), para 7.4.

[168] See, eg IMO Doc LEG 107/8 (n 22), para 28, vaguely referring to 'joint interpretation'.

[169] See, eg IMO Doc MSC 102/5/19 (n 148), para 8; IMO Doc MSC 102/5/20 (n 164), para 8; and IMO Doc LEG 107/8/2 (n 149), para 8.

[170] See, eg IMO Doc LEG 107/8/2 (n 149), para 18.

[171] See section 7.4 above.

[172] As regards the powers of IMO organs, in the context of amendments adopted under the tacit acceptance procedure, see n 81 above.

[173] IMO, 'Comments on Documents LEG 107/9, LEG 107/9/1 and LEG 197/INF.5' (24 January 2020) IMO Doc LEG 107/9/2, para 16.

[174] Proshanto K Mukherjee and Mark Brownrigg, *Farthing on International Shipping* (4th edn, Springer 2013) 276.

[175] Kirgis, 'Shipping' (n 9) 742.

[176] Mukherjee and Brownrigg (n 174) 276.

[177] Jacobsson (n 22) 282.

[178] See text accompanying n 134.

way. The International Law Commission (ILC) defines interpretation as 'the process by which the meaning of a treaty, including of one or more of its provisions, is clarified'.[179] Clarification of norms occurs, for example, in the process of applying the law to a specific case (interpretation *in concreto*). The content of instruments embodying such interpretation—say, a judgment or the view of a supervisory body—is not general-abstract, but instead could be considered individual-concrete. Thus, it is not 'law' as defined here.[180] Norms are, however, also interpreted in isolation from specific cases (interpretation in the *abstract*). If the result of this interpretative process is enshrined in an informal instrument directed at an indeterminate number of persons, and susceptible of repeated application—that is, one of a general-abstract character—it can be deemed to amount to 'law'.

UIs fall into the latter category of interpretation, as they are adopted 'to ensure uniform application of technical requirements containing vague expressions or other vague wording open to divergent interpretations, or to provide more specific guidance on certain provisions'[181] absent any link with a concrete situation. Rather, they are 'normatively worded' and could, theoretically, form part of the treaty they complement. The description of UIs by Mukherjee and Brownrigg as 'detailed supplementary texts' that 'serve as an interpretive tool' for those tasked with applying relevant provisions of the Convention[182] is, therefore, quite fitting.

The general-abstract character is even more pronounced when it comes to guidelines. Unlike UIs, these are usually not limited to the clarification of a specific treaty term. Rather, they are self-standing regulatory instruments that specify, or even develop, certain aspects or themes appearing in one or several treaties. Thus, for instance, the IMO Guidelines for the Use of Electronic Certificates,[183] which are referenced in the RSE as a regulatory model for addressing the horizontal issue of certificates in the context of MASS,[184] address the use of electronic certificates in a rather comprehensive fashion. After stating the purpose of the guidance and defining key terms, these guidelines stipulate rules on the features of electronic certificates and the verification of their content, as well as the notification and acceptance of their use. Since the concept of certificates appears in a range of IMO treaties,[185] the guidelines display their interpretative effect 'horizontally'. By contrast, UIs hone in on a very specific aspect of a treaty with the aim of clarifying and specifying it, and, thus, operate 'vertically'.

The MSC, FAL, and MEPC have approved a significant number of UIs in the past,[186] while the LEG has not yet done so.[187] However, the LEG has developed interpretations that were ultimately adopted in the form of Assembly resolutions.[188] It did so in cases where

[179] ILC, 'Draft Conclusions on Subsequent Agreements and Subsequent Practice in relation to the Interpretation of Treaties, With Commentaries' in *Yearbook of the International Law Commission*, vol II, pt 2 (2018) 43.

[180] See Shelton (n 67), and text of n 67, on 'secondary soft law', which is excluded from the definition used in this chapter.

[181] IMO Doc LEG 107/9/2 (n 173), para 16.

[182] Mukherjee and Brownrigg (n 174) 276.

[183] IMO, 'Guidelines for the Use of Electronic Certificates' (20 April 2016) IMO Doc FAL.5/Circ.39/Rev.2, Annex.

[184] IMO Doc LEG 107/8/2 (n 149), para 18.

[185] See IMO Doc FAL.5/Circ.39/Rev.2 (n 183), Annex, r 6, referring to three circulars listing the (many) certificates that ships must carry by virtue of different IMO treaties.

[186] IMO Doc LEG 107/9/2 (n 173), para 16.

[187] ibid, para 17.

[188] ibid.

'differing interpretations' existed in relation to a treaty[189] or a specific provision,[190] with the aim of 'remov[ing] ambiguity', and assisting states to apply the treaty 'in a uniform manner'.[191] As per the IMO secretariat, 'these resolutions do not generally use declaratory interpretative language'.[192] Indeed, in contrast to UIs and guidelines, not all recommendations comprised in this type of resolution are structured like 'law',[193] and some, instead, solicit conduct from state parties that furthers the correct implementation of the treaty.[194] Generally speaking,[195] both UIs and guidelines of the sort being considered here clearly fulfil the second criterion of our informal law definition—being 'law'—while interpretative Assembly resolutions may have a mixed character. In sum, all three IMO acts considered here—UIs, guidelines, and interpretative Assembly resolutions—may be characterized as informal law instruments. This conclusion broaches the subject of their potential function and weight in the interpretative process.

Articles 31 and 32 of the Vienna Convention on the Law of Treaties (VCLT)[196] do not expressly refer to informal law as a means of interpretation, yet doctrine and practice lend support to the idea that such law informs the interpretative process in a number of ways.[197] First of all, informal law instruments may embody 'a subsequent agreement between the parties regarding the interpretation of the treaty', in the sense of Article 31(3)(a) of the VCLT. In accordance with the ILC, such agreements 'contribute, in their interaction with other means of interpretation, to the clarification of the meaning of a treaty'.[198] Such clarification may, notably, consist of narrowing or widening the range of possible interpretations,[199] and indicating whether the parties intended to provide a given term with a meaning 'capable of evolving over time'.[200] Since subsequent agreements are 'objective evidence of the understanding of the parties as to the meaning of the treaty',[201] they are considered to be authentic interpretations.[202] As a result, although not being conclusive, in the sense of overriding all other means of interpretation,[203] they play an 'important role'[204] and

[189] Eg, IMO, 'Issue of Bunkers Certificates to Ships that are also Required to Hold a CLC Certificate' (20 December 2011) IMO Doc A 27/Res.1055, preambular para 6.

[190] Eg, IMO, 'Issue of Bunkers Certificates to Bareboat-registered Vessels' (18 January 2010) IMO Doc A 26/Res. 1028.

[191] ibid, preambular paras 4-6; IMO Doc A 27/Res.1055 (n 189), preambular para 7.

[192] IMO Doc LEG 107/9/2 (n 173), para 17, referring, inter alia, to the instruments cited in nn 189 and 190.

[193] 'Law'-like is, eg IMO Doc A 27/Res.1055 (n 189), para 1.2, recommending that states parties 'require ships ... to be insured and to hold a bunkers certificate as prescribed by the Bunkers Convention even when the ships concerned already hold a CLC certificate'.

[194] See, eg IMO Doc A 27/Res.1055 (n 189), para 1.3, recommending that states parties 'avoid taking action that could cause unnecessary bureaucracy'.

[195] Ultimately, each instrument must be considered separately, to assess whether its content amounts to 'law'.

[196] Vienna Convention on the Law of Treaties (adopted 23 May 1969, entered into force 27 January 1980) 1155 UNTS 331 (hereafter 'VCLT').

[197] André Nollkaemper, 'The Distinction between Non-legal and Legal Norms in International Affairs: An Analysis with reference to International Policy for the Protection of the North Sea from Hazardous Substances' (1998) 13(3) IJMCL 355, 364.

[198] ILC, 'Draft Conclusions' (n 179) 51, Conclusion 7(1).

[199] ibid.

[200] Ibid 64, Conclusion 8.

[201] ibid 23, Conclusion 3.

[202] Robert Kolb, *The Law of Treaties* (Edward Elgar 2016) 130–31: authentic in the narrow sense, meaning interpretations adopted jointly by all parties to the treaty.

[203] As per art 31(3) VCLT (n 196), they shall solely 'be taken into account' in the interpretation of the treaty, which consists of a 'single combined operation' with no hierarchy among the various means of interpretation mentioned in the provision: ILC, 'Draft Conclusions' (n 179) 17, Conclusion 2(5), 24–25, and 51.

[204] ILC, 'Draft Conclusions' (n 179) 23.

'possess a specific authority' in discerning the meaning of the treaty.[205] As a rule of thumb, the greater their clarity and specificity, the more interpretative weight they have.[206]

To determine whether UIs, guidelines, and interpretative Assembly resolutions qualify as subsequent agreements, three elements must be considered, which relate to the issuer, the agreement, and the time. As regards the latter, only 'subsequent' agreements fall under Article 31(3)(a) of the VCLT, that is those reached after the text of the treaty to be interpreted has been established as definitive.[207] Since the RSE relates to treaties already adopted or in force, potential prospective interpretations clearly fulfil this temporal requirement. The crux, rather, lies in the issuer of the interpretations. The wording of Article 31(3)(a) of the VCLT indicates that the agreement must be reached between all the parties to the treaty in question,[208] although the ILC acknowledges that decisions adopted by a conference of states parties—representing a 'particular form of action by States'[209]—may also embody a subsequent agreement.[210] Yet, only conferences where states act on their own behalf qualify, not conferences that are actually an organ of an IO in which states act in their capacity as members of that organ.[211] Unlike other international institutions, where there is complete convergence between the members of the organ and the states parties to the treaty establishing the organ,[212] the two circles do not overlap in this case, as none of the IMO treaties have been ratified by all 174 IMO members, and some by only a very small fraction of members.[213] Thus, the difference between the two potential adopters of interpretations not only exists conceptually, but materially as well. In IMO practice, UIs, guidelines, and Assembly resolutions are approved by the Organization's organs, and not by the states parties to the treaty subject to interpretation.[214] Thus, they cannot amount to subsequent agreements, in the sense of Article 31(3)(a) of the VCLT.[215] However, various treaties for which the IMO is responsible foresee conferences of the former type where states, in their capacity as parties to the relevant treaty, meet for purposes of its implementation and development.[216] Some conferences have issued interpretative resolutions in the past that the IMO secretariat qualified as subsequent agreements.[217] In a nutshell, to amount to a subsequent agreement, in the sense of Article 31(3)(a) of the VCLT, an interpretative resolution must be reached by the states parties of the treaty to be interpreted, rather than the IMO organ. However, to keep organizational efforts reasonable, such conferences of states parties

[205] ibid 24.

[206] ibid 70, Conclusion 9(1).

[207] ibid 27; agreements concluded in close temporal connection with the treaty itself fall under art 31(2)(a) VCLT (n 196).

[208] ILC, 'Draft Conclusions' (n 179) 28. On authentic interpretation being a prerogative of the parties to the treaty, see Oliver Dörr, 'Article 31' in Oliver Dörr and Kirsten Schmalenbach (eds), *Vienna Convention on the Law of Treaties: A Commentary* (2nd edn, Springer 2018) 570.

[209] ILC, 'Draft Conclusions' (n 179) 82.

[210] ibid, Conclusion 11(2).

[211] ibid 82–83.

[212] Eg, the International Whaling Commission, which the ILC considers to be 'a borderline case' between the two categories of conferences explained earlier: ibid 83.

[213] Thus, eg only seventeen states are party to the Convention Relating to Civil Liability in the Field of Maritime Carriage of Nuclear Material: see IMO, 'Status of Conventions' (n 106).

[214] For UIs specifically, see IMO Doc LEG 107/9/2 (n 173), para 16.

[215] ibid, para 18.

[216] See, eg art 18 of the 1996 Protocol to the Convention on the Prevention of Marine Pollution by Dumping of Wastes and Other Matter (opened for signature 7 November 1996, entered into force 24 March 2006) 36 ILM 1.

[217] Georg Nolte, 'Part 5: Reports for the ILC Study Group on Treaties over Time, Report 3: Subsequent Agreements and Subsequent Practice of States Outside of Judicial and Quasi-judicial Proceedings' in Georg Nolte (ed), *Treaties and Subsequent Practice* (OUP 2013) 370.

could be held in conjunction with a session of the IMO committee under the purview of which the respective treaty falls. Importantly, however, when adopting the respective decision in question, states must cast their vote as a member of the conference of states parties, rather than as a member of the respective IMO organ.[218]

Leaving aside the question of the issuer, we briefly turn to the agreement itself. From a formal point of view, an agreement in the sense of Article 31(3)(a) of the VCLT 'may, but need not, be legally binding', and can, thus, be an informal law instrument.[219] However, such agreement must be reached, thus presupposing a 'deliberate common act'[220] about which the parties are aware, and which they accept.[221] Importantly, consensus—the dominant decision-making mode in the IMO context[222]—only implies that the act was endorsed through non-objection, which does not necessarily mean that there is unanimity regarding its content.[223] From a substantive point of view, the agreement must relate to the interpretation of the treaty,[224] hence the parties must intend to clarify the meaning of a treaty.[225] The closer an agreement is intertwined with a treaty—for instance, by a reference linking the two[226]—the easier it is to argue that it *relates* to the interpretation of a treaty, and the higher its interpretative weight.[227] As regards UIs, in addition to their denomination pointing to their interpretative character, their title and introductory paragraphs generally mention the treaty (and at times even the provision) to which they relate and, moreover, indicate that the purpose of their approval is to provide guidance in the application of the respective provision.[228] Assuming, *arguendo*, they are adopted by the states parties to the treaty in question, rather than by an IMO organ,[229] they can be said to embody the 'common understanding regarding the interpretation of a treaty which the parties are aware of and accept'.[230] Consequently, and not least because of their high degree of clarity and specificity, they would have considerable weight in the interpretative process. Guidelines of the sort discussed here, by contrast, generally do not interpret a specific provision or treaty term, but, rather, set out fine-grained rules on a specific problem. Thus, they do not, primarily, have a post-law function (let alone reach the status of subsequent agreements),[231] but, rather, a pre- or even para-law function.[232] Finally, interpretative Assembly resolutions clarify issues in relation to a specific treaty; yet, as per the IMO secretariat, they 'never clearly indicate that they express the agreement of the parties or that they are adopted by them'.[233] Even

[218] IMO Doc LEG 107/9/2 (n 173), para 18.

[219] ILC, 'Draft Conclusions' (n 179) 75, Conclusion 10(1); see 92–93 with regard to interpretative resolutions by Conferences of States Parties specifically.

[220] ibid 30.

[221] ibid 75, Conclusion 10(1).

[222] Henry (n 79) 18.

[223] ILC, 'Draft Conclusions' (n 179) 90–1.

[224] ibid 43, Conclusion 6(1).

[225] ibid 30–31.

[226] ibid 31.

[227] ibid 45.

[228] See, eg IMO, 'Unified Interpretations of the IGC Code (as Amended by Resolution MSC.370(93))' (28 November 2016) IMO Doc MSC.1/Circ.1559, para 1.

[229] Currently, a discussion is taking place in the LEG as to whether a UI on the test for breaking the owner's right to limit liability should be adopted by the LEG, or by the states parties: see IMO Doc LEG 107/WP.1 (n 55), para 9.11–9.14.

[230] ILC, 'Draft Conclusions' (n 179) 75, Conclusion 10(1).

[231] But see below on VCLT (n 196), art 31(3)(c).

[232] See, eg IMO Doc FAL.5/Circ.39/Rev.2 (n 183), Annex, r 2.

[233] IMO Doc LEG 107/9/2 (n 173), para 17.

if, *arguendo*, the states parties to a treaty would have adopted them, rather than an IMO organ, their content has not been such, in the past, as to amount to a subsequent agreement in the sense of Article 31(3)(a) of the VCLT. Yet, they may, nevertheless, be considered in the interpretative process—notably as supplementary means in the sense of Article 32 of the VCLT—[234] which the interpreter, however, is not obliged to take into account.[235]

Moreover, informal law instruments adopted by the IMO may enter the interpretative process through Article 31(3)(c) of the VCLT, which stipulates that 'any relevant rules of international law applicable in relations between the parties' shall be taken into account. This norm, which lays the groundwork for the systemic approach to interpretation by referring to the entire international legal system as part of the context,[236] is construed very narrowly by some, and quite broadly by others. Understood in an orthodox fashion, the words 'rules of international law' refer only to formal sources of international law;[237] by contrast, parts of the international judicial system[238] and various commentators[239] include informal law. It seems, though, that the word 'rule' in Article 31(3)(c) of the VCLT dictates that only instruments of general-abstract character that are self-standing, such as the IMO guidelines considered above, qualify. UIs and interpretative Assembly resolutions, however, are linked to the treaty to be interpreted and, therefore, do not amount to rules *external* to the treaty to be interpreted.

To conclude, it has been demonstrated that informal law instruments of the IMO—notably UIs, guidelines, and interpretative Assembly resolutions—inform the interpretative process in a number of ways and, thus, have an important post-law function. As the methodology of the RSE comprises, in addition to 'developing interpretations', the options of 'amending existing instruments' and 'developing new instruments' as possibilities for addressing legal issues raised by MASS, the following section now turns, as a final step, to this scenario. Concretely, it sketches the role informal law may play in paving the way for the enactment of new, formal rules (pre-law function), and to what extent it may even substitute formal law altogether (para-law function).

7.5.2 Pre- and Para-law Function of Informal Law: Paving the Way for, or even Replacing, Treaties

To overhaul the IMO's legal framework in a timely and sensible fashion, as to accommodate the turn to MASS, is a daunting challenge.[240] As demonstrated earlier, the regulation of MASS is far from obvious, as they involve not one, but several, emerging technologies, each of which features a high degree of complexity, is inchoate, and is moving through the various innovation stages at a fast pace.[241] As a consequence, determining what, when, and

[234] ILC, 'Draft Conclusions' (n 179) 90.
[235] See VCLT (n 196), art 32: 'Recourse may be had . . .'.
[236] Dörr (n 208) 603.
[237] See, eg Mark E Villiger, *Commentary on the 1969 Vienna Convention on the Law of Treaties* (Martinus Nijhoff Publishers 2009) 433.
[238] For examples, see Dörr (n 208) 608.
[239] See, eg Anne Peters, 'The Refinement of International Law: From Fragmentation to Regime Interaction and Politicization' (2017) 15(3) ICON 671, 693 (no conclusive stance).
[240] Smeele (n 26) 70.
[241] See section 7.2 above.

how to regulate is formidably difficult.[242] Moreover, as 'technological transition is going to be a permanent state in the age of disruptive innovation',[243] the law must also be updated continuously to keep abreast of change. This scenario seems to suggest that, at least to some extent, recourse is to be had to regulatory processes and techniques that are characterized by their speed, adaptability, and flexibility.

The identification of the technology to be regulated—the 'what question'—is far from evident in the context of emerging technologies.[244] For MASS specifically, it is too early, at the current juncture, for a reliable forecast about the ultimate results of the technological transition, notably as regards the level of autonomy and forms of MASS that will become the industry standard.[245] Experience with this new kind of vessel is still very limited,[246] as too is our imagination.[247] As a result, it is hard to foresee the type and scope of issues that the construction and operation of MASS will ultimately raise.[248] For the time being, it thus seems impossible to regulate MASS at the 'front end'[249] by pursuing a fully fact-based approach.[250] This is also the case for other emerging technologies.

The next step, which is as difficult as the identification of the technology to be regulated, and is closely connected with it, is the determination of the timing of a regulatory intervention: the 'when question'.[251] Premature regulation carries the risk of rules that are poorly aligned with the ultimate technology, and may 'inappropriately "lock in" inferior technological choices'.[252] Moreover, the rules may already be 'ossified',[253] and in need of an update at the very moment of their entry into force, as they relate to an anticipated rather than eventual result of a given technological transition.[254] Smeele describes the problem by drawing on maritime metaphors, and writes that '[i]n the absence of the ... dot on the horizon to navigate toward, at present it seems premature to embark upon a comprehensive overhaul of maritime law'.[255] Engaging in such an endeavour now may entail the risk that 'the beacons are moved too early and will have to be moved again before long'.[256] Timing is further complicated by the fact that regulation requires a certain sense of imminence. Sufficient support for regulation can usually only be garnered once the use of a given technology is considered to be forthcoming, and thus jolted 'from the abstract into the concrete'.[257] Yet, within the IMO, this sense of imminence may vary starkly between member states, and may explain why states at the helm of MASS development were among the first

[242] Fenwick, Kaal, and Vermeulen (n 7) 561.
[243] ibid 573.
[244] ibid 571.
[245] Smeele (n 26) 70.
[246] Jacobsson (n 22) 283.
[247] Fenwick, Kaal, and Vermeulen (n 7) 574.
[248] Smeele (n 26) 70.
[249] See Marchant, 'Addressing the Pacing Problem' (n 35) 201.
[250] See Fenwick, Kaal, and Vermeulen (n 7) 576–77.
[251] ibid 571–72.
[252] Gary E Marchant, 'The Growing Gap between Emerging Technologies and the Law' in Gary E Marchant, Braden R Allenby, and Joseph R Herkert (eds), *The Growing Gap between Emerging Technologies and Legal-ethical Oversight: The Pacing Problem* (Springer 2011) 27.
[253] See ibid 24.
[254] See Fenwick, Kaal, and Vermeulen (n 7) 572.
[255] Smeele (n 26) 70.
[256] ibid.
[257] Neil C Renic, 'Autonomous Weapons Systems: When is the Right Time to Regulate?' (26 September 2019) Hum L & P <https://blogs.icrc.org/law-and-policy/2019/09/26/autonomous-weapons-systems-right-time-regulation/> accessed 1 April 2021.

to voice the need for timely regulation.[258] All in all, it seems well advised for the IMO not to engage in any rash regulatory action. Yet, at the same time, a delayed regulatory response equally harbours risks. A 'Wild West' of regulatory uncertainty[259] may notably impede research and hamper innovation,[260] which, in turn, may delay or block new (beneficial) technologies.[261] Moreover, regulation currently in force may prohibit the introduction of a new technology altogether, though this seems to be rare with regard to IMO treaties.[262] Still, if there is no prospect for timely regulation, flag states leading the development of MASS may adopt their own guidelines,[263] or partake in regional regulatory initiatives,[264] which may jeopardize the leadership role of the IMO[265] and the required harmonization of shipping regulation.[266] In addition, the time necessary to integrate MASS into the IMO's legal framework—estimates range from eight to twenty years[267]—must also be factored in when discussing timing. There is, thus, much to suggest that there is no time to waste. To conclude, the IMO is—paradoxically—being advised, simultaneously, to wait and to hurry.[268]

Turning to the 'how question', the foregoing suggests that the governance of emerging technologies requires regulatory processes and tools that allow for permanent re-evaluation and revision, in order to integrate new facts and relevant experience.[269] Formal lawmaking, which, in our context, means treaty-making by states that use the governance structures of the IMO is hardly suitable to ensure the 'adaptivity and responsiveness'[270] of the law.[271] Rather, making and amending treaties is a notoriously slow and rigid process, which is no different for the IMO,[272] as has been highlighted in the context of MASS regulation specifically.[273] By contrast, informal lawmaking is associated with the characteristics of adaptive governance,[274] which also hold true for informal law of the IMO,[275] despite its rather low degree of informality.[276] Compared with formal law, its amendment is considered to be faster and easier, thus making it a suitable means for a 'continuing dialogue'.[277] Such continuity is necessary if we subscribe to the ideas that technical transition will be a permanent state, and that MASS do not belong to those technologies that are stable and will not change considerably after their introduction to the market, such as, for instance, the 'game-changing' innovation of containers.[278] Moreover, at times, the informal law instrument itself foresees

[258] See, eg the states that proposed the RSE: IMO Doc MSC 98/20/2 (n 46).
[259] Hagemann, Huddleston Skees, and Thierer (n 10) 96.
[260] A concern expressed in IMO Doc MSC 98/20/2 (n 46), para 11.
[261] Marchant, 'The Growing Gap Between Emerging Technologies and the Law' (n 252) 25.
[262] See text accompanying n 160.
[263] According to IMO Doc MSC 98/20/2 (n 46), para 9, this has already happened to some extent.
[264] Henrik Ringbom, 'Legalizing Autonomous Ships' (2020) 34 Ocean YB 431, 447–48.
[265] This role is stressed in, eg IMO Doc A 30/Res. 1110 (n 35), Annex, para 2.
[266] See, eg IMO Doc MSC 98/20/2 (n 46), para 19.
[267] Liu (n 24) 493; Smeele (n 26) 70.
[268] Smeele (n 26) 70.
[269] Marchant, 'Addressing the Pacing Problem' (n 35) 201–02.
[270] ibid 200.
[271] See, eg Gregory C Shaffer and Mark A Pollack, 'Hard versus Soft Law in International Security' (2012) 52(4) BCL Rev 1147, 1163.
[272] Even though the tacit acceptance procedure (see n 81) has 'greatly sped up the amendment process': Lost-Sieminska (n 13) 917.
[273] See, eg Robert Veal and Michael Tsimplis, 'The Integration of Unmanned Ships into the *Lex Maritima*' [2017] LMCLQ 303, 333; Chircop, 'Testing International Legal Regimes' (n 1) 31.
[274] See, eg Shaffer and Pollack (n 271) 1163.
[275] Lefebvre-Chalain (n 83) 235.
[276] See text accompanying n 139.
[277] Hagemann, Huddleston Skees, and Thierer (n 10) 104.
[278] See text accompanying nn 30–34.

its own review: with this, the instrument is set in motion, allowing it to move forward along with the technological transition. Thus, for instance, the MSC agreed 'to keep the Interim Guidelines under review and to amend them in view of the experience gained with their application'.[279] In light of these characteristics, it is just a small step to conclude that 'the age of "hard law" governance of new technologies will continue to wane, and soft law governance will become the new norm for many technologies',[280] or that '[t]he era of hard law governance appears to be fading and the age of soft law is firmly underway'.[281]

Indeed, the characteristics ascribed to informal law make it a regulatory tool capable of mitigating—albeit not necessarily solving—problems associated with the regulation of emerging technologies. To begin with, an informal lawmaking process is a tool to get the normative ball rolling. As Boyle has noted, it provides an 'effective starting point when States need reassurance before commencing novel and previously unregulated activities',[282] as seems to be the case for the construction and operation of MASS.[283] Moreover, informal law is praised as a means to 'consolidate political opinion',[284] and find 'common ground',[285] as regards the need for action in a new field.[286] This may be necessary in the present context, since views among states about the need to establish new rules for MASS differ at times.[287] In this vein, it has been argued that one of the benefits of the adoption of the IMO Interim Guidelines for MASS Trials, in June 2019, is that they impliedly recognize the advent of this new type of vessel, and that existing law does not fully accommodate them.[288] By paving the way for a (thicker) normative framework applying to MASS, informal law emerges here in its pre-law function.

Further, informal law is a tool that allows experiences to be collected in a new field, which can later be used to adapt and enhance the regulatory framework accordingly. In the IMO context, specifically, informal instruments often serve as 'testing grounds for regulatory concepts', which, if successful, may later be imported into formal law.[289] In order to ensure this 'feedback loop' function of informal law, IMO instruments, at times, expressly invite relevant actors to report back 'the results of the experience gained from the use' of the respective instrument.[290] Informal law, thus, has the potential to compensate, at least to some extent, for the lack of experience, both as regards the technology and the best way(s) to regulate it, and this is another facet of its pre-law function.

Informal law is, moreover, understood as a temporary solution until firmer commitment is possible,[291] be it in the form of more detailed informal law, or even formal law. Hence, for instance, in the process leading to the adoption of the Interim Guidelines for MASS Trials, it was argued that the instrument may amount to 'a potential interim first step to new

[279] IMO Doc MSC.1/Circ.1604 (n 89), para 2.
[280] Hagemann, Huddleston Skees, and Thierer (n 10) 38; on the 'governance shift', see also ibid 40–42.
[281] ibid 129.
[282] Boyle, 'Soft Law in International Law-making' (n 62) 130.
[283] See IMO, 'Comments and Proposals for Interim Guidelines for MASS Trials' (28 February 2019) IMO Doc MSC 101/5/1, para 3.
[284] Shelton (n 67) 72.
[285] Lefebvre-Chalain (n 83) 240 ('*terrain d'entente*').
[286] Birnie (n 96) 32.
[287] See, eg IMO Doc LEG 107/8/5 (n 166), para 9.
[288] Smeele (n 26) 73.
[289] Lampe (n 83) 318.
[290] See, eg IMO Doc FAL.5/Circ.39/Rev.2 (n 183), para 4.
[291] Lefebvre-Chalain (n 83) 240.

international regulations' in the field.[292] The preliminary results of the RSE equally demonstrate that informal instruments are, inter alia, perceived as an 'interim measure' on the path leading to a comprehensive and detailed regulation of MASS.[293] Indeed, in the past, the IMO repeatedly relied on informal law to regulate, temporarily, new types of crafts not previously addressed by the Organization's legal framework, until the time for a treaty solution was ripe. This strategy pre-empted diverging flag state solutions,[294] which is seen as a risk in the context of MASS, if the IMO does not regulate them in a timely fashion. Being a first step towards a bolstered legal framework, and in functioning as a placeholder, informal law not only has a pre- but also a para-law function.

However, relegating the para-law function of informal law to the role of providing solely temporary solutions seems mistaken. Rather, there are prospects that it will, to some extent, substitute formal law altogether, and take a firm place in the regulation of MASS. The RSE foreshadows various scenarios of how informal law could complement the body of IMO treaties, which seamlessly fit into the Organization's previous use of, and reliance on, internal and external informal law.[295] For one, it is suggested to accommodate MASS through the development of non-mandatory instruments by the IMO itself, notably in the form of guidelines[296] or codes.[297] Yet, external informal instruments elaborated by private actors could play an equally important role, if not take centre stage entirely. As noted, the IMO deploys various 'endorsement' techniques to link private rules with its own rules, without changing their informal nature. While the inclusion of references in IMO treaties to external informal law is one option, the Organization has established a systematic relationship between its treaties and private informal law, through the GBS framework.[298] With regard to MASS—as holds true for other emerging technologies[299]—high hopes are placed on a goal-based approach to regulation, which is deemed more likely to withstand the passage of time than prescriptive rules.[300] Indeed, the Organization has been urged to develop a goal-based understanding of the main regulatory issues pertaining to MASS.[301] Classification societies are likely to be one of the main providers of rules, having been quick to embrace this new type of vessel, and they have already issued various sets of rules relating to MASS.[302] Increased reliance on GBS could give classification societies, including the IACS, considerable weight in the regulation of MASS.

[292] IMO Doc MSC 101/5/1 (n 283), para 3.

[293] See, eg IMO Doc MSC 102/5/3 (n 19), para 36.3.

[294] Henry (n 79) 76, providing the example of dynamically supported crafts.

[295] See section 7.4 above.

[296] See, eg IMO Doc LEG 107/8/2 (n 149), para 18.

[297] See, eg IMO, 'Summary of the Results of the Second Step of the RSE for SOLAS chapter XII and Associated Standards' (17 February 2020) IMO Doc MSC 102/5/22, para 9.

[298] See text accompanying nn 128–32.

[299] See, eg Martin Ebers, 'Regulating AI and Robotics: Ethical and Legal Challenges' in Martin Ebers and Susana Navas (eds), *Algorithms and Law* (CUP 2020) 97.

[300] IMO, 'Strategic Themes in MASS Perspective' (10 March 2020) IMO Doc MSC 102/INF.17, para 7.

[301] IMO, 'List of Common Potential Gaps/Themes Identified during the First Step of RSE for STCW Convention and Code, STCW-F, SOLAS, ISM Code, TONNAGE 1969, LL 1966, LL PROT 1988, IS Code, III Code, COLREG and SAR 1979' (10 February 2020) IMO Doc MSC 102/5/7, paras 11–12, 15, and 17.

[302] See, eg Class NK, *Guidelines for Automated/Autonomous Operation on Ships* (January 2020); Bureau Veritas, *Guidelines for Autonomous Shipping* (October 2019); China Classification Society, *Guidelines for Autonomous Cargo Ships* (October 2018); DNV GL, *Class Guideline: Autonomous and Remotely Operated Ships* (September 2018).

7.6 Conclusion

Given its characteristics, informal law seems, in various respects, suitable—often more so than formal law—to respond to legal issues raised by emerging technologies in general, and by MASS specifically. As demonstrated, beyond its potential to pave the way for a timely and sensible regulation of this new type of vessel in the long run, it is very likely that informal law will be a cornerstone of this legal framework. In addition, informal law informs the interpretative process in a number of ways, which is yet another approach for contributing to the quest of keeping IMO treaties abreast of new developments. All things considered, the answer to the question raised in the title of this chapter is somewhat self-evident: it is more than likely that unconventional law will play a key role in the regulation of unconventional ships, to which MASS certainly belong—at least for the time being.

8

The Use of Informal Agreements to Enhance Navigational Safety

*Natalie Klein**

8.1 Introduction

Navigation is one of the oldest and most important uses of the oceans. The UN Convention on the Law of the Sea (LOSC)[1] is important for establishing the legal framework for the exercise of navigational rights in different maritime zones, as well as for affirming and developing standards relevant for navigational safety.[2] The LOSC reflects provisions from the 1958 law of the sea conventions,[3] and accounts for numerous conventions, as well as guidelines and recommendations, concerning maritime safety that were adopted under the auspices of the International Maritime Organization (IMO).[4] While international navigation is, thus, highly regulated by formal international law, states have also utilized agreements that are not legally binding to address navigational issues that arise.[5] Generally, informal agreements[6] seek to augment international cooperation in response to perceived problems;[7] this central goal is evident in the realm of navigational safety.

Informal agreements on navigational safety have been used for practical reasons, as they may set out logistical or technical arrangements that states intend to put in place domestically to facilitate cooperation on a matter of concern. Setting out agreed modes of behaviour for when certain events occur may also create predictability and stability where tensions might otherwise have resulted from misunderstandings.

* I very gratefully acknowledge the research assistance of Priscilla Rivas and the editorial assistance of Jack McNally. I would also like to thank Millicent McCreath, Priscilla Rivas, and Jack McNally for very helpful substantive comments on the draft of this chapter. Any remaining errors are, of course, my own. Research for this chapter was supported by an Australian Research Council Future Fellowship award.

[1] United Nations Convention on the Law of the Sea (adopted 10 December 1982, entered into force 16 November 1994) 1833 UNTS 397 (hereafter 'LOSC').

[2] See, eg ibid, art 94.

[3] See, eg Convention on the High Seas (adopted 29 April 1958, entered into force 30 September 1962) 450 UNTS 1, art 10; Convention on the Territorial Sea and the Contiguous Zone (adopted 29 April 1958, entered into force 10 September 1964) 516 UNTS 205, art 15(2).

[4] For a listing of these treaties, see IMO, 'List of IMO Conventions' (2020) <http://www.imo.org/en/About/Conventions/ListOfConventions/Pages/Default.aspx> accessed 15 July 2021.

[5] See, eg IMO, 'Assuring Safety during Demonstrations, Protests or Confrontations on the High Seas' (17 May 2010) IMO Res MSC.303(87).

[6] For further discussion on terminology, see, eg Kal Raustiala, 'Form and Substance in International Agreements' (2005) 99 AJIL 581, 586–91; Gregory C Shaffer and Mark A Pollack, 'Hard vs. Soft Law: Alternatives, Complements, and Antagonists in International Governance' (2010) 94 Minn L Rev 706, 712–17.

[7] For discussion of the advantages of informal agreements, see Shaffer and Pollock (n 6) 719. See also Kenneth W Abbott and Duncan Snidal, 'Hard and Soft Law in International Governance' (2000) 54 Intl'l Org 421, 423; Charles Lipson, 'Why are some International Agreements Informal?' (1991) 45 Intl'l Org 495, 514–17; Alan Boyle, 'Some Reflections on the Relationship of Treaties and Soft Law' (1999) 48 ICLQ 901, 903.

Natalie Klein, *The Use of Informal Agreements to Enhance Navigational Safety* In: *Unconventional Lawmaking in the Law of the Sea.* Edited by: Natalie Klein, Oxford University Press. © Natalie Klein 2022. DOI: 10.1093/oso/9780192897824.003.0008

As discussed in Chapter 1, beyond the actual output, informal lawmaking can create shared expectations as to the standard of conduct in relation to specific international issues. Informal lawmaking, as a process, allows for relevant actors, such as regulators or industry groups, to assemble and share expertise and information, learn more about an issue, and bargain on what standards of behaviour will be acceptable, in the future, to address that issue.[8] Normative values may emerge through this engagement with legal processes and discourse,[9] even if there is no intent to create a binding legal commitment. Those values may have a 'normative effect', that is the agreements establish standards against which behaviour is assessed. The extent of the normative effect of informal lawmaking, including its possible impact on treaty interpretation, will be examined in this chapter, in the context of navigational safety.

This chapter considers informal lawmaking in relation to three examples of non-binding instruments relevant to navigational safety to assess the purpose of these instruments and their significance in international law. Much work has been undertaken within the IMO on navigational safety, and the lawmaking role of the IMO is discussed in other chapters of this volume,[10] and in the literature.[11] The examination of informal instruments relating to navigational safety in this chapter, thus, does not purport to be exhaustive;[12] instead, observations are made in relation to some examples beyond the IMO context, responding to recent confrontations that put navigational safety at risk in different ways.

First, emerging from diverse challenges in the South China Sea, including but not limited to navigational safety concerns, the Association of South East Asian Nations (ASEAN) and China adopted a Declaration of Conduct (DOC) in 2002 that affirms the freedom of navigation enshrined in the LOSC,[13] as well as setting out a variety of measures for the concerned states to better regulate their maritime activities in the South China Sea.[14] These states are currently negotiating a code of conduct, which, at present, seems most likely to be another informal agreement rather than a binding legal instrument.[15] Second, this chapter examines the Code for Unplanned Encounters at Sea (CUES).[16] The CUES was adopted by the Western Pacific Naval Symposium in 2014, and has been considered for application by

[8] 'Cross-border cooperation between public authorities, with or without the participation of private actors and/or international organizations, in a forum other than a traditional international organization (process informality), and/or as between actors other than traditional diplomatic actors (such as regulators or agencies) (actor informality) and/or which does not result in a formal treaty or other traditional source of international law (output informality).': Joost Pauwelyn, 'Informal International Lawmaking: Framing the Concept and Research Questions' in Joost Pauwelyn, Ramses A Wessel, and Jan Wouters (eds), *Informal International Lawmaking* (OUP 2013) 22.

[9] Abbott and Snidal (n 7) 422.

[10] See chapters by Sun and Petrig (Chapters 6 and 7, respectively) in this volume.

[11] See, eg James Harrison, *Making the Law of the Sea: A Study in the Development of International Law* (CUP 2011) 154–99.

[12] Navigational safety can encompass all shipping standards to do with the seaworthiness of ships, collision avoidance and ship routeing, and crew standards, as well as navigational aids. For a general discussion of the laws across all of these dimensions, see RR Churchill and AV Lowe, *The Law of the Sea* (3rd edn, Manchester UP 1999) 265–72.

[13] LOSC (n 1) arts 87 and 58.

[14] Declaration on the Conduct of Parties in the South China Sea (4 November 2002) <https://asean.org/?static_post=declaration-on-the-conduct-of-parties-in-the-south-china-sea-2> accessed 15 July 2021 (hereafter 'DOC').

[15] See, eg Viet Hoang, 'The Code of Conduct for the South China Sea: A Long and Bumpy Road' (*The Diplomat*, 28 September 2020)<https://thediplomat.com/2020/09/the-code-of-conduct-for-the-south-china-sea-a-long-and-bumpy-road/> accessed 15 July 2021.

[16] Western Pacific Naval Symposium, 'Code for Unplanned Encounters at Sea: Version 1.0' (22 April 2014) (hereafter 'CUES') <http://www.ions.global/sites/default/files/CUES-10-Approvedat-the-14th-WPNS-2014422.pdf> accessed 15 July 2021.

navies operating in other regional settings.[17] Finally, the chapter examines specific bilateral agreements between China and the United States: the Memorandum of Understanding regarding Rules of Behavior for Safety of Air and Maritime Encounters,[18] as well as a supplement (Behavior MoU),[19] and the Memorandum of Understanding on Notification of Major Military Activities Confidence-building Measures Mechanism (Notification MoU).[20] These instruments are generally intended to provide clarity for navies about, inter alia, signalling, communication, and manoeuvring during naval encounters, as a means of reducing or eliminating risks to the vessels, and those on board, during varied missions.

The aim of this chapter is, therefore, to consider for what purposes these informal agreements have been adopted, and to reflect on the significance of any informal lawmaking for international laws related to navigational safety. In considering the significance, the analysis will briefly step beyond the bounds of international law, and ask if other explanatory paradigms may be applicable. While there are many possible theories, it is notable that security studies literature may consider informal agreements responding to situations of political tension as confidence-building measures. What confidence-building measures might mean for international law will, thus, be assessed. An alternative explanation may be found in theories of governance, such as experimentalist governance, which allows for broader consideration of the principles, actors, and processes that may be brought to bear in managing a specific situation and, hence, may be an appropriate means to better understand the purposes of different informal instruments. The analysis below, thus, considers experimentalist governance as another frame for consideration.

To this end, the chapter proceeds as follows. Section 8.2 sets out the existing legal framework for navigational safety, and highlights why there is a role for informal agreements. Section 8.3 examines in more detail the aforementioned informal agreements relating to navigational safety: The DOC and possible code of conduct, the CUES, and the bilateral MoUs between China and the United States. These analyses focus on the possible intersections of each with international law. Section 8.4 proceeds to explore the alternative explanatory paradigms for understanding these agreements: the role of confidence-building measures, and the theory of experimentalist governance. Section 8.5 concludes the analysis with a cautionary note about what can be expected of these agreements relating to

[17] Notably ASEAN, with an agreement between ASEAN and China as to its application in the South China Sea: Joint Statement on the Application of the Code for Unplanned Encounters at Sea in the South China Sea (7 September 2016) <https://asean.org/wp-content/uploads/2016/09/Joint-Statement-on-the-Application-of-CUES-in-the-SCS-Final.pdf> accessed 15 July 2021 (hereafter '2016 Joint Statement'). The Indian Ocean Naval Symposium has also contemplated adopting a version of the CUES: see Gurpreet S Khurana, 'A New Beginning for "Code of Conduct" in South China Sea: Is one Required for the Indian Ocean?' (*National Maritime Foundation,* 8 September 2017) <https://www.maritimeindia.org/View%20Profile/636404436943047639.pdf> accessed 15 July 2021.

[18] Memorandum of Understanding between the Department of Defense of the United States of America and the Ministry of National Defense of the People's Republic of China regarding the Rules of Behavior for Safety of Air and Maritime Encounters (10 November 2014) <https://archive.defense.gov/pubs/141112_MemorandumOfUnderstandingRegardingRules.pdf> accessed 15 July 2021 (hereafter 'Behavior MoU').

[19] Supplement to the Memorandum of Understanding on the Rules of Behavior for Safety of Air and Maritime Encounters between the Department of Defense of the United States of America and the Ministry of National Defense of the People's Republic of China (2015). The Supplement addresses air-to-air encounters, and is of less relevance for present purposes because it falls more within the freedom of overflight.

[20] Memorandum of Understanding between the United States of America Department of Defense and the People's Republic of China Ministry of National Defense on Notification of Major Military Activities Confidence-building Measures Mechanism (31 October and 4 November 2014) <https://archive.defense.gov/pubs/141112_MemorandumOfUnderstandingOnNotification.pdf> accessed 15 July 2021 (hereafter 'Notification MoU').

navigational safety and signals, and what more might be required to meet the needs and expectations of diverse stakeholders in maintaining international legal rights and duties that enhance navigational safety.

8.2 Formal Law Regulating Navigational Safety

When considering the risks to navigational safety that have arisen in recent confrontations in locations such as the South China Sea and the Strait of Hormuz,[21] the relevant legal framework that formally binds the states concerned is the LOSC and customary international law, as well as treaties adopted under the auspices of the IMO. These formal sources of international law allocate rights and duties to different states within each of the maritime zones. Depending on the maritime zone and the navigational rights that exist therein, states may have different responsibilities in relation to navigational safety. In addition, there is an important body of law regulating what might be considered the core of navigational safety: seaworthiness of vessels, crewing, and safe navigation. This law is derived primarily from the LOSC, customary international law, and IMO treaties. These legal rules are introduced briefly in this section, and provide an important background to the informal agreements, discussed in section 8.3, that cut across these different dimensions of the navigational safety legal framework.

8.2.1 The LOSC and Customary International Law

As an initial matter, navigational rights and duties vary depending on where a vessel is situated relative to the coast of a state, and to what state the vessel is flagged. Also relevant is whether a vessel is privately owned or a state vessel: the latter vessels typically enjoy sovereign immunity.[22] Closest to the coast lies the territorial sea, comprised of the seabed, the water therein, and airspace above, up to twelve nautical miles from a state's coast, over which the coastal state exercises sovereignty.[23] The sovereignty of the coastal state is subject to a right of innocent passage that is enjoyed by the ships of all other states that are traversing the territorial sea.[24] The right of innocent passage also exists through internal waters that have been enclosed by straight baselines, in accordance with Article 7 of the LOSC.[25] The LOSC also sets out rules for transit passage in certain international straits,[26] and, further, creates a regime of archipelagic sea lanes passage, which is similar to transit passage, for vessels traversing archipelagic states.[27]

Within the exclusive economic zone (EEZ)—a maritime area extending up to 200 nautical miles from a state's coast—a balance is to be struck between the sovereign rights and jurisdiction allocated to the coastal state under Article 56 of the LOSC for economic

[21] See Cameron Moore, *Freedom of Navigation and the Law of the Sea: Warships, States and the Use of Force* (Routledge 2021) 2–6.

[22] LOSC (n 1) arts 32, 95, and 236.

[23] ibid, art 2.

[24] ibid, art 17.

[25] ibid, art 8(2).

[26] ibid, pt III.

[27] ibid, art 53.

activities, and the rights of all other states as recognized under Article 58 of the LOSC. Article 58 grants, to all states, the freedom of navigation and overflight, and of the laying of submarine cables and pipelines, 'and other internationally lawful uses of the sea related to these freedoms, such as those associated with the operation of ships, aircraft and submarine cables and pipelines, and compatible with the other provisions of this Convention'. Critical in this balance is that users of the EEZ must show due regard to the rights of other users in the exercise of their respective rights and duties.[28] The exact meaning of 'due regard' is not articulated in the LOSC.[29] The freedom of navigation is enjoyed by all states on the high seas,[30] although this freedom must also be exercised with due regard for the interests of other states.[31]

Beyond the rights and duties associated with navigation within the different maritime zones, there are safety requirements and permissible activities that may occur during the course of a journey, such as anchoring for repairs, undertaking a search and rescue, or operating standard equipment for navigational purposes. Article 94 of the LOSC requires states to take measures necessary to ensure safety at sea for their vessels.[32] In taking these measures, 'each State is required to conform to generally accepted international regulations, procedures and practices and to take any steps which may be necessary to secure their observance'.[33] This so-called 'rule of reference' necessitates that states adhere to both binding and non-binding standards, as a requirement of the LOSC.[34]

The LOSC also addresses the use of sea lanes and traffic separation schemes in straits used for international navigation, as well as in the territorial sea, to enhance navigational safety.[35] Article 41(3) of the LOSC anticipates that such schemes 'shall conform to generally accepted international regulations'. Navigational safety in the territorial sea further requires that foreign ships exercising their right of innocent passage comply with coastal state laws and 'generally accepted international regulations relating to the prevention of collisions at sea'.[36] The possibility, thus, exists that informal agreements take on a formally binding status under the requirements of the LOSC, if 'generally accepted'.[37]

When states exercise law enforcement powers at sea, any use of force must be reasonable, proportionate, and necessary.[38] The LOSC requires compensation to be paid to ships for any loss or damage sustained when a state's exercise of the right of visit or the right of hot pursuit was not justified.[39] Under the LOSC, states are also proscribed from endangering

[28] ibid, arts 56(2) and 58(3).

[29] The flexible meaning of the term was observed in the *Chagos Marine Protected Area Arbitration (Mauritius v United Kingdom)* (Award of 18 March 2015) PCA Case No 2011-03, paras 571-72. In this regard, the tribunal stated: 'the extent of the regard required by the Convention will depend upon the nature of the rights held by Mauritius, their importance, the extent of the anticipated impairment, the nature and importance of the activities contemplated by the United Kingdom, and the availability of alternative approaches.'

[30] LOSC (n 1) art 87(1).

[31] ibid, art 87(2).

[32] ibid, art 94(3).

[33] ibid, art 94(5).

[34] Yoshifumi Tanaka, *The Law of the Sea* (CUP 2012) 35–36 ('legal instruments can be incorporated into provisions of the LOSC via the "rules of reference" ').

[35] LOSC (n 1) arts 22(1), and 41(1).

[36] ibid, art 21(4).

[37] See Lene Korseberg, 'The Law-making Effects of the FAO Deep-sea Fisheries Guidelines' (2018) 67 ICLQ 801, 805–06.

[38] *M/V 'Saiga' (No 2) (Saint Vincent and the Grenadines v Guinea)* (Judgment) ITLOS Reports 1999, 10, 61–62, para 155; *The Arctic Sunrise Arbitration (Netherlands v Russia)* (Award on the Merits of 14 August 2015) PCA Case No 2014-02, 285, para 283.

[39] LOSC (n 1), arts 110(3) and 111(8).

navigational safety in the exercise of their enforcement powers for the protection and preservation of the marine environment.[40] Both the International Court of Justice and the International Tribunal for the Law of the Sea have affirmed that 'elementary considerations of humanity' apply at sea.[41] This principle should be considered a fundamental precept to requirements relating to navigational safety.

8.2.2 COLREGS and other International Treaties

As mentioned at the outset, the IMO has played a critical role in the development and revision of international treaties addressing navigational safety. Foremost among these is the International Convention for the Safety of Life at Sea (SOLAS Convention), which is the primary legal instrument dealing with seaworthiness of vessels, as well as traffic separation schemes, crewing standards, and maritime security.[42] The Load Lines Convention also holds importance for seaworthiness standards.[43] Crewing standards are dealt with in more detail in the International Convention on Standards of Training, Certification and Watchkeeping for Seafarers.[44]

When considering the suite of IMO instruments that address different aspects of navigational safety, it is notable that many of the current treaties found their genesis in, or have incorporated, informal instruments.[45] For example, the SOLAS Convention incorporated the Code for the Construction and Equipment of Ships carrying Dangerous Chemicals in Bulk, which was originally a non-binding Assembly resolution.[46] Routeing and traffic separation schemes, which have been critical in reducing collisions, were originally the subject of non-binding IMO recommendations, but became mandatory under the Convention on the International Regulations for Preventing Collisions at Sea (COLREGS).[47]

The COLREGS provide, inter alia, standards of behaviour for ships to steer so as to avoid dangerous interactions at sea, and require assessments of the risks of collision and the steps to be taken to mitigate those risks.[48] Rules 13 to 15 of the COLREGS, for example, set out what steps are needed in situations where one vessel is overtaking a slowing craft, to avoid head-on collisions, and where vessels are crossing. Other parts of the COLREGS deal with standards for lights and shapes to make vessels recognizable at a distance, as well as sound and light signals to relay manoeuvring and warning intentions, to facilitate quick communication. The COLREGS apply to warships and submarines, as well as commercial vessels.[49]

[40] ibid, art 225.

[41] *Corfu Channel Case (UK v Albania) (Merits)* [1949] ICJ Rep 4, 22; *'Juno Trader' (Saint Vincent and the Grenadines v Guinea-Bissau)* (Prompt Release, Judgment) ITLOS Reports 2004, 17, para 77.

[42] International Convention for the Safety of Life at Sea (adopted 1 November 1974, entered into force 25 May 1980) 1184 UNTS 1.

[43] International Convention on Load Lines (adopted 5 April 1966, entered into force 21 July 1968) 640 UNTS 133.

[44] International Convention on Standards of Training, Certification and Watchkeeping for Seafarers (adopted 7 July 1978, entered into force 28 April 1984) 1361 UNTS 2.

[45] See Harrison (n 11) 164–65.

[46] IMO, 'Code for the Construction and Equipment of Ships Carrying Dangerous Chemicals in Bulk' (12 October 1971) IMO Res A.212(VII).

[47] Convention on the International Regulations for Preventing Collisions at Sea (adopted 20 October 1972, entered into force 15 July 1977) 1050 UNTS 16 (hereafter 'COLREGS'). See Churchill and Lowe (n 12) 267.

[48] See Churchill and Lowe (n 12) 267.

[49] COLREGS (n 47) r 1(a).

The connection of the COLREGS with the LOSC was made in the *South China Sea Arbitration*. In that case, the Philippines claimed that China had utilized its law enforcement vessels 'in a dangerous manner causing serious risk of collision to Philippine vessels navigating in the vicinity of Scarborough Shoal'.[50] In the course of assessing China's conduct, the tribunal observed that the COLREGS were binding on parties to the LOSC by virtue of Article 94 of the LOSC,[51] and hence fell within the tribunal's jurisdiction. Article 94, as noted previously, sets out the duties of flag states, and requires them to conform to generally accepted international regulations, which include the COLREGS. The tribunal determined that the actions of Chinese law enforcement vessels in not yielding when required, progressing at higher speeds than were safe, and failing to maintain safe distances as needed, violated rules within the COLREGS and, hence, breached Article 94 of the Convention.[52] Chinese scholars have, instead, suggested that when law enforcement vessels are in the midst of law enforcement operations, the strictures of the COLREGS are necessarily inapplicable.[53]

Law enforcement operations may be regulated under treaties that respond to specific maritime security threats.[54] For instance, where states anticipate that a right of visit may be exercised, the flag state commonly has authority to set conditions for the exercise of this visit.[55] In addition, among the many safeguards anticipated with the right of visit, there are duties to ensure the safety and security of the ship and its cargo.[56]

8.3 Informal Agreements on Navigational Safety and their Intersection with Existing Legal Principles

The DOC, CUES, and China–US MoUs are informal agreements relating to navigational safety that intersect with the formal sources of international law addressed in section 8.2 in various ways. In examining these informal agreements, this intersection emerges in three, often distinct, ways. First, there is a deliberate disavowal of lawmaking. It may be observed, however, that a lack of normative intent does not entirely negate normative effect. Second, there is a repetition of existing norms, which mostly serves a diplomatic purpose, but also underlines adherence to existing formal agreements. Third, the informal agreements provide some modest elaboration of the content of ambiguous norms. The discussion below

[50] *South China Sea Arbitration (Philippines v China)* (Award of 12 July 2016) PCA Case No 2013-19, para 1044.

[51] ibid, paras 1082–83.

[52] ibid, paras 1105 and 1109. The tribunal did not directly address the question as to whether Article 94 necessarily applies within the territorial sea, despite the stipulation in Article 86 that it does not.

[53] Chinese Society of International Law, 'The South China Sea Arbitration Awards: A Critical Study' (2018) 17 Chinese JIL 207, para 843.

[54] See, eg Protocol against the Smuggling of Migrants by Land, Sea and Air, supplementing the United Nations Convention against Transnational Organized Crime (adopted 15 November 2000, entered into force 28 January 2004) 2241 UNTS 507 (hereafter 'Migrant Smuggling Protocol'); United Nations Convention against Illicit Traffic in Narcotic Drugs and Psychotropic Substances (adopted 20 December 1988, entered into force 11 November 1990) 1582 UNTS 95; Convention for the Suppression of Unlawful Acts against the Safety of Maritime Navigation (adopted 10 March 1988, entered into force 1 March 1992) 1678 UNTS 221, as amended by the Protocol of 2005 to the Convention for the Suppression of Unlawful Acts against the Safety of Maritime Navigation (adopted 14 October 2005, entered into force 28 July 2010) IMO Doc LEG/CONF.15/21 (hereafter '2005 SUA Convention').

[55] See, eg Migrant Smuggling Protocol (n 54) art 2(5); 2005 SUA Convention (n 54) art 8*bis* (5)(c).

[56] See, eg Migrant Smuggling Protocol (n 54) art 2(5); 2005 SUA Convention (n 54) art 8*bis* (10)(a). See, further, Douglas Guilfoyle, *Shipping Interdiction and the Law of the Sea* (CUP 2009) 266–67.

highlights the connection of these agreements to international law, and considers to what extent, and in what ways, normative effect may be attributed to the agreements.

8.3.1 Declaration of Conduct and Code of Conduct

Central to the relationships between the littoral states in the South China Sea has been an effort between ASEAN and China to establish key principles and frameworks for regulating action taken in disputed maritime areas. While a series of bilateral initiatives has been put in place between the coastal states in the South China Sea, including bilateral treaties and informal agreements,[57] a key point of reference has been the DOC. The DOC emerged when tensions escalated between the littoral states of the South China Sea in the 1990s. At that time, both ASEAN and China developed their own draft codes of conduct, but disagreement emerged in relation to geographic scope, construction on islands, military activities, and detention of fishers in disputed waters.[58] Instead, the parties reached a compromise with the 2002 adoption of the DOC.

The DOC states that, '[t]he Parties reaffirm their respect for and commitment to the freedom of navigation in and overflight above the South China Sea as provided for by the universally recognized principles of international law, including the [LOSC]'.[59] This language is in line with previous ASEAN communications that stressed the importance of the freedom of navigation.[60] There is no further reference in the DOC to navigational rights (such as innocent passage), but only a suggestion about cooperation in responding to issues such as conducting search and rescues, combating transnational crime, and 'safety of navigation and communication at sea'.[61] A voluntary obligation to notify of military exercises is recorded,[62] within a general admonition that the parties 'undertake to exercise self-restraint in the conduct of activities that would complicate or escalate disputes'.[63]

Regarding the implementation of the DOC, it is worth noting that two mechanisms were established. The first was the ASEAN–China Senior Officials Meeting on the Implementation of the DOC, an ad hoc mechanism to review the implementation process, and the second was the ASEAN–China Joint Working Group on the Implementation of the DOC, meeting twice a year under the direction of the ASEAN–China Senior Officials

[57] An example is the Agreement on Basic Principles Guiding the Settlement of Sea-related Issues between Vietnam and China (11 October 2011) <http://vietnamembassy-usa.org/news/2011/10/vn-china-basic-principles-settlement-sea-issues> accessed 15 July 2021. See Carlyle A Thayer, 'South China Sea Tensions: China, the Claimant States, ASEAN and the Major Powers' in Tran Truong Thuy and Le Thuy Trang (eds), *Power, Law and Maritime Order in the South China Sea* (Lexington Books 2015) 8.

[58] Carlyle A Thayer, 'ASEAN, China and the Code of Conduct in the South China Sea' (2013) 33 SAIS Rev Int Aff 75, 76–7.

[59] DOC (n 14) art 3.

[60] See, eg 1999 Chairman's Statement of the 6th Meeting of the ASEAN Regional Forum, Singapore (26 July 1999), para 11; 2000 Joint Communiqué of the 33rd ASEAN Ministerial Meeting, Bangkok (24–25 July 2000), para 25; 2000 Chairman's Statement of the 7th Meeting of the ASEAN Regional Forum, Bangkok (27 July 2000), para 19; 2001 Joint Communiqué of the 34th ASEAN Ministerial Meeting, Ha Noi (23–24 July 2001), para 20; 1995 Joint Communiqué of the 28th ASEAN Ministerial Meeting, Bandar Seri Begawan (29–30 July 1995), para 9. These documents are all reproduced in Centre for International Law, National University of Singapore, 'Documents on ASEAN and South China Sea' <https://cil.nus.edu.sg/wp-content/uploads/2011/06/Documents-on-ASEAN-and-South-China-Sea-as-of-June-2011-pdf.pdf> accessed 15 July 2021.

[61] DOC (n 14) art 6.

[62] ibid, art 5(c).

[63] ibid, art 5.

Meeting.[64] Some projects were agreed within the frame of these meetings,[65] which also discussed the drafting of the code of conduct. The inclusion of mechanisms to review commitments under the DOC, as well as to facilitate the implementation of projects envisaged within that instrument, reflects an important practical consequence for this informal agreement, as it gives some priority to the structure of the agreement as one of the design elements.[66]

Views on the significance of the DOC have varied. It has been seen as having only a short-lived impact for reducing tension and conflict in the South China Sea.[67] There has, instead, been an increasing number of incidents occurring that would seem to run contrary to the commitments set out in the DOC.[68] The DOC has remained a point of reference for ASEAN members and China in diplomatic dialogues, but the generality of its provisions does not establish clear standards of behaviour beyond those that already exist under international law.

The legal relevance of the DOC received some attention in the *South China Sea Arbitration*. China, for example, argued that the Philippines could not proceed to arbitration under the LOSC because of the obligation to negotiate that was enshrined in the DOC.[69] China considered that the undertaking to settle disputes by negotiation in the DOC constituted a formal promise.[70] The Philippines, instead, argued that the DOC was decidedly a political, non-binding document when regard was had to its aspirational language, the circumstances of its adoption as a 'stop-gap measure' to reduce tensions, and the subsequent conduct of the parties.[71] The tribunal agreed with the Philippines, noting that much of the DOC seeks to 'reaffirm' existing international obligations.[72] The language of the DOC, the intentions of the parties (including contemporaneous statements by Chinese officials), and the circumstances at the time of adoption, along with subsequent conduct, all affirmed to the tribunal the political nature of the agreement.[73]

The DOC also affirmed that the parties would work towards the adoption of a code of conduct in the South China Sea.[74] In the *South China Sea Arbitration*, the tribunal noted the intention to proceed to a code of conduct, and considered that aspect as another marker of the informal nature of the document.[75] In this regard, the DOC aligns with one purpose

64 Keyuan Zou, 'Managing Biodiversity Conservation in Disputed Maritime Areas: The Case of the South China Sea' (2015) 18 JIWLP 97, 104.

65 See, eg Yann-Huei Song, 'The Declaration on the Conduct of Parties and a Code of Conduct in the South China Sea: Recent Actions taken by ASEAN' in Seokwoo Lee and Hee Eun Lee (eds), *Northeast Asian Perspectives on International Law: Contemporary Issues and Challenges* (Brill 2013) 46; Termsak Chalermpalanupap, 'Review of the ASEAN–China Declaration on the Conduct of Parties in the South China Sea and Prospects of a Code of Conduct in the South China Sea' in Tran Truong Thuy and Le Thuy Trang (eds), *Power, Law and Maritime Order in the South China Sea* (Lexington Books 2015) 40–41.

66 Raustiala (n 6) 585. Abbott and Snidal also recognized 'delegation' as a further characteristic in assessing different international instruments. See Abbott and Snidal (n 7) 422.

67 See Stein Tønnesson, 'The 2002 Declaration on the Conduct of the Parties in the South China Sea: Why has it not Brought more Peace and Cooperation?' in Tran Truong Thuy and Le Thuy Trang (eds), *Power, Law and Maritime Order in the South China Sea* (Lexington Books 2015) 91.

68 Incidents occurring between 2007 and 2011 are detailed in Song (n 65) 31–38. Song concludes that these tensions highlight the ineffectiveness of the DOC.

69 DOC (n 14) art 4.

70 *South China Sea Arbitration (Philippines v China)* (Award on Jurisdiction and Admissibility of 29 October 2015) PCA Case No 2013-19 (hereafter '*South China Sea Jurisdiction Award*'), para 203.

71 ibid, para 208.

72 ibid, para 215.

73 ibid, paras 217–18.

74 DOC (n 14) art 10.

75 *South China Sea Jurisdiction Award* (n 70) para 215.

commonly attributed to informal agreements: that of providing a basis for subsequent formal obligations. The informal agreement can provide the parties with an opportunity to test the standards and socialize the behaviours expected of the main actors. In this setting, reaching agreement on a treaty may be easier when there is existing familiarity with the proposed rules. However, as noted above, the standards set out in the DOC pertaining to navigation are not at all prescriptive, and the DOC, thus, reduces opportunities to test standards properly.

As a precursor to the development of the code of conduct, ASEAN and China took steps to implement the DOC. To this end, Guidelines on the Implementation of the Declaration of Conduct were adopted in 2011.[76] The guidelines anticipated that expert committee meetings would be held on marine scientific research, environmental protection, search and rescue, and transnational crime, in line with the cooperative endeavours envisaged in the DOC. However, as Thayer has noted, 'no expert committee on safety of navigation and communication at sea was established due to its contentious nature'.[77] Moreover, in accordance with these guidelines, any implementation of concrete measures had to occur on the basis of consensus among all the states concerned.[78] Again, these efforts have had minimal practical relevance and normative effect, in relation to navigation.

Pending the conclusion of a code of conduct, members of ASEAN have sought to agree terms on what would further develop the DOC. An ASEAN-led initiative was thwarted in the final stages of the 2012 ASEAN ministerial meeting—[79]some have argued that this outcome was because of China's influence over the Cambodian chair at the time—but, instead, prompted the issuance of a Six-Point Statement on the South China Sea.[80] This statement reiterated broad obligations that had been included in the 1976 Treaty of Amity and Cooperation,[81] rather than developing any new understanding of pre-existing obligations.[82]

Discussions on the code of conduct commenced in 2013, and have been protracted, with ASEAN formulating its own proposed elements for discussion.[83] However, China has commented that '[s]ome countries are looking for a quick fix [to the disputes] and are hoping to thrash out a code in a day; this approach is neither realistic nor serious'.[84] There has been some commentary about proposed provisions within the Code of Conduct, particularly as to what dispute settlement mechanisms might be included.[85] In relation to navigation, it

[76] 2011 Guidelines for the Implementation of the Declaration of Conduct on the South China Sea (20 July 2011) <https://cil.nus.edu.sg/wp-content/uploads/2019/10/2011-DOC-Guidelines.pdf> accessed 15 July 2021 (hereafter 'Guidelines').

[77] Thayer, 'ASEAN, China and the Code of Conduct in the South China Sea' (n 58) 77.

[78] Guidelines (n 76) para 6.

[79] See Sheldon W Simon, 'Conflict and Diplomacy in the South China Sea' (2012) 52 Asian Survey 995, 1015–16; Thayer, 'ASEAN, China and the Code of Conduct in the South China Sea' (n 58) 78.

[80] ASEAN's Six-Point Principles on the South China Sea (20 July 2012) <https://www.asean.org/storage/images/AFMs%20Statement%20on%206%20Principles%20on%20SCS.pdf> accessed 15 July 2021.

[81] Treaty of Amity and Cooperation in Southeast Asia (adopted 24 February 1976, entered into force 15 July 1976) 1025 UNTS 297.

[82] See Simon (n 79) 1017.

[83] See Tran Truong Thuy, 'Code of Conduct and the Prevention and Management of Incidents in the South China Sea' in Tran Truong Thuy and Le Thuy Trang (eds), *Power, Law and Maritime Order in the South China Sea* (Lexington Books 2015) 318.

[84] Cited in James W Houck and Nicole M Anderson, 'The United States, China, and Freedom of Navigation in the South China Sea' (2014) 13 Wash U Global Stud L Rev 441, 451.

[85] See, eg Mark J Valencia, 'What the 'Zero Draft' Code of Conduct for the South China Sea Says (and doesn't Say)' (*Global Asia*, March 2013) <https://www.globalasia.org/v8no1/feature/what-the-zero-draft-code-of-conduct-for-the-south-china-sea-says-and-doesnt-say_mark-j-valencia> accessed 15 July 2021; Tran (n 83) 323–25.

can be noted that an early Indonesian proposal would have included detailed provisions, drawn from the COLREGS, for preventing incidents and collisions at sea.[86]

The engagement of ASEAN and China to address navigational concerns through the DOC and subsequent instruments has, thus, been quite minimal. At most, the statements, to date, reaffirm binding obligations, which include an obligation of cooperation in semi-enclosed seas under Article 123 of the LOSC. The reaffirmation of binding obligations does not have any separate normative effect, but at least performs a diplomatic function of reminding states of, and reinforcing, their pre-existing obligations. The DOC does not encapsulate any detail as to how the freedom of navigation may be exercised in diverse settings; even the implementation of the DOC has not progressed questions related to navigational safety. ASEAN and China have affirmed the need to maintain terminology that is consistent with the LOSC and other relevant IMO treaties.[87] Simply asserting the importance of the freedom of navigation does little to elucidate the content of the associated rights and duties that are found within that freedom.[88] The existence of the mechanisms to oversee the implementation of the DOC seemingly had the capacity to build on the political commitments, but this potential has not, to date, been realized. The practical significance of the DOC is also diminished when actions appear contrary to the goals set out in the agreement. The normative effect of the DOC is, thus, extremely limited.

8.3.2 Code for Unplanned Encounters at Sea

While the DOC contains broad statements on the freedom of navigation, and cooperation on navigational safety, more details relating to navigational safety appear in the 2014 Code for Unplanned Encounters at Sea (CUES). As noted above, the CUES was adopted by the Western Pacific Naval Symposium, which is a meeting of the professional chiefs of the navies of the region. A first version of the CUES was adopted in 2003,[89] though an earlier form dates to 2000.[90] In September 2016, ASEAN members and China adopted the Joint Statement on the Application of the Code for Unplanned Encounters at Sea (CUES) in the South China Sea.[91]

The CUES 'offers a means by which navies may develop mutually rewarding international cooperation and transparency and provide leadership and broad-based involvement

[86] Thayer, 'ASEAN, China and the Code of Conduct in the South China Sea' (n 58) 79.

[87] Plan of Action to Implement the Joint Declaration on ASEAN–China Strategic Partnership for Peace and Prosperity (29 November 2004) <https://asean.org/?static_post=plan-of-action-to-implement-the-joint-declaration-on-asean-china-strategic-partnership-for-peace-and-prosperity> accessed 15 July 2021, para 1.5, cited in Song (n 65) 44.

[88] One could, potentially, argue that the ongoing recognition of the freedom of navigation means that no littoral state is permitted to declare the South China Sea as waters over which it exercises sovereignty (as opposed to sovereign rights). Such a claim of sovereignty is manifestly untenable, and it does not presently appear that China has been arguing for it over the maritime area within its claimed nine-dash line.

[89] Western Pacific Naval Symposium, 'Code for Unalerted Encounters at Sea' (June 2003) reproduced in (2012) 4 Aust J Marit & Ocean Aff 126, 126–30.

[90] Cameron Moore, 'The Arbitral Award in the Matter of the South China Sea between the Philippines and China: What are the Implications for Freedom of Navigation and the Use of Force?' (2017) 2 Asia-Pac J Ocean L & P 117, 137 (hereafter Moore, 'The Arbitral Award'). See also Anh Duc Ton, 'Code for Unplanned Encounters at Sea and its Practical Limitations in the East and South China Seas' (2017) 9 Aus J Marit & Ocean Aff 227, 229 (referring to a 1999 version adopted by the Australian Chief of Navy).

[91] 2016 Joint Statement (n 17).

in establishing international standards in relation to the use of the sea'.[92] The two main aspects of the CUES are to set out safety procedures, and to provide communications procedures. These procedures are supplemented by Annex A, which contains 'Elected Signals Vocabulary and Basic Manoeuvring Instructions'. The safety procedures begin with a statement that navies are to comply with the COLREGS, and aspects of the procedures that follow rely explicitly on rules encapsulated in the COLREGS.[93] The safety procedures address the measures that should be taken to avoid collision (including the need for safe distance and safe speed),[94] in case of breakdown,[95] when encountering vessels in formation or in convoy,[96] and forestalling the conduct of manoeuvres in traffic separation schemes.[97]

Notable is the list of measures that 'the prudent commander might generally avoid', which include simulating attacks; discharging weapons or other objects; or using lasers in a harmful manner, or in the direction or vicinity of the vessels or aircrafts encountered.[98] Arguably, from a legal perspective, these activities might indicate a failure to show due regard to other users of the seas. The due regard requirement is reflected in Articles 56 and 58 of the LOSC, as well as rule 2 of the COLREGS. COLREGS provides, in rule 2(b), that 'due regard shall be had to all dangers of navigation and collision and to any special circumstances, including the limitations of the vessels involved'. These actions to avoid may help to inform the content of this due regard obligation. As such, informal agreements may be able to add content to otherwise broader—perhaps ambiguous—formal obligations, and enhance the implementation of those formal obligations.

The scope of application of the CUES has been criticized. When a proposal was first advanced to adopt the 2003 version of the CUES, China objected to its application to the territorial sea, and to public vessels other than naval warships and naval aircraft.[99] The CUES does not specifically refer to its geographic scope of application, but, instead, uses a reference to 'at sea', which is utilized in the COLREGS to indicate the high seas and 'all waters connected therewith navigable by seagoing vessels'.[100] The latter phrase has been understood to include the territorial sea and EEZ.[101]

There has since been discussion as to whether the CUES should extend beyond navies to encompass interactions between law enforcement agencies in the region.[102] This inclusive approach, found in the 2003 version of the CUES, was dropped in the adoption of the CUES in 2014.[103] Kraska has described the application to warships only as 'the greatest shortfall' in the CUES (as well as in the China–US MoUs discussed below).[104] Ton has also pointed out

92 CUES (n 16) para 1.1.1.
93 Such as COLREGS (n 47) rr 6, 8, 10, 27(a), 34(a)–(b).
94 CUES (n 16) paras 2.1, 2.5, and 2.6
95 ibid, para 2.2.
96 ibid, para 2.3.
97 ibid, para 2.4.
98 ibid, para 2.8.1.
99 Ton (n 90) 230.
100 COLREGS (n 47) r 1(a).
101 See Ton (n 90) 231.
102 Yan Yan, 'Maritime Confidence-building Measures: Assessing China–US MOU on Notification of Major Military Activities and Rules of Behavior' in Gordon Houlden and Nong Hong (eds), *Maritime Order and the Law in East Asia* (Routledge 2018) 185.
103 Ton (n 90) 230.
104 'Perhaps the greatest shortfall in CUES and the US–China bilateral MOUs is that none of them apply to non-naval assets. Beijing employs a fleet of fishing vessels and other civil craft and coast guard ships to promote and enforce its maritime claims, and these lie outside the new agreements.': James Kraska, 'Maritime Confidence-building Measures for Navigation in the South China Sea' (2017) 32 IJMCL 268, 294.

that the 'majority of incidents which have occurred in the East and South China Seas have involved non-naval maritime law enforcement vessels such as coast guard vessels, marine surveillance ships and fishery patrol vessels'.[105] Moore, though, has noted that the limitation to warships makes sense when it is considered that the greatest risk of lethal force lies with warships rather than coastguard or fishing vessels.[106]

In addition, the CUES does not address naval vessels or aircraft engaged in surveillance, as agreement could not be reached on the inclusion of a provision on surveillance that was in the initial version of the CUES, and had been included in an earlier bilateral agreement between the United States and the then-Soviet Union.[107] A further shortcoming associated with the CUES is that, by design, it refers to unplanned encounters, but commentators have observed that some of the incidents arising between China and the United States are deliberate, constituting 'unfriendly' action to respond to what are perceived to other 'unfriendly' acts.[108] These limitations may restrict the effectiveness of the CUES in its operation. From a legal perspective, beginning with a narrower scope has provided an opportunity for the parties to consider the implications of this scope, and lay down the groundwork of understanding for any future agreement that may address these points. Having precise rules that are not legally binding may be useful for the parties to see the consequences of the rules set out, without having to take the risk of being formally bound by obligations that may carry unanticipated costs.[109]

Although the CUES has as its purpose 'establishing international standards', the document is very clear as to its non-binding status .[110] Whether navies adopt the CUES or not is a discretionary matter, but, if they do, it is on a 'voluntary and non-binding basis'.[111] Where questions of state responsibility might arise, it is explicitly provided that the 'CUES does not constitute an international agreement or treaty, and as such, is not legally binding under international law'. In light of this language, the intention of the drafters could not be plainer.

To the extent that there is an interrelationship between the CUES and international law, it is only through its replication of rules that are sourced from formal sources, such as the COLREGS or the LOSC. The relevance of international treaties to the CUES is manifest, in that terms in the CUES are to draw their definitions from the COLREGS. Even if there was any suggestion of the CUES having a formal legal status, the CUES does not supersede any existing international treaties or agreements. Moreover, the CUES does not supersede 'international law' writ large. Kraska has observed, moreover, that '[i]t is hard to find anything new in CUES, but to the extent that it reminds states of their pre-existing legal obligations, it may produce some benefit even if it is legally superfluous'.[112]

The legal status of the CUES is, therefore, clear. It does not create distinct legal standards to which states must adhere. Does that necessarily mean that it is entirely devoid of legal consequence? The manifest status of the CUES indicates that it cannot constitute any

[105] Ton (n 90) 232.

[106] Moore 'The Arbitral Award' (n 90) 136.

[107] Ton (n 90) 231. The bilateral agreement between the United States and the Soviet Union is discussed further below: see nn 114–16 and accompanying text.

[108] Mark J Valencia, 'The US–China MOU on Air and Maritime Encounters' (*The Diplomat*, 17 November 2014) <https://thediplomat.com/2014/11/the-us-china-mou-on-air-and-maritime-encounters/> accessed 15 July 2021.

[109] Abbott and Snidal (n 7) 442.

[110] 'The document is not legally binding; rather, it's a coordinated means of communication to maximise safety at sea.': CUES (n 16) para 1.1.1.

[111] ibid, para 1.4.1.

[112] Kraska (n 104) 284.

crystallization of customary international law, or contribute to its development, as there is evidently no *opinio juris*. The standards set out in the CUES are to be followed on a voluntary basis to enhance maritime safety between navies, and not because there is a belief that the navies are legally required to do so. At most, the CUES could facilitate the interpretation of broad obligations such as 'due regard', bearing in mind the elaboration in the COLREGS, and the articulation of actions a prudent commander should avoid, in the CUES. Consistent action in line with the CUES may count as subsequent practice for the purposes of treaty interpretation,[113] even if those actions cannot necessarily build towards customary international law.

8.3.3 China–US MoUs

The navigational encounters between China and the United States have led to these states seeking different means to de-escalate tensions, and the China–US MoUs are one such initiative. The arrangements between the United States and China have, occasionally, been compared to an earlier arrangement put in place between the United States and the Soviet Union in the early 1970s: the Agreement on the Prevention of Incidents On and Over the High Seas (INCSEA).[114] The INCSEA was considered to have contributed to the decline in the number and severity of incidents.[115] However, there are differences between the INCSEA and the more recent arrangements between the United States and China. These distinctions have been attributed to the disparity in naval power between the two states, as compared to the situation that existed between the United States and the Soviet Union at the time the INCSEA was adopted.[116] Pedrozo has argued that a binding agreement similar to the INCSEA is not needed between the US and China for the additional reasons that the encounters are not usually navy–navy but navy–law enforcement; the two states do not share the same interests and understanding in the freedom of navigation; and that China is an unreliable actor for the purposes of an agreement.[117] Kraska has, similarly, questioned whether a binding agreement is essential in a situation where China, from his perspective, does not abide by existing international treaties.[118] From the Chinese perspective, one scholar has described the maritime incidents between the United States and China as 'non-intentional, non-violent, non-strategic and non-challenging', and opined that, as they did

[113] Vienna Convention on the Law of Treaties (adopted 23 May 1969, entered into force 27 January 1980) 1155 UNTS 331 (hereafter 'VCLT'), art 31(3)(b). Although the more limited participation in the CUES, as compared to the LOSC, may count against this use.

[114] Agreement between the Government of the United States of America and the Government of the Union of Soviet Socialist Republics on the Prevention of Incidents on and over the High Seas (adopted 25 May 1972, entered into force 25 May 1972) 852 UNTS 151 (hereafter 'INCSEA').

[115] Timothy J Nagle, 'The Dangerous Military Activities Agreement: Minimum Order and Superpower Relations on the World's Oceans' (1990) 31 Va J Intl L 125, 130. A later agreement with similar effect was the 1989 Jackson Hole Agreement, which reduced tensions between the United States and the then-Soviet Union in the Black Sea: Agreement and Joint Statement on Uniform Interpretation of the Rules of International Law Governing Innocent Passage (23 September 1989) 28 ILM 1444. For discussion, see William J Aceves, 'Diplomacy at Sea: US Freedom of Navigation Operations in the Black Sea' (1993) 46(2) Naval War Coll Rev 59, 73–75.

[116] Yan (n 102) 180–81.

[117] See Pete Pedrozo, 'The US–China Incidents at Sea Agreement: A Recipe for Disaster' (2012) 6 JNSLP 207, 209.

[118] Kraska (n 104) 274, 295. See also ibid 209.

not present issues for core interests they, hence, did not warrant a binding legal agreement equivalent to the INCSEA.[119]

The China–US MoUs sit within a legal framework established by a 1998 bilateral treaty entitled 'Agreement on Establishing a Consultation Mechanism to Strengthen Military Maritime Safety (MMCA)'.[120] This agreement was very much about modalities of communication, and does not directly have a bearing on the freedom of navigation, or inform responses to navigational incidents.[121] The consultations envisaged in the MMCA could cover diverse topics, and include 'measures to promote safe maritime practices and establish mutual trust as search and rescue, communications procedures when ships encounter each other, interpretation of the Rules of the Nautical Road and avoidance of accidents-at-sea'.[122] Most notably, for present purposes, the MMCA sought to promote 'common understandings regarding activities undertaken by their respective maritime and air forces when operating in accordance with international law, including the principles and regimes reflected in [the LOSC]'.[123] The MMCA led to the adoption of the Behavior MoU and Notification MoU.

As an initial matter, it can be noted that, while some standards are set out, neither of these MoUs seek to specify the corresponding maritime area in which they apply.[124] This feature may be both a strength and a weakness. The strength is that the working assumption might be that the expected behaviours are applicable throughout the South China Sea without regard to questions of territorial sovereignty, or the existence of territorial sea or EEZ maritime areas. Instead, the MoUs apply wherever the two navies encounter each other. The weakness might be the opportunity that is created for either party to negate the application of the standards of behaviour in specific maritime areas as suits their political preferences in addressing (or redressing) a military encounter. This weakness is seemingly compounded by the ongoing disagreements between China and the United States over issues like military activities in the EEZ, and what constitutes use of maritime areas for 'peaceful purposes'.[125]

8.3.3.1 Behavior MoU

The Behavior MoU, adopted in 2014, recognizes, in its preamble, several multilateral treaties that deal with questions of behaviour with regards to the safety of air and maritime encounters , as well as the adoption of the CUES. The Behavior MoU is, thus, cast as 'an effort to strengthen adherence to existing international law and norms'.[126]

The legal status of the Behavior MoU is set out clearly in Section V, which provides that:

> This Memorandum is not intended to be binding under international law.

[119] Cited in Yan (n 102) 182 (but not indicating which Chinese scholar is quoted).

[120] Agreement between the Department of Defense of the United States of America and the Ministry of National Defense of the People's Republic of China on Establishing a Consultation Mechanism to Strengthen Military Maritime Safety (adopted 19 January 1998, entered into force 19 January 1998) 37 ILM 530 (hereafter 'MMCA').

[121] The MMCA has been criticized because of its failure to address standards of behaviour in the face of military manoeuvres: see Yan (n 102) 177. Ji has also noted that the MMCA was 'shelved' by the Bush Administration in 1998. See Ji Guoxing, 'Rough Waters in the South China Sea: Navigation Issues and Confidence-building Measures' (2001) 53 Asia Pac I 1, 2.

[122] MMCA (n 120) art II(1).

[123] ibid, art I.

[124] Yan (n 102) 186.

[125] ibid 187.

[126] Behavior MoU (n 18) s I. A goal that is undermined by the fact that China and the United States disagree on the meaning of existing international law in relation to military activities in the EEZ. See Valencia, 'The US–China MOU' (n 108).

> This Memorandum is not intended to affect the rights or obligations of either Side under relevant international agreements or customary international law.
>
> This Memorandum is made without prejudice to either Side's policy perspective on military activities in the Exclusive Economic Zone.[127]

In this context, the intention of both states as to the legal character of the agreement is manifest. It does beg the question as to why such a firm position on the legal status of the agreement was necessary. This question is especially pertinent when considering the text of Annexes I and II of the Behavior MoU, including its use of legal definitions, as well as the replication of provisions enshrined in treaties and the CUES, and the prescriptive nature of the provisions when it comes to regulating encounters between military vessels and aircraft (nominated as 'rules').

The Behavior MoU contains provisions that address general navigational safety rules, rules for specially designated areas, and rules 'for establishing trust at sea'.[128] These rules draw heavily from the CUES, COLREGS, the International Code of Signals, the LOSC, and also a Manual on Maritime Safety Information prepared jointly by the International Hydrographic Organization, the IMO, and the World Meteorological Organization. The Behavior MoU, thus, draws on both formal and informal agreements. Repeating current treaty obligations, where the same language is involved, arguably does no more than reaffirm the existence of that obligation. Where language of informal agreements is repeated, that does not necessarily transform them into legally binding agreements.[129] The repetition of expected standards of behaviour may, though, potentially have relevance for treaty interpretation as subsequent state practice.[130]

The use of these different sources may be seen in various ways within the Behavior MoU. For example, the rules on specially designated areas anticipate appropriate warnings or warning areas being established for activities that may affect the safety of nearby military vessels or military aircraft. This situation may require active notification, in accordance with the CUES and the International Code of Signals, as well as the provision of timely hazard warnings, which aligns with the International Code of Signals and the Manual on Maritime Safety Information.[131] In this situation, the military vessels or aircraft of the other party are to refrain from interfering with activities in a declared warning area, albeit while still enjoying the freedom of navigation, in line with Articles 56 and 58 of the LOSC.[132]

To the extent that questions might arise as to whether due regard is shown, it is interesting to note a similar approach to the CUES whereby the rules for establishing mutual trust list actions that a 'prudent commander ... or master generally should avoid'.[133] These actions include simulation of attacks, the discharge of signal rockets or weapons (unless in distress), illumination of the navigation bridges of military vessels, the harmful use of lasers, the unsafe approach by one side's small craft to another side's vessel, and '[o]ther actions that may pose a threat to the other Side's military vessels'.[134] As noted above,[135] these

[127] Behavior MoU (n 18) s V.

[128] ibid, ss II–IV.

[129] *South China Sea Jurisdiction Award* (n 70) para 244.

[130] VCLT, art 31(3)(b) (n 113). Although the impact of a bilateral informal agreement may be more limited in this regard.

[131] Behavior MoU (n 18) Annex II, s VI.

[132] ibid, Annex II, s V(i)(3).

[133] ibid, s VI(ii).

[134] ibid, Annex II, s VI(ii).

[135] See n 97 and accompanying text.

actions may help to determine whether an actor has shown the requisite due regard in the exercise of the freedom of navigation.

Where there is a collision following an encounter at sea, the Behavior MoU indicates that the two sides:

> should separate immediately after damage control and life-saving measures are taken and should avoid taking any action that leads to escalation of the situation. Both Sides should conduct active rescue of personnel as required by international law and in the spirit of safety of life at sea, as their capacity allows. However, one Side may not board or salvage the other Side's military vessel or military aircraft without prior explicit consent.[136]

The note to this rule indicates that it is predicated on Articles 32, 58(2), 95, and 236 of the LOSC, which address the sovereign immunity of warships. On this basis, it is arguable that this provision of the Behavior MoU provides some details as to the appropriate or expected standard of behaviour for meeting these immunity requirements under the LOSC (or customary international law), in the context of a collision resulting from an encounter at sea.

The lack of legal status of the Behavior MoU may well augur against the use of any standards of conduct set out within the MoU in interpreting or applying formal legal obligations under the LOSC, customary international law, or the COLREGS, in the relations between the parties. The disavowal of legal status necessitates giving pause in this regard. On the other hand, where there is a need to determine if the United States or China is acting consistently with broad obligations concerned with due regard, or affecting the immunities of warships, the Behavior MoU assists in providing an agreed benchmark and, thus, should at least be taken into consideration.

8.3.3.2 Notification MoU

The Notification MoU is focused on determining when notifications of military activities are necessary, and underlining the exchange of information relating to each side's security policy, strategy, and intent.[137] The preamble highlights the strengthening of mutual trust and confidence through reciprocal notifications and information sharing. The purpose of the Notification MoU is to create a frame for specific notification activities. Annex I is focused on the voluntary exchange of information through briefings and information about speeches, announcements, and government publications.[138] Annex II seeks to promote the use of military observers at both sides' exercises, as a further means of reducing misunderstanding and miscalculation.[139] In each instance, an annual assessment working group meets to review progress, and consult on improvements for future implementation of this confidence-building mechanism.[140]

The normative effect of the Notification MoU is not immediately apparent. The significance of this agreement rests in the creation of the mechanism to monitor behaviour and exchange information. The existence of what may loosely be described as a compliance mechanism facilitates the governance arrangements around military encounters between

[136] Behavior MoU (n 18) Annex II, s VI(iv)(2).
[137] Notification MoU (n 20) Annex 1, s I.
[138] ibid, Annex I, s II.
[139] ibid, Annex II, s I.
[140] ibid, s III.

China and the United States. The existence of such processes enhances the likelihood that standards agreed between the parties will be followed as promised, because there is a means against which to assess performance if the parties wish to do so.

As Yan comments, '[i]t seems that both countries do not want to have a legally binding agreement to restrain them from possible future dangerous activities at sea'.[141] Indeed, Kraska has been critical of the China–US MoUs on the basis that the non-binding terms diminish obligations that are mandatory, as set out in binding treaties, or as part of customary international law, and, hence, are binding on both states.[142] The United States would seem to prefer that existing international agreements be applied, rather than developing a new agreement.[143] In this instance, it is arguable that the addition of the informal agreements may be antagonistic to the core elements of the formal agreements that were already in place between the parties.[144]

In sum, the discussion of each of these informal agreements has sought to provide indications of how they intersect (or not) with international law, observing that, at most, the standards of behaviour set out in the informal agreements may have some interpretative value. This relevance arises from the detail that is sometimes provided on what conduct should occur in different situations, and how those expectations fit within broader requirements enshrined in international treaties or customary international law. While the significance of these agreements for international law is worth contemplating, the normative effect should not be overstated. The limitations in their impact for international law, therefore, prompt consideration as to what other reasons may be provided for the existence and significance of these informal agreements. To this end, the following section explores the political characterization of these agreements, as well as a governance framework.

8.4 Alternative Explanatory Paradigms for Informal Agreements on Navigational Safety

In light of the clear disavowal of the legal status of the informal agreements examined above, and the concomitant constrained relevance under international law, it should be asked whether there are alternative ways to explain the role of these informal agreements. It is evident that, from a strategic perspective, informal agreements provide a means to accommodate power differentials and different policy preferences. States may be willing to pursue informal agreements as a strategic choice where they expect to improve their own situation in expectation of reciprocal changes by others.[145] Moreover, the process of reaching agreement as to shared expectations about behaviour may count in diffusion of tension in the immediate aftermath of the adoption of the agreement, as well as providing a testing ground for further agreement in the future. Moreover, less precise language in an agreement still allows a party some room to manoeuvre if adverse circumstances develop in the future.[146]

[141] Yan (n 102) 185.

[142] Kraska (n 104) 287–89, 291–92.

[143] Mira Rapp-Hooper and Bonnie Glaser, 'In Confidence: Will we Know if US–China CBMs are Working?' (*Asia Maritime Transparency Initiative*, 4 February 2015) <https://amti.csis.org/in-confidence-will-we-know-if-us-china-cbms-are-working/> accessed 15 July 2021.

[144] Shaffer and Pollack (n 6) 790–91.

[145] Lipson (n 7) 500.

[146] See Abbott and Snidal (n 7) 435.

As such, it is necessary to go beyond the strict parameters of international law and its formal sources and rules for lawmaking.

An alternative frame for understanding these agreements, and the processes by which they were reached, is within the political sphere of confidence-building measures (CBMs). Perhaps there is no lawmaking but, simply, political agreements. The first section below contemplates the use of CBMs, and their possible interrelationship with international law. The second section considers a more holistic account of law and politics in exploring a contemporary theory of governance—experimentalist governance—which seeks to explain the incentives for, and influence of, informal lawmaking in describing state action.

8.4.1 Confidence-building Measures

CBMs have featured in security studies,[147] and have been defined broadly as 'measures that address, prevent, or resolve uncertainties among states'.[148] More specifically in this context, CBMs can provide reassurance 'that certain legitimate military activities undertaken by potential adversaries are not intended as threatening'.[149] The reassurance must be credible.[150] As such, CBMs are designed to prevent escalation of hostilities and build mutual trust, especially in the face of a long-term irreconcilable problem, and can take many forms,[151] and may contain declaratory statements, or anticipate the taking of, or abstaining from, certain actions.[152] The functions of CBMs differ, but most commonly address information, notification, observation, and stabilization.[153] These features are evident in the Notification MoU, which is expressly designated as a CBM.

Desjardins has noted that those favouring CBMs over formal international law find CBMs politically attractive because they 'require only a minimum of political will, they imply reciprocity, they are initially nonconstraining and they involve no legally binding obligations'.[154] Each of the informal agreements examined in the previous section would fit within this frame. Another advantage to CBMs is that they do not necessarily deal with the root cause of the existing problems but, instead, focus on how the parties may gain greater confidence in understanding each other.[155] Understood in this context, the informal agreements discussed above may be seen as laying the groundwork for future, potentially binding, agreements.[156]

[147] They were initially proposed within the context of the Helsinki Conference on Security and Cooperation in Europe in the early 1970s.

[148] Yan (n 102) 176.

[149] Jonathan Alford, 'Confidence-building Measures in Europe: The Military Aspects' (1979) 149 Adelphi Pap 4, 4. CBMs 'are able to affect perceptions of danger in relation to military activities, they embody and project notions of shared interest—a concept of common security'. Johan Jørgen Holst, 'Confidence-building Measures: A Conceptual Framework' (1983) 25 Surv 2, 5.

[150] Alford (n 149) 5.

[151] Yan (n 102) 176.

[152] Holst further observes that these actions may be procedural or substantive in nature: Holst (n 149) 4.

[153] ibid.

[154] Marie-France Desjardins, *Rethinking Confidence-building Measures* (Routledge 2014) 24.

[155] See Simon JA Mason and Matthias Siegfried, 'Confidence Building Measures (CBMs) in Peace Processes' in *Managing Peace Processes: Process Related Questions. A Handbook for AU Practitioners* (African Union and the Centre for Humanitarian Dialogue 2013) 58.

[156] Ji has argued that 'confidence-building efforts aimed more narrowly—on practical navigation issues and managing "incidents at sea"—offer a starting point for first bilateral and then multilateral agreements': Ji (n 121) 1. See also Rapp-Hooper and Glaser (n 143).

CBMs do not usually have normative intent, given their political nature, and, especially in the context of the South China Sea, the informal agreements have been responsive to tensions arising because of disputed territorial sovereignty, and because of opposing views on rights and duties relating to navigation. As non-legally binding instruments, the intention is not to solve legal or geopolitical differences, but to provide a modus operandi to address issues of common concern (such as transnational crime, navigational safety, and search and rescue). The informal agreements, largely, do not resolve the core problems, but in maintaining this status quo, they endeavour to ameliorate conditions. Whether confidence is truly being built in the face of conduct that is inconsistent with the standards set out in the informal agreements may well be questioned. A political realist may dismiss CBMs as a form of appeasement to, or perhaps a distraction for, domestic or other constituencies that are insisting on any action being taken to respond to a perceived problem. CBMs may, thus, not achieve the substantial results that are sought, despite the time and effort involved in devising them in the first place.[157]

Characterizing these informal agreements as CBMs does provide some explanation for their initiation. Although there was no normative intent, the previous section has indicated that these CBMs may still give rise to normative effect in limited ways. States do give assurances, with varying degrees of precision, as to how they intend to behave in relation to specific issues and, thereby, create expectations in the conduct of international relations, even if those expectations are not associated with binding legal commitments.[158] The relevance of these commitments is underlined when there are also mechanisms put in place to assess the conduct, in line with these non-legally binding commitments.[159] A theory of CBMs, therefore, provides only part of the story in understanding the role for informal agreements in addressing navigational safety.

8.4.2 Experimentalist Governance

If we consider that CBMs may reflect informal agreements, and that confidence-building was a reason to create these agreements, we still need to explore the evolutionary process that sometimes follows the conclusion of the agreements. This perspective is not intended to suggest that all CBMs evolve into something more. Indeed, the DOC is so vague, from a normative perspective, that it does little to evolve much of anything. Can we find another way of understanding what might be happening here? Theories of governance may have some utility because they can capture the principles, processes, actors, and institutions involved in regulating conduct, and that have developed in different forms. Global governance recognizes that 'novel forms of regulation are developing alongside more traditional forms of international law'.[160] International relations theorists have progressed their

[157] See, generally, Desjardins (n 154). Kraska has questioned whether the measures put in place should be considered as CBMs, when taking into account the offset strategies that are being deployed in the region instead: see Kraska (n 104) 277.

[158] See Michael Bothe, 'Legal and Non-legal Norms—A Meaningful Distinction in International Relations' (1980) 11 NYIL 65, 70–71.

[159] ibid 78.

[160] Gráinne de Búrca, Robert O Keohane, and Charles Sabel, 'New Modes of Pluralist Global Governance' (2013) 45 NYU J Intl'l L & Pol 723, 725.

interpretation of international behaviour from regime theory to regime complexity,[161] but have needed to go further to capture how governance architecture might cope with rapidly changing environments in the face of uncertainty.[162]

Reflecting on these new forms of cooperation, especially in the absence of one dominant hegemon, or a monopolistic international institution, scholars have developed the concept of 'experimentalist governance', which:

> represents a form of adaptive, open-ended, participatory, and information-rich cooperation in world politics, in which the local and the transnational interact through the localized elaboration and adaption of transnationally agreed general norms, subject to periodic revision in light of knowledge locally generated.[163]

The concept of experimentalist governance has been used fruitfully to investigate an array of regulatory domains.[164] Adopting and building on new approaches to global governance could assist in discerning the future direction of ocean governance.

Experimentalist governance anticipates the use of informal agreements in: (1) setting overarching goals; (2) providing flexibility in how those goals might be reached by varied actors; (3) allowing for some sort of reporting mechanism; and (4) occasional revision of what was agreed in response to identified problems and possibilities.[165] In some respects, these elements of experimentalist governance align with the identified design elements of informal agreements.[166] Each of the informal agreements under discussion in this study may be tested against the experimentalist governance framework.

First, in relation to the DOC, the generality of the provisions, coupled with the intention to create a framework for improved cooperation in addressing differences that arise in the South China Sea may be construed as reflecting the establishment of framework goals and indicators to achieve those goals. As the terms of the DOC are quite broad, the states concerned retain flexibility in how they meet the varied goals. Arguably, this flexibility was manifest in the Philippines' decision to pursue arbitration under the LOSC, beyond the undertaking to negotiate differences pursuant to the DOC. The Senior Officials Meeting and the Joint Working Group seemingly provided a mechanism to show performance, and permit peer review of actions taken. As for the revision of the goals, it could be argued that the development of the code of conduct is the process that facilitates this dimension. There is a prima facie fit with experimentalist governance, but the DOC should not be examined in isolation from the actual conduct undertaken within the South China Sea, the limited activity of the Joint Working Group in implementing the DOC, and the glacial pace of negotiations on the code of conduct.

[161] See, eg Robert O Keohane and David G Victor, 'The Regime Complex for Climate Change' (2011) 9 Perspect Politics 7; Kal Raustiala and David G Victor, 'The Regime Complex for Plant Genetic Resources' (2004) 58 Intl'l Org 277, 279.

[162] Christine Overdevest and Jonathan Zeitlin, 'Assembling an Experimentalist Regime: Transnational Governance Interactions in the Forest Sector' (2014) 8 Reg & Gov 22, 26.

[163] de Búrca, Keohane, and Sabel (n 160) 726–27.

[164] See, eg Charles F Sabel and Jonathan Zeitlin, 'Learning from Difference: The New Architecture of Experimentalist Governance in the EU' (2008) 14 ELJ 271; Chiara Armeni, 'Global Experimentalist Governance, International Law and Climate Change Technologies' (2015) 64 ICLQ 875.

[165] Overdevest and Zeitlin (n 162) 44.

[166] Raustiala (n 6).

Second, the CUES also has the overriding objectives, as mentioned above, of developing 'mutually rewarding international cooperation and transparency', and providing 'leadership and broad-based involvement in establishing international standards in relation to the use of the sea'.[167] The voluntary nature of the CUES could align with the flexibility in implementation. In terms of a review mechanism, the Western Pacific Naval Symposium 'will accept recommendations from any competent source for development of CUES to improve its effectiveness, examine proposals for developing high levels of safety in maritime operations and for improvements to communications'.[168] As indicated in the discussion on the CUES, consideration has already emerged on enlarging the scope of application beyond naval vessels.

Third, the China–US MoUs align with the experimentalist governance criteria for the bigger goals relating to behaviour for the safety of maritime and air encounters between their respective defence forces. Similarly to the CUES, the prescriptive nature of some of the rules may remove some flexibility, but the voluntary nature of the agreements, the reservation of policy positions, and the ambiguity occasionally left within the agreements allows for different views in operation. The Notification MoU and the overarching MMCA ostensibly provide recourse for review and modifications. The latter dimension appears to have been minimally achieved.

Elements of experimentalist governance may, thus, be discerned from these informal agreements addressing navigation, when examined individually. Yet, examination in isolation does not provide a complete account of the governance framework influencing behaviour towards navigational safety.[169] When taken together, the state-centred nature of the agreements reduces elements of participation and transparency that otherwise contribute to the creation of 'compliance pull',[170] and to good governance. The review mechanisms that have the potential to provide information have performed modestly, if at all, to date. For navigational safety to be enhanced, let alone other aspects of navigation, stronger adherence to monitoring the standards set out, and to revising those standards when necessary, is essential.[171] While there are no sanctions that result from a review of conduct, an increased sharing of information would allow for learning, and should provide opportunities to socialize the expected behaviours within domestic decision-making structures.[172] Some of these dimensions are better met through formal law. By placing only the informal agreements within this frame, their shortcomings, from a governance perspective, are apparent. These 'novel forms of regulation'[173] would, thus, seem to need to operate in tandem with formal legal obligations in order to achieve better governance outcomes.

[167] CUES (n 16) para 1.1.1.

[168] ibid, para 1.6.2.

[169] Raustiala has noted the need to 'pay more attention to the complex architecture of agreements and treat their design holistically': Raustiala (n 6) 609.

[170] See Lipson (n 7) 500–01.

[171] In this vein, Pauwelyn, Wessels, and Wouters have observed the need for 'serious thought [as] to what legal effects it [an informal agreement] may still have and how to control these effects. Checks and balances are needed which should involve an examination of (i) the source, respectability, and authority of the norm-creating body, (ii) transparency, openness, and neutrality in the norm's procedural elaboration, and (iii) the substantive quality consistency, and overall acceptance (consensus of the norm)': Joost Pauwelyn, Ramses A Wessel, and Jan Wouters, 'When Structures Become Shackles: Stagnation and Dynamics in International Lawmaking' (2014) 25 EJIL 733, 757.

[172] See Raustiala (n 6) 607.

[173] de Búrca, Keohane, and Sabel (n 160) 725.

8.5 Concluding Remarks

The reality is that the informal agreements addressing navigational safety addressed in section 8.3 serve both political and legal ends. They have political effect as CBMs, and in diplomatic discourse. Informal agreements like the CUES and the Behavior MoU provide useful tools for decision-making in operational contexts in the day-to-day functions of vessels. Reaching agreement, as reflected in the DOC, the CUES, and the bilateral MoUs between China and the United States, may also have provided some political respite, in at least presenting a solution to a perceived problem in the short term. The future code of conduct may also be viewed in the latter vein.

These informal agreements also have normative effect in the limited ways identified in this discussion. They have this effect because the informal lawmaking process established shared expectations on the relevant standards of behaviour in different situations, or at least reaffirmed the importance of international law as a totem in resolving differences that emerge in ocean use. Arguably, these informal agreements have, in their development, further served as responses to perceived legal transgressions, and as forms of restoring situations that previously existed, which aligns with the concept of reparations for state responsibility.

Neither dimension can be overinflated to suggest that more is being delivered than the concerned parties intended. This caution is needed because the reality is that navigational contestations remain and have, indeed, been exacerbated in recent times. Nonetheless, these informal agreements should serve as starting points for improving the current situation.[174] What we know from experimentalist governance is that there are tools that could be added or strengthened to these agreements to provide them with more meaning in moderating state conduct.[175] In the context of the South China Sea, it would seem that incrementalism is inevitable.

The United States and other like-minded states may be concerned that China's incrementalism is deviating away from the navigational rights and duties as understood at the time the LOSC was adopted. If so, those states should engage more in articulating and adhering to those treaty and customary international law standards, if informal agreements are not to be antagonistic to the existing law.[176] Adherence to certain standards will also be greater if the states concerned are prepared to have stronger monitoring and review mechanisms in place,[177] as well as opportunities for learning and changing of goals as the situation shifts.

This chapter has sought to show the normative effect of a small number of informal agreements pertaining to navigational safety. It has also sought to progress this understanding by placing these agreements in the alternative explanatory paradigms of CBMs and experimentalist governance. A greater appreciation of all of these dimensions will, hopefully, contribute to the potential of informal agreements that enhance navigational safety being fully realized.

[174] '[An informal agreement] offers more effective ways to deal with uncertainty, especially when it initiates processes that allow actors to learn about the impact of agreements over time.': Abbott and Snidal (n 7) 423.

[175] To test experimentalist governance, the informal agreements can be assessed for their coherence, accountability, determinacy, sustainability, epistemic quality, and fairness: Keohane and Victor (n 161) 8.

[176] A phenomenon recognized in Shaffer and Pollack's work. See Shaffer and Pollack (n 6) 790–91.

[177] Allowing for structural mechanisms to disperse information, and allow strategies of reciprocity to operate, can contribute positively to the effectiveness of informal agreements. See Raustiala (n 6) 605.

PART IV

MARINE RESOURCES, RESEARCH, AND TECHNOLOGY

9

Unconventional Lawmaking in the Offshore Energy Sector

Flexibilities and Weaknesses of the International Legal Framework

Seline Trevisanut

9.1 Introduction

Offshore exploitation of oil and gas started in the 1930s, and thousands of installations are distributed around the world. Offshore installations threaten the environment, not only when it comes to oil spills—which are the most visible example, but, admittedly, rare—but also in relation to their contribution to marine debris, pollution by dumping, and greenhouse gas emissions.[1] Nonetheless, the construction, operation, and decommissioning of offshore installations, in the energy sector and beyond, is one of the maritime economic activities that has not yet been comprehensively regulated at the global level. The relevant international legal framework consists of a plethora of instruments adopted at the global, regional, and supranational level, which have developed in different institutional settings, and in different formats. The result is, first, that there is no specialized framework convention and, consequently, the legal framework is fragmented at the sectoral, institutional, geographical, and issue-related levels. Second, the legal framework is weak because of the non-binding nature of many of the instruments that are the outcome of unconventional lawmaking[2] processes. Third, the lawmaking processes in this field seem to be industry-led because of the important role the industry plays in unconventional lawmaking, both within and outside conventional fora.[3]

[1] 'Over 65 per cent of the ocean area is now experiencing cumulative impacts from human activities, including direct exploitation, in particular, overexploitation of fish, shellfish and other organisms, land- and sea-based pollution and land- and sea-use change, including coastal development for infrastructure and aquaculture. More food, energy and materials are being supplied than ever before, but increasingly at the expense of the planet's ability to contribute to future generations': UN, *Oceans and the Law of the Sea*, Report of the Secretary-General, UNGA Res 74/350 (11 September 2019) UN Doc A/74/350, para 54. Concerning the specific impact of deep-water oil and gas drilling, see Erik E Cordes and others, 'Environmental Impacts of the Deep-water Oil and Gas Industry: A Review to Guide Management Strategies' (2016) 4(58) Front Environ Sci.

[2] The expression 'unconventional lawmaking' builds on the concept of 'informal lawmaking', which, according to Pauwelyn, consists of international cooperation to reach agreements (other than treaties) between public authorities, with or without the participation of private actors or international organizations, in varied institutions and networks: Joost Pauwelyn, 'Informal International Lawmaking: Framing the Concept and Research Questions' in Joost Pauwelyn, Ramses Wessel, and Jan Wouters (eds), *Informal International Lawmaking* (OUP 2013) 13. Unconventional lawmaking, however, does not follow the methodology proposed by Pauwelyn, and, for instance, focuses on the 'normative intent' and the 'normative output' of the lawmaking process, beyond the formality of the actors and the process itself. For further information, see Klein, in Chapter 1 of this volume.

[3] The present author uses the expression 'conventional fora' to refer to entities created by treaty, at the global or regional level, and that consist of the institutional settings within which unconventional lawmaking takes place. By

Seline Trevisanut, *Unconventional Lawmaking in the Offshore Energy Sector* In: *Unconventional Lawmaking in the Law of the Sea*. Edited by: Natalie Klein, Oxford University Press. © Seline Trevisanut 2022. DOI: 10.1093/oso/9780192897824.003.0009

While unconventional lawmaking processes guarantee flexibility, and the necessary timeliness of regulatory efforts for a sector in continuous development and expansion, they do not necessarily allow for safeguarding or ensuring the coherence of the legal framework. Moreover, the processes might be abused to push forward the agenda of the strongest actors, at the expense of global commons such as the marine environment and climate. In order to support these submissions, the present chapter will proceed in four steps.

First, it will briefly introduce the existing conventional legal framework, and highlight its fragmentation at the material and geographical levels. Special attention will be dedicated to the mechanisms for the further development of the law contained in the analysed instruments, for example rules of reference and monitoring mechanisms. Second, the analysis will concentrate on unconventional lawmaking performed by conventional actors, namely competent international organizations and treaty bodies, with a focus on the standards for the conduct of environmental impact assessments. Third, the chapter will analyse the role of private actors, namely the industry, in unconventional lawmaking. Self-regulation plays an important role in the offshore energy sector. Codes of conduct adopted by multinational corporations, and guidelines and recommendations drafted by professional associations, highly influence the legal framework at the international level. A special mention will be made here of the renewable energy sector, and the role of the International Renewable Energy Agency (IRENA) as an example of an industry-led international organization that has only produced unconventional law, so far. Fourth, the legal nature of the outcomes of unconventional lawmaking will be analysed in light of their relationship to the existing conventional instruments. Specifically, it will be considered whether the unconventional lawmaking in the offshore energy sector has an autonomous normativity,[4] or whether the legal status of the resulting instruments derives from the instruments' function as interpretative tools of applicable binding instruments. Some concluding remarks will be presented, in order to highlight how unconventional lawmaking contributes to the fragmented and weak nature of the existing international legal framework.

9.2 The Fragmented Legal Framework

The offshore energy sector has expanded considerably in the last thirty years. Commentators talk about an 'offshorization'[5] of energy production. The expansion of the sector has multiplied the risks associated with this activity, especially when we consider the increased exploitation of deep-water resources.[6] The *Deepwater Horizon* disaster in April

contrast, 'unconventional fora' are non-treaty based institutional settings, for instance a professional association or a non-governmental organization (NGO).

[4] Considering the focus on lawmaking in the present volume, the analysis in this chapter strives to distinguish, as much as possible, between the making of law and the making of interpretative tools, through informal processes. Interpretative tools, such as guidelines or recommendations, can become law through practice and gain a certain normative autonomy.

[5] Tarik Dahou, 'La politique des espaces maritimes en Afrique. Louvoyer entre local et global' (2009) 116 Pol Afr 10.

[6] See, for instance, the debates concerning the exploitation of oil and gas in the deep waters of the Arctic Ocean: Will Amos, 'Development of Canadian Arctic Offshore Oil and Gas Drilling: Lessons from the Gulf of Mexico' (2011) 20 RECIEL 39; Rachael L Johnstone, *Offshore Oil and Gas Development in the Arctic under International Law: Risk and Responsibility* (Brill 2015); Karen N Scott, 'Drilling at the Poles: Environmental

2010[7] is, of course, a clear example of the risks associated with deep-water oil and gas exploitation. As mentioned above, no framework convention regulates the offshore energy sector. The legal framework has, instead, developed in a fragmented manner, following a problem-based approach at the global level, and a geographical approach at the regional level.

9.2.1 The *Ratione Materiae* Fragmentation at the Global Level

The United Nations Convention on the Law of the Sea (LOSC or the Convention)[8] contains a series of obligations that set the jurisdictional framework for conducting offshore energy activities, and for the protection of the marine environment. Pursuant to Articles 60 and 80, coastal states have exclusive rights to authorize the construction of, and exclusive jurisdiction over, installations in, respectively, their exclusive economic zone (EEZ) and continental shelf. The coastal state has an obligation to give due notice of the construction of any such installation, of the presence of any such installation at any time, and, where necessary, it can establish a safety zone around it. The safety zone in the LOSC has a double purpose: to ensure the safety of both navigation within the zone, and the installation.[9] The safety zone aims at avoiding any undue interference with the equipment that could jeopardize the security of the installation and the continuation of the economic activity.

The LOSC further contains, in Part XII, a series of obligations for the protection of the marine environment. First, while exercising their sovereign rights pursuant to Article 193, states shall comply with 'the obligation to protect and preserve the marine environment', as set out in Article 192, and take the necessary measures to prevent, reduce, and control pollution.[10] Coastal states have a duty to ensure that pollution arising from activities within their jurisdiction and control does not extend beyond those areas.[11] If there is an imminent

Protection in the Antarctic and the Arctic' in Malgosia Fitzmaurice, David M Ong, and Panos Merkouris (eds), *Research Handbook on International Environmental Law* (Edward Elgar 2010) 654–79.

[7] The *Deepwater Horizon* was a mobile offshore drilling unit that was operated at a depth of more than 1500 m in the Gulf of Mexico. Following an explosion in April 2010, killing eleven crew members, the rig sank, and an oil spill affected more than 1000 km of coastline. See Ruwantissa Abeyratne, 'The Deepwater Horizon Disaster—Some Liability Issues' (2010) 35 Tul Mar L J 125>. It severely damaged the environment and caused immense costs for the private economy in the region: John Mervin, 'Counting the Cost of the BP Disaster One Year' on (*BBC News*, 20 April 2011) <https://www.bbc.com/news/business-13120605> accessed 4 April 2021; Pacific States/British Columbia Oil Spill Task Force, *Deepwater Horizon Oil Spill, Incident Specific Preparedness Review (ISPR)* (2011) <www.uscg.mil/foia/docs/dwh/bpdwh.pdf> accessed 4 April 2021.

[8] United Nations Convention on the Law of the Sea (adopted 10 December 1982, entered into force 16 November 1994) 1833 UNTS 397 (hereafter 'LOSC').

[9] For further details on the legal regime of safety zones, see, inter alia, Stuart Kaye, 'International Measures to Protect Oil Platforms, Pipelines, and Submarine Cables from Attack' (2006–2007) 31 Tul Mar L J 377; Alex Oude Elferink, 'The *Arctic Sunrise* Incident: A Multi-faceted Law of the Sea Case with a Human Rights Dimension' (2014) 29 IJMCL 244; Sebastian Tho Pesch, 'Coastal State Jurisdiction around Installations: Safety Zones in the Law of the Sea' (2015) 30 IJMCL 512.

[10] LOSC (n 8) art 194. For a recent interpretation of the articles mentioned, in relation to the construction of installations and artificial islands, see *South China Sea Arbitration (Philippines v China)* (Award of 12 July 2016) PCA Case No 2013-19, spec. paras 983 ff.

[11] LOSC (n 8) art 194(2). This LOSC provision reaffirms the well-established customary norm prohibiting transboundary pollution. First affirmed in the *Trail Smelter* case (*United States v Canada* (Award of 11 March 1941)) RIAA 1941 vol III, 1905, the International Court of Justice (ICJ) has provided that, 'The existence of the general obligation of States to ensure that activities within their jurisdiction and control respect the environment of other States or of areas beyond national control is now part of the corpus of international law relating to the environment.': ICJ, *The Legality of the Threat or Use of Nuclear Weapons* (Advisory Opinion of 8 July 1996), para 29. See also Younna Lyons, 'Transboundary Pollution from Offshore Oil and Gas Activities in the Seas of the Southeast

risk of damage to the marine environment, the coastal state has an obligation to notify any other state that might be affected by such damage.[12]

Article 208 of the LOSC then specifically regulates the prevention, reduction, and control of the pollution from seabed activities subject to national jurisdiction, for instance the pollution generated by the offshore oil and gas industry located in the EEZ or continental shelf. Coastal states are required to adopt laws, regulations, and measures that 'shall be no less effective than *international rules, standards and recommended practices and procedures*'.[13] Moreover, states, 'acting especially through *competent international organizations or diplomatic conference*, shall establish global and regional rules, standards and recommended practices and procedures to prevent, reduce and control pollution of the marine environment referred to in paragraph 1'.[14] This provision builds an important 'bridge' between the LOSC and other relevant normative sources, which do not necessarily generate from treaties, but derive from the work of relevant actors, such as international organizations,[15] diplomatic conferences, and professional associations.[16]

The integration, within the LOSC, of future development in the field of environmental protection is also guaranteed by Article 237 of the LOSC, which consists of a specific compatibility clause between the Convention and obligations deriving from other agreements on the protection and preservation of the marine environment.[17] This provision facilitates the application of the LOSC in the relevant normative context, and of environmental law instruments in the context of marine environment protection.[18] Many international instruments are relevant for the protection of the marine environment in the context of offshore energy activities. There are instruments tackling a particular source of pollution and its consequences, for example the 1972 London Convention on the Prevention of Marine

Asia' in Robin Warner and Simon Marsden (eds), *Transboundary Environmental Governance: Inland, Coastland and Marine Perspective* (Ashgate 2012) 167.

[12] LOSC (n 8) art 198.

[13] ibid, art 208(3) (emphasis added). The LOSC does not define concepts such as 'international rules', 'standards', and 'recommended practices and procedures', which also remain vague in practice: Bernard H Oxman, 'The Duty to Respect Generally Accepted International Standards' (1991–92) 24 NYU JILP 109 ff; Seline Trevisanut, 'La Convention des Nations Unies sur le droit de la mer et le droit de l'environnement: développement intrasystémique et renvoi intersystémique' in Hélène Ruiz Fabri and Lorenzo Gradoni (eds), *La circulation des concepts juridiques: le droit international de l'environnement entre mondialisation et fragmentation* (Société de législation comparée 2009) (hereafter, Trevisanut, 'La Convention') 416.

[14] LOSC (n 8) art 208(5) (emphasis added).

[15] On the role of the International Maritime Organization (IMO) in the implementation of Art 208 of the LOSC, see J Ashley Roach, 'International Standards for Offshore Drilling' in Myron H Nordquist, John Norton Moore, Aldo Chircop, and Ronán Long (eds), *The Regulation of Continental Shelf Development, Rethinking International Standards* (Martinus Nijhoff 2013) 105.

[16] Catherine Redgwell, 'Mind the Gap in the GAIRS: The Role of other Instruments in LOSC Regime Implementation in the Offshore Energy Sector' in Nigel Bankes and Seline Trevisanut (eds), *Energy from the Sea: An International Law Perspective on Ocean Energy* (Brill 2015) 40.

[17] LOSC (n 8) art 237:

'1. The provisions of this Part are without prejudice to the specific obligations assumed by States under special conventions and agreements concluded previously which relate to the protection and preservation of the marine environment and to agreements which may be concluded in furtherance of the general principles set forth in this Convention.
2. Specific obligations assumed by States under special conventions, with respect to the protection and preservation of the marine environment, should be carried out in a manner consistent with the general principles and objectives of this Convention.'

[18] Trevisanut, 'La Convention' (n 13) 414 ff.

Pollution by Dumping of Waste and other Matter (London Dumping Convention)[19] and the 1996 Protocol thereto,[20] the 1969 Convention on Civil Liability for Oil Pollution Damage,[21] and the 1971 Convention on the Establishment of an International Fund for Compensation for Oil Pollution Damage.[22] Moreover, the London Dumping Convention is of particular importance in relation to the safety of the cessation of oil and gas activities, as it covers the disposal and dumping of oil and gas platforms and related material.[23] Moreover, the 1973 International Convention for the Prevention of Pollution from Ships, as amended by its 1978 Protocol (MARPOL),[24] also applies to 'fixed and floating platforms'.[25] However, it expressly excludes from its scope of application 'the release of harmful substances directly arising from the exploration, exploitation and associated offshore processing of sea-bed mineral resources'. This exclusion significantly limits the regulatory reach of this instrument for oil and gas operations.[26]

Then there are instruments that regulate wider questions relevant to the protection of the environment, and provide for specific obligations concerning the protection of the marine environment. For instance, the United Nations Framework Convention on Climate Change (UNFCCC)[27] and the 1992 Convention on Biological Diversity (CBD)[28] apply in areas subject to the jurisdiction of the coastal state, ie its continental shelf and EEZ, and integrate principles such as the precautionary principle and sustainable development into the context at stake. Article 14 of the CBD, and the 1991 Convention on Environmental Impact Assessment in a Transboundary Context (Espoo Convention),[29] a regional UNECE agreement now open to all states, both contain clear obligations relating to environmental impact assessment, which also apply to the offshore energy sector.

The duty to perform an environmental impact assessment (EIA) represents one of the restrictions on how states may treat their natural resources.[30] An EIA can be defined as 'a governmentally controlled procedure by which scientific assessments are made – together with public participation – of the proposed activity the impacts of which may be harmful.

[19] 1972 London Convention on the Prevention of Marine Pollution by Dumping of Waste and Other Matter (adopted 13 November 1972, entered into force 30 August 1975) 1046 UNTS 120 (hereafter 'London Dumping Convention').

[20] 1996 Protocol to the London Dumping Convention (adopted 7 November 1996, entered into force 24 March 2006) (1997) 36 ILM 1.

[21] 1969 Convention on Civil Liability for Oil Pollution Damage (adopted 29 November 1969, entered into force 19 June 1975) 973 UNTS 3.

[22] 1971 Convention on the Establishment of an International Fund for Compensation for Oil Pollution Damage (adopted 18 December 1971, entered into force 16 October 1978) 1110 UNTS 57.

[23] On the decommissioning, abandonment, and disposal of oil and gas installations, see Robert Beckman, 'Global Legal Regime on the Decommissioning of Offshore Installations and Structures' in Nordquist and others (eds) (n 15) 259; Lyons (n 11) 480; Leon Möller, 'UN Law on Decommissioning Offshore Installations' in Mark Hammerson (ed), *Oil and Gas Decommissioning* (Global Business Publishing 2013) 33.

[24] Protocol of 1978 relating to the International Convention for the Prevention of Pollution from Ships (adopted 17 February 1978, entered into force 2 October 1983) 1340 UNTS 61 (hereafter 'MARPOL').

[25] ibid, art 2(3).

[26] Lorenzo Schiano di Pepe, 'Offshore Oil and Gas in the Mediterranean Sea: Regulatory Gaps, Recent Developments and Future Perspective' in Juste Ruiz and Valentin Bou French (eds), *Derecho del Mar y Sostenibilidad en El Mediterraneo* (Tirant 2014) 370.

[27] United Nations Framework Convention on Climate Change (adopted 9 May 1992, entered into force 21 March 1994) 1771 UNTS 107.

[28] Convention on Biological Diversity (adopted 5 June 1992, entered into force on 29 December 1993) 1760 UNTS 79.

[29] Convention on Environmental Impact Assessment in a Transboundary Context (adopted 25 February 1991, entered into force 10 September 1997) 1989 UNTS 309 (hereafter 'Espoo Convention').

[30] Richard Barnes, *Property Rights and Natural Resources* (Hart 2009) 234–40.

Its goals include improving the quality of the information to enable decision-makers to make better decisions from the viewpoint of the environment and raise in general the level of public participation in environmental decision-making'.[31] It is now considered an obligation, under customary international law, to perform an EIA in relation to any activity that might have a significant impact on the environment.[32] This duty not only entails proceeding to an EIA before the activity in question has begun, but also requires that, 'once operations have started and, where necessary, throughout the life of the project, continuous monitoring of its effects on the environment shall be undertaken'.[33] A failure to conduct an EIA amounts to a failure to exercise due diligence,[34] which states are compelled to exercise on the basis of the general obligation to protect and preserve the marine environment.[35]

The LOSC provides for the direct obligations[36] to conduct an EIA, and to monitor operations , in Articles 204, 205, and 206. Article 206, in particular, provides that, when states have 'reasonable grounds for believing that planned activities under their jurisdiction or control may cause substantial pollution of or significant and harmful changes to the marine environment, they shall, as far as practicable, assess the potential effects of such activities on the marine environment'. States are also supposed to monitor the risks and effects of pollution resulting from activities under their jurisdiction,[37] and to communicate the results of such assessment and monitoring.[38] Starting from the assumption that 'harm to the marine environment is a matter of global interest', some scholars infer from this broad obligation of transparency that 'all States have equal access to information respecting potential harms'.[39]

Under the Espoo Convention,[40] parties have a duty to require an EIA, in order to 'prevent, reduce and control significant adverse transboundary environmental impact from proposed activities'.[41] State parties must also establish procedures that permit public participation. Pursuant to the Espoo Convention Guidance, a non-binding instrument adopted by the meeting of the parties in 2004,[42] the domestic EIA procedure should include the necessary provisions so that:

[31] Timo Koivurova, 'Could the Espoo Convention become a Global Regime for Environmental Impact Assessment and Strategic Environmental Assessment?' in Warner and Marsden (eds) (n 11) 326.

[32] *Pulp Mills on the River Uruguay (Argentina v Uruguay)*, Judgment, 20 April 2010, paras 205 ff; *Responsibilities and Obligations of States Sponsoring Persons and Entities with Respect to Activities in the Area*, Advisory Opinion (1 February 2011), para 145; *Construction of a Road in Costa Rica along the San Juan River (Nicaragua v Costa Rica)*, Judgment, 16 December 2015, para 161.

[33] *Pulp Mills* (n 32) para 205.

[34] Joanna Mossop, 'The Legal Framework for the Regulation of Safety and Environmental Issues on the Outer Continental Shelf' in Nordquist and others (n 15) 187. On due diligence, see also *Pulp Mills* (n 32) para 197; *Responsibilities and Obligations of States Sponsoring Persons and Entities* (n 32) para 120.

[35] LOSC (n 8) art 192.

[36] 'It should be stressed that the obligation to conduct an environmental impact assessment is a direct obligation under the Convention and a general obligation under customary international law.': *Responsibilities and Obligations of States Sponsoring Persons and Entities* (n 32) para 145.

[37] LOSC (n 8) art 204.

[38] ibid, art 205.

[39] Laura Pineschi, 'The Duty of Environmental Impact Assessment in the First ITLOS Chamber's Advisory Opinion: Towards the Supremacy of the General Rule to Protect and Preserve the Marine Environment as a Common Value?' in Nerina Boschiero, Tullio Scovazzi, Cesare Pitea, and Chiara Ragni (eds), *International Courts and the Development of International Law, Essays in Honour of Tullio Treves* (Springer 2013) 434, referring to Neil Craik, *The International Law of Environmental Impact Assessment: Process, Substance and Integration* (CUP 2008) 145.

[40] Espoo Convention (n 29).

[41] ibid, art 2(1).

[42] Meeting of the Parties to the Convention on Environmental Impact Assessment in a Transboundary Context, Guidance on Public Participation in Environmental Impact Assessment in a Transboundary Context, Decision III/8, Report of the Third Meeting, ECE/MP.EIA/6 (13 September 2004), Annex VIII.

(a) the public is informed on any proposals relating to an activity with potential adverse environmental impacts in cases subject to an EIA procedure in order to obtain a permit for a given activity; (b) the public in the areas likely to be affected is entitled to express comments and opinions on the proposed activity when all options are open before the final decision on this activity is made; (c) reasonable time-frames are provided allowing sufficient time for each of the different stages of public participation in the EIA procedure; (d) in making the final decision on the proposed activity, due account is taken of the results of the public participation in the EIA procedure.[43]

The 2003 Protocol on Strategic Environmental Assessment (SEA)[44] to the Espoo Convention allows the public to be involved in the decision-making process earlier than in the general EIA procedure. A SEA involves 'the evaluation of the likely environmental, including health, effects, which comprises the determination of the scope of an environmental report and its preparation, the carrying out of public participation and consultations, and the taking into account of the environmental report and the results of the public participation and consultations in a plan or programme'.[45]

The Espoo Convention and its SEA Protocol enhance transparency in the performance of the assessment and monitoring obligations, by opening these procedures to non-state actors. Thus, they enhance the safety of oil and gas operations by guaranteeing better control over the planned and performed activities, due to the participation of unconventional actors. Their reach is, however, limited to transboundary situations. Moreover, the Espoo Convention and its SEA Protocol have not yet been widely ratified,[46] and have not yet contributed to fostering a uniform practice in this respect. The existing regional instruments take diverse approaches to the conduct of EIAs.

9.2.2 The Geographical Fragmentation at the Regional Level

In the absence of a solid global legal framework, or maybe as a result of such an absence, several instruments have been adopted in the last twenty years addressing safety in offshore energy operations, within the framework of regional seas programmes, within and outside those sponsored by the United Nations Environment Programme (UNEP). The type of instruments adopted and their content varies significantly, depending on the level of cooperation and integration in the observed regional context.

The global legal framework, specifically Part XII of the LOSC, accommodates those regional efforts through Article 237, mentioned above,[47] and Article 311, which is the LOSC's

[43] ibid, para 14. For a comment, see, inter alia, Jonas Ebbesson, 'A Modest Contribution to Environmental Democracy and Justice in Transboundary Contexts: The Combined Impact of the Espoo Convention and the Aarhus Convention' (2011) 20 RECIEL 248–57.

[44] Protocol on Strategic Environmental Assessment to the Convention on Environmental Impact Assessment in a Transboundary Context (adopted 21 May 2003, entered in force 10 July 2010) 2685 UNTS 140 (hereafter 'SEA Protocol').

[45] ibid, art 2(6).

[46] As of June 2021, the number of state parties to the Espoo Convention and its SEA Protocol were, respectively, forty-five and thirty-three: see the United Nations Treaty Collection <https://treaties.un.org/Pages/ViewDetails.aspx?src = TREATY&mtdsg_no = XXVII-4&chapter = 27&clang = _en> and <https://treaties.un.org/Pages/ViewDetails.aspx?src = TREATY&mtdsg_no = XXVII-4-b&chapter = 27&clang = _en >, respectively, accessed 5 June 2021.

[47] See LOSC, art 237 (n 17).

general compatibility clause, and gives the Convention pre-eminence over other agreements. The LOSC not only accommodates regional agreements but, sometimes, demands that states enter into regional cooperation For instance, article 208(5) provides that: 'States, acting especially through competent international organizations or diplomatic conference, *shall* endeavour to establish global and *regional rules, standards and recommended practices and procedures* to prevent, reduce and control [pollution from seabed activities].'[48]

Some mechanisms of regional cooperation predate the LOSC and its entry into force. Under selected regional legal instruments, the situation certainly seems more advanced than at the global level.[49] Four regional sea conventions have a protocol or annex specifically dedicated to offshore activities. First, Annex III on the Prevention and Elimination of Pollution from Offshore Sources, of the Convention for the Protection of the Marine Environment of the North-east Atlantic (OSPAR Convention),[50] Article 2, requires states to use 'best available techniques' and 'best environmental practices' when adopting measures and programmes pursuant to the same annex. The annex also contains a specific provision, Article 5, on the management of disused installations and pipelines. This article was, subsequently, modified by *OSPAR Decision 98/3 on the Disposal of Disused Offshore Installations*,[51] which requires the full removal of any disused equipment with a residual possibility of abandonment, pursuant to a case-by-case evaluation.

Second, Annex VI on the Prevention of Pollution from Offshore Activities, to the Helsinki Convention on the Protection of the Marine Environment of the Baltic Sea Area,[52] obliges contracting parties to make use of best available techniques and practices. Annex VI contains a very detailed provision on EIA and monitoring.[53] Regulation 8 obliges states to perform an impact assessment before an offshore activity is permitted to start, and another after the exploration phase has begun.[54] Moreover, '[i]n order to monitor the consequent effects of the exploitation phase of the offshore activity studies ... shall be carried out *before* the operation, at *annual intervals* during the operation, and *after* the operation has been concluded'.[55] Regulation 8 is, at the moment, the most detailed international provision regulating EIA in the offshore oil and gas sector.

Third, the Offshore Protocol to the Barcelona Convention for the Protection of the Mediterranean Sea [56] consists of a quite detailed instrument that aims at covering the

[48] For instance, Article 208(5) provides that, 'States, acting especially through competent international organizations or diplomatic conference, *shall* endeavour to establish global and *regional rules, standards and recommended practices and procedures* to prevent, reduce and control [pollution from seabed activities], emphasis added.

[49] Schiano di Pepe (n 26) 371.

[50] Convention for the Protection of the Marine Environment of the North-east Atlantic (adopted 22 September 1992, entered into force 25 March 1998) 2354 UNTS 67.

[51] Commission of the Convention for the Protection of the Marine Environment of the North-east Atlantic, OSPAR 98/14/1-E, 22–23 July 1998, Annex 33.

[52] Convention on the Protection of the Marine Environment of the Baltic Sea Area (adopted 22 March 1974, entered into force 3 May 1980) 1507 UNTS 166. The Helsinki Convention has been amended many times since 1992. Any references made in the present text refer to the last version, as in force in 2008, and as available on the website on the Baltic Marine Environment Protection Commission—Helsinki Commission (HELCOM) at <https://helcom.fi> accessed 14 April 2021. Annex VI of the Helsinki Convention concerns the prevention of pollution from offshore activities and is available at <https://helcom.fi/about-us/convention/annexes-to-the-convention-2/annex-vi/> accessed 1 June 2021.

[53] Annex VI of the Helsinki Convention concerns the prevention of pollution from offshore activities, reg 8.

[54] ibid, reg 8, paras 1 and 3.

[55] Emphasis added.

[56] Protocol for the Protection of the Mediterranean Sea against Pollution Resulting from Exploration and Exploitation of the Continental Shelf and the Seabed and its Subsoil to the Convention for the Protection of the Mediterranean Sea Against Pollution (adopted 14 October 1994, entered into force 24 March 2011) 2742 UNTS 77 (hereafter 'Barcelona Offshore Protocol').

complete life cycle of an offshore operation. In setting a number of mandatory requirements for the authorization procedure,[57] the protocol focuses on the roles of both the authorizing states and the industry (ie the operator) in assessing the environmental impact of a planned activity, monitoring it, and reacting to possible emergencies.[58] The central role of the industry is also evident in Section IV of the Barcelona Offshore Protocol on safeguards, namely on safety measures, contingency plans, and emergency responses.[59] The Mediterranean Action Plan,[60] adopted in the framework of the Offshore Protocol, aims, in particular, at encouraging the adoption of further safety measures at the regional level, over the timeframe of 2016 to 2024. These measures should include, '[s]etting-up a governance framework to support the implementation of the Action Plan and the adoption, enforcement and monitoring of regional standards, procedures and rules', '[d]efining commonly agreed regional offshore standards and guidelines', and developing 'a regional commonly agreed reporting and monitoring for the Action Plan'.[61] The Action Plan then lists possible measures to be adopted in order to realize these three general objectives. In relation to the development of regional standards and guidelines, the document emphasizes the need for common rules on EIAs,[62] highlighting, in this way, the shortcomings of the global legal framework, and the crucial importance of such procedures.

Fourth, the Offshore Protocol to the Kuwait Regional Convention for Co-operation on the Protection of the Marine Environment from Pollution,[63] unfortunately, does not contain a clear and general obligation of EIA, as it allows contracting parties not to require such an assessment before a new activity starts. When the contracting state decides not to request an EIA, it 'shall consider' performing a survey of the marine environment.[64] Contracting parties, then, have a wide margin of discretion under this instrument, which is, however, limited by the global legal framework analysed above. Article VI of the Kuwait Protocol also asks states to 'take all practicable measures to ensure that every offshore installation ... is certified by a Certifying Authority or its designee [to be] safe and fit for the purpose for which it is to be used so as to ensure that it will not cause accidental damage to the marine environment'. Here, again, contracting parties retain discretion on when to request such a certificate, and on its content.

The regional fragmentation of the legal framework, on the one hand, allows for it to complement the weak global framework, but, on the other hand, hampers the development of coherent global rules. Some of the regional instruments considered here consist of binding applicable law, and their autonomous normativity directly shapes any further conventional or unconventional legal development at the global level.

[57] ibid, arts 4–7.

[58] Seline Trevisanut, 'The Role of Private Actors in the Offshore Energy Industry' (2014) 29 IJMCL 645.

[59] Barcelona Offshore Protocol (n 56) arts 15–21.

[60] Mediterranean Offshore Action Plan in the Framework of the Protocol for the Protection of the Mediterranean Sea against Pollution resulting from Exploration and Exploitation of the Continental Shelf and the Seabed and its Subsoil, UNEP(DEPI)/MED IG.22/28 <https://wedocs.unep.org/rest/bitstreams/8381/retrieve> accessed 14 April 2021.

[61] ibid 214.

[62] ibid 220.

[63] Protocol Concerning Marine Pollution resulting from Exploration and Exploitation of the Continental Shelf (adopted 29 March 1989, entered into force 17 February 1990) 2065 UNTS 68.

[64] ibid, art IV(2).

9.3 Unconventional Lawmaking in Conventional Fora

The implementation and development of the law of the sea are tightly interlinked with technological development. The legal framework needs to be both highly specialized and flexible. The specialization[65] is guaranteed by the sectoral fragmentation at the global level, and the geographical fragmentation at the regional level. The flexibility is pursued through unconventional lawmaking by international organizations and treaty bodies, at both global and regional levels.

9.3.1 Unconventional Lawmaking by the International Maritime Organization and Global Treaty Bodies

Many international institutions participate in the development of the legal framework at the global and regional levels, and they often do so by adopting informal instruments, and by entering into dialogue with the stakeholders in the relevant economic sector. Informal instruments[66] have, mainly, been adopted in order to set some common standards in the field of safety and pollution prevention, control, and reduction.[67] At the global level, the International Maritime Organization (IMO) has dealt with issues of security and the safety of installations, and partly with pollution produced by offshore installations, even though the focus of the IMO mandate remains on shipping.[68] The IMO has, in particular, taken the lead with regard to both the treatment of disused installations, and pollution by dumping. It has elaborated some guidelines for the removal of installations,[69] and is the depositary of the London Dumping Convention.[70] However, its role in the development of the regulatory framework in relation to the offshore oil and gas industry has raised some criticism.[71] The

65 '[S]pecialisation accommodates various needs and concerns if the states engage in international law-making, and states perceive that their individual positions are better respected in these special regimes than in a global one.': Gerhard Hafner, 'Pros and Cons ensuing from Fragmentation of International Law' (2004) 25 Michigan JIL 858–59.

66 See, in particular, the instruments elaborated by the IMO, which has taken the lead in recent years concerning the elaboration of standards and best practice related to the offshore industry, eg IMO, 'Guidelines for Safety Zones and the Safety of Navigation around Offshore Installations and Structures', IMO Doc SN.1/Circ.295, 7 December 2010.

67 Art 208(5) of the LOSC provides that:

> 'States, acting especially through competent international organizations or diplomatic conference, shall establish global and regional rules, standards and recommended practices and procedures to prevent, reduce and control pollution of the marine environment referred to in paragraph 1 [namely, the pollution arising from, or in connection with, seabed activities subject to their jurisdiction, and from artificial islands, installations, and structures under their jurisdiction, pursuant to Articles 60 and 80]. Such rules, standards and recommended practices and procedures shall be re-examined from time to time as necessary.'

According to Roach, there is a hierarchy among the actions that states are required ('shall establish') to adopt on the basis of this provision: legally binding rules, non-legally binding standards, and recommended practices. So far, states, also within the IMO, have preferred to elaborate non-legally binding instruments, and have not yet reached an agreement upon the adoption of a legally binding instrument regulating seabed activities: Roach (n 15) 107.

68 For a general treatise on the expansion of the IMO mandate, see, inter alia, Aldo Chircop, 'The IMO's Work on Environmental Protection and Global Governance' in David J Attard (ed), *The IMLI Treatise on Global Ocean Governance, vol III: IMO and Global Ocean Governance* (OUP 2018) 173.

69 IMO, Resolution A.672 (16) of 19 October 1989.

70 London Dumping Convention (n 19).

71 Some states and commentators have raised several points of criticism about the role of the IMO in the development of rules and standards concerning offshore installations. The details of such debate are beyond the scope of the present chapter. For a critical voice, refer to Roach (n 15) 107. See also Francesca Romanin Jacur, 'Formalism and Law-making in Treaty-based Ocean Governance: Limits and Challenges' in Seline Trevisanut,

IMO mandate, as amended, includes 'the general adoption of the highest practicable standards in matters concerning *maritime safety* ... and prevention and control of *marine pollution from ships*'.[72] Notwithstanding this, the IMO Legal Committee has pointed out that, 'while pollution directly arising from exploration/exploitation is however not of direct concern of IMO, the Organization may contribute to the establishment of international regulations'.[73] The IMO Legal Committee, in particular, supports the development of guidance for states in their efforts to conclude arrangements, at the bilateral and regional levels, on liability and compensation issues connected to transboundary pollution damage resulting from offshore oil exploration and exploitation.[74] Not all IMO contracting parties, however, support what they perceive as an unjustified extension of the IMO mandate.[75] This criticism undermines the 'generally accepted' character of the rules and standards that the organization elaborates.

General acceptance needs, then, to be assessed on the basis of the subsequent practice of states. Consequently, the 1989 IMO Guidelines and Standards for the Removal of Offshore Installations and Structures on the Continental Shelf and in the Exclusive Economic Zone (1989 IMO Guidelines)[76] are considered as generally accepted international rules and standards (GAIRS).[77] Within the London Dumping Convention system, Lyons, for instance, suggests that, unlike the 1972 London Convention, its 1996 Protocol does not yet qualify as a global rule under the LOSC, because it has gained general acceptance only in some regions of the world.[78] This limitation also suggests that the 1996 Protocol may be regarded as falling within the scope of GAIRS in some areas of the world where the majority of relevant states have ratified it, and so as regional GAIRS and not global rules. The 1996 Protocol could also fall within the definition of best environmental practices, as required by some regional instruments analysed below, namely the OSPAR and Helsinki Conventions.

Aside from the IMO, the treaty bodies of the Convention on Biological Diversity[79] have played an important role in the regulation of the offshore energy sector, specifically concerning the EIA procedures. Article 14 of the CBD provides for an international obligation to submit to EIA procedure any activity that might significantly impact biodiversity, whether internally or in a transboundary situation.[80] In order to support the integration of biodiversity considerations in EIA procedures, the Conference of the Parties (COP) of the CBD adopted, in 2006, the Voluntary Guidelines on Biodiversity-inclusive Impact

Nikolaos Giannopoulos, and Rozemarijn Roland Holst (eds), *Regime Interaction in Ocean Governance: Problems, Theories and Methods* (Brill 2020) 156 ff.

[72] Convention on the International Maritime Organization (adopted 6 March 1948, entered into force 17 March 1958) 289 UNTS 3 (emphasis added).

[73] See 'Implications of the United Nations Convention on the Law of the Sea for the International Maritime Organization' IMO Doc. LEG/Misc.7 Annex (19 January 2012) 18.

[74] See IMO Doc. LEG 99/14, 24 April 2012, at para 13.16.

[75] Roach (n 15) 105. See also Aldo Chircop, 'The International Maritime Organization' in Donald R Rothwell, Alex G Oude Elferink, Karen N Scott, and Tim Stephens (eds), *The Oxford Handbook of The Law of the Sea* (OUP 2015) 429.

[76] IMO, Resolution A.672 (16), 19 October 1989.

[77] Lyons (n 11) 495. By Contrast, see Alexander Proelss, *United Convention on the Law of the Sea: A Commentary* (Beck Hart Nomos 2017) 464.

[78] Lyons (n 11) 510.

[79] Convention on Biological Diversity (n 28).

[80] For a detailed analysis of Art 14, see, inter alia, Neil Craik, 'Biodiversity-inclusive Impact Assessment' in Michael Faure (ed), *Elgar Encyclopedia of Environmental Law*, vol III (Edward Elgar 2017) 431–44.

Assessment.[81] The lawmaking powers of COPs within multilateral environmental agreements (MEAs) are highly debated, and beyond the scope of the present chapter.[82] What is important here is the assessment of the normative value of the non-binding instrument that is the outcome of the decision-making process. Although not formally binding, the 2006 Voluntary Guidelines are considered to have 'high normative value because they have been negotiated under the auspices of the CBD and adopted by the [COP]'.[83] Of less normative value, for instance, and according to Craik, is the Draft Guidance on Biodiversity-inclusive Strategic Environmental Assessment (SEA Draft Guidance).[84] The SEA Draft Guidance 'was not "adopted" by the parties, but rather the document produced by the Secretariat was "endorsed", indicating agreement with the content but an unwillingness to give the document greater normative status'.[85] The instruments adopted by the parties through the COP, and, thus, whose content was 'subscribed' to by the parties, could even amount to 'subsequent agreements by which the underlying treaty is interpreted in the sense of Art. 31.3(a)'[86] of the Vienna Convention on the Law of Treaties (VCLT).[87] Moreover, the 2006 Voluntary Guidance benefits from the external support of other guideline documents with a similar content, such as the resolutions of the Conference of the Parties of both the Ramsar Convention ,[88] and the Convention on Migratory Species.[89] These documents 'operate collectively to reinforce the principles associated with biodiversity-inclusive impact assessment'[90] and, consequently, increase each other's normative value.

Unconventional lawmaking also allows biodiversity-inclusive EIAs to be linked with human rights law. Relevant instruments, in this regard, include the International Finance Corporation Performance Standards and related guidance notes,[91] the UN Guiding Principles on Business and Human Rights,[92] and the OECD Guidelines for Multinational

[81] COP 8 Decision VIII/28, 31 March 2006. SEA means 'the evaluation of the likely environmental, including health, effects, which comprises the determination of the scope of an environmental report and its preparation, the carrying out of public participation and consultations, and the taking into account of the environmental report and the results of the public participation and consultations in a plan or programme': SEA Protocol (n 44).

[82] COPs do not possess international legal personality, and are not considered international organizations. Whether their lawmaking powers can be justified on the basis of the theory of 'implied powers' is, thus, contested. For a treatise on the issue, see, inter alia, Jutta Brunné, 'COPing with Consent: Law-making under Multilateral Environmental Agreements' 2002 15 LJIL 1; Francesca Romanin Jacur, *The Dynamics of Multilateral Environmental Agreements, Institutional Architectures and Law-making Processes* (Editorial Scientifica 2013) 161 ff; Geir Ulfstein, 'Treaty Bodies' in Daniel Bodansky, Jutta Brunnée, and Ellen Hey (eds), *The Oxford Handbook of International Environmental Law* (OUP 2007) 877.

[83] Craik (n 80) 436.

[84] CBD Executive Secretary (2006), Voluntary Guidelines on Biodiversity-inclusive Impact Assessment, Annex II, UN Doc. UNEP/CBD/COP/8/27/Add.2

[85] Craik (n 80) 437–38.

[86] Georg Nolte, 'Role of Subsequent Agreements and Subsequent Practice in relation to the Interpretation of Constituent Instruments of International Organizations. Proposal for Draft Conclusion 11, Third Report of the Special Rapporteur', ILC Report, A/70/10 (2015), ch VIII, paras 118–29.

[87] Vienna Convention on the Law of Treaties (adopted 23 May 1969, entered into force 27 January 1980) 1155 UNTS 331.

[88] Ramsar Convention Conference of the Parties, 'Environmental Impact Assessment and Strategic Environmental Assessment: Updated Scientific and Technical Guidance', Resolution X.17, annex, 28 October to 4 November 2008.

[89] Convention on Migratory Species Conference of the Parties, 'Impact Assessment and Migratory Species', Resolution 7.2, 18–24 September 2002.

[90] Craik (n 80) 436.

[91] See, in particular, Performance Standard 6 on Biodiversity Conservation and Sustainable Management of Living Natural Resources: <https://www.ifc.org/wps/wcm/connect/topics_ext_content/ifc_external_corporate_site/sustainability-at-ifc/policies-standards/performance-standards/ps6> accessed 14 April 2021.

[92] UNHCHR, 'Guiding Principles on Business and Human Rights: Implementing the United Nations "Protect, Respect and Remedy" Framework', 2011 <https://www.ohchr.org/documents/publications/guidingprinciplesbusinesshr_en.pdf> accessed 14 April 2021.

Enterprises.[93] These instruments are also relevant for the offshore energy industry, when considering the impact of the sector on indigenous and local communities. Unconventional lawmaking, in this context, also allows the lack of will surrounding SEA, outside the regional context of the Espoo Convention, to be circumvented, given that the aforementioned instruments have a global ambition, and aim at integrating social considerations into the applicable legal framework.

9.3.2 Unconventional Lawmaking by Regional Seas Treaties Bodies

The regional seas treaties play an important role in regulating the offshore energy sector, in the absence of a specialized global instrument. Regional seas treaties are MEAs, and are, accordingly, supported by active and strong treaty bodies. The institutional framework is, however, very diverse, in line with the very different levels of integration in different regions.

The OSPAR Commission and the Helsinki Commission (HELCOM) are strong treaty bodies that can adopt binding decisions, and extensively use non-binding instruments to regulate, in particular, the protection of the marine environment. A clear example is the OSPAR Guidance on Environmental Considerations for Offshore Windfarm Development.[94] The OSPAR Guidance complements the relevant obligations of the Espoo Convention,[95] offering valuable guidance on the minimum content of EIAs for all stages of the lives of offshore wind farms, from selecting locations to decommissioning. Also, HELCOM Recommendation 18/2 on Offshore Activities[96] has reiterated that, for offshore oil and gas exploitation activities, it is necessary for states to assess the environmental status of the area in which the project is proposed to be located before any activity takes place. While the requirements set under Annex VI of the Helsinki Convention should apply as a minimum standard, the Recommendation highlights that, when the nature of the area so requires, states must apply more stringent requirements.

Little has, so far, come out of the Barcelona and Kuwait Conventions' treaty bodies, which do not have the same institutional features as the OSPAR Commission and the HELCOM. The Kuwait Convention and its protocols are implemented by the Regional Organization for the Protection of the Marine Environment (ROPME).[97] The ROPME is in charge of developing guidelines for assisting contracting states, but no guidelines are available on the ROPME official website. Thus, it does not appear that the ROPME has, so far, exercised its recommendatory functions.

93 OECD, 'OECD Guidelines for Multinational Enterprises', 2011 <http://mneguidelines.oecd.org/guidelines/> accessed 14 April 2021.

94 OSPAR Guidance on Environmental Considerations for Offshore Wind Farm Development, reference number 2008–3.

95 Similarly, wind farms are also included in the amended Annex of the Espoo Convention.

96 HELCOM Recommendation 18/2, adopted 12 March 1997, Attachment, para (a).

97 The ROPME was created in 1979, pursuant to art XVI of the Kuwait Convention. According to the information available on its official website (<http://ropme.org/1_WhoWeAre_EN.clx#> accessed 2 June 2021), '[t]he main objective of ROPME is to coordinate efforts of the eight Member States towards [the] protection [of] the marine and coastal environment and ecosystems in the ROPME Sea Area against marine pollution and stressors that might be induced from developmental activities or/and other drivers of change'.

In the Mediterranean context, the institutional framework of the Barcelona Convention consists of several bodies,[98] including a Meeting of the Parties (MOP), and the Barcelona Convention Offshore Oil and Gas Group (BARCO OFOG), the latter having been created in 2014. The BARCO OFOG is a technical body for the exchange of best practices, knowledge, and experiences between members, to assist the parties in promulgating international rules, standards, and recommended practices and procedures pursuant to Article 23 of the Barcelona Offshore Protocol.[99] Also, it is to undertake the periodic examination and review of the Offshore Action Plan, adopted by the MOP in 2016.[100] The Offshore Action Plan aims at operationalizing the harmonization of regional practices in the implementation of the Barcelona Offshore Protocol considering 'relevant existing standards and guidelines in this field'.[101] One of the outputs of the Action Plan is the adoption by the MOP, in 2019, of the Mediterranean Offshore Guidelines and Standards on the Disposal of Oil and Oily Mixtures.[102]

The normative value of these guidelines relies on two arguments, invoked in the document containing the guidelines. First, the Barcelona MOP adopted the guidelines pursuant to the specific objectives of the Action Plan, and, thus, pursuant to a mandate agreed by the contracting parties.[103] Second, '[t]his guidance has been derived from international best practices as outlined by organisations and institutions such as the Secretariat of the Convention for the Protection of the Marine Environment of the North-east Atlantic (OSPAR), International Finance Corporation (IFC)/World Bank and the International Association of Oil and Gas Producers (IOGP), as well as from countries with mature oil and gas industry with well-developed regulatory frameworks, such [as] the UK, Norway, the Netherlands and the US'.[104] As mentioned above, in relation to the guidelines adopted by some global treaty bodies, the cross-referencing of other instruments reinforces the principles enshrined in the guidelines, and increases each set of principles' normative value. The same can be concluded at the regional level, where a certain regional cross-fertilization is occurring. This cross-fertilization has the potential to limit the negative effects of geographical fragmentation on the coherence and strength of the global legal framework.

[98] For a complete overview of the Barcelona Convention bodies, see UNEP Mediterranean Action Plan, 'Governing and Subsidiary Bodies' <https://www.unenvironment.org/unepmap/who-we-are/governing-and-subsidiary-bodies> accessed 2 June 2021.

[99] Decision IG.21/8 (2014), Follow-up Actions regarding the Offshore Action Plan, UNEP/MED.IG.21/9, Annex.

[100] Decision IG/22/3 (2016), Mediterranean Offshore Action Plan in the Framework of the Protocol for the Protection of the Mediterranean Sea against Pollution resulting from Exploration and Exploitation of the Continental Shelf and the Seabed and its Subsoil, DOC UNEP/MED IG.22.

[101] ibid, s II.2.2, Specific Objectives 7 and 8, 220 ff.

[102] Decision IG.24/9 (2019), Mediterranean Offshore Guidelines and Standards: (a) Common Standards and Guidance on the Disposal of Oil and Oily Mixtures and the Use and Disposal of Drilling Fluids and Cuttings; (b) Common Standards and Guidelines for Special Restrictions or Conditions for Specially Protected Areas (SPA) within the Framework of the Mediterranean Offshore Action Plan, UNEP/MED IG.24/22, 471 ff. The Barcelona Secretariat is also finalizing the Guidelines for the Conduct of Environmental Impact Assessment (EIA), mandated by the Offshore Action Plan (Specific Objective 8), which were supposed to be submitted for the consideration of the next OFOG meeting during the first year of the 2020–2021 biennium, for submission to the Twenty-second Meeting of the Contracting Parties (COP 22). Unfortunately, due to the COVID-19 global pandemic in 2020, the meeting could not take place.

[103] ibid 471–72.

[104] ibid 476.

9.4 Unconventional Lawmaking by Unconventional Actors

The expansion of the offshore sector has buttressed the role of private actors at the international level. These actors are not only increasingly involved in the implementation and enforcement of international rules, but also in lawmaking processes. On the one hand, civil society—in particular local communities—can actively impact the decision-making processes thanks to their participation rights, guaranteed, inter alia, by the Aarhus Convention[105] and the Espoo Convention.[106] On the other hand, private actors financially involved in the activities, for example investors and insurance companies, bear (indirect) obligations under specific international instruments, such as the above- mentioned Barcelona Offshore Protocol,[107] and the 1989 IMO Guidelines.[108]

The latter element is particularly problematic because international law does not have 'teeth' to act directly against private actors, and private actors might disguise reality.[109] For instance, before the *Deepwater Horizon* incident, BP had a very good reputation for its environmental standards: it was considered a safe company. Self-regulation by private actors can allow for self-promotion. Nonetheless, the BP National Commission encourages 'self-regulation and co-regulation following the example of other economic sectors, such as fisheries, chemical industry, [and the] nuclear power industry'.[110] It justifies this approach by affirming that 'governments cannot compete with private-sector salaries for the most talented experts'.[111] Creutz has observed that 'self-regulation is an instrument whose very rationale is versatility; it can be portrayed as nonlaw, as soft law, and even as law. Thus, the character of regulation becomes decisive, not the content of the rules'.[112] However, self-regulation should not become 'a substitute of government but ... an important supplement to government oversight'.[113]

It has been noted that 'firms are no longer simply accountable under local law, but to international norms and standards, such as those promulgated by the International Labour Organization (ILO), the Universal Declaration of Human Rights (UDHR), and corporate best practices'.[114] In the offshore energy sector, this accountability is not as straightforward as just mentioned. Companies have, however, developed a 'green sensibility', and have invested in 'greening' their images, and declaring their respect for international law obligations. Several oil and gas companies have, in particular after the *Deepwater Horizon* disaster,

[105] Aarhus Convention on Access to Information, Public Participation in Decision-making and Access to Justice in Environmental Matters of the United Nations Economic Commission for Europe (adopted 25 June 1998, entered into force 30 October 2001) 2161 UNTS 450. The Aarhus Convention has been implemented at the EU level by Directive 2003/4/EC (OJ L 41/26, 14 February 2003).

[106] Espoo Convention (n 29).

[107] Barcelona Offshore Protocol (n 56).

[108] 1989 IMO Guidelines (n 76).

[109] '[E]ntity self-generated standards empower them to manage the data-driven construction of their reality': Larry Catá Backer, 'Transparency and Business in International Law: Governance between Norm and Technique' in Andrea Bianchi and Anne Peters (eds), *Transparency in International Law* (CUP 2013) 499.

[110] BP National Commission, 'Industry's Role in Supporting Health, Safety and Environmental Standards: Options and Models for the Offshore Oil and Gas Sector (Staff Working Paper No. 9)' 2.

[111] ibid.

[112] Katja Creutz, 'Law versus Codes of Conduct: Between Convergence and Conflict' in Jan Klabbers and Touko Piiparinen (eds), *Normative Pluralism and International Law: Exploring Global Governance* (CUP 2013) 167.

[113] BP National Commission, *Final Report* (2011), ch 8, 'Safety and Industry' 234.

[114] World Bank Group, Corporate Social Responsibility Practice, *Company Codes of Conduct and International Standard: An Analytical Comparison*, pt I (October 2003), 1 <https://documents1.worldbank.org/curated/en/416281468096001385/pdf/346620v10CompanyCodesofConduct.pdf> accessed 2 June 2021.

adopted codes of conduct where they affirm their recognition of international norms for the protection of the marine environment.[115] The internal codes of conduct are certainly not binding, but they can produce normative effects. In fact, they consist of a sort of declaration that the company is aware of the existing legal framework, and could be considered as relevant practice when assessing the content of the applicable due diligence obligations. Moreover, the codes of conduct, as relevant practice, can consist of 'best available practice', thus deepening the international legal framework, and clarifying the meaning of certain obligations.

The codes of conduct also contribute to 'corporate ocean responsibility' (COR), and specifically an ocean-focused corporate social responsibility (CSR). There is no agreed definition of COR or CSR. According to the World Bank, CSR is '[t]he commitment of business to contribute to sustainable economic development working with employees, their families, the local community, and society at large to improve their quality of life, in ways that are both good for business and good for development'.[116] Accordingly, COR could be defined as the commitment of business to contribute to the sustainable use of the oceans, working with employees, their families, local communities, and society at large, to improve the quality of the oceans in ways that are good for business, for development, and for the environment. The COR legal framework is composed of different categories of standards, and 'embodies non-binding general principles of responsible conduct and technical guidelines … directly addressing business operators, and those formally addressing States with recommendations to be complied with by private operators'.[117] Similarly to CSR, COR aims to fill in the details of international legal principles, either conventional or customary, that provide for the protection of common concerns such as the environment, and to focus the private companies' attention on the needs of the society in which they operate. COR can, thus, play an important role in preventing pollution and environmental disasters by pushing companies to set in place the necessary prevention mechanisms. It can also be a tool for mitigating damage and compensating losses, once a disaster has occurred.[118]

Private actors in the offshore energy sector not only include individual companies, but also professional associations. In the United States, for instance, the American Petroleum Institute (API) has played a dominant role in developing safety standards. However, it has also regularly resisted 'agency rulemakings that government regulators believe would make those operations safer', and has favoured 'rulemaking that promotes industry autonomy from government oversight'.[119] At the EU level, the pressure exercised by some

[115] See, inter alia, the commitment to respect the environment affirmed by Shell (<https://www.shell.com/sustainability/environment/respecting-nature.html#iframe = L3dlYmFwcHMvUG93ZXJpbmdQcm9ncmVzc19FbnZpcm9ubWVudEZyYW1ld29yay8> accessed 2 June 2021) and the environmental policy of BP (<https://www.bp.com/content/dam/bp/business-sites/en/global/corporate/pdfs/sustainability/bp-environmental-policy-2021.pdf> accessed 2 June 2021).

[116] World Bank Group, Corporate Social Responsibility Practice, *Strengthening Implementation of Corporate Social Responsibility in Global Supply Chains* (October 2003), 1 <https://documents1.worldbank.org/curated/en/910481468324044035/pdf/346640Strengthening1Implementation.pdf> accessed 2 June 2021.

[117] Angelica Bonfanti and Francesca Romanin Jacur, 'Energy from the Sea and the Protection of the Marine Environment: Treaty-based Regimes and Ocean Corporate Social Responsibility' in Bankes and Trevisanut (eds) (n 16) 73–74

[118] Ibid 78 ff.

[119] BP National Commission (n 113) 225.

representatives of the industry, such as Oil and Gas UK,[120] contributed to the decision to change the proposed instrument from a regulation to a directive.[121]

Professional associations play different roles in the international legal framework. They can guarantee a certain level of safety. The Offshore Pollution Liability Association (OPOL),[122] for instance, is a private agreement between certain European states[123] and the major participants in their offshore industries. Most participating states now require applicants for offshore exploration, exploitation, and pipe-laying licences to be parties to OPOL. Industry is also important for collecting high-quality and comprehensive data to ensure science-based standards setting.[124] The International Regulators' Forum (IRF) is a group of offshore health and safety regulators for the oil and gas industry, created in order to promote information sharing and collaboration though joint programmes. The participants in the International Regulators' Forum (IRF) Global Offshore Safety are: Australia (National Offshore Petroleum Safety Authority and Environmental Management Authority); Brazil (National Agency of Oil, Gas and Biofuels); Canada (Canada-Newfoundland and Labrador Offshore Petroleum Board, Canada-Nova Scotia Offshore Petroleum Board and Canada Energy Regulator); Denmark (Danish Working Environment Authority); Ireland (Commission for Regulation of Utilities); Mexico (National Agency for Safety, Energy and Environment of Mexico); The Netherlands (State Supervision of Mines); New Zealand (WorkSafe New Zealand); Norway (The Petroleum Safety Authority); United Kingdom (Health and Safety Executive and Offshore Petroleum Regulator for Environment and Decommissioning); and United States (Bureau of Safety and Environmental Enforcement). While IRF is a very important network for information exchange and data collection, it consists of very different administrations, with different mandates and priorities, at different regulatory levels, and with different expertise. Consequently, the type and quality of data might diverge. There is no guarantee of coherence, at the domestic level, concerning the standard-setting activity that such a network generates.[125]

Another interesting recent example is the International Renewable Energy Agency (IRENA). According to Article 2 of IRENA's statute, its objective is to promote the adoption and sustainable use of all forms of renewable energy, including marine renewable energy. The IRENA does not have the competence to issue legally binding standards on the

[120] 'We [Oil and Gas UK] believe the EC would best achieve its goal through a properly worded Directive, instead of Regulation.... A properly worded Directive would encourage member states which do not currently achieve the recognised high standards present in the North Sea, to do so in a way which blends with their established legislation. This would protect the existing strong safety regime in the UK, minimise disruption to operators and regulators and eliminate the additional risk that the Regulation presents': Oil and Gas UK, *Proposed Regulation on Offshore Safety* <http://www.oilandgasuk.co.uk/ProposedEURegulation.cfm> accessed 14 April 2021.

[121] A regulation is a binding legislative act, which is applicable across the European Union. Conversely, a directive is a legislative act which sets objectives that EU member states are supposed to achieve within a certain period of time, which is set by the same directive. Member states then have discretion on how to attain the objectives at the domestic level. For a comment concerning the negotiation of the 2013 EU Offshore Safety Directive, see Schiano di Pepe (n 26) 379.

[122] Under the Offshore Pollution Liability Agreement (concluded on 4 September 1974), operating companies agree to accept strict liability for pollution damage and the cost of remedial measures with only certain exceptions, up to a maximum of US $250,000,000 per incident. Within this limit there may also be included the cost of remedial measures undertaken by the party to OPOL involved in the incident. For more information, see OPOL <www.opol.org.uk> accessed 14 April 2021.

[123] The European states in which OPOL applies are: United Kingdom (including the Isle of Man), Denmark (including Faroe Islands and Greenland), Germany, France, Ireland, the Netherlands, and Norway.

[124] BP National Commission, 'Collecting High Quality, Objective, Comprehensive Data' (Staff Working Paper No 18).

[125] Trevisanut, 'The Role of Private Actors in the Offshore Energy Industry' (n 58).

operation of marine renewables, but can be a starting point for providing advice and monitoring in relation to policy, capacity-building, and collaboration, and it can function as a clearing house for research and best practices used in different regions.[126] In that sense, the IRENA, in collaboration with renewable energy professional associations such as the International Electrotechnical Commission (IEC), has collected renewable energy standards and relevant patents.[127] Furthermore, it has published renewable energy technology briefs relating to ocean thermal energy conversion, salinity gradient energy, and tidal and wave energy.[128] While these briefs outline the environmental impact of these marine renewable energy activities, they are not aimed at providing environmental standards to inform the due diligence standards of states in regulating and monitoring these activities. Consequently, none of these documents provide any international standards within the meaning of Article 208 of the LOSC.

The IRENA collaborates with specialized professional associations in the development of standards of operation specifically tailored for offshore renewable energy devices.[129] Aside from these technical standards and guidelines, the implementation of the UN Sustainable Development Goals promotes the strong engagement of non-state actors and the offshore industry.[130] In general, these standards are not legally binding on either states or the industry. However, their embeddedness in the international legal framework can upgrade their normative impact on state or industry conduct.[131] Depending on their institutional source, and the form and procedure by which they are adopted, these legally non-binding pronouncements may become relevant as interpretative guidance, or as standards of proof that a state has shown due diligence.

9.5 Concluding Remarks: Unconventional Law or Conventional Means of Interpretation

Redgwell has remarked that the LOSC 'was never intended to be a "one stop shop" for the regulation of all offshore activities'.[132] As a framework convention, it accommodates necessary changes and developments, either by referring explicitly to external sources of law (ie the GAIRS), or by using generic terms. In the latter case, the International Court of Justice has affirmed that, 'where the parties have used generic terms in a treaty, the parties

[126] Glen Wright, 'The International Renewable Energy Agency: A Global Voice for the Renewable Energy Era?' (2011) 2 REL P 267.

[127] IRENA, 'Irena Platform Supports Renewable Energy Innovation, Quality and Collaboration' <http://www.irena.org/newsroom/pressreleases/2015/Jul/New-IRENA-Platform-Supports-Renewable-Energy-Innovation-Quality-and-Collaboration> accessed 5 June 2021.

[128] IRENA, *Ocean Energy: Technologies, Patents, Deployment Status and Outlook* (August 2014) <https://www.irena.org/publications/2014/Aug/Ocean-Energy-Technologies-Patents-Deployment-Status-and-Outlook > accessed 5 June 2021.

[129] IRENA, *International Standardization in the Field of Renewable Energy*, March 2013, <http://www.irena.org/-/media/Files/IRENA/Agency/Publication/2013/Inventory_renewable_energy_standards.pdf?la = en&hash = 9E18027869BB956421143C768963EE945FAE7926> accessed 5 June 2021.

[130] See Stuart Bruce and Sean Stephenson, 'Issue Brief: SDG 7 on Sustainable Energy for All: Contributions of International Law, Policy and Governance' (August 2016), available at SSRN <https://ssrn.com/abstract = 2824835> accessed 4 June 2018,

[131] See, further, Telesetsky, in Chapter 14 of this volume.

[132] Catherine Redgwell, 'The Never Ending Story: The Role of GAIRS in UNCLOS Implementation in the Offshore Energy Sector' in Jill Barrett and Richard Barnes (eds), *Law of the Sea: UNCLOS as a Living Treaty* (BIICL 2016) 184.

necessarily having been aware that the meaning of the terms was likely to evolve over time, and where the treaty has been entered into for a very long period or is "of continuing duration", the parties must be presumed, as a general rule, to have intended those terms to have an evolving meaning'.[133] The LOSC was negotiated almost forty years ago, and has been in force for twenty-six years, at time of writing. Many of the other aforementioned treaties have also come to a certain phase of maturity in their lives, and need to evolve in light of new circumstances.

GAIRS create 'a degree of dynamism, as the standards may change over time, without having to amend the Law of the Sea Convention'.[134] However, the GAIRS are, at times, difficult to identify, and there is some disagreement over which rules and standards amount to GAIRS. Moreover, they might not be enough. It is not only the LOSC provisions, which explicitly contain a rule of reference, that need updating. The entire system, including the connected treaties, needs to be able to evolve, and needs to have a certain flexibility, especially in highly technology-dependent sectors such as offshore energy production.

Unconventional lawmaking guarantees this flexibility by its informality, which allows faster decision-making processes and, at times, a broader scope of intervention.[135] Moreover, unconventional lawmaking allows actors to intervene at different levels of governance (global, regional, and national), and to involve a variety of stakeholders that might not otherwise have an undisputed seat at the negotiation table (for example, professional associations). A key question, however, remains, concerning the legal value, i.e. the normativity, of the outcomes of unconventional lawmaking in the offshore energy sector.

Many of the instruments analysed above, developed either at a regional or global level, can possess a normativity in their own right, but that is mainly the case when the relevant treaty formally grants this status to the outputs of the treaty bodies:[136] the content of the instrument can then be directly applicable. Some others consist of either subsequent agreements or subsequent practice pursuant to Article 31(2)(a) and (b) of the VCLT. Acts of COPs or MOPs, for instance the CBD 2006 Voluntary Guidance,[137] or the 2019 Mediterranean Offshore Guidelines and Standards,[138] could fit this category. In this case, rather than lawmaking, the documents in question consist of authoritative interpretation of the law, or of conventional means of treaty interpretation.

The lawmaking of unconventional actors struggles to find its place within the general rules of interpretation. Its normativity is, however, not completely 'treaty-independent'. As mentioned above, private actors have a key role in developing best practices and applicable standards in the offshore energy sector. Some of the documents produced by recognized professional associations can mutually reinforce each other, and amount to GAIRS, acquiring binding effect through the LOSC rules of reference.[139]

The multiplicity of actors, the variety of involved fora, and the resulting scattered legal framework raise some concerns about the effectivity of the legal framework, and the coherence of its future developments. The School of Reims[140] affirmed that, by focusing on the

[133] *Dispute regarding Navigational and Related Rights (Costa Rica v Nicaragua)*, Judgment, 13 July 2009, para 66.
[134] James Harrison, *Making the Law of the Sea: A Study on the Development of International Law* (CUP 2014) 171
[135] See above, on the connection with human rights instruments (nn 91–92, and 114, for instance).
[136] See above the instruments elaborated by the OSPAR Commission (nn 51, 94, for instance).
[137] 2006 Voluntary Guidelines (n 84).
[138] Mediterranean Offshore Guidelines and Standards (n 102).
[139] Bonfanti and Romanin Jacur (n 117) 73–74.
[140] Monique Chemillier-Gendreau, 'Contribution of the Reims School to the Debate on the Critical Analysis of International Law: Assessment and Limits' (2011) 22 EJIL 649.

forms of expression of the legal rule, positivism overshadowed the concrete realities and actual functions of international law.[141] Unconventional lawmaking in the offshore energy sector is deeply anchored to reality, but does not necessarily fulfil the expected functions of international law.

[141] '[E]n se concentrant sur les formes d'expression de la règle de droit, le positivime aurait occulté les réalités concrètes sous-jacentes, de même que la function dévoulue au droit international.': Mohammad Bennouna, *Le Droit international entre la lettre et l'esprit* (Brill 2017) 31.

10

Formal and Informal Lawmaking by the International Seabed Authority

An Artificial Distinction?

Tara Davenport

10.1 Introduction

Intergovernmental organizations (IOs) have not, traditionally, been perceived as makers of international law.[1] They did not exist independently from the will of states, and were not typically granted the power to issue binding decisions.[2] Moreover, the various instruments issued by IOs, whether regulations, recommendations, standards, guidelines, or declarations,[3] did not fit neatly within the formal sources of international law set out in Article 38(1) of the Statute of the International Court of Justice (ICJ).[4] However, the exponential growth in the number and types of IOs has challenged orthodox conceptions of the sources and makers of international law.[5] It is now accepted that IOs engage in some form of lawmaking, not only by providing a framework for negotiation of formal sources of law, like treaties, but also by adopting legal instruments that have a normative, transnational impact on other actors.[6] Indeed, it has been argued that any distinction between formal law (outputs that are intended to be binding on states) and informal law (outputs that are intended to be non-binding)[7] is neither 'conclusive as to what constitutes institutional legislation nor is it decisive in considering compliance by member states in practice'.[8] Undoubtedly, in certain IOs, the difference between formal and informal law may be marginal,[9] and their outputs are all assumed to have normative effect capable of shaping the behaviour of the

[1] Ramses A Wessel, 'Institutional Lawmaking: The Emergence of a Global Normative Web' in Catherine Brolmann and Yannick Radi (eds), *Research Handbook on the Theory and Practice of International Lawmaking* (Edward Elgar 2016) 179, 183.

[2] ibid.

[3] Henry G Schermers and Niels M Blokker, *International Institutional Law: Unity within Diversity* (5th edn, Martinus Nijhoff 2011) 755–833.

[4] Ingo Venzke, 'Contemporary Theories and international Lawmaking' in Brolmann and Radi (eds) (n 1) 66, 66.

[5] José E Alvarez, 'International Organizations: Then and Now' (2006) 100 AJIL 324, 324.

[6] Wessel (n 1) 183.

[7] Pauwelyn has defined *formal lawmaking* as characterized by: (1) output formality, in that it is binding on states, and based on state consent; (2) process formality, in that it occurs in traditional forums; and (3) actor formality, in that it involves states and *informal lawmaking*, as dispensing with formalities associated with outputs, processes, and actors: see Joost Pauwelyn, 'Informal International Lawmaking: Framing the Concept and Research Question' in Joost Pauwelyn, Ramses Wessel, and Jan Wouters (eds), *Informal International Lawmaking* (OUP 2012) 13, 15–20. This chapter's definition focuses on *output informality* and, as will be explained below, perceives informal law as outputs that are non-binding and lacking in normative intent, but which still have normative effect.

[8] Nigel White, 'Lawmaking' in Jacob Katz Cogan, Ian Hurd, and Ian Johnstone (eds), *The Oxford Handbook of International Organizations* (OUP 2017) 559, 561.

[9] Schermers and Blokker (n 3) 825.

Tara Davenport, *Formal and Informal Lawmaking by the International Seabed Authority* In: *Unconventional Lawmaking in the Law of the Sea*. Edited by: Natalie Klein, Oxford University Press. © Tara Davenport 2022. DOI: 10.1093/oso/9780192897824.003.0010

intended addressees. This assumption is grounded in a conception of law that goes beyond the strict confines of formal sources, to encompass 'any kind of governance activity by international institutions [including informal networks of fora] ... [which] determines individuals, private associations, enterprises, states or other public institutions'.[10] Such conceptions eschew binary notions of law for broader conceptions that perceive 'legal normativity on a sliding scale'.[11]

This chapter examines the International Seabed Authority (ISA or the Authority)—the only IO established under the 1982 United Nations Convention on the Law of the Sea (LOSC)—[12] through the prism of formal and informal lawmaking. Forged in the crucible of North–South debates on who should have access to, and control over, resources beyond the jurisdiction of any state,[13] the ISA's establishment reflected a 'highpoint in international communitarian governance'.[14] Part XI of the LOSC, as modified by the 1994 Agreement relating to the Implementation of Part XI of the LOSC (1994 Agreement),[15] establishes a detailed regime for the exploration and exploitation of resources of the Area ('activities in the Area'),[16] which are designated, along with the Area, as the common heritage of mankind (hereafter referred to as the 'common heritage of humankind' or 'CHH').[17] The ISA organizes, carries out, and controls activities in the Area for and on behalf of humankind. Exploration and exploitation of CHH resources are conducted by contractors, consisting of states and non-state actors (state-owned enterprises and private entities, provided they are sponsored by states parties to the LOSC) pursuant to a contract with the ISA.[18]

To fulfil its mandate, the ISA has been given 'competence and regulatory control to an extent so far unparalleled in international law'.[19] The LOSC only sets out the core elements of the deep seabed regime, 'leaving the ISA with a significant degree of operational competence to further develop governance arrangements'.[20] The first phase of the ISA's work focused on the regulation of exploration,[21] and the second phase is currently focused on the regulation of exploitation of CHH resources.[22] It is envisaged that the 'whole of the

[10] Armin von Bogdandy, Philipp Dann, and Matthias Goldmann, 'Developing the Publicness of Public International Law: Towards a Legal Framework for Global Governance Activities' (2008) 9 GLJ 1375, 1380.

[11] Catherine Brolmann and Yannick Radi, 'Introduction: International Lawmaking in a Global World' in Brolmann and Radi (eds) (n 1) 1, 2.

[12] United Nations Convention on the Law of the Sea (adopted 10 December 1982, entered into force 16 November 1994) 1833 UNTS 397 (hereafter 'LOSC').

[13] Surabhi Ranganathan, 'Global Commons' (2016) 27(3) EJIL 693, 694.

[14] Richard Collins and Duncan French, 'A Guardian of Universal Interest or Increasingly out of its Depth? The International Seabed Authority Turns 25' (2019) 17(3) Intl Org L Rev 1, 2.

[15] Agreement relating to the Implementation of Part XI of the United Nations Convention on the Law of the Sea of 10 December 1982 (adopted 28 July 1994, entered into force 16 November 1994) 1836 UNTS 3 (hereafter '1994 Agreement').

[16] Resources refers to 'all solid, liquid or gaseous mineral resources *in situ* in the Area at or beneath the seabed, including polymetallic nodules': LOSC (n 12) art 133(a). The Area is defined as 'the seabed and ocean floor and subsoil thereof beyond the limits of national jurisdiction': LOSC (n 12) art 1(1).

[17] LOSC (n 12) art 136.

[18] ibid, art 153(2).

[19] Collins and French (n 14) 3.

[20] ibid 24.

[21] The ISA has issued three sets of regulations on exploration: Regulations on Prospecting and Exploration for Polymetallic Nodules in the Area (13 July 2000), Doc No ISBA/6/A/18 (13 July 2000) ('Nodules Regulations'); Regulations on Prospecting and Exploration for Polymetallic Sulphides in the Area, Doc No ISBA/16/A/12/Rev.1 (7 May 2010) ('Sulphides Regulations'); Regulations on Prospecting for Cobalt-rich Ferromanganese Crusts in the Area, Doc No ISBA/19/C/17 (22 July 2013) ('Cobalt Crust Regulations') (collectively the 'Exploration Regulations').

[22] See ISA, 'Note on Public Information on Plans of Work for Exploration' <https://www.isa.org.jm/legal-instruments/ongoing-development-regulations-exploitation-mineral-resources-area> accessed 4 March 2021. The

comprehensive set of rules, regulations and procedures issued by the [ISA] to regulate prospecting, exploration and exploitation of marine minerals'[23] will constitute the Mining Code. The ISA has employed a variety of regulatory outputs to govern activities in the Area. However, with exploitation said to be imminent, the legal nature of these instruments has become a recurring issue in the development of the exploitation regulations. This is unsurprising given that the normative intent (whether it is stated to be binding or non-binding) and normative effect (whether it is capable of shaping the conduct of its addressees) of these outputs may have significant implications for the governance of the CHH.[24] ISA organs, contractors, member states, and sponsoring states need a predictable legal system that sets out their rights and obligations in a clear and coherent manner, particularly when a failure to comply with these rights and obligations may have serious ramifications for the marine environment and entail liability.

However, determining the normative intent and normative effect of an ISA output has its challenges. First, the constituent documents of the ISA, namely the LOSC and the 1994 Agreement, do not always clearly state the legal nature of the outputs that are intended to regulate activities in the Area, and, in certain cases, the outputs themselves do not expressly state whether they are binding. Second, the evolutionary and incremental approach that the ISA has taken to administering activities in the Area, necessitated by constantly evolving knowledge of the deep seabed and technology, means that new forms of outputs may need to be developed that do not fit strictly into what was envisaged in the LOSC or the 1994 Agreement. Third, the legal regime governing exploitation is still in its nascent stages, and several of the outputs under discussion have not yet been adopted, and so it is impossible to know with certainty what their normative effect will be.

Notwithstanding the above difficulties, this chapter proposes a framework for classifying ISA regulatory outputs as formal or informal law. Informal law is understood as outputs that are intended to be non-binding (and lack normative intent), but may still have normative effect in shaping the conduct of their intended addressees. This normative effect may be on a 'sliding scale' of normativity.[25] Based on this conception, this chapter categorizes ISA's lawmaking as formal (section 10.2) or informal (section 10.3) and, within each category, analyses: (1) the source of the ISA's authority to adopt the output; (2) the process of adoption; (3) the participants; (4) the normative intent; and (5) the normative effects of such outputs, subject to the caveat that these are preliminary conclusions on *potential* normative effects, using some of the factors highlighted in Chapter 1. These factors include whether the output has been complied with (where possible); whether a violation of the relevant output entails legal consequences; whether the output is relevant in the interpretation of particular international obligations, including due diligence obligations; and/or whether the output informs, or is implemented in, domestic laws. The aim of this analysis is to examine whether (as is the case with many IOs) there are any real normative differences in formal and informal lawmaking by the ISA. Ultimately, this chapter argues that increasing convergences in formal and informal lawmaking processes at the ISA, coupled

Legal and Technical Commission (LTC) has issued draft exploitation regulations: see ISA, 'Draft Regulations on Exploitation of Mineral Resources in the Area' (22 March 2019) ISBA/25/C/WP.1 (hereafter '2019 DER').

23 ISA, 'The Mining Code' <https://www.isa.org.jm/mining-code> accessed 4 March 2021.

24 This chapter adopts the nomenclature on normative intent and normative effect utilized in Chapter 1.

25 See n 7.

with the potential normative effects of the ISA's informal outputs, means that the distinction between formal and informal lawmaking is more apparent than real. Nonetheless, this chapter hypothesizes that informal law still remains an important tool in the ISA's regulatory arsenal, due to the particular lawmaking dynamics at the ISA.

10.2 Formal Lawmaking by the ISA

As noted above, formal lawmaking is characterized by output formality (binding outputs and based on state consent), process formality (traditional forums), and actor formality (involving states or diplomatic actors representing states).[26] Accordingly, this section analyses two regulatory outputs (regulations and standards) that are the outcome of formal lawmaking, in that they have been adopted by the most formal ISA processes involving state actors, and that they are either explicitly or implicitly characterized as binding.

10.2.1 Source of Authority

10.2.1.1 Regulations

All rights in the resources of the Area (polymetallic nodules, polymetallic sulphides, and cobalt-rich crusts) are vested in humankind as a whole, on whose behalf the ISA is to act.[27] The overarching mandate of the ISA is to serve as the organization through which states parties organize, carry out, and control exploration and exploitation of CHH resources on behalf of, and for the benefit of, humankind.[28] The ISA's powers and functions are those expressly conferred upon it by the LOSC, and 'such incidental powers, consistent with this Convention, as are implicit in and necessary for the exercise of those powers and functions with respect to activities in the Area'.[29] The ISA has express powers and incidental powers, but they must be exercised only in relation to 'activities in the Area'.[30] In addition, the LOSC grants the ISA relatively extensive enforcement powers: the ISA 'shall exercise such control over activities in the Area as is necessary for the purpose of securing compliance with the relevant provisions of this Part and the Annexes relating thereto, and the rules, regulations and procedures of the Authority, and the plans of work approved in accordance with [Article 153(3) of the LOSC]'.[31] Further, the ISA 'shall have the right to take at any time any measures provided for under [Part XI] to ensure compliance with its provisions and the exercise of the functions of control and regulation assigned to it thereunder or under any contract'.[32]

26 Pauwelyn (n 7) 15–20.
27 LOSC (n 12) art 137(1).
28 ibid, arts 137(1), 153(1), and 157(1).
29 ibid, art 157(2).
30 This imposes both geographical and subject-matter limits on the ISA's authority. The Area refers to the seabed and ocean floor in areas beyond national jurisdiction: LOSC (n 12) art 1(1). The Seabed Disputes Chamber (SDC) has given a detailed definition of 'activities in the Area': SDC, 'Responsibilities and Obligations of States with respect to Activities in the Area' (Advisory Opinion) ITLOS Reports 2011, 10, paras 82–97 (hereafter 'SDC Advisory Opinion').
31 LOSC (n 12) art 153(4).
32 ibid, art 153(5).

Pursuant to its mandate of organizing, controlling, and administering activities in the Area, the ISA has been conferred with general authority to adopt 'rules, regulations and procedures' to govern activities in the Area,[33] and specific competences to adopt rules, regulations, and procedures on: (1) the system of exploration and exploitation;[34] (2) the protection of the marine environment from harmful effects arising from activities in the Area;[35] (3) the protection of human life vis-à-vis activities in the Area;[36] (4) the prevention of interference with other activities in the marine environment;[37] (5) the equitable sharing of financial and other economic benefits derived from activities in the Area;[38] and (6) the distribution of revenues to states parties from the exploitation of the outer continental shelf.[39] The ISA has adopted exploration regulations (pursuant to which it has entered into thirty exploration contracts with states, state-owned enterprises, and private entities).[40] Draft exploitation regulations ('2019 Draft Exploitation Regulations') have been issued by the Legal and Technical Commission (LTC), and are currently under consideration by the Council (the exploration regulations and exploitation regulations will, hereinafter, collectively be described as 'Regulations').

10.2.1.2 Standards

The ISA has the authority to adopt and uniformly apply rules, regulations, and procedures, on 'mining standards and practice, including those relating to operational safety, conservation of the resources and protection of the marine environment'.[41] The ISA's initial approach was to have all matters reflected in the exploitation regulations, albeit in two different sets with one specifically addressing environmental matters.[42] However, the ISA's current approach is to have one overarching set of exploitation regulations supplemented by 'Standards and Guidelines',[43] prompted by concerns relating to duplication, ambiguity, and a lack of consistency between separate sets of exploitation regulations.[44] The rationale for such standards is to 'ensure a level playing field across the [c]ontractor base and consistent treatment of specific risks',[45] and to 'facilitate flexibility in amending future guidance in the light of improved knowledge or technology, together with the development of more prescriptive regulations, as time and knowledge advance'.[46] Accordingly, the 2019 Draft Exploitation Regulations provide that the exploitation regulations are to be 'supplemented by Standards and Guidelines, as referred to in these Regulations and the Annexes thereto, as well as by further rules, regulations and procedures of the Authority, in particular on

[33] ibid, art 137.
[34] ibid, arts 153(1), 160(2)(f)(ii) and 162(2)(o)(ii); Annex III, art 17(1).
[35] ibid, arts 145, 209(1); Annex III, arts 17(1)(b)(xii) and 17(2)(f).
[36] ibid, art 146.
[37] ibid, art 147; Annex III, art 17(1)(b)(ix).
[38] ibid, arts 140(2), 160(2)(f), and 162(o)(i).
[39] ibid, art 82(4).
[40] ISA, Exploration Regulations (n 21); ISA, 'Status of Exploration Contracts' (17 December 2019) ISBA/26/C/4.
[41] LOSC (n 12) Annex III, art 17(1)(b)(xii).
[42] ISA, 'Discussion Paper on Development and Drafting of Regulations on Exploitation for Mineral Resources in the Area (Environmental Matters)' (January 2017) <https://www.isa.org.jm/files/documents/EN/Regs/DraftExpl/DP-EnvRegsDraft25117.pdf> accessed 4 March 2021.
[43] ISA, 'Note by the Secretariat' (10 August 2017) ISBA/23/C/12.
[44] ISA, 'Report of the LTC Chair' (9 August 2017) ISBA/23/C/13, para 17.
[45] ISA, 'Note by the Secretariat' (17 December 2018) ISBA 25/C/3, para 1.
[46] ISA, 'Note by the Secretariat' (10 August 2017) ISBA/23/C/12, para 3.

the protection and preservation of the marine environment'.[47] Standards will relate to, inter alia, operational safety, conservation of resources, and marine environment protection.[48]

10.2.2 Process of Adoption

10.2.2.1 Regulations

The ISA's main organs are: (1) the Assembly, composed of all states parties to the LOSC, including the European Union; (2) the Council, with thirty-six members; and (3) a Secretariat. There are also subsidiary bodies made up of experts, such as the LTC and the Finance Committee, which are responsible to the Council and Assembly, respectively. The ISA has a mining arm, the Enterprise, to carry out activities in the Area on behalf of humankind (currently non-operational),[49] and a judicial arm, the Seabed Disputes Chamber (SDC) of the International Tribunal for the Law of the Sea (ITLOS), to resolve disputes on activities in the Area.

For present purposes, this chapter focuses on the three main arenas that are engaged in the adoption of laws governing activities in the Area, namely the Assembly, the Council, and the LTC.[50] The Assembly is the supreme organ of the ISA, consisting of all parties to the LOSC and the 1994 Agreement.[51] The other principal organs are accountable to it, as specifically provided for in the LOSC, and the Assembly 'shall have the power to establish general policies in conformity with the relevant provisions of this Convention on any question or matter within the competence of the Authority'.[52] That said, the 1994 Agreement considerably reduced the Assembly's autonomy by curtailing its decision-making powers, consistent with the wishes of developed states.[53] Most policies adopted, or decisions taken by the Assembly, have to be made in conjunction with the Council.[54]

The Council is the executive organ of the ISA. Its primary function is to supervise and coordinate the implementation of Part XI on all matters within the competence of the Authority.[55] While it must act in accordance with the general policies established by the Assembly, the Council has significant powers over a range of matters set out in Article 162 that are not constrained by the Assembly.[56] The Council consists of thirty-six member states

[47] 2019 DER (n 22) regs 1(5) and 94(1).

[48] ibid, reg 94(1).

[49] Under the 1994 Agreement, the Enterprise's functions have been conferred on the Secretariat until such time as the Council issues a directive permitting the Enterprise to function independently: 1994 Agreement (n 15) s 2(1).

[50] The Finance Committee may also be involved in the adoption of laws, as it has been given authority to prepare draft financial rules, regulations, and procedures on the equitable sharing of financial and other economic benefits derived from exploitation of CHH resources: 1994 Agreement (n 15) s 9(7). However, this is still in the nascent stages, and the Finance Committee's role will be excluded from discussion for present purposes. The SDC, while in principle tasked with resolving disputes relating to activities in the Area, including disputes over the interpretation or application of the relevant provisions of the LOSC, will inevitably be engaged in some form of lawmaking. However, discussion on its lawmaking role is excluded, as the focus of this chapter is institutional lawmaking rather than possible judicial lawmaking.

[51] LOSC (n 12) arts 159(1) and 160(1).

[52] ibid, art 160.

[53] Aline L Jaeckel, *The International Seabed Authority and the Precautionary Principle: Balancing Deep Seabed Mineral Mining and Marine Environmental Protection* (Brill 2017) 92.

[54] 1994 Agreement (n 15) ss 3(1), 3(4), and 3(7).

[55] LOSC (n 12) art 162(2)(a).

[56] Michael Lodge, 'The Deep Seabed' in Donald R Rothwell, Alex G Oude Elferink, Karen N Scott, and Tim Stephens (eds), *The Oxford Handbook of the Law of the Sea* (OUP 2014) 226, 234.

elected by the Assembly for a four-year term,[57] divided into five groups: Group A (four members from the consumer/importer states); Group B (four members from investor states); Group C (four members from major producer or exporter states); Group D (six members from developing states representing special interests); and Group E (eighteen members elected according to the principle of ensuring an equitable geographical distribution of Council seats). Decisions are to be made by consensus, as a first step,[58] and decisions on questions of substance shall be taken either by consensus or by two-thirds majority.[59] The 1994 Agreement established four chambers for voting: Group A (consumer/importer states), Group B (investor states), and Group C (major producer/exporter states) make up one voting chamber each, and Group D (developing states representing special interests) and Group E (equitable geographical representation), together, make up the fourth voting chamber.

The LTC has a range of critical responsibilities.[60] Most of the substantive matters before the Council, except for financial and budgetary matters, necessitate the LTC's prior consideration and, on a number of important issues, the Council is required to act on the recommendations of the LTC.[61] The LTC consists of thirty members elected by the Council. Members are required to have appropriate qualifications, such as those 'relevant to exploration for and exploitation and processing of mineral resources, oceanology, protection of the marine environment, or economic or legal matters relating to ocean mining and related fields of expertise'.[62] The LTC is in principle a technical and advisory body, but the LOSC does not mention whether members are serving in their personal capacities or representing their states.[63] Members have included persons affiliated with a government institution or an entity that has an exploration contract with the ISA.[64]

The process of adoption of Regulations by the ISA is divided between the LTC, Council, and Assembly. First, the LTC formulates, and submits to the Council, draft texts of the Regulations.[65] Once the LTC has completed the draft, it adopts the draft Regulations by consensus, where possible, or by majority vote, if necessary.[66] The draft is then submitted to the Council for consideration.[67] The Council will then review the draft texts (taking into account the recommendations of the LTC), and can suggest amendments to the LTC.[68] The

[57] LOSC (n 12) art 162(1).
[58] 1994 Agreement (n 15) s 3(2).
[59] Consensus on decisions is required on certain specified issues: 1994 Agreement (n 15), s 3(5), read with LOSC (n 12) arts 161(8)(d), 162(2)(m) and (o). There is an exception for decision-making procedures on approvals of plans of work submitted by prospective contractors: 1994 Agreement (n 15) s 3(11).
[60] LOSC (n 12) art 165(2).
[61] ibid, art 162(2)(o)(ii); Lodge (n 56) 235.
[62] LOSC (n 12) art 165(1).
[63] Eg, the LOSC requires that members of the Commission on the Limits of the Continental Shelf (CLCS) 'shall serve in their personal capacities': LOSC (n 12), Annex II, art 2(1). There is no equivalent obligation for the LTC, although, in practice, its members make a sworn statement attesting to their independence, including a declaration of no financial interests, as required by art 163(8) of the LOSC.
[64] Jaeckel (n 53) 96.
[65] LOSC (n 12) art 165(f).
[66] 1994 Agreement (n 15) ss 3(2) and 3(13); ISA, 'Rules of Procedure of the Legal and Technical Commission' (hereafter 'LTC Procedures'), r 44 <https://www.isa.org.jm/files/documents/EN/Regs/ROP-LTC.pdf> accessed 19 March 2021.
[67] LOSC (n 12) art 162(o)(ii).
[68] Jaeckel (n 53) 101–02.

Council then adopts the Regulations by consensus, and there must be no formal objections by any of the thirty-six members.[69]

After the Council has approved the draft Regulations, they are sent to the Assembly for final approval. If the Assembly requires changes, it has to return the matter to the Council for further consideration.[70] Even if the Assembly does not approve them, the Regulations will still apply provisionally indefinitely, as there is no time limit by which the Council has to reconsider the Regulations.[71] The Assembly approves the Regulations by consensus and, where consensus cannot be reached, the Assembly may adopt the Regulations by a two-thirds majority.[72]

10.2.2.2 Standards

The Council has requested the LTC to undertake work on standards as a matter of priority, to ensure that they are in place before the exploitation regulations are adopted.[73] The LTC has recommended a three-phase approach, the three phases being standards that are deemed necessary to have in place either: (1) by the time of adoption of the exploitation regulations; or (2) prior to the receipt of an application of a plan of work for exploitation; or (3) before commercial mining activities commence in the Area.[74]

The current process for adoption of standards, in the 2019 Draft Exploitation Regulations, mirrors the procedures for the adoption of Regulations (outlined above), with some modifications. The LTC makes recommendations to the Council on the adoption and revision of standards.[75] The Council considers and approves the standards, provided that they are consistent with the intent and purpose of the LOSC, the 1994 Agreement, and the Regulations.[76] If the Council does not approve such standards, the Council shall return the standards to the LTC for reconsideration. The Assembly does not have a role in current procedures for the adoption of standards, presumably to avoid the additional time it would take to get Assembly approval. However, at a 2019 workshop on standards and guidelines,[77] participants pushed for greater formality and transparency in the adoption of standards. For example, it was suggested that when new standards are developed, there should be clear reasons and terms of reference for their development, and ideas on their designs and contents should be put before the Council before proceeding.[78] The participants suggested that, after the Council approves and provisionally applies the standards, the standards be sent to the Assembly for approval,[79] making the process identical to that applicable to the adoption of Regulations.

[69] 1994 Agreement (n 15), ss 3(2), and 3(6); LOSC (n 12), art 161(8)(d)(e). The LOSC and 1994 Agreement provide for procedures if consensus is not reached: LOSC (n 12), art 168(8)(e); 1994 Agreement (n 15) s 3(6).

[70] 1994 Agreement (n 15) s 3(4).

[71] James Harrison, *Making the Law of the Sea: A Study in the Development of International Law* (CUP 2011) 126.

[72] LOSC (n 12) art 159(8); 1994 Agreement (n 15) s 3(3).

[73] See ISA, 'Stakeholder Consultations on Draft Standards and Guidelines to Support the Implementation of the Draft Regulations for Exploitation of Mineral Resources in the Area' <https://www.isa.org.jm/stakeholder-consultations-draft-standards-and-guidelines-support-implementation-draft-regulations> accessed 4 March 2021.

[74] ibid.

[75] 2019 DER (n 22) reg 94(1).

[76] ibid, reg 94(2).

[77] ISA, 'Workshop on the Development of Standards and Guidelines for the Mining Code 13–15 May 2019: Background Information Note' (1 May 2019) <https://www.isa.org.jm/files/files/documents/bkgrnd.pdf> accessed 4 March 2021.

[78] ibid 16.

[79] ibid 17.

10.2.3 Participants

10.2.3.1 Regulations

States parties to the LOSC are clearly the dominant actors in the formal processes for the adoption of Regulations, acting primarily through the Council (and, to a more limited extent, through the Assembly). The various interests of states parties broadly correspond to the composition of the groups in the Council, namely the consumer states, investor states, land producers, and developing states. Another important participant is the ISA secretariat, which provides both administrative and technical expertise to ISA organs. It plays an indirect role in lawmaking through agenda-setting, and preparing informative background papers or notes that can influence discussion on certain topics.

Non-state actors are another group of important participants and, consistent with trends seen in other IOs,[80] the ISA has been a forum for state and non-state actors to interact with each other, inevitably shaping ISA lawmaking. The most important non-state actors for present purposes are the *non-state contractors* (presently consisting of eleven state-owned enterprises and five private entities) and the *non-governmental organizations* (NGOs) (there are presently thirty NGOs registered as observers, although there are more that can participate informally).[81]

Like the majority of IOs, non-state actors do not have the direct right to vote in the decision-making processes of the ISA.[82] However, non-state actors have other avenues to shape the adoption of Regulations by the ISA. First, certain non-state actors can participate in the meetings of the LTC, Council, and Assembly. Both state contractors and non-state contractors may be invited to attend LTC meetings for purposes of consultation and collaboration, where the LTC considers this appropriate.[83] NGOs, however, do not have the right to participate in LTC meetings. State contractors are able to participate in the Council, either in Group A (consumer/importer states) or Group B (investor states),[84] as well as in the Assembly. Non-state contractors do not participate in Council or Assembly meetings, but, arguably, their interests are represented by their sponsoring states having seats in Groups A or B in the Council.[85] NGOs recognized by the UN Economic and Social Council (ECOSOC) or 'other non-governmental organizations invited by the Assembly which have demonstrated their interest in matters under consideration by the Assembly'[86] have certain

[80] While there are variations in the extent to which different IOs permit non-state actor participation, their participation in the decision-making of IOs is recognized as a principle of both environmental governance (see, eg UN, 'Report of the United Nations Conference on Environment and Development' (3–14 June 1992) UN Doc A/CONF.151/26 (Vol. I), Annex I: Rio Declaration on Environment and Development, Principle 10; and the Convention on Access to Information, Public Participation in Decision-making and Access to Justice in Environmental Matters (opened for signature 25 June 1998, entered force 30 October 2001) 2161 UNTS 450 (hereafter 'Aarhus Convention')) and global governance (see Patrizia Nanz and Klaus Dingwerth, 'Participation' in Katz Cogan, Hurd, and Johnstone (eds) (n 8) 1126, 1126).

[81] ISA stakeholder surveys usually attract submissions by NGOs that have not been registered as observers.

[82] Richard Stewart, 'Remedying Disregard in Global Regulatory Governance: Participation and Responsiveness' (2014) 108(2) AJIL 211, 225.

[83] LTC Procedures (n 66) r 53(1).

[84] State contractors such as Korea, India, Russia, and Poland would have seats in Group A (consumer/importer states) or Group B (investor states) in the Council.

[85] The interests of sponsoring states and non-state contractors may not be identical, given that sponsoring states are often concerned about their own responsibilities and liabilities vis-à-vis their sponsored contractor's activities, as well as vis-à-vis the ISA.

[86] ISA, 'Rules of Procedure of the Assembly' (7 July 1994) ISBA/A/6 (hereafter 'Assembly Procedures'), r 82(1)(e). The Assembly has adopted guidelines for observer status of NGOs with the ISA: ISA, 'Decision of the Assembly

limited rights of participation in Assembly and Council meetings. NGOs can attend the meetings of the Assembly and Council, but can only make oral statements at the invitation of the President of the Assembly and Council,[87] and only on questions affecting them, or within the scope of their activities.[88]

The second avenue for non-state actor participation is through the regular workshops organized by the ISA, in which experts, including independent academics, scientists, and researchers can participate in discussions.[89] The results of these workshops are reflected in reports that are considered by the LTC in their development of the Regulations.[90] The development of the Regulations has also benefitted from briefing papers and technical studies prepared either by experts individually, or in collaboration with the ISA.[91] While the initial workshop processes were relatively ad hoc, it appears that the Secretariat is formalizing the procedure, by providing terms of reference and processes for how participants in the workshop are selected.[92]

Third, the ISA has engaged in consultations with non-state actors in the development of the exploitation regulations. In 2011, the ISA recognized that it needed to enable public participation in environmental decision-making procedures in accordance with the Aarhus Convention[93] and its own rules and procedures.[94] On the Council's suggestion,[95] a series of 'stakeholder surveys' were held from 2014 to 2019.[96] Stakeholders were, initially, loosely defined as 'contractors, international organizations, non-government organizations, scientific institutions, and universities, private entities and individuals',[97] but have now been described in the 2019 Draft Exploitation Regulations as 'natural or juristic person[s] or an association of persons with an interest of any kind in, or who may be affected by, the proposed or existing Exploitation activities under a Plan of Work in the Area, or who [have]

on the Guidelines for Observer Status of Non-governmental Organizations with the ISA' (26 July 2019) ISBA/25/A/16.

[87] Assembly Procedures (n 86) rr 83(3)–(6); ISA, 'Rules of Procedure of the Council' (3 December 1996) ISBA/C/12 (hereafter 'Council Procedures'), r 75.

[88] Assembly Procedures (n 86) r 82(5); Council Procedures (n 87) r 75.

[89] See, eg the ISA, 'Workshops' <https://www.isa.org.jm/events/workshops> accessed 4 March 2021.

[90] Eg, in 2006, workshops on prospects for mining cobalt-rich crusts and polymetallic sulphides in the Area were organized, to examine proposals for regulations that had been prepared by the LTC: See ISA, 'Possible Adjustments to the Draft Regulations for Prospecting and Exploration of Cobalt-rich Ferromanganese Crusts and Polymetallic Sulphides Suggested by the Workshop on Technical and Economic Considerations relating to Mining Polymetallic Sulphides and Cobalt-rich Crusts in the Area with respect to Polymetallic Sulphides' (8 August 2006) ISBA/12/C/7.

[91] See ISA, 'Draft Exploitation Regulations' <https://www.isa.org.jm/mining-code/ongoing-development-regulations-exploitation-mineral-resources-area> accessed 4 March 2021.

[92] Eg, most of the recent workshops have had provisions on terms of reference, and calls for nominations for participants: See, eg ISA, 'Workshop on the Development of a REMP for the Area of the Northern Mid-Atlantic Ridge, 23 November 2020–4 December 2020' <https://www.isa.org.jm/event/workshop-remp-area-northern-mid-atlantic-ridge> accessed 4 March 2021.

[93] Aarhus Convention (n 80).

[94] This was in the context of one of the guiding principles for the adoption of the Environmental Management Plan for the Clarion-Clipperton Zone: See ISA, 'Environmental Management Plan for the Clarion-Clipperton Zone' (13 July 2011) ISBA/17/LTC/7.

[95] ISA, 'Statement of the President of the Council on the work of the Council during the Nineteenth Session' (24 July 2013) ISBA/19/C/18, para 19.

[96] See, generally, ISA, 'Draft Exploitation Regulations' <https://www.isa.org.jm/mining-code/ongoing-development-regulations-exploitation-mineral-resources-area> accessed 4 March 2021.

[97] ISA, 'Developing a Regulatory Framework for Mineral Exploitation in the Area: Report to Members of the Authority and all Stakeholders' (March 2015) 2 <https://www.isa.org.jm/files/documents/EN/Survery/Report-2015.pdf> accessed 4 March 2021.

relevant information or expertise'.[98] In a separate process, the Secretariat has established an informal consultation process with contractors (including the non-state contractors) to get their input on the Draft Exploitation Regulations.[99]

10.2.3.2 Standards

Participants in the adoption of standards are almost the same as those in the adoption of Regulations (LTC and Council members plus stakeholders, with the exclusion of the Assembly). The LTC has taken the opportunity to formalize engagement and consultations with non-state actors, including technical experts, in the development of standards. Regulation 94 of the 2019 Draft Exploitation Regulations explicitly mentions the involvement of 'recognized experts' and 'recognized stakeholders'. The 2019 standards and guidelines workshop suggested that these experts could include professional standard-setting organizations and technical working groups, but the involvement of these actors should be subject to prior review and approval by the Council in each instance.[100]

10.2.4 Normative Intent

10.2.4.1 Regulations

The Regulations are, unquestionably, binding on the ISA itself and ISA organs.[101] While neither Annex III of the LOSC nor the Regulations, per se, bind the non-state contractors,[102] the contract between the ISA and the contractors contains standard terms that oblige contractors to 'comply with the Regulations, as well as other Rules of the Authority, as amended from time to time, and the decisions of the relevant organ of the Authority', and to carry out their obligations with 'due diligence, including compliance with rules, regulations and procedures adopted by the Authority to ensure effective protection for the Marine Environment'.[103] Further, the contract is governed by the 'the terms of this contract, the rules, regulations and procedures of the Authority, Part XI of the Convention, the Agreement and other rules of international law not incompatible with the Convention'.[104]

Are the Regulations binding on the 168 members of the ISA, including sponsoring states? Both the Exploration Regulations and 2019 Draft Exploitation Regulations contain direct obligations on ISA members and sponsoring states.[105] The Regulations are items of 'secondary legislation' that were envisaged by the drafters of the Convention to be subsidiary

[98] 2019 DER (n 22) sch 1.

[99] ISA, 'Annual ISA Deep-sea Exploration Contractors Meetings Conclude in China' (15 October 2019) <https://www.isa.org.jm/node/19320> accessed 4 March 2021.

[100] ISA, 'Workshop Report: Development of Standards and Guidelines for Activities in the Area, Pretoria, South Africa' (hereafter 'Standards and Guidelines Workshop Report') 18 <https://www.isa.org.jm/files/files/documents/pretoria_workshop_report-final.pdf>.

[101] See Schermers and Blokkers (n 3) 829, para 1327.

[102] Markos Karavias, *Corporate Obligations under International Law* (OUP 2013) 123.

[103] See, eg Nodules Regulations (n 21) Annex IV, s 13; 2019 DER (n 22) Annex X, ss 3.3(a) and (d). 'Rules of the Authority' is defined in the 2019 DER, sch 1.

[104] LOSC (n 12) Annex III, art 21; Nodules Regulations (n 21) Annex IV, s 27.1.

[105] Member states of the ISA and flag states, even when not directly involved in activities in the Area, have certain obligations under the Draft Exploitation Regulations: 2019 DER (n 22) regs 3, 31(2), and 96(2). Sponsoring states have direct obligations in both the Explorations Regulations and DER (see, eg Nodules Regulations (n 21) reg 31(2); 2019 DER (n 22) regs 3(b), 3(e), and 44(a).

and supplementary to the LOSC.[106] However, although not explicitly mentioned, these Regulations are said to be legally binding on all member states.[107] The LOSC recognizes the binding nature of the Regulations, in Article 137, which states that the 'minerals recovered from the Area, however, may only be alienated in accordance with this Part and *the rules, regulations and procedures of the Authority*', and in Article 153, which states that activities in the Area shall be carried out and controlled by the ISA 'in accordance' with 'relevant provisions of this Part and the relevant Annexes and the *rules, regulations and procedures* of the Authority'.[108] The Regulations are said to be binding on all members irrespective of whether they have been implemented in domestic law.[109] The SDC has also observed that the Exploration Regulations contain direct obligations on sponsoring states, without having any corresponding obligation in the LOSC, and that they are 'binding texts negotiated by States and adopted through a procedure similar to that used in multilateral conferences'.[110]

The ISA's authority to adopt such binding Regulations has been described as an 'unprecedented experiment in international law-making',[111] in that the Regulations are drafted by the LTC, and adopted by a mere thirty-six states in the Council.[112] They are not like 'generally accepted international rules and standards' that are indirectly binding on LOSC states parties through rules of reference only if they reach the vague threshold of being 'generally accepted', but are directly binding on ISA member states.[113] Further, unlike other IOs that, typically, allow states to opt out of instruments adopted by them,[114] there is no equivalent mechanism for Regulations. Their legitimacy as *law* is derived from their endorsement by the Council, which, for all intents and purposes, is recognized by the LOSC and 1994 Agreement as having the authority to act on behalf of states parties to the LOSC. Jaeckel observes that these far-reaching powers are explicable on the basis that the ISA's mandate is to administer, organize, and control the CHH, and that, if states were allowed to opt out, 'it would compromise the common heritage of mankind'.[115] Arguably, the mandatory nature of the Regulations was implicitly influenced by the politics prevailing at the time of adoption of the LOSC and, particularly, the practice of the developed states in adopting unilateral legislation on deep seabed mining, outside the LOSC framework.

[106] The Secretariat of the Preparatory Commission noted that the 'rules, regulations and procedures are subsidiary and supplementary to the Convention and are required to be drafted in greater detail and structured in such a way that they become in fact the day-to-day working instruments of the Authority': Preparatory Commission for the ISA and ITLOS (8 March 1984) UN Doc LOS/PCN/SCN.3/WP.1; SDC Advisory Opinion (n 30) para 93.

[107] Jaeckel (n 53) 145.

[108] ibid (emphasis added).

[109] ibid 149.

[110] SDC Advisory Opinion (n 30) para 60. The SDC, accordingly, used the Vienna Convention on the Law of Treaties as guidance for the interpretation of the Regulations.

[111] Harrison (n 71) 151–56.

[112] Jaeckel (n 53) 147.

[113] The LOSC contains several rules of reference, ranging from a direct obligation to adopt and follow 'generally accepted international rules and standards' (GAIRS), or to at least take them into account. It has been said that GAIRS apply to the LOSC states parties concerned by virtue of LOSC itself, and not the relevant instrument in question, avoiding the need for another binding instrument to be negotiated and agreed by the parties. However, it has not been definitively determined what it means for an instrument to be 'generally accepted': See Jill Barrett, 'UNCLOS: A "Living" Treaty?' in Jill Barrett and Richard Barnes (eds), *Law of the Sea: UNCLOS as a Living Treaty* (BIICL 2016) 20–23.

[114] See, eg the Convention on International Civil Aviation (adopted 7 December 1944, entered into force 4 April 1947) 15 UNTS 295, arts 12, 38; Constitution of the World Health Organization (adopted 22 July 1946, entered into force 7 April 1948) 14 UNTS 185.

[115] Jaeckel (n 53) 148.

10.2.4.2 Standards

Under regulation 94 of the 2019 Draft Exploitation Regulations, 'Standards adopted by the Council shall be legally binding on Contractors and the Authority and may be revised every 5 years from the date of their adoption or revision, and in the light of improved knowledge or technology.'[116] The standards and guidelines workshop observed that standards, as part of the Mining Code, are intended to be 'binding on Member States, Contractors, and the Authority'.[117] The workshop suggested that a document should be mandatory when it was necessary in order to ensure a level playing field for contractors, to set performance outcome thresholds for contractors, to ensure effective protection of the marine environment, or to set rules for the format of data/reports from the contractors that the ISA needs to receive in a consistent way in order to function effectively.[118] Some stakeholders also suggested that all issues related to environmental matters be made in standards.[119] It is clear that standards are intended to flesh out the substantive content of the Regulations. Arguably, like the Regulations, it is important for standards to be binding, so as not to compromise the implementation of the CHH, and to minimize any opportunity for contractors to justify non-compliance with such standards.

10.2.5 Normative Effect

The Regulations and standards have similar processes of adoption, involve similar participants, and are intended to be binding law vis-à-vis the ISA organs, the contractors, ISA member states, and sponsoring states. Prima facie, the Regulations and standards should also have normative effect on the ISA organs and contractors, being the primary documents that govern the relationship between them. The contractors have undertaken to comply with the 'rules, regulations and procedures of the ISA' as well as the decisions of ISA organs,[120] and, while it is not explicitly stated that 'standards' will be considered part of the 'rules, regulations and procedures of the ISA', it is a reasonable assumption to make, in view of the explicitly binding nature of standards, and the fact that it they are endorsed by a decision of the Council. Regulations and standards will be used by ISA organs and contractors to determine whether they have fulfilled their respective obligations, and, for contractors, breaches of the Regulations and standards may constitute a ground for the imposition of monetary penalties[121] or the termination of their contract.[122] The SDC and commercial arbitral tribunals have jurisdiction, under the LOSC, over disputes between the ISA and contractors relating to 'the interpretation or application of a relevant contract or a plan of work',[123] which incorporates the Regulations as well as standards (assuming that the standards are deemed part of the rules, regulations and procedures of the ISA).[124] Further, both

[116] 2019 DER (n 22) reg 94(4).
[117] Standards and Guidelines Workshop Report (n 100) 4.
[118] ibid 15.
[119] ISA, 'Note by the Secretariat, Comments on the Draft Regulations on the Exploitation of the Mineral Resources in the Area' (4 December 2019) ISBA/26/C/2.
[120] Nodules Regulations (n 21) Annex IV, s 13.1; 2019 DER (n 22) Annex X, s 3.3.
[121] 2019 DER (n 22) reg 103(6).
[122] See, eg Nodules Regulations (n 21) Annex IV, s 21.1(a); 2019 DER (n 22) reg 103(5).
[123] LOSC (n 12) arts 187(c)(i) and 188(2).
[124] Nodules Regulations (n 21) Annex IV, s 13.2(b); 2019 DER (n 22) Annex X, s 3.3(a).

the SDC and commercial arbitral tribunals can use the Regulations and standards as benchmarks to determine whether the contractor or ISA has committed a 'wrongful act' in the conduct of its operations or exercise of its powers and functions, so as to warrant a finding of liability for damage arising from activities in the Area.[125]

It is, of course, important that both the Regulations and standards have normative intent and effect. However, a question might be raised as to the retrospective application of standards, or changes in standards vis-à-vis the contractor after the signing of the contract with the ISA. While the objective of the standards being adopted separately from the Regulations was to facilitate the flexibility to accommodate developments in technology and knowledge of the marine environment, it is also important that standards 'should remain stable and avoid frequent changes in content, so as not to arbitrarily increase the burden on Contractors'.[126] Indeed, the contract between the ISA and the contractor cannot be amended without the consent of both parties,[127] and a question remains whether each time new standards are adopted subsequent to the contract, there needs to be a renegotiation between the parties,[128] or whether the new standards automatically apply.[129]

The normative effect of Regulations and standards on ISA member states and sponsoring states is less clear-cut. It is true that the LOSC dispute settlement system envisages that the ISA can initiate proceedings in the SDC against state parties (including member states and sponsoring states) for their acts or omissions in violation of the 'rules, regulations and procedures' of the ISA.[130] However, doubts have been expressed by certain sponsoring states on whether sponsoring states' obligations 'should be prescribed for in a set of regulations that regulates principally the relationship between a contractor and the Authority'.[131] This ambivalence about the Regulations could have implications for their normative effect vis-à-vis sponsoring states, and whether sponsoring states believe that the Regulations are binding on them, notwithstanding the fact that the Regulations can be enforced against LOSC state parties.

A more important issue on the normative effect of Regulations and standards relates to sponsoring states' due diligence obligations to take necessary and appropriate measures within their legal systems to ensure that contractors comply with their obligations under: (1) the relevant provisions of Part XI; (2) Annexes III and IV of the LOSC; (3) the rules, regulations, and procedures of the ISA; (4) plans of work approved by the LTC; (5) terms of their contracts; and (6) LOSC obligations.[132] These necessary and appropriate measures consist

[125] LOSC (n 12) Annex III, art 22.

[126] ISA, 'Statement by the President of the Council on the Work of the Council during the First Part of the Twenty-fifth Session' (18 March 2019) ISBA/25/C/17 (hereafter 'Council President's Statement 2019'), para 16.

[127] Nodules Regulations (n 21) Annex IV, s 24; 2019 DER (n 22) Annex X, s 16.

[128] Art 19(1) of Annex III of the LOSC notes that when circumstances have arisen, or are likely to arise, which, in the opinion of either party, would render the contract inequitable or make it impracticable or impossible to achieve the objectives set out in the contract or in Part XI, the parties shall enter into negotiations to revise it accordingly.

[129] In 2013, the Nodules Regulations were amended to enhance environmental standards and obligations, but instead of renegotiating each contract, the ISA requested that pending exploration contracts for polymetallic nodules incorporate the changes (ISA, 'Decision of the Council relating to Amendments to the Regulations on Prospecting and Exploration for Polymetallic Nodules in the Area and related Matters' (22 July 2013) ISBA/19/C/17, para 3), which led to a situation where contractors that had obtained their contracts prior to July 2013 were not bound by the amended higher environmental standards in the newly amended Nodules Regulations: See Jaeckel (n 53) 207.

[130] LOSC (n 12) art 187(b)(i).

[131] ISA, 'Briefing Note to the Council on the Submissions to the Draft Regulations on Exploitation of Mineral Resources in the Area' (21 February 2018) ISBA/24/C/CRP.1, Annex III.

[132] SDC Advisory Opinion (n 30) paras 103–06.

of 'laws and regulations, and ... administrative measures which are, within the framework of its legal system, reasonably appropriate for securing compliance by persons under its jurisdiction'.[133] The content, scope, and extent of the laws and regulations and administrative measures required depend upon the legal system of the sponsoring state, and policy choices on such matters are to be made by the sponsoring state.[134] The Regulations and standards have a normative effect, in that sponsoring states must adjust their national laws to fulfil their obligations under the LOSC, and will use the Regulations and standards as guidance for their own national laws. What is unclear, however, is the extent to which sponsoring states' national laws can depart from the content of Regulations and standards. Article 21(3) of Annex III of the LOSC states that, '[n]o State Party may impose conditions on a Contractor that are inconsistent with Part XI'. Nonetheless, the application of environmental or other laws and regulations more stringent than those in the Regulations dealing with the protection of the marine environment shall not be deemed inconsistent with Part XI.[135] This raises a question on whether sponsoring states can impose *non-environmental laws* that are more stringent to, or which depart from, the Regulations and Standards in any way. Another issue that implicates the sponsoring states' due diligence obligations is how to ensure that their national laws place a continuing obligation on sponsored contractors to comply with Regulations and standards, even as they may be amended.[136]

10.3 Informal Lawmaking by the ISA

Unlike conventional conceptions of informal lawmaking (characterized by process informality and actor informality), the outputs analysed in this section have been adopted by processes and actors on different spectrums of formality, ranging from the most formal (involving the LTC and the Council), to semi-formal (LTC only), to informal (no ISA organ or body involved). However, as discussed above, they fall within the scope of informal lawmaking, as the outputs of these processes are explicitly or implicitly characterized as non-binding, and have normative effect, albeit on a sliding scale.

10.3.1 Formal Processes Leading to Informal Outputs: Regional Environmental Management Plans

In 2012, the Council adopted the ISA's first Regional Environmental Management Plan (REMP) for the Clarion-Clipperton Zone (CCZ REMP).[137] The REMPs' purposes are, inter

[133] LOSC (n 12) Annex III, art 4(4); SDC Advisory Opinion (n 30), paras 216–17.

[134] SDC Advisory Opinion (n 30) para 218.

[135] ibid, para 240.

[136] See, eg Code Project, 'Template National Sponsorship Law for Seabed Mining beyond National Jurisdiction' (October 2020) <https://www.pewtrusts.org/-/media/assets/2020/09/seabed_mining_white_paper.pdf> accessed 5 March 2021, where 'Rules of the ISA' has been defined as any rules, regulations, procedures or *other standards* [instruments] adopted by the ISA pursuant to powers conferred on the ISA by [the LOSC] that are from time to time in force and intended to be legally binding upon States or Sponsored Parties, and any contractual terms contained in a plan of work in the form of a contract between the ISA and a Sponsored Party relating to ISA Seabed Mineral Activities' (emphasis added).

[137] ISA, 'Decision of the Council relating to an Environmental Management Plan for the Clarion-Clipperton Zone' (26 July 2012) ISBA/18/C/22.

alia, to provide 'the relevant organs of the ISA, as well as contractors and their sponsoring states, with proactive environmental management measures and tools, including area-based management tools, to support informed decision-making that balances resource development with the protection of the marine environment at a regional scale'.[138] A central feature of the CCZ REMP is that it designates nine 'Areas of Particular Environmental Interest' (APEIs) where no exploration or exploitation can be conducted for five years, or until further review by the LTC, although marine scientific research is permitted.[139] The Council called upon the LTC, in 2014, to consider further REMPs.[140] There are currently plans underway to develop REMPs in other regions where exploration is currently occurring.[141]

10.3.1.1 Source of Authority

The authority of the LTC to make recommendations on REMPs, including the designation of APEIs, and the Council to adopt such recommendations, is not explicitly stated in the LOSC. However, as explored elsewhere,[142] the ISA has the authority to do so under various provisions of the LOSC[143] and the exploration regulations.[144] The 2019 Draft Exploitation Regulations also affirm that REMPs are part of the ISA's environmental policy.[145]

10.3.1.2 Process of Adoption

There are no stated processes, in the LOSC, the Exploration Regulations, or the 2019 Draft Exploitation Regulations, for the adoption of REMPs. The CCZ REMP arose from a research project where external scientists suggested the establishment of marine protected areas as an option to manage biodiversity, which led to a workshop in 2007 that proposed the establishment of the nine APEIs.[146] The LTC convened another workshop with scientists, contractors, and LTC members to further study the proposal.[147] The outcome was a draft environmental management plan that was adopted by the LTC in a recommendation to the Council to adopt a 'provisional plan to give effect to the precautionary approach called for by the regulations'.[148] The Council adopted the CCZ REMP in 2012.

[138] ISA Secretariat, 'Guidance to Facilitate the Development of Regional Environmental Management Plans (REMPs)' (November 2019) (hereafter 'REMP Guidance') <https://www.isa.org.jm/files/files/documents/remp_guidance_.pdf> accessed 5 March 2021.

[139] See ISA, 'Environmental Management Plan for the Clarion-Clipperton Zone' (13 July 2011) ISBA/17/LTC/7.

[140] ISA, 'Statement of the President of the Council on the Work of the Council during the Nineteenth Session' (24 July 2013) ISBA/19/C/18, para 13; UNGA Res 69/245 (29 December 2014) UN Doc A/Res/69/245, para 51.

[141] See ISA, 'Environmental Management Plan' <https://www.isa.org.jm/minerals/environmental-management-plan-clarion-clipperton-zone> accessed 5 March 2021; ISA, 'Report of the Secretary-General, Preliminary Strategy for the Development of Regional Environmental Management Plans for the Area' (16 January 2018) ISBA/24/C/3; ISA, 'Report of the Secretary-General, Implementation of the Authority's Strategy for the Development of Regional Environmental Management Plans for the Area' (28 January 2019) ISBA/25/C/13.

[142] For a discussion on the authority of the ISA to declare marine protected areas, see Jaeckel (n 53) 169–73.

[143] LOSC (n 12) arts 145, 162(2)(x), and 165(2)(l).

[144] Nodules Regulations (n 21) regs 21(6) and 31(4); Sulphides Regulations and Crust Regulations (n 21) regs 23(6) and 33(4).

[145] 2019 DER (n 22) regs 2(e) and 15(2)(c).

[146] ISA, 'Rationale and Recommendations for the Establishment of Preservation Reference Areas for Nodule Mining in the Clarion-Clipperton Zone, Summary Outcomes of a Workshop to Design Marine Protected Areas for Seamounts and Abyssal Nodule Province in Pacific High Seas, held at the University of Hawaii, Manoa, Hawaii, USA, 23–26 October 2007' (28 March 2008) ISBA/14/LTC/2.

[147] ISA, 'Summary Report of the LTC Chairman on the Work of the Commission during the Fifteenth Session' (27 May 2009) ISBA/15/C/5, paras 7–12.

[148] ISA, 'Summary Report of the LTC Chairman on the Work of the Commission during the Seventeenth Session' (13 July 2011) ISBA/17/C/13. The LTC adjusted the size and location of the APEIs initially proposed, to accommodate pre-existing exploration contracts: see Jaeckel (n 53) 206–08; Rosemary Rayfuse, 'Crossing the

The Secretariat issued guidance on REMPs in 2019, which stated that the LTC is responsible for preparing REMPs and making recommendations to the Council for approval, and the Council is responsible for approving the draft REMPs recommended by the LTC.[149] The Secretariat proposed that the process for drafting REMPs should begin with workshops convened by the Secretariat under the auspices of the ISA, and then post-workshop processes will focus on preparing draft REMP documents drawing on the results of the workshops, and these will then be available for stakeholder review and subsequent consideration by the LTC.[150] However, concerns were raised by Germany, the Netherlands, and Costa Rica that a standardized approach concerning the development and contents of REMPs had not been explicitly clarified and agreed upon.[151] After a 2019 workshop, it was suggested that: (1) the Council should be responsible for the initiation of the REMP; (2) the Council, acting on a recommendation of the LTC, should establish an ad hoc expert committee, as a technical body of the LTC, to develop a REMP for a specific region; (3) the expert committee should consist of experts that have specific expertise relevant to REMPs, and should be appointed in line with relevant guidelines and UN procurement processes; (4) the expert committee, working with the Secretariat, should organize expert workshops to develop the first draft of the relevant REMP; (5) the LTC should then consider the draft REMP (which should describe the process undertaken and stakeholders engaged in its development); (6) the draft REMP should then be subject to formal stakeholder consultation; (7) thereafter, a recommendation should be made by the LTC to the Council (which should be accompanied by a justification for that recommendation, a description of the development process, and the report of the expert committee); and (8) the Council should either approve the REMP or ask the LTC to task the expert committee with making specific revisions.[152] The Council requested the LTC to further develop the Secretariat's guidance on REMPs, with a view to recommending to the Council a standardized approach, including a template with indicative elements.[153]

10.3.1.3 Participants

Under both the existing ad hoc processes and the proposed new processes, states parties (acting through the Council), the LTC, and non-state actors (including non-state contractors, experts, and NGOs) participate in the development of REMPs through the workshop process, as well as commenting on draft proposals for REMPs. The Secretariat has noted, however, that participants in the workshops will be invited through the ISA's official nomination/selection process, according to a set of selection criteria, so as to ensure the effective participation of relevant stakeholders, and experts in relevant fields.[154]

Sectoral Divide: Modern Environmental Law Tools for Addressing Conflicting Uses on the Seabed' in Catharine Banet (ed), *The Law of the Seabed* (Brill 2020) 527, 541.

[149] REMP Guidance (n 138) 7–8.

[150] ibid 11–12. Jaeckel observes that 'the push towards an environmental management plan for the Mid-Atlantic Ridge is being generated by external scientists, not the ISA': see Jaeckel (n 53) 209.

[151] 'Procedure for the Development, Approval and Review of Regional Environmental Management Plans' (6 January 2020) ISBA 26/C/6, submitted by the delegations of Germany and the Netherlands, with co-sponsorship by Costa Rica.

[152] ibid.

[153] ISA, 'Decision of the Council concerning a Standardized Approach for the Development, Approval and Review of Regional Environmental Management Plans in the Area' (21 February 2020) ISBA 26/C/10.

[154] REMP Guidance (n 138) 11.

10.3.1.4 Normative Intent

The normative intent of REMPs is not stated in the CCZ REMP. During the stakeholder submissions on the 2019 Draft Exploitation Regulations, some had proposed that the REMPs be binding, and that they should be made a condition for the approval of contracts to contractors, whereas other submissions noted that the REMPs were non-legally binding policy instruments.[155] Indeed, the Secretariat has observed that the REMPs 'are themselves not legal instruments but rather instruments of environmental policy'.[156] It went on to state:

> Rather, they clarify how the Council intends to apply those rules, regulations and procedures in light of the need to take a precautionary approach to the development of activities in the Area. Similarly, the plan for the Clarion-Clipperton Zone spells out the various activities that should be undertaken by various actors, including the secretariat, contractors, sponsoring States and scientific researchers, in order to develop, for example, sound scientific baselines. Such recommendations are not expressed in the form of binding legal obligations and, in fact, it would not be possible to do so.[157]

Further, the Secretariat commented that 'it is difficult to require contractors to comply with regional environmental management plans since such plans are not binding legal instruments and therefore, do not impose legal obligations on contractors'.[158] At the same time, the exploration contract and the draft exploitation contract, between the ISA and contractors, both specifically require contractors to 'comply with ... the decisions of the relevant organs of the Authority',[159] which include the Council's decision to adopt a REMP, suggesting that there is some uncertainty in the normative intent of the REMPs. That said, the Secretariat's view that the REMPs are non-binding is consistent with general practice on the adoption of criteria for area-based management tools such as marine protected areas, which are usually reflected in non-binding guidelines or criteria.[160] Such guidelines are non-binding for a variety of reasons, including the fact that they are too technical to form the basis for prescriptive, norm-creating obligations; that it is not feasible to agree on binding rules or obligations, given the evolving understanding of the marine environment; and, lastly, that it is necessary for the guidelines to be easily adaptable. These features could partially explain why REMPs are considered by the Secretariat as non-binding policy instruments.

155 ISA, 'Note by the Secretariat, Comments on the Draft Regulations on the Exploitation of Mineral Resources in the Area' (4 December 2019) ISBA/26/C/2, para 18.

156 ISA, 'Note by the ISA Secretariat, Relationship between the Draft Regulations on Exploitation of Mineral Resources in the Area and the Regional Environmental Management Plans' (20 December 2018) ISBA/25/C/4, para 4; REMP Guidance (n 138) 13.

157 ISA, 'Note by the ISA Secretariat' (n 156) para 4.

158 ibid, para 7.

159 Nodules Regulations (n 21) Annex IV, s 13(2)(b); 2019 DER (n 22) Annex X, s 3.3(b).

160 See, eg Food and Agriculture Organization (FAO), 'International Guidelines for the Management of Deep-sea Fisheries in the High Seas' (Rome 1999) <http://www.fao.org/3/i0816t/i0816t00.htm>; Convention on Biological Diversity (CBD), 'Report of the Ninth Meeting of the Conference of the Parties to the Convention on Biological Diversity' (9 October 2008) UN Doc UNEP/CBD/COP/9/29, Decision IX/20: Marine and Coastal Biodiversity, Annex I: Scientific Criteria for Identifying Ecologically or Biologically Significant Marine Areas in Need of Protection in Open-ocean Waters and Deep-sea Habitats. See also Scott, in Chapter 16 of this volume.

10.3.1.5 Normative Effect

Despite the (arguably) non-binding nature of the REMPs, there are several reasons why they may have normative effect. First, the REMPs are endorsed by a decision of the Council, which is perceived as representing the consensus of state parties to the LOSC, and adds to its normative value. Second, their process of adoption (either under the current ad hoc procedures, those proposed by the Secretariat, or the workshop proposal) also adds a layer of legitimacy, through the interaction between the contractors, technical experts, NGOs, and the LTC in generating the content of the REMPs. As noted by Brunée, non-binding norms gain normative value through the interactional processes of international law, where 'patterns of social practice emerge and increasingly influential mutual expectations and shared understandings of actors evolve'.[161] Third, the REMPs will be used to assess the contractors' environmental management and monitoring plans (EMMPs), and, if these do not contribute to the REMP's objectives, the contractors' EMMPs would need to be revised or rejected as inadequate.[162] As has been argued with non-binding guidelines adopted in other contexts, the REMPs will inform the ISA and contractors' due diligence obligations relating to the protection of the marine environment.[163]

The uncertainty on the normative intent of the REMPs, however, may raise several questions on the consequences of the contractors' non-compliance with a REMP (an extreme example is if a contractor did conduct activities in the APEI). The ISA can suspend or terminate a contract with the contractor for 'serious, persistent and wilful violations of the fundamental terms of the contract, Part XI [LOSC], the 1994 Agreement or the Regulations',[164] or impose monetary penalties for violations not amounting to 'serious, persistent and willful violations' of these instruments.[165] A breach of the non-binding REMP may not warrant the imposition of these penalties, although it will ultimately be up to the Council to decide. The ISA can initiate proceedings against the contractors before: (1) the SDC and commercial arbitral tribunals on disputes concerning either the interpretation or application of a relevant contract or plan of work; or (2) just the SDC on disputes concerning the contractors' acts or omissions relating to activities in the Area, and directed to the other party, or directly affecting its legal interests.[166] The subject-matter jurisdiction is, arguably, wide enough to encompass violations of REMPs on the basis that they either form part of the contract (the contractors undertake to comply with the decisions of the ISA), or that the violation consists of an act relating to activities in the Area, and affects the legitimate interests of the ISA. Whether contractors would have a valid defence on the basis that REMPs are non-binding remains to be seen.

[161] Jutta Brunnée, 'COPing with Consent: Law-making under Multilateral Environmental Agreements' (2002) 15(1) LJIL 2, 34.

[162] ISA, Note by the ISA Secretariat (n 156) para 7.

[163] Lene Korseberg, 'The Law-making Effect of the FAO Deep-sea Fisheries Guidelines' (2018) 67 ICLQ 801.

[164] LOSC (n 12) Annex III, art 18(1); Nodules Regulations (n 21) Annex IV, s 21.1; 2019 DER (n 22) Annex X, s 12.1.

[165] LOSC (n 12) Annex III, art 18(2); Nodules Regulations (n 21) Annex IV, s 21.6; 2019 DER (n 22) Annex X, s 12.6.

[166] LOSC (n 12) arts 187(c) and 188(2).

10.3.2 Semi-formal Processes Leading to Informal Outputs: Recommendations and Guidelines

This section considers recommendations (issued by the LTC under the Exploration Regulations) and guidelines (issued by the LTC under the 2019 Draft Exploitation Regulations) that do not require approval or endorsement by the Council. Processes that only require LTC approval are deemed 'semi-formal', to reflect the fact that these outputs are adopted by an ISA subsidiary body, but that this body consists of technical experts (ostensibly) not representing the interests of states,[167] and so the outputs do not have the same formality in adoption as Regulations and standards.

10.3.2.1 Source of Authority

Under the Exploration Regulations, the LTC may adopt 'recommendations of a technical or administrative nature for the guidance of contractors to assist them in the implementation of the rules, regulations and procedures of the Authority'.[168] This authority is not expressly provided for in the LOSC,[169] but would, presumably, come under the ISA's incidental powers necessary to perform its functions. The LTC has adopted five sets of recommendations, all directed at contractors, and one of which is directed at the sponsoring state.[170]

'Guidelines' have replaced recommendations in the 2019 Draft Exploitation Regulations.[171] Guidelines are intended to support the implementation of the Exploitation Regulations from an administrative and technical perspective, including on the impact of exploitation on the economies of developing states that are land-based producers of minerals,[172] harm to the marine environment,[173] training plans,[174] review of environmental plans,[175] qualifications on financial and technical qualifications of prospective contractors,[176] or the use of contract as security.[177]

10.3.2.2 Process of Adoption

The processes for adoption of recommendations and guidelines are similar, but not identical. The LTC develops recommendations, whereas, under the 2019 Draft Exploitation Regulations, either the LTC *or* the Secretary-General can issue guidelines of a technical or administrative nature, taking into account the views of the relevant stakeholders.[178] Both recommendations and guidelines are reported to the Council. Should the Council find

[167] See text accompanying n 64.
[168] Nodules Regulations (n 21) reg 39(1).
[169] The LOSC provides that the LTC can make recommendations on the protection of the marine environment, taking into account the views of recognized experts in that field, although it is not clear that this would be the explicit basis for the LTC's authority to adopt recommendations that do not deal with the marine environment: LOSC (n 12) art 165(2)(e).
[170] ISA, 'The Mining Code: Recommendations' <https://www.isa.org.jm/mining-code/recommendations> accessed 5 March 2021.
[171] 2019 DER (n 22) reg 95; ISA, 'Secretariat Note, Draft Regulations on the Exploitation of Mineral Resources in the Area' (25 May 2018) ISBA/24/LTC/6.
[172] 2019 DER (n 22) reg 3(g).
[173] ibid, reg 4(4).
[174] ibid, reg 7(g).
[175] ibid, reg 11(a).
[176] ibid, reg 13.
[177] ibid, reg 22(4)(b).
[178] ibid, reg 95. For a definition of 'stakeholders', see text accompanying n 98.

that a recommendation is inconsistent with the intent and purpose of the Exploration Regulations, or that a guideline is inconsistent with the intent and purpose of the LOSC, 1994 Agreement, and the Regulations, it may request that the recommendation or guideline be modified or withdrawn.[179] Recommendations are to be reviewed, to take into account the current state of scientific knowledge and information, at least every five years.[180] In contrast, the LTC or Secretary-General are to keep guidelines under review in light of improved knowledge or information.[181]

10.3.2.3 Participants

The process for the formulation of some, but not all, recommendations begins in workshops. For example, the first set of recommendations relating to environmental impact assessments (EIAs) were based on a workshop convened by the ISA in June 1998, and subsequent reviews of the EIA recommendations have all been guided by various workshops.[182] Indeed, the EIA recommendations explicitly state that the ISA should convene workshops, at appropriate intervals, in which the members of the LTC, contractors, and recognized experts from the scientific community, international and governmental organizations, and NGOs are invited to participate.[183]

The 2019 Draft Exploitation Regulations provide that the LTC or Secretary-General should take into account the views of relevant stakeholders. The 2019 standards and guidelines workshop reflected a consensus from participants that the guidelines also needed to incorporate open consultation with stakeholders, and the opportunity for expert independent review.[184] Thus, the workshop report suggested that, when draft guidelines are published for stakeholder consultations and submissions, the LTC or Secretary-General should incorporate comments as appropriate, and issue guidelines with a report summarizing feedback and reasons for decisions.[185]

10.3.2.4 Normative Intent

The recommendations are intended to be non-binding. The standard terms for exploration contracts, which require contractors to 'comply with the relevant Exploration Regulations', only require them 'to observe, *as far as reasonably practicable*, any recommendations which may be issued from time to time by the LTC.'[186] Unlike standards, the 2019 Draft Exploitation Regulations do not explicitly state whether the guidelines are binding or not. In 2018, the Secretariat noted that, while standards were in principle mandatory in nature, and guidelines were recommendatory, the legal status of each will be determined by their content.[187] However, the 2019 standard and guidelines workshop stated that 'guidelines' should refer to recommendatory documents.[188] It was suggested that indicators of whether

179 Nodules Regulations (n 21) reg 39(2); 2019 DER (n 22) reg 95(2).

180 ISA, 'Recommendations for the Guidance of Contractors for the Assessment of Possible Environmental Impacts Arising from Exploration for Marine Minerals in the Area' (30 March 2020) ISBA/25/LTC/6/Rev.1 (hereafter 'EIA Recommendations'), para 7.

181 2019 DER (n 22) reg 95(3).

182 For a history of the workshop processes, see EIA Recommendations (n 180) paras 3–4.

183 ibid, para 7.

184 Standards and Guidelines Workshop Report (n 100) 18.

185 ibid 9.

186 See, eg Nodules Regulations (n 21) Annex IV, s 13.2(e) (emphasis added).

187 ISA, Secretariat Note, Draft Regulations on the Exploitation of Mineral Resources in the Area (n 171) para 18.

188 Standards and Guidelines Workshop Report (n 100) 15.

a document should be recommendatory, rather than mandatory, would include the document providing a suggested way, but not the only way, to achieve compliance with a regulation or contractual requirement.[189] Factors that may *not* necessarily be relevant are whether the subject is controversial, whether the matter is urgent, or whether the documents require periodic updating to reflect new knowledge (which may be easier if the document was recommendatory rather than mandatory).[190]

10.3.2.5 Normative Effect

Do the LTC recommendations and guidelines have normative effect capable of shaping the conduct of the various actors despite their characterization as non-binding? First, as is the case with the REMPs, the fact that they are adopted by the LTC (an ISA subsidiary body, although arguably not representing state parties) in a process that involves various stakeholders giving their input may add to their normative value. Indeed, in the recent EIA reports submitted by two contractors, it was noted that, in preparing these EIA reports, they sought to follow the recommendations although they are not mandatory.[191]

Second, the recommendations and guidelines may be relevant in the interpretation of the obligations of contractors (or other addressees). For example, the SDC observed that, while general international law did not specify the scope and content of EIAs, and Article 206 of the LOSC only gives a few indications of this scope and content, 'the indications in the Regulations, and *especially in the Recommendations* ... add precision and specificity to the obligation as it applies in the context of activities in the Area'.[192] The participants in the 2019 standards and guidelines workshop also noted that, while the guidelines are not mandatory, 'adherence to their content or recommendations may be an indicative factor in demonstrating Contractor compliance with the regulations of the Authority',[193] and that guidelines could perform a 'due diligence' role, ie. that contractors can take comfort that adherence to the process or methodology set out in the document will result in compliance with the relevant requirement.[194] Conversely, the fact that contractors do not comply with recommendations and guidelines could be an indication that they did not meet their due diligence obligations under their contract with the ISA. Accordingly, a LOSC court or tribunal may very well consider such recommendations and guidelines in determining whether certain acts of contractors (or other addressees like the ISA) can be considered 'wrongful acts'[195] that warrant the imposition of liability on either actor.[196]

However, the lack of normative intent of the recommendations and guidelines may also have implications for the sponsoring states' due diligence obligation to ensure contractors' compliance with their obligations under the relevant instruments, including the contract

[189] ibid.
[190] ibid.
[191] GSR, 'Environmental Impact Statement' (1 April 2018) <https://economie.fgov.be/sites/default/files/Files/Entreprises/deep-see-mining/isa-eia-2018-gsrnod-2019.pdf> accessed 5 March 2021; BGR, 'Environmental Impact Assessment' (15 February 2018) <https://isa.org.jm/files/files/documents/EIA_BGR_0.pdf> accessed 5 March 2021.
[192] SDC Advisory Opinion (n 30) 45 (emphasis added).
[193] Standards and Guidelines Workshop (n 100) 4.
[194] ibid 15.
[195] LOSC (n 12) Annex III, art 22.
[196] Eg, the ICJ noted that recommendations adopted by International Whaling Commission may be relevant to the interpretation of the International Convention for the Regulation of Whaling: see *Whaling in the Antarctic (Australia v Japan: New Zealand intervening)* (Judgment) [2014] ICJ Rep 226, para 46.

and the Regulations.[197] It could be argued that non-binding recommendations and guidelines issued by the LTC are adopted pursuant to the Regulations, and that the sponsoring state, consequently, has a due diligence obligation to adopt national legislation to ensure that contractors comply with ISA recommendations and guidelines. Some sponsoring states have authorized their own national agencies to issue guidelines, which may include the recommendations of any ISA organ.[198] On the other hand, it could also be argued that ensuring compliance with non-binding recommendations and guidelines is not part of the sponsoring states' due diligence obligations. For example, the model sponsorship law proposed by the Code Project appears to limit the sponsoring states' obligations to ensuring compliance with only the ISA outputs that are legally binding.[199] This issue warrants further clarity.

Further, because the recommendations and guidelines are not binding, questions on enforceability, in cases of non-compliance, arise (as is the case with REMPs). As noted above, serious, persistent, and wilful violations of the fundamental terms of contract between the ISA and the contractor, Part XI of the LOSC, the 1994 Agreement, or the Regulations will warrant suspension or termination of the contract,[200] and violations not amounting to 'serious, persistent and wilful violations' can attract the imposition of monetary penalties.[201] Whether a breach of the recommendations or guidelines can be penalized by the ISA will depend on whether either are considered part of the fundamental terms of the contract or the Regulations, and what weight the Council (ultimately responsible for the imposition of penalties) places on the fact that these outputs are non-binding. The same arguments made in Section 10.3.1.5 on whether the ISA can initiate dispute settlement proceedings before the SDC or commercial arbitral tribunals for breaches of REMPs, would also apply to recommendations and guidelines.

10.3.3 Informal Processes Leading to Informal Outputs

The ISA is considering completely informal outputs that do not require adoption by the LTC, the Council, or the Assembly. As these outputs are still under consideration, it is not possible to utilize the framework of analysis that was used for the other outputs (ie source of authority, process of adoption, participants, and normative intent), and a few general comments will have to suffice.

The 2019 Draft Exploitation Regulations envisage outputs such as 'good industry practices',[202] as well as 'best environmental practices'.[203] 'Good industry practices' have been defined as 'the exercise of skill, diligence, prudence and foresight which would reasonably and ordinarily be expected to be applied by a skilled and experienced person engaged in the

[197] See discussion on sponsoring states' due diligence obligations, in section 10.2.5 above.

[198] See Seabed Minerals Act 2017 (Kiribati), s 18; Seabed Minerals Act 2014 (Tonga), s 17.

[199] See definition of 'ISA Rules' in Code Project (n 136).

[200] LOSC (n 12), Annex III, art 18(1); Nodules Regulations (n 21) Annex IV, s 21.1; 2019 DER (n 22) Annex X, s 12.1.

[201] LOSC (n 12) Annex III, art 18(2); Nodules Regulations (n 21) Annex IV, s 21.6; 2019 DER (n 22) Annex X, s 12.6.

[202] Good Industry Practice is used frequently in the DER, see, eg 2019 DER (n 22) regs 2(c), 13(2)(b)(iv), 13(3)(a), 13(3)(c), 25(1), 25, 28(1), 32, 36, 47(3)(d), 48(3)(c), 53(1)(a), and 59.

[203] See, eg 2019 DER (n 22) regs 3(e), 13(3)(c), 32, 44, 47(d), 51(c), 53, and 59.

marine mining industry and other related extractive industries worldwide'.[204] 'Best environmental practices' have been defined as 'the application of the most appropriate combination of environmental control measures and strategies that will change with times in light of improved knowledge, understanding or technology, taking into account the guidance set out in the applicable Guidelines'.[205] The obligation to apply best environmental practices is also a direct obligation on sponsoring states.[206] The Secretariat has said that sources of good industry practices can be found in 'laws and regulations, regulatory guidelines, international, regional and national standards, industry codes of practice and procedures of individual operators', and has listed certain examples of good industry practices such as those of the International Finance Corporation, International Organization Standards, and the International Marine Minerals Society.[207] However, the 2019 Draft Exploitation Regulations do not specify how good industry practices will be developed. The underlying assumption is that this is a form of self-regulation that contractors will be responsible for formulating, taking into account guidelines issued by the LTC.[208] The same assumption applies for best environmental practices.[209]

Deep seabed mining in the Area is a new, untested 'frontier' industry, involving the 'application of new technologies coupled with scientific uncertainty regarding future environmental impacts of the mining methods to be used'.[210] Existing industry or environmental practices may not be directly applicable to activities in the Area, and may have to be developed.[211] At the same time, if the list of practices is left open-ended, a number of good practices could, theoretically, be applied by contractors to demonstrate compliance with these practices.[212] Moreover, it has been highlighted that 'it is essential for regulatory purposes to ensure that clear reference is made to the party that is responsible for adopting and implementing the proposed practices, even though they may be intended to act as guidelines', as a gap might lead to regulatory uncertainty.[213] In this regard, it has been suggested by some scholars that the best regulatory approach is for good industry practices and best environmental practices to be explicitly adopted or endorsed by the ISA. Having a single source (for example, a restricted list adopted by the ISA) creates regulatory certainty, and decreases the need for the ISA, contractors, and sponsoring states to 'continuously evaluate the appropriateness of and applicability of newly established or evolved third-party developed standards to the marine mining sector'.[214] The fact that contractors are allowed to give input on the regulations, standards, and guidelines should 'mitigate concerns regarding regulatory uncertainty and the threat of future regulatory overburden'.[215]

[204] ibid, sch.
[205] ibid.
[206] SDC Advisory Opinion (n 30) para 136.
[207] 2019 DER (n 22) Annex IV; ISA, 'Note by the Secretariat, Key Terms: Distinguishing between Good Industry Practice and Best Practices under the Draft Regulations on Exploitation of Mineral Resources' (19 January 2019) ISBA/25/C/11, paras 6–11 and 22.
[208] ISA, 'Note by Secretariat, Content and Development of Standards and Guidelines for Activities in the Area under Authority's Framework' (17 December 2018) ISBA/25/C/3, para 13.
[209] The definition of 'Best Environmental Practices' in the DER expressly refers to 'Guidelines'.
[210] Leonardus J Gerber and Renee L Grogan, 'Challenges of Operationalizing Good Industry Practice and Best Environmental Practice in Deep Seabed Mining Regulation' (2020) 114 Mar Pol'y 1, 3.
[211] ibid 4.
[212] ibid.
[213] ibid.
[214] ibid.
[215] ibid 5.

Both best environmental practices and good industry practices could serve as references against which an assessment may be made as to whether a contractor is fulfilling its due diligence obligations under a contract for exploitation.[216] Arguably, this is the paragon of informal law: adopted in informal forums by informal actors, without any of the formalities associated with formal lawmaking by the ISA, although, as discussed above, there have been calls for more formality in the adoption of such self-regulatory instruments. While good industry practices and best environmental practices may be references for the due diligence obligations of the contractors (as is the case with recommendations and guidelines, discussed above), breach of such outputs may not warrant the imposition of monetary penalties, or the suspension or termination of the contract.

10.4 Conclusions

This chapter attempted to illustrate the dynamic nature of lawmaking by the ISA, through the lens of formal and informal lawmaking. The ISA is a particularly interesting laboratory for international lawmaking, due to the wide discretion it has been given to execute its mandate under the LOSC, the constantly evolving technology and understanding of science and the marine environment, the involvement of state and non-state actors (some of whom have competing interests that the ISA has to mediate), and the subject matter of regulation: the arguably controversial, but communitarian, concept of the CHH. Having preliminarily classified outputs of the ISA as 'formal law' or 'informal law,' this chapter will now extract some general (tentative) conclusions on formal and informal lawmaking by the ISA.

First, ISA lawmaking is, slowly but steadily, evolving to incorporate greater transparency, as well as participation by non-state actors, either through the workshop processes leading to the majority of these outputs, or the stakeholder consultations. The 2019 Draft Exploitation Regulations have affirmed and formalized this participation, and there have been further calls for the LTC to summarize stakeholder comments, and give reasons for why it has adopted certain provisions in the standards and guidelines.[217] This democratization of lawmaking is inevitable, and partially attributable to the enhanced role that NGOs play in the ISA. It may also, arguably, mitigate concerns from some quarters that ISA lawmaking is dominated by a handful of states.[218]

Second, like most IOs, the ISA uses a mix of formal and informal law to govern. The legal authority for adopting formal law such as the Regulations and standards has some basis in the LOSC, whereas the legal authority for adopting or using informal law such as the REMPs, the recommendations, guidelines, good industry practices, and best environmental practices stem from the Regulations (ie subsidiary legislation). The legal authority to adopt such informal outputs, although not expressly mentioned in the LOSC, can be justified by reference to incidental powers and specific competencies that the ISA has under the LOSC.

216 ISA, 'Note by the Secretariat, Key Terms: Distinguishing between Good Industry Practice and Best Practices under the Draft Regulations on Exploitation of Mineral Resources' (n 207) para 13.

217 Standard and Guidelines Workshop Report (n 100) 8–9.

218 See, generally, Collins and French (n 14).

Third, informal law, although non-binding, may have normative effect on the various actors engaged in activities in the Area. For outputs such as the REMPs, recommendations, and guidelines, the normative effect is attributable to both the organ that adopted them, and the processes used to develop them. The democratization of the lawmaking process has added to the normative value of these informal outputs, in that stakeholders interact with each other and give their input, cementing the idea that these informal outputs are based on some form of consensus. The normative effect lies in the fact that these informal outputs elaborate on obligations contained in formal outputs, and provide benchmarks that determine whether the relevant actor has fulfilled its obligations, particularly its due diligence obligations. However, the lack of normative intent of these outputs may have implications on whether breaches of these outputs can trigger enforcement consequences from the ISA, either in the form of termination or suspension of contracts, the imposition of monetary penalties, or the initiation of dispute settlement proceedings. Whether the enforcement consequences or dispute settlement will take place depends on the interpretation of 'contract' and 'rules, regulations and procedures', and, particularly, whether REMPs, recommendations, and guidelines are considered to fall within these definitions. It will also depend on the weight given to the fact that these informal outputs were stated to be non-binding.

Fourth, it is not possible to ascertain with certainty when formal outputs, such as Regulations and standards, will be used, and when informal outputs, such as the recommendations, guidelines, good industry practices, and best environmental practices will be used. The 2019 workshop on standards and guidelines engaged in discussion on when a document should be mandatory or recommendatory, with different views being put forth on the relevant indicators, but with the general understanding that binding standards would, at least, include processes and performance outcome thresholds for contractors, whereas recommendatory documents such as guidelines would identify recommended paths for implementing the Mining Code.[219] Some indicators were suggested (which have been discussed above, in the relevant sections), but it is not clear whether there will ever be any official guidance given on this issue. For example, during the standards and guidelines workshop, participants were asked to discuss which obligations or procedures should be reflected in standards or guidelines, and there was a diversity of views from the participants.[220] Indeed, it is most likely that the choice of formal or informal law will be decided on a case-by-case basis, depending on the needs, circumstances, and priorities at the time.

Fifth, is there any real difference between formal and informal lawmaking by the ISA? In terms of processes of adoption, as well as actors, there appears to be an increasing convergence between the processes for adoption of formal and informal law. The development of formal law (Regulations and standards) and informal law (REMPs, recommendations, and guidelines) involves non-state actors, be it through the workshop processes or stakeholder consultations, and the LTC and Council still play a role in the adoption of both, albeit in different ways. There are calls for even more formalized processes for the adoption of non-binding outputs, such as the proposal from Germany and the Netherlands on the adoption of REMPs, suggestions that the procedures for adoption of recommendations and guidelines be set out clearly, and that good industry practices should be endorsed by the Council

219 Standards and Guidelines Workshop Report (n 100) 4, 14–15.
220 ibid.

to give them a level of legitimacy and certainty. Indeed, the purported advantages of informal law over formal law (discussed in Chapter 1): to avoid formal adoption procedures, to give greater flexibility, and time and efficiency savings, are, arguably, not as obvious for informal law adopted, or to be adopted, by the ISA. Apart from processes of adoption and actors involved, both formal and informal law have similar normative effects, in that they will both be used as benchmarks to determine whether the conduct of the relevant actor is compliant with that actor's obligations under the LOSC and related instruments. That said, the difference between formal and informal law is more obvious when looking at consequences for non-compliance. The non-binding nature of informal law creates uncertainty on whether the consequences for non-compliance (termination or suspension of contract, monetary penalties, and/or dispute settlement proceedings) can be triggered.

Arguably, this is why the distinction between formal and informal lawmaking, in the context of ISA lawmaking, remains important. Unlike other IOs that make a 'conscious effort to side-step the question of binding effect in favor of standard-setting that intentionally lies along a spectrum of authority from binding to non-binding',[221] there is a concerted push (from states and stakeholders alike) to have clarity on which instruments are binding, and which are not. Indeed, the normative ambiguity of the outputs of many IOs does not seem to sit well in the context of the governance of the CHH. This state of affairs may be attributable to the particular dynamics of lawmaking in the ISA, which is increasingly seeing the economic value of the exploitation of CHH resources being pitted against the potential ramifications that such exploitation will have on the marine environment. Thus, NGOs and other like-minded stakeholders wish to see environmental obligations being reflected in formal law, as the best way to increase compliance by contractors with their various obligations. On the other hand, there are other stakeholders who are conscious of the need to minimize undue regulatory burden on contractors and the sponsoring states that have an obligation to regulate them. The emphasis on the non-binding nature of some of these outputs may give some level of reassurance to contractors (and sponsoring states) that the legal regime is not unnecessarily burdensome or restrictive, is sufficiently flexible to accommodate changes in technology and the marine environment, and will not result in open-ended liability. Indeed, it was the overly prescriptive and technically detailed legal regime in Part XI of the LOSC that resulted in the Western industrial states (reportedly pushed by the corporations that had licences in the Area) deciding not to participate in the LOSC. Thus, while the distinction between formal law and informal law adopted by the ISA can be described as artificial, in that the adoption processes, participants, and normative effects are similar (although not identical), informal law still plays an important role in the governance of the CHH.

[221] See Jose Alvarez, *International Organizations as Law-makers* (OUP 2006) 222.

11

The Significance of Informal Lawmaking in International Fisheries Law

*Zoe Scanlon**

11.1 Introduction

Although a substantial body of formal, binding law exists in the international fisheries management sphere, numerous informal instruments have also been developed. This chapter explores the function of informal law instruments in a sector in which formal law is regularly developed at the regional level; where legal instruments are often technical, detailed, and specific to a region; technology, science, and realities change rapidly; and in which the legal framework must be flexible enough to adapt quickly.

This chapter provides an overview of the key binding instruments and informal instruments in this field, and considers the contribution of these informal instruments to international fisheries law. It highlights the roles that these instruments have played in incorporating modern approaches to fisheries management and global minimum standards into the legal framework, in establishing detailed guidance to facilitate the implementation of obligations, and as a catalyst for legal action. It also explores the prospect of such informal instruments constituting interpretative guidance in respect of key treaties, and whether they have contributed to the development of customary international law. How and why these instruments have been able to make this contribution—despite their non-binding status—is also explored, including whether their informal status has, at times, been an advantage, and the effect of their quality and development processes. Ultimately, the chapter concludes that, despite their non-binding nature, there is little doubt that informal instruments in this field have made a valuable contribution to international fisheries law.

11.2 The Formal Legal Framework in International Fisheries Law

The binding legal instruments in this sector must be considered at the outset, as these agreements comprise a significant legal framework that establishes the context in which the informal instruments exist. As a starting point, the United Nations Convention on the Law of the Sea (LOSC) contains some provisions on fisheries. It provides coastal states with sovereign rights for the purpose of exploring and exploiting, conserving, and managing the natural resources of their exclusive economic zone (EEZ), including fisheries.[1] It sets out,

* The views expressed in this chapter are the personal views of the author. They do not represent the views of any organization with which the author is or has been affiliated.

[1] United Nations Convention on the Law of the Sea (adopted 10 December 1982, entered into force 16 November 1994) 1833 UNTS 397 (hereafter 'LOSC'), art 56(1)(a).

Zoe Scanlon, *The Significance of Informal Lawmaking in International Fisheries Law* In: *Unconventional Lawmaking in the Law of the Sea.* Edited by: Natalie Klein, Oxford University Press. © Zoe Scanlon 2022. DOI: 10.1093/oso/9780192897824.003.0011

in relatively broad terms, coastal states' rights and obligations in respect of the conservation and utilization of living resources in the EEZ.[2] The LOSC contains relatively few provisions on fisheries management in respect of the high seas. These provisions are general, and allow parties significant discretion in how they implement their obligations. Article 87 of the LOSC establishes the freedoms of the high seas, which includes a freedom to fish. This freedom is subject to some limitations, but these limitations are also expressed in general terms. The freedom to fish on the high seas must be exercised with due regard for the interests of other states,[3] subject to any treaty obligations,[4] subject to duties and interests of coastal states for particular fish stocks,[5] and subject to the special obligations established for straddling stocks and highly migratory species.[6]

The LOSC anticipates that state parties will need to take additional measures to meet conservation and management obligations. Articles 63 and 64 of the LOSC require states to cooperate to agree measures to ensure the conservation of straddling stocks and highly migratory stocks. Article 117 outlines a duty to cooperate to manage and conserve high seas resources,[7] and Article 118 sets out a duty to make use of international fisheries commissions.[8] Importantly, for present purposes, Article 119 requires parties to take into account 'any generally recommended international minimum standards' when implementing measures in pursuit of the conservation of living resources.

To address the generality of some of the LOSC's provisions on fishing, the UN Fish Stocks Agreement (FSA) was adopted.[9] Its binding nature was not insignificant, with chairperson Satya Nandan articulating his sense during negotiations that there was a 'widespread and substantial view' in the conference that a binding instrument was essential for effective conservation and management. [10] The FSA gives practical effect to the broad 'duty to cooperate' in the LOSC by providing a framework for cooperation, and setting out principles for conservation and management. The FSA details global minimum standards for the conservation and management of straddling and highly migratory fish stocks, ensures that conservation and management measures for stocks present in EEZs and adjacent high seas areas are compatible, and requires mechanisms for compliance with, and enforcement of, those measures. It also outlines a system of Regional Fisheries Management Organisations (RFMOs). It requires the creation of RFMOs to manage highly migratory and straddling stocks, and, in essence, provides that if a state seeks to fish in an area regulated by an RFMO, it must join the relevant RFMO and abide by its conservation and management measures

[2] ibid, arts 61 and 62.
[3] ibid, art 87(2).
[4] ibid, art 116(a).
[5] ibid, art 116(b).
[6] ibid, art 118.
[7] ibid, art 117.
[8] ibid, art 118.
[9] Agreement for the Implementation of the Provisions of the United Nations Convention on the Law of the Sea of 10 December 1982 relating to the Conservation and Management of Straddling Fish Stocks and Highly Migratory Fish Stocks (FSA) (adopted 4 August 1995, entered into force 11 December 2001) 2167 UNTS 88 (hereafter 'FSA').
[10] Satya Nandan, 'Statement of the Chairman, Satya Nandan, upon the adoption of the FSA, at the UN Conference on Straddling Fish Stocks and High Migratory Fish Stocks' (26 August 1994), para 4. The chairperson stated, upon the FSA's adoption, that, 'if we had failed to adopt a strong and binding Agreement at this Conference, we would have failed the international community, and in so doing, would have contributed to the further demise of the major international fishery resources: Satya Nandan, 'Statement of the Chairman, Satya Nandan, upon the adoption of the FSA, at the UN Conference on Straddling Fish Stocks and High Migratory Fish Stocks' (4 August 1995) UN Doc A/CONF.164/35 (20 September 1995) 3.

(CMMs), or else it may not fish in that area.[11] The FSA, thus, anticipates further formal agreements for its implementation.

Several RFMOs have been established through international treaties in high seas areas, and these sometimes extend to areas under national jurisdiction. RFMO objectives are focused on the long-term conservation and sustainable use of the fishery resources, and, in some cases,[12] safeguarding the ecosystems in which those resources occur. RFMOs are intergovernmental organizations that, generally, hold annual meetings at which fisheries management decisions are made, informed by the advice of scientific advisory bodies. The CMMs adopted by RFMOs, pursuant to their constituent conventions, are wide-ranging, and include matters such as setting total allowable catches, limiting effort in a fishery, requiring or prohibiting the use of certain gear types, and banning or regulating the by-catch of incidentally caught species. CMMs are, generally, adopted by consensus, and are binding on all parties to the relevant RFMO convention, without the need for further approval, although they are often subject to an opt-out clause.[13]

Although there is increasingly a general perception that the development of formal international law is stagnating,[14] in part due to 'treaty fatigue,'[15] treaty saturation,[16] and increasing state reluctance to take on obligations considered an 'invasion' of domestic legal systems,[17] this phenomenon has not been apparent in fisheries management. New or amended CMMs, which apply to a particular region or fishery, tend to be adopted on an annual basis within RFMOs. In addition, other treaties have been developed, at the global level, for fisheries management, including the Compliance Agreement[18] and the Port State Measures Agreement (PSMA),[19] which were both developed within the UN Food and Agriculture Organization (FAO). The Compliance Agreement reiterates many provisions of the LOSC, but has a focus on flag state responsibility.[20] The PSMA seeks to prevent, deter, and eliminate illegal, unreported, and unregulated (IUU) fishing, through the implementation of effective port state measures. This sector may, therefore, be somewhat unique, as an area in which there is a substantial, detailed, and regularly updated body of formal, binding law.[21]

[11] FSA (n 9) art 8.

[12] Eg, the Convention on the Conservation and Management of High Seas Fishery Resources in the South Pacific Ocean (adopted 14 November 2009, entered into force 24 August 2012) 2899 UNTS 211 (hereafter 'SPRFMO Convention'), art 2; Convention on Cooperation in the Northwest Atlantic Fisheries (adopted 24 October 1978, entered into force 1 January 1979) 1135 UNTS 369, amendments in force 18 May 2017 (hereafter 'NAFO Convention'), art II.

[13] James Harrison, *Saving the Oceans through Law: The International Legal Framework for the Protection of the Marine Environment* (OUP 2017) 305.

[14] Joost Pauwelyn, Ramses A Wessel, and Jan Wouters, 'When Structures become Shackles: Stagnation and Dynamics in International Lawmaking' (2014) 25(3) EJIL 733.

[15] ibid 739.

[16] ibid.

[17] ibid 734.

[18] Agreement to Promote Compliance with International Conservation and Management Measures by Fishing Vessels on the High Seas (adopted 24 November 1993, entered into force on 24 April 2003) 2221 UNTS 91 (hereafter 'Compliance Agreement').

[19] Agreement on Port State Measures to Prevent, Deter and Eliminate Illegal, Unreported and Unregulated Fishing (adopted 22 November 2009, entered into force 5 June 2016) (hereafter 'PSMA'). There are sixty-two parties to the PSMA, at time of writing.

[20] There are forty parties to the Compliance Agreement at time of writing.

[21] Another area of ocean governance where this occurs is in relation to the instruments adopted under the auspices of the International Maritime Organization. For discussion, see Zhen, in Chapter 6 of this volume, and Petrig, in Chapter 7 of this volume.

11.3 Informal Instruments in the International Fisheries Sphere

A number of informal instruments have also been developed in the international fisheries sector. This section discusses some of the key informal instruments in this field, including the key drivers of their development, their core content, and the fora, actors, and processes involved in their development. It will later be argued that these key elements play an important role in their legitimacy and influence, and that, despite their non-binding nature, these instruments have made a valuable contribution to international fisheries law.

11.3.1 FAO Code of Conduct and Technical Guidelines for Responsible Fisheries

At the request of the FAO Committee on Fisheries (COFI) in 1991, the Code of Conduct for Responsible Fisheries (the Code) was developed under the auspices of the FAO, in light of concern at overfishing, ecosystem damage, and trade affecting sustainability of stocks.[22] Technical consultations and informal consultations with intergovernmental organizations and non-governmental organizations (NGOs) took place. The Code aims to establish principles for responsible fishing, as a reference for states to improve national fisheries management frameworks, and for international fisheries instruments.[23] It outlines international standards of behaviour for responsible fisheries practices, with a view to ensuring the effective conservation, management, and development of living aquatic resources, with due respect for ecosystems and biodiversity. The Code takes an all-encompassing approach, covering many aspects of fisheries management.

The Code is a long instrument that covers a breadth of areas, including general principles, fisheries management, fisheries operations, aquaculture development, integration of fisheries into coastal area management, post-harvest practices, and trade and fisheries research. The provisions of the Code are, mostly, broad principles, because it was not intended to be a stand-alone instrument. Consequently, many of its principles have been developed further by other informal instruments, including the FAO Technical Guidelines for Responsible Fisheries.[24] These guidelines provide detailed technical and operational guidance on the implementation of the Code, such as vessel monitoring systems, a precautionary approach to capture fisheries, fisheries management, managing fishing capacity, and the ecosystem approach to fisheries.[25]

11.3.2 IPOA–IUU

The International Plan of Action to Prevent, Deter and Eliminate Illegal, Unreported and Unregulated Fishing (IPOA–IUU) builds on the Code, and aims to combat IUU fishing

[22] FAO, 'Code of Conduct for Responsible Fisheries' (31 October 1995) <http://www.fao.org/tempref/docrep/fao/005/v9878e/v9878e00.pdf> accessed 15 March 2021 (hereafter 'Code').

[23] ibid, arts 2(a)–(d).

[24] FAO, 'Technical Guidelines for Responsible Fisheries' <www.fao.org/fishery/publications/technical-guidelines/en> accessed 15 March 2021.

[25] ibid.

by providing a 'toolkit' of measures for states.[26] It outlines specific measures to be taken by flag states, port states, and market states, and measures for all states, as well as setting out internationally agreed market-related measures, and measures on research and RFMOs. It contains general principles as well as prescriptive provisions. It is widely considered an important development that is among the most well-accepted voluntary instruments in this space.[27] It is said to have a greater practical impact than the Code, and that various of its measures to address IUU fishing have since been implemented.[28]

The IPOA–IUU was developed in response to a call from COFI in 1999. After an expert consultation and two technical consultations, it was adopted by the FAO Council in 2001. The IPOA–IUU reaffirms key provisions of the LOSC, the FSA, the Compliance Agreement, and the Code, and encourages implementation, as well as outlining useful steps for more effective management. It includes measures for improved cooperation between states, the development of monitoring, control, and surveillance (MCS) measures, and a requirement for national plans of action,[29] provisions on trade measures, port state controls, and controls over nationals.

11.3.3 Other IPOAs

Three other IPOAs have been developed—relating to seabirds, sharks, and fishing capacity—after COFI requested, in 1997, that the FAO address these issues. All three were elaborated within the framework of the Code,[30] build on its provisions, and were endorsed by the FAO Council in 1999.[31]

The objective of the International Plan of Action for Reducing Incidental Catch of Seabirds in Longline Fisheries (IPOA–Seabirds) is to reduce the incidental catch of seabirds in longline fisheries. The International Plan of Action for the Conservation and Management of Sharks (IPOA–Sharks) aims to ensure the conservation and management, and long-term sustainable use, of sharks. The objective of the International Plan of Action for the Management of Fishing Capacity (IPOA–Capacity) is for states and RFMOs to achieve efficient, equitable, and transparent management of fishing capacity, so that fishing

[26] FAO, 'International Plan of Action to Prevent, Deter and Eliminate Illegal, Unreported and Unregulated Fishing' (Rome 2001) (hereafter 'IPOA–IUU') <http://www.fao.org/3/y1224e/Y1224E.pdf> accessed 15 March 2021.

[27] William Edeson, 'The International Plan of Action on IUU Fishing: The Legal Context of a Non-legally Binding Instrument' (2001) 16 IJMCL 603, 603 (hereafter Edeson, 'The International Plan of Action'); Maryann Palma, Martin Tsamenyi, and William Edeson, *Promoting Sustainable Fisheries: The International Legal and Policy Framework to Combat Illegal, Unreported and Unregulated Fishing* (Martinus Nijhoff 2010) 20.

[28] Palma, Tsamenyi, and Edeson (n 27) 96.

[29] Some regional plans of action have also been developed: RPOA–IUU (South-East Asia), the European Union, ASEAN, APEC, and High Seas Task Force. See FAO, 'National and Regional Plans of Action to Prevent, Deter, and Eliminate Illegal, Unreported and Unregulated Fishing' <www.fao.org/fishery/topic/166341/en> accessed 15 March 2021.

[30] Code (n 22) art 2(d).

[31] FAO, 'International Plan of Action for the Conservation and Management of Sharks' (Rome 1999) (hereafter 'IPOA–Sharks') <http://www.fao.org/tempref/docrep/fao/006/x3170e/X3170E00.pdf> accessed 15 March 2021; FAO, 'International Plan of Action for the Management of Fishing Capacity' (Rome 1999) (hereafter 'IPOA–Capacity') <http://www.fao.org/tempref/docrep/fao/006/x3170e/X3170E00.pdf> accessed 15 March 2021; FAO, 'International Plan of Action for Reducing Incidental Catch of Seabirds in Longline Fisheries' (Rome 1999) (hereafter 'IPOA–Seabirds') <http://www.fao.org/tempref/docrep/fao/006/x3170e/X3170E00.pdf> accessed 15 March 2021.

capacity is progressively reduced in affected fisheries. Expert and technical consultations worked to develop these instruments, which outline actions to be taken, including assessments, adoption of national plans of action, mitigation measures, and procedures for review and reporting.

11.3.4 FAO Guidelines

Under the auspices of the FAO, several sets of voluntary guidelines have been developed that aim to assist states to implement and fulfil various international obligations. These instruments include the Voluntary Guidelines for Flag State Performance,[32] the Voluntary Guidelines for Catch Documentation Schemes,[33] the Voluntary Guidelines on the Marking of Fishing Gear,[34] and the Deep-sea Fisheries Guidelines.[35] These instruments are discussed in more detail below.

11.3.5 UN General Assembly Resolutions

Fisheries issues are regularly on the UN General Assembly's agenda. The General Assembly annually debates and adopts a resolution on sustainable fisheries,[36] and another on oceans and the law of the sea,[37] which includes fisheries issues. These resolutions are negotiated each year among UN member states, and tend to reiterate provisions in other instruments, encourage implementation of treaties, and outline emerging principles. The General Assembly also adopts resolutions on specific fisheries issues, several of which are discussed in more detail below. For instance, the General Assembly has adopted influential resolutions on important issues such as bottom fishing, protection for vulnerable marine ecosystems,[38] drift net fishing,[39] fisheries by-catch and discards,[40] and unauthorized fishing within national jurisdiction.[41]

[32] FAO, 'Voluntary Guidelines for Flag State Performance' (Rome 2015) <http://www.fao.org/3/a-i4577t.pdf> accessed 15 March 2021.

[33] FAO, 'Voluntary Guidelines for Catch Documentation Schemes' (Rome 2017) <http://www.fao.org/3/a-i8076e.pdf> accessed 15 March 2021.

[34] FAO, 'Voluntary Guidelines on the Marking of Fishing Gear' (Rome 2019) <http://www.fao.org/3/ca3546t/ca3546t.pdf> accessed 15 March 2021.

[35] FAO, 'International Guidelines for the Management of Deep-sea Fisheries in the High Seas' (Rome 1999) <http://www.fao.org/3/i0816t/i0816t00.htm> accessed 15 March 2021.

[36] Available at UN, 'Oceans and the Law of the Sea in the General Assembly of the United Nations: General Assembly Resolutions and Decisions' (2021) <https://www.un.org/depts/los/general_assembly/general_assembly_resolutions.htm> accessed 15 March 2021.

[37] ibid.

[38] See UNGA Res 59/25 (17 November 2004) UN Doc A/RES/59/25; UNGA Res 61/105 (8 December 2006) UN Doc A/RES/61/105; UNGA Res 64/72 (4 December 2009) UN Doc A/RES/64/72.

[39] See UNGA Res 44/225 (22 December 1989) UN Doc A/RES/44/225; UNGA Res 45/197 (21 December 1990) UN Doc A/RES/45/197; UNGA Res 46/215 (20 December 1991) UN Doc A/RES/46/215.

[40] UNGA Res 49/116 (19 December 1994) UN Doc A/RES/49/116.

[41] ibid.

11.4 The Contribution of Informal Fisheries Instruments to International Fisheries Law

There is a wide range of non-binding instruments in this field that vary in their purpose, form, and content. There is little doubt that, despite their non-binding nature, these informal instruments have made a valuable contribution to international fisheries law. This section discusses examples in which informal instruments have made such a contribution, by playing a role in incorporating modern approaches or global standards into formal law, by acting as a catalyst for the development of formal law, and by providing detailed guidance on the implementation of relevant legal obligations. It also considers their potential contribution to relevant treaties by serving as interpretive guidance in respect of such treaties, and the potential for such instruments to contribute to the development of new norms of customary international law.

11.4.1 The Incorporation of Modern Approaches into International Fisheries Law

Informal fisheries instruments have played an important role in incorporating modern approaches into the international legal framework. The instruments that have played this role range from broadly framed instruments like General Assembly Resolutions and the Code, to those that are more detailed, like FAO guidelines. As approaches to fisheries management have shifted throughout the decades to respond to evolving science and technology, informal fisheries instruments have reflected certain modern principles as they have developed,[42] and have, thereby, played a role in facilitating global acceptance of, and comfort with, these concepts, as well as acting as a conduit for the inclusion of such approaches in binding legal instruments. In this way, informal instruments have ultimately contributed to better conservation outcomes.

For instance, the move away from the concept of maximum sustainable yield (MSY) in modern instruments illustrates this contribution of informal agreements. The LOSC requires parties to take measures designed to maintain fish populations at, or restore them to, levels that can produce the MSY.[43] MSY is the maximum yield that can be removed from a stock over a period, under constant environmental conditions, without reducing its average size.[44] MSY was a well-established target for managing fisheries when the LOSC was negotiated, but, in recent decades, the concept has come under increasing criticism.[45] MSY ignores the size, age, and reproductive status of the fish captured,[46] and focuses solely on the targeted species, ignoring damage to the surrounding ecosystem and by-catch. Most

[42] See Edeson's discussion on this point, suggesting that some informal instruments have supported the evolution of certain modern principles: William Edeson, 'Closing the Gap: The Role of 'Soft' International Instruments to Control Fishing' (1999) 20 Aust YBIL 83, 102 (hereafter Edeson, 'Closing the Gap').

[43] LOSC (n 1) art 19.

[44] Patricia Birnie, Alan Boyle, and Catherine Redgwell, *International Law and the Environment* (3rd edn, OUP 2009) 150, 590–591 cited in Lene Korseberg, 'The Law-making Effects of the FAO Deep-sea Fisheries Guidelines' (2018) 67(4) ICLQ 801, 811.

[45] Yoshifumi Tanaka, *The International Law of the Sea* (2nd edn, CUP 2015) 236.

[46] See Louis Botsford, Juan Carlos Castilla, and Charles Peterson, 'The Management of Fisheries and Ecosystems' (1997) 277 Science 509, 512.

scholars now agree that MSY should be replaced with a more precautionary approach like sustainable use.[47] In recent decades, a stronger environmental and precautionary dimension has been incorporated into fisheries management frameworks, and informal instruments have played an important role in this development. For instance, in the Code, MSY is placed within the context of a precautionary and more environmentally focused approach to conservation.[48] The FSA takes the same approach, qualifying the requirement to design measures to maintain stocks capable of producing MSY with relevant environmental considerations.[49] The General Assembly's Resolution on Sustainable Fisheries,[50] and the IPOAs, focus on sustainable use rather than MSY.[51] RFMO conventions, which require conservation measures to be designed to reflect certain principles, have now also been adapted. Some have taken the same approach as the Code and the FSA, by qualifying references to MSY, often with the principle of 'sustainable use'.[52] In more modern RFMO conventions, however, MSY does not feature at all, and 'sustainable use' is a central principle.[53]

The concept of vulnerable marine ecosystems (VME) does not appear in the LOSC or the FSA, but has, subsequently, emerged through informal instruments to become an important concept in the regulation of deep-sea fishing. A series of General Assembly resolutions,[54] and the Deep-sea Fisheries Guidelines, raised concerns about the lack of protections for VMEs, and included calls for action to address this issue. Improved regulation of deep-sea fishing and protections for VMEs are now in place in many binding RFMO measures, as discussed further below. In many such instruments, the relevant General Assembly resolutions are referred to in preambular paragraphs, and the Deep-sea Fisheries Guidelines' definition of VME has been adopted in those binding measures.[55] The incorporation of this

[47] Tanaka (n 45) 236.

[48] Eg, art 7.2.1 of the Code (n 22) provides that, '[r]ecognizing that long-term sustainable use of fisheries resources is the overriding objective of conservation and management, States and subregional or regional fisheries management organizations and arrangements should, inter alia, adopt appropriate measures, based on the best scientific evidence available, which are designed to maintain or restore stocks at levels capable of producing maximum sustainable yield, as qualified by relevant environmental and economic factors.'

[49] Art 5(b) of FSA (n 9) (General Principles) provides that Parties must, 'ensure that such measures are based on the best scientific evidence available and are designed to maintain or restore stocks at levels capable of producing maximum sustainable yield, *as qualified by relevant environmental and economic factors*, including the special requirements of developing States, and taking into account fishing patterns, the interdependence of stocks and any generally recommended international minimum standards, whether subregional, regional or global' (emphasis added). Other general principles include the precautionary approach (art 5(c)), the ecosystem approach (art 5(d)), and the protection of biodiversity (art 5(g)).

[50] See UNGA Res 74/18 (10 December 2019) UN Doc A/RES/74/18, paras 1, 17, 47, 130, and 164.

[51] IPOA–Sharks (n 31) art 16; IPOA–Capacity (n 31) art 9(iv); IPOA–IUU (n 26) art 9(4).

[52] See, eg Convention on the Conservation and Management of Highly Migratory Fish Stocks in the Western and Central Pacific Ocean (adopted 5 September 2000, entered into force 18 June 2004) 2275 UNTS 43 (hereafter 'WCPFC Convention'), preamble; Convention for the Strengthening of the Inter-American Tropical Tuna Commission established by the 1949 Convention between the United States of America and the Republic of Costa Rica (adopted 27 June 2003, entered into force 27 August 2010) (hereafter 'Antigua Convention'), art VII(1)(c).

[53] Eg, SPRFMO Convention (n 12) art 3(1)(a)(ii).

[54] See UNGA Res 59/25 (n 38); UNGA Res 61/105 (n 38); UNGA Res 64/72 (n 38).

[55] Eg, see SEAFO, 'Conservation Measure 30/15 on Bottom Fishing Activities and Vulnerable Marine Ecosystems in the SEAFO Convention Area' (adopted 3 December 2015, entered into force 15 February 2016) CMM 30/15, art 2(g) <http://www.seafo.org/Management/Conservation-Measures> accessed 16 March 2021; SPRFMO, 'Conservation and Management Measure for the Management of Bottom Fishing in the SPRFMO Convention Area' (6 May 2021) CMM 03-2021, para 3 <https://www.sprfmo.int/assets/Fisheries/Conservation-and-Management-Measures/2021-CMMs/CMM-03-2021-Bottom-Fishing-12Mar2021.pdf> accessed 21 June 2021; SIOFA, 'Conservation and Management Measure for the Interim Management of Bottom Fishing in the Agreement Area (Interim Management of Bottom Fishing)' (10 October 2019) CMM 2019/01, para 3(a) <https://www.apsoi.org/node/460> accessed 16 March 2021.

globally-agreed definition plays an important role in helping to ensure that adequate protections are provided globally, through regional CMMs.

The precautionary approach is another example. The precautionary approach does not appear in the LOSC, but has since become a central principle in modern fisheries management. Reference to the precautionary approach is found in the Code,[56] some IPOAs,[57] and in General Assembly resolutions.[58] Its inclusion in the FSA[59] and many modern RFMO conventions[60] has formalized its place in law. However, its inclusion in informal instruments, many of which are referenced in the FSA and RFMO conventions, also clearly contributed to solidifying its role in modern fisheries management, particularly before the FSA entered into force.

The LOSC does not include an ecosystem approach to fisheries management, although this important principle has emerged in more recent decades. The Code seeks the application of the ecosystem approach,[61] as do the 2001 Reykjavik Declaration on Responsible Fisheries in the Marine Ecosystem,[62] the FAO Technical Paper on the Ecosystem Approach to Fisheries,[63] and the Johannesburg Plan of Implementation,[64] as well as the FSA.[65] Most modern RFMO conventions now require an ecosystem approach to be applied in the development of CMMs,[66] and some older RFMOs have modernized their conventions by renegotiating and adopting new conventions, which now also incorporate an ecosystem approach.[67] As with the precautionary approach, the consistent references to an ecosystem approach in informal instruments, over a period of several years, assisted in attracting broad acceptance of the approach, to help secure its place in binding instruments.

The PSMA focuses on another modern aspect of fisheries management—port state controls—and was developed directly from an informal instrument. The LOSC's enforcement focus is on flag and coastal state control.[68] However, it has become increasingly clear over the years that, in the context of fisheries management, the exercise of flag state jurisdiction has been plagued by shortcomings,[69] and enforcement gaps have undermined

56 Code (n 22) art 7.5.

57 IPOA–Sharks (n 31) para 14; IPOA–Capacity (n 31) para 9(iv).

58 See, eg throughout the UNGA Sustainable Fisheries Resolutions, eg UNGA Res 74/18 (n 50).

59 FSA (n 9) arts 5(c) and 6.

60 SPRFMO Convention (n 12) art 2, 3(1)(b); Southern Indian Ocean Fisheries Agreement (adopted 7 July 2006, entered into force 21 June 2012) 2835 UNTS 409 (hereafter 'SIOFA'), art 4(c), noting the inclusion of the principle in the FSA and the Code.

61 Code (n 22) arts 2(i), 6.1, 6.2, 6.4, and 6.8.

62 FAO, 'Reykjavik Declaration on Responsible Fisheries in the Marine Ecosystem' (Rome 2001) <http://www.fao.org/tempref/FI/DOCUMENT/reykjavik/y2198t00_dec.pdf> accessed 16 March 2021.

63 FAO, 'The Ecosystem Approach to Fisheries. Issues, Terminology, Principles, Institutional Foundations, Implementation and Outlook' (Rome 2003) <http://www.fao.org/3/a-y4773e.pdf> accessed 16 March 2021.

64 UN, 'Report of the World Summit on Sustainable Development' (26 August to 4 September 2002) UN Doc A/CONF.199/20, Annex: Plan of Implementation of the World Summit on Sustainable Development (Johannesburg Plan of Implementation).

65 FSA (n 9) art 5(d) and (e).

66 Eg, SPRFMO Convention (n 12) art 2, SIOFA (n 60) art 4; Convention on the Conservation of Antarctic Marine Living Resources (adopted 20 May 1980, entered into force 7 April 1982) 1329 UNTS 47 (hereafter 'CAMLR Convention'), art IX(2)(i); Antigua Convention (n 52) art 1(f); Convention on Future Multilateral Cooperation in North-East Atlantic Fisheries (adopted 18 November 1980, entered into force 17 March 1982) 1285 UNTS 129, art 4(2)(c); NAFO Convention (n 12).

67 NAFO Convention (n 12) arts II, III(d), and VIII(b); Antigua Convention (n 52) art 1(f).

68 LOSC (n 1) arts 61, 62, and 118–19.

69 Rosemary Rayfuse, *Non-flag State Enforcement in High Seas Fisheries* (Martinus Nijhoff 2004) 24.

the legal regime.[70] Accordingly, the international community has increasingly looked to create mechanisms for third state enforcement to conserve and manage fisheries, including through port state controls. The Code and IPOA–IUU both promote port state controls, for example.[71] On the recommendation of COFI, the non-binding Model Scheme on Port State Measures to Combat IUU Fishing[72] was developed, which was a comprehensive instrument recommending effective port state controls. However, it was eventually decided that a binding instrument was necessary,[73] and COFI decided to develop a treaty based on the Model Scheme.[74] The content of the PSMA and the Model Scheme is similar. They set out similar expectations for the information that port states should collect from vessels seeking to enter port, how to carry out port inspections, when to refuse entry into port, and the types of information to be shared, and with whom. This example highlights how the inclusion of a modern approach to fisheries management in an informal instrument paved the way for its inclusion in a binding agreement.

Neither the LOSC nor the FSA contain provisions on the trade of fish. However, as combatting IUU fishing has proven extremely challenging, controlling trade has increasingly become a focus of international fisheries management. The Code contains only high-level measures that go to maintaining liberalization of fish trade, and the IPOA–IUU is conservative, noting only that multilaterally agreed requirements are a possibility.[75] There has, however, been a shift, in recent years, to a greater openness towards more restrictive trade in fish, and better catch documentation. This focus seeks to emphasize the importance of market state controls in stopping fish products resulting from IUU fishing from entering the market, thereby removing the financial incentive for IUU fishing. Catch documentation schemes determine, throughout the supply chain, whether fish originate from catches that were compliant with applicable regulations. The Voluntary Guidelines for Catch Documentation Schemes were developed[76] in response to a call in the General Assembly's 2013 Sustainable Fisheries Resolution,[77] and were adopted by an FAO Conference in 2017. They are broad and outline principles, aimed at assisting states, RFMOs, and other organizations to develop, implement, review, or harmonize catch documentation schemes. Some RFMOs have catch documentation schemes in place,[78] and the European Union has also implemented such a scheme.[79] This area of fisheries management is developing, and it is

[70] Rosemary Rayfuse, 'The Anthropocene, Autopoiesis and the Disingenuousness of the Genuine Link: Addressing Enforcement Gaps in the Legal Regime for Areas Beyond National Jurisdiction' (2009) UNSW Law Research Paper No 2009-2, 1.

[71] Code (n 22) art 8.3; IPOA–IUU (n 26) paras 52–64.

[72] FAO, 'Model Scheme on Port State Measures to Combat Illegal, Unreported and Unregulated Fishing' (Rome 2007) <http://www.fao.org/3/a0985t/A0985T.pdf> accessed 16 March 2021.

[73] In 2006, the FSA Review Conference directed states and RFMOs to begin negotiations within FAO.

[74] FAO, 'Report of the 27th Meeting of the Committee on Fisheries' (5–9 March 2007) FIEL/R830, para 68.

[75] IPOA–IUU (n 26) para 69.

[76] An expert consultation was established, as well as a COFI subcommittee on fish trade, and a technical consultation.

[77] UNGA Res 68/71 (9 December 2013) UN Doc A/RES/68/71, para 68.

[78] These RFMOs include: Commission for the Conservation of Antarctic Marine Living Resources (CCAMLR), International Commission for the Conservation of Atlantic Tuna (ICCAT), and Commission for the Conservation of Southern Bluefin Tuna (CCSBT).

[79] EU, Council Regulation (EC) No 1005/2008 of 29 September 2008 Establishing a Community System to Prevent, Deter and Eliminate Illegal, Unreported and Unregulated Fishing, Amending Regulations (EEC) No 2847/93, (EC) No 1936/2001, and (EC) No 601/2004 and Repealing Regulations (EC) No 1093/94 and (EC) No 1447/1999 (OJ L 286, 29.10.2008, p 1); EU, Commission Regulation No 1010/2009 of 22 October 2009 Laying down Detailed Rules for the Implementation of Council Regulation (EC) No 1005/2008 Establishing a Community System to Prevent, Deter and Eliminate illegal, unreported and unregulated fishing.

hoped that RFMOs increasingly adopt catch documentation schemes by reference to the guidance in the Voluntary Guidelines on Catch Documentation Schemes, as these guidelines reflect agreed global standards and good practice.

The difficulty in moving away from a management approach set down in a governing text such as the LOSC or an RFMO convention is significant, as any subordinate instruments should take a consistent approach to a governing treaty. These informal instruments have played an important role in introducing more modern approaches to fisheries management, facilitating greater familiarization with those approaches, and assisting in modernizing fisheries management consistently with contemporary scientific advice. The greater acceptance of these modern approaches in informal instruments also appears to have facilitated their inclusion in formal instruments.

11.4.2 The Incorporation of Global Standards into Law, and a Catalyst for Legal Action

Informal fisheries instruments have further played a role in incorporating global minimum standards into formal legal frameworks across several areas of fisheries management. Establishing global minimum standards is among the express objectives of some such instruments, including the Code, and some FAO guidelines. These instruments reflect shared expectations, agreed at the global level, designed to be implemented by the diversity of states and regional organizations around the world. Establishing global standards in this field is important because they establish global minimum expectations on states and regional organizations when adopting binding management measures. This important role helps ensure that the binding regional instruments uphold standards that are not just developed between a small group of states with a particular interest in a fish stock, but, instead, uphold global standards agreed by all states within the auspices of a UN body, through an inclusive and transparent process. Regional management measures are updated frequently to account for evolving science, technology, and data. Having minimum global standards in place helps to ensure that, although these regional instruments are opened up for renegotiation frequently, the acceptable minimum standards should not be negotiable. Article 119 of the LOSC requires states parties to 'take into account' any 'generally recommended international minimum standards' when establishing conservation measures for living resources in the high seas, which leaves states with a great deal of discretion in the measures they decide to apply. In a similar, but more robust, approach, Article 10(c) of the FSA requires states parties, when participating in RFMOs, to 'adopt and apply generally recommended international minimum standards for the responsible conduct of fisheries operations'. Which standards and instruments these provisions capture is not clear. Some commentators consider that this effectively renders the Code and other FAO instruments binding.[80] Others note the lack of normativity of the provisions of such non-binding instruments, and consider that there is, accordingly, some discretion in respect of their implementation,

[80] Gerald Moore, 'The Code of Conduct on Responsible Fisheries' in Ellen Hey (ed), *Developments in International Fisheries Law* (Kluger Law International 1999) 89, cited in James Harrison, *Making the Law of the Sea* (CUP 2011) 226.

suggesting, rather, that these provisions setting out minimum standards should *inform* the development of national policies.[81]

Many informal instruments have also played a critical role as catalysts for binding legal action to address fisheries management issues. These highlight concerning issues at the global level, and place pressure on states and RFMOs to act. Some examples are discussed below. The calls to action and global standards set out in some of these instruments have influenced and guided the development of CMMs within RFMOs. This influence is often clear not only from the inclusion of standards in CMMs, but also because those CMMs 'note' or 'recall' these guiding instruments in preambles, acknowledging their role in the CMM's development.

For instance, in 2004, the General Assembly adopted Resolution 59/25 calling for urgent action and consideration of the interim prohibition of destructive fishing practices. In 2006, it adopted Resolution 61/105, which called on states and RFMOs to take urgent action to protect VMEs from the impacts of bottom fishing. Specifically, it called for impact assessments, improved scientific research, 'move-on' rules, and the closure of certain areas. In 2009, after reviewing progress, Resolution 64/72 recalled Resolution 61/105, deemed its implementation insufficient, and called on states to take immediate action to protect VMEs prior to authorizing bottom fishing in the high seas. The FAO Deep-sea Fisheries Guidelines were subsequently developed, within the FAO, at the request of the General Assembly,[82] to provide states with a regulatory framework for the management of deep-sea fisheries, and to develop standards and criteria to identify VMEs, as well as establishing standards for managing them. These guidelines have been described as 'internationally endorsed standards of conduct for deep-sea fisheries'.[83] They reiterate provisions in related instruments, but also contain unique aspects specific to deep-sea fisheries, and detail on environmental concepts that have emerged in recent years. They provide guidance on identifying VMEs, and assessing significant adverse impacts, best practice enforcement, and compliance measures (for example MCS measures, including observer programs, vessel monitoring systems (VMSs), and data collection), and management and conservation tools (for example area closures, precautionary effort limits, limiting the expansion of existing bottom fishing, and protocols and reporting in response to encounters with VMEs).

In response to the General Assembly resolutions and Deep-sea Fisheries Guidelines, several RFMOs have now adopted CMMs that regulate bottom fishing to protect VMEs, and many recall the General Assembly resolutions and the Deep-sea Fisheries Guidelines in their preambles, or acknowledge their influence elsewhere.[84] Some acknowledge that all UN

[81] Harrison, Making the Law of the Sea (n 80) 226.

[82] UNGA Res 61/105 (n 38).

[83] Korseberg (n 44) 804.

[84] Eg SPRFMO CMM 03-2021 (n 55); SIOFA CMM 2019/01 (n 55); North-east Atlantic Fisheries Commission (NEAFC), 'Recommendation on Area Management Measures for the Protection of Vulnerable Marine Ecosystems in the NEAFC Regulatory Area, as amended' (2014) Rec 19/2014 <https://www.neafc.org/rec/2014/19> accessed 17 March 2021; SEAFO CMM 30/15 (n 55); North Pacific Fisheries Commission (NPFC), 'Conservation and Management Measure for Bottom Fisheries and Protection of Vulnerable Marine Ecosystems in the Northwestern Pacific Ocean' (2019) CMM 2019-05 <https://www.npfc.int/cmm-2019-05-bottom-fisheries-and-protection-vmes-nw-pacific-ocean> accessed 17 March 2021; NPFC, 'Conservation and Management Measure for Bottom Fisheries and Protection of Vulnerable Marine Ecosystems in the Northeastern Pacific Ocean' (2019) CMM 2019-06 <https://www.npfc.int/cmm-2019-06-bottom-fisheries-and-protection-vmes-ne-pacific-ocean> accessed 17 March 2021; CCAMLR, 'Restrictions on the Use of Bottom Trawling Gear in High-seas Areas of the Convention Area' (2008) Conservation Measure 22-05 <https://www.ccamlr.org/en/measure-22-05-2008> accessed 17 March 2021; CCAMLR, 'Bottom Fishing in the Convention Area' (2019) Conservation Measure 22-06 <https://www.ccamlr.org/en/measure-22-06-2019> accessed 17 March 2021; CCAMLR, 'Interim Measure for Bottom Fishing

members joined consensually to adopt the resolutions,[85] and some directly implement the guidelines' definitions,[86] or directly require bottom fishing impact assessments, their consideration by scientific committees, or fishing determinations[87] to be conducted in accordance with the guidelines.[88] It has been said that the General Assembly resolutions played a significant role in the improvements in the management of deep-sea fisheries in areas beyond national jurisdiction, as well as the availability of information on deep-sea fishing and known or likely VMEs, the impact of gear types, and catch and by-catch data.[89] They clearly also played a catalysing role in highlighting the urgent need for action, and placing pressure on states and relevant RFMOs to act. RFMOs have been criticized for responding too slowly to the threat to VMEs, but it has also been noted that significant progress has been made in implementing the General Assembly resolutions[90] and that good practices for identifying and protecting VMEs are emerging.[91]

General Assembly resolutions have also been catalysts for state action in respect of drift net fishing. Serious concern about the increase in large-scale pelagic drift net fishing and its indiscriminate and harmful nature grew in the 1980s and 1990s, leading to General Assembly resolutions in 1990 and 1991 that called for a global moratorium on large-scale pelagic drift net fishing.[92] These calls have since been reiterated in subsequent resolutions,[93] urging states to take greater enforcement responsibility. Several RFMOs have since adopted CMMs that ban or regulate the use of drift nets and gill nets,[94] and make specific reference

Activities Subject to Conservation Measure 22-06 Encountering Potential Vulnerable Marine Ecosystems in the Convention Area' (2013) Conservation Measure 22-07 <https://www.ccamlr.org/en/measure-23-07-2013> accessed 17 March 2021; CCAMLR, 'Protection of Registered Vulnerable Marine Ecosystems in Subareas, Divisions, Small-scale Research Units, or Management Areas open to Bottom Fishing' (2012) Conservation Measure 22-09 <https://www.ccamlr.org/en/measure-22-09-2012> accessed 17 March 2021; Matthew Gianni and others, 'How Much Longer will it Take? A Ten-year Review of the Implementation of United Nations General Assembly Resolutions 61/105, 64/72 and 66/68 on the Management of Bottom Fisheries in Areas beyond National Jurisdiction' (*Deep Sea Conservation Coalition*, August 2016) 5 <http://www.savethehighseas.org/wp-content/uploads/2016/07/DSCC-Review-2016_Launch-29-July.pdf> accessed 18 June 2021.

[85] See, eg CCAMLR Conservation Measure 22-06 (n 84) in respect of UNGA Resolution 61/105 (n 38).

[86] Including the definitions of 'vulnerable marine ecosystem' and 'significant adverse impact'. See, eg SEAFO CMM 30/15 (n 55) art 2, which directly implements the Deep-sea Fisheries Guidelines definitions of 'VME' and 'significant adverse impact'.

[87] NPFC CMM 2019-06 (n 84) and NPFC, 'CMM 2021-05 for Bottom Fisheries and Protection of VMEs in the NW Pacific Ocean' (2021) Conservation Measure 2021-05 <https://www.npfc.int/cmm-2021-05-bottom-fisheries-and-protection-vmes-nw-pacific-ocean> accessed 21 June 2021.

[88] Eg, SIOFA CMM 2019/01 (n 55) para 26(a); NPFC CMMs 2019-05 and 2019-06 (n 84).

[89] Gianni and others (n 84) 4. See also Techera, in Chapter 13 of this volume.

[90] UNGA, 'Letter dated 9 September 2016 from the Moderator of the Workshop to Discuss the Implementation of Paragraphs 113, 117 and 119 to 124 of Resolution 64/72 and Paragraphs 121, 126, 129, 130 and 132 to 134 of Resolution 66/68 on Sustainable Fisheries, Addressing the Impacts of Bottom Fishing on Vulnerable Marine Ecosystems and the Long-term Sustainability of Deep-sea Fish stocks Addressed to the President of the General Assembly' (2016) UN Doc A/71/377 2.

[91] Jeff Ardron and others, 'The Sustainable Use and Conservation of Biodiversity in ABNJ: What can be Achieved Using Existing International Agreements?' (2014) 49 Mar Pol'y 98, 103.

[92] UNGA Res 44/225 (n 39); UNGA Res 45/197 (n 39) and UNGA Res 46/215 (n 39).

[93] UNGA Res 50/25 (5 December 1995) UN Doc A/RES/50/25; UNGA Res 51/36 (9 December 1996) UN Doc A/RES/51/36; UNGA Res 52/29 (26 November 1996) UN Doc A/RES/52/29; UNGA Res 53/33 (24 November 1998) UN Doc A/RES/53/33; UNGA Res 55/8 (30 October 2000) UN Doc A/RES/55/8; UNGA Res 57/142 (12 December 2002) UN Doc A/RES/57/142.

[94] See, eg SIOFA, 'Conservation and Management Measure regarding the Use of Large-scale Pelagic Driftnets and Deepwater Gillnets in the Southern Indian Ocean Fisheries Agreement Area (Pelagic Driftnets and Deepwater Gillnets)' (18 October 2016) CMM 2016/05; IOTC, 'Resolution 17/07 on the Prohibition to Use Large-scale Driftnets in the IOTC Area' (1 December 2017) Res 17/07; WCPFC, 'Conservation and Management Measure to Prohibit the Use of Large Scale Driftnets on the High Seas in the Convention Area' (2008) CMM 2008-04.

to these resolutions in their preambles. There have been regular reports to the General Assembly on the use of drift nets, noting a significant reduction in their usage. These resolutions have, thus, played an important role in encouraging states and RFMOs to take action in this area.

The definition of IUU fishing, which, arguably, now sets a global standard for unacceptable fishing conduct, was also negotiated in an informal context, but has subsequently made its way into the formal legal framework. The concept of IUU fishing did not exist at the time of the LOSC or FSA negotiations, but began to appear in informal instruments from the late 1990s onwards: in the Rome Declaration on Responsible Fisheries,[95] and in General Assembly resolutions.[96] The only significant attempt to define IUU fishing internationally was in the IPOA–IUU, which outlines a description of fishing activities considered illegal, unregulated, or unreported.[97] Defining the term at the global level was important, as it set the standard for the conduct that the international community, as a whole, considered unacceptable: a standard that has since been upheld in regional CMMs. The IPOA–IUU definition is the most frequently referred to definition of IUU fishing and, subsequently, many international, regional, and domestic instruments now define IUU fishing by reference to it,[98] including several RFMO instruments,[99] regional instruments,[100] and domestic legislation and policies,[101] as well as the PSMA.[102]

Several other CMMs adopted within RFMOs have clearly been influenced by the calls for action and standards set out in informal fisheries instruments. For example, many RFMOs have adopted CMMs to minimize the by-catch of seabirds by fishing vessels, and many of these CMMs make reference to the IPOA–Seabirds or the FAO Technical Guidelines for Responsible Fishing.[103] Some RFMOs have adopted CMMs on the conservation of sharks that refer to informal instruments, including the IPOA–Sharks and relevant General Assembly resolutions.[104] Most RFMOs have adopted CMMs that establish IUU vessel

[95] FAO, 'The Rome Declaration on the Implementation of the Code of Conduct for Responsible Fisheries' (Rome 1999), para 2, 12(j) <http://www.fao.org/3/X2220e/X2220e00.htm> accessed 17 March 2021.

[96] As early as 2000. See, eg UNGA Res 55/7 (30 October 2000) UN Doc A/RES/55/7, preamble, para 24.

[97] IPOA–IUU (n 26) para 3.

[98] See PSMA (n 19) art 1(e). See, further, the discussion in *Request for Advisory Opinion Submitted by the Sub-regional Fisheries Commission* (Advisory Opinion) ITLOS Reports 2015, 4, para 92.

[99] Eg, SPRFMO Convention (n 12) art 1(j); WCPFC, 'Conservation and Management Measure on Minimum Standards for Port State Measures' (2018) CMM 2017-02.

[100] Eg, RPOA–IUU, 'Listing Procedure', para 2 <http://www.rpoaiuu.org/listing-procedure/> accessed 17 March 2021.

[101] Eg, Australian Government Department of Agriculture, 'Australia's Second National Plan of Action to Prevent, Deter and Eliminate Illegal, Unreported and Unregulated Fishing' (2014), para 2 <https://www.agriculture.gov.au/sites/default/files/sitecollectiondocuments/fisheries/iuu/aus-second-npoa-iuu-fishing.pdf>accessed 15 March 2021.

[102] PSMA (n 19) art 1(e).

[103] Eg SPRFMO, 'Conservation and Management Measure for Minimising Bycatch of Seabirds in the SPRFMO Convention Area' (2017) CMM 09-2017 <https://www.sprfmo.int/assets/Fisheries/Conservation-and-Management-Measures/CMM-09-2017-Seabirds-27Feb17.pdf> accessed 17 March 2021; SIOFA, 'Conservation and Management Measure on Mitigation of Seabirds Bycatch in Demersal Longlines and other Demersal Fishing Gears Fisheries (Mitigation of Seabirds Bycatch)' (2019) CMM 2019/13 <https://www.apsoi.org/sites/default/files/documents/cmm/CMM%202019_13%20Mitigation%20of%20seabirds%20bycatch.pdf> accessed 17 March 2021; SEAFO, 'Conservation Measure 25/12: On Reducing Incidental By-catch of Seabirds in the SEAFO Convention Area' (2012) CMM 25/12 <http://www.seafo.org/Management/Conservation-Measures> accessed 17 March 2021; CCAMLR, 'Combating Illegal, Unreported and Unregulated Fishing in the Convention Area by the Flag Vessels of Non-contracting Parties' (2006) Res 22/XXV <https://www.ccamlr.org/en/resolution-25/xxv-2006> accessed 17 March 2021. Seabirds measures have also been adopted in IOTC, IATTC, ICCAT, and WCPFC.

[104] Eg SIOFA, 'Conservation and Management Measure for Sharks' (2019) CMM 2019/12 <http://www.apsoi.org/sites/default/files/documents/cmm/CMM%202019_12%20Sharks.pdf> accessed 17 March 2021; CCAMLR, 'Conservation of Sharks' (2006) CMM 32-18 <https://www.ccamlr.org/en/measure-32-18-2006> accessed 17

lists, and refer to the recommendation to do so in the IPOA–IUU.[105] Several RFMOs have adopted CMMs encouraging members to take action against vessels without nationality that undertake IUU fishing on the high seas, many of which refer to the recommendation to do so in the IPOA–IUU.[106] More generally, the IPOA–IUU is seen as having provided renewed focus for states and RFMOs to address concerns about IUU fishing.[107]

11.4.3 Detailed Guidance on Implementation

Another manner in which some informal instruments contribute to international fisheries law is through the detailed practical guidance that they provide to states and RFMOs on the implementation of broad principles and treaty provisions into domestic law or regional CMMs. The impetus for developing these instruments has been the ongoing failings in respect of fisheries management despite the existence of various binding instruments governing these matters. Efforts have, therefore, been made to inform, and provide more guidance to, states on how to meet the obligations set out in the binding instruments discussed above.

This role is especially evident for more detailed instruments like the FAO guidelines, including the FAO Technical Guidelines for Responsible Fishing, or the Voluntary Guidelines on Flag State Performance. These instruments assist states and RFMOs in transforming broad principles into specific legal provisions, and provide guidance on appropriate standards to clarify how states can better comply with their obligations. The objective of such instruments does not appear to be that *all* provisions are implemented by all states. Rather, their purpose is to compile and clarify existing obligations, and to provide practical guidance on how to implement these obligations, thereby providing a 'toolkit' of measures for

March 2021; IOTC, 'Resolution 18/02 on Management Measures for the Conservation of Blue Shark Caught in Association with IOTC Fisheries' (2018) Res 18/02 <https://www.iotc.org/cmm/resolution-1802-management-measures-conservation-blue-shark-caught-association-iotc-fisheries> accessed 17 March 2021 (noting UNGA Res 62/177 (18 December 2007) UN Doc A/RES/62/177; UNGA Res 63/112 (5 December 2008) UN Doc A/RES/63/112; UNGA Res 64/72 (n 38); UNGA Res 65/38 (7 December 2010) UN Doc A/RES/65/38; UNGA Res 66/68 (6 December 2011) UN Doc A/Res/66/68; UNGA Res 67/79 (11 December 2012) UN Doc A/RES/67/79; UNGA Res 68/71 (n 77); UNGA Res 69/109 (9 December 2014) UN Doc A/RES/69/109; UNGA Res 70/75 (8 December 2015) UN Doc A/RES/70/75; and UNGA Res 71/123 (7 December 2016) UN Doc A/RES/71/123.

[105] Eg SPRFMO, 'Conservation and Management Measure Establishing a List of Vessels Presumed to have Carried out Illegal, Unreported and Unregulated Fishing Activities in the SPRFMO Convention Area' (2020) Conservation Measure 04-2020 <https://www.sprfmo.int/assets/Fisheries/Conservation-and-Management-Measures/2020-CMMs/CMM-04-2020-IUU-Vessel-List-31Mar20.pdf> accessed 21 June 2021; WCPFC 2010-06; SIOFA 2018/10-08.

[106] Eg SIOFA, 'Conservation and Management Measure on Vessels without Nationality (Vessels without Nationality)' (2016) CMM 2016/04 <https://www.apsoi.org/sites/default/files/documents/cmm/CMM%202016_04%20Vessels%20without%20Nationality%20%282016.10.18%29%20edited%202017.pdf> accessed 17 March 2021 <; IOTC, 'Resolution 16/05 on Vessels without Nationality' (2016) Res 16/05 <https://www.iotc.org/cmm/resolution-1605-vessels-without-nationality> accessed 17 March 2021; SPRFMO, 'Conservation and Management Measure on Vessels without Nationality' (2016) CMM 15-2016 <https://www.sprfmo.int/assets/Fisheries/Conservation-and-Management-Measures/2019-CMMs/CMM-15-2016-Stateless-Vessels-FormattedMay2019.pdf> accessed 17 March 2021.

[107] Edeson, The International Plan of Action (n 27) 622. Some consider that the IPOA–IUU set the international standards for the regulation of IUU fishing at the national level. See, eg Dikdik Mohamed Sodik, 'Non-legally Binding International Fisheries Instruments and Measures to Combat Illegal, Unreported and Unregulated Fishing' (2008) Aust Intl'l L J 129, 131.

states and RFMOs, particularly those whose fisheries management systems are less developed. Some examples of such practical guidance are outlined immediately below.

Under the auspices of the FAO, voluntary guidelines have been developed that are designed to assist states in implementing their fisheries management obligations. The Voluntary Guidelines on Flag State Performance seek to prevent, deter, and eliminate IUU fishing through effective implementation of flag state responsibilities, and provide practical guidance on how these responsibilities will be realized. For instance, the LOSC requires flag states to maintain a register of flagged vessels that should contain 'names and particulars',[108] but does not provide any further guidance. These guidelines and the IPOA–IUU provide other details that should be recorded, such as, inter alia, any previous names of the vessel; the name, address, and nationality of the owner, manager, and any beneficial owners; the vessel dimensions; and any alterations.[109] Similarly, the Voluntary Guidelines on Flag State Performance include implementation guidance on a fishing authorization regime for flagged vessels. The LOSC requires parties to effectively exercise jurisdiction and control in administrative, technical, and social matters over flagged vessels,[110] and the FSA only allows flag states to authorize vessels to fish on the high seas where they can exercise their responsibilities effectively.[111] The IPOA–IUU and Voluntary Guidelines on Flag State Performance provide more detailed guidance on how to comply with these obligations. They outline details to be included in any authorization, including, inter alia, scope, area, species, gear, and any applicable measures for the authorized fishing.[112] These instruments detail conditions that might be applied to any authorization, such as, inter alia, VMS, catch reporting, observer coverage, logbook requirements, and compliance with applicable measures.[113]

The FSA requires parties to minimize catch by lost or abandoned gear,[114] and requires flag states to develop requirements for marking gear for identification, in accordance with internationally recognizable vessel and gear marking systems.[115] The IPOA–IUU requires gear to be marked in accordance with such standards before vessels are authorized to fish,[116] but there were no such internationally recognized markings. In 2018, COFI adopted the Voluntary Guidelines on the Marking of Fishing Gear, due to concern about 'ghost fishing' by abandoned, lost, or discarded fishing gear. These guidelines aim to assist states and RFMOs to develop gear-marking systems to facilitate the location and identification of ownership of such gear, frameworks for risk assessment, and regulations designed to minimize abandoned and lost gear, and encourage its recovery. They provide practical guidance on how to implement the more general obligations in the LOSC and the FSA, and the provisions of the IPOA–IUU.[117] For example, they recommend that markings match vessel

[108] LOSC (n 1) art 94(2(a)). The Code (n 22) also provides that flag states should maintain a vessel list that should include details of vessel, ownership, and authorization (para 8.2.1).

[109] IPOA–IUU (n 26) paras 42–42.6; FAO, Voluntary Guidelines for Flag State Performance (n 32) para 25.

[110] LOSC (n 1) art 94.

[111] FSA (n 9) art 18(2).

[112] IPOA–IUU (n 26) para 46; FAO, Voluntary Guidelines for Flag State Performance (n 32) para 29.

[113] IPOA–IUU (n 26) para 47; FAO, Voluntary Guidelines on Flag State Performance (n 32) para 29(c)(iv), Annex 1.

[114] FSA (n 9) art 5(f).

[115] ibid, art 18(d).

[116] IPOA–IUU (n 26) para 47.8.

[117] The Voluntary Guidelines on the Marking of Fishing Gear (n 34) note (at para 1) that the guidelines are expected to assist states in implementing their international obligations.

registration details,[118] that if gear is to be used by a commercial group, a common mark can be issued to a company,[119] and that gear markings be documented in a gear record or license authorization system.[120]

11.4.4 Informal Instruments as Interpretive Guidance

As an increasing body of informal law is developed in fisheries management, how these instruments might serve as interpretive guidance in respect of the treaties in this field, especially the LOSC and the FSA, must be examined. Article 31 of the Vienna Convention on the Law of Treaties governs this question, and provides that the terms of a treaty shall be interpreted in good faith in accordance with their ordinary meaning, in context, and in light of the treaty's object and purpose.[121] It provides that, together with the treaty text and its preamble and annexes, the context is comprised of any subsequent agreement between the parties regarding the interpretation of the treaty, or the application of its provisions, any subsequent practice in the application of the treaty that establishes the agreement of the parties regarding its interpretation, and any relevant rules of international law applicable in the relations between the parties.[122] Accordingly, where informal fisheries instruments fall into these categories, they may constitute 'context', for the purposes of the Vienna Convention, and, thereby, constitute interpretative guidance. However, Article 31(3) necessarily bears a high threshold.

In *Whaling in the Antarctic*, the International Court of Justice found that, where resolutions of the International Whaling Commission were not adopted by *all* parties to the International Convention on the Regulation of Whaling, they were not sufficient to satisfy Articles 31(3)(a) or (b).[123] The Court did state, however, that recommendations adopted by consensus in the International Whaling Commission might be relevant to interpreting the Convention, despite being non-binding.[124] The International Law Commission has, similarly, acknowledged the capacity for decisions adopted within a Conference of State Parties framework to embody a subsequent agreement or subsequent practice, in some circumstances,[125] also noting that this could be the case if the relevant decision of the Conference of State Parties 'is based on a unanimous vote in which all parties participate'.[126]

On this analysis, it appears that, even if it were accepted that informal instruments could satisfy one of the limbs of Article 31(3) in any given scenario, whether the group of parties to the treaty and the informal instrument in question were the same would need to be examined closely. Further, however, the connection between the subject matter of the

[118] ibid, para 24. The vessel registration details are a number designated by the IMO.
[119] ibid, para 25.
[120] ibid, para 27.
[121] Vienna Convention on the Law of Treaties (adopted 23 May 1969, entered into force 27 January 1980) 1155 UNTS 331, art 31(1).
[122] ibid, art 31(3)(a)–(c).
[123] *Whaling in the Antarctic (Australia v Japan: New Zealand intervening)* (Judgment) [2014] ICJ Rep 226, para 83.
[124] ibid, para 46.
[125] International Law Commission, 'Draft Conclusions on Subsequent Agreement and Subsequent Practice in relation to the Interpretation of Treaties with Commentaries' (2018) UN Doc A/73/10, Conclusions 11(3), and 66.
[126] ibid, Conclusion 74.

two instruments and the structure of the surrounding legal framework would need to be considered. Recommendations adopted within an RFMO, for example, despite their non-binding nature, might meet this threshold vis-à-vis the convention of that RFMO, as those instruments address the same subject matter, form part of the same legal framework, and tend to be adopted by consensus. However, for many of the other instruments discussed above, whether such informal instruments would satisfy Article 31(3) seems less likely. Even if the parties to, for example, the LOSC and a particular FAO instrument overlapped, it is not clear that those instruments could be said to address the same specific subject matter, and whether, given the separate legal frameworks, processes, and parties, such instruments could satisfy Article 31(3). Furthermore, given that Article 31(3)(c) of the Vienna Convention applies to relevant *rules* of international law, it seems doubtful that provisions in non-binding instruments would satisfy this article.[127]

11.4.5 The Development of Customary International Law?

In light of the varied ways that informal instruments have contributed to the international fisheries law framework, a final consideration is their potential to contribute to the development of customary international law, as another formal source of international law. There are, undoubtedly, numerous examples of domestic legislation, policy, and practices in fisheries management that implement provisions of these informal instruments, in some cases due to the practical implementation guidance they provide, which may contribute to a body of state practice. States' endorsement of informal instruments could also, potentially, constitute state practice in support of certain provisions. In particular, several informal fisheries instruments replicate treaty or other informal law provisions. Although these instruments are sometimes criticized for this repetition,[128] states' endorsements of such text could constitute state practice, for the purposes of the development of a norm of custom, which requires 'evidence of a general practice accepted as law'.[129] For this reason, the repetition of such provisions potentially strengthens the volume of state practice, particularly given the large numbers of endorsing states for many of the instruments discussed above. Indeed, instruments of this kind—those developed within international organizations—are recognized as increasingly contributing to the development of custom.[130]

However, there are significant limitations on the potential for informal instruments to contribute to the development of customary international law. First, there is a question as to whether the duration and consistency of any state practice—a key element in the formation of a customary norm[131]—is sufficient to support its development. Second, whether

[127] The position on this is not clear. See the discussion in Richard Gardiner, *Treaty Interpretation* (OUP 2008) 268–69.

[128] See, eg Edeson, Closing the Gap (n 42).

[129] Statute of the International Court of Justice, art 38(1)(b).

[130] See, in particular, Treves's view that 'the intensification of practice within international organisations and conferences . . . has contributed to the acceleration of the formation of customary rules': Tullio Treves, 'Customary International Law' in *Max Planck Encyclopaedia of Public International Law* (2006), paras 2 and 25.

[131] *North Sea Continental Shelf cases (Germany v Denmark; Germany v Netherlands)* [1969] ICJ Rep 3, para 72.

any provision in question is 'of a fundamentally norm-creating character'[132] must be considered. Although some provisions of informal fisheries instruments are specific and detailed, several are vague and general, and, without adequate specificity or clarity, these may not be of a norm-creating character. Some commentators have suggested that, for this reason, it is doubtful that some informal instruments have contributed to crystallizing new rules of custom.[133]

Finally, and significantly for informal instruments, whether any state practice would be accompanied by the requisite *opinio juris* necessary for the development of a customary norm is doubtful. Given the non-binding nature of these instruments, in many cases *opinio juris* is likely to be lacking. In light of these issues, whether any particular provisions of the informal instruments discussed above could develop into norms of customary law must be examined on a case-by-case basis, requiring a detailed analysis of the consistency and character of any state practice and *opinio juris*.

11.5 The Capacity of Informal Instruments to Influence International Fisheries Law

As illustrated above, informal fisheries instruments are varied. Some are comprehensive and cover a broad range of topics, while others relate to a specific issue. Some contain vague or aspirational principles or calls to action, while others include specific, instructive provisions that are highly practical. Some contain a combination of these types of provisions. Some seem to embody a long-term vision,[134] while others reflect an expectation of more immediate action. Some provide a 'toolkit' of measures, where it is not necessarily envisaged that endorsing states will implement all provisions, and others set out shared, globally agreed standards. Almost all were developed under the auspices of the UN, within the General Assembly or the FAO, through rigorous, transparent, and consistent processes, with the involvement of large groups of states, and, in some cases, a variety of other actors. These instruments, generally, have the endorsement of more states than the key treaties in this field.[135]

The value of these instruments is significant and varied. Many are broadly endorsed, widely respected, and have contributed to international fisheries law in several different ways. As discussed in the previous section, they act as a catalyst for states and regional organizations to develop binding instruments to address priority issues that reflect globally agreed modern standards in fisheries management. They have also, more generally, influenced and shaped the policies of states, and the operation and decisions of regional organizations in this field. Although not binding, the informal instruments in this area have played an important role in shaping the concepts, standards, and expectations in international fisheries law, and their influence is often acknowledged. This part of the chapter explores why these instruments have had this degree of influence.

[132] ibid.

[133] See, eg Harrison, Making the Law of the Sea (n 80) 218 (in respect of the Code).

[134] Eg IPOA–IUU (n 26) para 9.2 describes 'phased implementation'.

[135] Eg, at time of writing, the FSA (n 9) has ninety parties, the Compliance Agreement (n 18) has forty parties, and the PSMA (n 19) has sixty-four parties.

11.5.1 The Non-binding Nature of Informal Instruments

A clear limiting factor in the legal significance of these instruments is their non-binding nature. Quality and acceptance aside, there is no formal obligation on endorsing states to implement the provisions of these instruments, domestically or otherwise, to comply with them. Despite this characteristic, however, many of these instruments have proven influential, and as illustrated above, have had a clear impact on the legal framework for fisheries conservation and management.

In fact, informal instruments have a number of advantages. It is, in part, on account of their non-binding nature that they are able to make such a significant contribution to the law in this area. First, without the complexities of lengthy deliberations and formal ratification processes that states must undertake for treaties, informal instruments can be developed quickly. This shorter time frame is, in part, due to states being more likely to agree to support instruments when they are not legally bound to comply with the standards therein, and there are no associated compliance mechanisms. Without a formal commitment to uphold certain standards, lengthy domestic ratification processes are not necessary. This factor can be critical when an urgent issue needs to be addressed. For example, the General Assembly resolutions on drift net fishing and bottom fishing were able to be adopted quickly, whereas agreement to similar instruments in binding form would, presumably, have been very difficult, and would have required lengthy negotiations. These instruments, however, paved the way for subsequent formal legal action at the regional and national level, as well as, most likely, some change in practice.

Second, informal instruments are more likely to include higher standards, or clear and ambitious standards, than binding instruments.[136] States are more inclined in binding instruments to agree only to standards that are modest or ambiguous,[137] whereas the absence of a legal commitment or risks associated with non-compliance, in an informal instrument, may increase willingness to endorse non-binding instruments. Informal instruments in this field include relatively ambitious global standards that may not have been supported by states if a binding instrument had, instead, been pursued. The flexibility of informal instruments allows states to support higher standards without the risks of non-compliance, while working towards full compliance over time. For example, it has been suggested that, in the case of most of the IPOAs, and the Code, states would not have agreed to such ambitious provisions in a binding instrument.[138]

11.5.2 Influence Derived from Development Process and Quality

Further, despite being non-binding, other characteristics of these instruments, such as the quality of their provisions, and the inclusiveness of their development processes, have played a significant role in establishing their influence. Non-binding instruments may attract legitimacy through factors other than formality, such as their development processes,

[136] It has been observed that states 'seem more willing to adopt clear and ambitious commitments when they are in non-binding form' in Dinah Shelton (ed), *Commitment and Compliance: The Role of Non-binding Norms in the International Legal System* (OUP 2000) 11; see also Harrison, Making the Law of the Sea (n 80) 218.

[137] Shelton (n 136) 12.

[138] Edeson, Closing the Gap (n 42) 103.

transparency, and inclusion, and the involvement of a wide range of actors.[139] In this regard, they may even be 'normatively superior' to some binding instruments,[140] particularly those binding instruments developed behind closed doors, through discussions between small groups of government officials, with very little transparency.[141]

The development of many of these instruments was at the direction of a large, unified group of states, through well-established and respected UN bodies such as COFI or the General Assembly, with near-universal membership, illustrating comprehensive support for their development. Many were negotiated under the auspices of the FAO[142]—a UN specialized agency with near-universal membership—[143]with a senior FAO body endorsing both their development process and the final text.[144] Support for their standards and provisions is, therefore, not limited to those states with a direct interest in a particular fishery or issue. This facilitates a truly universal approach. The FAO's work is held in high esteem, due to its broad membership and recognized role in the development of fisheries law: thus, its consensus-based instruments carry substantial weight.[145]

Many of these instruments were developed through similar processes within the FAO. These processes involved 'expert consultations' comprised of experts from states, the FAO, NGOs, regional organizations, and industry, who presented issues papers, and negotiated draft text or reports.[146] Then, 'technical consultations'[147] made up of state representatives, with NGOs and regional organizations as observers, would negotiate a final text to present to a senior FAO body for adoption. In general, the inclusiveness and transparency of these processes are commended: they facilitate contributions from a diversity of voices and perspectives, bringing depth of expertise and operational experience to shaping these instruments. In this way, they reflect the interests and needs of the international community.[148] The inclusivity, transparency, rigour, and formality of these development processes have also contributed to their influence. Edeson hints at the early appreciation of the significance of the IPOA–IUU, noting that, despite its non-binding status, the text was negotiated as if it may become a binding text, 'or at the very least that it might have an impact on binding legal instruments or even on the evolution of customary international law'.[149]

[139] Pauwelyn, Wessel, and Wouters (n 14) 747, 749. Shelton suggests there is a perception that soft law allows greater participation for non-state actors, extending a role that is rarely possible in treaty negotiations (n 136) 13.

[140] Pauwelyn, Wessel, and Wouters (n 14) 734, 749.

[141] ibid. Shelton suggests that this was particularly the case historically (n 136) 13.

[142] Eg IPOA–IUU (n 26); Code (n 22); IPOA–Seabirds (n 31); IPOA–Sharks (n 31); IPOA–Capacity (n 31); FAO, Voluntary Guidelines for Flag State Performance (n 32); FAO, Voluntary Guidelines on the Marking of Fishing Gear (n 34); FAO, Voluntary Guidelines for Catch Documentation Schemes (n 33).

[143] 194 states, at time of writing.

[144] Generally, FAO Conference, FAO Council, or COFI.

[145] Korseberg (n 44) 825. Harrison notes that the FAO has 'actively developed international fisheries law through the use of non-binding instruments that have served to crystallise international support for new principles that can be applied to the conservation and management of fisheries': Harrison, Making the Law of the Sea (n 80) 234.

[146] See, eg a list of experts from the IPOA–IUU Expert Consultation: FAO, 'Appendix B. List of Experts' <http://www.fao.org/3/Y3274E/y3274e03.htm#bm03.2> accessed 17 March 2021.

[147] See, eg FAO, 'Report of the Technical Consultation on Illegal, Unreported and Unregulated Fishing' (2–6 October 2000) FAO Fisheries Report No 634 <http://www.fao.org/3/X8623E/X8623E.htm#_Toc497551966> accessed on 15 March 2021.

[148] Harrison, Making the Law of the Sea (n 80) 234.

[149] Edeson, The International Plan of Action (n 27) 604.

11.6 Conclusion

Although the informal instruments examined in this chapter are non-binding, there is little doubt that they have made a valuable contribution to international fisheries law. In particular, the examples highlighted in this chapter demonstrate the ways in which these instruments have acted as a catalyst for states and regional organizations to take action to implement globally agreed standards and modern concepts in fisheries management into binding legal instruments. Even where their provisions have not been directly implemented into binding law, these instruments have often been influential, through, for example, modern approaches to fisheries management, increasing the international community's familiarity and comfort with such standards generally, and shaping the policies and decisions of states and regional organizations.

While, in other fields, informal instruments are, at times, adopted where 'treaty fatigue' has led to an unwillingness to adopt binding instruments, in fisheries management frameworks, binding legal instruments are adopted and updated frequently, particularly at the regional level. In this sphere, informal instruments are also adopted, but often at the global level. They play a critical role in incorporating appropriate modern concepts, and setting minimum acceptable standards. This critical role helps to ensure that binding regional instruments incorporate standards and principles that are not just developed between a small group of states with an interest in the fishery being managed, but, rather, they uphold global standards agreed by all states within a UN body, with the involvement of a broad range of actors. Although binding law in this field is constantly developing, the surrounding informal instruments help shape it, sometimes drive it, and help to uphold acceptable standards.

Although the non-binding nature of informal instruments is a clear limitation in the effectiveness of these instruments, it has, in other respects, also been an advantage. Their informal nature has played a critical role in their contribution to the legal framework, as it is unlikely that their ambitious provisions, their swift negotiation and adoption, and their near-universal support would have been possible through binding instruments. Further, their influence also stems, in part, from the rigour in their development processes. The legitimacy that these instruments derive from their inclusiveness, transparency, and quality has allowed them to make a valuable contribution to international law.

Yet, it must be acknowledged that, despite the comprehensive legal framework in this field, problems in fisheries management have persisted across many parts of the world. The FAO's 2020 State of the World's Fisheries (SOFIA) report found that 34.2% of fish stocks are now fished at biologically unsustainable levels, and this figure is not improving, globally.[150] This finding illustrates the ongoing need for a sharp improvement in fisheries management. Although a lack of implementation and enforcement of legal frameworks likely plays a significant role in these failings, establishing a sound legal framework is, nonetheless, critical to improving the state of fisheries. As set out in this chapter, informal law has already made an important contribution towards this objective. In light of their influence to date, and noting that, within the General Assembly and the FAO, there is existing architecture and processes in place to develop such instruments, it is likely that informal instruments in

[150] FAO, 'The State of World Fisheries and Aquaculture 2020' (Rome 2020) <www.fao.org/documents/card/en/c/ca9229en> accessed 17 March 2021.

fisheries management will continue to be influential, and contribute to the legal framework, into the future.

International fisheries law is constantly evolving, and as new science, technology, and management approaches emerge, new informal instruments will be needed to reflect these developments. These instruments will, surely, continue to have significance for international fisheries law, and the normative value of the informal instruments in this field has enhanced, and will continue to enhance, global efforts to improve fisheries management and conservation into the future.

12

Marine Scientific Research and Informal Lawmaking

Chie Kojima

12.1 Introduction

Science has contributed to understanding the oceans, including the living and non-living marine resources, marine ecology and ecosystems, and oceanography. It has also helped reveal how various anthropogenic activities on land, and at sea, have influenced the marine environment and its ecosystems. While scientific findings, such as those demonstrating the adverse effects of global climate change on the oceans, have influenced the behaviour of policymakers at both international and domestic levels, further research activities are needed in order to gather more scientific data to continue assessing the healthiness of the oceans, and to predict what environmental risks may exist in the future. Up-to-date scientific data is necessary for governments to take appropriate measures for the protection and conservation of the marine environment, from both short-term and long-term perspectives. Marine scientific research is also important in assessing the environmental impact of increasing anthropogenic activities, including new uses of the non-renewable and renewable resources of the oceans. These developments are accelerating, as resources become scarcer, and blue economy policies are promoted.

Marine scientific research takes place not only in the marine areas under coastal state jurisdiction, such as the territorial sea, the exclusive economic zone (EEZ), and the continental shelf, but also in areas beyond national jurisdiction. Historically, marine scientific research was not a concern for international regulation, as research in the territorial sea and internal waters was considered to be within a coastal state's sovereignty.[1] This situation has changed since states began to claim their sovereign rights over continental shelves, and to explore and exploit resources therein. A new question then arose, relating to how to balance the rights of coastal states and the right to marine scientific research enjoyed by all states on the high seas.[2] The 1982 United Nations Convention on the Law of the Sea ('LOSC')[3] maintains this balance by providing, for the first time in a multilateral treaty, the right to marine scientific research enjoyed by all states and international organizations, and coastal state jurisdiction to regulate marine scientific research activities within the territorial sea, the EEZ, and the continental shelf.

[1] Nele Matz-Lück, 'Article 238 Right to Conduct Marine Scientific Research' in Alexander Proelss (ed), *United Nations Convention on the Law of the Sea: A Commentary* (Beck Hart Nomos 2017) 1607.

[2] ibid 1607–08.

[3] United Nations Convention on the Law of the Sea (adopted 10 December 1982, entered into force 16 November 1994) 1833 UNTS 3 (hereafter 'LOSC').

Chie Kojima, *Marine Scientific Research and Informal Lawmaking* In: *Unconventional Lawmaking in the Law of the Sea.* Edited by: Natalie Klein, Oxford University Press. © Chie Kojima 2022. DOI: 10.1093/oso/9780192897824.003.0012

Part XIII of the LOSC is praised for its comprehensiveness, but criticized for leaving a 'legal grey area'.[4] In particular, the lack of a definition of 'marine scientific research' creates uncertainty about the applicability of the provisions under Part XIII to a wide range of research activities at sea, as well as to an increasing range of activities that use new technologies, such as remote sensing, from which certain data can be used for marine scientific research.[5] When scientific and technological innovations occur much faster than government efforts to regulate those activities, unknown risks of harm to the marine environment, or security concerns, might arise.

On the other hand, a generic term such as 'marine scientific research' leaves enough flexibility to address future developments in science and technology, as well as new human activities in the oceans that emerge from societal, economic, and environmental changes. Such developments are, in reality, often 'unevenly distributed' among states.[6] While all states, irrespective of their geographical location, are entitled to exercise the right to conduct marine scientific research, under Article 238 of the LOSC, actual participants in marine scientific research have been limited mostly to developed states, as well as the scientists and private companies based in those developed states. This situation is, of course, due to an easier access to advanced technologies, and the capacity to afford the high costs of marine scientific research. Although it can be said that marine scientific activities have become increasingly global in recent decades,[7] enhanced international cooperation is still needed for states to share scientific information and implement their obligations under the LOSC in a unified manner, including in relation to the obligation to protect and preserve the marine environment.

In order to ensure that developments in marine scientific research are reflected in universally accepted rules under Part XIII of the LOSC, international cooperation is inevitable. In this regard, the duty to cooperate through competent international organizations, as provided under Part XIII of the LOSC, is an important tool for shaping the interests and expectations of the international community in the conduct of marine scientific research. Not only state actors, but also non-state actors, including research institutions and groups of scientists, are involved in processes of international cooperation in marine scientific research, and these various actors contribute to the development of international law on marine scientific research, in the frameworks of both Part XIII of the LOSC and general international law. As a framework agreement, the LOSC does not specify the means for cooperation, and the implementation of the duty to cooperate may rely on informal processes.

Informal processes may ultimately have an important role to play in resolving textual ambiguities, and elaborating on the content of some obligations. One reason why informal lawmaking may have this role is because, under the LOSC regime, some of these issues cannot fully be assessed, in light of existing legal rules, by relying solely on the interpretations provided by an arbitral tribunal or international court. This examination is precluded because the coastal state's denial of consent for marine scientific research in its EEZ, or on

[4] Paul Gragl, 'Marine Scientific Research' in David Joseph Attard, Malgosia Fitzmaurice, and Norman A Martinez Gutierrez (eds), *The IMLI Manual on International Maritime Law, vol I: The Law of the Sea* (OUP 2014) 398.

[5] See Techera, in Chapter 13 of this volume.

[6] Emmanuella Doussis, 'Marine Scientific Research: Taking Stock and Looking Ahead' in Gemma Andreone (ed), *The Future of the Law of the Sea* (Springer 2017) 100.

[7] Luis Valdes (ed), *Global Ocean Science Report: The Current Status of Ocean Science around the World* (IOC–UNESCO 2017) 149.

the continental shelf, is not subject to compulsory dispute settlement under Article 297(2) of the LOSC.[8] It is equally unlikely that the freedom of marine scientific research will be tested before an arbitral tribunal or international court under the general provisions of the LOSC, unless an agreement outside the LOSC stipulates both specific obligations in conducting research on the high seas, and the procedure for international dispute settlement. In this regard, roles for formal and informal lawmaking, as well as the development of consistent state practice, become even more important for integrating new developments into the LOSC regime on marine scientific research.[9] These limitations under the LOSC regime, however, do not prevent the development of international law concerning marine scientific research by international courts' decisions with respect to the application and interpretation of other international conventions, as was evident in the *Whaling in the Antarctic* case.[10] Lowe and Tzanakopoulos succinctly write that not only the international and domestic 'adjudicators', but also non-governmental 'codifiers', international organizations as 'regulators', and states as 'law-makers', all contribute to the development of the law of the sea.[11]

The purpose of this chapter is to discuss in what forms informal lawmaking exists in marine scientific research, and how informal lawmaking interacts with the LOSC. First, the chapter highlights some key issues relating to the international regime of marine scientific research under the LOSC, which leaves room for future developments. It then examines some examples of informal lawmaking by international and regional institutions, as well as examples of standard making by private actors who engage in marine scientific research, and their significance in the international context. It is necessary, for the purposes of this section, to consider informal lawmaking as various processes towards sharing expectations among stakeholders, and shaping standards concerning various research activities at sea.[12] Finally, it concludes with some observations concerning the relationship between the LOSC and informal lawmaking, by demonstrating that informal lawmaking processes in marine scientific research have provided means and networks for cooperation that not only complement the LOSC, but also work towards better ocean governance.

12.2 The LOSC Framework on Marine Scientific Research

Part XIII of the LOSC is clear with regard to the consent regime on marine scientific research in maritime areas under coastal state jurisdiction. All states, irrespective of their geographical location, and competent international organizations, have the right to conduct

[8] Gragl (n 4) 398–99; Tim Stephens and Donald R Rothwell, 'Marine Scientific Research' in Donald R Rothwell, Alex G Oude Elferink, Karen N Scott, and Tim Stephens (eds), *The Oxford Handbook of the Law of the Sea* (OUP 2015) 566.

[9] Gragl (n 4).

[10] *Whaling in the Antarctic (Australia v Japan: New Zealand intervening)* (Judgment) [2014] ICJ Rep 226. The court declined to give a definition of 'scientific research', but interpreted the meaning of the phrase 'for the purpose of scientific research' under Article VIII of the International Convention for the Regulation of Whaling. In the judgment, the court stated that recommendations adopted by consensus, or by a unanimous vote, within the International Whaling Commission may be relevant for the interpretation of the International Convention for the Regulation of Whales.

[11] Vaughan Lowe QC and Antonios Tzanakopoulos, 'The Development of the Law of the Sea by the International Court of Justice' in Christian J Tams and James Sloan (eds), *The Development of International Law by the International Court of Justice* (OUP 2013) 179–85.

[12] See Klein, in Chapter 1 of this volume.

marine scientific research,[13] subject to the rights and duties of other states, including coastal states' rights to regulate, authorize, and conduct marine scientific research in their territorial seas, EEZs, and continental shelves.[14] States and international organizations that intend to undertake marine scientific research in the EEZ or continental shelf of a coastal state not only have to obtain the consent of that coastal state, but also provide it with information relating to their research project at least six months prior to the commencement of the project.[15]

In maritime areas beyond national jurisdiction, all states enjoy the freedom to conduct marine scientific research in the high seas, under Article 87(1)(f) of the LOSC. This freedom is reflected in the right of all states and international organizations to conduct marine scientific research in the water column beyond the limits of the EEZ, under Article 257, as well as their right to conduct marine scientific research in the Area, under Article 256 of the LOSC. Marine scientific research in the Area should be carried out exclusively for peaceful purposes, and for the benefit of humankind as a whole.[16] The International Seabed Authority is under the obligation not only to promote and encourage the conduct of marine scientific research in the Area, but also to coordinate and disseminate the results of research and analysis.[17]

While these basic rights and obligations concerning marine scientific research, stipulated in the LOSC, are comprehensive, and considered to be a 'major advance' in the regulation of marine scientific research compared to the 1958 Geneva regime, where no mention was made of marine scientific research,[18] this frame does not mean that states have implemented their rights and duties in a unified manner. In particular, the consent regime for marine scientific research in the EEZ is 'controversial and unevenly interpreted by the international community'.[19] While some researching states are reluctant to follow the procedures for the implied consent regime under Article 252 of the LOSC, some coastal states apply more stringent rules on marine scientific research than others.[20] However, Part XIII includes undefined terms, and leaves room for evolutionary interpretation, depending on future developments in science, technologies, and environmental changes, as well as room for interaction with other parts of the LOSC, such as Part XII on the protection and preservation of the marine environment. Furthermore, fulfilling the duty to cooperate stipulated under Parts XII and XIII may supplement the shortcomings of inconsistent state practice, and contribute to achieving a common goal of promoting the study of the marine environment, by the international community, in addressing global environmental challenges.

The major issues that are open for future development include: (1) the definition of 'marine scientific research'; (2) the definition of 'competent international organizations'; and (3) the relationship between Part XIII on marine scientific research and Part XII on the protection and preservation of the marine environment of the LOSC. These issues are

[13] LOSC (n 3) art 238.
[14] ibid, arts 245, 246.
[15] ibid, art 248.
[16] ibid, art 143(1).
[17] ibid, art 143(2).
[18] Donald R Rothwell and Tim Stephens, *The International Law of the Sea* (2nd edn, Bloomsbury 2016) 347.
[19] Sam Bateman, 'Security and the Law of the Sea in East Asia: Navigational Regimes' in David Freestone, Richard Barnes, and David M Ong (eds), *The Law of the Sea: Progress and Prospects* (OUP 2006) 381.
[20] ibid.

discussed immediately below, to highlight the potential for informal lawmaking processes to complement the LOSC.

12.2.1 Definition of Marine Scientific Research

The LOSC provides no definition of 'marine scientific research'. During the Third United Nations Convention on the Law of the Sea (UNCLOS III), the delegations could not agree on whether marine scientific research should be limited to pure research, or should mean all scientific research, including applied research for industrial purposes.[21] The drafting history of the LOSC rather indicated a general understanding that a distinction between pure scientific research and industrial research for economic purposes was not possible. The efforts to define the term 'marine scientific research' ended with the Informal Single Negotiating Text issued in 1976, which defined marine scientific research as 'any study or related experimental work designed to increase mankind's knowledge of the marine environment'.[22] This background implies that the LOSC 'deliberately' left the term undefined, in order not to limit its meaning only to pure research.[23] It is, however, generally understood among scholars that the definition of marine scientific research under the LOSC comprises, at least, areas of marine science such as physical oceanography, marine biology, marine geology, and geophysics.[24]

Whether hydrography is included in the definition is controversial because, under Article 21(1)(g), hydrographic surveying is listed separately from marine scientific research, as one of the matters over which coastal states exercise their jurisdiction relating to innocent passage through their territorial seas.[25] This distinction raises the question of whether survey activities that are not resource-related should be separated from the definition of marine scientific research.[26] Not only survey activities, but also prospecting, exploration, and exploitation of marine resources are 'primarily' dealt with in other parts of the LOSC, such as Parts II, III, and XI, and Annex III.[27]

The Agreement relating to the Implementation of Part XI of the United Nations Convention on the Law of the Sea of 10 December 1982,[28] and the Regulations on Prospecting and Exploration for Polymetallic Nodules in the Area, adopted in 2000,[29] are

[21] UN DOALOS, *Marine Scientific Research: A Revised Guide to the Implementation of the Relevant Provisions of the United Nations Convention on the Law of the Sea* (2010) (hereafter 'DOALOS Guide') 4–6.

[22] ibid.

[23] Gragl (n 4) 403.

[24] Tullio Treves, 'Marine Scientific Research' in Rüdiger Wolfrum (ed), *Max Planck Encyclopedia of International Law* (OUP 2012), para 1.

[25] State practice is divergent as to whether coastal states may require consent from other states conducting hydrographic surveys conducted in their EEZ or other states may conduct such surveys freely as they are not resource-related. See Bateman, 'Security and the Law of the Sea in East Asia: Navigational Regimes' (n 19) 382.

[26] For more discussion, see Sam Bateman, 'Hydrographic Surveying in the EEZ: Differences and Overlaps with Marine Scientific Research' (2005) 29 Mar Pol'y 163.

[27] UN DOALOS Guide (n 21) 6.

[28] Agreement relating to the Implementation of Part XI of the United Nations Convention on the Law of the Sea of 10 December 1982 (adopted 28 July 1994, entered into force provisionally 16 November 1994 and definitively 28 July 1996) 1836 UNTS 3.

[29] ISA, 'Regulations on Prospecting and Exploration for Polymetallic Nodules in the Area' <https://www.isa.org.jm/files/documents/EN/Regs/PN-en.pdf> accessed 26 July 2021.

also relevant to understanding any definition of marine scientific research. Viewed from a formalistic perspective, survey activities, prospecting, exploration, and exploitation of marine resources may be excluded from the regime under Part XIII of the LOSC.[30] Whether or not these activities are excluded from the application of Part XIII is, however, not only a matter of interpretation of the text of the LOSC in light of its drafting process. How the term is understood may also be discerned from the subsequent practice of states, and the treatment of scientific activities within different organizations, or in other settings. Viewed from such a dynamic perspective, informal lawmaking through international organizations may play a role in further contributing to subsequent state practice for the purposes of treaty interpretation, or supporting the development of a customary international rule in this respect.

12.2.2 Definition of 'Competent International Organizations'

Article 238 of the LOSC explicitly confers the right to conduct marine scientific research on all states, regardless of whether they are coastal, landlocked, or geographically disadvantaged states, and on competent international organizations. However, the LOSC does not identify which organizations are qualified as 'competent international organizations' to enjoy the right to conduct marine scientific research.

Although some controversies exist, it is generally understood by formalists that 'competent international organizations', under Article 238 of the LOSC, refers only to intergovernmental organizations, and excludes non-governmental organizations.[31] These intergovernmental organizations are given, by their member states, the mandate to undertake, coordinate, promote, or facilitate the development of marine scientific research. Examples of such intergovernmental organizations are the United Nations and its specialized agencies and associated programmes, as well as the Intergovernmental Oceanographic Commission (IOC) of the United Nations Educational, Scientific and Cultural Organization (UNESCO), the International Seabed Authority, and the European Union.[32]

The LOSC further refers to competent international organizations in Article 251, stipulating states' obligation to work with competent international organizations for the establishment of general criteria and guidelines in marine scientific research. Such criteria and guidelines cannot be established without scientific expertise. As examined below, a variety of non-governmental organizations, research institutions, and groups of scientists participate in the process of informal lawmaking as important actors. This engagement in informal lawmaking may indicate a broader interpretation of 'competent international organizations' than the formalists would, otherwise, have anticipated.

[30] See Treves (n 24).
[31] Matz-Lück (n 1) 1613, fn 59.
[32] Gragl (n 4) 413.

12.2.3 Relationship with Part XII of the LOSC on the Protection and Preservation of the Marine Environment

The LOSC recognizes the importance of the marine environment, and indicates, in its preamble, that the parties are to promote the 'study, protection and preservation of the marine environment'. Article 240(d) of the LOSC also stipulates that marine scientific research should be conducted in compliance with all relevant regulations adopted in conformity with the LOSC, including those for the protection and preservation of the marine environment. Needless to say, marine scientific research is increasingly gaining importance for the protection of the marine environment, in the context of global environmental changes threatening the marine ecosystems and increasing anthropogenic activities at sea. Marine scientific research, whether pure or applied, also identifies new non-renewable and renewable resources of the oceans, to facilitate the pursuit of sustainable development.

The duty to cooperate, stipulated repeatedly under the LOSC, plays an important role in connecting marine scientific research and the protection and preservation of the marine environment. Under Part XII of the LOSC on the protection and preservation of the marine environment, Article 197 requires states to cooperate on a global or regional basis, 'directly or through competent international organizations, in formulating and elaborating international rules, standards and recommended practices and procedures' for the protection and preservation of the marine environment. Furthermore, Article 200 recognizes the need for marine scientific research in the protection of the marine environment from pollution, and stipulates the duty to cooperate 'for the purpose of promoting studies, undertaking programmes of scientific research and encouraging the exchange of information and data acquired about pollution of the marine environment'. International courts and tribunals have recognized that the duty to cooperate is 'a fundamental principle in the prevention of pollution of the marine environment under Part XII of the Convention [LOSC] and general international law'.[33]

Similarly, provisions under Part XIII of the LOSC, namely Articles 242 to 244, promote international cooperation in marine scientific research. Article 242(2) stipulates that states should allow other states a reasonable opportunity to obtain 'information necessary to prevent and control damage to the health and safety of persons and to the marine environment'. While this provision originally envisaged the prohibition of transboundary pollution,[34] it could be interpreted evolutionally, in parallel with Part XII of the LOSC, for instance in the context of the protection of the marine environment from adverse effects of climate change.[35] Article 243 obliges states and competent international organizations to cooperate, through the conclusion of bilateral and multilateral agreements, for the purposes of creating

[33] *MOX Plant* (*Ireland v United Kingdom*), Provisional Measures, Order of 3 December 2001, ITLOS Reports 2001, 95, 110, para 82; *Land Reclamation in and around the Straits of Johor* (*Malaysia v Singapore*), Provisional Measures, Order of 8 October 2003, ITLOS Reports 2003, 10, 25, para 92; *Request for Advisory Opinion submitted by the Sub-Regional Fisheries Commission* (*SRFC*), Advisory Opinion, 2 April 2015, ITLOS Reports 2015, 4, 43, para 140; *South China Sea Arbitration* (*Republic of the Philippines v People's Republic of China*), Award, 12 July 2016, PCA Case No. 2013-19, 376, para 946.

[34] Irini Papanicolopulu, 'Article 242 Promotion of International Cooperation' in Alexander Proelss (ed), *United Nations Convention on the Law of the Sea: A Commentary* (Beck Hart Nomos 2017) 1632.

[35] See, eg Chie Kojima, 'Climate Change and the Protection of the Marine Environment: Food Security, Evolutionary Interpretation, and the Novel Application of Dispute Settlement Mechanisms under the United Nations Convention on the Law of the Sea' in Neil Craik, Cameron Jeffries, Sara Seck, and Tim Stephens (eds), *Global Environmental Change and Innovation in International Law* (CUP 2018) 138.

favourable conditions for the conduct of marine scientific research in the marine environment, and integrating the efforts of scientists in studying the marine environment. Article 244 further provides that states should:

> actively promote the flow of scientific data and information and the transfer of knowledge resulting from marine scientific research, especially to developing States, as well as the strengthening of the autonomous marine scientific research capabilities of developing States through, inter alia, programmes to provide adequate education and training of their technical and scientific personnel.

This provision is closely linked to Part XIV of the LOSC on the transfer of marine technology, as it comprises the duty to engage in capacity-building in marine scientific research.[36]

The duty to cooperate in marine scientific research existed in other international environmental conventions, even before the adoption of the LOSC. For example, the 1972 Convention on the Prevention of Marine Pollution by Dumping of Wastes and other Matter and its 1996 Protocol, in Article VIII, provides for the duty to cooperate in the field of monitoring and scientific research.[37] The 1959 Antarctic Treaty also promotes scientific research for peaceful purposes in Article I, and international cooperation in scientific investigation in Antarctica through the exchange of scientific personnel and scientific results under Article III.[38] The Convention on Biological Diversity (CBD),[39] adopted after the LOSC, not only highlights the contracting parties' obligations to promote international cooperation in marine science and technology, especially with developing states, but also their obligations to implement the CBD consistently with the rights and obligations under the law of the sea.[40]

Despite these frequent references, it is not stipulated in these formal instruments how a state can fulfil the duty to cooperate in marine scientific research in the context of the protection of the marine environment. The LOSC is similarly devoid of detail in this regard. Considering the procedural nature of the duty to cooperate developed in the marine environmental law context,[41] informal lawmaking, which engages multiple actors in its processes, may be counted as one of the strategies that states can take to fulfil the obligation.

[36] For discussion concerning how informal law can assist capacity-building by facilitating the transfer of marine technology and data sharing, see Techera, in Chapter 13 of this volume.

[37] Convention on the Prevention of Marine Pollution by Dumping of Wastes and other Matter and its 1996 Protocol (adopted 7 November 1996, entered into force 24 March 2006) 1046 UNTS 120. Article VIII reads:

> 'In order to further the objectives of this Convention, the Contracting Parties with common interests to protect in the marine environment in a given geographical area shall endeavour, taking into account characteristic regional features, to enter into regional agreements consistent with this Convention for the prevention of pollution, especially by dumping. The Contracting Parties to the present Convention shall endeavour to act consistently with the objectives and provisions of such regional agreements, which shall be notified to them by the Organisation. Contracting Parties shall seek to co-operate with the Parties to regional agreements in order to develop harmonized procedures to be followed by Contracting Parties to the different conventions concerned. Special attention shall be given to co-operation in the field of monitoring and scientific research.'

[38] Antarctic Treaty (adopted 1 December 1959, entered into force 23 June 1961) 402 UNTS 71.

[39] Convention on Biological Diversity (adopted 5 June 1992, entered into force 29 December 1993) 1760 UNTS 79. The CBD refers, in Article 22(2), to the rights and obligations under the law of the sea.

[40] ibid, arts 12, 16, 18, and 22(2).

[41] See, generally, Chie Kojima, 'The Duty to Cooperate in the Protection and Preservation of the Marine Environment' in Myron H Nordquist, John Norton Moore, and Ronan Long (eds), *Cooperation and Engagement in the Asia-Pacific Region* (Brill 2019) 125.

12.3 Examples of Informal Lawmaking in Marine Scientific Research

Informal lawmaking is one of the means available to fill in the gaps between the text of the LOSC and actual practice in marine scientific research, and to provide details where the LOSC includes only general provisions. While marine scientific activities have become increasingly global, the regulatory frameworks are fragmented because of the sector-oriented management of ocean activities such as fishing, shipping, and offshore energy.[42] It follows that ocean science matters are discussed at multiple forums, at the national, regional and international levels, including intergovernmental, non-governmental, and multi-stakeholder forums and coalitions.[43] Moreover, as noted previously, difficulties arise when scientific and technological innovations occur much faster than government efforts to regulate marine scientific research. In this situation, existing sector-oriented regional and international rules cannot effectively or comprehensively address new situations that arise from such innovations. One result is that no overarching informal instrument has been developed to deal holistically with questions of marine scientific research, as has occurred in other areas of the law of the sea.[44]

Furthermore, as also noted at the outset, the consent regime under Part XIII of the LOSC is not interpreted and implemented by states in a coherent manner, despite the recognized importance of promoting marine scientific research. These diverse interpretive approaches, coupled with the fragmented regulatory mechanisms on marine scientific research in international law, could, thus, provide opportunities for informal solutions to improve coherence among the actions of non-state actors, such as individual scientists, scientific communities, and corporations, to enhance adherence to basic principles under the LOSC, including the protection and preservation of the marine environment. Examples of efforts in informal lawmaking are examined, from this perspective, below.

12.3.1 Informal Lawmaking on Marine Scientific Research by International Organizations

Informal lawmaking on marine scientific research, at the level of intergovernmental organizations, includes various activities such as the issuance of non-binding documents to assist states in implementing Part XIII of the LOSC domestically in a unified manner, the adoption of non-binding declarations to call for international cooperation, and the adoption of criteria and guidelines in conducting scientific research when the organization itself is involved in a research project.

12.3.1.1 Division for Ocean Affairs and the Law of the Sea of the United Nations

The Division for Ocean Affairs and the Law of the Sea (DOALOS) of the Office of Legal Affairs in the United Nations, the secretariat of the LOSC, has issued guides on marine scientific research, in 1991 and 2010, for the purpose of promoting the uniform and consistent

[42] See, generally, Luis Valdés, Jan Mees, and Henrik Oksfeldt Enevoldsen, 'International Organizations Supporting Ocean Science' in Luis Valdes (ed), *Global Ocean Science Report: The Current Status of Ocean Science around the World* (IOC–UNESCO 2017) 148–69.

[43] ibid 149.

[44] As in relation to fisheries, for example. See Scanlon, in Chapter 11 of this volume.

application of the LOSC. The 1991 guide, entitled 'Marine Scientific Research: A Guide to the Implementation of the Relevant Provisions of the United Nations Convention on the Law of the Sea', was intended to advise states about coastal and researching states' means of implementing the LOSC . The revised 2010 guide was based on the outcome of a 2009 meeting of experts, and integrated some new trends in marine data acquisition, marine data dissemination, and international collaborative programmes.[45]

These guides provide a detailed explanation of the provisions on marine scientific research in the LOSC, and give states practical advice for the implementation of Part XIII of the LOSC. The revised guide not only gives reliable guidance on the interpretation and application of the relevant provisions of the LOSC, but also provides valuable information as to the existence or non-existence of state practice in marine scientific research. For example, it noted that there was little evidence of any particular landlocked or geographically disadvantaged states being involved in marine scientific research activity,[46] and that there was little information about state practice regarding marine scientific research beyond areas of national jurisdiction at that time.[47] The information on state practice in the revised guide was gathered from the results of member state responses to questionnaire no. 3 on marine scientific research and transfer of marine technology of the Advisory Body of Experts on the Law of the Sea of the Intergovernmental Oceanographic Commission, and the experience of the group of experts who met for the purpose of revising the guide.

The question as to what kinds of activities constitute marine scientific research under the LOSC remains unanswered in the guides, however. With regard to the term 'competent international organizations', the revised guide only suggests that the term generally includes 'inter-governmental organizations which are empowered by their constituting instruments or other rules to undertake, coordinate, or promote and facilitate the development and conduct of marine scientific research', by referring to the list of organizations provided in Annex VIII to the LOSC.[48] However, it is noteworthy that, in the part related to international cooperation, the revised guide recognizes informal forms of international cooperation, as follows:

> [M]any non-governmental organizations, including professional societies, also facilitate cooperation in marine scientific research. States, through their formal or informal participation in these organizations and negotiation of bilateral and regional partnerships to address marine scientific issues of common interest, are also building capacity for a better understanding of the oceans' environment.[49]

On the question of marine scientific research, in relation to Part XII of the LOSC, the revised guide clarifies the content of the LOSC. By explicitly stating that the provisions of Part XII apply to the conduct of marine scientific research,[50] the guide suggests that environmental impact assessments may be required under national regulations.[51] From an example of state

45 DOALOS Guide (n 21), iii and v.
46 ibid 30.
47 ibid 32.
48 ibid 7.
49 ibid 27–28.
50 ibid 21.
51 ibid 31.

practice relating to the undertaking of marine scientific research in marine protected areas, and in light of the trends of increasing designation of offshore marine protected areas by coastal states, the guide recommends that researching states should bear such constraints in mind when conducting marine scientific research.[52] Thus, while the guides have no formal status under international law, the information and analysis contained therein may assist in the interpretation and application of LOSC provisions.

12.3.1.2 Intergovernmental Oceanographic Commission of the United Nations Educational, Scientific and Cultural Organization

The Intergovernmental Oceanographic Commission (IOC) of the United Nations Educational, Scientific and Cultural Organization (UNESCO) was established in 1960,[53] and has 150 state parties, as of 2020. The IOC is recognized as a competent international organization, for the purposes of Parts XIII and XIV of the LOSC.[54] The IOC promotes international cooperation, and coordinates programmes in marine scientific research, and in the transfer of marine technology, as well as supporting its member states to build their scientific and institutional capacity in implementing Parts XIII and XIV of the LOSC.

The IOC contributes to building general criteria and guidelines in marine scientific research and the transfer of technology. For example, the IOC Advisory Body of Experts on the Law of the Sea, established in 1997, adopted guidelines for the legal regulation of Argo profiling float deployments on the high seas.[55] The Argo floats project is a pilot project within the Global Ocean Data Assimilation Experiment, being a part of the Global Ocean Observing System (GOOS). The project collects and shares data on the temperature and salinity of the seawater, contributing to understanding the effects of climate change on the oceans, and estimating possible changes to the oceans in the future. Even though the project was endorsed by the Fourth Conference of the Parties to the United Nations Framework Convention on Climate Change, the efforts to regulate the project under the guidelines raised controversies as to whether the deployment of Argo floats is to be governed by Part XIII of the LOSC.[56]

The IOC Advisory Board of Experts, further, published the IOC Criteria and Guidelines on the Transfer of Marine Technology in 2005. In the criteria and guidelines, marine technology was defined as 'instruments, equipment, vessels, processes and methodologies required to produce and use knowledge to improve the *study and understanding of the nature and resources of the ocean and coastal areas*'.[57] In 2007, the IOC adopted a procedure for the

[52] ibid.

[53] The IOC was established as a mechanism to facilitate the development of the International Indian Ocean Expedition (IIOE), the largest multinational research endeavour in oceanography at that time.

[54] Rothwell and Stephens, The International Law of the Sea (n 18) 352. The Intergovernmental Oceanographic Commission of UNESCO is listed as one of the 'competent or relevant international organizations' of LOSC under the list provided by the Division for Ocean Affairs and the Law of the Sea of the Office of Legal Affairs at the United Nations: DOALOS, Law of the Sea Bulletin no 31 (1996) 79–80.

[55] The 'Argo floats' project is explained as 'an international program that collects information from inside the ocean using a fleet of robotic instruments that drift with the ocean currents and move up and down between the surface and a mid-water level.... The data that Argo collects describes the temperature and salinity of the water and some of the floats measure other properties that describe the biology/chemistry of the ocean'. See, further, Argo, 'About' <https://argo.ucsd.edu/about/> accessed 22 January 2021.

[56] Aurora Mateos and Montserrat Gorina-Ysern, 'Climate Change and Guidelines for Argo Profiling Float Deployment on the High Seas' (2010) 14(8) ASIL 8.

[57] Intergovernmental Oceanographic Commission, 'IOC Criteria and Guidelines on the Transfer of Marine Technology' (2005) IOC/INF-1203 9 (emphasis added). See, further, Techera, in Chapter 13 of this volume.

application of Article 247 of the LOSC on special procedures regarding research projects under the auspices of, or undertaken by, international organizations.[58] Article 247 leaves discretion to each organization to adopt its own internal procedure, on the basis of its own constituent instrument and any relevant rules adopted by the organization, in conducting marine scientific research under Part XIII of the LOSC.[59] Informal lawmaking, thus, provides an opportunity to elaborate on this LOSC provision.

Moreover, the IOC coordinates capacity-building programmes in areas related to scientific research. Such programmes are not intended to be lawmaking, but they can be seen as contributing to the fulfilment of the obligations relating to international cooperation stipulated under the LOSC. Nonetheless, it was on the IOC's initiative that the UN General Assembly declared, in 2017, the UN Decade of Ocean Science for Sustainable Development, for 2021 to 2030.[60]

The purpose of the Decade is to achieve the 2030 Agenda for Sustainable Development,[61] particularly Goal 14 on the conservation and sustainable use of the ocean and its resources, by strengthening partnerships among all communities.[62] The Decade calls upon the scientific community, policymakers, the private sector, and civil society to work together to ensure the sustainable development of the ocean. The Decade is designed to facilitate global communication and mutual learning across research and stakeholder communities, and to mobilize such partnerships to assist states—especially small island developing states, and the least developed countries—with limited capacity.

An example of such collaboration is the drafting of 'Ocean Decade—Arctic Action Plan', in which all relevant actors from governments, businesses, science communities, and the public, from both Arctic and non-Arctic states, were encouraged to discuss existing challenges, and to formulate proposals for actions to be taken in support of the Ocean Decade.[63] Another example of implementing the Decade is the partnership platform created by the IOC and the DOALOS.[64] Although formal lawmaking arising out of the Ocean Decade is not envisaged, the 2030 Agenda for Sustainable Development itself can be regarded as a form of informal law,[65] and the Decade provides a vehicle for informal lawmaking processes by helping to shape expectations across communities.

[58] Intergovernmental Oceanographic Commission, 'Procedure for the Application of Article 247 of UNCLOS by the Intergovernmental Oceanographic Commission of UNESCO—Marine Scientific Research: A Guide to the Implementation of the Relevant Provisions of UNCLOS' IOC/INF-1222 (2007).

[59] ibid 9.

[60] UN Doc A/RES/72/73 (5 December 2017).

[61] Transforming our World: The 2030 Agenda for Sustainable Development, UN Doc A/RES/70/1 (21 October 2015).

[62] In particular, SDG Target 14.a calls on states to '[i]ncrease scientific knowledge, develop research capacity and transfer marine technology, taking into account the Intergovernmental Oceanographic Commission Criteria and Guidelines on the Transfer of Marine Technology, in order to improve ocean health and to enhance the contribution of marine biodiversity to the development of developing countries, in particular small island developing States and least developed countries'.

[63] See Ocean Decade 2021–2030 <https://www.oceandecade.dk> accessed 8 May 2021.

[64] See UN, 'Promote and Facilitate the Conduct of Marine Scientific Research (MSR) under the United Nations Convention on the Law of the Sea (UNCLOS)' <https://sustainabledevelopment.un.org/partnership/?p = 7819> accessed 8 May 2021.

[65] For more discussions on Sustainable Development Goals (SDGs), see Telesetsky, in Chapter 14 of this volume.

12.3.1.3 International Seabed Authority

The International Seabed Authority (ISA or Authority) facilitates international cooperation among states carrying out marine scientific research in the Area, developing states, and technologically less-developed states. It does so both by coordinating marine scientific research in the Area, and disseminating the results of such research. Article 143 of the LOSC stipulates that the Authority is to develop international programmes in which states participate to promote international cooperation in marine scientific research. Such programmes are organized for the benefit of developing states and technologically less- developed states, in order to strengthen their research capabilities, to train their personnel and the personnel of the Authority in the techniques and applications of research, and to foster the employment of their qualified personnel in research in the Area.

The ISA launched the DeepData database in 2019, which gathers all deep seabed-related data submitted and collected by contractors through their exploration activities. The database contains biological, physical, and geochemical parameters of the marine ecosystems from the seafloor to the ocean surface, including maps, photographs, videos, graphics, and relevant publications in peer-reviewed journals.[66] Sharing the results of marine scientific research through the database helps the ISA to regulate activities in the Area for the benefit of humankind, and to protect the marine environment at the same time. The database itself is, of course, not an informal agreement, but establishing and operating the database is a process towards the implementation of the ISA's obligations under the LOSC, for which certain informal rulemaking is necessary as to the protection of the data, and the procedures on how to use the database.

The ISA developed a Draft Action Plan on Marine Scientific Research in 2020, with a view to implementing the 2017 UN Decade of Ocean Science for Sustainable Development.[67] The Draft Action Plan includes a set of strategies, and serves as a tool for coordinated action among international organizations. As with the capacity-building programmes of the IOC, the Draft Action Plan may not constitute an informal agreement, but it offers a vehicle for informal lawmaking in the future.

12.3.2 Extending Formal Law for the Participation of Non-state Actors in Marine Scientific Research

The practice of the Arctic states offers a unique example of defining what constitutes 'scientific activities', and allowing participation of non-state actors from the non-contracting parties under a formal agreement. The governments of Canada, Denmark, Finland, Iceland, Norway, the Russian Federation, Sweden, and the United States of America signed the Agreement on Enhancing International Arctic Scientific Cooperation in 2017.[68] The agreement facilitates access by scientists of the eight Arctic governments to Arctic areas that each government has identified, including entry and exit of persons, equipment, and materials;

[66] See ISA, 'Marine Scientific Research' <https://www.isa.org.jm/marine-scientific-research> accessed 22 January 2021.

[67] ISA, 'Action Plan of the International Seabed Authority in Support of the United Nations Decade of Ocean Science for Sustainable Development', 26 May 2020, ISA Doc ISBA/A/26/4.

[68] Agreement on Enhancing International Arctic Scientific Cooperation (signed 11 May 2017, entered into force 23 May 2018) <http://hdl.handle.net/11374/1916> accessed 26 July 2021.

access to research infrastructure and facilities; and access to data. The agreement also calls for the parties to promote education, career development and training opportunities, and encourages activities associated with traditional and local knowledge.

The agreement adopts a very broad definition of 'science activities' as 'efforts to advance understanding of the Arctic through scientific research, monitoring and assessment'.[69] These activities include:

> planning and implementing scientific research projects and programs, expeditions, observations, monitoring initiatives, surveys, modelling, and assessments; training personnel; planning, organizing and executing scientific seminars, symposia, conferences, workshops, and meetings; collecting, processing, analyzing, and sharing scientific data, ideas, results, methods, experiences, and traditional and local knowledge; developing sampling methodologies and protocols; preparing publications; and developing, implementing, and using research support logistics and research infrastructure.[70]

These activities are not limited to activities taking place under the jurisdiction of the contracting parties to the agreement. They include science activities by the non-contracting states and their scientists.

While the Agreement is open only to the eight Arctic states, the parties have the discretion to extend benefits under the agreement to noncontracting parties, including Arctic Council observer states, when they cooperate with Arctic states.[71] In the Agreement, participants are defined as 'the Parties' scientific and technological departments and agencies, research centers, universities and colleges, and *contractors, grantees and other partners acting with or on behalf of any Party or Parties*, involved in Scientific Activities under this Agreement'.[72] From the negotiating history of the agreement, this definition may be understood to include research institutes and scientists of non-contracting parties to the agreement, irrespective of their nationalities or their places of establishment, on the condition that they cooperate with the parties to the agreement.[73] Shibata argues that the agreement can be regarded as 'a unique implementing agreement at a regional level', under Article 243 of the LOSC, which requires states and competent international organizations to cooperate to create favourable conditions for the conduct of marine scientific research.[74]

This unique practice can be considered as a form of informal lawmaking, as standards are being set through the articulation of the meaning of scientific activities, and benefits are given to participants from non-contracting parties to the agreement. The rights and duties enshrined in the agreement are not formally guaranteed under international law, because the agreement does not confer on the non-contracting parties the right to claim such benefits, on behalf of their nationals, that the Arctic states may give their nationals.[75] Instead,

[69] ibid, art 1.
[70] ibid.
[71] Senior Arctic Officials' Report to Ministers, Fairbanks, Alaska, United States (11 May 2017) 79.
[72] Agreement on Enhancing International Arctic Scientific Cooperation (n 68) art 1 (emphasis added).
[73] Akiho Shibata, 'The Arctic Science Cooperation Agreement: A Perspective from Non-Arctic Actors' in Akiho Shibata, Leilei Zou, Nikolas Sellheim, and Marzia Scopelliti (eds), *Emerging Legal Orders in the Arctic: The Role of Non-Arctic Actors* (Routledge 2019) 218–19.
[74] ibid 215.
[75] ibid 220.

there is informal regulation of scientific activity beyond the formal rights and duties enshrined in the agreement.

12.3.3 Influence of Voluntary Standard-setting by Non-state Actors on Informal Lawmaking

The actual conduct of marine scientific research is not limited to states themselves, but also includes natural or juridical persons under their jurisdiction, such as individual scientists, research institutes, and corporations. Activities of these non-state actors go beyond inter-state cooperation, as there are no borders in science.

Informal lawmaking by international organizations, or by treaty bodies, is often influenced by voluntary standards developed by non-state actors. As one example, the commission established under the Convention for the Protection of the Marine Environment of the North-east Atlantic (OSPAR) adopted the OSPAR Code of Conduct for Responsible Marine Research in the Deep Seas and High Seas of the OSPAR Maritime Area in 2008. The code of conduct is based on the Statement of Commitment to Responsible Research Practices at Deep-sea Hydrothermal Vents, issued by a non-profit organization called InterRidge, and an unofficial translation of the German Marine Consortium KDM's Commitment to Responsible Marine Research. The code of conduct was developed through the work of the OSPAR Biodiversity Committee, in consultation with a number of deep-sea scientists and experts. The code of conduct further incorporates comments from the International Council for the Exploration of the Sea (ICES), and elements of the International Research Ship Operators' Meeting Code of Conduct for Marine Scientific Research Vessels, proposed by the Marine Board of the European Science Foundation.[76]

Although it is often said that assessing the effectiveness and impact of such codes is very difficult,[77] the role of standard setting by non-state actors can be evaluated as a process-oriented approach that reflects the fact that formal laws are not the only means to effectively control various activities at sea. Formal laws often leave grey areas, due to uncertainties at the time of drafting, and, as noted previously, science and technologies may advance much faster than the revision of existing formal laws. Recent studies, therefore, increasingly focus on the standard-setting activities of both state and non-state actors, in connection with the notion of global governance.[78] From the perspective of global governance, regulatory tools include 'not only formal laws, but also informal rules and standards involving all societal actors and expanding to all levels of governance, from local, sectoral, public to global governance'.[79] Standard setting by non-state actors becomes relevant to global governance when the standards are complied with, and the non-state actor's authority to set standards may be a key factor in generating effectiveness.[80] Voluntary measures adopted by non-state

[76] See Introduction, OSPAR Code of Conduct for Responsible Marine Research in the Deep Seas and High Seas of the OSPAR Maritime Area, OSPAR 08/24/1, Annex 6, 2008-1 (24 January 2008).

[77] Harriet Harden-Davies, 'The Regulation of Marine Scientific Research: Addressing Challenges, Advancing Knowledge' in Robin Warner and Stuart Kaye (eds), *Routledge Handbook of Maritime Regulation and Enforcement* (Routledge 2016) 219.

[78] See, generally, Anne Peters, Lucy Koechlin, Till Förster, and Gretta Fenner Zinkernagel, *Non-state Actors as Standard Setters* (CUP 2009).

[79] ibid 17–18.

[80] ibid 24–25.

actors in marine scientific research, therefore, may become an important source of informal lawmaking when they induce compliance among relevant participants.

12.4 Conclusions

Stephens and Rothwell presented a realistic view on marine scientific research in the LOSC, as follows: 'while the LOSC places significant emphasis on the desirability of [marine scientific research], for the most part the LOSC has played a relatively low-key role in facilitating scientific research or in regulating its conduct. Instead, many of the most significant developments in recent decades have been outside the LOSC'.[81] The question remains as to how these developments outside the LOSC can be linked to the LOSC, without creating fragmentation. While fragmented regulatory mechanisms in international law, on marine scientific research, remain, informal lawmaking of a non-binding or voluntary nature plays an important role in improving ocean governance across different sectors. From this perspective, the examples of informal lawmaking and its processes in marine scientific research, as examined in this chapter, and the formal laws, including the LOSC, do not necessarily conflict with each other. Those informal lawmaking and its processes examples do not exist completely outside the LOSC either. Informal lawmaking under the auspices of international organizations aims to implement obligations under the LOSC, such as the duty to cooperate, by virtue of the reference to 'competent international organizations' in the LOSC's text. Informal lawmaking may exist under the purview of formal law, as in the case of the Agreement on Enhancing International Arctic Scientific Cooperation. Informal standard setting by non-state actors may promptly supplement gaps that emerge between the LOSC and scientific and technological innovations. Informal solutions, if accompanied by certain conditions, may become immediately effective for individual scientists, scientific communities, and corporations, which is particularly important in protecting and preserving the marine environment. These solutions may provide the impetus for informal lawmaking in the future as observed in the case of OSPAR Code of Conduct.

A question remains as to how to assess the disparities of state practice in marine scientific research in the context of the law of the sea. Treves writes that, '[a]lthough the principle of consent of the coastal State is by and large now a part of or in the process of becoming part of customary international law, most of the detailed provisions spelled out in the UN Convention on the Law of the Sea are not, and because of their precision, are unlikely to become so'.[82] Gragl also points to the fact that a lack of state practice exists with regard to provisions relating to the rights of landlocked and geographically disadvantaged states, rules on dispute settlement, and the period of notice and implied consent.[83] The impact of any informal lawmaking effort may be limited if there is insufficient engagement across a sufficiently broad range of stakeholders.

[81] Stephens and Rothwell, Marine Scientific Research (n 8) 581. The *Whaling in the Antarctic* case and other treaty regimes such the 1996 London Protocol and the deep seabed mining system administered by the ISA are noted by the authors as developments outside the LOSC, which imply processes for increasing oversight in marine scientific research.

[82] Treves (n 24) para 16.

[83] Gragl (n 4) 422.

Nonetheless, it is readily apparent that states are no longer the only subjects involved in the making, and implementation processes, of international law. The undefined or imprecise terms found in Part XIII of the LOSC resulted from the UNCLOS III negotiations, and do not prevent a process of international lawmaking where formal and informal laws interact, and diverse actors participate towards better ocean governance. Concepts of global governance may better account for the engagement of diverse actors, the development of shared understandings of critical terms, and the evolving and responsive regulatory regime for marine scientific research. Considering the rapid changes in the current global environment, Part XIII of the LOSC should not only be perceived and implemented in relation to the established consent regime, but should also be interpreted progressively, to better account for the diverse formal and informal lawmaking that is being undertaken in intergovernmental, non-governmental, and multi-stakeholder fora.

13

The Role of Informal Lawmaking in Facilitating Marine Technology Transfer and Data Sharing

Erika Techera

13.1 Introduction

From the creation of the earliest fish hooks[1] to the development of deep-sea aquatic drones,[2] human ingenuity has continuously been applied to the ocean environment. Law can provide invaluable frameworks to take advantage of the opportunities that new marine technologies offer, and to manage the risks they create.[3] Yet, new technologies are being developed at an ever-increasing rate, challenging law to keep pace with this innovation.[4] Against this backdrop, this chapter explores how the law of the sea accounts for marine technologies and related data. It commences by highlighting the range of technologies and technological data related to oceans, and then outlines the relevant provisions of the United Nations Convention on the Law of the Sea (LOSC)[5] that provide a foundation of obligations with respect to the use, development, and transfer of marine technologies, as well as access to, and sharing of, data. Thereafter, the role and effect of informal lawmaking on technologies is examined. The particular focus is on the transfer of technologies and sharing of technological data: issues where implementation has tended to lag behind other areas.[6] The final two sections analyse the various ways that informal law has been utilized in these areas, the strengths and weaknesses of these contributions, and the areas in which opportunities remain for enhanced informal lawmaking in the future.

[1] The earliest definitive evidence of fishing technology is the fish hooks that were discovered in Timor-Leste, estimated to be 42,000 years old: Charles Q Choi, 'World's Oldest Fish Hooks Show Early Humans Fished Deep Sea' (*Live Science*, 24 November 2011) <https://www.livescience.com/17186-oldest-fish-hooks-early-humans.html>accessed 2 October 2020. It is likely that much earlier tools existed, though evidence of them has been lost in the mists of time.

[2] European Commission Joint Research Centre, 'New Technologies in the Ocean Energy Sector' (20 October 2018) <https://phys.org/news/2018-10-technologies-ocean-energy-sector.html> accessed 2 October 2020; Michele Debczak, '7 Technologies that are Revolutionizing Ocean Exploration' (*Mental Floss*, 9 March 2018) <https://www.mentalfloss.com/article/534827/technologies-that-are-revolutionizing-ocean-exploration> accessed 2 October 2020.

[3] 'New Technology Allows Fleets to Double Fishing Capacity—and Deplete Fish Stocks Faster' (*Science Daily*, 16 September 2019) <https://www.sciencedaily.com/releases/2019/09/190916160819.htm> accessed 2 October 2020.

[4] Erika Techera, 'Is Environmental Law Keeping Pace with Innovation?' (2019) 34(1) Aust Envtl Rev 8.

[5] United Nations Convention on the Law of the Sea (adopted 10 December 1982, entered into force 16 November 1994) 1833 UNTS 3 (hereafter 'LOSC').

[6] Elisa Morgera and Mara Ntona, 'Linking Small-scale Fishers to International Obligations on Marine Technology Transfer' (2018) 93 Mar Pol'y 295; Harriet Harden-Davies and Paul Snelgrove, 'Science Collaboration for Capacity Building: Advancing Technology Transfer through a Treaty for Biodiversity Beyond National Jurisdiction' (2020) 7 Front Mar Sci 1.

Erika Techera, *The Role of Informal Lawmaking in Facilitating Marine Technology Transfer and Data Sharing*
In: *Unconventional Lawmaking in the Law of the Sea*. Edited by: Natalie Klein, Oxford University Press.
DOI: 10.1093/oso/9780192897824.003.0013

The LOSC does not define 'data', 'technology', or 'technology transfer'. For the purposes of this chapter, 'marine technologies' are defined as 'instruments, equipment, vessels, processes and methodologies' used in the maritime domain.[7] The focus, therefore, is squarely upon technologies themselves, rather than marine scientific research more broadly, or the provision of technical assistance, although it is acknowledged that there are clear links between these.[8] Marine technologies have widespread application and include, or are associated with, fishing gear, geoengineering projects, naval architecture, navigational instrument design, seabed mining equipment, remote sensing, and Earth observation devices, as well as data collection, processing, and analysis using tools such as artificial intelligence, machine learning, and algorithms.[9] Clearly, the development and utilization of marine technologies is a mammoth topic, given the range of human activities in the oceans, and innovations employed within them.

This chapter explores a subset of these technologies by focusing specifically on fishing. This fisheries lens is appropriate for three main reasons. First, fisheries regulation is an area where the LOSC includes explicit legal provisions that provide a firm foundation of formal law upon which informal law has been built. Secondly, there is a long history of technological developments, and regulatory responses, in the fisheries sector, providing a rich array of examples for analysis. Finally, many fish stocks are now fully utilized or overfished, resulting, in part, from the use of marine technologies, and data availability on probable fish stock locations. Marine technologies, and data in particular, are routinely being applied to assess and better manage these stocks. Remote sensing, information communication, and data processing technologies are increasingly being deployed for monitoring and enforcement, including to address the perennial challenge of illegal fishing. Fisheries governance, therefore, provides a valuable lens through which to examine the utilization, development and transfer of marine technology, and access to, and sharing of, data. This chapter is not intended to be an exhaustive examination of the legal governance of all fishing-related marine technologies, but, rather, the purpose is to highlight the spectrum of approaches, instruments, actors, and goals that have resulted in informal laws that add to the provisions of the LOSC and other treaty law. This chapter demonstrates that informal law has played, and continues to play, a vital supporting role in facilitating the use, development, and transfer of new technologies and their outputs.

13.2 The Marine Technology Landscape

Marine technologies are relevant to the fishing sector in a variety of ways. Most importantly, they are used to enhance socio-economic outcomes and commercial efficiencies. For example, innovations in ship design and advanced navigation equipment allow vessels to

[7] UNESCO IOC Advisory Body of Experts on the Law of the Sea, 'IOC Criteria and Guidelines on the Transfer of Marine Technology (CGTMT)' (hereafter 'IOC Guidelines') 9. Notably, the LOSC does not define 'marine technology' or 'fishing technologies'.

[8] Marine scientific research is the subject of Part XIII of the LOSC, and technical assistance features in several other articles of the LOSC: arts 202, 203, 266, 269, and 274. For discussion on informal lawmaking and marine scientific research, see Kojima, in Chapter 12 of this volume.

[9] Pierre Girard and Thomas Du Payrat, 'Issue Paper: An Inventory of New Technologies in Fisheries' (GGSD Forum, OECD, Paris, 2017) <https://www.oecd.org/greengrowth/GGSD_2017_Issue%20Paper_New%20technologies%20in%20Fisheries_WEB.pdf> accessed 2 October 2020.

operate in close to freezing conditions and extreme weather settings; echo locators and fish aggregation devices, along with netting technologies, facilitate larger harvests from deeper waters; and advances in factory ships, freezer technologies, and offshore floating processing facilities allow catches to be more effectively managed from net to market.[10] These technologies involve multiple fields, from naval architecture to remote sensing, and information technology to materials science. The purpose of highlighting these areas is to illuminate the extent of the relevant disciplines and sectors, and, therefore, the range of actors involved in marine technologies. Significantly, the marine technologies listed above are focused on maximizing catches of wild fish with the least fishing effort, with wholesale use of such equipment often resulting in indiscriminate harvests, significant wastage of by-catch, and incidental marine environmental damage.[11] Interestingly, on land, technological developments have also focused on efficiencies, but technologies have assisted farmers to generate higher yields in more targeted ways, at less cost, in smaller land areas, and utilizing fewer resources.[12] The use of fishing technologies often poses greater ecological risks than similar terrestrial activities, because they can lead to overharvesting of target species, negative impacts on non-target animals, and degradation of habitats, including vulnerable marine ecosystems. Effective legal responses are vital in managing the marine technologies to maximize the benefits of their use, while also minimizing specific impacts and risks. Given the interconnectedness of ocean areas, with significant movement of marine species and vessels across jurisdictional boundaries, harmonized responses are needed to establish global standards and best-practice legal frameworks.

In addition to addressing current opportunities and risks, new technologies are being developed that could enhance marine protection and facilitate more sustainable utilization of wild fish stocks. These include, for example, advanced net design that discriminates between target and non-target species,[13] vessel tracking systems and remote sensing technologies to monitor legitimate fishing activities and detect illegal fishing and transhipments,[14] and on-board cameras and smart weighing systems to accurately calculate fish catches.[15] Some of these marine technologies can be deployed to assist with marine research, to learn more about the changing ocean and its resources, and to provide greater certainty about the status and health of fish stocks.[16] Other technologies, such as information communication

[10] ibid.

[11] For an overview, see Jacob Hill, 'Environmental Consequences of Fishing Practices' (*Environmental Science*) <https://www.environmentalscience.org/environmental-consequences-fishing-practices> accessed 2 October 2020.

[12] See Geoffrey Ling and Blake Bextine, 'Precision Farming Increases Crop Yields' (*Scientific American*, 26 June 2017) <https://www.scientificamerican.com/article/precision-farming/> accessed 2 October 2020. cf Martin Føre and others, 'Precision Fish Farming: A New Framework to Improve Production in Aquaculture' (2018) 173 Bio Eng 176, 176–193.

[13] Roger Harrabin, 'Can New Technology Save Fish?' (*BBC News*, 25 February 2013) <https://www.bbc.com/news/science-environment-21500701> accessed 2 October 2020.

[14] 'Transparent Transhipping: Detecting Illegal Fishing with Satellite Data' (*Ship Technology*, 20 August 2018) <https://www.ship-technology.com/features/global-fishing-watch/> accessed 2 October 2020.

[15] Darcy Bradley and others, 'Opportunities to Improve Fisheries Management through Innovative Technology and Advanced Data Systems' (2019) 20(3) Fish Fish 564, 564–83.

[16] See, eg Digna T Rueda-Roa, Tal Ezer, and Frank E Muller-Karger, 'Description and Mechanisms of the Mid-year Upwelling in the Southern Caribbean Sea from Remote Sensing and Local Data' (2018) 6(2) J Mar Sci Eng 36. These uses of marine technologies are not new, and have been employed for twenty years: Michael JA Butler, M-C Mouchot, V Barale, and C LeBlanc, *The Application of Remote Sensing Technology to Marine Fisheries: An Introductory Manual* (FAO Fisheries Technical Paper 295, 1988); Arthur P Cracknell (ed), *Remote Sensing Applications in Marine Science and Technology* (Springer 1983).

and data processing tools—including blockchain, algorithms, machine learning in the analysis of fisheries and oceans data, and use of artificial intelligence—have significant potential to enhance compliance and enforcement.[17] These technologies are largely being developed in the global North and, if the risks and rewards of these advances are to be tackled, cooperation and collaboration with developing states is critical. These developments emphasize the need for legal frameworks to facilitate the sustainable development and use of marine technologies, address potential risks, and provide a vehicle for sharing knowledge, expertise, and data with the global South. As will be seen below, both formal and informal law exists in all of these areas.

Hard law, in the international context, takes the form of treaties and other binding legal agreements between states, as well as customary international law. Binding laws are needed to set standards and provide certainty and clarity in relation to rights and obligations that are legally enforceable. Informal law comes in an infinite variety of forms.[18] Informal law, with respect to marine technology, includes United Nations General Assembly (UNGA) resolutions, international plans of action, codes of conduct, guidelines, targets, and indicators. Some commentators have postulated that informal law is superior to hard law in many respects, particularly given its ability to respond more quickly to the rapidly evolving technological landscape, to involve end users, to provide flexible, non-binding guidance, and to communicate in much more user-friendly formats.[19] Informal legal approaches do have limitations, though, and have attracted scholarly criticism.[20] Less supportive commentators argue that informal law is 'regulatory dark matter',[21] with quasi-legal status but little in the way of procedural safeguards, and that, in large volumes, it can add to complexity and uncertainty.[22]

For the purposes of this chapter, it is clear that informal law can play three key roles in the global governance of marine technologies. First, it can be additive, filling gaps in the law of the sea and international fisheries regulation.[23] Sometimes this role can be a stepping stone to hard law, but in other cases informal law can achieve goals without becoming legally binding.[24] Secondly, informal law can also 'thicken' the hard law by providing much needed

[17] Ketil Malde and others, 'Machine Intelligence and the Data-driven Future of Marine Science' (2019) 77(4) ICES J Mar Sci 1274, 1274–85; CSIRO, 'Artificial Intelligence' <https://www.csiro.au/showcase/ai%20> accessed 2 October 2020.

[18] RR Baxter, 'International Law in "Her Infinite Variety"' (1980) 29(4) ICLQ 549, 549–66.

[19] Richard Morrison, 'Limits of "Soft Law" Approach to Tech Regulation' (*Competitive Enterprise Institute*, 9 August 2019) <https://cei.org/blog/limits-soft-law-approach-tech-regulation> accessed 2 October 2020; Mara Ntona, 'The Transfer of Marine Technology as Benefit-sharing' (*Benelex Blog*, 4 November 2015) <https://benelexblog.wordpress.com/2015/11/04/the-transfer-of-marine-technology-as-benefit-sharing/> accessed 2 October 2020. For a discussion of the benefits of soft law more generally, see Kenneth W Abbott and Duncan Snidal, 'Hard and Soft Law in International Governance' (2000) 54(3) Intl'l Org 421.

[20] See, eg Prosper Weil, 'Towards Relative Normativity in International Law?' (1983) 77(3) AJIL 413; Gregory C Shaffer and Mark A Pollack, 'Hard vs. Soft Law: Alternatives, Complements, and Antagonists in International Governance' (2010) 94(3) Minn L Rev 706.

[21] Competitive Enterprise Institute, 'Regulatory Dark Matter' <https://cei.org/content/regulatory-dark-matter> accessed 2 October 2020.

[22] Morrison (n 19). While many international informal instruments include vague and unclear wording, there are also similar examples in binding instruments where the precise requirements are difficult to determine. See, eg LOSC (n 5) art 200, which requires states to 'endeavour to participate actively in regional and global programmes'. Nevertheless, it is equally apparent that, where there is international support for the subject matter of the informal law, it can be highly effective. See, eg FAO Code of Conduct for Responsible Fisheries, discussed further below.

[23] Ulrich Fastenrath, 'Relative Normativity in International Law' (1993) 4(3) EJIL 305.

[24] See, eg FAO Code of Conduct for Responsible Fisheries, discussed further below.

detail where it is absent from the binding instrument.[25] As will be seen below, this contribution has been a fruitful area in the governance of marine technologies, where informal law has fleshed out the high-level obligations in the LOSC. Thirdly, informal law can play a broadening role by involving multiple stakeholders, beyond state actors, to expand regulatory regimes.[26] Again, examples are highlighted in the sections that follow.

This short summary highlights the need for further exploration and analysis of what formal and informal law exists to govern fishing-related marine technologies, and an examination of the broader issues that the use of these different legal approaches raises. In particular, the fisheries sector provides a rich landscape from which to draw examples of informal lawmaking related to new technologies, further justifying the focus of this chapter.[27] In relation to marine technologies, the law has tended to divide attention between the use of marine technologies and the development of new innovations and transfer of technology. Access to, and sharing of, data is considered separately. The sections that follow adopt these divisions, and outline the binding legal obligations under the LOSC and subsequent instruments, before examining the informal laws in each of these three areas. The final sections reflect upon the roles that informal law is playing, and where gaps remain that informal law might fill.

13.3 The Use of Marine Technologies for Fishing

13.3.1 The LOSC Framework

'Technology' or 'technologies' are mentioned in eighteen articles of the LOSC, but 'fisheries technologies' only once.[28] As noted above, the use of marine technologies can have negative impacts upon the marine environment, as well as benefits. The LOSC seeks to address both aspects, albeit in different ways. It requires, in Article 62, that:

> Nationals of other States fishing in the exclusive economic zone shall comply with the conservation measures and with the other terms and conditions established in the laws and regulations of the coastal State. These laws and regulations ... may relate, inter alia, to the following:
>
> (a) ... *equipment and technology relating to the fishing industry*;
>
> ...
>
> (j) ... and the *transfer of fisheries technology*, including enhancement of the coastal State's capability of undertaking fisheries research.[29]

[25] Annecoos Wiersema, 'The New International Law-makers? Conferences of the Parties to Multilateral Environmental Agreements' (2009) 31 Mich J Intl'l L 231.

[26] Abbott and Snidal (n 19). See also Hannah Cole, 'Contemporary Challenges: Globalisation, Global Interconnectedness and that "there are *not* plenty more Fish in the Sea": Fisheries, Governance and Globalisation: Is there a Relationship?' (2003) 46 Ocean Coastal Mgmt 77.

[27] See also Scanlon, in Chapter 11 of this volume.

[28] 'Technology' or 'technologies' are referred to in LOSC (n 5), arts 62(4)(a), 144, 150, 155, 170, 196, 266, 267, 268, 269, 270, 271, 272, 273, 274, 275, 276, and 277; 'fisheries technologies' are mentioned in art 62(4)(j). In this chapter, the provisions in relation to the Area and the International Seabed Authority are not explored, as they relate to non-living resource exploration and extraction.

[29] ibid, art 62(4) (emphasis added).

Article 62 of the LOSC clearly acknowledges the sovereign right of states to impose conservation measures to which licensed foreign fishers must adhere, with fishing technology and equipment as one form of payment for such rights. There is no provision, however, requiring coastal states to adopt laws relating to technology or its transfer. In terms of positive obligations, Article 61, for example, requires coastal states to maintain stocks and prevent over-exploitation of living resources in their exclusive economic zones (EEZs) through proper 'conservation and management measures', taking into account the 'best scientific evidence' available.[30] A similar provision could have been included in the LOSC, encouraging the development, and mandating the use, of best practice marine technologies. The absence of such a provision creates the opportunity for informal law to fill the gap. Article 62 also recognizes the needs of developing countries—those offering the right to fish in their EEZs—with respect to fishing technology, and serves to encourage its transfer. The provision does not directly address the use of marine technology in the fishing industry and, therefore, is not considered further here, but is explored again below.

The only place where the LOSC specifically considers the risks posed by the use of marine technologies is in Article 196. States are obliged to 'take all measures necessary to prevent, reduce and control pollution of the marine environment resulting from the use of *technologies* under their jurisdiction or control'.[31] Fishing technologies can pollute in different ways: nets and equipment can be deliberately or accidentally discarded, creating 'ghost nets' and a marine debris problem; even the most technologically advanced vessels can discharge oil and other substances into the water column; and ballast water and biofouling can introduce invasive alien species. Article 196 creates a general obligation, but the detail is absent, once again leaving the door open for informal law to 'thicken' the hard law provision. Yet, pollution is not the only issue resulting from the use of technologies. Over-exploitation of species, by-catch, damage to habitats, and degradation of the ocean environment more broadly, are also concerns. The LOSC is silent with reference to the specific use of technology in these areas, and states have only general obligations under Article 192 to 'protect and preserve the marine environment' in all maritime zones. Again, informal law has a role to play in filling the lacuna with respect to both technology and data.

The basic LOSC provisions have facilitated further hard law developments that expand upon the obligation to conserve and manage, and which do refer to fishing technologies. The most significant is the 1995 Fish Stocks Agreement (FSA), which provides that:

> In order to conserve and manage straddling fish stocks and highly migratory fish stocks, coastal States and States fishing on the high seas shall, in giving effect to their duty to cooperate in accordance with the Convention:
>
> ...
>
> (k) promote and conduct scientific research and *develop appropriate technologies in support of fishery conservation and management*;[32]

[30] ibid, art 61(2).

[31] ibid, art 196 (emphasis added).

[32] Agreement for the Implementation of the Provisions of the UN Convention on the Law of the Sea of 10 December 1982 Relating to the Conservation and Management of Straddling Fish Stocks and Highly Migratory Fish Stocks (adopted 4 August 1995, in force 11 December 2001) 34 ILM 1542 (hereafter 'FSA'), art 5 (emphasis added).

The only other relevant reference in this instrument relates to cooperation with developing states that should 'include ... assistance relating to ... *transfer of technology*',[33] with such assistance being directed towards 'monitoring, control, surveillance, compliance and enforcement, including ... *access to technology* and equipment'.[34]

Other binding international law instruments, such as the 1993 Food and Agriculture Organization of the United Nations (FAO) Agreement to Promote Compliance with International Conservation and Management Measures by Fishing Vessels on the High Seas,[35] do not explicitly refer to marine technologies and data, only requiring parties to cooperate to provide technical and other assistance to developing countries in order to fulfil their obligations.[36]

Later hard law developments have reacted to the need to control and manage damaging fishing technologies and methods. Few of these developments are global, but they are multilateral, and targeted at prohibiting the most harmful technologies. For example, the Convention for the Prohibition of Fishing with Long Driftnets in the South Pacific (Wellington Agreement) recognizes the importance of marine living resources, the damage done to stocks by pelagic drift nets, and the obligations under the LOSC.[37] It prohibits drift net fishing in the South Pacific.[38] A binding prohibition has not been adopted worldwide, although informal law has added to the legal landscape, as discussed further below.[39]

13.3.2 Informal Law and the Use of Marine Technology

It is clear that informal law has played a part in filling gaps in the LOSC framework with respect to the use and abuse of fishing technologies. A critical informal instrument that added to the LOSC provisions is the 1995 FAO Code of Conduct for Responsible Fisheries (Code of Conduct), which seeks to set international standards to ensure effective conservation, management, and development of marine living resources.[40] One of its core objectives is to 'establish principles, in accordance with the relevant rules of international law, for responsible fishing and fisheries activities, taking into account ... technological ... aspects'.[41] The needs of developing countries are specifically noted:

> States, relevant intergovernmental and non-governmental organizations and financial institutions should work for the adoption of measures to address the needs of developing

[33] ibid, art 25(2) (emphasis added).

[34] ibid, art 25(3)(c) (emphasis added).

[35] Agreement to Promote Compliance with International Conservation and Management Measures by Fishing Vessels on the High Seas (adopted 24 November 1993, in force 24 April 2003) 33 ILM 368 (hereafter 'FAO Compliance Agreement').

[36] ibid, art VII.

[37] Convention for the Prohibition of Fishing with Long Driftnets in the South Pacific (adopted 29 November 1989, in force 17 May 1991) 29 ILM 1449, Preamble.

[38] ibid, art 2.

[39] UNGA Res 44/225 (22 December 1989) UN Doc A/RES/44/225 (non-binding moratorium on the use of drift nets), and the prohibition of such nets, by 31 December 1992, in UNGA Res 46/215 (20 December 1991) UN Doc A/Res/46/215, which is still not binding, but was adopted without vote, with all states (and Taiwan) agreeing to abide by it.

[40] FAO, 'Code of Conduct for Responsible Fisheries' (Rome 1999) (hereafter 'Code of Conduct') <http://www.fao.org/3/v9878e/V9878E.pdf> accessed 2 October 2020.

[41] ibid, art 2(a).

> countries, especially in the areas of ... *technology transfer*, to develop their own fisheries as well as to participate in high seas fisheries, including access to such fisheries.[42]

The Code of Conduct stops short of setting out a list of options for inclusion in legal frameworks for technology transfer. A further article in the Code of Conduct relates to LOSC obligations to prevent marine pollution:

> States should cooperate to develop and apply technologies, materials and operational methods that minimize the loss of fishing gear and the ghost fishing effects of lost or abandoned fishing gear.[43]

Here, the Code of Conduct is much more specific. Yet, other forms of pollution, identified above, including the incidental introduction of chemicals and oil pollutants, are not referred to. This oversight may be because there is hard law in this space, yet invasive species are not mentioned either, and this is an area where binding law is limited.

The Code of Conduct further addresses the LOSC obligation to adopt conservation and management measures incorporating best scientific evidence, by requiring states to 'promote the adoption of appropriate technology, taking into account economic conditions, for the best use and care of the retained catch'.[44] Again, this is just one issue associated with conservation and management, but the Code of Conduct goes on to require that:

> States, with relevant groups from industry, should encourage the development and implementation of technologies and operational methods that reduce discards. The use of fishing gear and practices that lead to the discarding of catch should be discouraged and the use of fishing gear and practices that increase survival rates of escaping fish should be promoted.[45]

First, this provision broadens the stakeholders to include industry. Second, it envisages technologies such as turtle excluder devices (TEDs), now mandated in many domestic jurisdictions.[46] As noted above, fishing technologies in the form of nets, gear, and equipment have also been the focus of specific informal law developments. For example, the global moratorium on the use of large-scale pelagic drift nets is only contained in informal law (UNGA resolutions), and has, effectively, resulted in a ban on the use of this equipment, given its broad endorsement and support.[47] In contrast to this example is the use of bottom trawling fishing gear, the risks of which include over-harvesting of deep seas species, habitat loss, and indiscriminate taking of non-target species.[48] A series of UNGA resolutions call

[42] ibid, art 5.2 (emphasis added).

[43] ibid, art 8.4.6.

[44] ibid, art 8.4.4.

[45] ibid, art 8.4.5.

[46] See, eg US Code of Federal Regulations Title 50 Part 223 – §223.205 Sea Turtles and §223.207 Approved TEDs; NOAA, 'Turtle Excluder Device Regulations' <https://www.fisheries.noaa.gov/southeast/bycatch/turtle-excluder-device-regulations> accessed 2 October 2020. TEDs are also mandatory in some Australian prawn fisheries: AFMA, 'Turtle Excluder Devices' <https://www.afma.gov.au/environment-and-research/reducing-bycatch/bycatch-reduction-devices/turtle-excluder-devices> accessed 2 October 2020.

[47] UNGA Res 46/215 (20 December 1991) UN Doc A/RES/46/215.

[48] Lissette Victorero and others, 'Out of Sight, But within Reach: A Global History of Bottom-trawled Deep-sea Fisheries From >400 m Depth' (2018) 5 Front Mar Sci 1.

on high seas fishing states and regional fisheries management organizations (RFMOs) to take action to protect vulnerable marine ecosystems from destructive fishing practices, including bottom trawl fishing.[49] Yet, the practice has not ceased, and subsequent calls for a permanent ban have not been heeded. This example of restrictions on the use of marine technologies remaining informal shows how their effectiveness is limited by the non-binding nature of the provisions. In the case of bottom trawling, there can be some beneficial as well as detrimental impacts, and, therefore, it is likely that the complexity of the issue has impeded further binding legal developments.[50]

In relation to fishing operations, the Code of Conduct makes it clear that 'States should not link access to markets to the purchase of specific technology'.[51] This innovative approach seeks to expand the law to cover a new issue—markets—and to reduce the risks of any perverse outcomes from positively requiring, or subsidizing, the use of certain technologies.

Another area where informal law has played additive and broadening roles is in addressing the critical issue of illegal, unreported, and unregulated (IUU) fishing. This issue provides a plethora of examples of informal lawmaking,[52] with specific references to marine technologies and subsequent data-sharing arrangements. The FAO International Plan of Action to Prevent, Deter and Eliminate Illegal, Unreported and Unregulated Fishing (IPOA–IUU) expands upon the Code of Conduct. This instrument is, essentially, a global plan of action on IUU fishing, with a strong focus on enforcement. It calls upon states to adopt national legislation addressing 'evidentiary standards and admissibility including, as appropriate, the use of electronic evidence and new technologies'.[53] The IPOA–IUU also encourages cooperation to deter IUU fishing through, inter alia, 'transferring expertise and technology',[54] and the development of monitoring, control, and surveillance, including 'promoting ... real time catch and vessel monitoring systems, [and] other new technologies'.[55] The IPOA–IUU, in addition to the LOSC, the FAO Compliance Agreement, the FSA, and the Code of Conduct, led to the development of further informal law, as well as hard law: the Model Scheme on Port State Measures to Combat IUU Fishing,[56] and the subsequent, binding Port State Measures Agreement.[57] In this sense, the informal law has filled gaps in the hard law, and has also been a stepping stone to the development of binding law.

[49] UNGA Res 59/25 (17 November 2004) UN Doc A/Res/59/25; UNGA Res 61/105 (8 December 2006) UN Doc A/Res/61/105; UNGA Res 64/72 (4 December 2009) UN Doc A/Res/64/72; UNGA Res 66/68 (6 December 2011) UN Doc A/Res/66/68.

[50] Some research points to increased fish production where sanded seabeds are stirred up, while in other (reef) environments, significant habitats can be lost: Imants Priede, 'A Bottom-trawling Ban could See Fish Stocks Fall' (*The Conversation*, 6 September 2013) <https://theconversation.com/a-bottom-trawling-ban-could-see-fish-stocks-fall-17807> accessed 19 March 2021.

[51] Code of Conduct (n 40) art 11.2.8.

[52] See, further, Scanlon, in Chapter 11 of this volume.

[53] FAO, 'International Plan of Action to Prevent, Deter and Eliminate Illegal, Unreported and Unregulated Fishing' (Rome 2001) (hereafter 'IPOA–IUU') , para 17 <http://www.fao.org/3/y1224e/Y1224E.pdf> accessed 5 March 2021.

[54] ibid, para 28.4

[55] ibid, para 80.7.

[56] FAO, 'Model Scheme on Port State Measures to Combat Illegal, Unreported and Unregulated Fishing' (2007) <http://www.fao.org/3/a0985t/a0985t00.pdf> accessed 2 October 2020.

[57] Agreement on Port State Measures to Prevent, Deter and Eliminate Illegal, Unreported and Unregulated Fishing (adopted 22 November 2009, entered into force 5 June 2016) 2167 UNTS 3 (hereafter 'Port State Measures Agreement').

13.4 Development and Transfer of Marine Technologies

13.4.1 The LOSC Framework

Development and transfer of technologies are dealt with together, under Part XIV of the LOSC. This Part contains much more expansive provisions than the use and protection measures, including provisions on maximizing the benefits of new technologies through sharing, and facilitating the means by which they might be developed. The more detailed provisions on development and sharing versus those on use and protection, are, perhaps, a reflection of attitudes towards progress, technology, and scientific innovation, which are generally seen as beneficial.[58]

The LOSC seeks to support marine technologies in different ways: (1) by encouraging the transfer of existing technology;[59] and (2) by facilitating future marine scientific research.[60] Particular emphasis is placed on cooperation through international organizations,[61] and the establishment of regional centres for technological research.[62]

The overarching LOSC provision requires that:

> 1. States, directly or through competent international organizations, shall cooperate in accordance with their capabilities to *promote actively the development and transfer of... marine technology.*
>
> ...
>
> 3. States shall endeavour to foster favourable economic and *legal conditions for the transfer of marine technology* for the benefit of all parties concerned on an equitable basis.[63]

This latter provision creates a specific role for law in technology transfer, yet little international law has emerged in response. Obligations extend to promoting the development of:

> *technological capacity* of States ... with regard to the exploration, exploitation, conservation and management of marine resources, the protection and preservation of the marine environment, marine scientific research and other activities ... with a view to accelerating the social and economic development of the developing States.[64]

This provision is broadly worded, and encompasses the opportunities and risks posed by marine technologies. It is the only article in the LOSC that explicitly refers to assisting developing states with technologies to protect and preserve the marine environment. Safeguards

58 An examination of the philosophical aspects of this focus are beyond the scope of this chapter.
59 LOSC (n 5) arts 266–74.
60 ibid, arts 275–76.
61 See, eg ibid, art 268.
62 ibid, arts 275 and 276.
63 ibid, art 266 (emphasis added).
64 ibid, art 266(2) (emphasis added). 'Capacity' and 'capacity-building' are not defined in the LOSC.

are, of course, put in place for rights-holders, and the LOSC does not displace intellectual property laws, or other property laws.[65]

The basic objectives of Part XIV are set out in Article 268:

States, directly or through competent international organizations, shall promote:

(a) the acquisition, evaluation and dissemination of marine technological knowledge and facilitate access to such information and data;
(b) the development of appropriate marine technology;
(c) the development of the necessary *technological infrastructure* to facilitate the transfer of marine technology.[66]

In relation to the last of these sub-provisions, what this infrastructure might involve, and whether it includes legal architecture, is unclear. Some guidance is given in Article 269, which sets out that measures to achieve the objectives include:

(a) [establishing] programmes of technical cooperation for the effective transfer of all kinds of marine technology to States which may need and request technical assistance in this field . . . which have not been able either to establish or develop their own technological capacity in marine science and in the exploration and exploitation of marine resources or to develop the infrastructure of such technology;

. . .

(c) [holding] conferences, seminars and symposia on scientific and technological subjects, in particular on policies and methods for the transfer of marine technology;[67]

Measures also include technological cooperation programmes, promotion of favourable contractual provisions, and the undertaking of joint ventures and multilateral cooperation.[68] Therefore, Articles 268 and 269 appear to envisage law and policy developments. Added to these are the Article 62 encouragements, noted above, to utilize the transfer of technology as a means of compensation or remuneration.

The LOSC specifically envisages the development of informal law, by promoting 'the establishment of generally accepted *guidelines, criteria and standards* for the transfer of marine technology on a bilateral basis or within the framework of international organizations'.[69] As will be seen below, this work has subsequently occurred, albeit to a limited extent.

[65] See ibid, art 267.
[66] ibid, art 268 (emphasis added).
[67] ibid, art 269.
[68] ibid, art 268.
[69] ibid, art 271 (emphasis added).

13.4.2 Informal Law Supporting the Development and Transfer of Technology

With respect to the development and transfer of technology, informal law has, again, contributed to the area in various ways. The Code of Conduct, for example, includes relevant provisions:

> International cooperation should be encouraged with respect to research programmes for fishing gear selectivity, and fishing methods and strategies, dissemination of the results of such research programmes and the transfer of technology.[70]

Research is also covered, with the Code of Conduct requiring states to 'ensure that appropriate research is conducted into all aspects of fisheries including … technology'.[71] This expectation includes practical aspects, by encouraging 'States and relevant organizations … [to] sponsor research in fish technology', particularly with reference to 'post-harvest handling of fish'.[72]

In relation to technology transfer, the Code of Conduct plays a thickening role, providing some detail to the general LOSC obligations, requiring states to 'promote the development and transfer of technology in relation to energy optimization within the fisheries sector'.[73] In addition, the Code of Conduct obliges states to 'ensure that [fish] processing, transporting and storage methods are environmentally sound' by 'facilitating the development and transfer of appropriate technologies'.[74] Yet, the Code of Conduct does not go so far as to provide practical guidance on how technology transfer is to be achieved. In this regard, one particularly significant informal law development is the UNESCO Intergovernmental Oceanographic Commission (IOC) Criteria and Guidelines for the Transfer of Marine Technology (IOC Guidelines).[75] The IOC Guidelines were developed and adopted specifically to apply the provisions of Part XIV of the LOSC.[76] The scope includes:

(a) Information and data, in a user-friendly format, on marine sciences and related marine operations and services;
(b) Manuals, guidelines, criteria, standards, reference materials;
(c) Sampling and methodology equipment;
(d) Observation facilities and equipment;
(e) Equipment for in situ and laboratory observations, analysis and experimentation;
(f) Computer and computer software, including models and modelling techniques; and
(g) Expertise, knowledge, skills, technical/scientific/legal know-how and analytical methods related to marine scientific research and observation.[77]

70 Code of Conduct (n 40) art 8.5.4.
71 ibid, art 12.1. That includes traditional fisheries technologies (ibid, art 12.12).
72 ibid, art 11.1.6.
73 ibid, art 8.6.2.
74 ibid, art 11.1.7.
75 IOC Guidelines (n 7).
76 ibid, para A.1. Indeed, IOC is the competent international organization with respect to implementing Part XIV of the LOSC (Development and Transfer of Marine Technology). See IOC, *Medium-term Strategy 2014–2021* (UNESCO 2014).
77 IOC Guidelines (n 7) para A.2.

The criteria adopted include that transfer of technology should enable all parties to 'benefit on an equitable basis from developments in marine science-related activities'.[78] In particular, the criteria set out that legal, financial, and scientific schemes should be developed,[79] transfer should be 'done free of charge or at a reduced rate',[80] and that due regard should be given to the 'needs and interests of developing States ... which have not been able to develop their own capabilities ... and related technology', other legitimate interests, and the importance of transferring 'environmentally sound technologies'.[81] The final criterion notes that transfers should take advantage of 'new, existing or expected co-operation schemes'.[82] In this way, the IOC Guidelines have directly responded to the LOSC provisions calling for the development of criteria.[83]

The IOC Guidelines themselves are set out clearly and concisely, and cover five substantive matters. The first guideline relates to what the IOC should do,[84] which, essentially, is to create a clearing-house mechanism to encourage national representatives of IOC member states to include their plans and strategies around transfer of marine technology,[85] to promote the establishment of regional and subregional focal points,[86] to organize conferences and seminars,[87] and to seek financial contributions to the IOC Trust Fund or Voluntary Co-operation Fund to promote and facilitate transfer of marine technologies.[88] Relevantly, the second guideline establishes a practical mechanism to apply for the transfer of technology: the Transfer of Marine Technology Application.[89] The third and fourth guidelines detail the procedure for examining the transfer application.[90] A similar guideline could also have been developed in relation to a model law. The fifth guideline sets out that the IOC shall provide technical assistance with implementing a marine technology project, and promote and facilitate the involvement of scientists from the recipient country in technology development and research.[91]

The guidelines, therefore, 'thicken' the law by providing much needed detail in response to the LOSC obligations. Nevertheless, the IOC Guidelines do not appear to have built legal capacity, for example, for states seeking to establish domestic law to facilitate technology transfer. Although the IOC was to prepare a clearing house of national and regional rules, it is unclear that this task has been done. Such a resource would be of obvious benefit to states seeking to implement LOSC obligations. This failure highlights that implementation of law is critical to its success, regardless of whether it is hard or informal. The challenge has led to further informal law to enforce the importance of the IOC Guidelines document, with

[78] ibid, para B.
[79] ibid, para B(a).
[80] ibid, para B(b).
[81] ibid, para B(c).
[82] ibid, para B(d).
[83] LOSC (n 5) art 271.
[84] IOC Guidelines (n 7) para C.1(a). These activities include listing government or non-governmental entities interested in participating as donors of marine technology, opportunities for transfer-related projects, sources of technological information, and university and other organization funding, a directory of marine research institutes and experts, offers of cruises for studies, *preparing a study of transfer-related national and regional rules*, and making links and agreements with other repositories of information and expertise (emphasis added).
[85] ibid, para C.1(b).
[86] ibid, para C.1(c).
[87] ibid, para C.1(d).
[88] ibid, para C.1(e).
[89] ibid, para C.2. The form is set out in the Annex.
[90] ibid, para C.3. and 4.
[91] ibid, para C.5.

a UNGA resolution calling for ongoing dissemination and implementation of the guidelines,[92] as well as the transfer of 'environmentally sound technologies' more broadly.[93]

Another relevant informal law development that is linked to the LOSC and the IOC Guidelines is the Sustainable Development Goals (SDGs). The SDGs were adopted as part of Agenda 2030—the outcome document of the Rio+20 Conference—and build on the former Millennium Development Goals (MDGs).[94] Significantly, SDG 14 includes a set of goals focused on oceans— 'Life Below Water'—absent from the earlier MDGs. SDG 14.a makes specific reference to the IOC Guidelines by establishing the goal to:

> Increase ... [the] transfer [of] marine technology, taking into account the Intergovernmental Oceanographic Commission Criteria and Guidelines on the Transfer of Marine Technology, in order to improve ocean health and ... enhance the conservation of marine biodiversity.[95]

The relevant indicator is the proportion of total research budget allocated to the field of marine technology.[96] The SDGs are valuable, as they thicken the law by providing details missing from other instruments: in this case, targets and indicators. Although there are no explicit legal indicators to facilitate any lawmaking in relation to marine technology transfer or data sharing, SDG 14.c calls on states to '[e]nhance the conservation and sustainable use of oceans and their resources by implementing international law as reflected in UNCLOS'. Therefore, in combination, 14.a and 14.c ought to provide impetus for further action, including informal lawmaking, related to the LOSC obligations set out above. Although some scholars have questioned whether the SDGs are powerful enough to achieve articulated outcomes,[97] they have triggered voluntary commitments, such as the Division for Ocean Affairs and the Law of the Sea (DOALOS)/IOC partnership on promoting and facilitating the conduct of marine scientific research.[98] SDG 14.a makes specific reference to technology transfer and the IOC Guidelines, with two capacity-building projects focusing on training courses, and an online portal to create a community of practice. Neither project specifically refers to building legal capacity for technology transfer, and, therefore, it is unclear whether these initiatives might lead to further informal lawmaking.

In summary, the LOSC has provided a foundation for the transfer of marine technologies and data sharing, setting out what should be done, when, and by whom. In addition, the

[92] UNGA Res 59/24 (17 November 2004) UN Doc A/Res/59/24, para 11.

[93] ibid, para 10.

[94] For details of the SDGs, see United Nations Dept of Economic and Social Affairs, Sustainable Development, 'The 17 Goals' <https://sdgs.un.org/goals> accessed 2 October 2020. See also Telesetsky, in Chapter 14 of this volume.

[95] United Nations Department of Economic and Social Affairs, Sustainable Development 'Goal 14' <https://sdgs.un.org/goals/goal14> accessed 2 October 2020. SDG 17.7 calls on states to '[p]romote the development, transfer, dissemination and diffusion of environmentally sound technologies to developing countries on favourable terms, including on concessional and preferential terms, as mutually agreed': United Nations Department of Economic and Social Affairs, Sustainable Development 'Goal 17' <https://sdgs.un.org/goals/goal17> accessed 2 October 2020.

[96] SDG indicator 14.a.1: United Nations Department of Economic and Social Affairs, Sustainable Development 'Goal 17' <https://sdgs.un.org/goals/goal17> accessed 2 October 2020.

[97] Joyeeta Gupta and Courtney Vegelin, 'Sustainable Development Goals and Inclusive Development' (2016) 16(3) Intl'l Env't A 433, 433–48, quoted in Morgera and Ntona (n 6).

[98] Sustainable Developmental Goals Knowledge Platform, '#SDGACTION7819' <https://sustainabledevelopment.un.org/partnership/?p = 7819> accessed 2 October 2020.

FSA creates obligations for states to 'develop appropriate technologies in support of fishery conservation and management', as noted above.[99] Nevertheless, detail is missing in relation to how the obligations are to be fulfilled. Rather than further hard law progressions, there have tended to be more significant informal legal developments.

13.5 Exchange and Sharing of Data

13.5.1 The LOSC Framework

The LOSC was adopted well before the rapid increase in data that occurred after technological developments in the 1990s. Nevertheless, the LOSC makes relevant reference to data in nine articles.[100] Article 61(5) encourages the regular exchange of 'scientific information, catch and fishing effort statistics and other data relevant to the conservation of fish stocks'. A similar provision is set out in relation to the exchange of data in relation to living resources on the high seas, to determine the allowable catch and any conservation measures.[101] Other relevant fishery provisions include Article 62(4)(f), which requires foreign fishers to comply with laws and regulations of the coastal state, when fishing in its EEZ, including reporting of scientific data. A similar provision requires states to provide access to data derived from marine scientific research conducted in the EEZ of another state.[102]

Article 200 of the LOSC requires states to cooperate to encourage the exchange of data about marine pollution. This provision would, presumably, apply to marine debris such as ghost fishing nets. Article 201 builds on this provision by requiring states to use the data acquired to develop 'rules, standards and recommended practices and procedures for the prevention, reduction and control of pollution'. This provision envisages the use of data for future lawmaking, but not the development of laws about the data itself.

A broader requirement to 'promote the flow of scientific data and information and the transfer of knowledge resulting from marine scientific research' is set out in Article 244(2). Similarly, Article 268 requires states to facilitate access to marine technological data, directly or through international organizations. Finally, Article 277 focuses on regional centres with functions including 'acquisition and processing of marine scientific and technological data and information'. This provision is the only reference to data processing in the LOSC, perhaps because computer-based analysis was nascent at the time the treaty was negotiated.

13.5.2 Informal Law on Data Collection and Sharing

In general, there is much less informal law in relation to data sharing and processing than the previous two areas explored. Nevertheless, the Code of Conduct notes that:

[99] FSA (n 32) art 5.

[100] LOSC (n 5) arts 61, 62, 119, 200, 201, 244, 249, 268, and 277. There are other references to data in the LOSC, unrelated to fishing.

[101] ibid, art 119(2).

[102] ibid, art 249.

> States and relevant international organizations should promote and enhance the research capacities of developing countries, inter alia, in the areas of *data collection and analysis*, information, science and technology.[103]

Some informal law has established partnerships with non-state actors that broaden the scope of the law. One specific example involves the satellite data-sharing agreements, such as the Japan Fisheries Research and Education Agency (FRA)/Global Fishing Watch/ANCORS arrangement.[104] This formal collaboration, via a memorandum of understanding (MoU), is aimed at strengthening governance and addressing IUU fishing. The MoU provides that the partners share vessel movement data, catch data, and satellite imagery, and collaborate on research activities, to assess the impacts of IUU fishing. In this sense, the informal instrument does not add to the law, but, rather, broadens the collaborating stakeholder group, and extends the law beyond international cooperation as envisaged in the LOSC.

In conclusion, there is, clearly, an expanded role for law (including informal law) in the area of data collection, sharing, and analysis. For example, legal frameworks could set standards for data formats, build capacity in data analysis and processing, and provide mechanisms for equitable access to data and the sharing of it. This area is one in which law must respond swiftly to rapidly evolving technologies.

13.6 Analysing the Significance of Informal Law Relating to Fishing Technologies

As with the broader debate on the role of informal law, explored throughout this volume, scholars are not aligned on its value vis-à-vis hard law in relation to marine technologies.[105] Regardless, it is clear that informal law is playing a part in the use, development, and transfer of marine technologies and technological data.

In reflecting on the exploration of hard and informal law for marine technologies and data sharing, several observations can be made. First, the field of fisheries law provides ample examples of each of these types of law in relation to fishing-related marine technologies and data, such as: (1) non-binding instruments that seek to restrict the use of marine technologies that are harmful; (2) guideline documents focused on the development and transfer of marine technologies; and (3) MoUs that involve non-state actors in data sharing. The first example is, arguably, filling in the gaps in the LOSC, where it provides only the broadest obligations to conserve and protect the marine environment. In this sense, the informal law is additive, creating detailed rules where none existed before. The challenge, though, is that informal law is not legally binding. So, to the extent that this gap-filling adds to existing obligations, it relies on later 'hardening' in international law, or domestic implementation, to become enforceable. The second example is informal lawmaking catalysed by the LOSC, and which is additive, and provides much needed detail about specific

[103] Code of Conduct (n 40) art 12.18 (emphasis added).

[104] Sara Bladen, 'New Research Partnership to Investigate Illegal Fishing in the North Pacific Ocean' (*Global Fishing Watch*, 13 September 2018) <https://globalfishingwatch.org/press-release/new-research-partnership-to-investigate-illegal-fishing-in-the-north-pacific-ocean/> accessed 2 October 2020.

[105] Dimitra Kourmatzi (2017) 'Soft Law Plays Hard Ball in the Maritime Industry' (Human Rights at Sea Legal Research Programme, Legal Research Paper 02/17).

obligations envisaged in that treaty. Informal law could be highly effective, particularly in terms of setting standards that harmonize the law and achieve best practice. In the third case, the informal law has a broadening role, which is critically important in the area of technology and data, where private industries and non-governmental actors are frequently the developers and/or operators of technology, and providers of raw data and/or data processing and analysis services.

Second, exploring marine technologies through a fisheries lens serves to highlight the successes of informal lawmaking (such as the worldwide drift net prohibition) and its failures (including the lack of a ban on bottom trawling), as well as particular strengths (the adoption of, and integrated references to, the IOC Guidelines). Nevertheless, the development of informal law appears to have been selective, and there are obvious gaps remaining. This weakness is clear from the sections above that highlight piecemeal references to particular forms of pollution from fishing with little attention paid to other impacts. For example, informal law is needed to set standards for the use of fish aggregation devices, which can maximize catches, but also attract non-target species, including marine mammals.[106] These devices are widely utilized, but prohibited in some jurisdictions, and regulated by some RFMOs; informal law could play a role in strengthening and harmonizing the law. Another gap appears to be the proactive development of new marine technologies, and the role that informal law could play in terms of a road map for the future. Furthermore, some existing informal law does not always incorporate sufficient detail to support the implementation of new marine technologies, where they do exist. For example, the Voluntary Guidelines for Catch Documentation Schemes is an international instrument that seeks to provide guidelines to support sustainable fisheries management. It makes only limited reference to technology, requiring:

> technology transfer and training for developing states in order to achieve the objectives of these Guidelines and to support its effective implementation, especially regarding issuance of electronic catch certificates.[107]

Perhaps most significant are the gaps in informal laws that assist in developing legal frameworks to facilitate the transfer of marine technology and data sharing. Whilst the LOSC provides broad state obligations, and the Code of Conduct adds some detail, informal law could assist further in legal capacity-building. For example, Article 266(3) of the LOSC requires states to endeavour to foster legal conditions that facilitate technology transfer. The clearing house of rules envisaged by the IOC Guidelines would be invaluable in achieving this goal.

Third, the above analysis exposes the issue of the 'fuzzy' border between informal law focused on the governance of marine technologies and data sharing, on the one hand, and programmes of action involving these technologies, on the other, with little legal connection beyond the link to general hard law obligations. While each is important, the former goes to development of the legal landscape, and the latter to the effectiveness of the regulatory

[106] MRAG, 'An Analysis of the Uses, Impacts and Benefits of Fish Aggregating Devices (FADs) in the Global Tuna Industry' (*WWF UK*, 2017) <https://www.wwf.org.uk/sites/default/files/publications/Mar17/Tuna%20fisheries%20FADs%20report%20-%20MRAG_WWF.pdf> accessed 2 October 2020.

[107] FAO, 'Voluntary Guidelines for Catch Documentation Schemes' (Rome 2017), para 1.5 <http://www.fao.org/3/a-i8076e.pdf> accessed 5 March 2021. Electronic systems are referred to again, in para 4.6.

framework. This distinction is not a new issue, and many scholars have addressed the spectrum of instruments and approaches in the context of seeking clarity around definitions of 'soft law'.[108] While it is accepted that law is not a simple binary,[109] not all informal instruments could be said to contribute to informal lawmaking. It is clear that declarations, non-binding agreements, and codes of conduct are, squarely, informal law. Projects focused on implementation, and capacity-building programmes involving the application and use of law are, arguably, not informal lawmaking. In this sense, the IOC Guidelines are something of a paradox. They are envisaged in the LOSC, and specifically referred to in the SDGs. Yet, beyond encouraging the IOC to create a clearing house of technology transfer rules, it is difficult to see how they develop the legal landscape. Added to this discourse is the issue of whether an informal instrument is used to strengthen the law, reiterate key provisions of it, or support a focused programme of action.[110] An example of the last of these is FISH-i Africa, which provides a platform and tools to support cooperation in addressing IUU fishing, but does not create any new law.[111] The Joint Group of Experts on the Scientific Aspects of Marine Environmental Protection (GESAMP)[112] is another body whose work could, sometimes, be considered to be informal lawmaking and, in other cases, as adding to knowledge and expertise regarding marine technologies. GESAMP was established in 1969, and is sponsored by ten UN agencies.[113] It comprises a group of experts who provide scientific advice to the UN, organizations, and governments, in relation to the protection and sustainable use of the marine environment. GESAMP certainly facilitates the implementation of the LOSC by undertaking research in relation to marine technologies: for example, its High Level Review of a Wide Range of Proposed Marine Geoengineering Techniques.[114] This report, however, does not fit the criteria for informal law, in that it adds knowledge, but does not, directly, fill gaps in the law, or provide detail to existing legal provisions. The report on methodology for the evaluation of ballast water management systems using active substances, on the other hand, arguably does 'thicken' the law, by providing critical detail needed to implement the International Convention for the Control and Management of Ships' Ballast Water and Sediments.[115] It remains difficult, therefore, to determine the boundaries of what is included as informal law for marine technologies and data.

[108] Abbott and Snidal have sought to 'explain' soft law as beginning with a weakening of 'obligation, precision, and delegation', which can occur to 'varying degrees': Abbott and Snidal (n 19) 422. Klabbers highlights the breadth of 'soft law', which is sometimes used to describe any legal instrument falling short of hard law, and, in other instances, is said to include non-legal (politically or morally binding) agreements: Jan Klabbers, 'The Redundancy of Soft Law' (1996) 65 Nord J Intl'l L 167.

[109] Klabbers (n 108).

[110] See, eg Agenda 21, which reiterates the call for marine technology transfer and the establishment of regional centres: United Nations Conference on Environment and Development, 'Agenda 21' (1992), ch 17.119(d).

[111] FISH-i Africa, 'Our Future' <https://fish-i-network.org/> accessed 2 October 2020.

[112] See the GESAMP home page <www.gesamp.org> accessed 2 October 2020.

[113] GESAMP, 'About: History' <http://www.gesamp.org/about/history> accessed 2 October 2020.

[114] GESAMP, 'High Level Review of a Wide Range of Proposed Marine Geoengineering Techniques' (IMO/FAO/UNESCO-IOC/UNIDO/WMO/IAEA/UN/UN Environment/UNDP/ISA GESAMP, 2019) Rep Stud GESAMP No 98 <http://www.gesamp.org/publications/high-level-review-of-a-wide-range-of-proposed-marine-geoengineering-techniques> accessed 2 October 2020.

[115] GESAMP, 'Methodology for the Evaluation of Ballast Water Management Systems using Active Substances' (IMO/FAO/UNESCO-IOC/UNIDO/WMO/IAEA/UN/UN Environment/UNDP/ISA GESAMP, 2019) Rep Stud GESAMP No 101 <http://www.gesamp.org/publications/methodology-for-the-evaluation-of-ballast-water-management-systems-using-active-substances> accessed 2 October 2020.

13.7 Concluding Remarks

The LOSC remains the most critically relevant legal instrument for oceans governance. Yet it does not, and cannot, provide all the necessary legal detail. Informal lawmaking contributes significantly to global fisheries governance, and is, itself, a complex and evolving field. In relation to fishing technologies, informal law has a crucial role to play, as technological developments, and their outputs in the form of data, are rapidly expanding, and law must respond swiftly.

This chapter has demonstrated three distinct ways in which informal law is playing a vital part in the use, development, and transfer of marine technologies, and access to, and sharing of, data. It demonstrates the distinct value that informal lawmaking brings to an ever busy and complex space, but also how much remains to be achieved. Informal lawmaking is likely to remain important in the future, yet it appears clear that there is little centralized oversight that might encourage systematic development of the law. If law is to keep pace with rapid technological and data developments, ways must be found to efficiently address legal weaknesses, to facilitate best practice in the use, development, and transfer of marine technologies, and to optimize data sharing arrangements. Lessons may be learnt from other areas of international law, such as environmental and climate change law.[116] It is clear that the advantages of informal law—including the ability to develop swiftly, incorporate quasi-legal elements, and involve a broader range of stakeholders—mean that it has a critical supporting role to play in the good governance of marine technology and data.

[116] The Clean Development Mechanisms under the Kyoto Protocol, for example, provide an example of a legal mechanism to facilitate transfer of technology from developed to developing countries. Kyoto Protocol to the United Nations Framework Convention on Climate Change (adopted 11 December 1997, entered into force 16 February 2005) 2303 UNTS 162.

PART V
MARINE ENVIRONMENT

14

The Sustainable Development Goals and Informal Lawmaking Processes

How a Voluntary Initiative Sets International Standards for Governments and the Private Sector

Anastasia Telesetsky

14.1 Introduction

International lawmaking has, historically, been the realm of states, where diplomats and other political authorities formally negotiate treaties using familiar intergovernmental mechanisms. While these traditional state-based approaches to lawmaking have been perceived to be at the core of what constitutes international law, informal international lawmaking has also been proliferating in the shadows. This core and shadow metaphor would seem to suggest that traditional lawmaking continues to dominate international implementation efforts. However, this chapter will argue that the formal lawmaking process has proven too inflexible for many states, while, at the same time, lacking in credibility for other social actors, such as sub-national government bodies, corporations, and civil society groups. Formal international lawmaking has failed to deliver intended lawmaking effects, particularly in the realm of ocean governance. The assumption that public governance would efficaciously curtail private activities rests on faulty beliefs, given the difficulty of regulating activities across areas that are only loosely bounded and surveilled. It is not particularly surprising that piracy persists, that overfishing is the rule and not the exception in many fisheries, and that pollution is pervasive.

In reaction to lukewarm performance on ocean governance indicators, states are trying new approaches to lawmaking, particularly in the field of sustainability. There is an increasing shift away from multilateral treaty-making, where states hotly contest the means to achieve negotiated objectives, towards what might be characterized as multilateral, goal-driven 'project management'. The 2015 Sustainable Development Goals (SDGs) are part of this new project management trend, but that does not mean that the general goals, with their various instrumental targets, are mere pledges.[1] Instead, as will be suggested below, the SDG targets have become international standards that have been internalized and 'legalized' by both states and private actors, in the form of state law and company policy, respectively. In spite of being clearly labelled as voluntary commitments, the SDGs are part of a process of informal lawmaking that has normative effect, where states and companies

[1] Kal Raustiala, 'Form and Substance in International Agreements' (2005) 99 AJIL 581 (arguing that states make a choice between either a pledge—an informal written accord—and a contract, during international negotiations).

Anastasia Telesetsky, *The Sustainable Development Goals and Informal Lawmaking Processes* In: *Unconventional Lawmaking in the Law of the Sea*. Edited by: Natalie Klein, Oxford University Press. © Anastasia Telesetsky 2022.
DOI: 10.1093/oso/9780192897824.003.0014

now measure and adjust their performance in a variety of ocean management arenas, on the basis of the negotiated SDG targets.

This chapter will begin with a brief history of the SDGs, with a focus on SDG 14, which focuses attention on the conservation and sustainable use of the oceans, seas, and marine resources. The original contribution of this chapter will be to argue that many of the targets set by the SDGs are more than simply political aspirations. They have become de facto international standards, and manifest normative effect, even though states and private actors continue to emphasize that the goals are non-binding. In support of this argument, the chapter will examine some state responses following the adoption of the SDGs to the target on marine protected areas; corporate responses to combatting overfishing; and corporate responses to reducing marine debris. In each of these cases, states and companies have explained their actions as contributing directly to the achievement of particular SDG targets. Finally, the chapter will ask what the implications of the SDG process are for informal lawmaking. Beyond the actual adoption of laws, a legitimate legal process requires implementation of the law, plus accountability for how a given law is implemented, or not implemented. Will the adopted laws and corporate policies that meet the SDG standards be implemented to further the spirit of the SDGs? Or are the laws and policies adopted in response to the SDGs expedient but empty pledges?

14.2 Sustainable Development Goals and Goal 14

The SDGs, including Goal 14 for the oceans, represent a departure from traditional international lawmaking approaches. While states have historically made pledges to act in a variety of contexts, the SDGs differ by trying to find a common language for states and stakeholders to create ambitious change. Civil society and private enterprise engagement were an essential part of the drafting of the goals, targets, and indicators. Through a dialogic process, proponents of the SDGs hoped to be able to transform normative ambitions. Thus, while the SDGs were never conceived of as having any normative intent, they have, as will be explained, generated a normative effect.

The genesis of the SDGs was the conclusion of the 2012 UN Conference on Sustainable Development. The global leaders that assembled in Rio de Janeiro in 2012, unlike their predecessors at the 1992 UN Conference on Environment and Development, did not finalize an array of formal international lawmaking documents, such as the Convention on Biological Diversity[2] or the UN Framework Convention on Climate Change.[3] Instead, the 2012 leaders drafted a single outcome document titled *The Future We Want*, calling for the need to 'mainstream sustainable development at all levels',[4] and recognizing the 'diversification of actors and stakeholders'.[5] In many respects, it was a weak outcome for a critical

[2] Convention on Biological Diversity (adopted 5 June 1992, entered into force 29 December 1993) 1760 UNTS 79 (hereafter 'CBD').

[3] United Nations Framework Convention on Climate Change (adopted 9 May 1992, entered into force 21 March 1994) 1771 UNTS 107 (hereafter 'UNFCCC').

[4] UN General Assembly, 'The Future We Want', UNGA Res 66/288 (27 July 2012) UN Doc A/RES/66/288, para 3.

[5] ibid, para 19.

meeting, with states, in general terms, calling upon each other, and a broader set of stakeholders, to 'do better'.

Oceans and seas were a major subject for *The Future We Want*, wherein international decision-makers recognized the UN Convention on the Law of the Sea (LOSC) as 'the legal framework for the conservation and sustainable use of the oceans and their resources', but also recognized the existing limits of the LOSC in addressing a variety of issues, including ocean acidification, coastal erosion, and ocean fertilization.[6] Seeking urgent action, states drafted language in support of meeting existing global fisheries targets, as already adopted under the Johannesburg Plan of Implementation,[7] but also urged states to do more to implement science-based management plans. While states understood that implementing existing ocean laws would not be enough to address contemporary concerns, there was no interest in tailoring any new international regulations at the 2012 meeting.

Instead, the 2012 outcome document called for the development of a set of 'sustainable development goals' that would be 'action-oriented, concise and easy to communicate, limited in number, aspirational, global in nature and universally applicable to all countries while taking into account different national realities, capacities and levels of development and respecting national policies and priorities'.[8] Negotiation between international stakeholders, including private sector actors, transpired over the next three years, until the SDGs were unanimously adopted in 2015 by 193 countries, as part of the 2030 Agenda for Sustainable Development. The 2030 Agenda included 17 Sustainable Development Goals and 169 targets, expected to be achieved by 2030. In a departure from previous cooperative goal-setting efforts, such as the Millennium Development Goals, the SDGs were understood to be universal, applying to all states and other stakeholders, and interconnected, such that there would be no hierarchy among the goals.

The most interesting component of the SDG process was the setting of multiple targets for each goal. The SDG drafters understood that they were not drafting a formal treaty, like the LOSC, that would evolve over time, but were, instead, creating a set of somewhat flexible international standards on what constitutes sustainability (for example, outcomes of the targets), with some agreed-upon practices for achieving those standards (for example, action required to achieve the outcome of the targets). As will be suggested below, in more detail, the SDG targets, adopted by all states, are part of an informal lawmaking process. The SDGs, which were always intended to be aspirational, have, in practice, become a project with normative effect, in light of the new laws and policies adopted directly in response to the SDG targets.

While the SDGs are a vision of 'the future we want', the targets are 'action-oriented', requiring states that have adopted the SDGs to do more than simply give lip service to the targets that standardize the goals. While there are no sanctioning mechanisms, there is some limited public accountability for the promises made by states, which follows from the annual Secretary-General's progress report, and the Global Sustainable Development Report

[6] United Nations Convention on the Law of the Sea (adopted 10 December 1982, entered into force 16 November 1994) 1833 UNTS 397 (hereafter 'LOSC'), arts 158, 165–67.

[7] UN, 'Report of the World Summit on Sustainable Development' (26 August to 4 September 2002) UN Doc A/CONF.199/20, Annex: Plan of Implementation of the World Summit on Sustainable Development (hereafter 'Johannesburg Plan of Implementation').

[8] ibid 247.

issued by a group of independent scientists.[9] In September 2019, after these reports were published, states convened a high-level political meeting, and issued a political declaration, *Gearing up for a Decade of Action and Delivery for Sustainable Development*, calling on states to invest more effort in achieving the SDGs.[10] While the declaration from 2019 is not a binding declaration, the subsequent convening of the meeting to improve performance on sustainable development, and the issuance of the declaration, suggest that the SDGs are regarded by states as something more than just empty political pledges.

14.2.1 History of Goal 14

Sustainable Development Goal 14, Life below Water, calls upon states to 'conserve and sustainably use the oceans, seas and marine resources for sustainable development'. When the SDG negotiation process began, the idea for a goal focused on ocean protection and restoration was not contemplated. The topic of 'oceans and seas' was not considered by the Open Working Group on the Sustainable Development Goals until February 2014.[11] The government of Palau had, in 2013, proposed a goal to 'achieve healthy, productive, and resilient oceans', and offered a series of targets related to sustainable fishing and protecting the marine environment, including several concepts that were, eventually, adopted in the final targets, including elimination of subsidies, and adaptation to ocean acidification.[12] Momentum grew around the idea of an ocean-specific SDG, resulting in support from a number of countries and civil society groups, coalescing around a distinct goal for oceans that would be connected to other goals.

14.2.2 Targets under Goal 14

States set ten targets, reproduced in Table 14.1 below. Reviewing the list of targets, four observations about the targets, as a group, are worth noting, when thinking about what these targets represent, from a governance perspective. First, a number of the targets set more ambitious dates than the 2030 Agenda for Sustainable Development might otherwise have encouraged, with many of the targets to be evaluated five to ten years after the goals were adopted. Second, achieving most of the targets depends on national responses, because of the references, in particular, to coastal ecosystems and coastal areas that are wholly under the jurisdiction of individual coastal states. Third, the targets acknowledge common but differentiated responsibilities. Finally, the targets embed themselves explicitly within the pre-existing international legal framework of the LOSC and other formal efforts to improve

[9] See, eg UN, 'Report of the Secretary-General on SDG Progress 2019: Special Edition' (2019) <https://sustainabledevelopment.un.org/content/documents/24978Report_of_the_SG_on_SDG_Progress_2019.pdf> accessed 30 June 2021; UN, 'Global Sustainable Development Report 2019, The Future is Now: Science for Achieving Sustainable Development' (2019) <https://sustainabledevelopment.un.org/content/documents/24797GSDR_report_2019.pdf> accessed 30 June 2021.

[10] UNGA Res 74/4 (21 October 2019) UN Doc A/Res/74/4, 'Annex: Gearing up for a Decade of Action and Delivery for Sustainable Development: Political Declaration of the Sustainable Development Goals Summit' (hereafter 'Gearing up for a Decade of Action').

[11] UNGA, 'Report of the Open Working Group of the General Assembly on Sustainable Development Goals' (12 August 2014) UN Doc A/68/970.

[12] Palau Mission to the UN, 'Toward an Ocean SDG' (17 April 2013).

Table 14.1 Goal 14: Targets and Global Indicators*

Goal 14: Conserve and Sustainably Use the Oceans, Sea and Marine Resources for Sustainable Development	
Target 14.1	By 2025, prevent and significantly reduce marine pollution of all kinds, in particular from land-based activities, including marine debris and nutrient pollution. *Global Indicator*: Index of coastal eutrophication and floating plastic debris density.
Target 14.2	By 2020, sustainably manage and protect marine and coastal ecosystems to avoid significant adverse impacts, including by strengthening their resilience, and take action for their restoration, in order to achieve healthy and productive oceans. *Global Indicator*: Proportion of national exclusive economic zones managed using ecosystem-based approaches.
Target 14.3	Minimize and address the impacts of ocean acidification, including through enhanced scientific cooperation at all levels. *Global Indicator*: Average marine acidity (pH) measured at agreed set of sampling stations.
Target 14.4	By 2020, effectively regulate harvesting, and end overfishing, illegal, unreported, and unregulated fishing, and destructive fishing practices, and implement science-based management plans, in order to restore fish stocks in the shortest time feasible, at least to levels that can produce maximum sustainable yield as determined by their biological characteristics. *Global Indicator*: Proportion of fish stocks within biologically sustainable levels.
Target 14.5	By 2020, conserve at least 10% of coastal and marine areas, consistent with national and international law, and based on the best available scientific information. *Global Indicator*: Coverage of protected areas in relation to marine areas.
Target 14.6	By 2020, prohibit certain forms of fisheries subsidies which contribute to overcapacity and overfishing, eliminate subsidies that contribute to illegal, unreported, and unregulated fishing, and refrain from introducing new such subsidies, recognizing that appropriate and effective special and differential treatment for developing and least- developed countries should be an integral part of the World Trade Organization fisheries subsidies negotiation. *Global Indicator*: Degree of implementation of international instruments designed to combat illegal, unreported, and unregulated fishing.
Target 14.7	By 2030, increase the economic benefits to small island developing States and least- developed countries from the sustainable use of marine resources, including through sustainable management of fisheries, aquaculture, and tourism. *Global Indicator*: Sustainable fisheries as a proportion of gross domestic product in small island developing States, least-developed countries, and other countries
Target 14.a	Increase scientific knowledge, develop research capacity, and transfer marine technology, taking into account the Intergovernmental Oceanographic Commission Criteria and Guidelines on the Transfer of Marine Technology, in order to improve ocean health, and to enhance the contribution of marine biodiversity to the development of developing countries, in particular small island developing States and least-developed countries. *Global Indicator*: Proportion of total research budget allocated to research in marine technology.

Continued

Table 14.1 *Continued*

Goal 14: Conserve and Sustainably Use the Oceans, Sea and Marine Resources for Sustainable Development	
Target 14.b	Provide access for small-scale artisanal fishers to marine resources and markets. *Global Indicator*: Progress by countries in the degree of application of a legal/regulatory/policy/institutional framework that recognizes and protects access rights or small-scale fisheries.
Target 14.c	Enhance the conservation and sustainable use of oceans and their resources by implementing international law as reflected in the United Nations Convention on the Law of the Sea, which provides the legal framework for the conservation and sustainable use of oceans and their resources, as recalled in paragraph 158 of *The Future We Want*. *Global Indicator*: Number of countries making progress in ratifying, accepting, and implementing, through legal, policy, and institutional frameworks, ocean-related instruments that implement international law, as reflected in the United Nations Convention on the Law of the Sea, for the conservation and sustainable use of the oceans and their resources.

*UNGA Res 71/313 (6 July 2017) UN Doc A/RES/71/313, 'Annex: Global Indicator Framework for the Sustainable Development Goals and Targets of the 2030 Agenda for Sustainable Development'.

ocean governance. In the context of the LOSC as a multilateral treaty, the targets become an informal, yet focused, extension of the implementation of those parts of the LOSC that support conservation and the sustainable use of the oceans.

14.3 SDGs Operating as Standards for Implementing the Law of the Sea

The SDGs were never intended to be binding, because states and other actors did not have normative intent to create a legal agreement when they commenced negotiations and charged the Open Working Group with preparing a proposal for draft language. The creation of the SDGs was viewed as an exercise in cooperation, expressing a long-term vision of 'the future we want'. This lack of normative intent was expressed explicitly in the Report of the Open Working Group on the SDGs, where the drafters note that '[t]argets are defined as aspirational global targets, with each Government setting its own national targets guided by the global level of ambition, but taking into account national circumstances'.[13]

However, implicit within the SDGs is an expectation that the goals will have a normative effect. The Open Working Group did not intend for the goals to be purely aspirational, because the participants understood that the implementation of the goals would require partnerships between public and private actors and, even more significantly, 'a robust mechanism to review implementation'.[14] If the goals and targets were ambitious, but merely political pledges, then there would be no need to 'review implementation'.

The SDGs reflect more than simply a way-post for global leaders to celebrate sustainable development as a concept: this is reflected in the 2019 declaration that states will take

[13] UN, 'Report of the Secretary-General on SDG Progress 2019: Special Edition' (n 9).
[14] ibid.

concrete steps to 'implement' the 2030 Agenda.[15] In 2019, the UN Secretary-General's office reported that the 142 'voluntary national reviews' submitted to the UN 'show that Governments have prioritized integration of the Sustainable Development Goals into their national plans and policies and are creating the institutional arrangements that will help drive and also monitor progress towards the transformation needed in their economies and societies'.[16] This conclusion suggests that states have taken what are otherwise soft declarations and hardened them into operational plans, policies, and institutional changes. The report notes that parliaments have taken a lead role, in part through the adoption of budgets to implement the SDGs, and that, in some countries, the parliaments are involved 'in the implementation, monitoring and review of the Goals, although this is far from widespread'.[17] Even though there is not universal domestication of SDG goals, a number of national parliaments have taken seriously this responsibility to translate the content of the SDGs into actionable legislation. In 2015, the Inter-Parliamentary Union (IPU), which represents 173 national parliaments, adopted the Hanoi Declaration on the SDGs, and emphasized the need for governments to fulfil their public commitment to the SDGs.[18]

States have relied on certain SDG targets as standards against which to measure performance. The targets, some of which build on the pre-existing expectations and obligations of states, have, through use, become a set of performance standards for ocean management, providing for additional specificity on how to implement certain obligations under the LOSC. For example, Target 14.1 provides additional specification for state parties as to how they can comply with Article 207 of the LOSC, which requires states to prevent, reduce, and control land-based source pollution. Target 14.1 specifies that states are expected to 'significantly' reduce marine pollution, particularly marine debris (for example, plastics) and nutrient pollution. Targets 14.4 and 14.6 offer specific standards for implementation of Articles 61 and 62 of the LOSC on conservation and utilization of marine living resources in exclusive economic zones (EEZs), as well as Article 119 on conservation on the high seas. In particular, these targets expect science-based management plans, designed 'to restore fish stocks in the shortest time feasible, at least to levels that can produce maximum sustainable yield', and end the use of perverse fisheries subsidies that contribute to overcapacity and overfishing.

The SDGs also introduce new shared standards that implement the LOSC's general marine protection obligations, such as Article 192's duty to protect and preserve the marine environment. For example, Target 14.2 calls upon states and other actors to mainstream restoration, as part of marine and coastal management. Target 14.3 calls for international, regional, and public–private cooperation to address the drivers and impacts of ocean acidification. Each target, therefore, provides direction for state legislators and enforcement agencies as to how their international obligations are to be interpreted and applied.

[15] Gearing up for a Decade of Action (n 10) paras 2 and 16 (acknowledging 'that the Sustainable Development Goals are increasingly incorporated in national policies, plans, budgets and development cooperation efforts'), and para 27(C) (states 'pledge to lift the level of ambition of our national responses to the implementation of the 2030 Agenda, while respecting national processes and ensuring ownership. To this end, we aim to proactively mainstream the 2030 Agenda into our national planning instruments, policies, strategies and financial frameworks').

[16] UN, 'Report of the Secretary-General on SDG Progress 2019: Special Edition' (n 14).

[17] ibid 33.

[18] Inter-Parliamentary Union, 'Hanoi Declaration: The Sustainable Development Goals: Turning Words into Action' (1 April 2015) <http://archive.ipu.org/conf-e/132/rpt-gendebate.htm> accessed 30 June 2021 ('Our responsibility is clear: to hold governments accountable for the goals they have subscribed to, and to make sure that enabling laws are passed and budgets adopted.').

14.3.1 Target 14.5 (Increase Waters under Marine Protection)

From a flexible framework of relatively general targets (for example, 'address the impacts of ocean acidification'), states have responded, in some instances with formal lawmaking, in relation to those targets that appear easier to legislate some action that can be quantified and reported back to the SDG committee. Notably, Target 14.5 on marine protected areas (MPAs), which also supports a commitment under the Aichi Targets for Biodiversity,[19] has been a subject of significant legislative action since the adoption of the SDGs. In 2019, the UN reported that the proportion of waters under national jurisdiction classified as MPAs in 2018 had increased by about 5% since 2015, so that 17.2% of waters under national jurisdiction were now protected.[20] UN research estimated that, in the year of 2017 alone, voluntary commitments in response to the SDGs accounted for a 2.85% increase in global MPA coverage.[21] Examples of national responses, after the adoption of the SDGs in 2015, that involved adopting new legislation or implementing new regulations to broaden MPAs include the following:

- Argentina implemented two MPAs through the Yaganes National Park and the Namuncurá–Burdwood Bank II, under a law adopted in December 2018. This law added 98,000 square kilometres of ocean habitat to Argentina's protected areas, increasing the area of Argentina's MPAs more than four-fold from 28,000 square kilometres to 126,000 square kilometres.[22]
- In 2018, Brazil's president approved two decrees to create large environmental protection areas/national monuments in the Tridade e Martim Vaz archipelago and the São Pedro e São Paulo archipelago, covering more than 100,000 square kilometres of no-take areas.[23]
- In 2017, Micronesia adopted a law on MPAs, to apply to almost 200,000 square kilometres of marine environment.[24]
- In 2016, Russia extended the Russian Arctic (Russkaya Arktika) National Park to include Franz Josef Land, expanding its no-take marine protection.[25]
- In 2016, South Africa issued a draft regulatory notice to announce twenty-one new MPAs, as part of Operation Phakisa: Oceans Economy Marine Protected Area Network, to form the basis of an ecologically representative system of South African

[19] CBD, 'Decision X/2: The Strategic Plan for Biodiversity 2011–2020 and the Aichi Biodiversity Targets' (29 October 2010) UN Doc UNEP/CBD/COP/DEC/X/2, Aichi Target 11: 'By 2020, at least ... 10 per cent of coastal and marine areas, especially areas of particular importance for biodiversity and ecosystem services, are conserved through effectively and equitably managed, ecologically representative and well-connected systems of protected areas and other effective area-based conservation measures, and integrated into the wider landscape and seascape.'

[20] UN, 'Report of the Secretary-General on SDG Progress 2019: Special Edition' (n 9) 24. Notably, more than 60% of the oceans are not under national jurisdiction, and only 1% of this ocean space is protected.

[21] UN DESA, Division for Sustainable Development, 'In-depth Analysis of Ocean Conference Voluntary Commitments to Support and Monitor their Implementation' (2017) 42, fig 35 <https://sustainabledevelopment.un.org/content/documents/17193OCVC_in_depth_analysis.pdf> accessed 30 June 2021.

[22] Ley No 27.490 (13 December 2018) <http://servicios.infoleg.gob.ar/infolegInternet/anexos/315000-319999/317651/norma.htm> accessed 30 June 2021.

[23] Decree Nos 9312 and 9313 (19 March 2018).

[24] Congressional Act #19-176 (18 April 2017).

[25] 'Russia Expands National Park to Protect Frank Josef Land Archipelago' (*National Geographic Society Newsroom*, 26 August 2016) <https://blog.nationalgeographic.org/2016/08/29/russia-expands-national-park-to-protect-franz-josef-land-archipelago/> accessed 30 June 2021.

MPAs.[26] As of 2019, management plans had been legally adopted for MPAs covered by Operation Phakisa.[27]

- In 2016, the United Kingdom invested £20 million in its Blue Belt Programme to protect more than four million square kilometres of marine environment associated with UK Overseas Territories by 2020. Legislation has been adopted by some of the overseas territories, such as the Pitcairn Islands Marine Protected Area Ordinance (2016), covering the EEZ and the territorial seas of Pitcairn, Henderson, Ducie, and Oeno Islands.[28] Under the 2016 Environmental Protection Ordinance, the government of St Helena adopted a Marine Protected Area Management Plan for 445,000 square kilometres.[29] Additional funding has been promised to support implementation of the Blue Belt Programme.
- The United States expanded Papahanaumokuakea Marine National Monument in 2016.[30]

While it appears that the existence of the SDGs may be informing some recent lawmaking efforts in relation to the creation of new MPAs since 2015, it is less clear to what extent the SDGs have operated as informal lawmaking mechanisms independent of other drivers, such as the Aichi Biodiversity Targets concluded under the Convention on Biological Diversity.[31] While correlation between the adoption of SDG 14 targets and a particular piece of formal legislation may not be readily traceable, what is clear is that informal lawmaking mechanisms—either the SDG targets or the Aichi targets—have created national momentum, leading to formal legal instruments involving MPAs. Informal lawmaking may, therefore,

[26] National Environmental Management: Protected Areas Act 2003, Draft Notices (February 2016) <https://www.environment.gov.za/sites/default/files/gazetted_notices/nempaa57of2003_draftregulations_newproposedmarineprotectedarea1_gg39646.pdf> accessed 30 June 2021 (covering 70,000 km^2 of ocean).

[27] Government of South Africa National Environmental Management: Protected Areas Act (57 of 2004) Regulations (23 May 2019): Management of Addo Elephant National Park Marine Protected Area (42479—GN 777); Management of Amathole Offshore Marine Protected Area (42479—GN 778); Management of Agulhas Front Marine Protected Area (42479—GN 779); Management of Agulhas Bank Complex Marine Protected Area (42479—GN 780); Management of Aliwal Shoal Marine Protected Area (42479—GN 781); Management of Benguela Muds Marine Protected Area (42479—GN 782); Management of Browns Bank Corals Marine Protected Area (42479—GN 783); Management of Cape Canyon Marine Protected Area (42479—GN 784); Management of Childs Bank Marine Protected Area (42479—GN 785); Management of Namaqua Fossil Forest Marine Protected Area (42479—GN 786); Management of Namaqua National Park Marine Protected Area (42479—GN 787); Management of iSimangaliso Marine Protected Area (42479—GN 788); Management of Port Elizabeth Corals Marine Protected Area (42479—GN 789); Management of Uthukela Marine Protected Area (42479—GN 790); Management of Orange Shelf Edge Marine Protected Area (42479—GN 791); Management of Southeast Atlantic Seamounts Marine Protected Area (42479—GN 792); Management of Protea Marine Protected Area (42479—GN 793); Management of Robben Island Marine Protected Area (42479—GN 794); Management of South West Indian Seamount Marine Protected Area (42479—GN 795); Management of Agulhas Muds Marine Protected Area (42479—GN 796).

[28] Pitcairn Islands Marine Protected Area Ordinance CAP. 48 2017 Rev Ed <http://www.government.pn/Laws/Cap%2048%20-%20Pitcairn%20Islands%20Marine%20Protected%20Area%202017%20Rev%20Ed.pdf> accessed 30 June 2021.

[29] St Helena Extraordinary Gazette No 91 of 2016, Management Plan for a Marine Protected Area (16 September 2016).

[30] Proclamation No 9478, 81 FR 60225 (26 August 2016) Papahanaumokuakea Marine National Monument Expansion <https://www.federalregister.gov/documents/2016/08/31/2016-21138/papahamacrnaumokuamacrkea-marine-national-monument-expansion> accessed 14 July 2021.

[31] See, eg 'Belize's Voluntary National Review for the Sustainable Development Goals 2017' 45 <https://sustainabledevelopment.un.org/content/documents/16389Belize.pdf> accessed 30 June 2021 (noting that Belize has surpassed Target 14.5, and also met the Aichi Target, through the establishment of the Turneffe Atoll Marine Reserve in 2012, and the expansion of Hoi Chan Marine Reserve in 2015, which puts over 20% of Belize's jurisdictional waters into marine protected status).

serve an important function in catalysing otherwise disparate efforts to achieve harmonized outcomes. Targets articulated as a product of informal lawmaking are particularly interesting in stimulating government action through friendly national competition to avoid future shaming during review processes. Arguably, the existence of the intergovernmental review process has catalysed domestic legal efforts that might not otherwise have materialized.

The goals that lack normative intent have ended up having a normative effect for certain ends. The SDGs have had synergistic consequences for the fuller implementation of the law of the sea, by taking specific obligations where states were underperforming and providing criteria and standards against which a state can measure its own success. A country that takes legal steps, domestically, to conserve at least 10% of coastal areas to implement a science-based management plan, or to eliminate certain types of fisheries subsidies, can be considered by other countries to have achieved at least part of Goal 14.

Whether this type of target-driven process is qualitatively desirable may be a different matter. Countries may claim to have achieved Goal 14 through restoration efforts that are, largely, window dressing, or poorly funded science-based management plans. Countries that wish to continue status quo subsidy policies may try to obfuscate these subsidies within a complex regulatory system, rather than actually eliminating the existing subsidies. There is no third-party substantive review or verification process. Unlike a more formal treaty process, parties cannot depend upon the protection of good faith in the form of *pacta sunt servanda*, since the drafters of the SDGs were quite explicit about the intended aspirational quality of the goals and targets. While a regular reporting mechanism does offer a limited degree of accountability, by giving an opportunity for the public to review a state report, there is no obvious forum for challenging a state's self-reporting on achievement of SDGs. While academic scholars or non-governmental organization (NGO) activists may contest the content of a report based on different data sets, there is no obligation under the SDG process for states to respond to such challenges. While most states are likely to use similar methodologies to calculate information to measure target indicators, there is no requirement for all states to apply the same methodologies in measuring progress towards targets.[32]

Informal lawmaking mechanisms triggering formal lawmaking are, unfortunately, not a panacea for the magnitude of challenges facing the ocean environment. Even with the relatively quick expansion of MPAs, implementing MPAs has not been enough to address more pressing ocean protection issues, including increasing ocean acidification and illegal fishing, because many of the MPAs continue to have weak governance schemes. Many of the other SDG 14 targets have not yet been leveraged to create new national legislation, or to reform existing legislation.

As part of a process of informal lawmaking, the SDG targets represent, at best, a patchwork, with some targets assuming more legalistic qualities and being adopted into legislative frameworks, while other targets remain aspirational. One of the challenges with informal

[32] The UN has provided some direction in how to calculate indicators, and offers capacity- building to assist states, but the information provided on applying measurements has been advisory, and not mandated. See, eg UN, 'Goal 14—Conserve and Sustainably Use the Oceans, Sea, and Marine Resources for Sustainable Development' (7 April 2016) <https://unstats.un.org/sdgs/files/metadata-compilation/Metadata-Goal-14.pdf> accessed 30 June 2021. See also Intergovernmental Oceanographic Commission, 'Measuring Progress on SDG 14 Indicators' (31 January 2019) <http://www.unesco.org/new/en/natural-sciences/ioc-oceans/single-view-oceans/news/measuring_progress_on_sdg_14_indicators/> accessed 30 June 2021.

lawmaking processes is the substantive content of the law. For example, while most states have accepted that the SDG 14.5 target for MPAs is 10% of the coastal and marine area, and have reacted to that target, at least one country has set itself a different target. Vietnam, in its 2019 voluntary review, notes that it has established 10 MPAs, covering 0.24% of its sea area, and proceeds to reference SDG 14.5 with an explanation that "Up to 2030, the coastal and marine protected areas will account for 3–4 per cent of the natural areas." '[33] Vietnam is, therefore, striving towards a meaningful target, but not the one shared by most of the other countries participating in the SDG process. This interpretation of SDG 14.5 raises questions about the SDG process. Presumably, when a state commits to the SDGs, it generally commits itself to the targets established. Vietnam has, unilaterally, reduced its goal to less than half of the published target. Perhaps Vietnam is relying on the principle of common but differentiated responsibility to eventually achieve a 10% target for MPAs, or perhaps it is simply being more realistic about what it expects to be able to achieve by 2030. This example from Vietnam is illustrative of one of the major limitations of informal lawmaking. Where there is no requirement to share a legal lexicon of obligations, as there is with a treaty, states and others working within the framework have discretion about how to interpret a given goal, target, or principle.

14.3.2 Target 14.c

Beyond the responses focused on MPAs, another interesting standard emerging from the SDGs is participation in international institutions. Target 14.c calls for states to join 'regional and international regimes for the conservation and sustainable use of oceans and their resources by their parties'. While most states were already party to the LOSC, there has been some activity in joining the Fish Stocks Agreement,[34] with a number of new states, including Chile, Ecuador, Ghana, Thailand, Benin, St Kitts and Nevis, Vanuatu, Vietnam, and Cambodia joining after the adoption of the SDGs.

Even where there continue to be shortfalls, targets for governments still have value because of their informal nature, for at least three reasons. First, they offer a rapid-response policy tool, particularly where the policy object is under the control of states, as in the case of some sources of land-based pollution, or the designation of an MPA. In contrast to treaty negotiations, there is no need for states to deliberate, and potentially disagree, over textual language, as occurs when negotiators grapple with trying to create a new binding instrument to address areas beyond national jurisdiction. States can, instead, move towards identifying where implementation of a target exists, where gaps exist, and where best practices might be appropriate. While the level of detail of the 142 'voluntary national reviews' varies, all of the submissions demonstrate a concerted effort to at least compare national policies with the specific SDG targets and, in many instances, to initiate or continue national policies

[33] 'Vietnam's Voluntary National Review on the Implementation of the Sustainable Development Goals' (June 2018) <https://sustainabledevelopment.un.org/content/documents/19967VNR_of_Viet_Nam.pdf> accessed 30 June 2021.

[34] Agreement for the Implementation of the Provisions of the United Nations Convention on the Law of the Sea of 10 December 1982 Relating to the Conservation and Management of Straddling Fish Stocks and Highly Migratory Fish Stocks (adopted 4 August 1995, entered into force 11 December 2001) 2167 UNTS 3 (hereafter 'Fish Stocks Agreement').

intended to achieve the targets.[35] Second, the targets offer a shared standard for governments to build the rule of law around ocean governance. While there are certain benefits for investing in the SDG targets of combatting illegal, unregulated, or unreported (IUU) fishing and reducing land-based pollution these benefits are further multiplied by having a critical mass of states coordinating efforts. Finally, some states are more willing to be honest about their shortcomings because there are no sanctions. In 2020, during the First Global Workshop for the Voluntary National Reviews, representatives from one country indicated that their government was attempting to make an honest assessment of their 'progress' by doing a gap analysis to assess where the country was 'falling short in SDG implementation'.[36]

As an informal lawmaking tool, the SDGs apply not only to states. As encouraged in *The Future We Want*, SDG 17 contemplates involvement from civil society, academia, and private enterprise, through global partnerships for sustainable development. The next section explores how the private corporate sector has interacted with SDG 14, and internalized certain targets from the SDG into its business activities.

14.4 Role of Private Sector in Implementing SDG14 and Informal Lawmaking by Private Business Sector

As part of *The Future We Want*, state policymakers understood that policies would continue to fail without a holistic approach. They called for better integration between public and private governance.[37] Throughout the process, it was understood that private actors, ranging from civil society groups, to universities, to businesses, must be integrated into implementation efforts. In addition to the possibility of public–private partnerships, states called for more 'regulatory and policy frameworks that enable business to advance sustainable development initiatives', as well as more 'responsible business practices, such as those promoted by the United Nations Global Compact'.[38]

After states adopted the SDGs in 2015, conversations began almost immediately about what types of partnerships might be productive to achieve targets. For achieving certain SDG 14 targets, the response of the private sector becomes critical, because many existing ocean challenges are driven by private actions that may, or may not, be regulated, and which range from maritime transport, fishing, energy extraction, and mining, to waste production. In 2017, the UN Global Compact, representing the interests of 4,658 national and multinational companies, published a Blueprint for Business Leadership on the SDGs, calling upon company leaders to take business actions aligned with SDG targets.[39]

[35] It may be noted that Belize, in 2017, intended, in response to SDG 14, to enact and implement a new Fisheries Bill by 2018, and to develop a national marine fisheries policy by 2020. Belize had not implemented a Fisheries Bill, as of November 2019, but the Belize Fisheries Department made a public commitment, at the 2017 Ocean Conference, to implement a new fisheries bill, and work still appears to be under way, in spite of the delays.

[36] 'First Global Workshop for the Voluntary National Reviews to be presented at the UN High-Level Political Forum on Sustainable Development in 2020' (19–20 November 2019) <https://sustainabledevelopment.un.org/content/documents/25466Summary_of_the_first_Global_VNR_Workshop_Oslo.pdf> accessed 30 June 2021.

[37] UN General Assembly, 'The Future We Want' (n 4) paras 46–47.

[38] ibid, para 46.

[39] UN Global Compact, 'How Business Leadership can Advance Goal 14 on Life Below Water' (2017) <http://blueprint.unglobalcompact.org/sdgs/sdg14/#business-actions> accessed 30 June 2021. 75% of business leaders who were surveyed in 2017 indicated that they were taking action on the SDGs as part of business practice; only 12% of these leaders are taking actions on SDG 14: UN Global Compact, 'United Nations Global Compact Progress

Table 14.2 Business Actions and Corporate Accountability Measures

Business Action from SDG Blueprint	Corporate Accountability Measures
1. 'Implement policies and practices to protect ocean ecosystems that are affected by business and supply chain activities.'	Put in place social safeguards and manage negative impacts. Ensure 'meaningful engagement with potentially affected populations', to respect and protect human rights. Monitor and report on progress towards SDGs.
2. 'Research, develop, and deploy products, services, and business models which negate impacts on ocean ecosystems and contribute to their restoration.'	Manage economic and social risks associated with introducing new products, services, and business models.
3. 'Galvanize finance for the protection and further development of ocean ecosystems and water system flows.'	Manage risks with adequate safeguards in place for local communities and other stakeholders, where financial flows are altered.
4. 'Design and implement solutions to accurately value and respect natural capital, and drive wider adoption of these solutions.'	Provide newly acquired information to the public on the negative and positive impacts of natural capital.

Recognizing that '[a]ll businesses have a responsibility to abide by environmental law and international treaties on the protection of marine ecosystems',[40] the Blueprint calls upon corporate actors to take actions, including to 'protect ocean ecosystems', 'develop products that restore oceans', 'finance the protection of water systems', and 'design solutions that value natural capital'.[41]

Within the Blueprint context, engaged companies are expected to achieve 'accountability' for their actions in support of the SDGs. The choice of the word 'accountability' by the Blueprint authors suggests that the SDGs reflect something more than an aspiration for corporate governance. Instead, the SDGs represent standards against which a corporation can measure its performance. The following table, Table 14.2, provides text describing SDG 14's business actions, plus accountability measures for companies adhering to the Blueprint.

From the perspective of informal lawmaking, the adoption of Business Action 1 is perhaps the most interesting, because it acknowledges the direct role that private environmental governance and, particularly, supply chain decisions play in marine protection. Companies, through pursuit of various certification schemes, such as the Marine Stewardship Council's (MSC) certification for certain fisheries, understand the power of informal lawmaking in their industries. The MSC has set the standards by which company players who hope to be certified are trying to change their fishing practices.[42] While the MSC standards have

Report: Business Solutions to Sustainable Development' (2017) 9<https://www.unglobalcompact.org/docs/publications/UN%20Impact%20Brochure_Concept-FINAL.pdf> accessed 30 June 2021.

[40] UN Global Compact, 'How Business Leadership can Advance Goal 14 on Life Below Water' Business Action 1.

[41] ibid, Business Actions 2, 3, and 4.

[42] Marine Stewardship Council, 'The MSC Fisheries Standard' <https://www.msc.org/standards-and-certification/fisheries-standard> accessed 30 June 2021.

no basis in formal law, they incorporate the Food and Agriculture Organization's Code of Conduct for Responsible Fishing (also an informal lawmaking tool), and are now informally incentivizing formal changes to business operations.

In response to the Blueprint, companies participating in the Global Compact are now expected to consider 'policies and practices' that incorporate actions that further the achievement of the SDGs. Just as there is some expectation that states will participate in voluntary reporting, companies are also expected to report. In 2017, the Global Compact issued a document to assist businesses with reporting on corporate progress towards achieving the SDGs, in order to create a 'common disclosure set'.[43] Also in 2017, the Global Compact published a business progress report, with one of its focus areas being 'saving our oceans: everybody's business', where it called on its members to take specific business operation actions, including implementing the circular economy, reducing carbon emissions, banning bottom trawling, and removing plastics from products.[44] This effort was followed up by the Global Compact's Action Platform on ocean stewardship, which calls for specific actions for both states and companies to deliver on the SDGs, including some important and interesting legalistic suggestions.[45] In 2020, the Global Compact published the 'Sustainable Ocean Principles', offering a private sector commitment framework for furthering the achievement of SDG 14.[46] Notably, in 'practical guidance', the Global Compact offers a number of specific recommendations for industry sectors to move 'beyond minimum requirements set by laws and regulations'.[47] What these commitments mean, from an informal lawmaking perspective, is that principles like the Sustainable Ocean Principles, which are explicitly identified as aspirational (rather than operational), may actually achieve lawmaking outcomes, if sectors implement the 'practical guidance' so that a sector such as the aquaculture sector may create for itself new, generally accepted international regulations and standards, such as obligations to report publicly on social and environmental impacts associated with business activities, to certify facilities to a particular set of sustainability criteria, or to conduct human rights assessments across a supply chain.[48]

The SDG targets are, arguably, having an impact on business because of the perception that they are setting the agenda for government regulators. Given the potential cost of being regulated, many companies will choose to work with governments on creating

[43] UN Global Compact, 'Business Reporting on the SDGs: An Analysis of the Goals and Targets' (2017) <https://www.unglobalcompact.org/docs/publications/GRI_UNGC_SDG_Reporting_An_Analysis_of_Goals_and_Targets_2017.pdf> accessed 30 June 2021.

[44] UN Global Compact, 'United Nations Global Compact Progress Report: Business Solutions to Sustainable Development' (2017) (n 40) 74.

[45] UN Global Impact, 'Action Platform: Sustainable Seafood' (2020) <https://unglobalcompact.org/take-action/ocean/communication/sustainable-seafood> accessed 30 June 2021 ('All seafood traded internationally in 2030 should be required by law to be accompanied by standardized traceability data that consumers can trust.'); UN Global Impact, 'Action Platform, Decarbonizing Shipping' (2020) <https://unglobalcompact.org/take-action/ocean/communication/decarbonizing-shipping> accessed 30 June 2021 ('International regulations to reduce shipping emissions: IMO members, Governments and the industry must support proposed regulatory measures, the timelines and the proposed stringency levels.').

[46] UN Global Compact, 'Sustainable Ocean Principles' <https://d306pr3pise04h.cloudfront.net/docs/publications%2FSustainable + Ocean+Principles.pdf> accessed 30 June 2021 (including participation from seventy companies, from a variety of ocean-related sectors).

[47] UN Global Compact, 'Sustainable Ocean Business Action Platform, Practical Guidance for the UN Global Compact Sustainable Ocean Principles: Aquaculture' 13 <https://ungc-communications-assets.s3.amazonaws.com/docs/publications/UN-Global-Compact-Sustainable-Ocean-Principles-%20Aquaculture.pdf> accessed 30 June 2021.

[48] ibid 9, 16–17.

functioning regulatory frameworks.[49] As with states, various companies have, in response to the SDG targets, made public commitments.[50] As some of these commitments are specific to supply chains, the commitments have direct implications for key aspects of private environmental governance. As of December 2020, various stakeholders had entered 16,333 commitments to achieve SDG 14.[51] Of these commitments, 118 were made by the private sector.[52] Many of these commitments were made at a high-level UN Conference to Support the Implementation of Sustainable Development Goal 14, also known as 'The Ocean Conference'. The following subsections provide two illustrations of how the SDG targets, perceived to be a legitimate expression of governments' expectations for private industry, may have triggered internal corporate changes as a result of public commitments made by private actors in the context of SDG 14.

14.4.1 Fisheries Commitment towards MSC Certification

In April 2019, the Organization of Associated Producers of Large Tuna Freezers (OPAGAC), which has, historically, been responsible for handling 6% of the world's tuna catch from the Atlantic, Indian, and Pacific Oceans, entered a commitment to ensure that tuna handled by members of the organization would be responsibly fished. This commitment was, partially, in response to Target 14.4, calling upon states to regulate harvesting, and end overfishing, in conformity with the LOSC obligations to manage fisheries sustainably.[53]

As part of this commitment, OPAGAC members have agreed to adhere to a standard (UNE 195006), developed by the Spanish Association for Standardization, for tuna purse seiners, covering fishing activity, crew safety, and maritime health, as well as ensuring a chain of custody between seiners and processing plants. OPAGAC members who comply with the standard are eligible for certification by AENOR, a business association member of the UN Global Compact. Also partnering with the World Wildlife Fund on a global tuna fisheries improvement project, OPAGAC has agreed to work towards achieving certification under MSC standards.

What makes these commitments interesting, from an informal lawmaking perspective, is that OPAGAC, as a sizeable industry player, is now requiring its members to comply with an industry standard, UNE 195006, to demonstrate progress towards Target 14.5. OPAGAC described its commitment to both the UNE standard and the MSC standard as achieving 'a fisheries certification that will include the environmental and social sustainability of the tuna fisheries as a global standard'.[54] In making a more formal and public SDG 14 commitment, OPAGAC identified numerous targets that were covered by their sustainability

[49] ibid, Principle 5 ('Engage responsibly with relevant regulatory or enforcement bodies on ocean-related laws, regulations, and other frameworks.').

[50] See, eg UN Global Compact, 'Signatories to the Sustainable Ocean Principles' <https://www.unglobalcompact.org/take-action/ocean/signatories> accessed 30 June 2021.

[51] Ocean Conference, 'Registry of Voluntary Commitments' (30 December 2020) <https://oceanconference.un.org/commitments/> accessed 30 June 2021.

[52] ibid.

[53] OPAGAC, 'OPAGAC Signs the UN Global Compact's Sustainable Ocean Principles to Promote Responsible Practices in the Fishing Industry' (10 June 2020) <http://opagac.org/en/opagac-signs-the-un-global-compacts-sustainable-ocean-principles-to-promote-responsible-practices-in-the-fishing-industry/> accessed 30 June 2021.

[54] OPAGAC, 'Tuna from Responsible Fishing' <https://oceanconference.un.org/commitments/?id = 31754> accessed 30 June 2021.

efforts, including ecosystem management (SDG Target 14.2), ending overfishing (SDG Target 14.4), increasing benefits to small island developing states (SDG Target 14.7), improving marine scientific research and technology transfer (SDG Target 14.a), and improving the rule of law (SDG Target 14.c). OPAGAC's articulated contribution to the rule of law is quite interesting, as the organization drafted three points to describe the context for its commitment to the rule of law, namely:

- activities to develop the capacity of States towards broader participation in and effective implementation of UNCLOS and its implementing Agreements
- strengthening ocean governance
- development of necessary infrastructure and/or enforcement capabilities to comply with international law, as reflected in UNCLOS and as complemented by other ocean-related instruments[55]

With the exception of 'strengthening ocean governance', OPAGAC's rule of law commitments describe efforts that are usually considered to be state-led, namely the implementation of treaty commitments, and their enforcement. This example represents an interesting blurring of the lines between state responsibilities and private activities. Moreover, OPAGAC's SDG commitment reflects a strong showing of private environmental governance in an industry where private involvement is essential to improve compliance, given the difficulties of detecting IUU fishing. Arguably, the designation of SDG 14 has catalysed informal lawmaking processes, propelling entities like OPAGAC to accelerate sustainability efforts.

14.4.2 Marine Plastic Pollution

In response to Target 14.1, a number of companies have become increasingly vocal about their efforts to change internal policies and practices to address marine pollution, thereby further implementing the LOSC. With the year 2025 approaching, an increasing number of large companies are making packaging changes intended to reduce marine debris. Some of these companies are announcing their commitments within the context of the SDGs. For example, Coca-Cola Japan entered an SDG partnership commitment in 2018, and shared its 2030 packaging vision, which includes a series of milestones, such as recycling 50% of PET plastic by 2022, introducing all-recyclable materials for packaging by 2025, reducing materials for bottles by 35% by 2030, and using 100% sustainable materials (for example, recycled plastics or plant-based plastics) by 2030, including no fossil fuel feedstocks in producing PET packaging.[56] Whether these goals are ambitious enough to stem the tide of trash entering the oceans remains to be seen, but what is interesting about this commitment is Coca-Cola Japan's internalization of the target into its business operations.

Other supply chain-centred commitments that further progress the achievement of Target 14.1 include the Dell computer company's investment in a new supply chain that collects and reuses ocean-bound plastics for production components. In 2017, Dell entered

[55] ibid.

[56] UN, 'World Without Waste' (2018) SDG Action 34140 <https://sustainabledevelopment.un.org/partnership/?p=34140> accessed 2 July 2021.

a commitment to use 16,000 pounds of 'ocean-bound plastic' obtained from ghost fishing gear and other sources, with a goal of diverting 3 million pounds of plastics between 2017 and 2022.[57]

14.5 Concluding Thoughts about SDGs as an Informal Lawmaking Process

While SDG 14 is a non-binding goal with no normative intent, this chapter has argued that the targets designed under SDG 14 have had normative effect, and have generated formal legal and governance responses from both national governments and multinational corporations. In some cases, governments are partnering with multinational corporations to achieve ocean-related targets, as exemplified by the Maldives' collaboration with Parley for the Oceans, to create a nationwide plan to respond to a number of the ocean-related goals, including creating and scaling up new non-toxic marine materials for a blue economy.[58] While the responses to the SDG targets have taken different formats—from the introduction of laws, for some states, to changes in supply chains, for private corporations—all of the responses suggest that the targets are functioning as informal lawmaking measures, catalysing ongoing implementation of the law of the sea, including the LOSC.

In some respects, in the context of ocean governance, the informal lawmaking process associated with SDG 14 is serving 'as a crude global system of checks and balances',[59] by compelling states to take stock of their existing governance responses, and to make reforms, as necessary, to conform with the targets, as well as bringing corporate players out of the shadows. The current structure of the SDGs, as an informal lawmaking process, encourages rudimentary 'checks and balances' based on social and reputational accountability, rather than sanctioned accountability. All of the targets of the SDGs are published on multiple public platforms, and have been translated into multiple languages. As a result, the literate public can query governments on domestic implementation efforts.

Under the SDG framework, there are five additional mechanisms that serve limited accountability functions. First, states have agreed to submit voluntary national reviews that provide more detailed information about what they are doing to achieve the SDGs. These reports are publicly available for review.[60] Second, the UN Secretary-General's office has published an annual report, based on the voluntary state reports, that describes progress towards the various goals, and areas where more effort from actors is needed.[61] In the case

[57] UN, 'Dell Commits to Scaling Commercial Use of Ocean bound Plastic' (2017) Ocean Action 37851 <https://oceanconference.un.org/commitments/?id=37851#:~:text=Dell%20Commits%20to%20Scaling%20Commercial%20Use%20of%20Ocean%20Bound%20Plastic&text=Our%20commitment%20in%20support%20of,based%20on%20our%202017%20baseline> accessed 2 July 2021.

[58] Parley for the Oceans, 'The Maldives Join Parley for the Oceans as Founding Member of "Future Island Nation" Program' (*Global Recycling*, 26 September 2019) <https://global-recycling.info/archives/3318> accessed 2 July 2021.

[59] Mark Pollack and Gregory Shaffer, 'The Interaction of Formal and Informal Lawmaking' in Joost Pauwelyn, Ramses A Wessel, and Jan Wouters (eds), *Informal International Lawmaking* (OUP 2012) 28.

[60] For links to Voluntary National Reviews, see, generally, UN Sustainable Development Goals Knowledge Platform, 'States Members of the United Nations and States Members of Specialized Agencies' <https://sustainabledevelopment.un.org/memberstates> accessed 2 July 2021.

[61] For links to UN Secretary-General's Sustainable Development Goals Reports, see, generally, UN, 'Sustainable Development Goals Report' <https://www.un.org/sustainabledevelopment/progress-report/> accessed 2 July 2021.

of SDG 14, for example, the Secretary-General's 2019 report drew attention to the fact that 20% of countries, particularly in Oceania and Central/South Asia, have a low to medium level of implementation of regulatory and institutional frameworks to protect small-scale fisheries.[62] Third, for each promise made by a state, company, or NGO, the SDG knowledge platform provides a web page, with a symbolic 'traffic light' indicating steps taken towards achieving the goal. This visual cue provides all interested actors with a signal of whether an actor has achieved its pledge, and so this tool may have implications for reputational integrity. Fourth, UN member states are hosting an 'Ocean Conference' every few years. The events are designed to keep the focus on the goals and targets, and to seek additional partnerships for science-based solutions to ocean challenges. A number of the corporate commitments discussed above were made at the 2017 Ocean Conference. Finally, in order to keep attention focused on ocean matters, the UN has declared 2021 to 2030 to be the UN Decade of Ocean Science for Sustainable Development, and has called upon partners to participate in a decade-long process to develop 'ocean decade' objectives and actions, responsive to the SDGs and regional and global policy frameworks.[63]

There is an unprecedented degree of interest in the oceans, and so the acceleration of informal lawmaking processes to achieve quantitative and qualitative standards is not surprising. However, this chapter closes with a cautionary statement. The nature of the SDGs as standards does not offer a unitary approach, but, instead, a flexible approach intended to ensure the broadest participation possible by social actors. Yet, the flexible nature of the standards may also compromise the targets as standards. If every country and concerned actor freely interprets the relatively open-ended standards, this fragmentation may ultimately lead to less ambition than a more traditional lawmaking instrument. States with extremely biodiverse coastlines and marine areas may be fully satisfied with protection for just 10% of their marine area, and companies who have changed their packaging will be content that they have 'significantly' reduced a source of marine pollution. Without visionary leadership at the international level, there will be progress in addressing ocean governance issues, but only up to a certain politically or economically convenient point. States and companies can prove this fear wrong in the coming decade, but once performance standards are negotiated, only a few actors will be likely to outperform the standards.

While the standards may produce a 'medley' approach to marine governance, it remains clear that the standards are catalysing states to act more quickly, and more publicly. In 2019, at the Our Ocean conference, which was a multi-stakeholder annual conference sponsored by various states to assess solutions for better ocean governance, eleven states committed to creating new MPAs.[64] Even though the SDG targets alone would never be sufficient as the basis of an ocean governance structure, they are part of a 'bottom-up' process that may eventually contribute to full implementation of the LOSC.

[62] UN, 'Report of the Secretary-General on SDG Progress 2019: Special Edition' (n 9).

[63] UN, 'The United Nations Decade of Ocean Science for Sustainable Development (2021–2030): Implementation Plan Summary' (2021) 8 <https://oceandecade.org/resource/109/Summary—Version-20-of-the-Ocean-Decade-Implementation-Plan> accessed 14 July 2021 (just as SDG Goal 14 is situated within the existing legal structure of the LOSC, so too is 'the Ocean Decade … implemented on a voluntary basis within the legal framework of the United Nations Convention on the Law of the Sea').

[64] Government of Norway, 'Our Ocean' (Oslo 2019) <https://ourocean2019.no/wp-content/uploads/2019/12/Report_OurOcean_Oslo_2019_UU.pdf> accessed 2 July 2021 (Belgium (protect 30% of ocean by 2030), Canada, Indonesia (700,000 hectares of marine conservation areas by 2020), Mozambique (increasing protected areas from 3% to 7%), Namibia, Norway, Pakistan, Panama, Poland, Spain, and United Arab Emirates).

From the perspective of informal lawmaking, the SDGs reflect a paradox of sorts. On the one hand, the SDGs are explicitly non-binding, and are not legal instruments. How is it, then, that a non-legal instrument can operate in a lawmaking fashion? What is surprising is that, even though the SDGs are 'no stakes' in terms of their legal consequences, the very negotiation of the SDGs has compelled a wide spectrum of states to take legal actions, as states have sought, in public venues, to boost state authority by announcing legislative actions in response to SDG targets. As the SDG 14 targets have contributed to the interpretation of what is expected of states under the LOSC, the SDGs have operated as a 'commitment club' for states that are implementing legislative reforms that they are not legally obliged to undertake. While one may be sceptical of the SDGs as offering 'too little, too late' on tackling complex socioecological challenges, what is clear is that the informal structure of the SDGs has catalysed immediate and visible legislative and policy action from a diverse set of states, rather than the inertia sometimes associated with post-treaty adoption as states seek ratifications.[65] What remains to be seen is whether the legislative commitments made by states in response to the SDG targets are actually qualitatively significant in achieving shared ocean governance goals. More structures of formal accountability may still be needed, but perhaps the reputational gains possible under the SDGs will translate into long-term and meaningful legal and normative changes.

[65] The SDGs have received attention in a variety of state-oriented venues, including the G20, which publishes annual updates on the Action Plan on the Sustainable Development Goals. Notably, the potential lawmaking capacity of Goal 14 is a view not uniformly shared across international organizations.

15

Informal International Lawmaking as a Panacea in the Absence of Regime Focus? Marine Debris, Plastics, and Microplastics

Rosemary Rayfuse

15.1 Introduction

In 2019, scientists discovered a plastic bag on the seafloor at the bottom of the Mariana Trench, nearly eleven kilometres below the surface of the ocean.[1] While most plastic in the ocean floats on the surface, discarded plastic litter has increasingly been found in the deep sea, at depths down to 7,000 metres and beyond.[2] As well-represented in the notorious 'garbage patches' now circulating in the world's oceans, the amount of anthropogenic debris in the marine environment, in particular the amount of plastics and microplastics, continues to increase exponentially.[3] It has been estimated that, by 2050, the weight of plastics in the ocean will exceed that of fish.[4] Entanglement in, and ingestion of, plastics is known to account for the deaths of millions of marine organisms, including seabirds, marine mammals, turtles, and fish, annually. In addition to plastic litter, ingestion of microplastics, produced either for industrial purposes or as a by-product of the breakdown of larger pieces of plastic, poses a serious threat to both marine biota and humans, although the full extent of the adverse impacts, and their downstream impacts on human health, are not yet completely understood.[5]

Of course, plastic is not the only type of marine debris (or litter, as it is also referred to). Marine debris, as a category of marine pollution, includes other substances, such as wood, glass, metal, and any other substances made, or used, by humans that make their way, either directly or indirectly, into the marine environment.[6] However, with between 8 million and

[1] Rebecca Morelle, 'Mariana Trench: Deepest-ever Sub Dive Finds Plastic Bag' (*BBC News*, 13 May 2019) <https://www.bbc.com/news/science-environment-48230157> accessed 27 July 2021.

[2] Sanae Chiba and others, 'Human Footprint in the Abyss: 30 Year Records of Deep-sea Plastic Debris' (2018) 96 Mar Pol'y 204–12. See also AJ Jamieson and others, 'Microplastics and Synthetic Particles Ingested by Deep-sea Amphipods in Six of the Deepest Marine Ecosystems on Earth' (2019) 6 Royal Soc'y Open Sci 180667.

[3] UN, 'Report on the Work of the United Nations Open-ended Informal Consultative Process on Oceans and the Law of the Sea at its Seventeenth Meeting' UN Doc A/71/204, 25 July 2016, para 15.

[4] World Economic Forum, 'The New Plastics Economy: Rethinking the Future of Plastics' (January 2016) 7 <http://www3.weforum.org/docs/WEF_The_New_Plastics_Economy.pdf> accessed 27 July 2021; Jenna R Jambeck, 'Plastic Waste Inputs from Land into the Ocean' (2015) 6223 Science 347.

[5] PJ Kershaw and CM Rochman (eds), 'Sources, Fate and Effects of Microplastics in the Marine Environment: Part Two of a Global Assessment' (GESAMP 2016) (IMO/FAO/UNESCO–IOC/UNIDO/WMO/IAEA/UN/UNEP/UNDP Joint Group of Experts on the Scientific Aspects of Marine Environmental Protection) Reports & Study Series, GESAMP No 93.

[6] UNEP defines marine litter as 'any persistent, manufactured or processed solid material discarded, disposed of or abandoned in the marine and coastal environment', and notes that it 'consists of items that have been made or used by people and deliberately discarded into the sea or rivers or on beaches; brought indirectly to the sea with

Rosemary Rayfuse, *Informal International Lawmaking as a Panacea in the Absence of Regime Focus? Marine Debris, Plastics, and Microplastics* In: *Unconventional Lawmaking in the Law of the Sea*. Edited by: Natalie Klein, Oxford University Press. © Rosemary Rayfuse 2022. DOI: 10.1093/oso/9780192897824.003.0015

12 million tonnes of plastic ending up in the ocean each year, plastic accounts for up to 80% (and, in some places, as much as 95%) of the total amount of marine debris entering the ocean.[7] The vast majority of this plastic enters the ocean from land.[8] However, up to 20% of marine plastic litter results from sea-based activities, such as fishing, aquaculture, shipping, ocean dumping, and other ocean-based activities.[9] Of particular concern is the problem of abandoned, lost, or discarded fishing gear (ALDFG), which consists mostly of plastic and synthetic materials that do not degrade in seawater. ALDFG is estimated to account for up to 60% of ship-source plastic debris,[10] and one tenth, by volume, of all marine debris.[11]

By far the most pervasive form of ocean pollution, marine plastic debris is now recognized as a serious global environmental problem, negatively affecting the entire marine ecosystem and all ocean users,[12] and posing a potential planetary boundary threat.[13] The environmental, economic, and social impacts of marine debris, in general, and marine plastic debris, in particular, have been well documented in recent years. However, the ubiquitous origins and global effects of marine plastic debris make it difficult to regulate and control, in the context of a state-based, sectoral approach to oceans management.

The Law of the Sea Convention (LOSC)[14] requires states to protect the marine environment, including through the adoption of laws and regulations aimed at preventing, reducing, and controlling marine pollution from all sources. At the global level, a number of binding international agreements address various aspects of ship-source plastic pollution. However, while the law of the sea can provide guidance in the context of marine-based sources, notably only three of the 320 provisions in the LOSC refer specifically to land-based sources of pollution.[15] This lack of 'regime focus' in the LOSC is hardly surprising, given the LOSC's role as the 'constitution for the oceans'.[16] However, when combined with the multiplicity of anthropogenic land-based sources of marine debris, this lack of regime focus results not only in the need for cross-sectoral cooperation and collaboration within

rivers, sewage, storm water or winds; accidentally lost, including material lost at sea in bad weather (fishing gear, cargo); or deliberately left by people on beaches and shores': UNEP, *Marine Litter: A Global Challenge* (United Nations Environment Programme Nairobi 2009) (hereafter UNEP, 'Marine Litter') 13.

[7] Florian Thevenon, Chris Carroll, and Joao Sousa (eds), *Plastic Debris in the Ocean: The Characterization of Marine Plastics and their Environmental Impacts, Situation Analysis Report* (IUCN 2014) 19. See also Michelle Allsopp, Adam Walters, David Santillo, and Paul Johnston, *Plastic Debris in the World's Oceans* (Greenpeace 2006).

[8] Julien Boucher and Damien Friot, *Primary Microplastics in the Oceans: A Global Evaluation of Sources* (IUCN 2017).

[9] GESAMP, 'Sea-based Sources of Marine Litter—A Review of Current Knowledge and Assessment of Data Gaps: Second Interim Report of GESAMP Working Group 43' (2020) <http://www.gesamp.org/work/groups/wg-43-on-sea-based-sources-of-marine-litter> accessed 27 July 2021.

[10] Carmen Morales-Caselles, Josue Viejo, Elisa Martí, and others, 'An Inshore–Offshore Sorting System Revealed from Global Classification of Ocean Litter' (2021) 4 Nat Sustain 484–93 <https://doi.org/10.1038/s41893-021-00720-8> accessed 27 July 2021.

[11] Graeme Macfadyen, Tim Huntington, and Rod Cappell, *Abandoned, Lost or Otherwise Discarded Fishing Gear* (FAO Fisheries and Aquaculture Technical Paper No 523, 2009).

[12] UNEP, Marine Litter (n 6); UNEP, Resolution on Marine Plastics and Microplastics, UNEP/EA.4/L.7, 14 March 2019; UN, Report of the Secretary-General on Oceans and the Law of the Sea, UN Doc A/71/74, 22 March 2016.

[13] Patricia Villarrubla-Gómez, Sarah E Cornell, and Joan Fabres, 'Marine Plastic Pollution as a Planetary Boundary Threat—The Drifting Piece in the Sustainability Puzzle' (2018) 96 Mar Pol'y 213.

[14] United Nations Convention on the Law of the Sea (adopted 10 December 1982, entered into force 16 November 1994) 1833 UNTS 31363 (hereafter 'LOSC').

[15] ibid, arts 194, 207, and 213.

[16] Usually attributed to Tommy Koh, this term was, in fact, used earlier by Elisabeth Mann Borgese: Elisabeth Mann Borgese, 'A Constitution for the Oceans' in Elisabeth Mann Borgese and David Krieger (eds), *The Tides of Change: Peace, Pollution and the Potential of the Oceans* (Mason/Charter 1975) 340.

the law of the sea, but also the need for broader coordinated approaches beyond the law of the sea, involving state and non-state actors, the private sector, and civil society.

This chapter examines the role of informal international lawmaking, in the context of the control of marine plastic debris. The chapter focuses, in particular, on the International Maritime Organization (IMO) and the Global Programme of Action for the Protection of the Marine Environment from Land-based Activities (GPA) as illustrations of two possible roles for informal lawmaking: the 'thickening' of existing hard-law obligations, and the filling of gaps in relation to complex large-scale global issues that affect the oceans, but that lie beyond the formal limits of the LOSC. The chapter begins with a brief description of the increasing international recognition of the problem of marine plastic debris, before turning to the definition of informal lawmaking and an analysis of its application in the contexts of ship-source, and land-based sources of, marine plastic debris. The chapter concludes with some observations on the significance of informal lawmaking and its role in filling the void between the law of sea and the control of marine plastic pollution from land-based sources.

15.2 International Recognition of the Problem of Marine Plastic Debris

Plastic has been recognized as a serious marine pollutant since at least the 1960s; early concerns relating to the problem of ingestion by, and entanglement of, marine species soon giving way to increasing concerns over dangerous chemical compounds such as PCBs entering the marine, and ultimately human, food chain. Initial international efforts to deal with the problem of marine plastic debris focused on the regulation of ship-source plastic pollution. The London Convention, adopted in 1972, explicitly prohibits the deliberate disposal of dangerous wastes, including 'persistent plastics and other persistent synthetic materials, such as netting or ropes, that float or remain suspended in marine waters in a way that may materially interfere with fishing, navigation, and other legitimate uses of the sea'.[17] The London Protocol, adopted in 1996, goes further, by banning all dumping of all substances, except for those specifically listed, of which plastic is not one.[18] A major limitation of the London Convention, and the subsequent London Protocol, is, however, that they do not regulate waste generated during the normal operation of ships. In other words, they permit the deliberate disposal of ship wastes, including plastics and other garbage generated in the day-to-day operations of ships, as well as the disposal of synthetic fishing gear from fishing vessels, since such actions are, arguably, 'incidental to, or derived from the normal operations of vessels'.[19]

The limitations of the London Convention were addressed in Annex V to the International Convention for the Prevention of Pollution from Ships (known as the MARPOL Convention or MARPOL).[20] MARPOL applies to the discharge of all harmful substances from ships,

[17] Convention on the Prevention of Marine Pollution by Dumping of Waste and other Matter (opened for signature 29 December 1972, entered into force 30 August 1975) 1046 UNTS 120, Annex 1(4) (hereafter 'London Convention').

[18] Protocol to the Convention on the Prevention of Marine Pollution by Dumping of Wastes and other Matter (opened for signature 7 November 1996, entered into force 24 March 2006) 36 ILM 1 (hereafter 'London Protocol').

[19] London Convention (n 17) art III (1)(b)(i).

[20] Annex V [Regulations for the Prevention of Pollution by Garbage from Ships] to International Convention for the Prevention of Pollution from Ships (as Modified by the Protocol of 1978 Relating thereto) (adopted 2 November 1973, entered into force 2 October 1983) 1340 UNTS 184 (hereafter 'MARPOL Annex V').

including operational discharges, except those from dumping, seabed exploration and exploitation, and from legitimate scientific research into pollution abatement. The MARPOL Convention contains provisions dealing with national law, certificates and inspections, and enforcement of standards. The details of these standards are then set out in six annexes, of which Annex V deals with garbage. Annex V expressly prohibits all ships from discharging any plastics into marine waters, including such debris as synthetic ropes, synthetic fishing nets, and plastic garbage.[21] It also severely restricts the discharge of certain other ship-generated wastes.[22] Importantly, Annex V applies to all ships, of any size, including fishing vessels, as well as to floating platforms and oil rigs,[23] although exceptions are made in respect of ship safety and accidental loss of synthetic fishing nets or synthetic rope.[24] Requirements for information placards, garbage management plans, and the keeping of a garbage record book vary, depending on the size of a ship.[25] Port states are to provide adequate garbage reception facilities and they can also inspect foreign-flagged ships, in certain circumstances, to ensure that adequate shipboard procedures are in place.[26]

Although adopted in 1978, MARPOL Annex V did not enter into force until 1988, in part due to concerns regarding requirements relating to the provision of port waste reception facilities, the existence and/or adequacy of which were lacking in most states.[27] In the intervening years, attention focused, increasingly, on the problem of ALDFG and, in particular, on the use of large-scale pelagic drift nets. The use, and often loss or abandonment, of these 'ghost nets' was stripping the ocean of both target and non-target species, including marine mammals, birds, and other living marine resources, which were either injured or killed. Gear set with the original intention of retrieval, but later abandoned, or lost due to conflict, bad weather, or snagging, did not meet the definition of dumping under the London Convention. Likewise, the exceptions in MARPOL Annex V regarding ship safety and accidental loss provided a significant loophole.

In 1985, the problem of discarded or lost fishing gear was recognized as a particular concern by the Food and Agriculture Organization (FAO) Committee on Fisheries (COFI), who noted the lack of success of MARPOL Annex V in dealing with the issue, and pointedly encouraged further work to be undertaken by the IMO and other treaty bodies.[28] In 1989, the UN General Assembly (UNGA) went further, noting the highly indiscriminate and wasteful method of large-scale pelagic drift net fishing, expressing concern over the entanglement—including in lost or discarded nets—of marine living resources, resulting in injury or death, and calling for the adoption of a global moratorium on all large-scale pelagic drift net fishing.[29]

In 2002, the UNGA recognized the continuing and increasingly pressing need to address the issue of marine debris derived from both land-based and ship-generated sources

[21] ibid, reg 3.

[22] 'Garbage' is defined as including 'all kinds of victual, domestic and operational wastes excluding fresh fish and parts thereof, generated during the normal operation of the ship' (ibid, reg 1).

[23] ibid, reg 1.

[24] ibid, reg 6.

[25] ibid, reg 9.

[26] ibid, reg 8.

[27] National Research Council, *Clean Ships, Clean Ports, Clean Oceans: Controlling Garbage and Plastic Wastes at Sea* (The National Academies Press 1995) 166.

[28] FAO, 'Report of the 16th Session of the Committee on Fisheries' (FAO Fisheries Report no 339, 2009), paras 69–72 <http://www.fao.org/3/am682e/am682e.pdf> accessed 27 July 2021.

[29] UNGA Res 44/225 (22 December 1989) UN Doc A/RES/44/225, para 4.

of pollution.[30] The general topic of 'marine debris' first appeared on the UNGA's agenda in 2004, where it was selected as a topic for consideration by the UN Informal Consultative Process on Oceans and the Law of the Sea (UNICPOLOS) in 2005.[31] In its report to the UNGA, UNICPOLOS noted that, although discharge of plastics at sea was prohibited under MARPOL Annex V, levels of marine plastic debris were increasing in some parts of the world. Inadequate waste management, in particular poorly managed landfills, waste carried by wind from urban areas and by sewage systems and rivers into the ocean, and deficiencies in the implementation of MARPOL Annex V were identified as the main reasons for the increase in marine debris, with ALDFG being identified as the most harmful debris to ocean life.[32]

The issue of marine debris has been addressed annually in the UNGA resolutions on the oceans since 2005, where, in line with the emerging recognition of the particular problems posed by plastics and microplastics, the terminology has developed to include specific reference to plastics and microplastics. In 2012, specific reference to marine plastic debris appeared in the outcome document of the Rio+20 Conference on Sustainable Development, *The Future We Want*, in which states noted 'with concern that the health of the oceans and marine biodiversity are negatively affected by marine pollution, including marine debris, especially plastic', and committed 'to take action to reduce the incidence and impacts of such pollution on marine ecosystems, including through the effective implementation of relevant conventions adopted in the framework of the International Maritime Organization, and the follow-up of relevant initiatives such as the Global Programme of Action for the Protection of the Marine Environment from Land-based Activities, as well as the adoption of coordinated strategies to this end'.[33] They further committed 'to take action, by 2025, based on collected scientific data, to achieve significant reductions in marine debris to prevent harm to the coastal and marine environment'.[34] In 2013, the UNGA reiterated these concerns, and recognized the need for better understanding of the sources, amounts, pathways, distribution trends, nature, and impacts of marine debris.[35] To that end, in 2014, it assigned the topic of 'marine debris, plastics and microplastics' to UNICPOLOS, for consideration in 2016.[36]

In 2015, the UNGA adopted the Sustainable Development Goals, Goal 14.1 of which calls on states 'by 2025, to prevent and significantly reduce marine pollution of all kinds, in particular from land-based activities, including marine debris and nutrient pollution'.[37] While SDG 14.1 does not, explicitly, mention plastics, both plastics and microplastics are specifically referred to in subsequent UNGA resolutions. In 2016, the UNGA had before it the report of the discussions in UNICPOLOS on marine debris, plastics, and microplastics, which highlighted the exponential growth of the problem, and the need for prevention,

[30] UNGA, 'Large-scale Pelagic Drift-net Fishing, Unauthorized Fishing in Zones of National Jurisdiction and on the High Seas/Illegal, Unreported and Unregulated Fishing, Fisheries By-catch and Discards, and other Developments' (12 December 2002) UN Doc A/57/142.

[31] UNGA Res 59/24 (17 November 2004) UN Doc A/RES/59/24.

[32] UN, 'Report on the Work of the United Nations Open-ended Informal Consultative Process on Oceans and the Law of the Sea at its Sixth Meeting' (7 July 2005) UN Doc A/60/99.

[33] Endorsed by the UNGA in 'The Future we Want', UNGA Res 66/288 (27 July 2012) UN Doc A/RES/66/288.

[34] ibid, para 163.

[35] UNGA Res 68/70 (9 December 2013) UN Doc A/RES/68/70, para 152.

[36] UNGA Res 69/245 (29 December 2014) UN Doc A/RES/69/245, para 298.

[37] UN, 'Transforming Our World: The 2030 Agenda for Sustainable Development', UNGA Res 70/1 (25 September 2015) UN Doc A/RES/70/1, Goal 14.1, 23.

emphasizing the need to address the issue, 'both downstream, through improved mechanisms for waste management, disposal and recycling, and upstream, by addressing consumption and production patterns, including through awareness-raising campaigns'.[38] To that end, the UNGA encouraged states to 'further develop partnerships with industry and civil society to raise awareness of the extent of the impact of marine debris' on the marine environment, and consequent economic loss, and 'to cooperate, as appropriate, to address marine debris and microplastics in the marine environment'.[39] In 2017, the UNGA called on states to 'accelerate actions to prevent and significantly reduce marine pollution of all kinds, particularly from land-based activities, including marine debris, plastics and microplastics'.[40] Annual oceans resolutions since have reiterated the need for better understanding of the sources, amounts, pathways, distribution, trends, nature, and impacts of marine debris, have repeated the encouragement to develop partnerships with industry and civil society to raise awareness of the problem, and have urged states to integrate the issue of marine debris into national and regional strategies dealing with waste management.[41]

For its part, the United Nations Environment Assembly (UNEA), created in 2012 in response to calls during Rio+20 for the strengthening and upgrading of the United Nations Environment Programme (UNEP), has continued UNEP's focus on the topic of 'marine plastic litter and microplastics'. At its first session, in 2014, UNEA requested that a study be undertaken to identify the key sources of plastic debris, identify the best available techniques and environmental practices to prevent their accumulation, and to recommend the most urgent actions and specific areas in need of further research.[42] The report[43] was considered during the second session of UNEA, in 2016, and further study of the effectiveness of international governance strategies, to identify gaps and options for addressing the problem of marine plastic litter and microplastics, was requested.[44] This gap analysis[45] was considered at the third session of UNEA, in 2017, and states were encouraged to engage in a number of actions, including the development of action plans to prevent marine litter, the development of common definitions and harmonized standards for measurement and monitoring of marine litter. UNEA also decided to establish 'an open-ended ad hoc expert group to further examine the barriers to and options for combating marine plastic litter and microplastics from all sources, especially land-based sources', and to identify the full range of national, regional, and international response options, including voluntary and legally binding governance strategies and approaches.[46] At the fourth session, in 2019, the mandate of the group was extended for two years, and it was further tasked with taking stock

[38] UNICPOLOS, Report on the Work of the United Nations Open-ended Informal Consultative Process on Oceans and the Law of the Sea at its Seventeenth Meeting' (25 July 2016) UN Doc A/71/20.

[39] UNGA Res 71/257 (23 December 2016) UN Doc A/RES/71/257, para 209.

[40] UN, 'Our Ocean Our Future: Call for Action', UNGA Res 71/312 (6 July 2017) UN Doc A/RES/71/312, para 13(g).

[41] See UNGA Res/72/73 (5 December 2017) UN Doc A/RES/72/73, paras 209–14; UNGA Res/73/124 (11 December 2018) UN Doc A/RES/73/124, paras 207–15; UNGA Res/74/19 (20 December 2019) UN Doc A/RES/74/19, paras 218–24; UNGA Res/75/239 (31 December 2020) UN Doc A/RES/75/239, paras 217–26.

[42] UNEP, 'Marine Plastic Debris and Microplastics' UNEP/EA.1/Res.6 (27 June 2014).

[43] UNEP, *Marine Plastic Debris and Microplastics: Global Lessons and Research to Inspire Action and Guide Policy Change* (UNEP 2016).

[44] UNEP, 'Marine Plastic Litter and Microplastics' UNEP/EA.2/Res.11 (27 May 2016).

[45] UNEP, *Combating Marine Plastic Litter and Microplastics: An Assessment of the Effectiveness of Relevant International, Regional and Subregional Governance Strategies and Approaches* UNEP/EA.3/INF.5, 5 October 2017.

[46] UNEP, 'Marine Litter and Microplastics' UNEP/EA.3/Res.7 (6 December 2017).

of all existing activities and actions to reduce marine plastic litter, and with analysing the effectiveness of existing and potential response options.

Despite the growing recognition of the need to take action , and the existence of a formal legal framework in respect of ship-source plastic debris, however, the problem of marine plastic debris has not only persisted, but has increased exponentially.[47] It is in this context that the role of informal lawmaking becomes relevant. Before examining its role, however, it is useful to explain what is meant, for the purposes of this chapter, by informal lawmaking, and to apply that definition to the UNGA and UNEA resolutions discussed above.

15.3 Defining 'Informal International Lawmaking'

Informal international lawmaking, as defined in the introduction to this book, 'involves international cooperation to reach agreements (other than treaties) between public authorities, with or without the participation of private actors or international organizations, in varied institutions or networks'.[48] This definition is derived from that crafted by Pauwelyn, who defines informal lawmaking as:

> Cross-border cooperation between public authorities, with or without the participation of private actors and/or international organisations, in a forum other than a traditional international organisation (*process informality*), and/or asbetween actors other than traditional diplomatic actors (such as regulators or agencies) (*actor informality*) and/or which does not result in a formal treaty or other traditional source of international law (*output informality*).[49]

As is apparent from both definitions, anything short of a formal treaty or treaty-making process constitutes informal law or informal lawmaking. Interestingly, while recognizing that informality may result in something less than formal treaty status, Pauwelyn does not equate output informality, necessarily, with non-legally binding. Rather, he notes that non-treaty outputs (or outputs that result in non-traditional sources of international law) may also have binding force. The determining factor is the normative effect of an output, by which he means that it 'steers behaviour or determines the freedom of actors'.[50] In this respect, informal law appears to go beyond the notion of 'soft law', defined by Boyle as a 'variety of non-legally binding but normatively worded instruments used in contemporary international relations by States and international organisations'.[51] On Boyle's definition, while soft law may have normative intent, it lacks binding effect. According to Pauwelyn, however, informal law may have binding, or at least regulatory, effect. In other words, informal lawmaking processes need not necessarily result only in 'soft law'. Rather, they may result in outputs that determine the freedom of actors in such a way as to operate as

[47] UNICPOLOS (n 38).

[48] See Klein, in Chapter 1 of this volume.

[49] Joost Pauwelyn, 'Informal International Law-making: Framing the Concept and Research Questions' in Joost Pauwelyn, Ramses A Wessel, and Jan Wouters (eds), *Informal International Law-making* (OUP 2012) 13, 22.

[50] ibid.

[51] Alan Boyle, 'Soft Law in International Law-making' in Malcolm D Evans (ed), *International Law* (5th edn, OUP 2018) 119, 121.

quasi-binding obligations. Thus, the key characteristics of informal law appear to be either normative intent or normative effect—or both.

Pauwelyn's definition also distinguishes between processes within traditional international organizations and those outside them, equating international organizations with formal, rather than informal, processes. This distinction is not to suggest that informal lawmaking cannot occur in international organizations, but, rather, that within international organizations only two types of informality are possible: actors and outputs. In other words, while international organizations may be considered formal processes under Pauwelyn's definition, consultation and decision-making processes within those organizations may, nevertheless, engage in informal lawmaking as informal actors, or by producing informal outputs of a regulatory character. Indeed, the subsidiary bodies of international organizations may (and often do) engage in informal lawmaking, including through the involvement and participation of a wide range of state and non-state actors, and the adoption of non-legally binding outputs that are, nevertheless, intended to—and do—steer behaviour. Obvious examples are the adoption, by international organizations, of guidelines, resolutions, or recommendations not intended to be binding, but intended to have a regulatory character that guides or otherwise influences the behaviour of the members of an organization in the implementation of their treaty obligations. Beyond the confines of formal international organizations, a wide range of informal processes and actors may engage in informal lawmaking, resulting in an equally broad range of informal outputs short of a treaty or other traditional source of international law that, nevertheless, have either normative intent or normative effect, or both. In this case, all three types of informality can present themselves: process, actors, and outputs.

Applying this to the discussion of UNGA and UNEA resolutions above, it is clear that neither UNGA nor UNEA resolutions are binding. However, they can reflect a common concern among states that normative developments, including those incorporating binding outcomes, may be desirable. Thus, while the resolutions themselves may not be binding, they may have either the normative intent or the normative effect, or both, required for informal lawmaking, and may even lead to binding developments elsewhere. A prime example of this evolution is the adoption, by the UNGA, of the global moratorium on large-scale pelagic drift net fishing, which came into effect in 1992.[52] The moratorium called upon all states to prevent such fishing operations on the high seas, and established the responsibility of all states to prohibit such activities and to take such actions as may be necessary to prevent their occurrence. While the legal status of the moratorium was the subject of much debate at the time, both its normative intent and its normative effect were clear. States parties to the North Pacific Anadromous Fish Commission relied on the moratorium to support enforcement actions against non-party vessels engaged in large scale drift net fishing in the North Pacific.[53] The prohibition on drift net fishing was also embodied in formal treaties, and in conservation measures adopted by a number of regional fisheries management organizations that are binding on the members of those organizations.[54] Indeed, by

[52] UN, 'Large-scale Pelagic Drift-net Fishing and its Impact on the Living Marine Resources of the World's Oceans and Seas' UNGA Res 46/215 (20 December 1991) UN Doc A/RES/46/215, calling for the moratorium to come into effect from 31 December 1992.

[53] Rosemary Rayfuse, *Non-flag State Enforcement in High Seas Fisheries* (Brill 2004) 134–36.

[54] See, further, Scanlon, in Chapter 11 of this volume.

1994, commentators were suggesting that its status as customary international law had been confirmed.[55]

Nevertheless, a signal feature of the UNGA resolutions on marine debris, plastics, and microplastics is their apparent lack of both normative intent and normative effect. While noting the adverse impacts of marine debris, the focus of these resolutions is to encourage studies to be undertaken to examine the sources and impacts of marine debris, and to encourage states to develop public and private partnerships aimed at cleaning up marine debris. States are merely urged to cooperate, as appropriate, to address the problems of marine debris, with no guidance as to what that cooperation might entail. Similarly, the UNEA resolutions are aimed at framing consensus around practical rather than normative actions to be taken, and helping to coordinate, rather than regulate, development and technical assistance. This is not to suggest that informal lawmaking is not occurring in the marine debris context, but, rather, that we must look beyond the UNGA and UNEA.

The following sections explore informal lawmaking in the context of ship-source marine plastic debris, on the one hand, and marine plastic debris from land-based sources, on the other. In the former case, we observe a formal legal framework that is supplemented, bolstered, and influenced—or 'thickened'—by informal actors and outputs. In the latter, we see informal processes, involving both formal and informal actors, producing informal outputs very clearly intended to steer the behaviour, or determine the freedom, of actors, although that effect may not yet be fully realized.

15.4 Informal Lawmaking and Ship-source Marine Plastic Debris

As noted in section 15.2, a formal legal framework for addressing ship-source marine plastic debris already exists. This framework has been adopted under the auspices of the International Maritime Organization (IMO), which is responsible for the administration of the MARPOL and London Conventions, and the London Protocol. It is important to note that the IMO itself does not possess general 'formal' lawmaking powers. The powers of the organization extend only to the making of 'recommendations'.[56] Formal treaty-making power rests with the member states that ultimately adopt the recommendations of the IMO in a treaty, such as the London Convention, the London Protocol, or the MARPOL Convention, or in a treaty amendment, an obvious example of which is the IMO's International Code for Ships Operating in Polar Waters (the Polar Code),[57] which is made mandatory through amendments to MARPOL, the International Convention for the Safety of Life at Sea, and the International Convention on Standards of Training, Certification and Watchkeeping for Seafarers. Thus, to the extent that the IMO engages in lawmaking, its lawmaking is 'informal'. Of course, not every IMO recommendation will constitute informal lawmaking. Only those having a regulatory character intended to 'steer behaviour or determine the freedom of actors' will be relevant.

[55] Grant J Hewison, 'The Legally Binding Nature of the Moratorium on Large Scale High Seas Driftnet Fishing' (1994) 25(4) J Mar L & Com 557.

[56] Convention on the International Maritime Organization (adopted 6 March 1948, entered into force 17 March 1958) 289 UNTS 3, arts 2(a) and (d).

[57] IMO, '2015 Guidelines for Exhaust Gas Cleaning Systems' IMO Res MEPC.259(68), Annex 10, 3 <https://www.imo.org/en/MediaCentre/HotTopics/Pages/Polar-default.aspx> accessed 27 July 2021.

In the context of prevention and control of pollution from ships, the work of the IMO is, primarily, conducted in the Marine Environmental Protection Committee (MEPC). All 174 member states, representing more than 97% of global merchant shipping tonnage, are represented in the MEPC, together with any non-member states that are party to the relevant treaty (in the case of marine plastics, MARPOL). A significant number of non-governmental organizations representing both industry and environmental interests have been granted consultative status with the IMO, and are also represented in the MEPC, as are a significant number of intergovernmental organizations. In addition to formal meetings, held at least once a year, the MEPC works through correspondence groups, intersessional meetings, and other structured formal work programmes in which all members and interested stakeholders can participate. Although not without its critics,[58] the inclusive nature of the IMO regulatory structure is, generally, considered to be a highly authoritative, albeit 'informal', regulatory model.[59]

As described by the IMO, the MEPC is 'concerned with the adoption and amendment of conventions and other regulations and measures to ensure their enforcement'.[60] A signal feature of its work is, thus, its normativity. Proposals for amendment of the formal law are negotiated by a combination of formal (state) and informal (non-state) actors within the MEPC. Those proposals, however, even once adopted by the MEPC, constitute informal law until such time as they are formally adopted as amendments to the relevant treaty by the states parties. In 2005, the UNGA called on the IMO to review MARPOL Annex V, and to assess its effectiveness.[61] While the IMO could not be accused of having acted with alacrity, the MEPC did take up the task, eventually adopting a revised version of Annex V in 2011, which, after the expiration of the tacit amendment procedure time frame, formally came into force in 2013.[62] However, the informal lawmaking activities of the MEPC go beyond the negotiation of treaty amendments. With respect to MARPOL Annex V, this work has centred around the adoption of guidelines for the implementation of Annex V, and for ensuring the adequacy of port waste reception facilities.

Guidelines for the Implementation of MARPOL Annex V were, originally, adopted by MEPC in 1988, at the time the Annex entered into force, and have since been revised regularly.[63] Indeed, the IMO refers to these guidelines as 'a living document', the purpose of which is 'to assist governments, ships and port operators in implementing relevant requirements under MARPOL Annex V'.[64] An important feature of these guidelines is their contribution, not only to the interpretation and implementation of Annex V, but also to its ongoing amendment. In 2012, revised guidelines were adopted, setting out in greater

[58] Harilos N Psaraftis and Christos A Kontovas, 'Influence and Transparency at the IMO: The Name of the Game' (2020) 22 Marit Econ Logist 151–72.

[59] Rosalie P Balkin, 'The IMO and Global Ocean Governance: Past, Present, and Future' in David J Attard, Rosalie P Balkin, and Donald W Greig (eds), *The IMLI Treatise on Global Ocean Governance, vol III: The IMO and Global Ocean Governance* (OUP 2018) 10.

[60] See IMO, 'Structure of IMO' <https://www.imo.org/en/About/Pages/Structure.aspx#4> accessed 27 July 2021.

[61] UNGA Res 60/30 (29 November 2005) UN Doc A/RES/60/30.

[62] IMO, 'Amendments to the Annex of the Protocol of 1978 Relating to the International Convention for the Prevention of Pollution from Ships, 1973 (Revised MARPOL Annex V)' (adopted on 15 July 2011, entered into force 1 January 2013) IMO Res MEPC.201(62).

[63] IMO, 'Guidelines for the Implementation of Annex V of MARPOL 73/78)' (1 January 1988) IMO Res MEPC.59(33).

[64] See IMO, 'Prevention of Pollution by Garbage from Ships' <https://www.imo.org/en/OurWork/Environment/Pages/Garbage-Default.aspx> accessed 27 July 2021.

detail the types of actions, both practical and regulatory, that states parties are required to engage in when implementing their obligations under the Annex.[65] In their most recent iteration, the 2017 Guidelines specifically stipulate one of their main objectives as being 'to assist Governments in developing and enacting domestic laws which implement MARPOL Annex V'.[66] In other words, they are intended to provide guidance on required normative developments (normative intent), and to 'steer the behaviour' of states parties to the Annex (normative effect). Importantly, the guidelines fill interpretational holes in Annex V, providing much needed detail as to what behaviour is to be 'steered', and in what manner.

A similar effect can be seen in the Guidelines for Ensuring the Adequacy of Port Waste Reception Facilities.[67] If discharges from ships are prohibited, then provision of adequate waste reception facilities is crucial for the effective implementation of MARPOL Annex V. Indeed, the requirement for all states parties to ensure the provision of reception facilities was included in Regulation 7 of the original Annex V. The guidelines urge the proper planning and establishment of 'adequate' reception facilities, detailing what that adequacy requires. In 2006, the MEPC adopted an action plan, aimed at improving both the provision and use of 'adequate' port reception facilities, lack of technical and financial capacity having been recognized as two of the main inhibiting factors.[68] Interestingly, both the requirement of 'adequacy' and the recognition of the possible use of regional, rather than national reception facility arrangements, to accommodate technical and financial concerns of developing states, were, subsequently, specifically included in the 2012 Revised Annex V, showing the influence of the guidelines on the development of the formal law. The MEPC has also adopted a number of guidance documents, consolidated in 2018 in the Revised Consolidated Guidance for Port Reception Facility Providers and Users, which further details proposed methods to comply with the guidelines.[69] Collectively, the guidelines and the consolidated guidance provide detailed provisions, aimed at steering the behaviour of the states parties, and influencing their freedom of action. In this regard, they can certainly be said to have at least normative intent.

Particularly germane in the context of increasing concern over the incidence of plastics and microplastics in the marine environment, and the target set by SDG 14, is the IMO Action Plan to Address Marine Plastic Litter From Ships, adopted by the MEPC in 2018.[70] The action plan is intended to 'enhance existing regulations and introduce measures to reduce and prevent marine plastic litter entering the oceans through ship-based activities'.[71] To that end, it recommends specific measures aimed at, among other things, reducing plastic litter from ships, including fishing vessels, improving the effectiveness of port reception facilities, and understanding both the contribution of ships to marine plastic litter and the regulatory framework and regulatory needs associated with it. In addition to measures

[65] IMO, '2012 Guidelines for the Implementation of MARPOL Annex V' (2 March 2012) IMO Res MEPC.219(63).

[66] IMO, '2017 Guidelines for the Implementation of MARPOL Annex V' (7 July 2017) IMO Res MEPC.295(71).

[67] IMO, 'Guidelines for Ensuring the Adequacy of Port Waste Reception Facilities' (13 March 2000) IMO Res MEPC.83(44).

[68] IMO, 'Action Plan to Tackle the Inadequacy of Port Reception Facilities' (2006) IMO Res MEPC.23(55). See also IMO, 'Reception Facilities' <https://www.imo.org/en/OurWork/Environment/Pages/Port-Reception-facilities.aspx> accessed 27 July 2021.

[69] IMO, 'Consolidated Guidance for Port Reception Facility Providers and Users' (1 March 2018) IMO Res MEPC.1/Circ.834/Rev.1.

[70] IMO, 'Action Plan to Address Marine Plastic Litter from Ships' (26 October 2018) IMO Res MEPC.310(73).

[71] ibid, para 2.

aimed at increasing understanding and awareness of the problem, specific measures are identified, such as, for example, promoting the reporting of loss of fishing gear, facilitating the delivery of retrieved fishing gear to shore facilities, and making marking of fishing gear mandatory. Clearly, the action plan is intended to steer behaviour (normative intent). In terms of its normative effect (the extent to which it actually does steer behaviour), actions taken by the MEPC, to date, have mainly focused on improving scientific knowledge of the contribution of ships to marine plastic litter, and preparation of a regulatory gap analysis.[72] However, work is progressing, in the MEPC, on a draft strategy on more substantive matters relating to ship-source plastic litter, including reporting mechanisms for lost fishing gear, which are recognized as among the most effective tools for preventing the occurrence of ALDFG.

Work on designing the actual standards for marking fishing gear has taken place within the FAO. Like the IMO, the FAO does not, itself, possess general formal lawmaking powers. Its functions are, rather, to collect, analyse, interpret, and disseminate information, to provide technical assistance, and to promote and recommend policy and legal developments.[73] As such, its work is inherently 'informal', although a number of formal agreements have been adopted under its auspices. The FAO Voluntary Guidelines for the Marking of Fishing Gear are aimed at assisting states and regional fisheries bodies in developing and applying a system for the marking of fishing gear and related measures to address ALDFG.[74] The expectation is that the non-binding prescriptions set out in the guidelines will be implemented through the provision of technical assistance and the adoption of domestic law. In this respect, the guidelines are clearly intended to steer the behaviour of states, both individually and collectively, and, thus, can be said to meet the criteria of informal law. Indeed, the MEPC has sought advice from the FAO on whether such measures should be made mandatory, and, if so, what the most appropriate FAO or IMO instrument might be for introducing such a requirement. In the meantime, the IMO and the FAO have partnered in the GloLitter Partnerships project,[75] aimed at supporting developing countries to implement both practical and regulatory steps to address the issues identified in the IMO Action Plan and the FAO Guidelines, further demonstrating the normative effect of these instruments.

Admittedly, the MEPC operates within the framework of the established international legally binding instruments that the IMO is tasked with administering. In this respect, its work reveals one of the key functions of informal lawmaking: the 'thickening' of existing formal law through the development of agreed requirements for the interpretation, application, and implementation of treaty obligations, as a result of negotiation with interested stakeholders beyond the states parties themselves. As discussed in the following section, this role is in contradistinction to informal lawmaking in the context of land-based sources of marine plastic debris.

72 GESAMP, 'Sea-based Sources of Marine Litter' (n 9).

73 See FAO, 'Constitution of the Food and Agriculture Organization of the United Nations' (16 October 1945), available at <http://www.fao.org/3/K8024E/K8024E.pdf> accessed 27 July 2021.

74 FAO, 'Voluntary Guidelines on the Marking of Fishing Gear', 5 April 2019 <http://www.fao.org/fishery/nems/41168/en> accessed 27 July 2021.

75 See IMO, 'GloLitter Partnerships Project' <https://www.imo.org/en/OurWork/PartnershipsProjects/Pages/GloLitter-Partnerships-Project-.aspx> accessed 27 July 2021.

15.5 Informal Lawmaking and Land-based Sources of Marine Plastic Debris

In contrast to the ship-source context, there is no binding global legal framework for which reduction of land-based sources of marine pollution, in general, let alone marine plastic pollution, specifically, is a primary objective. The only global obligation is found in Article 207 of the LOSC, which merely requires states to 'take into account' internationally agreed rules, standards, and recommended practice and procedures, and simply to 'endeavour' to establish such rules and standards. In short, under the LOSC, states retain their freedom of regulatory action in balancing environmental measures against their economic needs and desires, subject only to their other treaty obligations.[76] Beyond the LOSC, a complex and fragmented labyrinth of multilateral environmental agreements are relevant, either directly or indirectly, to the regulation of land-based sources of marine pollution.[77] However, in none of these agreements is there a specific regime focus on land-based sources of marine pollution, let alone on marine plastic debris, although a number of regional seas agreements do have protocols on the prevention of pollution from land-based activities.[78]

The lack of any comprehensive global agreement on plastics is hardly surprising. Reducing plastic pollution from land-based sources requires action by many actors, and in respect of a myriad of land-based activities, including waste management, recycling, and packaging strategies, to name but a few. This dynamic requires exploration of a wide-ranging array of legislative and regulatory measures, and policy responses, at the local, regional, and global level, that go well beyond the law of the sea. As a result, some countries and commentators have called for the adoption of a global, legally-binding agreement to coordinate action against plastic litter in the oceans.[79] Others, however, dispute the need for, and desirability of, such negotiations, suggesting, for example, that improving waste management is the fastest way to achieve the goal of eliminating plastic litter in the oceans.[80] Still others suggest the complete reframing of the issue of 'plastic pollution', to address both its increasing production and consumption, and the global regulatory actions needed to ensure its global reduction.[81] It is in this context that informal lawmaking takes on importance.

Informal international lawmaking in response to land-based sources of marine debris, including marine plastic debris, has, predominantly, occurred under the auspices of

[76] Frank Wacht, 'Article 207: Pollution from Land-based Sources' in Alexander Proelss (ed), *United Nations Convention on the Law of the Sea: A Commentary* (Beck Hart Nomos 2017) 1378–90, 1380–81.

[77] UNEP, 'Combating Marine Plastic Litter and Microplastics' (n 45).

[78] See, eg Protocol for the Protection of the Mediterranean Sea against Pollution from Land-based Sources and Activities (LBS Protocol) (as amended 7 March 1996) (signed 17 May 1976, entered into force 11 May 2008), to the Convention for the Protection of the Mediterranean Sea Against Pollution (adopted 16 February 1976, entered into force 12 February 1978) 1102 UNTS 27 ('Barcelona Convention') <https://www.unep.org/unepmap/who-we-are/barcelona-convention-and-protocols> accessed 27 July 2021.

[79] See, eg Karen Raubenheimer, Alistair McIlgorm, and Nilüfer Oral, 'Towards an Improved International Framework to Govern the Life Cycle of Plastics' (2018) 27 RECIEL 210–21; Marcus Haward, 'Plastic Pollution of the World's Seas and Oceans as a Contemporary Challenge in Ocean Governance' (2018) 9 Nat Comm 667 DOI: 10.1038/s41467-018-03104-3; UNEP, 'Proceedings of the United Nations Environment Assembly at its Fourth Session' (22 March 2019) UNEP/EA.4/2 (hereafter 'UNEA Proceedings'), para 61.

[80] See UNEA Proceedings (n 79) paras 62–66; Laura Parker, 'The World Agrees there's a Plastic Waste Crisis—Can it Agree on a Solution?' (*National Geographic*, 25 March 2019) <https://www.nationalgeographic.com/environment/article/un-environment-plastic-pollution-negotiations> accessed 27 July 2021.

[81] Giulia Carlini and Konstantin Kleine, 'Advancing the International Regulation of Plastic Pollution beyond the United Nations Environment Assembly Resolution on Marine Litter and Microplastics' (2018) 27 RECIEL 234–44.

UNEP, in the context of the Global Programme of Action for the Protection of the Marine Environment from Land-based Activities (GPA). Established in 1972 to promote international cooperation and the acquisition of knowledge and information, and to provide policy guidance on environmental matters, UNEP has been described as having 'played a significant catalytic role in the development of treaties and soft law rules'.[82] Like both the IMO and the FAO, UNEP has no general formal lawmaking powers, although it does provide a forum for discussion, as well as secretariat services to a number of multilateral environmental agreements. Nevertheless, UNEP can, and often does, engage with both formal (state) and informal (non-state) actors in the negotiation, development, and adoption of both formal (ie legally binding) and informal (ie non-legally binding) outputs.

The issue of protection of the marine environment from land-based activities has been a focus in UNEP since 1982. In 1985, UNEP adopted its first instrument applicable exclusively to land-based sources of marine pollution. Presented as 'a check list of basic provisions rather than a model agreement, from which Governments may select, adapt, or elaborate, as appropriate to meet the needs of specific regions' when developing bilateral, regional, and multilateral agreements, and national legislation, the Montreal Guidelines for the Protection of the Marine Environment from Land-based Sources[83] can be said to have some normative, if not entirely prescriptive, intent. Guideline 7, in particular, provides that states should 'take all appropriate measures ... to protect certain areas to the fullest possible extent from pollution, including from land-based sources'. The specific strategies to be adopted by states are detailed in Annex I, while requirements relating to the classification of substances, and monitoring and data management, are set out in two further annexes. Although the guidelines do not specifically mention plastics, they do suggest that 'persistent synthetic materials which may seriously interfere with any legitimate use of the sea' should be placed on a blacklist of substances, pollution from which should be eliminated.[84] The guidelines were reviewed in 1991,[85] and strategies for their more extensive implementation were, subsequently, included in Chapter 17 of Agenda 21, adopted in Rio in 1992,[86] ultimately leading to the convening of the Washington Conference in November 1995, at which the Washington Declaration on Protecting the Marine Environment from Land-based Sources,[87] and the GPA,[88] were adopted.

Adopted by 108 states, and the European Commission, in 1995, the GPA is a non-legally binding intergovernmental mechanism 'aimed at preventing the degradation of the marine environment from land-based activities by facilitating the realization of the duty of States to preserve and protect the marine environment', and 'designed to assist States in taking

[82] Philippe Sands and Jacqueline Peel, *Principles of International Environmental Law* (4th edn, CUP 2018) 63.

[83] Montreal Guidelines for the Protection of the Marine Environment from Land-based Sources (24 May 1985) Call Number UNEP(092)/E5 (hereafter 'Montreal Guidelines').

[84] ibid, Annex II, s 1.

[85] UNEP, 'Review of Developments and Activities since 1985: Note by the Secretariat' (6 February 1997) UN Doc UNEP/MG/IG/I/2.

[86] UN, 'Report of the United Nations Conference on Environment and Development' (3–14 June 1992) UN Doc A/CONF.151/26/Rev.1 <https://www.un.org/esa/dsd/agenda21/res_agenda21_00.shtml> accessed 27 July 2021.

[87] UNEP, 'Washington Declaration on Protecting the Marine Environment from Land-based Sources' (1995), available at <https://wedocs.unep.org/bitstream/handle/20.500.11822/13421/WashingtonDeclaration.pdf?sequence = 1&isAllowed = y> accessed 27 July 2021.

[88] Global Programme of Action for the Protection of the Marine Environment from Land-Based Activities (5 December 1995) UN Doc UNEP(OCA)/LBA/IG.2/7 (hereafter 'GPA'), available at <https://wedocs.unep.org/bitstream/handle/20.500.11822/13422/GPAFullTextEn.pdf?sequence = 1&isAllowed = y> accessed 27 July 2021.

actions individually or jointly within their respective policies, priorities and resources, which will lead to the prevention, reduction, control and/or elimination of the degradation of the marine environment, as well as to its recovery from the impacts of land-based activities'.[89] The GPA is designed to be a source of both 'conceptual and practical guidance to be drawn upon by national and/or regional authorities in devising and implementing sustained action to prevent, reduce, control and/or eliminate marine degradation from land-based activities'.[90] Specific targets and actions are suggested in relation to nine source categories, one of which is litter, where the focus is on reduction of waste, provision of disposal facilities, awareness and education campaigns, and improved local planning and management programmes.[91] Since 2012, the GPA has focused its attention on three of the nine source categories only, including the category of marine debris/litter, which includes marine plastic debris and microplastics.[92]

Institutionally, UNEP provides secretariat services through the GPA Coordination Office, and parties to the GPA meet every five years in an intergovernmental review (IGR) meeting to assess progress in implementation. Over the years, implementation of the GPA has, essentially, formed part of UNEP's work programme, with the Coordination Office assisting in the provision of reports and policy advice, technical assistance, and capacity-building programmes, aimed specifically at implementation of the GPA.

At the national level, the GPA urges states to adopt national programmes of action, the detailed parameters of which are set out in the GPA, and which should include provisions for the following: identification and assessment of problems; establishment of priorities for action; setting management objectives for priority problems; identification, evaluation, and selection of strategies and measures, including management approaches; criteria for evaluating the effectiveness of strategies and programmes; and programme support elements, such as financing, and legal and enforcement mechanisms.[93] At the regional level, states are urged to strengthen existing regional conventions and programmes, to consider negotiating new ones, and to adopt regional action plans reflecting the parameters set out for national action plans.[94] At the international level, the GPA recommends international cooperation aimed at enhancing capacity-building, technology transfer, and financial support; assigns the secretariat role to UNEP, which is urged to provide GPA implementation through a revitalized Regional Seas Programme; and requires the convening of periodic intergovernmental review meetings to assess progress on the implementation of the GPA.[95]

With respect to marine litter, in particular, the specifics of possible approaches have been elaborated in the UNEP Guidelines on the Survey and Monitoring of Marine Litter,[96] and in

[89] ibid, para 3.
[90] ibid, para 14.
[91] ibid, paras 140–48.
[92] See UNEP, 'Report of the Third Session of the Intergovernmental Review Meeting on the Implementation of the Global Programme of Action for the Protection of the Marine Environment from Land-based Activities' (26 January 2012) UN Doc UNEP/GPA/IGR.3/6, Annex. The other focus areas are nutrient management and waste water management. The focus areas were reaffirmed by parties to the GPA in November 2018, in UNEP, 'Bali Declaration on the Protection of the Marine Environment from Land-based Activities' (1 November 2018) UN Doc UNEP/GPA.4/6.
[93] GPA (n 88) para 18.
[94] ibid, paras 96–97.
[95] ibid, paras 51, 74–77.
[96] UNEP/IOC, 'Guidelines on the Survey and Monitoring of Marine Litter' (2009) <https://wedocs.unep.org/xmlui/handle/20.500.11822/13604> accessed 27 July 2021.

the Guidelines on the Use of Market-based Instruments to Address the Problem of Marine Litter, both of which aim to provide the parties to the GPA (and others) with standardized operational guidelines for marine litter survey and monitoring programmes, and practical reference guides on how, when, and why economic tools to address problems with marine litter should be selected, applied, and implemented.[97] The GPA Coordination Office was also instrumental in the adoption of the Honolulu Commitment,[98] which outlines twelve actions to be taken by states to reduce marine debris, and the Honolulu Strategy,[99] which provides a detailed set of goals and strategies for collaborative efforts aimed at implementing the Honolulu Commitment, in order to reduce the impacts of marine debris worldwide. Specifically, the purposes of the Honolulu Strategy are 'to describe and catalyze the multi-pronged and holistic response required to solve the problem of marine debris', and 'to guide monitoring and evaluation of global progress on specific strategies at different levels of implementation—including local, national, regional, and international efforts and achievements'.[100] Developed in consultation with a wide range of stakeholders, the Honolulu Strategy is intended to motivate actors across the 'full spectrum of civil society, government and intergovernmental organizations, and the private sector'.[101] The Honolulu Strategy was endorsed by the parties to the GPA at the third IGR, in 2012,[102] at which they launched the Global Partnership on Marine Litter (GPML), 'a voluntary open-ended partnership aimed at increasing collaboration and cooperation among international agencies, governments, businesses, academia, local authorities, nongovernmental organizations and individuals in reducing marine litter and particularly marine plastic litter'.[103] The aims of the GPML are to engage all interested stakeholders in finding solutions to the problem of marine litter and microplastics, to identify gaps and emerging issues, and to create the awareness required for behavioural change.[104] In 2017, building on the GPML, UNEP launched its Clean Seas Campaign, which is 'aimed at connecting and rallying individuals, civil society groups, industry and governments for catalyzing change and transforming habits, practices, standards and policies around the globe to dramatically reduce marine litter and its negative impacts'.[105] In 2018, the parties to the GPA affirmed the value of, and the need for strengthening, global partnerships, including the GPML, to deal with the problem of marine (plastic) litter and microplastics.[106]

[97] UNEP, 'Guidelines on the Use of Market-based Instruments to Address the Problem of Marine Litter' (April 2009) <https://wedocs.unep.org/handle/20.500.11822/2435> accessed 27 July 2021.

[98] 'The Honolulu Commitment' (March 2011) Adopted at the 5th International Marine Debris Conference <https://5imdc.files.wordpress.com/2011/03/honolulucommitment.pdf> accessed 27 July 2021.

[99] UNEP/NOAA, 'Honolulu Strategy: A Global Framework for Prevention and Management of Marine Debris' (25 March 2011) <https://wedocs.unep.org/bitstream/handle/20.500.11822/10670/Honolulu%20strategy.pdf?sequence = 1&isAlloisA = y> accessed 27 July 2021.

[100] ibid 1.

[101] ibid, ES-1.

[102] UNEP, 'Report of the Third Session of the Intergovernmental Review Meeting on the Implementation of the Global Programme of Action for the Protection of the Marine Environment from Land-based Activities' (26 January 2012) UN Doc UNEP/GPA/IGR.3/6.

[103] See UNEP, 'Global Partnership on Marine Litter' <https://www.gpmarinelitter.org/> accessed 27 July 2021.

[104] See UNEP, 'Progress on the Implementation of the Global Programme of Action for the Protection of the Marine Environment from Land-based Activities at the National, Regional and International Levels during the Period 2012–2018' (25 September 2018) UN Doc UNEP/GPA/IGR.4/2/Rev.1.

[105] See Clean Seas, 'The Campaign' <https://www.cleanseas.org/about> accessed 27 July 2021.

[106] UNEP, 'Report of the Fourth Session of the Intergovernmental Review Meeting on the Implementation of the Global Programme of Action for the Protection of the Marine Environment from Land-based Activities' (7 March 2019) UN Doc UNEP/GPA/IGR.4/5.

As an agreement other than a treaty involving international cooperation between states outside the confines of an international organization, the GPA certainly meets the criteria of being an informal output of an informal process. The participation of non-governmental stakeholders in its implementation, and in the IGR process, as well as in the GPML, suggests that the GPA can also meet the third criterion of actor informality. The question is, however, whether the GPA constitutes informal lawmaking, in the sense that it has either normative intent or normative effect, or both.

In terms of normative intent, a key feature of the GPA is that it calls for the further adoption of both binding and non-binding measures to achieve its objectives, although it does not prescribe any particular measures beyond requiring that such measures should achieve the objectives of the GPA. It also lacks any mechanisms to ensure that any actions are, in fact, taken. In this respect, it is difficult to maintain that the GPA determines the freedom of its members. Rather, it provides a suggestive and non-prescriptive smorgasbord of choices from which parties can choose, should they feel so inclined. On this reading, its intent is merely programmatic rather than normative. Nevertheless, the GPA clearly envisages that both practical and normative developments will be necessary in order to achieve its goals, and it attempts to steer and define for parties what those developments will entail. In particular, the GPA emphasizes the key principles that should underlie all national and regional action, including precaution, pollution prevention, public participation, integrated coastal area management, and intergenerational equity. Moreover, the whole point of the GPA is to inspire 'new approaches by, and new forms of collaboration among' multiple stakeholders at all levels of governance.[107] In short, the GPA could be said to offer up a new vision of normativity, involving multiple optional, rather than singular, prescriptive approaches to dealing with an issue.

In terms of normative effect, review of the implementation of the GPA indicates that, at the national level, more than 100 national programmes of action have been adopted pursuant to the GPA,[108] although not all of these necessarily target marine litter or marine plastic debris. At least ten states have adopted national policy instruments specifically aligned with the Honolulu Strategy.[109] More than fifty governments have also joined the GPML campaign, and have made commitments, for example, to improve plastics management through reductions in the use of single-use plastics, and a global phasing-out of microplastics in personal care and cosmetics products.[110]

At the regional level, implementation of the GPA has, largely, occurred under the broad auspices of the UNEP Regional Seas Programme, through the adoption of protocols to regional seas conventions and action plans (RSCAPs), and other action plans. Eight regions have adopted protocols on land-based activities, and up to eleven regions have prepared assessments and established monitoring programmes for the collection of data on impacts, in addition to adopting regional plans of action on land-based activities.[111] Increasingly,

[107] GPA (n 88) para 15.

[108] UNEP, 'The Global Programme of Action for the Protection of the Marine Environment from Land-based Activities: A 20-year Perspective on a Unique Programme to Advance the Ocean Agenda' (4 September 2018) UN Doc UNEP/GPA/IGR.4/INF/3 (hereafter 'GPA 20-year Perspective'), para 119. See also UNEP, 'Progress on the Implementation of the Global Programme of Action' (n 104).

[109] GPA 20-year Perspective (n 108).

[110] UNEP, 'Contributions of the United Nations Environment Programme into the 2019 Report of The Secretary-General on Oceans and the Law of the Sea, pursuant to General Assembly Resolution A/73/124' <https://www.un.org/depts/los/general_assembly/contributions_2019/UNEP.pdf> accessed 27 July 2021.

[111] ibid.

parties to the RSCAPs are adopting further action plans that specifically address the issues of marine litter and marine plastic litter. Most notable among these is the legally binding Regional Plan on Marine Litter Management in the Mediterranean, adopted by the parties to the Convention for the Protection of the Mediterranean Sea Against Pollution (Barcelona Convention) in 2013, which came into force in 2014, and has been the impetus for the adoption of a range of measures at the regional and national levels relating to, among other things, reduction of single-use plastics and microplastics.[112] Other marine litter action plans specifically targeting plastics and microplastics, and aligned with the Honolulu Strategy, include those adopted by the OSPAR Commission, the Baltic Marine Environment Protection Commission (HELCOM), the Commission on the Protection of the Black Sea Against Pollution, the parties to the Cartagena Convention on the Wider Caribbean Region, the Coordinating Body of the Seas of East Asia (COBSEA), and the parties to the Northwest Pacific Action Plan (NOWPAP).[113]

At the global level, the GPA has supported development of a global strategy on the reduction of marine litter, the establishment of the GPML, and the multi-stakeholder partnerships aimed at achieving its objectives. Notably, the work of the GPA Coordination Office on marine litter is also credited with influencing the adoption, in 2014, of UNEA's Resolution 1/6 on marine plastic debris and microplastics, and its subsequent iterations.[114]

Like its intent, the effect of the GPA is, arguably, programmatic rather than normative. Nevertheless, it seems fair to say that implementation of the GPA has provided a platform for regulatory and policy developments at the national, regional, and global levels, aimed at addressing the problem of land-based generation of marine litter, in general, and marine plastic debris, in particular. In this respect, it can be said to have had some normative effect, although, given the ever-increasing problem of marine plastic pollution, it can hardly be said to have been a success.

In truth, gauging the actual contribution of the GPA is extremely difficult, given the complexity of the problem of land-based sources of marine pollution, and the plethora of states, institutions, and non-state actors that must be involved in addressing it. Indeed, it seems unlikely that any single overarching regulatory or programmatic approach can ever adequately address the problem, which is precisely why the focus has shifted to looking at specific pollutants such as plastics. However, even with plastics—or, perhaps, particularly with plastics—the problem is complex and large-scale, and requires multifaceted solutions across the full range of human activities, and involving all states and non-state actors. These dimensions have implications for both the efficacy and the future of the GPA, the membership of which is not universal.

In 2013, all UN member states automatically became members of UNEP and its new plenary body, the UNEA,[115] which, as noted in section 15.2 above, has taken an active

[112] UNEP, 'Regional Plan on Marine Litter Management in the Mediterranean in the Framework of Article 15 of the Land Based Sources Protocol' (2011) UN Doc UNEP(DEPI)/MED IG.21/9, Annex II <https://wedocs.unep.org/bitstream/handle/20.500.11822/6012/13ig21_09_annex2_21_07_eng.pdf?sequence = 1&isAllowed = y> accessed 27 July 2021.

[113] For information, see UNEP, 'Progress on the Implementation of the Global Programme of Action' (n 104); UNEP, 'Contributions of the United Nations Environment Programme' (n 110). See also UNEP, 'Implementation of the Global Programme of Action by the Regional Seas Conventions and Action Plans between 2012 and 2017' (2019) UN Doc UNEP/GPA/IGR.4/INF/8 <https://www.un.org/depts/los/general_assembly/contributions_2019/UNEP.pdf> accessed 27 July 2021.

[114] GPA 20-year Perspective (n 108)

[115] UNGA Res 67/213 (21 December 2012) UN Doc A/RES/67/213; UNGA Res 67/251 (13 March 2013) UN Doc A/RES/67/251.

interest in addressing the problem of marine plastic litter and microplastics. It is, thus, not surprising that, in 2018, the parties to the GPA agreed to explore options for its future, and deferred any discussion on its future programme of work, pending a decision on its future.[116] Whether the GPA will be wound down, or subsumed fully into the work of the UNEA, remains to be seen. In the meantime, the GPA stands as an illustration of a second function of informal lawmaking: that of gap-filling, in the absence of a formal legal framework for the implementation of Article 207 of the LOSC, and the obligation to protect and preserve the marine environment from activities occurring beyond the ocean but having a detrimental effect on it.

15.6 Conclusion

This chapter has examined the role of informal international lawmaking in the context of marine plastic debris, focusing on developments within the IMO relating to ship-source plastic pollution, and on the GPA relating to marine plastic pollution from land-based activities. In the former case, we observe an established global legal framework that is supplemented, bolstered, and influenced—or 'thickened'—by informal actors and outputs. In the latter case, and in the absence of any established global legal framework, we see informal processes involving both formal and informal actors producing informal outputs clearly intended to steer behaviour, although that effect has not yet been (fully) realized.

Given the ever-increasing prevalence of plastic and microplastic debris in the oceans, it would be tempting to label this second function of informal lawmaking as a chimera: a dizzying flurry of activity at the international level, involving continuing calls for information and action at the national level, providing merely the illusion—or perhaps delusion—of regulatory or normative progress. However, in contrast to the problem of ship-source debris, the number and complexity of land-based sources of marine plastic pollution make the negotiation of one comprehensive and effective global regime focused on the issue unlikely, both practically and substantively, at least in the near- to medium-term.[117] In this context, the significance of informal lawmaking, as reflected in the work of the GPA, lies in the role it has played in developing awareness of the problem, and in influencing attitudes and behaviour at the individual, local, national, and regional levels, and perhaps ultimately at the global level. While certainly no real panacea for the lack of regime focus, informal lawmaking is at least attempting to occupy the void between the law of the sea and the control of marine plastic pollution from land-based sources.

[116] See UNEP, 'Report of the Fourth Session' (n 106).

[117] This assessment may prove to have been too pessimistic. On 2 September 2021, after completion of this chapter, the UN Ministerial Conference on Marine Litter and Plastic Pollution, adopted a Ministerial Statement affirming the commitment of the signatories to work towards the timely establishment of an Intergovernmental Negotiating Committee on Marine Litter and Plastic Pollution. A draft resolution has been submitted by a number of states, for consideration at the resumed UNEA Fifth meeting (UNEA 5.2) to be held in Nairobi from 28 February to 2 March 2022, calling for the convening of the committee 'with a mandate to prepare an internationally legally binding instrument to address plastic pollution commencing its work in 2022 with the goal of completing by the sixth session of the Environment Assembly'. At time of writing, the outcome remains to be seen.

16

Unconventional Lawmaking in the Law of the Sea and Area-based Conservation Measures

Karen N Scott

16.1 Introduction

Area-based conservation in the marine environment is an important tool for implementing an ecosystem approach to protecting the marine environment and managing activities on an integrated, holistic basis. Area-based measures are now employed by institutions at all levels of governance, to support marine spatial planning, to protect species and ecosystems, and to manage activities such as fishing, minerals extraction, and even navigation. As will be demonstrated in this chapter, informal or unconventional lawmaking processes have been particularly significant in the context of area-based conservation, in terms of both the development and implementation of the law in this field. This chapter begins with a discussion of how 'unconventional' or 'informal' lawmaking is defined, for the purposes of subsequent analysis, before going on to define marine protected areas (MPAs) and area-based conservation more generally. Six categories of unconventional or informal lawmaking are identified, focusing on instruments that are characterized by informality with respect to actors, processes, or outputs, but which are, nevertheless, normative in purpose and effect. This chapter briefly considers the role played by these instruments in developing and implementing the law relating to area-based conservation, and its relationship with formal law. The chapter concludes with a short analysis of the potential impact of a new formal instrument, the international legally binding instrument under the 1982 United Nations Convention on the Law of the Sea (LOSC) on the conservation and sustainable use of marine biodiversity beyond national jurisdiction (the ILBI), on current and future informal or lawmaking processes related to area-based conservation.

16.2 'Unconventional' or 'Informal' Lawmaking and the Law of the Sea

'Unconventional' or 'informal' lawmaking is an inherently relational concept, contrasted with conventional or formal sources of law. In its most basic definition, unconventional law can be defined as including any 'law' not categorized as such by Article 38 of the 1945 Statute of the International Court of Justice (ICJ Statute) (under which 'law' comprises treaties, custom, general principles, judicial decisions and the writings of eminent publicists). Joost Pauwelyn, in his seminal work (with Ramses Wessel and Jan Wouters) on informal international lawmaking, takes a more sophisticated approach, and focuses on law

Karen N Scott, *Unconventional Lawmaking in the Law of the Sea and Area-based Conservation Measures*
In: *Unconventional Lawmaking in the Law of the Sea*. Edited by: Natalie Klein, Oxford University Press.
DOI: 10.1093/oso/9780192897824.003.0016

that 'dispenses with certain formalities' in relation to process, actors or output.[1] Much work on unconventional lawmaking concerns so-called 'soft law', defined by Alan Boyle as 'a convenient description for a variety of non-legally binding but normatively worded instruments used in contemporary international relations by States and international organizations'.[2] Soft law may be informal, in terms of the actors and/or processes involved in its creation, but it is, principally, characterized by informality in respect of its output. By contrast, unconventional lawmaking also encompasses legally binding—formal—outputs, created by informal actors, or processes such as treaty bodies or international organizations.[3]

Boyle's reference to 'norms' in his definition of soft law raises an important question as to the relationship between 'norms' and 'law'. Normative intent and/or normative effect are integral components of unconventional *lawmaking* for the purposes of this volume.[4] But while norms and law are both designed to influence the behaviour of legal actors, not all norms are law: '[t]he universe of norms is larger than the universe of law'.[5] Pauwelyn helpfully distinguishes between 'legal acts' and 'legal facts', both of which may have 'legal effects'.[6] He defines a legal act as having formalities and emanating from an entity with the capacity to act, whereas a legal fact can 'emanate from anyone and from anywhere'.[7] The legal effect of a legal act stems 'directly and independently from the legal act', whereas 'the legal effects of a legal fact stem not from the fact as such but from the application of a separate legal act whose application is triggered by this fact'.[8] Applied to area-based conservation measures, the Commission on the Conservation of Antarctic Marine Living Resources (CCAMLR) Conservation Measure 91-05 (2016), which established the Ross Sea region MPA,[9] is a legal act, whereas Sustainable Development Goal (SDG) 14.5, which establishes the target of protecting 10% of the marine and coastal environment by 2020,[10] is a legal fact. Both instruments are normative, and both have legal effects, but neither are necessarily 'law', as defined by conventional, or even unconventional, means.

The distinction between 'law' and 'non-law' has long exercised both academics and practitioners of international law. For commentators such as Prosper Weil and Jan Klabbers, there is a bright line between law and non-law, and the concepts of 'soft law' and, more generally, relative normativity, are roundly rejected.[11] Kal Raustiala makes a similar argument: '[t]hat many nonbinding commitments ultimately influence state behavior illustrates the complexity of world politics, not the character of those commitments'.[12] Other

[1] Joost Pauwelyn, 'Informal International Lawmaking: Framing the Concept and Research Questions' in Joost Pauwelyn, Ramses A Wessel, and Jan Wouters (eds), *Informal International Lawmaking* (OUP 2012) 13, 15.

[2] Alan Boyle, 'Soft Law in International Law-making' in Malcolm D Evans (ed), *International Law* (5th edn, OUP 2018) 119, 121.

[3] See Jutta Brunnée, 'COPing with Consent: Law-making Under Multilateral Environmental Agreements' (2002) 15 LJIL 1; Robin R Churchill and Geir Ulfstein, 'Autonomous Institutional Arrangements in Multilateral Environmental Agreements: A Little-noticed Phenomenon in International Law' (2000) 94 AJIL 623.

[4] See Klein, in Chapter 1 of this volume.

[5] Joost Pauwelyn, 'Is It International Law or Not, and Does It Even Matter?' in Pauwelyn, Wessel, and Wouters (n 1) 125.

[6] ibid 153–54.

[7] ibid 154.

[8] ibid.

[9] Discussed in section 16.5.1.2 below.

[10] 'Transforming Our World: The 2030 Agenda for Sustainable Development', UNGA Res 70/1 (25 September 2015) UN Doc A/Res/70/1. SDG 14.5 is discussed in section 16.5.4.1 below.

[11] Prosper Weil, 'Towards Relative Normativity in International Law' (1983) 77 AJIL 441; Jan Klabbers, 'The Redundancy of Soft Law' (1996) 65 Nordic JIL 167. See also Jean D'Aspremont, *Formalism and the Sources of International Law* (OUP 2011).

[12] Kal Raustiala, 'Form and Substance in International Agreements' (2005) 99 AJIL 581, 590.

scholars, by contrast, recognize the legal effects of unconventional instruments expressly[13] or implicitly. Kenneth Abbot and Duncan Snidal, for example, assert that '[c]ontemporary international relations are legalized to an impressive extent, yet international legalization displays great variety'.[14] This pluralization of international law may arise from a desire to recognize that unconventional instruments, in practice, have legal effect;[15] from a critique or dissatisfaction with conventional international lawmaking processes;[16] or from an ideology, such as the New Haven School of international law, which defines international law broadly, as a process of authoritative decision-making.[17]

For the purposes of this book, informal or unconventional lawmaking is defined by Klein, in the introduction, as 'the process of international cooperation to reach agreements (other than treaties) between public authorities, with or without the participation of private actors or international organizations, in varied institutions and networks. This cooperation typically entails "norm-setting or public policy making by public authorities" and, on this basis, warrants the description of "lawmaking"'.[18] Bearing in mind that informality may arise with respect to actors, process and/or outputs, and that unconventional law is characterized by normative intent or normative effect, or both, this chapter identifies the following categories of unconventional lawmaking in relation to area-based conservation measures. First, binding measures that are adopted by regional fisheries management organizations (RFMOs) and regional seas organizations. Examples are drawn from the CCAMLR and the OSPAR Commission (established by the 1992 Convention for the Protection of the Marine Environment of the North-east Atlantic). Second, binding measures that are adopted by the International Maritime Organization (IMO) and International Seabed Authority (ISA). Third, non-binding 'pledges'—to use Raustiala's term[19]—adopted by states through the United Nations General Assembly (UNGA), the 1992 Convention on Biological Diversity (CBD) and on a regional basis. In respect of the latter, the 2014 Declaration for the Conservation of the Sargasso Sea provides a contemporary, pertinent example. Fourth, non-binding guidelines or other initiatives adopted by international treaty bodies and other organizations. Relevant examples in this section include the work of the CBD, particularly in relation to ecologically or biologically significant areas (EBSAs), and the UN Food and Agricultural Organization (FAO), in relation to vulnerable marine ecosystems (VMEs). Finally, this chapter will examine non-binding guidelines and other initiatives adopted by a (quasi-)NGO, the International Union for the Conservation of Nature (IUCN). Examples in this section comprise the IUCN guidelines on protected areas and MPAs, the identification of Important Marine Mammal Areas (IMMAs) and the IUCN Global Standard for the Identification of Key Biodiversity Areas. It is acknowledged that this final category stretches the term 'public authorities', as set out by Klein in Chapter 1 of this volume, but the IUCN is a hybrid organization involving both states and NGOs, and its standards have had undeniable legal effects on the law relating to area-based conservation.[20]

[13] See, eg Christine Chinkin, 'The Challenge of Soft Law: Development and Change in International Law' (1989) 38 ICLQ 850.

[14] Kenneth W Abbott and Duncan Snidal, 'Hard and Soft Law in International Governance' (2000) 53 Intl'l Org 421, 421.

[15] See, eg Anthony Aust, 'The Theory and Practice of Informal International Instruments' (1986) 35 ICLQ 787.

[16] See, eg Geoffrey Palmer, 'New Ways to Make International Environmental Law' (1992) 86 AJIL 259.

[17] See, eg Rosalyn Higgins, *Problems & Process: International Law and How We Use It* (Clarendon Press 1994) 2.

[18] Klein, in Chapter 1 of this volume (footnotes omitted).

[19] Raustiala (n 12) 581.

[20] See, further, section 16.5.6 below.

The order in which these unconventional or informal examples of lawmaking are listed demonstrates a continuum of both conventionality (or informality) and lawmaking. Decisions establishing area-based conservation measures taken by institutions such as the IMO, RFMOs, regional seas organizations and the ISA are unconventional, in so far as they do not constitute treaties or custom, or are not otherwise covered by Article 38 of the ICJ Statute. However, the role of these organizations in developing the law of the sea is far from unconventional in 2021. As noted by James Harrison a decade ago, 'the creation of a universal legal order of the oceans has been significantly facilitated by the use of increasingly sophisticated law-making procedures involving international institutions'.[21] The status of pledges and non-binding targets is more complex. These are clearly normative in intent, in that they are designed to influence the behaviour of legal actors, and normative in effect (in that legal actors have changed their behaviour in response to these targets). They have legal effects, so might be described as 'lawmaking', but they are, arguably, not, in and of themselves, 'law'. Similar conclusions might be reached in relation to non-binding measures and initiatives developed by both treaty and international organizations and by other non-state actors. The roles played by these informal outputs may vary, however, depending on the formality of the actor and the process of norm creation. Pledges adopted by states collectively, or acting through an international organization, often seek to fill gaps in the law: to create standards—in relation to area coverage, for example—where none previously existed. Measures adopted by more informal actors, such as the CBD and the IUCN, largely serve to strengthen or 'thicken'[22] existing law, through the clarification of terms (such as an MPA), and the development of standards relating to the establishment and management of MPAs and other area-based conservation measures.

What cannot be denied, however, is that area-based conservation measures have, largely, been developed by informal or unconventional lawmaking processes. While treaty-based measures have been used in some fields, such as in relation to mitigating ship-based pollution and in whale conservation, it is institutions—state and non-state based—that have, to date, largely driven and developed the law and norms of area-based conservation. There is, however, no bright-line distinction between formal and informal law, and both exist side by side. Their relationship may be complementary or, occasionally, antagonistic,[23] but it is, indubitably, symbiotic. It is also dynamic While informal lawmaking has dominated area-based protection over the last decade or so, this situation may change if the negotiations for the ILBI are successful. Area-based protection is one of five substantive areas slated for inclusion within the ILBI, and the instrument may set out binding detailed standards and processes for the establishment and management of MPAs beyond national jurisdiction. As will be demonstrated in the final section of this chapter, however, informal or unconventional processes and instruments are contributing to the development of the ILBI regime, and are unlikely to be entirely replaced by it.

[21] James Harrison, *Making the Law of the Sea: A Study on the Development of International Law* (CUP 2011) 3.

[22] The term 'thicken' was identified by Rosemary Rayfuse at the 2019 workshop associated with this project.

[23] Mark A Pollack and Gregory C Shaffer, 'The Interaction of Formal and Informal International Lawmaking' in Pauwelyn, Wessel, and Wouters (n 1) 241

16.3 Defining Area-based Conservation Measures

There is no single definition of an MPA or an area-based conservation measure.[24] The most widely applied definition of an MPA was developed by the IUCN, and defines a protected area as 'a clearly defined geographical space, recognised, dedicated and managed, through legal or other effective means, to achieve the long-term conservation of nature with associated ecosystem services and cultural values'.[25] The IUCN has, more recently, clarified that 'only those sites where the main goal or outcome is conserving nature should be considered MPAs'.[26] The parties to the CBD[27] have adopted a similar definition of an MPA, as 'any defined area within or adjacent to the marine environment, together with its overlaying waters and associated flora, fauna and historical and cultural features, which has been reserved by legislation or other effective means, including custom, with the effect that its marine and/or coastal biodiversity enjoys a higher level of protection than its surroundings'.[28] The broader notion of the OECM ('other effective area-based conservation measure'), which was inserted into Aichi Biodiversity Target 11 in the final stages of negotiations,[29] has recently been defined by the parties to the CBD as 'a geographically defined area other than a Protected Area, which is governed and managed in ways that achieve positive and sustained long-term outcomes for the in situ conservation of biodiversity, with associated ecosystem functions and services and where applicable, cultural, spiritual, socio-economic, and other locally relevant values'.[30] The IUCN has, recently, opined that fishery management areas with no wider conservation aims, large areas protecting a particular species across a region, and areas that incidentally protect biodiversity while serving another purpose (such as managing offshore wind farm development) should be classified as OECMs.[31]

Applying these definitions, which, incidentally, were developed through informal or unconventional lawmaking processes, but are widely accepted, this chapter will discuss MPAs and OECMs established for conservation purposes. These include MPAs proper (such as the network developed by OSPAR), protected areas established for fisheries management purposes with a strong conservation objective (for example, the Ross Sea MPA established by CCAMLR), particularly sensitive sea areas (PSSAs), established under the auspices of the IMO, and areas of particular environmental interest identified by the ISA. This chapter will also include a brief discussion of guidelines and other processes associated with area-based conservation areas, as developed by the CBD, FAO and IUCN. This chapter will not

[24] See, generally, Petra Dranker, 'Marine Protected Areas in Areas beyond National Jurisdiction' (2012) 27 IJMCL 291; Kristina M Gjerde and Anna Rulska-Domino, 'Marine Protected Areas beyond National Jurisdiction: Some Practical Perspectives for Moving Ahead' (2012) 27 IJMCL 351; Karen N Scott, 'Conservation on the High Seas: Developing the Concept of the High Seas Marine Protected Area' (2012) 27 IJMCL 849; Tullio Scovazzi, 'Marine Protected Areas on the High Seas: Some Legal and Policy Considerations' (2004) 19 IJMCL 1.

[25] Nigel Dudley (ed), *Guidelines for Applying Protected Area Management Categories* (IUCN 2008) 8.

[26] Jon Day, Nigel Dudley, and Marc Hockings (eds), *Guidelines for Applying the IUCN Protected Area Management Categories to Marine Protected Areas* (2nd edn, IUCN 2019) 8 <https://www.iucn.org/content/guidelines-applying-iucn-protected-area-management-categories-marine-protected-areas-0> accessed 9 January 2021.

[27] Convention on Biological Diversity (adopted 5 June 1992, entered into force 29 December 1993) 1760 UNTS 79 (hereafter 'CBD').

[28] Report of the Ad Hoc Technical Expert Group on Marine and Coastal Protected Areas, of 13 February 2003 (doc. UNEP/CBD/SBSTTA/8/INF/7), para 30.

[29] Dan Laffoley and others, 'An Introduction to "Other Effective Area-based Conservation Measures" under Aichi Target 11 of the Convention on Biological Diversity: Origin, Interpretation and Emerging Ocean Issues' (2017) 27(S1) Aquat Conserv 130, 131.

[30] CBD Decision 14/8 *Protected Areas and other Effective Area-based Conservation Measures* (2018), para 2.

[31] Day, Dudley, and Hockings (n 26) 11.

address broader area-based processes such as spatial planning and integrated coastal zone management.

16.4 'Conventional' Sources of Area-based Conservation Measures

The LOSC[32] does not expressly provide for area-based protection. Nevertheless, parties to the Convention are subject to a general obligation to 'protect and preserve the marine environment',[33] and must take measures to 'protect and preserve rare and fragile ecosystems as well as the habitat of depleted, threatened or endangered species and other forms of marine life'.[34] A LOSC Annex VII Tribunal has recently confirmed that the designation of an MPA is a 'measure' for the purposes of Article 194(5) of the LOSC.[35] The LOSC is complemented by the CBD, which, in Article 8, requires parties, as far as possible and appropriate, to establish a system of protected areas, and to manage those areas in a manner consistent with the aims of conservation.

A number of global and regional instruments provide for the designation of MPAs and other area-based conservation measures within their treaty text. For example, Special Areas may be designated under MARPOL 73/78, within which there are operational constraints on vessels in respect of the discharge of oil, noxious liquid substances, sewage, garbage, and air pollution.[36] Twenty-four such Special Areas have been designated to date.[37] Under the 1946 International Convention on the Regulation of Whaling,[38] whale sanctuaries have been designated in the Southern and Indian Oceans.[39] The 1972 World Heritage Convention[40] provides for a detailed process for listing sites of natural heritage under the Convention,[41] and fifty listed sites currently comprise MPAs,[42] with the Great Barrier Reef in Australia being listed as early as 1981.[43] The 1971 Ramsar Convention,[44] similarly, provides for a listing process for important wetland areas which may include 'areas of marine water the depth of which at tide does not exceed six metres'.[45]

[32] United Nations Convention on the Law of the Sea (adopted 10 December 1982, entered into force 16 November 1994) 1833 UNTS 397 (hereafter 'LOSC').

[33] ibid, art 192.

[34] ibid, art 194(5).

[35] *Chagos Marine Protected Area Arbitration (Mauritius v United Kingdom)* (Award of 18 March 2015) PCA Case No 2011-03, para 538.

[36] International Convention for the Prevention of Pollution from Ships (as Modified by the Protocol of 1978 Relating Thereto) (adopted 2 November 1973, entered into force 2 October 1983) 1340 UNTS 184 (hereafter 'MARPOL 73/78'), Annexes I, II, IV–VI.

[37] IMO, 'Special Areas under MARPOL' <https://www.imo.org/en/OurWork/Environment/Pages/Special-Areas-Marpol.aspx> accessed 7 January 2021.

[38] International Convention for the Regulation of Whaling (adopted 2 December 1946, entered into force 10 November 1948) 161 UNTS 72 (hereafter 'ICRW').

[39] ibid, sch, [7(a)] and [7(b)]. The Schedule is an integral part of the Convention (ICRW (n 38) art 1(1)).

[40] Convention for the Protection of the World Cultural and Natural Heritage (adopted 16 November 1972, entered into force 17 December 1975) 1037 UNTS 151 (hereafter 'WHC').

[41] ibid, arts 2 and 11.

[42] UNESCO WHC, 'World Heritage List' <https://whc.unesco.org/en/list/?search=&themes = 7> accessed 7 January 2021.

[43] UNESCO WHC, 'Great Barrier Reef' <https://whc.unesco.org/en/list/154> accessed 7 January 2021.

[44] Convention on Wetlands of International Importance Especially as Waterfowl Habitat (adopted 2 February 1971, entered into force 21 December 1975) 96 UNTS 245 (hereafter 'Ramsar Convention').

[45] ibid, art 1(1).

At the regional level, the 1995 SPA Protocol[46] to the 1995 Barcelona Convention[47] explicitly provides for the designation of Specially Protected Areas of Mediterranean Importance (SPAMI),[48] with detailed criteria and processes for designation being set out in Annex I to the Protocol. There are thirty-nine SPAMIs currently listed under the Protocol, with one, the Pelagos Sanctuary for the Conservation of Marine Mammals, including an area of high seas.[49] In the Antarctic, Annex V of the 1991 Environmental Protocol[50] to the 1959 Antarctic Treaty[51] provides for the creation of Antarctic Specially Protected Areas (ASPAs) and Antarctic Specially Managed Areas (ASMAs) in the Antarctic Treaty Area, which extends south of 60 degrees south latitude.[52] Annex V expressly stipulates that protected areas may be established in any marine area,[53] although the designation of MPAs under the Environmental Protocol has been slow, with fewer than 20% of the ASPAs established having a marine component.[54] Although ASPAs and ASMAs are designated by separate Measures, decisions are taken on the basis of consensus, and Annex V to the Protocol sets out the detailed criteria and process for designation.

16.5 'Unconventional' Sources of Area-based Conservation Measures

As noted above, there is no bright-line distinction between conventional and so-called unconventional lawmaking. Where area-based conservation measures or very detailed guidelines and processes are set out within a treaty, as illustrated by the examples in the previous section, these can, uncontroversially, be categorized as conventional or formal law. Similarly, a non-binding pledge adopted through the UN with normative intent and normative effect can be considered an example of informal or unconventional lawmaking. But is the development of area-based conservation through decision-making within an international institution unconventional, and does it matter whether decisions are taken by consensus, or whether they build on a clear formal law base? For the purposes of this chapter, the current author has, for example, distinguished between the 1991 Environmental Protocol to the Antarctic Treaty, which sets out detailed criteria and processes for the establishment of protected areas within an Annex to the Protocol (an example of formal lawmaking), and

46 Protocol Concerning Specially Protected Areas and Biological Diversity in the Mediterranean (adopted 10 June 1995, entered into force 12 December 1999) (hereafter '1995 SPA Protocol').

47 Convention for the Protection of the Marine Environment and the Coastal Region of the Mediterranean (adopted 10 June 1995, entered into force 9 July 2004), amending Convention for the Protection of the Mediterranean Sea Against Pollution (adopted 16 February 1976, entered into force 12 February 1978) 1102 UNTS 27 (1995 Barcelona Convention). The consolidated text is available at UNEP, 'Barcelona Convention and Amendments' <https://wedocs.unep.org/bitstream/handle/20.500.11822/7096/BarcelonaConvention_Consolidated_eng.pdf> accessed 28 June 2021.

48 1995 SPA Protocol (n 46) art 8.

49 Specially Protected Areas Regional Activity Centre, 'SPAMIs' <https://www.rac-spa.org/spami> accessed 5 January 2021.

50 Protocol on Environmental Protection to the Antarctic Treaty (adopted 4 December 1991, entered into force 14 January 1998) 2941 UNTS 3 (hereafter '1991 Environmental Protocol').

51 The Antarctic Treaty (adopted on 1 December 1959, entered into force 23 June 1969) 402 UNTS 71.

52 ibid, art VI.

53 1991 Environmental Protocol (n 50) Annex V, art 2.

54 Karen N Scott, 'Marine Protected Areas in the Southern Ocean' in Alex Oude Elferink, Erik Molenaar, and Donald R Rothwell (eds), *The Law of the Sea and Polar Regions: Interaction between Global and Regional Regimes* (Martinus Nijhoff 2013) 113, 128.

the 1982 Convention for the Conservation of Antarctic Marine Living Resources (CAMLR Convention),[55] which provides a bare reference to measures that may be area-based, but which has developed a detailed set of criteria and processes for MPA designation through decisions of the Commission (an example of informal or unconventional lawmaking). But this distinction might, legitimately, be critiqued as arbitrary, with the difference between the two regimes being one of degree rather than of kind.

Nevertheless, using the criteria identified by Pauwelyn, Wessel and Wouters, noted above, namely, informality associated with actors, processes and/or outputs, as well as the requirement of normative intent or normative effect (or both), six categories of unconventional lawmaking in the context of area-based conservation have been identified for the purposes of this chapter. These range from binding (formal) outputs resulting from unconventional actors and processes (international institutions), to non-binding (informal) outputs created by formal actors (states) and informal actors (international and non-state institutions). All categories are characterized by both normative (although not necessarily lawmaking) intent and, to a greater or lesser extent, normative effect.

16.5.1 Binding Area-based Conservation Measures Adopted by RFMOs and Regional Seas Organizations

16.5.1.1 OSPAR

Annex V of the 1992 Convention for the Protection of the Marine Environment of the North-east Atlantic (OSPAR Convention)[56] permits the Commission to 'develop means, consistent with international law, for instituting protective, conservation, restoration or precautionary measures related to specific areas or sites or related to particular species or habitats'.[57] On the basis of this spare provision, the Commission has established a network of MPAs that cover 7% of the total OSPAR area and 8% of the OSPAR area beyond national jurisdiction (ABNJ).[58] The lawmaking mechanisms on which this MPA network was established comprise a combination of binding and non-binding decisions and recommendations. Recommendation 2003/3 (amended in 2010)[59] has no binding force,[60] but defines an MPA for the purposes of OSPAR,[61] and aimed to develop an ecologically coherent network by 2012, to be well managed by 2016. Detailed criteria, and the process for establishing MPAs, are set out in the Guidelines for the Identification and Selection of Marine Protected

[55] Convention on the Conservation of Antarctic Marine Living Resources (adopted 20 May 1980, entered into force 7 April 1982) 1329 UNTS 47 (hereafter 'CAMLR Convention').

[56] Convention for the Protection of the Marine Environment of the North-east Atlantic (opened for signature 22 September 1992, entered into force 25 March 1998) 2354 UNTS 67 (hereafter 'OSPAR Convention').

[57] ibid, Annex V, art 3(1)(b)(ii).

[58] OSPAR Commission, 'Key Figures of the MPA OSPAR Network' <https://mpa.ospar.org/home-ospar/key-figures> accessed 5 January 2021.

[59] OSPAR Commission, 'Recommendation 2003/03 on a Network of Marine Protected Areas' (23–27 June 2003) OSPAR Doc 03/17/1, Annex 9, amended by OSPAR Recommendation 2010/2 (OSPAR Doc 10/23/1, Annex 7).

[60] 1992 OSPAR Convention (n 56) art 13(5). Decisions and recommendations must be adopted on a unanimous vote unless unattainable, in which case they may be adopted on a three-quarters majority (ibid, art 13(1)).

[61] An MPA is defined as 'an area within the maritime area for which protective, conservation, restorative or precautionary measures, consistent with international law have been instituted for the purpose of protecting and conserving species, habitats, ecosystems or ecological processes of the marine environment'.

Areas in the OSPAR Maritime Area,[62] which is also a non-binding instrument. The network of (currently) seven high seas MPAs was established by virtue of binding decisions,[63] but the management plans associated with each MPA are set out in non-binding recommendations.[64] Non-state actors were heavily involved in developing the MPA network, with the WWF and the Netherlands co-supporting a proposal for a pilot MPA to be established for the Charlie-Gibbs Fracture Zone (in the ABNJ), as early as 2000.[65] The OSPAR Commission has not only been a pioneer in establishing MPAs beyond national jurisdiction, but has also developed innovative formal (but not binding) collaborative arrangements with relevant RFMOs (such as the North-east Atlantic Fisheries Commission (NEAFC)), as well as the ISA.[66]

Although the OSPAR MPA network has a clear formal legal basis in a treaty provision, the MPA regime has been developed by actors, and through processes, that are informal or unconventional, at least compared with 'conventional' sources of international law. Moreover, the outputs establishing the MPAs and associated measures are also informal, comprising decisions and recommendations. The decisions establishing the MPAs in ABNJ are clearly binding, but the criteria and process are set out in non-binding instruments. The intent, however, of all instruments, is normative, as is their effect. In practice, the OSPAR process for area-based conservation can legitimately be described as 'lawmaking', albeit of an informal or unconventional kind.

16.5.1.2 CCAMLR

CCAMLR is authorized to adopt conservation measures for the CAMLR Convention area, including the 'opening and closing of areas, regions or sub-regions for the purpose of

[62] OSPAR Agreement: 2003-17 as amended by OSPAR, 'Meeting of the Biodiversity Committee Summary Record' (26–30 March 2007) OSPAR Doc BDC 07/12/1-E, para 3.43b, and OSPAR 'Meeting of the Biodiversity Committee Summary Record' (29 February–4 March 2016) OSPAR Doc BDC 16/9/1, para 5.27 and Annex 13.

[63] OSPAR Commission, 'Decision 2010/1 on the Establishment of the Milne Seamount Complex Marine Protected Area' (2010) OSPAR Doc 10/23/1-E; OSPAR Commission, 'Decision 2010/2 on the Establishment of the Charlie-Gibbs South Marine Protected Area' (2010) OSPAR Doc 10/23/1-E, Annex 36; OSPAR Commission, 'Decision 2010/3 on the Establishment of the Altair Seamount High Seas Marine Protected Area (2010) OSPAR Doc 10/23/1-E, Annex 38; OSPAR Commission, 'Decision 2010/4 on the Establishment of the Antialtair Seamount High Seas Marine Protected Area' (2010) OSPAR Doc 10/23/1-E, Annex 40; OSPAR Commission, 'Decision 2010/5 on the Establishment of the Josephine Seamount High Seas Marine Protected Area' (2010) OSPAR Doc 10/23/1-E, Annex 43; OSPAR Commission, Decision 2010/6 on the Establishment of the Mid Atlantic Ridge North of the Azores High Seas Marine Protected Area' (2010) OSPAR Doc 10/23/1-E, Annex 44; OSPAR Commission, 'Decision 2012/1 on the Establishment of the Charlie-Gibbs North High Seas Marine Protected Area' (2012) OSPAR Doc 12/22/1, Annex 6. Decisions are binding by virtue of Article 13(2) of the 1992 OSPAR Convention, although states may opt out, provided they do so in writing.

[64] OSPAR Commission, 'Recommendation 2010/12 on the Management of the Milne Seamount Complex Marine Protected Area' (2010) OSPAR Doc 10/23/1-E, Annex 35; OSPAR Commission, 'Recommendation 2010/13 on the Management of the Charlie-Gibbs South Marine Protected Area' (2010) OSPAR Doc 10/23/1-E, Annex 37; OSPAR Commission, 'Recommendation 2010/14 on the Management of the Altair Seamount High Seas Marine Protected Area' (2010) OSPAR Doc 10/23/1-E, Annex 39; OSPAR Commission, 'Recommendation 2010/15 on the Management of the Antialtair Seamount High Seas Marine Protected Area' (2010) OSPAR Doc 10/23/1-E, Annex 41; OSPAR Commission, 'Recommendation 2010/16 on the Management of the Josephine Seamount High Sea Marine Protected Area' (2010) OSPAR Doc 10/23/1-E, Annex 43; OSPAR Commission, 'Recommendation 2010/17 on the Management of the Mid-Atlantic Ridge North of the Azores High Seas Marine Protected Area' (2010) OSPAR Doc 10/23/1-E, Annex 45; OSPAR Commission, 'Recommendation 2012/1 on the Management of the Charlie-Gibbs North High Seas Marine Protected Area' (2012) OSPAR Doc 12/22/1, Annex 7.

[65] B O'Leary and others 'The First Network of Marine Protected Areas (MPAs) in the High Seas: The Process, the Challenges and where Next' (2012) 36 Mar Pol'y 598, 599.

[66] See OSPAR Commission/NEAFC, 'Collective Arrangement between Competent International Organizations on Cooperation and Coordination regarding Selected Areas in Areas beyond National Jurisdiction in the North-east Atlantic' (2014) OSPAR Agreement 2014-09, updated 2018.

scientific study or conservation, including special areas for protection and scientific study' by the convention.[67] In contrast to the 1991 Environmental Protocol to the 1959 Antarctic Treaty, detailed provisions relating to the criteria for, and process of, area-based protection are not set out in the Convention itself. Rather, area-based conservation measures have been developed through a series of binding conservation measures.[68]

The general framework measure for the establishment of CCAMLR MPAs was adopted in 2011.[69] It endorsed area-based protection as an important tool to sustain ecosystem function particularly in light of climate change, while recognizing that rational use of marine resources is an objective of CCAMLR. Conservation Measure 91-04 (2011), surprisingly, does not define an MPA for the purposes of CCAMLR, but it sets out the purposes for which an MPA may be established by the Commission.[70] It also requires any MPA measure to include specific objectives and clear spatial boundaries, and to identify activities that are restricted, prohibited or managed, including any temporal or spatial limits on activities.[71] A skeleton management plan must be included in any measure establishing an MPA, as well as an outline of any administrative arrangements. There is no need for an MPA to be designated for a defined period. The general framework measure sets out the process for adopting a research and monitoring plan for the MPA, and the obligations of all parties associated with research, monitoring and review.[72] Provisions for cooperation with other institutions, including the 1991 Environmental Protocol, and the IMO, are provided for within the measure,[73] although the scope of CCAMLR measures is largely restricted to fishing and fishing research vessels.

In contrast to OSPAR, the process of designating MPAs, or, perhaps more accurately, area-based conservation measures under CCAMLR has, thus far, been politically (and legally) fraught. Currently, only two MPAs have been established.[74] The first CCAMLR MPA, and, indeed, the first MPA to be designated on the high seas, was established in 2009 as the South Orkney Islands Southern Shelf (SOISS) MPA.[75] The SOISS MPA covers 94,000 square kilometres, and is designed to establish a scientific reference area, conserve important predator foraging areas and include representative examples of pelagic and benthic bioregions.[76] All types of fishing, other than scientific research as agreed by the Commission, are prohibited within the MPA, and discharges and dumping from fishing vessels are also prohibited. Vessels transiting the MPA are encouraged to inform CCAMLR. The SOISS MPA has been designated for an indefinite duration, but is reviewed every five years. Notwithstanding its pioneering status as the first high seas MPA, the SOISS MPA has been subject to trenchant critique. Most significantly, the boundaries of the SOISS MPA

[67] CAMLR Convention (n 55) art IX(2)(g).

[68] ibid, art IX(6)(b). The Convention provides for a process whereby a member may object to, and thus be exempt from, binding conservation measures (art 6(c) and (d)).

[69] CCAMLR, 'General Framework for the Establishment of CCAMLR Marne Protected Areas' (2011) Conservation Measure 91–04.

[70] ibid, para 1.

[71] ibid, para 3(i), (ii), and (iii).

[72] ibid, para 5.

[73] ibid, para 10.

[74] CCAMLR's early spatial management initiatives focused on designating CCAMLR Monitoring Program (CEMP) sites, in order to gather data comparing fishing and non-fished areas, and cannot be considered as operating primarily for conservation purposes. See CCAMLR, 'Procedure for According Protection to CEMP Sites' (2004) Conservation Measure 91-01.

[75] CCAMLR, 'Protection of the South Orkney Islands Southern Shelf' (2009) Conservation Measure 91-03.

[76] ibid.

were adjusted during negotiation, to exclude a valuable commercial fishery,[77] and, moreover, the 'MPA was adopted without management, research or monitoring plans, leaving no mechanisms for implementation'.[78] The SOISS MPA was, of course, established prior to the adoption of the general framework conservation measure on MPAs, but subsequent attempts to harmonize Conservation Measure 91-03 (2009) with Conservation Measure 91-04 (2011) have proven unsuccessful. A draft Research and Monitoring Plan (RMP) for the SOISS MPA has been developed, to strengthen harmonization between these two measures, but, even though such a Plan is not required under Conservation Measure 91-03 (2009) (the general framework instrument), it has not been adopted by the Commission, as of 2020.[79]

The second CCAMLR MPA, adopted for the Ross Sea region in 2016,[80] has proven no less controversial. It took five years to negotiate,[81] and significant compromises were made, reducing its area coverage by almost 40 %, introducing a krill research zone, and inserting a clause limiting its duration to thirty-five years (subject to renewal). Nevertheless, at 1.55 million square kilometres, the Ross Sea region MPA comprises the largest high seas MPA, and 72% of its waters are closed to commercial fishing, although research fishing is permitted in the 'no-take' zone.[82] Conservation Measure 91-05 (2016) divides the Ross Sea MPA into three zones (the General Protection Zone, the Special Research Zone and the Krill Research Zone),[83] within which fishing is prohibited or restricted,[84] and sets out eleven objectives for the MPA, ranging from providing reference areas to monitor environmental (including climate) change, to protecting pelagic prey species and ecosystem processes.[85] In 2017, the Ross Sea region MPA (RSRMPA) RMP was endorsed by the CCAMLR Scientific Committee.[86] Nevertheless, there was disagreement among the CCAMLR members as to whether the RSRMPA RMP needed to be specifically adopted by the Commission (as advocated by China and Russia), or whether its endorsement by the Scientific Committee meant that it was already in effect, with no further action by the Commission required (as asserted by the United States).[87] Moreover, China and Russia criticized the extent to which the Scientific Committee had provided 'advice', as required by Conservation Measure 91-04,[88] and Russia also questioned the level of scientific information available to develop 'a scientifically based RMP in accordance with the aims and objectives of the MPA'.[89] This disagreement has yet to be resolved.

[77] CCAMLR, 'Report of the Twenty-eighth Meeting of the Commission' (26 October–6 November 2009) CCAMLR-XXVIII, paras 7.4 and 7.5.

[78] Cassandra M Brooks and others, 'Reaching Consensus for Conserving the Global Commons: The Case of the Ross Sea, Antarctica' [2019] Conserv Lett e12676, 1, 3.

[79] See CCAMLR, 'Report of the Thirty-eighth Meeting of the Commission' (21 October–1 November 2019) CCAMLR-XXXVIII, paras 6.31–6.32. There was no discussion of this proposal at the 2020 meeting, which was truncated, and was held online, owing to the COVID-19 pandemic.

[80] CCAMLR, 'Ross Sea Region Marine Protected Area' (2016) Conservation Measure 91–05.

[81] For an overview of this process, see Karen N Scott, 'Protecting the Commons in the Polar South: Progress and Prospects for Marine Protected Areas in the Antarctic' in Keyuan Zou (ed), *Global Commons and the Law of the Sea* (Brill Nijhoff 2018) 326.

[82] Julia Jabour and Danielle Smith, 'The Ross Sea Region Marine Protected Area: Can it be Successfully Managed?' (2018) 32 Ocean Y B 190, 192.

[83] CCAMLR Conservation Measure 91–05 (n 80) para 5.

[84] ibid, paras 6–8.

[85] ibid, para 3.

[86] CCAMLR, 'Report of the Thirty-sixth Meeting of the Scientific Committee' (16–20 October 2017) SC-CCAMLR XXXVI, para 5.45(iii).

[87] ibid, paras 5.76–5.82.

[88] ibid, paras 5.76–5.79.

[89] ibid, para 5.80.

There are three other MPAs under advanced negotiation within CCAMLR, but all are struggling to achieve the consensus needed for adoption.[90] More significantly, this process of informal lawmaking, in order to establish an MPA network has, arguably, damaged the efficacy of CCAMLR as a fisheries conservation institution. In a recent article, Brooks and others have concluded that the institutional conflict over MPAs has caused 'CCAMLR member states to disregard the best available science, distort the foundational rules of their convention, break trust, and threaten the integrity of one of the world's most well-regarded science-based multinational governance efforts'.[91] Some (although by no means all) of the conflict has arisen from disputes as to the legal basis for MPA designation under CCAMLR (and, indeed, more generally), and as to the processes associated with informal lawmaking.[92] However, it would be a mistake to attribute the MPA conflict within CCAMLR solely to the fact that it has been developed through informal, as opposed to formal, lawmaking processes, and it is worth noting that CCAMLR is far more functional than the International Whaling Commission, notwithstanding that the latter's rules relating to whaling are adopted through conventional treaty law mechanisms. Nevertheless, this example of informal lawmaking appears more functional in legal, as opposed to practical, terms.

16.5.2 Binding Area-based Conservation Measures Adopted by the IMO

The IMO makes a significant contribution to developing the law of the sea through formal law, primarily through facilitating the negotiation of treaties on shipping and associated environmental matters.[93] It has contributed to area-based conservation through the formal designation of Special Areas under MARPOL 73/78, as noted above. However, area-based conservation has been further developed by the IMO through unconventional means: the designation of particularly sensitive sea areas (PSSAs).[94] A PSSA is defined as 'an area that needs special protection through action by IMO because of its significance for recognized ecological, socio-economic, or scientific attributes where such attributes may be vulnerable to damage by international shipping activities'.[95] The IMO began work on PSSAs in 1978,[96] but it is generally agreed that the legal basis for their designation can be found in

[90] For an overview of the progress (or lack thereof) in establishing MPAs under CCAMLR, see Karen N Scott, 'MPAs in the Southern Ocean under CCAMLR: Implementing SDG 14.5' (2021) 9(1) Korean J Intl Comp L 84.

[91] Cassandra M Brooks and others, 'Science-based Management in Decline in the Southern Ocean' (2016) 364(6309) Science 185, 185.

[92] For example, during the negotiations for the Ross Sea region MPA, the Ukraine stated, in 2013, that '[t]he UN Convention on the Law of the Sea (ratified by Ukraine) provides the opportunity for establishing MPAs only within the coastal waters in the areas of jurisdiction of those countries. Therefore, at this stage we cannot see any legal possibility for establishing MPAs in the high seas of the World Ocean containing areas for which CCAMLR is responsible'. See CCAMLR, 'Report of the Second Special Meeting of the CCAMLR Commission' (15–16 July 2013) CCAMLR-SM-II, para 3.26. Russia has also disputed whether CCAMLR has a legal basis to establish MPAs. See VV Lukin, 'Russia's Current Antarctic Policy' (2014) 4 Polar J 199, 219.

[93] See, generally, James Harrison, *Making the Law of the Sea: A Study on the Development of International Law* (CUP 2011), ch 6. See also Sun, in Chapter 6 of this volume.

[94] See, generally, Julian Roberts, Aldo Chircop, and Siân Prior, 'Area-based Management on the High Seas: Possible Application of the IMO's Particularly Sensitive Sea Area Concept' (2010) 25 IJMCL 483.

[95] IMO, 'Guidelines for the Identification and Designation of Particularly Sensitive Sea Areas' (1 December 2005) IMO Res A.982(24), para 1.2.

[96] ibid, para 1.1.

Articles 194(5) and 211(6) of the LOSC. Nevertheless, the detailed criteria for, and process associated with, designating a PSSA are set out in non-binding IMO guidelines, originally adopted in 1991, and revised in 2005.[97] At the time of designation, an associated protective measure must be adopted and approved by the IMO, in order to prevent, reduce, or eliminate the threat or identified vulnerability of the PSSA.[98] PSSAs are established by IMO binding resolution,[99] although the legal effect of the PSSA on shipping results from the protective measure associated with the PSSA, adopted under relevant conventions such as SOLAS[100] or MARPOL, rather than the PSSA itself. Associated measures may include a routing system, area to be avoided, or compulsory pilotage. Sixteen PSSAs have been designated to date,[101] with the Great Barrier Reef being the first PSSA designated, in 1990 (extended in 2005 to include the Torres Strait), and the most recent, the Tubbataha Reefs Natural Park in the Sulu Sea, being designated in 2017.

The process of PSSA designation is informal, as it operates outside of conventional treaty processes, and involves state actors (who propose the PSSA), and the IMO, which approves both the PSSA and associated protective measures. The guidelines, which set out the substantive standards and processes, as applied to PSSAs, are, as their nomenclature implies, non-binding, but the PSSA is designated by a binding IMO resolution. Both the guidelines and associated resolutions are clearly normative in both intent and effect.

16.5.3 Binding Area-based Conservation Measures Adopted by the ISA

The ISA's designation of a representative network of areas of environmental interest in the Clarion-Clipperton zone is notable for the unconventionality of the lawmaking process.[102] Under Article 145 of the LOSC, the ISA has a mandate to take necessary measures for the protection of the environment of the Area,[103] including the prevention of damage to flora and fauna of the marine environment.[104] The ISA has implemented this mandate primarily through the development of the Mining Code, which regulates prospecting, exploring and exploitation of mineral resources in the Area.[105] Environmental protection is, principally, effected through environmental impact assessment and the development of regional

[97] IMO, 'Guidelines for the Designation of Special Areas and the Identification of Particularly Sensitive Sea Areas' (6 November 1991) IMO Res A.720(17), consolidated and revised by IMO, 'Guidelines for the Identification and Designation of Particularly Sensitive Sea Areas' (1 December 2005) IMO Res A.982(24), and IMO, 'Guidelines for the Designation of Special Areas under MARPOL 73/78 and Guidelines for the Designation of Particularly Sensitive Sea Areas' (29 November 2001) IMO Res A.927(22). See also IMO, 'Procedures for the Identification of Particularly Sensitive Sea Areas and the Adoption of Associated Protective Measures and Amendments to the Guidelines Contained in Resolution A.720(17)' (25 November 1989) IMO Res A.885(21).

[98] IMO Res A.982(24) (n 97) para 1.2.

[99] Eg, the most recent PSSA, Tubbataha Reefs Natural Park in the Sulu Sea (Philippines), was designated by IMO, 'Designation of the Tubbataha Reefs Natural Park as a Particularly Sensitive Sea Area' (7 July 2017) IMO Res MEPC.294(71).

[100] International Convention for the Safety of Life at Sea (adopted 1 November 1974, entered into force 25 May 1980) 1184 UNTS 278 (hereafter 'SOLAS').

[101] IMO, 'Particularly Sensitive Sea Areas' <https://www.imo.org/en/OurWork/Environment/Pages/PSSAs.aspx> accessed 8 January 2021.

[102] See, further, Davenport, in Chapter 10 of this volume.

[103] The Area is defined as the 'seabed and ocean floor and subsoil thereof beyond the limits of national jurisdiction', under art 1(1) of the LOSC (n 32).

[104] ibid, art 145 and, in particular, para (b).

[105] See ISA, 'The Mining Code' <https://www.isa.org.jm/mining-code> accessed 9 January 2021.

environmental management plans (REMP). It is through the latter that the ISA has begun the process of developing a network of protected areas. The first (and, thus far, only) REMP has been adopted for the Clarion-Clipperton Zone,[106] and the plan sets out, in detail, the location of, and justification for, a network of protected areas closed to mining, in order to protect and preserve the marine environment.[107] The ISA is in the process of adopting REMPs for other regions,[108] and the guidance to facilitate the development of REMPs, adopted by the ISA in 2019,[109] includes the objective:

> to provide the ISA with a clear and consistent mechanism to identify particular areas thought to be representative of the full range of habitats, biodiversity and ecosystem structures and functions within the relevant management areas and/or sites in need of protection to preserve ecological balance of the marine environment in the Area [and] to provide those areas with appropriate levels of protection.[110]

On the basis of Pauwelyn, Wessel and Wouters' criteria for informal lawmaking, discussed above, the network of areas of particular environmental interest developed by the ISA involves informal actors, informal processes and informal outputs. The principal actor is the ISA, comprising, largely, the Legal and Technical Commission and the Council, but the impetus for developing REMP actually derives from the work of scientists who, in 2007, proposed the development of a network of protected areas for conservation purposes.[111] The process of developing the plan is, undoubtedly, informal, as is the plan itself, notwithstanding that the plan is binding on LOSC parties and contractors by virtue of Article 162(o)(ii) of the Convention. The REMP, nevertheless, is normative in both intent and effect, and the process can, undoubtedly, be defined as lawmaking, albeit of an unconventional kind.

16.5.4 Non-binding 'Pledges' to Establish MPAs and other Area-based Conservation Measures

Whereas the previous section focused on area-based conservation, effected through binding or partially binding instruments, the following sections highlight instruments and mechanisms that are not binding, but, nevertheless, are normative in both intent and effect, and contribute, to varying extents, to lawmaking processes in the field of area-based conservation.

[106] ISA, 'Environmental Management Plan for the Clarion-Clipperton Zone' (13 July 2011) IBSA/17/LTC/7, para 21, formally endorsed by ISA, 'Decision of the Council Relating to an Environmental Management Plan for the Clarion-Clipperton Zone' (16–27 July 2012) ISBA/18/C/22. See, generally, Michael Lodge and others, 'Seabed Mining: International Seabed Authority Environmental Management Plan for the Clarion-Clipperton Zone. A Partnership Approach' (2014) 49 Mar Pol'y 66.

[107] ISA, Environmental Management Plan for the Clarion-Clipperton Zone (n 106) paras 21–42.

[108] See Aline Jaeckel, 'Strategic Environmental Planning for Deep Seabed Mining in the Area' (2020) 114 Mar Pol'y 103423.

[109] See ISA, 'Guidance to Facilitate the Development of Regional Environmental Management Plans (REMPs)' <https://www.isa.org.jm/files/files/documents/remp_guidance_.pdf> accessed 9 January 2021.

[110] ibid.

[111] Lodge and others (n 106) 68.

16.5.4.1 UN and CBD Targets to Protect 10% of the Oceans by 2020

One of the most visible initiatives in international environmental governance over the last decade has been the contribution of binding and non-binding global goals or targets to lawmaking processes. For example, the 2015 Paris Agreement commits parties to hold 'the increase in the global average temperature to well below 2°C above pre-industrial levels and [to pursue] efforts to limit the temperature increase to 1.5°C above pre-industrial levels'.[112] Also in 2015, the UNGA adopted the Sustainable Development Goals (SDGs),[113] which establish 17 goals and 169 targets across the areas of environment, development and social equality. Both instruments (notwithstanding that one is a binding treaty obligation and the other is a non-binding resolution) 'utilise goal-based targets, which provide states with significant flexibility in deciding how to meet those targets'.[114] This approach has been described as a '"novel" type of global governance',[115] but can also be categorized as an example of unconventional or informal lawmaking.

In the context of area-based conservation, the most influential target (or pledge) is the commitment to protect 10% of the marine environment by 2020. Originally adopted by the parties to the World Summit on Sustainable Development in 2002 (with a target date of 2012)[116] and endorsed by the parties to the CBD,[117] the target was revised in 2010, with a new target date of 2020, under the CBD Aichi Biodiversity Targets.[118] Aichi Biodiversity Target 11 also broadened the notion of protection to include 'other effective area-based conservation tools' in addition to MPAs. This target was repeated in SDG 14.5, as part of SDG 14, which seeks to achieve the conservation and sustainable use of the oceans, seas and marine resources.[119]

This target, to use the typology of Pauwelyn referred to above, constitutes a legal fact rather than a legal act, but it has, undoubtedly, had a legal (and normative) effect. It has galvanized states, international institutions and other actors into taking action to increase protected area coverage in the oceans, and the normative impact of this target can be assessed by its incorporation into, and provision of the impetus for, numerous instruments issued by states and international organizations, including all of those surveyed in this chapter.[120] In the context of lawmaking, it is significant that this target has been repeated and cross-referenced among multiple institutions. As asserted by Pierre-Marie Dupuy:

[112] Paris Agreement to the United Nations Framework Convention on Climate Change (adopted 12 December 2015, entered into force 4 November 2016) (2016) 55(4) ILM 740, art 1(1)(a).

[113] UN, 'Transforming Our World: The 2030 Agenda for Sustainable Development', UNGA Res 70/1 (25 September 2015) UN Doc A/Res/70/1.

[114] Karen N Scott and others , 'An Introduction to International Environmental Law' in Erika Techera and others (eds), *Routledge Handbook of International Environmental Law* (2nd edn, Routledge 2021) 1, 6.

[115] Frank Biermann, Norichika Kaine and Rakhyun E Kim, 'Global Governance by Goal-setting: The Novel Approach of the UN Sustainable Development Goals' (2017) 26 Curr Opin Environ 26.

[116] UNGA, 'Report of the World Summit on Sustainable Development' (26 August to 4 September 2002), UN Doc A/CONF.199/20, Annex: Plan of Implementation of the World Summit on Sustainable Development, para 31(c).

[117] CBD, 'Decision VII/28: Protected Areas (Articles 8 (A) to (E))' (13 April 2004) UN Doc UNEP/CBD/COP/DEC/7/28; CBD, 'Decision VII/5: Marine and Coastal Biodiversity' (13 April 2004) UN Doc UNEP/CBD/COP/DEC/VII/5, paras 18–31.

[118] CBD, 'Decision X/2: The Strategic Plan for Biodiversity 2011–2020 and the Aichi Biodiversity Targets' (29 October 2010) UN Doc UNEP/CBD/COP/DEC/X/2, Target 11.

[119] UN, 'Our Ocean, Our Future: Call for Action' UNGA Res 71/312 (6 July 2017) UN Doc A/RES/71/312. See also discussion by Telesetsky, in Chapter 14 of this volume.

[120] There is insufficient space to provide a thorough survey of relevant instruments that refer to one of more of these targets. One illustrative example is the reference to the WSSD target, and the aim of establishing a representative system of Antarctic MPAs, in the preamble to CCAMLR Conservation Measure 91-04 (n 69).

> [c]ross-references from one institution to another, the recalling of guidelines adopted by other apparently concurrent international authorities, recurrent invocation of the same rules formulated in one way or another to the universal, regional and more restricted levels, all tend progressively to develop and establish a common international understanding.[121]

This common understanding of the behavioural norm is integral to the process of lawmaking.

SDG 14 is notable in that, notwithstanding its non-binding status, it has been subject to development, and even review, through international fora: first, the High-level Political Forum on Sustainable Development, which was established in 2012, under the auspices of the UN Economic and Social Council,[122] and, second, the 2017 United Nations Conference to Support the Implementation of Sustainable Development Goal 14 (Oceans Conference). The Oceans Conference was particularly significant for two reasons. First, it adopted a declaration entitled 'Our Ocean, Our Future: Call for Action' (subsequently endorsed by the UNGA[123]), which, among other things, added 'conceptual clarity to the interpretation of SDG 14 targets by including reference to terms and instruments not previously incorporated into SDG 14'.[124] With respect to SDG 14.5, the Call for Action added precautionary and ecosystem-based approaches to the scope of Target 14.5, and expanded the target to include other area-based management tools, including integrated, cross-sectoral approaches; marine spatial planning (MSP); and integrated coastal zone management (ICZM).[125] Second, the 2017 Oceans Conference instituted a novel process whereby any stakeholder could register a voluntary commitment to support the implementation of SDG 14. As of 31 December 2020, of the 1,633 commitments made by governments, international organizations, NGOs and scientific groups, across all ten SDG 14 targets, 449 relate specifically to SDG 14.5. Of these, 177 have been made by governments, 177 by NGOs, scientific/academic/philanthropic institutions and 17 by the private sector.[126]

The extent to which these targets are lawmaking (as distinct from having legal and normative effects) is debatable.[127] It is also worth noting that—despite the apparent activity relating to SDG 14.5—as of January 2021, just 7.65% of the marine environment is subject to area-based protection.[128] Moreover, much of the area protected comprises very large-scale MPAs, which are not, necessarily, well-managed. It is estimated that ten large MPAs cover more than 50% of the total area protected,[129] and that international commitments

[121] Pierre-Marie Dupuy, 'Soft Law and the International Law of the Environment' (1991) 12 Mich J Intl'l L 420, 424.

[122] The High-level Political Forum on Sustainable Development replaced the UN Commission on Sustainable Development, and it reviewed SDG 14 in 2017 (in addition to SDGs 1, 2, 3, 5, and 9). See UN Sustainable Goals Knowledge Platform, 'High-level Political Forum 2017' <https://sustainabledevelopment.un.org/hlpf/2017> accessed 9 January 2021.

[123] UNGA Res 71/312 (n 119).

[124] Daniela Diz, Elisa Morgera and Meriwether Wilson, 'Marine Policy Special Issue: SDG Synergies for Sustainable Fisheries and Poverty Alleviation' (2019) 110 Mar Pol'y 102860, 2.

[125] UNGA Res 71/312 (n 119) para 13(j).

[126] UN Ocean Conference, 'Registry of Voluntary Commitments' <https://oceanconference.un.org/commitments/> accessed 31 December 2020.

[127] See, further, Telesetsky, in Chapter 14 of this volume.

[128] Protected Planet, 'Marine Protected Areas' <https://www.protectedplanet.net/en/thematic-areas/marine-protected-areas> accessed 9 January 2021.

[129] Bárbara Horta e Costa and others, 'A Regulation-Based Classification System for Marine Protected Areas (MPAs)' (2016) 72 Mar Pol'y 192, 192.

are leading to a 'race' towards MPA designation, with many MPAs established in remote locations, without management plans or monitoring, and permitting a variety of extractive activities.[130] Horta e Costa and others argue that this leads 'to a false sense of protection by society at large',[131] and undermines the efficacy of assessing 'conservation targets centred on area coverage alone'.[132] The development of targets through informal processes could, therefore, actually undermine formal law, if they are insufficiently or poorly developed, although such deficiencies are by no means confined to informal processes of lawmaking.

These reservations notwithstanding, pledges of this kind have clearly made an important contribution to the process of norm creation with respect to area-based conservation. The CBD/SDG 14.5 targets are not binding (or lawmaking), in and of themselves, but they have provided the catalyst or motivation for action, including lawmaking, at all levels of governance. Moreover, they can provide a platform from which to develop more sophisticated or ambitious targets. Notwithstanding the fact that the international community has failed to protect 10% of the marine environment by 2020, a new target—30% of areas protected by 2030—was announced in December 2020 by the High-level Panel for a Sustainable Ocean Economy (Ocean Panel).[133] The target is a global goal, and is not binding on states individually,[134] but is intended to be normative, and may yet have normative effect.

16.5.4.2 2014 Hamilton Declaration for the Conservation of the Sargasso Sea

The 2014 Hamilton Declaration for the Conservation of the Sargasso Sea[135] demonstrates the value and significance of instruments that can be described as informal, unconventional and normative, but not lawmaking. The Declaration is, unequivocally, non-binding but, nevertheless, establishes a Commission and a framework for cooperation in conserving the Sargasso Sea (beyond national jurisdiction), designed to guide the actions of the ten signatory states.[136] The Commission is built on the work of the Sargasso Sea Alliance, led by Bermuda, and the process has involved significant NGO and other non-state participation. The aims of the Declaration and the Commission are to protect the Sargasso Sea, using existing institutions and mechanisms, and, therefore, the Declaration deliberately refrained from any form of lawmaking. Nevertheless, it might be described as strengthening or 'thickening' existing law, in developing its application and potential extension to the Sargasso Sea.[137]

[130] ibid.
[131] ibid.
[132] ibid.
[133] High-level Panel for a Sustainable Ocean Economy, 'Transformations for a Sustainable Ocean Economy: A Vision for Protection, Production and Prosperity' (2020) <https://www.oceanpanel.org/ocean-action/files/transformations-sustainable-ocean-economy-eng.pdf> accessed 8 January 2021. The Ocean Panel is an initiative of fourteen world leaders, working with business and financial institutions, as well as the science community, and civil society, which has launched an ambitious, yet practical, oceans agenda.
[134] ibid.
[135] The text of the Declaration is available at: Sargasso Sea Commission, 'Hamilton Declaration on Collaboration for the Conservation of the Sargasso Sea' (2018) <http://www.sargassoseacommission.org/storage/Hamilton_Declaration_with_signatures_April_2018.pdf> accessed 8 January 2021.
[136] The signatory states are the Azores, Bermuda, Monaco, the United Kingdom, the United States, British Virgin Islands, the Bahamas, Canada, the Cayman Islands, and the Dominican Republic. Sargasso Sea Commission, 'About the Commission: The Hamilton Declaration' <http://www.sargassoseacommission.org/about-the-commission/hamilton-declaration> accessed 3 January 2021.
[137] See, further, David Freestone and Kate Killerlain Morrison, 'The Sargasso Sea Alliance: Seeking to Protect the Sargasso Sea' (2012) 27 IJMCL 647; and David Freestone and Faith Bulger, 'The Sargasso Sea Commission: An Innovative Approach to the Conservation of Areas beyond National Jurisdiction' (2016) 30 Ocean Y B 80.

16.5.5 Non-binding Guidelines and other Measures Adopted by International Organizations and Institutions

The fifth category of unconventional or informal lawmaking in the context of area-based conservation focuses on non-binding guidelines and other measures adopted by international organizations or treaty regimes. These measures are non-binding, but are, nevertheless, normative in both intent and effect, and are designed to develop and 'thicken' the law relating to area-based conservation. Two examples are highlighted below: the work of the CBD, particularly in relation to ecologically or biologically significant marine areas (EBSAs), and the work of the FAO in relation to vulnerable marine ecosystems (VMEs).

16.5.5.1 The CBD, Area-based Protection, and Ecologically or Biologically Significant Marine Areas (EBSAs)

Article 8(a) of the CBD requires contracting parties, as far as possible and appropriate, to 'establish a system of protected areas or areas where special measures need to be taken to conserve biological diversity'. Unsurprisingly, the CBD has been active in developing and promoting a range of initiatives relating to area-based protection, including developing valuable definitions of MPAs and other effective area-based conservation measures.[138] In 2008, the CBD adopted scientific guidance for establishing a network of MPAs in open-water and deep-sea habitats.[139]

One of the most influential developments, which was also initiated in 2008, was the adoption of criteria for the identification of Ecologically or Biologically Significant Marine Areas (EBSAs).[140] EBSAs are not, in and of themselves, MPAs, and there is no obligation to turn an EBSA into an MPA,[141] but they constitute 'a scientific process aiming, notably, to give support to and facilitate the designation of MPAs in ABNJ'.[142] Seven scientific criteria[143] have been established by the CBD as key to identifying EBSAs, and, through fifteen regional workshops, over 250 million square kilometres of ocean area (around two-thirds of the ocean) has been assessed, and 204 EBSAs described.[144] Thirty-one lie solely within ABNJ, and a further thirty-five straddle areas within and beyond national jurisdiction.[145]

While EBSAs are not solely focused on ABNJ, the tool has very much been designed to support biodiversity beyond national jurisdiction, and the development of area-based conservation, under the ILBI, in ABNJ.[146] Moreover, EBSAs have contributed to area-based

[138] See CBD Decision VII/5 (n 117); CBD, 'Report of the Ad Hoc Technical Expert Group on Marine and Coastal Protected Areas' (13 February 2003) UN Doc UNEP/CB/SBSSTA/8/INF/7; CBD, 'Decision 14/8: Protected Areas and other Effective Area-based Conservation Measures' (30 November 2018) UN Doc CBD/COP/DEC/14/8.

[139] CBD, 'Decision IX/20: Marine and Coastal Biodiversity' (9 October 2008) UN Doc UNEP/CBD/COP/DEC/IX/20, Annex II.

[140] ibid.

[141] DC Dunn and others 'The Convention on Biological Diversity's Ecologically or Biologically Significant Areas: Origins, Development and Current Status' (2014) 49 Mar Pol'y 137, 143.

[142] Marta Chantal Ribeiro, 'South Atlantic Perspectives on the Future International Legally Binding Instrument under the LOSC on Conservation and Sustainable Use of BBNJ' (2017) 32 IJMCL 733, 760.

[143] The criteria comprise: uniqueness or rarity; special importance for life-history stages of species; importance for threatened, endangered, or declining species or habitats; vulnerability, fragility, sensitivity, or slow recovery; biological productivity; biological diversity; and naturalness.

[144] NJ Bax and others, 'Results of Efforts by the Convention on Biological Diversity to Describe Ecologically or Biologically Significant Marine Areas' (2015) 30 Conserv Biol 571, 572.

[145] ibid 574.

[146] See Elisabeth Druel, 'Ecologically or Biologically Significant Marine Areas (EBSAs): The Identification Process under the Convention on Biological Diversity (CBD) and Possible Ways Forward' (2012) IDDRI Working Paper No 17/12, 19.

conservation lawmaking within a number of other global and regional institutions.[147] For example, the ISA environmental management plan for the Clarion-Clipperton Zone references EBSAs and the work of the CBD on area-based conservation more generally.[148] The IMO has deemed the EBSA guidelines a valuable reference tool to support the use of the revised PSSA guidelines,[149] and the Banc D'Arguin PSSA proposal from Mauritania (currently under discussion at the IMO) draws data from the EBSA described for the area.[150] The Sargasso Sea was, officially, described as an EBSA in 2012,[151] and this description underpins the aims and objectives of the 2014 Hamilton Declaration.

The EBSA process is, undoubtedly, informal or unconventional, with respect to actors (international institutions with significant input from scientific experts), process (a quasi-scientific description of an area) and output (a non-binding, non-normative description that can be used to support future normative measures). It is not lawmaking per se, but, rather, contributes to law-making processes in other institutions: a legal fact rather than a legal act, to use the terminology developed by Pauwelyn.

16.5.5.2 FAO and VMEs

The status attributed to EBSAs applies similarly to the concept of the VME, as developed by the UNGA and the FAO. A VME is, similarly to the EBSA, a quasi-scientific process, whereby vulnerable marine ecosystems are identified, and may, subsequently, become subject to area-based conservation measures such as closure to bottom trawling. Initially developed by the UNGA,[152] the concept of the VME was advanced and implemented by the FAO, in the 2009 International Guidelines for the Management of Deep-sea Fisheries in the High Seas.[153] Although non-binding, these guidelines are normative in intent and effect, and have led to significant areas of the seabed being closed to bottom trawling.[154] In addition to contributing to the lawmaking processes of states and RFMOs, the concept of the VME has also been referred to by other international institutions, including, for example, the ISA, in the Clarion-Clipperton environmental management plan.[155]

[147] See Piers K Dunstan and others, 'Using Ecologically or Biologically Significant Marine Areas (EBSAs) to Implement Marine Spatial Planning' (2016) 121 Ocean & Coastal Mgmt 116.

[148] ISA, Environmental Management Plan for the Clarion-Clipperton Zone (n 106) para 27. The Plan acknowledges that the EBSA criteria were not fully developed at the time of the adoption of the Plan, 'but the design [of the network] covers the key elements currently applicable to the Clarion-Clipperton Zone' (ibid, para 27), and that, as more information becomes available, 'the spatial management of mining activities may have to reflect' other EBSA factors (ibid, para 29).

[149] IMO, 'Report of the Marine Environmental Protection Committee on its Sixty-ninth Session' (17 May 2016) IMO Doc MEPC 69/21, paras 10.5–10.6.

[150] Daniela Diz and others, 'Mainstreaming Marine Biodiversity into the SDGs: The Role of other Effective Area-based Conservation Measures (SDG 14.5)' (2018) 93 Mar Pol'y 251, 255.

[151] Freestone and Bulger (n 137) 84.

[152] See UNGA Res 59/25 (17 January 2005) UN Doc A/Res/59/25, paras 67–69; UNGA Res 61/105 (6 March 2007) UN Doc A/Res/61/105, paras 80–81.

[153] FAO, 'International Guidelines for the Management of Deep-sea Fisheries in the High Seas' (Rome 2009) <http://www.fao.org/3/i0816t/i0816t00.htm> accessed 10 January 2021. These were endorsed in UNGA Res 67/79 (11 December 2012) UN Doc A/RES/67/79, para 134. See also Scanlon, in Chapter 11 of this volume.

[154] Diz and others (n 150) 256.

[155] ISA, Environmental Management Plan for the Clarion-Clipperton Zone (n 106) para 27(a).

16.5.6 Non-binding Guidelines and other Measures Adopted by the IUCN

The final category of unconventional or informal lawmaking comprises a range of initiatives associated with area-based conservation by the IUCN. This category takes an expansive view of the term 'public authority', as set out in the introduction to this volume, but the IUCN is a private actor with public elements. Over 200 states and governments are IUCN members, in addition to the more than 1,200 NGOs and indigenous peoples' groups.[156] Moreover, the IUCN Protected Area Guidelines, in particular, have had legal effects equivalent to many formal law examples, notwithstanding that they are, clearly, neither law nor lawmaking. Three IUCN initiatives developing formal and informal lawmaking in the context of area-based conservation are, very briefly, highlighted below.

16.5.6.1 IUCN Protected Area Guidelines

The current IUCN Guidelines for Applying Protected Area Management Categories were adopted in 2008,[157] and, as described above, set out a definition of a protected area and six related management categories. Guidelines clarifying the application of these categories to MPAs were adopted in 2019.[158] These guidelines are, clearly, neither binding, nor law, as such, but they have been widely adopted by states, and by international institutions, in their lawmaking processes. Most significantly, the IUCN definition and categories of MPAs have been recognized by the parties to the CBD as a basis for defining an MPA and types of management objectives.[159] The categories have also been adopted by the UN, in respect of the UN List of Protected Areas,[160] and have been used in a more limited way by the Intergovernmental Forum on Forests, and in respect of biosphere reserves.[161] They have been applied in the Conservation of Arctic Flora and Fauna (CAFF) Circumpolar Protected Areas Network (CPAN) Strategy and Action Plan 1996 and the 2003 revised African Convention on the Conservation of Nature and Natural Resources.[162] Controversially, CCAMLR categorized the entire CAMLR Convention area as an IUCN Category IV MPA in 2011,[163] although the authors of the IUCN protected area guidelines dispute whether the entire area meets the Category IV criteria.[164] The endorsement of the IUCN categories by CCAMLR has also had the unexpected effect of making the designation of MPAs within the CAMLR Convention area harder, as states opposed to further MPA initiatives challenge

[156] IUCN, 'IUCN, International Union for the Conservation of Nature' <https://www.iucn.org> accessed 9 January 2021.

[157] Nigel Dudley (ed), *Guidelines for Applying Protected Area Management Categories* (IUCN 2008) (hereafter 'IUCN 2008 Protected Area Guidelines') <https://portals.iucn.org/library/sites/library/files/documents/2008-106.pdf> accessed 9 January 2021. The first set of guidelines were adopted by the IUCN in 1994.

[158] Day, Dudley, and Hockings (n 26).

[159] CBD Decision VII/5 (n 117) para 10.

[160] M Deguignet and others, *2014 United Nations List of Protected Areas* (UNEP-WCMC 2014) 19.

[161] IUCN 2008 Protected Area Guidelines (n 157) 48.

[162] ibid.

[163] CCAMLR Conservation Measure 91-04 (n 69) preamble.

[164] Rob Nicoll and Jon C Day, 'Correct Application of the IUCN Protected Area Management Categories to the CCAMLR Convention Area' (2017) 77 Mar Pol'y 9. The authors assert that the CAMLR Convention Area does not meet the criteria of an IUCN Category IV MPA, as the area is not 'recognised, dedicated and managed to achieve the long-term conservation of nature' (ibid 11). The authors also argue that the Ross Sea MPA is not an MPA under the IUCN guidelines, as it is not managed in perpetuity, but that the SOISS MPA is an MPA according to the guidelines (ibid 11).

their necessity, on the basis of the IUCN Category IV designation.[165] Finally, the categories and definitions have been adopted in 10% of national protected area legislation since 1994, including in Australia, Brazil, Bulgaria, Cambodia, Cuba, Georgia, Hungary, Kuwait, Mexico, Niger, Slovenia, Uruguay and Vietnam.[166]

16.5.6.2 Important Marine Mammal Areas (IMMAs) and the IUCN Global Standards for the Identification of Key Biodiversity Areas (KBAs)

Two less well-known IUCN initiatives are directed at identifying areas important for biodiversity and, more particularly, marine mammals, in order to inform policymakers engaged in area-based conservation. The Important Marine Mammal Areas (IMMAs) is an initiative led by the Marine Mammal Protected Areas Task Force (MMPATF), which was created, in 2013, by the International Committee on Marine Mammal Protected Areas, the IUCN World Commission on Protected Areas vice chair, and members of the IUCN Species Survival Commission.[167] Like EBSAs, IMMAs are not MPAs, but are areas identified on the basis of selection criteria and regional workshops. One workshop, for the Mediterranean, has been held, to date.[168] The IUCN Global Standard for the Identification of Key Biodiversity Areas (KBAs)[169] was adopted in 2016, and, again, operates a little like an EBSA, in that KBAs are not protected areas, but are identified in order to inform protected area policy and frameworks. Key questions, on which there is currently little research, are how these various processes (EBSAs, VMEs, IMMAs and KBAs) support and/or undermine one another, and how they relate to other processes (such as IMO PSSAs, ISA areas of particular environmental interest and other MPA networks such as those established under the auspices of OSPAR and CCAMLR).

16.6 'Unconventional' Area-based Conservation Measures and the International Legally Binding Instrument for the Conservation and Sustainable Use of Biodiversity beyond National Jurisdiction (ILBI)

Two important themes have emerged in this chapter, thus far, from the discussion of unconventional lawmaking in the context of area-based conservation measures. First, that in contrast to many other areas of marine environmental protection, such as vessel-source pollution or dumping waste at sea, area-based conservation has, largely, been developed and implemented through informal rather than formal lawmaking mechanisms. Second, that there is a close and symbiotic relationship between formal and informal lawmaking in respect of area-based conservation, with the latter regularly expanding upon, and

[165] Eg, at the 2018 CCAMLR Meeting, China recalled that the CCAMLR Scientific Committee had advised that the CAMLR area was an IUCN Category IV MPA, and asserted that, '[t]hus, the special consideration of establishing additional MPAs within the Convention Area shall be further discussed and justified'. See CCAMLR, 'Report of the Thirty-seventh Meeting of the Commission' (22 October—2 November 2018) CCAMLR-XXXVII, para 6.21.

[166] IUCN 2008 Protected Area Guidelines (n 157) 48.

[167] Marine Mammal Protected Areas Task Force, 'Important Marine Mammals' https://www.marinemammalhabitat.org/immas/> accessed 8 January 2021.

[168] ibid.

[169] See IUCN, 'A Global Standard for the Identification of Key Biodiversity Areas: Version 1.0' (2016) <https://portals.iucn.org/library/node/46259> accessed 9 January 2021.

implementing, the former. In part, this consequence emerges because of a relative absence of formal lawmaking in the field of area-based conservation.

This scenario is, however, set to change in respect of ABNJ, on the assumption that the negotiations for the ILBI are successful. The ILBI will be a treaty—a legally binding instrument resulting from a formal lawmaking process—[170] and the final formal negotiating round was due to take place in 2020, but was postponed owing to the COVID-19 pandemic. Area-based conservation measures comprise one of five substantive areas slated to be covered by the ILBI,[171] and, for the first time, detailed criteria and processes for general area-based protection in ABNJ are likely to be included within a formal lawmaking instrument. This prospect raises interesting questions in respect of the relationship between informal (and indeed formal) MPA processes and the ILBI, and the future prospects for informal lawmaking in respect of area-based conservation.

The relationship between the ILBI, its institutions and processes, and existing global and regional institutions is proving challenging to negotiate, but the agreed-upon overarching principle is that the ILBI will be interpreted and applied in a manner that does not 'undermine relevant legal instruments and frameworks and relevant global, regional, subregional and sectoral bodies'.[172] This issue is particularly pressing with regard to area-based conservation, given the number of institutions and regimes already engaged in MPA and other related measures. In 2017, three approaches to the designation of area-based conservation measures were put forward.[173] One is the 'global model', whereby the ILBI would create a global, overarching framework for the identification, designation, management and enforcement of area-based management tools, including MPAs.[174] By contrast, the 'regional and/or sectoral model' would largely leave the development of area-based conservation measures to existing institutions, with the role of the ILBI confined to providing global-level general policy guidance to promote cooperation.[175] The 'hybrid model' attempts to provide a compromise between these two positions, and promotes a model under which regional and sectoral institutions would remain the principal actors in implementing area-based conservation measures, but the ILBI would provide oversight, in addition to general guidance.[176]

[170] In 2015, the UNGA took the decision to establish a formal preparatory committee for the purpose of developing a binding instrument, under the auspices of the LOSC, on the conservation and sustainable use of biodiversity beyond national jurisdiction, and formal negotiations were instituted in December 2017. See 'Development of an International Legally Binding Instrument under the United Nations Convention on the Law of the Sea on the Conservation and Sustainable Use of Marine Biological Diversity of Areas Beyond National Jurisdiction' UNGA Res 69/292 (19 June 2015) A/RES/69/292 and 'International Legally Binding Instrument under the United Nations Convention on the Law of the Sea on the Conservation and Sustainable Use of Marine Biological Diversity of Areas Beyond National Jurisdiction' UNGA Res 72/249 (24 December 2017) A/RES/72/249.

[171] The other issues comprise marine genetic resources, including questions on the sharing of benefits; environmental impact assessment; and capacity-building and transfer of technology. See UNGA Res 66/231 (24 December 2011) UN Doc A/RES/66/231, para 167.

[172] 'Revised Draft Text of an Agreement under the United Nations Convention on the Law of the Sea on the Conservation and Sustainable use of Marine Biological Diversity of Areas Beyond National Jurisdiction' (18 November 2019) UN Doc A/CONF.232/2020/3, art 4(3) (hereafter 'November 2019 Revised Draft Text').

[173] 'Chair's Streamlined Non-paper on Elements of a Draft Text of an International Legally-binding Instrument under the United Nations Convention on the Law of the Sea on the Conservation and Sustainable use of Marine Biological Diversity of Areas beyond National Jurisdiction' (2017), paras 94–97 <http://www.un.org/depts/los/biodiversity/prepcom_files/Chairs_streamlined_non-paper_to_delegations.pdf>.

[174] ibid, para 94.

[175] ibid, para 96.

[176] ibid, para 95.

As of June 2021, the negotiating states have yet to determine which model will be adopted. The current draft text (from November 2019) permits states, under the ILBI, to adopt conservation and, possibly, management measures to complement measures adopted under existing instruments, but it seems clear that the measures envisaged will not amount to area-based conservation per se.[177] Where there are no regional or relevant global instruments, the draft text provides two options. The first would permit ILBI parties to establish area-based conservation tools,[178] but the second merely encourages states to cooperate to establish relevant regional or global instruments.[179] The extent to which the ILBI will provide a framework for the substantive designation of MPAs, and other area-based conservation measures has, thus, yet to be agreed.

Notwithstanding, much of the draft text of Part III of the ILBI appears to proceed on the assumption that parties to the ILBI *will* have a role in establishing area-based conservation measures directly under the agreement. Draft Article 17, for example, sets out a process whereby states (and only states) may submit proposals for area-based management tools. Extensive guidance relating to consultation is provided for, under draft Article 18, and the process of decision-making by the conference of the parties on area-based management tools is articulated in draft Article 19. Draft Article 16 stipulates that:

> Areas requiring protection through the establishment of area-based management tools, including marine protected areas, shall be identified on the basis of the best available [science] [scientific information and relevant traditional knowledge of indigenous peoples and local communities], the precautionary [approach] [principle] and an ecosystem approach.[180]

The indicative criteria for the identification of areas are set out in Draft Annex I, and the seven criteria developed by the CBD in the context of EBSAs are included verbatim, in addition to fourteen other potential criteria. A number of the EBSA criteria, however, are currently in square brackets, so remain under negotiation, in terms of their potential inclusion.[181] The draft definition of an MPA draws significant inspiration from the IUCN definition of a protected area, in that it refers to an 'area that is designated and managed to achieve specific [long term biodiversity] conservation and sustainable use objectives [and that affords higher protection than the surrounding areas]'.[182] This definition is narrower than that adopted by the CBD, and, arguably, implies that MPAs should be established in perpetuity (as required by the IUCN definition), although the relevant phrase is currently in square brackets, indicating that the parties have yet to finally agree on this definition. The draft definition of an 'area-based management tool', under the ILBI, is currently rather different from the text (although not the spirit) of the CBD OECM, in that it includes an MPA, and refers to 'a geographically defined area through which one or several sectors or activities are managed with the aim of achieving particular conservation and sustainable use

[177] November 2019 Revised Draft Text (n 172), draft art 15(1)(b)(i).

[178] ibid, draft art 15(1)(b)[(ii)].

[179] ibid, draft art 15 [2. Alt to para 1(b)(ii)].

[180] ibid, draft art 16(1). The text in square brackets indicates alternative phrases still under negotiation.

[181] ibid, draft Annex I. The EBSA criteria, currently (as of December 2020) in square brackets, comprise uniqueness, rarity, biological productivity, and naturalness.

[182] ibid, draft art 1(10).

objectives [and affording higher protection than that provided in the surrounding areas]'.[183] This definition also appears to draw inspiration from the 2019 IUCN MPA guidelines clarifying the definition of MPAs and other area-based conservation measures for the purposes of the IUCN protected area categories.

The negotiators of the ILBI are, thus, using informal (non-binding) instruments in order to develop definitions and standards, and are not merely deriving inspiration from the work of the CBD, but also the unambiguously non-binding standards developed by the IUCN. Nevertheless, it is clear that states do not regard these instruments as binding, or as setting standards that must be followed, or otherwise engaged with, by the ILBI, and it is notable that the IUCN categories, which have been adopted by other parts of the UN, are not referred to, or otherwise included, in the ILBI draft text. Moreover, it is clear from the negotiations that states regard the principle relating to not undermining 'relevant legal instruments and frameworks and relevant global, regional, subregional and sectoral bodies'[184] as applying to informal lawmaking instruments such as PSSAs, ISA areas of particular environmental interest, and the MPA networks developed by OSPAR, CCAMLR and other regional bodies. While these area-based conservation measures may have been created by unconventional processes (outside of the categories listed in Article 38 of the ICJ Statute), they are, nevertheless, undoubtedly 'lawmaking' and, thus, must not be undermined for the purposes of the ILBI. It is, therefore, clear that the ILBI will complement rather than replace existing informal lawmaking processes in the context of area-based conservation. Whether the locus of developing the future law of area-based conservation shifts from informal bodies and processes to the more formal treaty bodies of the ILBI remains to be seen, and will depend, in part, on the powers ultimately granted to the parties and institutions under the ILBI.

16.7 Concluding Remarks

This chapter has demonstrated the fundamental importance of informal or unconventional lawmaking to area-based conservation in the marine environment. Using the typology of Pauwelyn, Wessel and Wouters, six categories of informal or unconventional lawmaking were identified on the basis of their normative intent and/or effect, and their informality in relation to actors, processes and/or outputs. The distinction between legal acts and legal facts adopted by Pauwelyn was employed to distinguish between instruments that have legal effects as a consequence of the act itself (such as a binding resolution) and instruments that have indirect legal effect through their adoption in other lawmaking processes (such as pledges and guidelines). In other words, whereas the former can be described as directly lawmaking, the latter are indirectly lawmaking or, possibly, not lawmaking at all. However these instruments are categorized, there is no doubt that, to date, area-based conservation has largely been developed through informal, as opposed to formal, processes. Thus, informal or unconventional lawmaking has served a valuable purpose in addressing gaps in the formal regime (such as providing definitions of MPAs and other forms of area-based conservation), creating new commitments (in relation to area coverage, for example) and

[183] ibid, draft art 1(3).
[184] ibid, draft art 4(3).

developing or 'thickening' existing laws (for example, in respect of modes of managing conservation areas).

There are, nevertheless, risks that come with informal or unconventional lawmaking processes. It is possible that states may view informal—particularly non-binding— commitments as a replacement for more formal law, notwithstanding that such commitments may, effectively, be unenforceable, leading to an accountability gap. Less thought may be given to the negotiation of instruments adopted through informal processes, leading to commitments that may undermine formal law, or which are inadequate in terms of addressing the risks or threats in question. As noted above, the various pledges to extend area coverage of MPAs to 10% of the ocean environment have been criticized for promoting a 'race' to establish large MPAs, with little thought to their effective management or enforcement. Where informal law is misapplied or inappropriately used, there may be an absence of appropriate mechanisms to correct the error. In the case of CCAMLR, for example, the designation of the entire CAMLR Convention area as an IUCN Category IV MPA has been disputed, but the description has yet to be reversed and, in fact, has been used by some states to resist the development of more appropriate MPA measures by the Commission. The proliferation of similar processes, such as those associated with the identification of areas to be protected, may lead to confusion, and an inefficient deployment of valuable scientific resources.

These issues notwithstanding, the advantages of unconventional or informal lawmaking processes for area-based conservation clearly outweigh the risks. Moreover, the ubiquitous nature of many of these processes is, arguably, challenging the categories of 'conventional' and 'unconventional' lawmaking, more generally. While decisions and resolutions of international organizations and treaty institutions clearly fall outside the parameters of Article 38 of the ICJ Statute, should they really be categorized as 'unconventional' sources of lawmaking in 2021? In the law of the sea, the initiation of negotiations for the ILBI is an increasingly rare example of formal lawmaking. Today, law is more commonly created through these 'unconventional' processes, which are, consequently, increasingly regarded as 'conventional'.

17

Sea Level Rise and the Law of the Sea

Filling the Legal Gaps through Informal Lawmaking

Nilüfer Oral and Tutku Bektaş

17.1 Introduction

Climate change-induced sea level rise will result in the partial or complete inundation of low-lying coastal areas and insular features.[1] Sea level rise can lead to the loss of baselines from which maritime zones are measured, the partial or complete inundation of islands, and the concomitant loss of valuable maritime entitlements in such cases. Undoubtedly, such impacts of sea level rise create uncertainty as to the validity of existing and future maritime delimitations. These impacts can have serious consequences for many states dependent on the resources derived from maritime entitlements, as well as on the delicate balance of certainty and stability of inter-state relations. Moreover, the current state of international law does not provide clear guidance on the status of existing maritime boundaries in the event that the baseline disappears, or islands become submerged, as a result of climate change-induced sea level rise, adding further to the uncertainty.

As it stands, there is a legal gap between the two main international legal regimes that are applicable to the challenge at hand.[2] The 1982 United Nations Convention on the Law of the Sea (LOSC), a comprehensive global instrument intended to address all matters related to the oceans, is silent on issues arising from climate change and sea level rise. The Convention was negotiated and adopted before climate change was recognized as a concern of the international community and, therefore, before its impact on rising sea levels was recognized.[3] On the other hand, the United Nations Framework Convention on Climate Change (UNFCCC), adopted in 1992, does not directly address the consequences of climate change on sea level rise for low-lying coastal areas, islands and maritime entitlements.[4] Partly because of this gap, there has been no formal lawmaking process, to date, to address the impacts of climate change-induced sea level rise on baselines, maritime entitlements, low-lying coastal areas, and islands.

In the absence of direct guidance on the topic from traditional sources of international law, the current legal regime on the law of the sea needs adjustments, either in the form

[1] Intergovernmental Panel on Climate Change, 'Climate Change 2013: The Physical Science Basis. Working Group I Contribution to the Fifth Assessment Report of the Intergovernmental Panel on Climate Change' (CUP 2013) 25 (hereafter IPCC, 'Fifth Assessment Report').

[2] Nilüfer Oral, 'Ocean Acidification: Falling between the Legal Cracks of UNCLOS and the UNFCCC' (2018) 45(1) Ecology LQ 9.

[3] United Nations Convention on the Law of the Sea (adopted 10 December 1982, entered into force 16 November 1994) 1833 UNTS 397 (hereafter 'LOSC').

[4] United Nations Framework Convention on Climate Change (adopted 9 May 1992, entered into force 21 March 1994) 1771 UNTS 107 (hereafter 'UNFCCC').

Nilüfer Oral and Tutku Bektaş, *Sea Level Rise and the Law of the Sea* In: *Unconventional Lawmaking in the Law of the Sea*. Edited by: Natalie Klein, Oxford University Press. © Nilüfer Oral and Tutku Bektaş 2022. DOI: 10.1093/oso/9780192897824.003.0017

of amendments, or creation of a new internationally binding instrument specifically addressing sea level rise. As an alternative, states and other stakeholders have already resorted to informal processes of lawmaking in relation to the legal problems expected from sea level rise. These informal processes and efforts differ in their goals, methodology, participants, desired outcomes, and in terms of their legal effects on the interpretation of existing treaties, and the formation of traditional sources of international law.

This chapter will analyse a variety of existing processes of informal lawmaking in the progressive development of international law and their ability to meet the challenges of the impacts of sea level rise on maritime boundaries and entitlements. The first part sets out and discusses the current legal gaps in the regime in relation to sea level rise. The second part analyses the informal lawmaking processes under the LOSC and the UNFCCC (including the Paris Agreement),[5] and related efforts by states, regional bodies, and international courts and tribunals. The chapter also discusses potential legal effects of such subsequent agreements and subsequent practice by states, international organizations, and non-state actors, under Article 31 of the Vienna Convention on the Law of Treaties (VCLT),[6] in relation to the interpretation of the LOSC and the UNFCCC.

While the current informal international lawmaking efforts are far from achieving definitive normative outcomes in the traditional sense, whether it be through amending the existing legal frameworks, or creating new internationally binding instruments, the current endeavours should, nonetheless, be viewed as igniters of momentum towards such normative outcomes. The complexity of the challenge at hand bars any quick fixes or short-term solutions. The high value of endeavours taken to date is undeniable, ranging from establishing new networks and tools of cooperation under existing legal frameworks, to forming expert study groups and achieving regional consensus among the states that are most vulnerable to rising sea levels. Such efforts are the first steps taken by the states, individually or collectively, to set out all potential recourse, and design a satisfactory and durable solution to the legal challenges posed by sea level rise.

17.2 Gaps in the Legal Regime in Relation to Sea Level Rise

As noted at the outset, climate change-induced sea level rise creates risks to existing baselines from which maritime zones are measured, the partial or complete inundation of islands, and the concomitant loss of valuable maritime entitlements. None of these problems were foreseen by the drafters of the LOSC.[7] This situation has created inadvertent legal lacunae in the international legal framework for the law of the sea applicable to the

[5] Paris Agreement to the United Nations Framework Convention on Climate Change (adopted 12 December 2015, entered into force 4 November 2016) (2016) 55(4) ILM 740 (hereafter 'Paris Agreement').

[6] Vienna Convention on the Law of Treaties (opened for signature 23 May 1969, entered into force 27 January 1980) 1155 UNTS 331 (hereafter 'VCLT').

[7] See David D Caron, 'When Law Makes Climate Change Worse: Rethinking the Law of Baselines in Light of a Rising Sea Level' (1990) 17 Ecology LQ 621 (hereafter Caron, 'When Law Makes Climate Change Worse'), 635–36: 'the 1982 Convention appears to provide that ... the outer boundary of the exclusive economic zone, the contiguous zone, and the territorial sea are ambulatory in that they will move with the baselines from which they are measured. Apparently, the conference of experts who met throughout the decade of the 1970s did not anticipate that there could be a significant global regression of coastlines'. See also AHA Soons, 'The Effects of a Rising Sea Level on Maritime Limits and Boundaries' (1990) 37 Netherlands Intl'l L Rev 207–32.

consequences of sea level rise.[8] David Caron, as early as 1990, warned of the risks created by this uncertainty, not only on the applicable legal framework, but also its potential to disrupt inter-state relations and pose significant economic costs for states, which may need to pursue negotiations and adjudication.[9] This section sets out legal uncertainties surrounding the effects of sea level rise on the baselines and the outer limits of the maritime spaces that are measured from the baselines, and on islands.

17.2.1 Legal Uncertainty Surrounding the Effects of Sea Level Rise on Baselines and the Outer Limits of the Maritime Spaces Measured from the Baselines

The rights and obligations of a state in different maritime zones are determined in accordance with the provisions of the LOSC and customary international law. The set of maritime zones created pursuant to the Convention includes territorial sea, contiguous zone, continental shelf (including the extended continental shelf), exclusive economic zone (EEZ), high seas, and the Area, as well as archipelagic waters for archipelagic states.[10] As the limits of these zones are drawn by measuring their distance from the baseline from which the territorial sea is measured, any change or loss of the baseline due to sea level rise may result in change, reductions, or even complete loss of maritime entitlements of a state over a particular maritime area. According to the IPCC Fifth Report on Climate Change, around 70 % of global coastlines are expected to experience sea level rise within 20 % of the global mean.[11]

According to Article 5 of the LOSC, the normal baseline 'is the low-water line along the coast as marked on large-scale charts officially recognized by the coastal State'.[12] On the other hand, in relation to straight baselines, Article 7 provides that '[i]n localities where the coastline is deeply indented and cut into, or if there is a fringe of islands along the coast in its immediate vicinity, the method of straight baselines joining appropriate points may be employed in drawing the baseline from which the breadth of the territorial sea is measured'. Article 14 recognizes that the coastal State may use any of the methods in the Convention to meet the different conditions.

A key debate with respect to the effects of sea level rise on baselines and outer limits of maritime spaces is whether baselines are ambulatory, requiring that they be redrawn in the event of changes. Consequentially, where a new baseline is drawn in a landward position, the existing seaward limits of various maritime zones, such as the territorial sea, the contiguous zone, and the EEZ, will move in the same direction as the new baseline.[13] In 2012,

[8] International Law Commission, 'First Issues Paper by Bogdan Aurescu and Nilüfer Oral, Co-chairs of the Study Group on Sea-level Rise in relation to International Law' (28 February 2020) UN Doc No A/CN.4/740 (hereafter ILC, 'First Issues Paper'), para 181.

[9] Caron, 'When Law Makes Climate Change Worse' (n 7); See also David D Caron, 'Climate Change, Sea Level Rise and the Coming Uncertainty in Oceanic Boundaries: A Proposal to Avoid Conflict' in Seoung-Yong Hong and Jon M Van Dyke (eds), *Maritime Boundary Disputes, Settlement Processes, and the Law of the Sea* (Brill 2009) 1–17.

[10] For an in-depth discussion on the maritime zones under the law of the sea, see ILC, 'First Issues Paper' (n 8) paras 152–71.

[11] IPCC, Fifth Assessment Report (n 1) 1140.

[12] LOSC (n 3) art 5.

[13] ILC, 'First Issues Paper' (n 8) paras 68–69. The same landward positioning of the baseline also occurs in the event of permanent inundation of the points used to draw the baselines in the cases of reefs (art 6), mouths of rivers (art 9), bays (art 10), low-tide elevations (art 13), and archipelagic baselines (art 47) (LOSC (n 3)).

the International Law Association (ILA)'s Baseline Committee adopted the view that baselines are ambulatory.[14] In 2018, the International Law Association's Committee on Sea Level Rise adopted a resolution recommending the maintenance of existing baselines and outer boundaries of maritime zones.[15] The problem is that there is no explicit legal provision in the LOSC, or rule of customary international law, that clearly addresses this critical matter.

The only instance of permanency of maritime boundaries is found in the case of the continental shelf. According to Article 76(9) of the LOSC, when the coastal State deposits charts and relevant information describing the outer limits of its continental shelf with the UN Secretary General, the description becomes permanent. This process would reasonably be interpreted to mean that the outer limits of the continental shelf cannot be altered due to sea level rise and its effects on the baselines, provided that the coastal State complies with the requirements established under the Convention.[16] Similarly, under Article 76(8), a coastal State may establish the outer limits of its continental shelf beyond 200 nautical miles on the basis of the recommendations of the Commission on the Limits of the Continental Shelf. The maritime limits established on the basis of the recommendations of the Commission are final and binding, meaning that sea level rise cannot result in a change on these limits.[17]

While the LOSC provides that the outer limits of the continental shelf are permanent, it is silent on whether the same applies to the outer limits of the EEZ or other maritime zones. Thus, in theory, if a new baseline is drawn in a landward position, the outer limits of the EEZ will also move in the same direction. Nevertheless, this situation causes difficulties in practice, due to the fact that the outer limits of the EEZ and those of the continental shelf often coincide.[18] This situation may lead to the loss of valuable entitlements of a coastal State in its EEZ and continental shelf, and bring considerable limitations to the scope of its permitted activities.[19]

Similarly, in the case of archipelagic States, the inundation of small islands or drying reefs may impact on the existing archipelagic baselines, resulting in the loss of archipelagic state status of baselines, provided that the water to land ratio exceeds 9:1. Moreover, sea level rise may also cause an appreciable departure from the general configuration of an archipelago, affecting the distance–percentage criteria for the archipelagic baselines in Article 47(2) of the LOSC.[20]

In relation to baselines, the first issues paper of the International Law Commission (ILC)'s Study Group on Sea level rise in relation to international law, underlined that the LOSC 'does not indicate *expressis verbis* that new baselines must be drawn, recognized (in accordance with article 5 of UNCLOS) or notified (in accordance with article 16 of

[14] ILA, 'Baselines Under the International Law of the Sea', Resolution 1/2012 (26–30 August 2012) <http://ilareporter.org.au/wp-content/uploads/2015/07/Source-2-Baselines-Resolution.pdf> accessed 17 July 2021.

[15] ILA, 'Committee on International Law and Sea Level Rise', ILA Resolution 5/2018 (19–24 August 2018) <https://www.ila-hq.org/images/ILA/Resolutions/ILAResolution_5_2018_SeaLevelRise.pdf> accessed 17 July 2021: 'ENDORSES the proposal of the Committee that, on the grounds of legal certainty and stability, provided that the baselines and the outer limits of maritime zones of a coastal or an archipelagic State have been properly determined in accordance with the 1982 Law of the Sea Convention, these baselines and limits should not be required to be recalculated should sea level change affect the geographical reality of the coastline.'

[16] Caron, 'When Law Makes Climate Change Worse' (n 7) 634–35.

[17] LOSC (n 3) art 76(8).

[18] ILC, 'First Issues Paper' (n 8) para 75.

[19] LOSC (n 3) art 77(1).

[20] Stuart Kaye, 'The Law of the Sea Convention and Sea Level Rise after the *South China Sea* Arbitration' (2017) 93 US Naval War Coll Intl'l L Stud. Series 423, 433–36.

UNCLOS) by the coastal State when coastal conditions change; and the same observation is valid also with regard to the new outer limits of maritime zones (which move when baselines move).'[21] In its role as the subsidiary body of the General Assembly for the progressive development of international law and its codification, the decision of the International Law Commission to place the topic of sea level rise in relation to international law on its active work programme, in 2018, has been lauded and welcomed by many member states of the Sixth Legal Committee of the United Nations during its seventy-fourth session.[22] The Commission, through the process of informal lawmaking, can contribute to the clarification of the important issues raised by sea level rise and provide guidance to states.

17.2.2 Legal Uncertainty Surrounding the Effects of Sea Level Rise on Islands

The continued physical existence of many islands and low-lying small island states is currently uncertain due to the effects of climate change and sea level rise. Under the LOSC, islands are entitled to the same maritime zones and entitlements as continental land territory, unless the feature is a rock or low-tide elevation. Article 121(3) provides that '[r]ocks which cannot sustain human habitation or economic life of their own shall have no exclusive economic zone or continental shelf'. In other words, an island is entitled to a full panoply of maritime entitlements, unlike rocks, which have only a territorial sea and contiguous zone. Moreover, the famously cryptic language as to whether the feature is 'capable of sustaining human habitation or economic life on its own' has, to date, been subject to much scholarly debate.[23] However, very little guidance on the provision has been received from international courts and tribunals, with the exception of the *South China Sea* arbitration.[24]

Arguably, the distinction between islands and rocks carries utmost significance, especially for low-lying island states such as Tuvalu, Kiribati, and Maldives, due to the prospect of sea level rise. The risks of partial or complete inundation of islands include complete disappearance of the islands, or them being rendered uninhabitable because of increased flooding due to elevated tides, infiltration of saltwater in freshwater supplies, or loss of

[21] ILC, 'First Issues Paper' (n 8) para 78.

[22] See statements made during the Sixth Committee on Report of the International Law Commission on the work of its seventy-second session, 5 November 2020: Tuvalu (on behalf of the Pacific Islands Forum) <https://www.un.org/en/ga/sixth/75/pdfs/statements/ilc/13mtg_pacificislans.pdf> accessed 10 January 2021; Belize (on behalf of the Alliance of Small Island States (AOSIS)), <https://www.un.org/en/ga/sixth/75/pdfs/statements/ilc/13mtg_aosis.pdf> accessed 10 January 2021; Papua New Guinea, <https://www.un.org/en/ga/sixth/75/pdfs/statements/ilc/13mtg_papuanewguinea.pdf> accessed 10 January 2021; New Zealand <https://www.un.org/en/ga/sixth/75/pdfs/statements/ilc/13mtg_newzealand.pdf> accessed 10 January 2021; Fiji (on behalf of the Pacific Small Island Developing States) <https://www.un.org/en/ga/sixth/75/pdfs/statements/ilc/13mtg_psids.pdf> accessed 10 January 2021; Micronesia (Federated States of), <https://www.un.org/en/ga/sixth/75/pdfs/statements/ilc/13mtg_micronesia.pdf> accessed 10 January 2021; Maldives <https://www.un.org/en/ga/sixth/75/pdfs/statements/ilc/13mtg_maldives.pdf> accessed 10 January 2021; Tonga <https://www.un.org/en/ga/sixth/75/pdfs/statements/ilc/13mtg_tonga.pdf> accessed 10 January 2021; Republic of Korea <https://www.un.org/en/ga/sixth/75/pdfs/statements/ilc/13mtg_rok.pdf> accessed 10 January 2021; Solomon Islands <https://www.un.org/en/ga/sixth/75/pdfs/statements/ilc/13mtg_solomonislands.pdf> accessed 10 January 2021.

[23] Clive Schofield, 'The Trouble with Islands: The Definition and Role of Islands and Rocks in Maritime Boundary Delimitation' in Seoung-Yong Hong and Jon M Van Dyke (eds), *Maritime Boundary Disputes, Settlement Processes, and the Law of the Sea* (Brill 2009) 19, 21; Jon M Van Dyke and Robert A Brooks, 'Uninhabited Islands: Their Impact on the Ownership of the Oceans' Resources' (1983) 12 ODIL 265, 271; Jonathan Charney, 'Rocks that cannot Sustain Human Habitation' (1999) 93 AJIL 863, 870–71.

[24] See, further, section 17.3.4 below.

agricultural land and food production.[25] As it stands, the LOSC provides no clear guidance on the legal consequences of an island being submerged in water and, thereby, losing its island status. Similarly, questions persist as to whether an island that is rendered uninhabitable due to the adverse impacts of climate change, hence acquiring the legal status of a rock, would then lose all its maritime zones and entitlements. Such legal reclassification would be catastrophic for the economic, social, and cultural viability and existence of low-lying island states, and would be likely to lead to economic waste and conflict.[26] Informal lawmaking at the state level, as well as the dicta of international courts and tribunals, are valuable in shaping a common approach on how to address this issue under international law in the coming years.

17.3 Current Processes for Informal Lawmaking for Sea Level Rise

Informal lawmaking efforts offer alternative means of filling the legal gaps, as opposed to formal law processes such as amending conventions, or negotiating new binding instruments. It can provide guidance for actions by states to ameliorate the harsh consequences of inaction, and also lay the future foundations for more formal lawmaking measures. Overall, informal lawmaking efforts in relation to the challenges posed by sea level rise are forward-looking exercises, aiming to provide greater clarity on how to develop existing frameworks to fill gaps and adequately respond to emerging issues. As seen below, informal lawmaking is also an important tool in strengthening cooperation among a broad and diverse network of actors, through dialogue and aligning the expectations of states. Cooperation among state actors, in particular, is important, as state practice is essential to addressing these legal gaps. However, a broad range of stakeholders engaged in informal lawmaking can serve as drivers. Moreover, where the action is taken by states or Conference of the Parties (COP), in the framework of the UNFCCC, or Conference of the Parties serving as the meeting of the Parties to the Paris Agreement (CMA), these subsequent agreements, and subsequent practice, carry the utmost significance in informing the interpretation of treaty provisions in light of rising sea levels.

17.3.1 Processes and Mechanisms under the UNFCCC and the Paris Agreement

Formal lawmaking, typically through negotiation of binding treaties, protocols, or amendments, requires a ratification process, and a minimum number of ratifications in order for the instrument to enter into force. Formal lawmaking, although preferred for creating legally binding instruments, does not always offer the most time-efficient, flexible, or detail-oriented process. Against this background, the UNFCCC, through the meetings of the COP, including the meeting of the Parties to the Paris Agreement (CMA), or the meeting of the Parties to the Kyoto Protocol (CMP), provides important informal lawmaking mechanisms

[25] The representative of Fiji, during the Sixth Committee meeting, stated that 'Fijian communities are experiencing the decline of food production due to saltwater intrusion': UN Doc A/C.6/73/SR.23, para 61.

[26] Caron, 'When Law Makes Climate Change Worse' (n 7) 636–41.

for taking measures to mitigate and adapt, thanks to its capacity to produce hundreds of highly technical and detailed decisions and recommendations. Moreover, these bodies are better situated to respond more immediately to the constant need to expand, adjust, and update responses to the growing and changing scientific knowledge.[27]

In regard to the UNFCCC, Article 2 provides that the ultimate objective is to stabilize the greenhouse gas concentrations in the atmosphere in a way that avoids the adverse effects of climate change.[28] In relation to oceans, Article 4 of the UNFCCC requires the Parties under the Convention to 'promote sustainable management, and promote and cooperate in the conservation and enhancement, as appropriate, of sinks and reservoirs of all greenhouse gases'.[29] However, there are no provisions relating directly to sea level rise.

Building on the UNFCCC, the Paris Agreement, which was adopted by the COP21 in December 2015,[30] reflects the common goal to combat the threat of climate change through strengthening global cooperation at both the international and national levels.[31] An important component is the objective of holding the increase in the global average temperature to well below 2°C above pre-industrial levels, and pursuing efforts to limit the temperature increase to 1.5°C above pre-industrial levels.[32] The Paris Agreement establishes a clear 'global goal on adaptation of enhancing adaptive capacity, strengthening resilience and reducing vulnerability to climate change, with a view to contributing to sustainable development and ensuring an adequate adaptation response in the context of the temperature goal referred to in Article 2'.[33] Without question, adaptation to sea level rise must be seen as an integral part of the climate regime, even though it is not expressly referred to.

Enhancing adaptation action under the UNFCCC has been carried out through COP decisions, which established the Cancun Adaptation Framework and the Warsaw International Mechanism for Loss and Damage.[34] In addition, the Paris Agreement created an innovative process that requires the Parties to submit nationally determined contributions (NDCs) of the mitigation measures they will take at domestic levels. These processes, put forth under the UNFCCC and the Paris Agreement, are each invaluable examples of informal lawmaking efforts that help to create shared expectations, and align a common approach, to combat the adverse impacts of climate change.[35]

17.3.1.1 Cancun Adaptation Framework and National Adaptation Plans

The Cancun Adaptation Framework was established by the COP in its sixteenth session, in Mexico in 2010. The Parties decided that adaptation to the impacts of climate change should be given the same level of priority as mitigation of such effects.[36] One tool established under the Cancun Adaptation Framework is the strategic process of national

[27] Joost Pauwelyn, Ramses A Wessel, and Jan Wouters, 'When Structures Become Shackles: Stagnation and Dynamics in International Lawmaking' (2014) 25(3) EJIL 740.

[28] UNFCCC (n 4) art 2.

[29] ibid, art 4(d).

[30] UNFCCC COP, 'Adoption of the Paris Agreement', Decision 1/CP.21 (30 November–13 December 2015).

[31] Paris Agreement (n 5) art 2.

[32] ibid, art 2(1)(a).

[33] ibid, art 7(1).

[34] UNFCCC COP, 'Warsaw International Mechanism for Loss and Damage Associated with Climate Change Impacts', Decision 2/CP.19 (11 November 2013); Paris Agreement (n 5) art 8.

[35] See, further, Klein, in Chapter 1 of this volume.

[36] UNFCCC COP, 'The Cancun Agreements: Outcome of the Work of the Ad Hoc Working Group on Long-term Cooperation Action under the Convention', Decision 1/CP.16 (29 November 2010).

adaptation plans (NAPs), which allows countries to identify their medium- and long-term adaptation needs, and to develop and implement necessary strategies and programmes to meet those needs.[37] In 2015, the Paris Agreement recognized the importance of NAPs in the global effort to address climate change.[38] Now, in 2021, the NAPs have become an ongoing exercise, with steady progress achieved in the formulation and implementation of NAPs worldwide.[39] Since successful NAPs create intentional and strategic linkages between national and subnational adaptation efforts, the process also plays a role in 'vertical integration', such as seeking to achieve coherence between the Paris Agreement, the 2030 Agenda for Sustainable Development,[40] the Sendai Framework,[41] and other global, regional, and national frameworks and agendas.

To date, the NAP process has allowed some countries to create adaptation projects to respond specifically to sea level rise. For instance, St Lucia plans to improve marine and terrestrial spatial planning, in order to balance rising sea level with its fishery needs, terrestrial development, and shoreline protection. Sri Lanka, on the other hand, is concentrating on reducing the impacts of sea level rise on agriculture in coastal zones.[42]

17.3.1.2 Warsaw International Mechanism for Loss and Damage

The Warsaw International Mechanism for Loss and Damage (WIM) was established by the COP in its nineteenth session, in 2013, with the objective of addressing loss and damage associated with the effects of climate change, including slow-onset events and extreme events. Slow-onset events, as initially defined by the Cancun Agreement, expressly refers to the risks and impacts associated with sea level rise.[43] The WIM recognizes that developing countries are particularly vulnerable to the impacts of climate change. The work of the WIM was, subsequently, adopted in Article 8 of the Paris Agreement,[44] and is implemented by the Executive Committee, which engages with, and involves, a broad range of communities and bodies. Three main functions of the WIM are to enhance knowledge and understanding of comprehensive risk management approaches; to strengthen dialogue, coordination, coherence, and synergies among relevant stakeholders; and to enhance action and support, including finance, technology, and capacity-building.[45]

[37] ibid, para 15. See also UNFCCC COP, 'National Adaptation Plans', Decision 5/CP.17 (28 November 2011).

[38] Art 7(9) of the Paris Agreement (n 5) provides that 'each party shall, as appropriate, engage in adaptation planning processes and the implementation of actions, including the development or enhancement of relevant plans, policies and/or contributions'. Evidently, the NAP process is central to meeting the goals of the agreement.

[39] As of December 2020, it was reported that 125 of the 154 developing countries have initiated NAP processes: SBI, 'Progress in the Process to Formulate and Implement National Adaptation Plans' (20 November 2020) UN Doc FCCC/SBI/2020/INF.13, para 16.

[40] 'Transforming our World: The 2030 Agenda for Sustainable Development' UNGA Res 70/1 (25 September 2015) UN Doc No A/RES/70/1.

[41] UNISDR (United Nations International Strategy for Disaster Reduction), Sendai Framework for Disaster Risk Reduction 2015–2030 (2015) <http://www.wcdrr.org/uploads/Sendai_Framework_for_Disaster_Risk_Reduction_2015-2030.pdf> accessed 20 November 2020.

[42] Contribution by the Secretariat of UNFCCC (2020) (hereafter 'Contribution by the Secretariat of the UNFCCC') 3 <https://www.un.org/Depts/los/consultative_process/contribution21/18UNFCCC.pdf> accessed 10 January 2021.

[43] UNFCCC COP, 'The Cancun Agreements: Outcome of the Work of the Ad Hoc Working Group on Long-term Cooperation Action under the Convention', Decision 1/CP.16 (29 November 2010), para 25.

[44] See also UNFCCC COP, 'Warsaw International Mechanism for Loss and Damage Associated with Climate Change Impacts', Decision 2/CP.21 (30 November–13 December 2015).

[45] MJ Mace and Roda Verheyen, 'Loss, Damage and Responsibility after COP21: All Options Open for the Paris Agreement' (2016) 25 RECIEL 197.

To this end, the mandate of the Executive Committee of the WIM, in relation to slow onset events, has been organized through five-year and a two-year work plans.[46] The current work plan seeks to assess and develop recommendations to improve the Parties' state of knowledge, and their capacity to address slow-onset events and their impacts. The WIM also seeks to inform the Parties of the capacities of regional agencies and relevant partners, and to help the Parties identify necessary and appropriate follow-up actions.[47] So far, the committee has created an invaluable online database on slow-onset events, in which it identified more than 160 organizations working on the issue, along with a synopsis of the organizations' mandates, scopes of work, and geographic coverage.[48] The committee also published a technical paper setting out existing approaches to slow-onset events, through planning and developing regulations at the national level, as well as methods and tools towards slowing down sea level rise.[49] Thirdly, the committee decided to establish a slow-onset event experts group, which was launched in 2020.[50]

Moreover, the COP25 foresaw the creation of the Santiago Network, which aims to catalyse the technical assistance of key partners for the implementation of approaches to loss and damage at the local, national, and regional levels, particularly in developing countries that are vulnerable to the adverse effects of climate change.[51] In this regard, as also mentioned in Article 8 of the Paris Agreement, the WIM serves as an important mechanism for facilitating collaboration between the existing Parties, bodies, and expert groups under the UNFCCC and the Paris Agreement, and other relevant organizations and expert bodies outside the Agreement.[52]

The question is whether the WIM provides the framework to respond to the gaps in the LOSC concerning baselines, maritime boundaries, the status of islands, and archipelagos. Its mandate is geared more towards developing adaptation support to vulnerable countries in relation to finance, technology, and capacity-building. Nonetheless, it can provide an important forum for including the risk of loss, in whole or in part, of existing maritime entitlements, as part of the loss and damage mechanism, and enhancing understanding of the implications of these losses, as well as developing risk management approaches, which could include preserving existing rights.

17.3.1.3 Nationally Determined Contributions

Pursuant to Article 4 of the Paris Agreement, the Parties are required to 'prepare, communicate and maintain nationally determined contributions [NDCs]', which are to be

[46] UNFCCC COP, 'Warsaw International Mechanism for Loss and Damage Associated with Climate Change Impacts' (1 December 2014) Decision 2/CP.20.

[47] Subsidiary Body for Scientific and Technological Advice, 'Report of the Executive Committee of the Warsaw International Mechanism for Loss and Damage Associated with Climate Change Impacts' (24 August 2017) UN Doc No FCCC/SB/2017/1/Add.1.

[48] UNFCCC, 'Addressing Slow Onset Events' <https://www4.unfccc.int/sites/NWPStaging/Pages/soe.aspx> accessed 30 September 2020.

[49] UNFCCC, 'Slow Onset Events: Technical Paper' (26 November 2012) UN Doc FCCC/TP/2012/7.

[50] UNFCCC COP, 'Warsaw International Mechanism for Loss and Damage Associated with Climate Change Impacts' (6–18 November 2017) Decision 5/CP.23, para 1; UN Doc FCCC/SB/2017/1 and Add.1, Annex 1: Activity 2 of strategic workstream (a) in the Excom's first five-year rolling work plan concerns the establishment of a technical expert panel/group on slow onset event (SOEs Expert Group). The terms of reference of the SOEs Expert Group were adopted at Excom 12 (October 2020).

[51] UNFCCC CMA, 'Warsaw International Mechanism for Loss and Damage Associated with Climate Change Impacts and its 2019 Review' (2–13 December 2019) Decision 2/CMA.2, para 43.

[52] UNFCCC (n 4) art 8.

implemented domestically.[53] NDCs are to be submitted every five years,[54] and each submission must represent progress over the previous submission.[55] Parties are also able to include intended measures for adaptation. Importantly, every five years (beginning in 2023), the COP will undertake a global stocktaking on the implementation of the Paris Agreement.[56] The NDCs will, clearly, be integral to the process and outcome of the stocktaking, which is to be reflected in the subsequent contributions of the Parties.

The NDCs and the global stocktaking are integral to how governments will achieve the objectives of the Paris Agreement. Also, they provide a possible informal lawmaking opportunity, through the feedback mechanism created by the global stocktaking process. Notably, as of June 2016, out of 161 governments that had filed NDCs, 103 NDCs focused on ocean-inclusive issues, such as climate change impacts, and adaptation needs in marine areas.[57] Over fifty Parties, in their NDCs, identified sea level rise and its impacts as a common concern and risk factor.[58] However, included among the fourteen coastal States that omitted the consideration of oceans in their NDCs are large ocean states such as Australia, Brazil, the United States, Russia, and Norway.[59] It would be interesting if states, in their updated or revised NDCs, were to include the preservation of maritime baselines and boundaries as part of their adaptation measures. If there was widespread acceptance of such declarations then, arguably, the seeds for the development of a new rule of customary international law could be sown.

17.3.1.4 Subsidiary Body for Scientific and Technological Advice and Oceans Dialogue

The UNFCCC has also established requirements and processes to enable the collection of long-term data sets to monitor global emission levels and impacts of climate change. Such activities take place under the Subsidiary Body for Scientific and Technological Advice (SBSTA) and its Global Climate Observing System (GCOS) implementation plan. The SBSTA is a subsidiary body to the UNFCCC, responsible for providing information and advice on scientific and technological matters, and enabling collaboration with organizations and key stakeholders. Its mandate allows for holding research dialogues, where the most recent information can be reported and discussed, with the aim of strengthening cooperation, and addressing gaps, and the needs of the Parties.

To this end, the COP25, in 2019, mandated the chair of the SBSTA to convene 'a dialogue on the ocean and climate change to consider how to strengthen mitigation adaptation action in this context', now known as the Oceans Dialogue.[60] Notably, submissions from both

[53] Paris Agreement (n 5) art 4 (2).
[54] ibid, art 4(9).
[55] ibid, art 4(3).
[56] ibid, art 14.
[57] Natalya D Gallo, David G Victor, and Lisa A Levin, 'Ocean Commitments under the Paris Agreement' (2017) 7 Nat Clim Change 833–38: 'The dominant concerns raised by governments were coastal impacts (95 NDCs), ocean warming impacts (77 NDCs), and fisheries impacts (72 NDCs).'
[58] Eg, the current NDC submitted by Tuvalu states, '[l]onger term impacts such as sea level rise could result in the unavoidable out-migration of some of Tuvalu's people, they have a right to pursue any and all means to ensure their nation survives and the legacy remains, with future generations living productive lives on these islands' (Contribution of the Secretariat of UNFCCC (n 42) 2).
[59] Gallo, Victor, and Levin (n 57) 833–38.
[60] UNFCCC COP, 'Chile/Madrid Time for Action', Decision 1/CP.25 (15 December 2019), para 31.

Parties and non-party stakeholders were invited.[61] The process was increasingly diversified in terms of actors, and may lead to new forms of cooperation, other than inter-state cooperation under traditional international lawmaking.

The Oceans Dialogue represented an important opportunity to discuss and formulate recommendations on strengthening existing processes, and to support action on adaptation and mitigation under the UNFCCC and the UN, improving both cross-cutting support for action, and action at national level.[62] Moreover, the dialogue brought together oceans and climate communities—which have, historically, developed independently, in separate international fora—[63] and aimed to promote enhanced interaction between them.[64] Notably, the participants also addressed the importance of linkages across multilateral agreements on the ocean and climate.[65] To this end, the Oceans Dialogue served to enhance the participants' and state Parties' understanding of existing international cooperation on the ocean, and how issues related to the ocean–climate nexus are being addressed within other international fora and bodies.

Currently, there are important ongoing international processes and discussions related to oceans, climate change, and biodiversity, including the renegotiation of goals and targets for the Convention on Biological Diversity, and the negotiation of an instrument, under the LOSC, on the conservation and sustainable use of marine biological diversity of areas beyond national jurisdiction.[66] Against this background, participation by representatives of these treaty bodies in the Oceans Dialogue helped with discussing how to promote complementarity among these multilateral processes. The outcome of the discussions on the existing mechanisms may serve as a useful indicator for the revisions to NDCs.[67] Overall, the Oceans Dialogue, as an informal lawmaking effort, represented a preliminary step towards responding to current challenges more holistically, taking account of multiple overlapping regimes. The normative effect of any outcome of this dialogue remains to be seen.

[61] As of 4 June 2020, pursuant to Decision 1/CP.25 paras 31 and 33–34, a total of forty-three parties, UN organizations, admitted non-governmental organizations, and non-admitted entities provided input to inform the dialogue on ocean and climate change to consider how to strengthen mitigation and adaptation action: UNFCC, 'Inputs to Inform the Dialogue on the Ocean and Climate Change to Consider how to Strengthen Mitigation and Adaptation Action in this Context' <https://unfccc.int/sites/default/files/resource/List%20of%20submissions%20 04.05.2020.pdf> accessed 14 September 2020.

[62] UNFCCC, 'Ocean and Climate Change Dialogue to Consider how to Strengthen Adaptation and Mitigation Action' (2–3 December 2020) <https://unfccc.int/event/ocean-and-climate-change-dialogue-to-consider-how-to-strengthen-adaptation-and-mitigation-action> accessed 10 January 2020. See also submissions by Belize, Australia, Canada, Natural Resources Defense Council, Pew Charitable Trust <https://unfccc.int/sites/default/files/resource/OceanDialogue_SubmissionsList.pdf> accessed 7 September 2020. Eg, Panama, Indonesia, and Fiji, as well as the Food and Agriculture Organization and Environmental Defence Fund suggested that the dialogue should discuss how to integrate oceans into national policies on national adaptation and mitigation processes, NDCs, and NAPs.

[63] See submissions by Norway, Canada, Costa Rica, and Natural Resources Defense Council <https://unfccc.int/sites/default/files/resource/OceanDialogue_SubmissionsList.pdf> accessed 7 September 2020.

[64] The consideration of ocean–climate issues is already being integrated, in different ways, into the UNFCCC, including under the Nairobi Work Programme, the work of the WIM, and the Marrakesh Partnership for Climate Action. Yet, the dialogue can raise the visibility of such work: see Submission by Canada <https://unfccc.int/sites/default/files/resource/OceanDialogue_SubmissionsList.pdf> accessed 7 September 2020.

[65] See submissions by Japan, Pew Charitable Trusts, Belize, Climate Action Network, Canada, and Costa Rica <https://unfccc.int/sites/default/files/resource/OceanDialogue_SubmissionsList.pdf> accessed 7 September 2020.

[66] 'Intergovernmental Conference on Marine Biodiversity of Areas beyond National Jurisdiction' <https://www.un.org/bbnj/> accessed 10 January 2021; CBD, 'Post-2020 Global Biodiversity Framework being Developed under the Convention on Biological Diversity (CBD)' <https://www.cbd.int/conferences/post2020> accessed 10 January 2021.

[67] See submission by Pew Charitable Trusts <https://unfccc.int/sites/default/files/resource/OceanDialogue_SubmissionsList.pdf> accessed 7 September 2020.

17.3.1.5 Nairobi Work Programme on Impacts, Vulnerability, and Adaptation to Climate Change

The Nairobi Work Programme (NWP) was established by the COP in its eleventh session, in 2005, to facilitate the development of information and dissemination of knowledge on the impacts of climate change, to inform and support existing adaptation policies and practices, especially in developing countries, and to bridge knowledge gaps. For example, the key input at the thirteenth Focal Point Forum of the NWP, held at COP25, was the scoping paper on 'Adaptation of the Ocean, Coastal Areas and Ecosystems'.[68] The paper contained recommendations for Parties and other stakeholders to address adaptation knowledge gaps, but also mentioned necessary reforms in institutional, legal, and governance structures. For example, in the context of sea level rise, the NWP paper stressed the need to ensure the compatibility of global agenda, and the mainstreaming of climate change within international ocean governance, to strengthen the international response to sea level rise. This approach encompasses the legal and governance regimes introduced by the UNFCCC, the Sustainable Development Goals, the Sendai Framework, the Convention on Biological Diversity, and the international legally binding instrument under the LOSC on the conservation and sustainable use of marine biological diversity of areas beyond national jurisdiction (BBNJ).[69]

17.3.2 Efforts under the Existing LOSC Regime

Many of the impacts of climate change-induced sea level rise are issues that fall directly under the scope of the LOSC. Notably, as discussed earlier, the impacts include those on baselines from which the territorial sea is measured, related maritime entitlements, possible risks to the use of archipelagic baselines, and the status of islands under Article 121 of the LOSC. However, unlike the UNFCCC regime, which has a robust process for adopting decisions that implement that Convention and other instruments adopted under it, the LOSC is quite limited. The Meeting of the State Parties to the Law of the Sea (SPLOS)[70] does not function as a decision-making body on the interpretation and application of the LOSC, in the same way as the process under the UNFCCC. It decides administrative and budgetary issues, and elects judges to the International Tribunal of the Law of the Sea (ITLOS), and members to the Commission on the Limits of the Continental Shelf.

There is, however, no legal impediment that would prevent SPLOS from developing an informal lawmaking function to allow it to operate along the same lines as the COP does under the UNFCCC system. Serious consideration should be given to including substantive matters related to the interpretation and application of the LOSC as part of the work of SPLOS. The need for this shift can be seen in some of the comments made by states during discussion of the ILC decision to undertake work on sea level rise. Concerns were raised that the work of the ILC should not undermine the LOSC.[71] Indeed, the Commission has

[68] UNFCC, 'Scoping Paper on the Topic of Adaptation Knowledge and Knowledge Gaps on the Ocean, Coastal Areas and Ecosystems' (2019) <https://unfccc.int/sites/default/files/resource/Scopingpaper_Finalest%20version.pdf> accessed 10 January 2021.

[69] Contribution of the Secretariat of UNFCCC (n 42) 2–3.

[70] Article 319(2)(e) of the LOSC provides that the Secretary-General shall 'convene necessary meetings of States Parties in accordance with this Convention'.

[71] ILC, First Issues Paper (n 8) para 13.

limited its work expressly so as not to propose modifications to the LOSC.[72] Given the challenges associated with formal lawmaking processes, such as amending the LOSC or adopting a new implementing agreement, SPLOS decisions could be a more efficient and state-driven method of filling these gaps.

One very interesting development came in 2019, when, for the first time in the history of the LOSC, a state party lodged an observation in relation to its deposit of charts and lists of geographical coordinates of points for maritime baselines and maritime zones, including territorial sea, contiguous zone, and EEZ, in accordance with the LOSC. The observation was submitted by the Federated States of Micronesia, a state made up of 607 islands, most of which are low-lying islands and atolls that are at risk from sea level rise. The Federated States of Micronesia communicated its understanding that it is not obliged to keep under review the maritime zones reflected in the official deposit, and noted its intention to maintain these maritime zones in line with that understanding, notwithstanding any change induced by sea level rise.[73]

17.3.3 Informal Lawmaking Efforts as Subsequent Agreements and Subsequent Practice

A number of the informal lawmaking efforts outlined above also carry legal importance under Article 31(3) of Vienna Convention on the Law of Treaties (VCLT), as elements of general treaty interpretation. Under Article 31, 'any subsequent agreement between the parties regarding the interpretation of the treaty or the application of its provisions' (Article 31(3)(a)), and 'any subsequent practice in the application of the treaty which establishes the agreement of the parties regarding its interpretation' (Article 31(3)(b)) can be taken into account, together with the context, for the purposes of treaty interpretation.[74] The role of subsequent agreements, and subsequent practice of the parties to a treaty, as elements of treaty interpretation are well-accepted in the jurisprudence of international courts and tribunals, with their customary international law status repeatedly being confirmed.[75] While subsequent agreements fall more into the field of formal lawmaking, subsequent practice allows for informal lawmaking.

In its seventieth session in 2018, the ILC adopted draft conclusions on subsequent agreements and subsequent practice in relation to the interpretation of treaties (Draft

[72] ibid.

[73] 'Observations by the Federal States of Micronesia in Connection with the Official Deposit of its Lists of Geographical Points of Coordinates, Accompanied by Illustrative maps, for Maritime Baselines and Maritime Zones in Accordance with the 1982 United Nations Convention on the Law of the Sea' <https://www.un.org/Depts/los/LEGISLATIONANDTREATIES/PDFFILES/DEPOSIT/communicationsredeposit/FSM_Observations.pdf> accessed 10 January 2021.

[74] VCLT (n 6) art 31. Villiger notes that subparagraphs 3(a) and (b) of Article 31, as well as Article 31(2), 'represent forms of authentic interpretation whereby all parties themselves agree on (or at least accept) the interpretation of treaty terms by means which are extrinsic to the treaty. As a result, the parties' authentic interpretation of the treaty terms is not only particularly reliable, it is also endowed with binding force': Mark E Villiger, *Commentary on the 1969 Vienna Convention on the Law of Treaties* (Brill 2009) 429.

[75] International Law Commission, 'Draft Conclusions on Subsequent Agreements and Subsequent Practice in relation to the Interpretation of Treaties, with Commentaries' (2018) UN Doc No A/73/10 (hereafter 'ILC Draft Conclusions'), Conclusion 2(1), fns 22–30. Its limits are also noted by the International Court of Justice (ICJ): see *Land, Island and Maritime Frontier Dispute (El Salvador v Honduras, Nicaragua intervening)* [1992] ICJ Rep 351, para 380.

Conclusions), offering rich guidance on the definition, scope, and legal effects of Article 31.[76] On the topic of the potential effects of subsequent agreements and subsequent practice, Conclusion 7 recognized that such conduct may contribute to 'the clarification of the meaning of a treaty', resulting in 'narrowing, widening, or otherwise determining the range of possible interpretations'.[77] The Commission noted, nevertheless, that the possibility of amending or modifying a treaty by subsequent practice of the parties has not been generally recognized.[78] In other words, the Draft Conclusions can be taken to affirm the legal interpretative value of some of the informal lawmaking efforts, in the context of the LOSC and the UNFCCC, under customary international law. Article 31 is, therefore, an important legal source for the purposes of clarifying the meaning of the LOSC or UNFCCC provisions that pose legal uncertainties in light of rising sea levels. This interpretative exercise, however, is limited, to the extent that it does not amount to modification or amendment of the treaty.[79]

One of the clearest examples of subsequent agreements and subsequent practice is provided by the decisions adopted within the framework of the COP to the UNFCCC.[80] The Draft Conclusions have expressly recognized that a COP decision would embody a subsequent agreement or subsequent practice, in so far as it 'expresses agreement in substance between the parties regarding the interpretation of a treaty, regardless of the form and the procedure by which the decision was adopted'.[81] In the context of sea level rise, the COP to the UNFCCC is the key body that continuously reviews and implements the obligations under the UNFCCC.[82] To date, COP decisions have established mechanisms and processes, such as the WIM, and the NAP process. Thus, under the Vienna Convention, and in light of Draft Conclusion 11, the subsequent outcomes and processes established by COP decisions can be taken into account in interpreting the UNFCCC and the Paris Agreement, as subsequent agreement or subsequent practice, depending on the circumstances.[83] Similarly, a pronouncement of an expert treaty body may, too, give rise to a subsequent agreement or subsequent practice by parties.[84] Notably, the outcomes produced by the technical expert

[76] ILC Draft Conclusions (n 75).

[77] ibid, Conclusion 7(1).

[78] ibid, Conclusion 7(3).

[79] Oliver Dörr, 'Interpretation of Treaties' in Oliver Dörr and Kirsten Schmalenbach (eds), *Vienna Convention on the Law of Treaties* (Springer-Verlag 2018) 595. See also Villiger (n 74) 429.

[80] COP is defined as 'a meeting of parties to a treaty for the purpose of reviewing or implementing the treaty'. The conclusion observes that the legal effect of a COP decision depends primarily on the treaty and applicable rules of procedure: ILC Draft Conclusions (n 75) Conclusion 11(2).

[81] ibid, Conclusion 11(3). See also Anthony Aust, *Modern Treaty Law* (3rd edn, CUP 2013) 191: '[p]rovided the purpose is clear, the agreement can take various forms, including a decision adopted by a meeting of the parties'.

[82] See also Volker Röben, 'Conference (Meeting) of States Parties' in *Max Planck Encyclopedia of Public International Law* (OUP 2010) 605; Robin R Churchill and Geir Ulfstein, 'Autonomous Institutional Arrangements in Multilateral Environmental Agreements: A Little-noticed Phenomenon in International Law' (2000) 94 AJIL 623–59; Annecoos Wiersema, 'The New International Law-makers? Conference of the Parties to Multilateral Environmental Agreements' (2009) 31 Mich J Intl'l L 231.

[83] This is subject to restrictions, however. A decision, despite having been adopted by consensus, may not represent a subsequent agreement under Article 31(3)(a), provided that an objection is recorded. Eg, in *Whaling in the Antarctic*, the ICJ observed, in principle, that the non-binding recommendations by the International Whaling Commission (IWC), when adopted by consensus or by a unanimous vote, may be relevant for the interpretation of the International Convention on the Regulation of Whaling. However, since many IWC resolutions were adopted without support of all state parties to that treaty, they could not be regarded as subsequent agreements or practice: *Whaling in the Antarctic (Australia v Japan: New Zealand intervening)* (Merits) [2014] ICJ Rep 226, paras 46 and 83.

[84] An expert body is defined as 'consisting of experts serving in their personal capacity, which is established under a treaty and is not an organ of an international organization'. However, silence by a party does not constitute

group on slow-onset events, established in 2020 under the decision of the WIM Committee, may be relevant in interpreting issues relating to loss and damage in Article 8 of the Paris Agreement.

With respect to the remaining efforts, three points need additional consideration. First, the conduct of non-state actors does not constitute subsequent practice, although it may be relevant in the context of assessing the subsequent practice of parties to a treaty.[85] Rather, the conduct of state parties 'in the application of a treaty, whether in the exercise of its executive, legislative, judicial or other functions' constitutes such practice.[86] The concept of 'practice' is construed widely, with no particular form required. Therefore, official statements, diplomatic correspondence, bilateral agreements, votes on resolutions in international organizations, or pledges taken, would be as relevant as national legislation and judicial decisions.[87] Similarly, subsequent agreements may include informal agreements that lack binding force.[88] Notably, the NDCs and NAPs can be considered among subsequent practices since, through such conduct, a state party incorporates and applies its international obligations into its domestic policies. Similarly, official statements and submissions by state Parties to the Oceans Dialogue conducted under the mandate of the SBSTA also hold interpretative value under the UNFCCC.

Second, the interpretative value of subsequent practice depends on the consistency of the acts.[89] The parties should demonstrate that their conduct falls within the scope of the application of the treaty concerned, and that they should be motivated in their subsequent practice by their treaty obligations.[90] The practice does not have to be engaged in by every single party to a treaty, and it would suffice if it was accepted by the remaining inactive parties.[91] Draft Conclusion 10(9) reaffirmed this position by recognizing that, '[s]ilence on the part of one or more parties can constitute acceptance of the subsequent practice when the circumstances call for some reaction'.[92] For example, the lack of focus, in some coastal States' NDCs, on ocean issues, as noted above, may not obstruct a finding of subsequent practice, as long as the practice is consistent, and the circumstances do not call for some reaction. Third, even if subsequent practice does not, specifically, refer to a particular provision of a treaty, it may, nevertheless, be taken into account in interpretation, if the practice relates to the treaty as a whole, or to some parts of it.[93]

subsequent practice, and the draft conclusion is without prejudice to the contribution that pronouncements of expert treaty bodies make to the interpretation of the treaties: ILC Draft Conclusions (n 75), Conclusion 13.

[85] ibid, Conclusion 5(2).

[86] ibid, Conclusion 5(1).

[87] ibid, Conclusion 6. See also Dörr (n 79) 597.

[88] The definition of 'agreement' is broad enough to cover a decision of a treaty organ, 'provided that it was taken unanimously by all States parties to the treaty or that parties that did not vote can at last be taken to have implicitly accepted the decision made': Dörr (n 79) 594–95.

[89] Dörr (n 79) 598; Villiger (n 74) 431.

[90] This stance is also confirmed by the ILC, in Conclusion 6, where 'a determination whether the parties, by an agreement or practice, have taken a position regarding the interpretation of the treaty' is noted to be necessary: ILC Draft Conclusions (n 75) Conclusion 6.

[91] Villiger (n 74) 431.

[92] ILC Draft Conclusions (n 75) Conclusion 10(2).

[93] Dörr (n 79) 598.

17.3.4 Regional Informal Lawmaking Processes for Sea Level Rise

17.3.4.1 Work Undertaken by the Pacific Islands Forum

While sea level rise and other impacts of climate change on maritime zones may affect many states globally, certain regions are more affected than others. The South Pacific Ocean, which is home to the majority of the world's low-lying atoll states and states dependent on coral islands and cays, is particularly affected. Thus, potential sea level rise trends could be devastating for the South Pacific states, as they are, predominantly, communities in close connection with coastal environments and the ocean. Established in 1971, the Pacific Island Forum (PIF) has eighteen members: Australia, Cook Islands, Federated States of Micronesia, Fiji, French Polynesia, Kiribati, Nauru, New Caledonia, New Zealand, Niue, Palau, Papua New Guinea, Republic of Marshall Islands, Samoa, Solomon Islands, Tonga, Tuvalu, and Vanuatu.[94] The PIF members have been active in developing frameworks and policies, undertaking projects, and issuing declarations relevant to the issue of sea level rise.

Among the priorities identified by the PIF members is the need to preserve existing maritime zones delineated in accordance with the LOSC, and the entitlements that flow from them. For example, the PIF leaders issued the Forum Leaders Communiqué in 2019, under which the leaders committed to collective efforts, including to develop international law, with the objective of ensuring that the maritime zones delineated in accordance with the LOSC should not be challenged or reduced as a result of sea level rise and climate change.[95] To this end, the leaders also discussed, and further encouraged, the negotiations undertaken by PIF members to conclude all outstanding maritime boundary claims and zones.[96] As of 2019, there were forty-eight shared or overlapping boundaries between the PIF members, and thirty-five of those boundaries had been formalized.[97] Importantly, the collective action of the PIF states has, possibly, given rise to an emerging regional state practice, as observed by the ILA and ILC.[98] Notably, in August 2021, the leaders of PIF issued a declaration on sea level rise and maritime zones, in which they affirmed that the LOSC imposes 'no affirmative obligation' to keep baselines and outer limits of maritime zones under review and made clear their position that they do not intend to do so as a consequence of sea level rise.[99] Members of PIF further proclaimed that the LOSC, and the legal principles underpinning it, support maintaining maritime zones established in accordance with the LOSC, and rights and entitlements that flow from them, notwithstanding sea level rise resulting from climate change.[100]

[94] The Pacific Islands Forum <https://www.forumsec.org/who-we-arepacific-islands-forum/> accessed 8 January 2020.

[95] PIF, 'Forum Communiqué' (Fiftieth Pacific Islands Forum, 13–16 August 2019)Doc No PIF(19)(14), para 26 <https://www.forumsec.org/wp-content/uploads/2019/08/50th-Pacific-Islands-Forum-Communique.pdf> accessed 10 January 2021.

[96] ibid, para 25.

[97] 'Pacific Islands Forum's Contribution to the Report of the United Nations Secretary-General on the Sea-level Rise and its Impacts', Open-ended Informal Consultative Process on Oceans and the Law of the Sea to be held in New York from 22–26 June 2020 <https://www.un.org/Depts/los/consultative_process/contribution21.html> accessed 20 August 2020.

[98] ILC, First Issues Paper (n 8) para 103; see Davor Vidas, David Freestone, and Jane McAdam (eds), *International Law and Sea Level Rise: Report of the International Law Association Committee on International Law and Sea Level Rise* (Brill 2019).

[99] Pacific Islands Forum Leaders, 'Declaration on Preserving Maritime Zones in the Face of Climate Change-Related Sea-Level Rise' (6 August 2021) <https://www.forumsec.org/wp-content/uploads/2021/08/Declaration-on-Preserving-Maritime.pdf> accessed 18 December 2021.

[100] ibid.

Previously, in the Forum Leaders' 2019 Kainaki II Declaration,[101] and Forum Leaders' 2014 Palau Declaration,[102] the PIF affirmed the importance of preserving their members' maritime zones once they have been delineated in accordance with the LOSC, and preventing any challenge or reduction in members' maritime zones as a result of climate change and sea level rise. The Framework for Pacific Oceanscape, in 2010, also noted, as a strategic priority, establishing jurisdictional rights and responsibilities over maritime zones. This priority consists of two actions for countries, namely: (1) formalizing their maritime boundaries and securing rights over their resources; and (2) undertaking regional efforts to fix baselines and maritime boundaries, so that sea level rise does not result in reduced jurisdiction.[103]

17.3.4.2 Efforts by Small Island Developing States and CARICOM

There have been a number of multilateral processes during which small island developing states (SIDS) have reiterated their particular vulnerability, caused by adverse impacts of climate change, including sea level rise. Among these processes, which set out programmes of international, regional, and national action, and measures to strengthen the resilience and adaptive capacity of SIDS, are the Programme of Action for the Sustainable Development of Small Island Developing States (1994),[104] the Mauritius Strategy for the Further Implementation of the Programme of Action for the Sustainable Development of Small Island Developing States (2005),[105] and the SIDS Accelerated Modalities of Action (SAMOA) Pathway (2014).[106]

The SAMOA Pathway, for example, is an international framework adopted at the Third International Conference on Small Island Developing States, in 2014. The Pathway document describes climate change as 'an immediate and urgent global priority',[107] and warns of its risks to the efforts of the SIDS in achieving sustainable development, as well as their survival and viability.[108] In this regard, the document was significant in stressing the leadership role of SIDS in furthering efforts to address climate change,[109] and the primary role of the COP to the UNFCCC as an international intergovernmental forum for negotiating the global response to climate change.[110] It further called for support for the efforts of SIDS in building resilience to the impacts of climate change, and enhancing their adaptation capacity through design and implementation of appropriate measures.[111]

[101] PIF, 'Kainaki II Declaration for Urgent Climate Change Action Now on Securing the Future of our Blue Pacific' (13–16 August 2019), para 14 <https://www.forumsec.org/wp-content/uploads/2019/08/50th-Pacific-Islands-Forum-Communique.pdf> accessed 10 January 2021.

[102] Pacific Islands Forum Leaders, 'Palau Declaration on "The Ocean: Life and Future", Charting a Course to Sustainability' (2014), para 10 <https://www.hokulea.com/wp-content/uploads/2016/08/Palau-Declaration-on-The-Ocean-Life-and-Future.pdf> accessed 10 January 2021.

[103] Cristelle Pratt and Hugh Govan, 'Framework for a Pacific Oceanscape: A Catalyst for Implementation of Ocean Policy' (November 2020), Strategic Priority 1, Action 1A and 1B, 57 <https://www.forumsec.org/wp-content/uploads/2018/03/Framework-for-a-Pacific-Oceanscape-2010.pdf> accessed 10 January 2021.

[104] Programme of Action for the Sustainable Development of Small Island Developing States, Report of the Global Conference on the Sustainable Development of Small Island Developing States, Bridgetown, Barbados (25 April–6 May 1994) (United Nations publication, Sales No E.94.I.18 and corrigenda), ch I, Res 1, Annex II.

[105] ibid.

[106] 'SIDS Accelerated Modalities of Action (SAMOA) Pathway', UNGA Res 69/15 (14 November 2014) UN Doc A/RES/69/15.

[107] ibid, para 32.

[108] ibid, paras 11 and 31.

[109] ibid, para 33.

[110] ibid, para 34.

[111] ibid, para 44.

The high-level meeting held in 2019 for the purposes of reviewing the progress made, and the implementation of the SAMOA Pathway, resulted in a political declaration that called for action to take urgent and ambitious global action, in line with the Paris Agreement, to enhance understanding, strengthen dialogue, and enhance action and support with respect to averting, minimizing, and addressing loss and damage, including under the WIM.[112] Similarly, the Caribbean Community (CARICOM) member states issued the 2015 CARICOM Declaration for Climate Action, urging all member states to the UNFCCC to adopt a new international legally binding agreement under the UNFCCC, which later became the Paris Agreement.[113]

17.3.5 International Courts and Tribunals

The judgments of international courts and tribunals are binding only on the parties, and are not considered as international lawmaking. Article 38(d) of the ICJ Statute lists judicial decisions, alongside the teachings of the most highly qualified publicists, as subsidiary means for the determination of rules of law. Nonetheless, such decisions, including those that are non-binding advisory opinions, often acquire a self-standing normative value through the iterative judicial process of referencing in legal arguments and awards, and in academic writings. In this regard, court decisions can be counted as part of the informal lawmaking process.[114]

The unresolved legal issues relating to sea level rise have not, to date, been directly addressed by international courts and tribunals.[115] For instance, the International Court of Justice (ICJ) has avoided providing clarification of the famously vague language in Article 121(3) of the LOSC on a feature that 'cannot sustain human habitation or economic life of [its] own'. The ICJ has issued judgments commenting that the size of an island alone is not determinative of its legal status in the 2001 *Qatar v Bahrain* maritime delimitation case,[116] and later reaffirmed this statement in the 2012 *Nicaragua v Colombia* case.[117] Other cases, such as *Eritrea v Yemen*,[118] and the *Black Sea (Romania v Ukraine)*,[119] missed the opportunity to meaningfully tackle the topic in depth. The arbitral award in the 2016 *South China Sea* arbitration between the Republic of the Philippines and the People's Republic of China

[112] 'Political Declaration of the High-level Meeting to Review Progress made in Addressing the Priorities of Small Island Developing States through the Implementation of the SIDS Accelerated Modalities of Action (SAMOA) Pathway', UNGA Res 74/3 (10 October 2019) UN Doc A/Res/74/3, para 30.

[113] CARICOM, 'CARICOM Declaration for Climate Action' (2–4 July 2015) <https://caricom.org/caricom-declaration-for-climate-action/> accessed 10 January 2021.

[114] See Thomas Buergenthal, 'Lawmaking by the ICJ and Other International Courts' (2009) 103 *Proceedings of the ASIL Annual Meeting* 403.

[115] For instance, although the decisions of the ICJ have no binding force, except between the parties, and in respect of the particular case, pursuant to Article 59 of its statute, the observations of the court tend to exert a significant influence over the interpretation and development of international legal norms.

[116] *Maritime Delimitation and Territorial Questions between Qatar and Bahrain (Qatar v Bahrain)* (Merits) [2001] ICJ Rep 97, 185. See also *Dubai–Sharjah Border Arbitration* (1981) 91 ILR 543.

[117] To date, the ICJ has expressly classified one feature to be a rock, under Article 121(3), in only one instance: *Territorial and Maritime Dispute between Nicaragua and Honduras in the Caribbean Sea (Nicaragua v Honduras)* (Merits) [2007] ICJ Rep 659, paras 139 and 177.

[118] *Award of the Arbitral Tribunal in the Second Stage of Proceedings between Eritrea and Yemen Arbitration (Maritime Delimitation)* (Decision of 17 December 1999), vol XXII RIAA 335, paras 147–48.

[119] *Maritime Delimitation in the Black Sea (Romania v Ukraine)* (Merits) [2009] ICJ Rep 61, para 187.

is the only case, to date, that has directly engaged with, and offered substantive analysis of, Article 121(3).[120]

On the topic of delimitation of maritime boundaries, the ICJ, in the *Black Sea* maritime delimitation case,[121] and the arbitral tribunal in relation specifically to future sea level rise, in the *Bay of Bengal Maritime Boundary Arbitration between Bangladesh and India*,[122] examined only the set of facts 'at the present time', stating that it was 'the physical reality at the time of the delimitation' that mattered. The latter tribunal expressly discounted taking into account possible future events, such as sea level rise, that could alter basepoints, stressing the importance of the stability of boundaries. In this regard, the tribunal stated that 'maritime delimitations, like land boundaries, must be stable and definitive to ensure a peaceful relationship between the States concerned in the long term'.[123] It referred specifically to climate change and its effects, including sea level rise, noting that '[i]n the view of the Tribunal, neither the prospect of climate change nor its possible effects can jeopardize the large number of settled maritime boundaries throughout the world. This applies equally to maritime boundaries agreed between States and to those established through international adjudication'.[124] As such, it is apparent that international courts and tribunals, in exercising their contentious jurisdiction, have not squarely addressed the legal challenges posed by sea level rise.

Seeking an advisory opinion from either the ICJ or ITLOS is one possible recourse for filling the gaps through informal lawmaking. These opinions are not binding, but would, nonetheless, offer authoritative guidance to states in developing legal responses to the pressing issues surrounding sea level rise.[125]

To date, several international campaigns, notably led by Pacific island states such as Vanuatu and Palau have sought to secure advisory opinions from the ICJ on issues of climate change, such as on states' obligations under the UNFCCC and the Paris Agreement,[126]

[120] The tribunal did not require actual habitation to fulfil the criteria of having capacity to sustain human habitation. It also assessed historical evidence of past human habitation and economic activities: 'the Tribunal should consider whether there is evidence that human habitation has been prevented or ended by forces that are separate from the intrinsic capacity of the feature. War, pollution, and environmental harm could all lead to the depopulation, for a prolonged period, of a feature that, in its natural state, was capable of sustaining human habitation. In the absence of such intervening forces, however, the Tribunal can reasonably conclude that a feature that has never historically sustained a human community lacks the capacity to sustain human habitation.' (*South China Sea Arbitration* (*Philippines v China*) (Award of 12 July 2016) PCA Case No 2013-19, para 549).

[121] *Romania v Ukraine* (n 119) para 131.

[122] Bangladesh had expressly raised the possible future impacts of sea level rise on the low tide elevations selected by India, and even the coastal locations of the basepoints chosen by Bangladesh, as these basepoints are susceptible to change or disappearance in the future, because of rising sea levels. However, the tribunal found that future events such as sea level rise were not relevant: *Bay of Bengal Maritime Boundary Arbitration* (*Bangladesh v India*) (Award of 7 July 2014) PCA Case No 2010-16, para 213–15.

[123] ibid, paras 216–17.

[124] ibid.

[125] UN Charter, art 96; ICJ Statute , ch IV, arts 65–68; Rules of Court (adopted on 14 April 1978 and entered into force on 1 July 1978), part IV, arts 102–09. See Annalisa Savaresi, Kati Kulovesi and Harro van Asselt, 'Beyond COP26: Time for an Advisory Opinion on Climate Change?', *EJIL:Talk! Blog of the European Journal for International Law* (17 December 2021) <https://www.ejiltalk.org/beyond-cop26-time-for-an-advisory-opinion-on-climate-change/> accessed 18 December 2021.

[126] Nataša Nedeski, Tom Sparks, and Gleider Hernández, 'Judging Climate Change Obligations: Can the World Court Raise the Occasion? Part II: What Role for International Adjudication?' (*Völkerrechtsblog*, 30 April 2020) <https://voelkerrechtsblog.org/judging-climate-change-obligations-can-the-world-court-raise-the-occasion-2/> accessed 1 September 2020; Margaretha Wewerinke-Singh and Diana Hinge Salili, 'Between Negotiations and Litigation: Vanuatu's Perspective on Loss and Damage from Climate Change' (2020) 20(6) Clim Pol'y 681; Daniel Bodanksy, 'The Role of the International Court of Justice in Addressing Climate Change: Some Preliminary Reflections' (2017) 49 Ariz St L J 659–712.

and on the assignment of responsibility for causing climate change.[127] The possibility of an advisory opinion was also considered at the 2019 meeting of the PIF in Tuvalu. The Forum Communiqué 'noted the proposal for a UN General Assembly Resolution seeking an advisory opinion from the International Court of Justice on the obligations of States under international law to protect the rights of present and future generations against the adverse effects of climate change'.[128] The most practical challenge is to persuade the majority of member states in the General Assembly to support the resolution requesting the advisory opinion.

In addition, ITLOS also has jurisdiction to render an advisory opinion. Under Article 21 of its statute, the tribunal's jurisdiction comprises 'all disputes and all applications submitted to it in accordance with this Convention and all matters specifically provided for in any other agreement which confers jurisdiction on the Tribunal'.[129] Article 138 of the rules state that ITLOS may deliver 'an advisory opinion on a legal question if an international agreement related to the purposes of [LOSC] specifically provides for the submission to the Tribunal of a request for such an opinion'.[130] While ITLOS's advisory jurisdiction was challenged in the *Request for an Advisory Opinion Submitted by the Sub-regional Fisheries Commission (SRFC Advisory Opinion)*, on the ground that neither the LOSC nor the ITLOS statute make express reference to ITLOS possessing advisory jurisdiction,[131] the tribunal found that the prerequisite for the exercise of the advisory jurisdiction under Article 138 was satisfied, because the dispute concerned an international agreement that was closely related to the purposes of the LOSC.[132] Similarly, a possible advisory opinion from ITLOS on the legal issues raised by rising sea levels is likely to be closely related to the provisions under the LOSC, whether it be under Article 121 on the status of islands, or under maritime entitlements, or under baselines and outer limits of maritime zones.

Significantly, on 31 October 2021, the governments of Antigua and Barbuda and Tuvalu signed an agreement to establish the Commission of Small Island States on Climate Change and International Law.[133] Notably, Article 2(2) of the Agreement, provides that the Commission 'shall be authorized to request advisory opinions from [ITLOS] on any legal questions within the scope of the 1982 [LOSC]'.[134] Such efforts highlight the efforts of small island states to further the progressive development of international law with regards to climate change, particularly the protection and preservation of the marine environment.

[127] Douglas A Kysar, 'Climate Change and the International Court of Justice', *Yale Law School Public Law Research Paper No 315* (15 August 2013).

[128] PIF, Forum Communiqué (n 95) para 16. However, the proposal was not expressly supported in the outcome document of the forum, due to the objection by the government of Australia.

[129] Statute of the International Tribunal for the Law of the Sea, LOSC (n 3) Annex VI, art 21.

[130] Rules of the Tribunal (adopted on 28 October 1997 and amended on 15 March 2001, 21 September 2001, 17 March 2009, 25 September 2018 and 25 September 2020), art 138.

[131] *Request for Advisory Opinion Submitted by the Sub-Regional Fisheries Commission* (Advisory Opinion) ITLOS Reports 2015, 4, para 40.

[132] ibid, paras 59–68.

[133] Agreement for the Establishment of the Commission of Small Island States on Climate Change and International Law (signed on 31 October 2021). See AN Honnibal, 'Antigua and Barbuda/Tuvalu: Accord to Establish Commission of Small Island States on Climate Change & International Law', *Maribus* (11 November 2021) <https://demaribus.net/2021/11/04/antigua-and-barbuda-tuvalu-accord-to-establish-commission-of-small-island-states-on-climate-change-international-law/> accessed 18 December 2021.

[134] Ibid.

17.4 Conclusion

This chapter has undertaken an overview of different sources of informal lawmaking in relation to addressing the gaps that exist under the LOSC in relation to the effects of sea level rise. Before assessing these sources, one question is whether there is a need for such informal lawmaking on this matter? Without question, there is. The many gaps that exist in the present framework for climate change and sea level rise demonstrate as much. Traditional lawmaking processes are time-consuming, considering the period between adoption and entry into force of treaties or amendments, and cannot guarantee the desired result. The LOSC took nine years to negotiate, another twelve to enter into force, and is replete with compromise text.

Sea level rise has its own challenges, presenting a situation where there are two regimes applicable simultaneously. While the LOSC applies directly to the law of the sea issues, such as baselines, maritime entitlements, and islands, it does not include climate change issues. By contrast, climate change forms the mandate of the UNFCCC regime, but has no direct application for the law of the sea. Informal lawmaking can provide a very functional method of bridging these gaps, and allowing for timely and focused solutions to the pressing needs of states facing the adverse impacts of sea level rise.

The UNFCCC regime provides multiple opportunities to contribute to informal lawmaking, through the COP (UNFCCC) or the CMA (Paris Agreement), and different specialized bodies such as the Cancun Adaptation Framework, the WIM, and the NWP. However, these specialized bodies, in light of their existing scope, they only provide for limited input within the framework, mostly in relation to adaptation measures, to fill the specific gaps in relation to the law of the sea and sea level rise. By contrast, the role of decisions adopted by the COP or CMA, if accepted as subsequent agreements or subsequent practice, under Article 31 of the Vienna Convention, can play a more direct role, through the flexible and dynamic process they offer, by building upon existing decisions, making adjustments where necessary, and, perhaps most importantly, responding to new issues. The consensus-driven aspect of UNFCCC COP/CMA/CMP decisions further adds to the informal lawmaking process, representing the position of some 197 Parties.[135] However, the scope of application of the UNFCCC and Paris Agreement to law of the sea issues is limited, and can only be through indirect measures related to mitigation and adaptation for marine and coastal ecosystems, or related to the ocean as a source of mitigation of greenhouse gases. In order to tackle the law of the sea issues in this setting, they would have to be framed within these parameters.

Nonetheless, the NDC process under the Paris Agreement does hold promise as an informal lawmaking tool. It allows individual states to construct their own responses to climate change, which can include sea level rise. States could include, as part of their adaptations, or even mitigations, measures on the practice of maintaining existing maritime boundaries. These NDCs, which are not legal instruments per se, could, collectively, create a certain standard of conduct and international recognition, and provide a potential source of informal lawmaking that, eventually, reflects the foundation for normative standards.

[135] UNFCCC, Status of Ratification of the Convention <https://unfccc.int/process-and-meetings/the-convention/status-of-ratification/status-of-ratification-of-the-convention> accessed 10 January 2020. Out of 197 parties, 196 are states, and the other is a regional economic integration organization (the European Union).

This result could be obtained through the global stocktaking process in which the NDCs will, collectively, be assessed. In this process, collective affirmation of the role, or perhaps the necessity, of measures taken to address sea level rise could pave the way for a normative outcome.

The LOSC, as it is currently implemented, provides fewer options for informal lawmaking, given the limited function of SPLOS to more administrative and budgetary issues. This situation can, and should, be revised. The 'observation' submitted by the Federated States of Micronesia, which is a form of interpretive statement, is another interesting development that could be emulated by other states. If these interventions are consistent and focused, such statements could also provide a source of informal lawmaking—as subsequent practice, even—to the interpretation of the relevant provisions of the LOSC. Moreover, states parties could seek an advisory opinion from ITLOS on these very specific issues, which could provide guidance for states to fill these gaps without having to embark upon formal treaty-making processes.

Small island developing states, particularly in the Pacific Island Forum, provide an example of structured and focused regional informal lawmaking that is advancing the necessary gap-filling of LOSC. However, it is important that the regional approach be broadened and emulated by other regions, to create a level of collective action that will trigger international recognition.

Rising sea levels represent an undeniable global challenge to the delicate balance of certainty and stability of inter-state relations, threatening the livelihoods of millions of people, and the sovereignty of numerous states. It is a global problem that has not been tackled in the existing legal frameworks of the LOSC and the UNFCCC, and, thus, necessitates cooperation at the international and regional levels. Through analyzing the gaps in the legal framework, this chapter has identified ongoing informal lawmaking efforts under the treaty frameworks, including decisions that could constitute subsequent agreements or practice under the VCLT, and regional organizations involving the participation of states, international organizations, non-governmental organizations, and international courts and tribunals.

This chapter has shown the challenges posed by sea level rise, which was an unforeseen event at the time the LOSC was adopted, to the ability of traditional lawmaking processes to respond. This lack of an immediate and effective response has been countered with piecemeal, in some cases short-term, informal lawmaking options or responses to different aspects of the challenge posed by sea level rise. Furthermore, this overview shows a rapidly forming momentum towards normative outcomes, through the efforts of a diverse set of actors seeking to establish greater cooperation and agreed responses and positions, even if not legally binding, to deal with different aspects of the challenge posed by sea level rise. However, such informal international lawmaking endeavours fall short of a full commitment to change, as they do not, at this juncture, provide clear normative solutions. Notably, at the global level, such efforts are restricted to the existing frameworks under the UNFCCC and the LOSC, where neither regime offers a comprehensive account of the problem, or any legal solution with an interdisciplinary approach. Nevertheless, one should not overlook the significance of current endeavours. The informal lawmaking efforts discussed in this chapter have placed the phenomenon of sea level rise on global agenda, built extensive knowledge networks on a complex phenomenon, and strengthened cooperation at national, regional, and international levels. Perhaps most importantly, current informal lawmaking efforts have paved the way for achieving clear legal results via the study of the matter by the International Law Commission, or its possible future consideration in an advisory opinion by the ICJ or ITLOS. The final result should be the recognition, by the international community as a whole, of a permanent legal solution that will achieve legal certainty, security, and peaceful relations, to the serious consequences of sea level rise on existing maritime boundaries, entitlements, and the statuses of islands, under international law.

PART VI
CONCLUSION

18
Informal Lawmaking and the Future of the Law of the Sea
Developing Legal Infrastructure and Regulating Human Activity

Ellen Hey

18.1 Introduction

Taking its cue from the previous chapters in this volume, this chapter departs from the premise that informal instruments will continue to be part of lawmaking processes in the law of the sea. This chapter seeks to identify the different ways in which informal instruments matter in the law of the sea. In this analysis, lawmaking is conceived as a process in which informal and formal instruments interact.[1] The analysis suggests that how informal and formal instruments interact, and how informal instruments matter, depends on context. In other words, informal instruments may have normative intent, but whether, and how, they influence the content of formal instruments depends on context.[2]

This chapter distinguishes between two types of lawmaking processes in the law of the sea: (1) developing the legal infrastructure, or the jurisdictional framework, of the law of the sea; and (2) regulating human activity. The former involves lawmaking processes in which decisions are taken regarding the competences of states and other actors to regulate human activities at sea and on land, for land-based activities that impact the marine environment. An example is the ongoing lawmaking process for a regime on the conservation and sustainable use of marine biodiversity of areas beyond national jurisdiction (BBNJ negotiations). This lawmaking process will determine *who* will be competent to regulate access to, and *who* will obtain benefits from, marine biodiversity in areas beyond national jurisdiction (ABNJ), as well as the contours of how access to, and obtaining benefits from such resources will be regulated. In other words, this lawmaking process will determine the competences of states and international organizations for regulating human activity involving the use of marine biodiversity in ABNJ.[3] If the BBNJ negotiations result in a new regime, its focus will be on *how* to regulate human activity within the agreed legal infrastructure.

The second type of lawmaking processes—those that focus on regulating human activity—involve standard setting within an agreed legal infrastructure. An example is the regulation of ship safety through the standards set in the 1974 Convention for the Safety of Life at Sea (SOLAS),[4] and within the legal infrastructure on flag and coastal state jurisdiction

[1] See Jutta Brunnée and Stephen J Toope, *Legitimacy and Legality in International Law* (CUP 2010).

[2] See Klein, in Chapter 1 of this volume, for the description of 'normative intent' as the contribution of informal instruments to the development of treaty or customary international law.

[3] For a more in-depth discussion of the BBNJ negotiations, see section 18.2.2.3 below.

[4] International Convention for the Safety of Life at Sea (adopted 1 November 1974, entered into force 25 May 1980) 1184 UNTS 1 (hereafter 'SOLAS').

Ellen Hey, *Informal Lawmaking and the Future of the Law of the Sea:* In: *Unconventional Lawmaking in the Law of the Sea.* Edited by: Natalie Klein, Oxford University Press. © Ellen Hey 2022. DOI: 10.1093/oso/9780192897824.003.0018

provided by the 1982 United Nations Convention on the Law of the Sea (LOSC)[5] and port state jurisdiction, based on a mixture of customary international law and treaty law.[6]

The chapter, first, discusses lawmaking processes that involve developing legal infrastructure. Thereafter, the focus is on the interaction between informal and formal instruments in regulating human activity. This chapter suggests that, in each of these contexts, informal and formal instruments interact in different ways.

18.2 Developing Legal Infrastructure

The lawmaking processes in which the legal infrastructure of the law of the sea is developed involve determining or changing the competences of states vis-à-vis each other, and of other actors. As a result, these lawmaking processes regularly involve significant political contestation. Think of the extension of the territorial sea to twelve nautical miles, which led to the development of the regime of transit passage for straits, in order to secure the navigational interests of, in particular, the United States and the then-Soviet Union.[7] Also, think of the developments in the deep seabed mining regime, discussed below.[8] This section analyses the interaction between informal and formal instruments in such contested situations, by focusing on the relationship between the global South and global North, and on how competences to exercise jurisdiction at sea have been developed.

18.2.1 Relations between the Global South and the Global North

Political contestation is manifest in the relations between the global South and the global North, in particular when it comes to the nature of the international economic system. It is evidenced by the 2018 United Nations (UN) General Assembly resolution entitled 'Towards a New International Economic Order' (NIEO), which was voted for only by developing states, with developed states either voting against or abstaining.[9] This contestation dates back to the mid twentieth century, when newly independent states joined the UN and, during the 1970s, sought to advance the NIEO.[10] Informal instruments, such as UN General Assembly resolutions, play a prominent role in this context.

Contestation between the global South and global North has also influenced the law of the sea ever since Pardo's famous speech to the UN General Assembly in 1967.[11] Given

[5] United Nations Convention on the Law of the Sea (adopted 10 December 1982, entered into force 16 November 1994) 1833 UNTS 397 (hereafter 'LOSC'). Relevant provisions include arts 17–26, 37–45, 53–54, 58, 87, and 94.

[6] See Cedric Ryngaert and Henrik Ringbom, 'Introduction: Port State Jurisdiction: Challenges and Potential' (2016) 31(3) IJMCL 379.

[7] John R Stevenson and Bernard Oxman, 'The Third United Nations Conference on the Law of the Sea: The 1974 Caracas Session' (1975) 69 AJIL 1, 14–15; William T Burke, 'Who Goes Where, When, and How: International Law of the Sea for Transportation' (1977) 31(2) Intl'l Org 267, 270–81.

[8] See section 18.2.1.2 below.

[9] UNGA Res 73/240 (20 December 2018) UN Doc A/RES/73/240.

[10] UN, 'Declaration on the Establishment of a New International Economic Order', UNGA Res S-6/3201 (1 May 1974) UN Doc A/RES/S-6/3201. For further information, see Mohammed Bedjaoui, *Towards a New International Economic Order* (UNESCO, Holmes & Meier Publishers 1979).

[11] UNGAOR, 1515th Session (1 November 1967) UN Doc A/C.1/PV.1515; UNGAOR, 1516th Session (1 November 1967) UN Doc A/C.1/PV.1516.

that the Third UN Conference on the Law of the Sea (UNCLOS III) was contemporaneous with efforts to establish the NIEO, the two lawmaking processes interacted.[12] In the law of the sea, informal instruments have reflected, and continue to reflect, this contestation. Informal instruments reflecting this contestation played a role in the decision-making process that was adopted for UNCLOS III, in the development of the deep seabed mining regime, and, to date, figure prominently in the regime for the transfer of marine technology. Each of these topics will be discussed below, after which this section will reflect, briefly, on the role of informal instruments in the context of relations between the global South and the global North.

18.2.1.1 Decision-making at UNCLOS III

In view of the large number of newly independent states participating in UNCLOS III, the conference adopted the 'Gentlemen's Agreement', in which it was agreed that every effort would be made to adopt decisions by consensus.[13] In addition, given the complexity of, and the interrelationships between, the issues at stake in the negotiations, the conference adopted the 'package deal approach'.[14] This approach meant that the final instrument resulting from UNCLOS III was to be adopted as a whole, and that reservations to it would not be allowed.[15] Together, these informal instruments were to govern the decision-making procedure for the adoption of the LOSC.

Both the Gentlemen's Agreement and the package deal approach, as mentioned above, were informal instruments, even if the Gentleman's Agreement was appended to the text of the Rules of Procedure for UNCLOS III, which themselves were deeply contested.[16] The agreed manner of proceeding governed the decision-making throughout UNCLOS III, even if the LOSC was ultimately adopted by a vote, at the request of the United States, because of its opposition to the deep seabed mining regime in Part XI of the LOSC.[17]

The decision-making process adopted for UNCLOS III was relatively new at the time. It replaced the 'one state, one vote' system, majority voting, and the acceptance of reservations, which, until UNCLOS III, had been the prevalent manner of proceeding at multilateral conferences for the negotiation of new treaty regimes.[18] Decision-making by consensus, and the non-allowance of reservations, have become generally accepted for the negotiation of, for example, multilateral environmental agreements (MEAs), such as the 1992 United Nations Framework Convention on Climate Change (UNFCCC),[19] the 1992 Convention

[12] Lawrence Juda, 'UNCLOS III and the New International Economic Order' (1979) 7(3-4) ODIL 221; Euripides L Evriviades, 'Third World's Approach to the Deep Seabed' (1982) 11(3-4) ODIL 201. See also Surabhi Ranganathan, 'Decolonization and International Law: Putting the Ocean on the Map' (2021) 23(1) Journal of the History of International Law 161.

[13] The text of the Rules of Procedure to which the Gentlemen's Agreement was appended were adopted on 27 June 1974, see UN Doc A/CONF.62/30/Rev.1: the Rules of Procedure are reproduced in (1974) 13(5) ILM 1199. See Edward Miles, 'The Structure and Effects of the Decision Process in the Seabed Committee and the Third United Nations Conference on The Law of the Sea' (1977) 31(2) Intl'l Org 159; Barry Buzan, 'Negotiating by Consensus: Developments in Technique at the United Nations Conference on the Law of The Sea' (1981) 75(2) AJIL 324.

[14] See Hugo Caminos and Michael R Molitor, 'Progressive Development of International Law and the Package Deal' (1985) 79(4) AJIL 871.

[15] LOSC (n 5) art 309.

[16] For the Rules of Procedure, see n 13. See also Miles (n 13) 180–85.

[17] See text at, and fn 55 to, the Final Act of UNCLOS III (1982) 21(6) ILM 1245. See also David L Larson, 'The Reagan Administration and the Law of the Sea' (1982) 11(3-4) ODIL 297.

[18] Buzan (n 13) 326–27.

[19] United Nations Framework Convention on Climate Change (adopted 9 May 1992, entered into force 21 March 1994) 1771 UNTS 107.

on Biological Diversity (CBD),[20] and the 2015 Paris Agreement.[21] However, the decision-making processes for the negotiation of MEAs have not adopted the package deal approach, which has been linked to the failure of the LOSC to attract universal ratification.[22] Instead, in negotiating MEAs, the 'framework convention protocol approach' has been adopted.[23] The lawmaking process developed for UNCLOS III has, however, resurfaced in the BBNJ negotiations.[24]

18.2.1.2 Developing the Deep Seabed Mining Regime

After the adoption of the LOSC, states—in particular, developed states, but also India and the Soviet Union—started prospecting parts of the Area, especially in the Clarion-Clipperton Zone in the Pacific Ocean.[25] Their aim was, at least for signatories to the LOSC, to secure registration as pioneer investors.[26] In order to avoid overlap between their claims, these states concluded a number of agreements.[27] The adopted agreements were of a formal nature, and legally bound their parties, including the United States, which was, and is, not a signatory to the LOSC. These agreements met with strong resistance from developing states, and from the Preparatory Commission (PrepCom)[28] that had started to develop the necessary measures to ensure the smooth entry into force of the LOSC.[29]

These agreements, together with additional informal instruments such as the 1986 Arusha Understanding,[30] probably had normative intent, and had normative effect in that they influenced the lawmaking process that developed the deep seabed mining regime after the adoption, and prior to the entry into force, of the LOSC. The contours of the amended deep seabed mining regime emerged in the 1986 New York Understanding, an informal instrument adopted by the PrepCom.[31] The New York Understanding was one

[20] Convention on Biological Diversity (adopted 5 June 1992, entered into force 29 December 1993) 1760 UNTS 79.

[21] Paris Agreement to the United Nations Framework Convention on Climate Change (adopted 12 December 2015, entered into force 4 November 2016) (2016) 55(4) ILM 740.

[22] See Christopher C Joyner and Elizabeth A Martell, 'Looking Back to See Ahead: UNCLOS III and Lessons for Global Commons Law' (1996) 27(1-2) ODIL 73, 81–82.

[23] Nele Matz-Lück, 'Framework Conventions as a Regulatory Tool' (2009) 1(3) Goettingen J Intl'l L 439; Joyner and Martell (n 22).

[24] 'International Legally Binding Instrument under the United Nations Convention on the Law of the Sea on the Conservation and Sustainable Use of Marine Biological Diversity of Areas beyond National Jurisdiction' UNGA Res 72/249 (24 December 2017) A/RES/72/249, para 2 (refers to the topics to be negotiated as 'the package'), and para 17 (on consensus).

[25] Note that the Indian claim was in the Indian Ocean.

[26] See Final Act of UNCLOS III (n 17) Resolution II on Governing Preparatory Investment in Pioneer Activities Relating to Polymetallic Nodules.

[27] Agreement concerning Interim Arrangements Relating to Polymetallic Nodules of the Deep Sea Bed (adopted 2 September 1982, entered into force 2 September 1982) (1982) 21 ILM 950; and Provisional Understanding Regarding Deep Seabed Matters (adopted 3 August 1984, entered into force 2 September 1984) (1987) 26 ILM 1502 were concluded by the above-mentioned states and Belgium, Italy, Japan, and the Netherlands. The complex of agreements and informal instruments is also known as 'the reciprocating states regime'.

[28] 'Declaration Adopted by the Preparatory Committee 30 August 1985' (1985) 6 LOSB 85.

[29] Final Act of UNCLOS III (n 17) Resolution I on Establishment of the Preparatory Commission for the International Sea-Bed Authority and for the Tribunal for the Law of the Sea.

[30] This understanding was concluded between India, Japan, France, and the Soviet Union, in 'Report on the Fourth Session of the Preparatory Commission for the International Sea-Bed Authority and for the International Tribunal for the Law of the Sea Kingston, 17 March–1 April 1986' (1986) 8 LOSB 35.

[31] United Nations Convention on the Law of the Sea: Understanding of the Preparatory Commission for the International Sea-Bed Authority and for the International Tribunal for the Law of the Sea for Proceeding with Deep Sea-Bed Mining Applications and Resolving Disputes of Overlapping Claims of Mine Sites (11 September 1986), reproduced in (1986) 25(5) ILM 1326.

of a series of informal instruments that 'adjusted' the deep seabed mining regime in Part XI of the LOSC, and the regime for pioneer investors in Resolution II of the Final Act of UNCLOS III.[32] Eventually, these instruments resounded in the 1994 Agreement Relating to the Implementation of Part XI of the LOSC of 10 December 1982 (Implementation Agreement).[33] As a result of this lawmaking process, developing states lost their preferential position in the deep seabed mining regime.[34]

18.2.1.3 Transferring Marine Technology

Part XIV of the LOSC, on the development and transfer of marine technology, does not formulate a hard duty on the part of developed states to transfer relevant technology to developing states.[35] It subjects the transfer of technology to the obligation of states to 'have due regard for all legitimate interests including, *inter alia*, the rights and duties of holders, suppliers and recipients of marine technology'.[36] A similar approach has been adopted in other formal instruments that address the transfer of technology.[37] Part XI of the LOSC is an exception: it contains a hard duty to transfer deep seabed mining technology to developing states and the Enterprise, but the Implementation Agreement transformed this hard duty into a soft commitment.[38] This soft approach to the transfer of technology is also reflected in Sustainable Development Goal (SDG) 14 on oceans, which does not provide a clear commitment on the part of developed states to transfer marine technology to developing states.[39] Target 14.a calls on states to :

> Increase scientific knowledge, develop research capacity and transfer marine technology, taking into account the Intergovernmental Oceanographic Commission Criteria and Guidelines on the Transfer of Marine Technology, in order to improve ocean health and to enhance the contribution of marine biodiversity to the development of developing countries, in particular small island developing States and least developed countries.[40]

The indicator for target 14.a is noteworthy.[41] Instead of providing a criterion related to the transfer of marine technology from developed to developing states, it refers to the

[32] See n 26.

[33] For further information on the negotiation process, as well as other informal instruments that played a role in it, see Moritaka Hayashi, 'Registration of the First Group of Pioneer Investors by the Preparatory Commission for the International Sea-Bed Authority and for the International Tribunal for the Law of the Sea' (1989) 20(1) ODIL 1; RR Churchill and AV Lowe, *The Law of the Sea* (3rd edn, Manchester University Press 1999) 232–38; Katherine Dixon, 'Law Of The Sea—Deep Seabed Mining—United States Position in Light of Recent Agreement and Exchange of Notes with Five Countries Involved in Preparatory Commission of United Nations Convention on the Law of the Sea' (1988) 18 Ga J Intl'l & Comp L 497.

[34] See DH Anderson, 'Resolution and Agreement Relating to the Implementation of Part XI of the UN Convention on the Law of the Sea: A General Assessment' (1995) 55 HJIL 275.

[35] See Techera, in Chapter 13 of this volume.

[36] LOSC (n 5) art 267.

[37] Irina V Shugurova and Mark V Shugurov, 'International Technology Transfer' (2015) 45(3-4) EP & L 133; Carlos M Correa, 'Innovation and Technology Transfer of Environmentally Sound Technologies: The Need to Engage in a Substantive Debate' (2013) 22(1) RECIEL 54.

[38] Compare LOSC (n 5) art 144 to Implementation Agreement, Annex, s 5: Agreement Relating to the Implementation of Part XI of the United Nations Convention on the Law of the Sea of 10 December 1982 (adopted 28 July 1994, entered into force 16 November 1994) 1836 UNTS 3; see also Anderson (n 34) 287.

[39] On the SDGs, see Telesetsky, in Chapter 14 of this volume.

[40] UN, 'Transforming Our World: The 2030 Agenda for Sustainable Development', UNGA Res 70/1 (25 September 2015) UN Doc A/Res/70/1.

[41] The indicators that accompany the SDG were adopted by UNGA Res 71/313 (6 July 2017) UN Doc A/RES/71/313, in order to facilitate the measurement of progress on the implementation of the SDGs.

'[p]roportion of total research budget allocated to research in the field of marine technology'.[42] In other words, the indicator does not relate to the transfer of marine technology.

The transfer of marine technology from developed to developing states is part of the wider contestation among developed and developing states about the transfer of technology.[43] It is related to the World Trade Organization (WTO) regime for the protection of intellectual property rights in the 1994 Agreement on Trade-related Aspects of Intellectual Property Rights (TRIPS Agreement).[44] Based on the TRIPS Agreement, intellectual property right-holders enjoy strong protections that hamper the transfer of technology.[45] Only if states, and developed states in particular, agree to change the transfer of technology regime embedded in the TRIPS Agreement are we likely to see real change in the law governing the transfer of marine technology.[46] By implication, it is the legal infrastructure protecting intellectual property rights that must change, before formal instruments containing hard obligations about the transfer of marine technology are likely to emerge.

When issues are politically contested, such as in the case of the transfer of technology, informal instruments might be characterized as, perhaps, pointing to best practices. However, informal instruments are unlikely to breach the divide, in this case between the global South and global North about the transfer of technology from the latter to the former. As a result, we are likely to continue to see provisions in formal instruments that include references to the transfer of technology being promoted, subject to the rights and duties of those who hold or supply technology. Informal instruments, such as UN General Assembly resolutions, do not, necessarily, include such explicit provisions,[47] even if some informal instruments do. The Intergovernmental Oceanographic Commission (IOC)'s Criteria and Guidelines on the Transfer of Marine Technology, referred to in SDG 14, provide an example of the latter.[48]

18.2.2 Informal Instruments in the Relationship between the Global South and Global North

The contestation between the global South and the global North has played, and continues to play, a prominent role in the law of the sea. The promise of the NIEO was never realized, and its strong reflection in a formal instrument—the deep seabed mining regime in

[42] ibid, Annex, indicator 14.1.a.

[43] Shugurova and Shugurov (n 37); Correa (n 37).

[44] Agreement on Trade-related Aspects of Intellectual Property Rights (adopted 14 April 1994, entered into force 1 January 1995) 1869 UNTS 299.

[45] On the transfer of technology, generally, see Andria Naudé Fourie, 'SDG 9: Build Resilient Infrastructure, Promote Inclusive and Sustainable Industrialization and Foster Innovation' in Jonas Ebbeson and Ellen Hey (eds), *The Handbook on the Sustainable Development Goals and International Law* (CUP forthcoming); Claude Henry and Joseph E Stiglitz, 'Intellectual Property, Dissemination of Innovation and Sustainable Development' (2010) 1(3) Global Pol'y 237.

[46] Klaus D Beiter, 'Reductionist Intellectual Property Protection and Expansionist (and "Prodevelopment") Competition Rules as Human Rights Imperative? Enhancing Technology Transfer to the Global South' (2021) 14(1) L Dev Rev 215.

[47] See UNGA Res 73/240 (n 9) para 13. However, the latest UNGA resolution on oceans, , ('Oceans and the Law of the Sea', UNGA Res 75/239 (31 December 2020) UN Doc A/RES/73/239, paras 14 and 21), as SDG 14, refers to the IOC's Criteria and Guidelines on the Transfer of Marine Technology.

[48] The IOC Criteria and Guidelines are available at <https://unesdoc.unesco.org/ark:/48223/pf0000139193.locale = en> accessed 16 July 2021. See, in particular, para B(c)(ii).

Part XI of the LOSC—was revoked by way of a series of interacting formal and informal instruments, culminating in the Implementation Agreement. As a result, the concept of the common heritage of humankind, which itself originated in an informal instrument,[49] has been significantly eroded, even if it is still part of the legal infrastructure of the law of the sea.[50] Informal instruments have not had a comparable normative effect on the regime for the transfer of marine technology. In this case, the legal infrastructure provided by the TRIPS Agreement is dominant. All of which goes to show, perhaps unsurprisingly, that political and economic power matter in determining the normative effect of informal instruments, when it comes to determining legal infrastructure.

An exception to the above conclusion, from outside the law of the sea, is provided by the International Court of Justice (ICJ)'s Advisory Opinion in *Chagos*.[51] In its ruling, the court attributed normative effect to UN General Assembly resolutions in order to find that Mauritius's decolonization process had not been concluded, because the United Kingdom had retained the administration of the Chagos Archipelago.[52] The court held that the decolonization process must be concluded based on the *erga omnes* right of peoples to self-determination, and that the continued administration of the Chagos Archipelago by the United Kingdom was unlawful.[53] International courts and tribunals may, then, given certain circumstances, attribute normative effect to instruments that are, as such, informal.

18.2.3 The Exercise of Jurisdiction at Sea

Developing the competences to exercise jurisdiction at sea, a central element of the infrastructure of the law of the sea, has been marked with controversy throughout the history of the law of the sea. Informal instruments, unilateral or multilateral, have played an important role in these controversies. This section, first, briefly discusses early examples of these types of instruments, and then focuses on three contemporary examples of lawmaking processes in which the legal infrastructure of the law of the sea is being developed. These examples are: (1) the role of informal instruments in stabilizing baselines, in view of sea level rise; (2) the BBNJ negotiations; and (3) combating piracy in the Somali territorial sea. Lastly, this section reflects on the legal effect of relevant informal instruments.

18.2.3.1 Early Examples

An early example of an informal multilateral instrument that was part of a lawmaking process that, eventually, contributed to changes in the law of the sea is the 1970 Montevideo Declaration on the Law of the Sea.[54] It was adopted by nine Latin American states, claiming extended coastal state jurisdiction over the water column, seabed, and subsoil out to 200 nautical miles.[55] This declaration, and others preceding it, clearly had normative intent, and

[49] UN, 'Declaration of Principles Governing the Sea-Bed and Ocean Floor, and the Subsoil thereof, beyond the Limits of National Jurisdiction', UNGA Res XXV/2749 (17 December 1970) UN Doc A/RES/XXV/2749, para 1.

[50] Implementation Agreement (n 38) preamble, para 2.

[51] *Legal Consequences of the Separation of the Chagos Archipelago from Mauritius in 1965* (Advisory Opinion) [2019] ICJ Rep 1.

[52] ibid, paras 163–69.

[53] ibid, paras 177–82.

[54] Montevideo Declaration on the Law of the Sea (8 May 1970) (1970) 9(5) ILM 1081.

[55] See LDM Nelson, 'The Patrimonial Sea' (1973) 22(4) ICLQ 668.

had normative effect by way of the incorporation of the regime of the exclusive economic zone (EEZ) in the LOSC,[56] and its recognition in customary international law by the ICJ in 1982.[57] Unilateral instruments with similar normative intent and effect include the 1945 Truman Proclamation on the Continental Shelf,[58] the extension of fisheries zones to twelve nautical miles, starting in the 1960s,[59] and the extension by Canada of its fisheries enforcement powers beyond 200 nautical miles, in 1994.[60] The Truman Proclamation found its way into the 1958 Geneva Convention on the Continental Shelf;[61] the extension of fisheries zones to twelve nautical miles was recognized as part of customary international law by the ICJ in 1974;[62] and the competence to exercise fisheries enforcement powers on the high seas by states other than the flag state was incorporated the UN Fish Stocks Agreement.[63]

Going back even further, we might ask ourselves how to assess Grotius's 1609 *Mare Liberum*.[64] In *Mare Liberum*, Grotius posited the freedom of the high seas, in the interest of the Dutch East India Company, supported by the then-government of the Netherlands.[65] Was this an informal instrument? It certainly had normative intent and, eventually, normative effect.

18.2.3.2 Stabilizing Baselines

A contemporary example of claims to the exercise of jurisdiction at sea is provided by the instruments that Pacific island states have adopted to stabilize their baselines and maritime zones in view of sea level rise due to climate change.[66] The LOSC provides that the

[56] LOSC (n 5) pt V on the EEZ.

[57] *Case concerning the Continental Shelf (Tunisia/Libyan Arab Jamahiriya)* (Judgment) [1982] ICJ Rep 18, para 100.

[58] Proclamation No 2667, 10 FR 12305 (28 September 1945) Policy of the United States with respect to the Natural Resources of the Subsoil and Sea Bed of the Continental Shelf <https://www.presidency.ucsb.edu/documents/proclamation-2667-policy-the-united-states-with-respect-the-natural-resources-the-subsoil> accessed 20 July 2021.

[59] Ludwik A Teclaff, 'Jurisdiction over Offshore Fisheries—How Far into the High Seas' (1967) 35 Fordham L Rev 409, 420.

[60] Canadian Coastal Fisheries Protection Act, Amendment of 12 May 1994 (SC 1994, c 14). See, in particular, ss 7 and 8 <https://www.un.org/Depts/los/LEGISLATIONANDTREATIES/PDFFILES/CAN_1994_Amendment.pdf> accessed 17 July 2021. David Freestone, 'Canada and the EU Reach Agreement to Settle the Estai Dispute' (1995) 10(3) IJMCL 397.

[61] Convention on the Continental Shelf (adopted 19 April 1958, entered into force 10 June 1964) 499 UNTS 311, art 2.

[62] *Fisheries Jurisdiction (United Kingdom v Iceland)* (Judgment) [1974] ICJ Rep 3, para 52. On the early history of the extension of coastal state jurisdiction for fisheries purposes, see, generally, Teclaff (n 59).

[63] Agreement for the Implementation of the Provisions of the United Nations Convention on the Law of the Sea of 10 December 1982 Relating to the Conservation and Management of Straddling Fish Stocks and Highly Migratory Fish Stocks (adopted 4 August 1995, entered into force 11 December 2001) 2167 UNTS 3 (hereafter 'UN Fish Stocks Agreement').

[64] For the original Latin text, and a new English translation, see Robert Feenstra and Jeroen Vervliet, *Hugo Grotius Mare Liberum 1609–2009* (Brill 2009). For further information, see Gustaaf van Nifterik and Janne Nijman, 'Mare Liberum Revisited (1609–2009)' (2009) 30 Grotiana 3.

[65] Nifterik and Nijman (n 64) 3–4.

[66] Eg, C Pratt and H Govan, 'Our Sea of Islands, Our Livelihoods, Our Oceania: Framework for a Pacific Oceanscape: A Catalyst for Implementation of Ocean Policy' (November 2010) <https://www.forumsec.org/wp-content/uploads/2018/03/Framework-for-a-Pacific-Oceanscape-2010.pdf> accessed 17 July 2021; Taputapuātea Declaration on Climate Change (Polynesian Leaders Group, 16 July 2015) <https://www.state.gov/wp-content/uploads/2019/03/248-Deep-Sea-Bed.pdf> accessed 17 July 2021; Delap Commitment on Securing our Common Wealth of Oceans (Parties to the Nauru Agreement, 2 March 2018), para 8 <https://www.pnatuna.com/sites/default/files/Delap%20Commitment_2nd%20PNA%20Leaders%20Summit.pdf> accessed 17 July 2021. See Oral and Bektaş, in Chapter 17 of this volume; Chris Armstrong and Jack Corbett, 'Climate Change, Sea Level Rise, and Maritime Baselines: Responding to the Plight of Low-lying Atoll States' (2021) 21(1) Glob Envt'l Polit 89; Clive Schofield and David Freestone, 'Islands Awash amidst Rising Seas: Sea Level Rise and Insular Status under the Law of the Sea' (2019) 34(3) IJCML 391.

normal baseline is the low-water line along the coast, as well as allowing for several exceptions where baselines other than the low-water mark may be used.[67] Yet, the situation of the Pacific island states is not included among the exceptions provided. In other words, Pacific island states are seeking to obtain support for adapting or interpreting the law of the sea in a manner that will accommodate their situation. The instruments adopted by Pacific island states are of an informal character, and clearly have normative intent, but they do not change the law of the sea, as such, even if they may be gaining support, and may ultimately acquire normative effect. In terms of gaining support, and perhaps also normative effect, the consideration of the topic by the International Law Association (ILA) and International Law Commission (ILC) is relevant.

In 2012, the ILA, a non-governmental organization (NGO) whose global membership consists of international lawyers—that is, experts—established the Committee on International Law and Sea Level Rise.[68] While the ILA committee reports might not have normative intent, as such, ILA resolutions, to which these reports might be annexed, clearly have normative intent. Moreover, ILA members are well aware of the potential normative effect of ILA resolutions, as evidenced by the following quotation from the 2018 Report of the ILA Committee on International Law and Sea Level Rise. The Committee:

> while deciding not to propose any specific option at this point, expressed the hope that a Resolution of the International Law Association might be the most effective first step in bringing its recommendations to a wider audience.[69]

In 2018, the ILA did, indeed, adopt Resolution 5/2018 on International Law and Sea Level Rise, which addressed the stabilization of baselines. The resolution not only supports the position of Pacific island states,[70] but also, and as evidence of its normative intent, requests the ILA Secretary-General to communicate the resolution to the UN Secretary-General, the parties to the LOSC, the ICJ, the Tribunal for the Law of the Sea (ITLOS), and the Permanent Court of Arbitration.[71]

In 2019, the ILC—the expert legal body of the United Nations that engages in the codification and progressive development of international law—established a Study Group on Sea Level Rise and International Law.[72] In their 2020 report, the co-chairs quoted ILA Resolution 5/2018 in positive terms.[73] The report, among other things, concludes the following:

[67] LOSC (n 5) arts 5–14.

[68] For information on the work of the committee, and relevant resolutions, see ILA, 'ILA Committees' <https://www.ila-hq.org/index.php/committees> accessed 17 July 2021. See also Schofield and Freestone (n 66) 400–04.

[69] ILA, 'Report of the Committee on International Law and Sea Level Rise' (2018) 19 <https://www.ila-hq.org/images/ILA/DraftReports/DraftReport_SeaLevelRise.pdf> accessed 17 July 2021.

[70] ILA, 'Committee on International Law and Sea Level Rise', ILA Resolution 5/2018, para 5 <https://www.ila-hq.org/images/ILA/Resolutions/ILAResolution_5_2018_SeaLevelRise.pdf> accessed 17 July 2021.

[71] ibid, para 9.

[72] For information on the study group, see ILC, 'Analytical Guide to the Work of the International Law Commission: Sea-Level Rise in relation to International Law' <https://legal.un.org/ilc/guide/8_9.shtml> accessed 17 July 2021.

[73] Bogdan Aurescu and Nilüfer Oral, 'Sea-Level Rise in relation to International Law: First Issues Paper by Bogdan Aurescu and Nilüfer Oral, Co-chairs of the Study Group on Sea-Level Rise in relation to International Law' (28 February 2020) UN Doc A/CN.4/740, para 82.

> Consequently, nothing prevents Member States from depositing notifications, in accordance with the Convention, regarding the baselines and outer limits of maritime zones measured from the baselines and, after the negative effects of sea-level rise occur, to stop updating these notifications in order to preserve their entitlements.[74]

The co-chairs of the ILC Study Group, as a preliminary conclusion, thus suggest that it would be sufficient for Pacific island and other states to register baselines and the outer limits of their maritime zones in accordance with the LOSC, to obtain the desired normative effect. That is, they suggest that amendment of the LOSC would not be required; instead, they point to the possible emergence of a rule of customary international law on the topic.[75]

What can be witnessed, in this case, is a lawmaking process consisting of informal instruments adopted by states, an instrument adopted by an NGO with expertise on international law (the ILA), and a report circulated within a UN expert body (the ILC). In other words, a lawmaking process that, to date, consists entirely of informal instruments to amend or adjust a fundamental aspect of the law of the sea: the determination of baselines. While it should be apparent that the lawmaking process in the ILC could not proceed if it were to meet with strong disapproval from relevant states, this, so far, does not seem to be the case.[76]

18.2.3.3 The BBNJ Negotiations

In the BBNJ negotiations, basic principles governing inter-state relations on the conservation and use of marine biodiversity in ABNJ are being negotiated.[77] The history of political contestation between the global North and the global South, as discussed above, has resurfaced in this lawmaking process.[78] It revolves around the very different implications that the principle of the freedom of the high seas, the principle of the common heritage of humankind, and the CBD have for how marine biological diversity will be accessed, and benefits obtained therefrom.[79] More concretely, it involves decisions on access to, and benefit sharing from, access to marine biological diversity, as well as the allocation of decision-making powers to global or regional institutions. In other words, states are involved in determining the legal infrastructure governing the conservation and sustainable use of marine biological diversity in ABNJ. This infrastructure will form the basis for regulating human activities in ABNJ, for example by way of marine protected areas (MPAs), or benefit-sharing arrangements.

74 ibid, para 104 (f).

75 ibid, para 104 (g)–(j).

76 See the comments submitted by states: ILC, 'Analytical Guide to the Work of the International Law Commission: Sea-Level Rise in relation to International Law' (n 72).

77 For information on the negotiations, see UN, 'Intergovernmental Conference on Marine Biodiversity of Areas beyond National Jurisdiction' <https://www.un.org/bbnj/> accessed 17 July 2021. For the latest draft text, see 'Revised Draft Text of an Agreement under the United Nations Convention on the Law of the Sea on the Conservation and Sustainable Use of Marine Biological Diversity of Areas beyond National Jurisdiction' (18 November 2019) UN Doc A/CONF.232/2020/3.

78 Ethan Beringen, Nengye Liu, and Michelle Lim, 'Australia as a Middle Power: Challenging the Narrative of Developed/Developing States in International Negotiations Surrounding Marine Genetic Resources' (2021) 52(2) ODIL 143.

79 Ellen Hey, 'Regime Interaction and Common Interests in Regulating Human Activities in Areas beyond National Jurisdiction' in Seline Trevisanut, Nikolaos Giannopoulos, and Rozemarijn Roland Holst (eds), *Regime Interaction in Ocean Governance* (Brill Nijhoff 2020) 106–10; Vito de Lucia, 'The Concept of Commons and Marine Genetic Resources in Areas beyond National Jurisdiction' (2018–19) 5 Mar Safety & Sec L J 1.

The BBNJ negotiations, as with most global negotiations, have given rise to NGOs developing initiatives to influence the lawmaking process. In addition, public actors, and international organizations in particular, have developed instruments that also seek to influence the negotiations. Both types of instruments are discussed below.

Multilateral negotiations, such as the BBNJ negotiations, trigger the development of draft provisions, or even full draft treaty texts, by non-state actors. In the case of the BBNJ negotiations, for example, the International Union for Conservation of Nature (IUCN) has provided detailed comments on the draft texts.[80] These comments clearly have normative intent, and may be more or less influential in the context of the negotiations. An example from outside the law of the sea is the set of draft articles submitted by the IUCN early on in the negotiation process for the CBD, which resounds in the CBD and, thus, might have had normative effect.[81]

The above-mentioned IUCN texts, even if informal in character, can, then, play a prominent role in lawmaking processes. Depending on who submits such instruments, and their content, they may have a lesser or greater normative effect. For example, the IUCN as an NGO, even if it has state agencies among its members, is known for its expertise in environmental and nature conservation matters, and may have considerable influence in the BBNJ negotiations. The role that the IUCN plays in the BBNJ negotiations might be compared to the role of the ILA in the lawmaking process to stabilize baselines, discussed above. Both organizations are influential because of their expertise. The development of the San Remo Manual on Naval Warfare, by a group of experts, seems to belong to the same category, even if this initiative is not a reaction to an ongoing lawmaking process, but seems to *be* the lawmaking process, even if informal.[82]

In the context of the BBNJ negotiations, and in terms of claims to changing competences in maritime areas, the 2014 Collective Arrangement, concluded by OSPAR and the North-East Atlantic Fisheries Commission (NEAFC), is noteworthy.[83] OSPAR is the regional seas body for the North-east Atlantic, and NEAFC is the regional fisheries management organization (RFMO) for the North-east Atlantic. The Collective Arrangement puts forward a claim that an RFMO and a regional seas body— or coastal states in the region through these bodies—have the competence to regulate human activities in ABNJ, including those of third parties. It is presented as 'a formal agreement between legally competent authorities managing human activities in … ABNJ in the North-East Atlantic'.[84] The Collective

[80] Comments are available at IUCN, 'Marine Biodiversity of Areas beyond National Jurisdiction (BBNJ)' <https://www.iucn.org/theme/environmental-law/our-work/oceans-and-coasts/marine-biodiversity-areas-beyond-national-jurisdiction-bbnj> accessed 17 July 2021. See also IUCN, 'Area-Based Management Tools in Marine Areas beyond National Jurisdiction: Building Ambition, Broadening Participation and Planning Ahead' (IUCN 2020) https://www.iucn.org/sites/dev/files/content/documents/iucn_abmt_-_report_final_web.pdf accessed 17 July 2021. On the role of NGOs in the preparatory process for the BBNJ negotiations, see Robert Blasiaka and others, 'The Role of NGOs in Negotiating the Use of Biodiversity in Marine Areas beyond National Jurisdiction' (2017) 81 Mar Pol 1.

[81] Françoise Burhenne-Guilmin and Susan Casey-Lefkowitz, 'The Convention on Biological Diversity: A Hard Won Global Achievement' (1992) 3 Yb Intl'l Env L 43, 46.

[82] Lijnzaad, in Chapter 2 of this volume.

[83] The Collective Arrangement (OSPAR Commission/NEAFC, 'Collective Arrangement between Competent International Organizations on Cooperation and Coordination Regarding Selected Areas in Areas beyond National Jurisdiction in the North-East Atlantic' (2014) OSPAR Agreement 2014-09, updated 2018) is available at OSPAR, 'Collective Arrangement' <https://www.ospar.org/about/international-cooperation/collective-arrangement#:~:text=The%20'Collective%20Arrangement%20between%20competent,of%20the%20Marine%20Environment%20of> accessed 17 July 2021; and at NEAFC, 'OSPAR/NEAFC Collective Arrangement' <https://www.neafc.org/collective-arrangement> accessed 17 July 2021.

[84] See websites cited in n 83, where the Collective Arrangement is presented.

Arrangement is grounded in legally binding decisions, that is formal instruments, adopted by OSPAR and NEAFC, respectively, instituting MPAs and closed areas for bottom trawling in ABNJ.[85]

Other international organizations with competences in the high seas areas in the North-east Atlantic—in particular the IMO, the International Seabed Authority (ISA), and the International Commission for the Conservation of Atlantic Tunas (ICCAT)—have been invited to join the Collective Arrangement,[86] but have not done so, to date. Instead, co-operation between OSPAR and the IMO, OSPAR and the ISA, and NEAFC and the IMO are based on Memoranda of Understanding (MoUs).[87] These MoUs focus on the exchange of information, and mutual recognition as observers at relevant meetings.[88] Annual meetings are held under the auspices of the Collective Arrangement.[89] These meetings serve as a forum for exchanging information among OSPAR and NEAFC, members of these two organizations, and other organizations, including the ISA.[90] In June 2017, OSPAR and NEAFC, under the Collective Arrangement, submitted a joint commitment under Target 14.c of SDG 14. The commitment aims 'to promote the benefits of the cross-sectoral work through [the] collective arrangement model', and also states that, '[w]e will aim to work with our sister intergovernmental organisation secretariats in other regions and other sectors to promote such collaboration'.[91] OSPAR and NEAFC, thus, clearly aim to propagate their manner of cooperation in respect of ABNJ, thereby showing normative intent. But how might the instruments involved in this ongoing lawmaking process be characterized?

The OSPAR and NEAFC decisions instituting measures in ABNJ are formal instruments that bind the parties to the OSPAR and NEAFC conventions.[92] The Collective Arrangement is presented as a formal agreement between the two organizations, presumably meaning that it is governed by the law on treaties between international organizations, as reflected in the 1986 Vienna Convention on the Law of Treaties between States and International Organizations or between International Organizations (VCLTIO).[93] If so, the Collective Arrangement, as such, would be a formal instrument, which, based on the law of treaties, would be binding on the two organizations.[94] While the Collective Arrangement, based on

[85] For NEAFC decision on bottom trawling, see Annex IA to the Collective Arrangement (n 83). NEAFC recommendations become binding on its members, subject to an opting-out procedure: see Convention on Future Multilateral Cooperation in North-East Atlantic Fisheries (adopted 18 November 1980, entered into force 17 March 1982) 1285 UNTS 129, arts 5(1) and 12. For OSPAR decisions on MPAs, see Annex 1B to the Collective Arrangement (n 83). OSPAR decisions become binding on its members, subject to an opting-out procedure: see Convention for the Protection of the Marine Environment of the North-East Atlantic (opened for signature 22 September 1992, entered into force 25 March 1998) 2354 UNTS 67, art 13(1).

[86] Collective Arrangement (n 83) art 3 and Annex 2.

[87] See Collective Arrangement (n 83) Annex 2.

[88] For information on OSPAR MoUs, see OSPAR Commission, 'Memoranda of Understanding & Cooperation Arrangements' <https://www.ospar.org/about/international-cooperation/memoranda-of-understanding> accessed 18 July 2021; and, on NEAFC MoUs, see NEAFC, 'Basic Texts' <https://www.neafc.org/basictexts> accessed 18 July 2021.

[89] For reports, search the OSPAR meeting archive at OSPAR Commission, 'Meeting Archive' <https://www.ospar.org/meetings/archive> accessed 18 July 2021.

[90] Reports of the annual meetings can be found at ibid.

[91] For the commitment under SDG 14, see UN, 'Commitment between the Secretariats of the North-East Atlantic Fisheries Commission and the OSPAR Commission under the Collective Arrangement' <https://oceanconference.un.org/commitments/?id = 21204> accessed 18 July 2021.

[92] See n 85.

[93] The VCLTIO has not entered into force: Vienna Convention on the Law of Treaties between States and International Organizations or between International Organizations (adopted 21 March 1986) (not in force).

[94] ibid, art 26.

the law of treaties, would not bind third parties, it is likely to have normative effect for the parties to OSPAR and NEAFC. However, the normative effect of the decisions adopted by OSPAR and NEAFC, and the Collective Arrangement, vis-à-vis third states is more complex. For parties to the UN Fish Stocks Agreement, the NEAFC decision on closed areas for bottom trawling, as with other high seas fisheries conservation measures adopted by RFMOs,[95] would qualify as a measure taken by an RFMO that flag states are to implement vis-à-vis their vessels.[96] However, beyond that, I suggest, the Collective Arrangement, as well as the OSPAR and NEAFC decisions, would, for third states, be better viewed as documents that clearly have normative intent, but whose normative effect in changing the law of the sea remains uncertain.

The normative intent of the Collective Arrangement for third states is best understood in the context of the ongoing BBNJ negotiations. In these negotiations, the roles, and competences of regional seas bodies and RFMOs currently remain contested.[97] If a treaty emerging from the BBNJ negotiations was to recognize a role for regional bodies, as is arguably the intention of the OSPAR/NEAFC initiative, the Collective Arrangement and the underlying decisions could have normative effect beyond the parties to the two conventions. This normative effect could be realized similarly to how the UN Fish Stocks Agreement integrates the decisions of RFMOs into its legal framework.[98] Alternatively, the OSPAR/NEAFC initiative might be followed by other RFMOs and regional seas bodies,[99] and become part of customary international law. What the discussion of the OSPAR/NEAFC initiative illustrates is that, while an instrument might have all the attributes of a formal instrument in one setting, it might, even if it is a formal instrument, have attributes similar to informal instruments with normative intent, in another setting.

18.2.3.4 Combating Armed Robbery and other Illicit Activities in the Territorial Sea of Somalia and the Gulf of Aden

Another example of how the law of the sea evolved in a specific situation, and by way of the interplay of formal and informal instruments, is the regime for addressing piracy and armed robbery off the coast of Somalia.[100] Clearly the LOSC does not entitle other states to act against armed robbery or piracy-like acts in the territorial sea of another state.[101] In this case, the competences of other states in the territorial sea of Somalia were extended by the UN Security Council to include combating armed robbery,[102] and later expanded to include combating other illicit activities.[103] The Security Council, in this case, clearly acted in view of the situation in Somalia, which it had identified as a threat to international peace and security.[104] The Security Council also stressed that the competences attributed to other states

[95] See Scott, in Chapter 16 of this volume.

[96] UN Fish Stocks Agreement (n 63) art 18.

[97] Nicola A Clark, 'Institutional Arrangements for the New BBNJ Agreement: Moving beyond Global, Regional, and Hybrid' (2020) 122 Mar Pol 104143.

[98] See text at n 96.

[99] See Scott, in Chapter 16 of this volume.

[100] See Jacobsson and Klein, in Chapter 3 of this volume, and Ishii, in Chapter 5 of this volume.

[101] In the territorial sea, the coastal state enjoys sovereignty (LOSC (n 5) art 2), subject to the right of innocent passage (LOSC (n 5) art 17), which prohibits ships from engaging in activities 'not having a direct bearing on passage' (LOSC (n 5) art 19(2)(l)). The definition of piracy is such that it is limited to acts on the high seas: 'a place outside the jurisdiction of any State' (LOSC (n 5) art 101(a)(i), and (ii)).

[102] UNSC Res 1816 (2 June 2008) UN Doc S/RES/1816.

[103] UNSC Res 1950 (23 November 2010) UN Doc S/RES/1950, paras 6 and 7.

[104] UNSC Res 733 (23 January 1992) UN Doc S/RES/733, preamble, para 4.

to act in the territorial sea of Somalia only apply in the Somali situation, and do not involve 'the rights or obligations or responsibilities of member states under international law', the LOSC, or the development of customary international law.[105]

A framework for implementing the relevant UN Security Council resolutions was, subsequently, developed by way of the informal Contact Group on Piracy off the Coast of Somalia and the Gulf of Aden,[106] and the IMO, in informal instruments, such as the 2006 Djibouti Code of Conduct, as amended by the 2017 Jeddah Amendment.[107] Several points are noteworthy in this context. First, to the extent that the Djibouti Code of Conduct permits activities in the territorial sea of another state, the consent of the coastal state seems to have been secured.[108] Second, in this case, the LOSC regime has been expanded upon in formal instruments—UN Security Council resolutions—which then served to legitimize their implementation by way of informal instruments. Yet, the implications thereof, at least so far, seem to be limited to efforts to address the threat to international peace and security that characterizes the situation in Somalia.

18.2.3.5 Legal Effect

The informal instruments discussed in this subsection, on their own, do not change the infrastructure of the law of the sea, as such. Instead, they become relevant in the context of other documents, that is in lawmaking processes, which may involve significant contestation. Think, for instance, of the ongoing BBNJ negotiations.

Yet, some of the informal instruments discussed may have one legal effect in common. Based on the principle of good faith and, related thereto, the doctrine of estoppel, the states or international institutions involved in propagating the intended changes to the infrastructure of the law of the sea, especially if they act thereon, are likely to be estopped from preventing other states or international institutions from acting similarly.[109] Thus, just as the United States, after issuing the Truman Proclamation on the Continental Shelf, would, probably, have been estopped from preventing other states from claiming continental shelves, Pacific island states are likely to be estopped from preventing other states from fixing their baselines and maritime zones, and the parties to OSPAR and NEAFC would be estopped from preventing other states, through regional seas bodies and RFMOs, from adopting area-based management measures in ABNJ. It is exactly this situation that the UN

[105] See, eg UNSC Res 1816 (n 102) para 9.

[106] Henk Swarttouw and Donna L Hopkins 'The Contact Group on Piracy off the Coast of Somalia: Genesis, Rationale and Objectives' in Thierry Tardy (ed), *Fighting Piracy off the Coast of Somalia: Lessons Learned from the Contact Group* (EU Institute for Security Studies 2014) 11–17; Anna Petrig and Robin Geiß, *Piracy and Armed Robbery at Sea: The Legal Framework for Counter-Piracy Operations in Somalia and the Gulf of Aden* (OUP 2011) 71–78.

[107] IMO, 'Code of Conduct concerning the Repression of Piracy and Armed Robbery against Ships in the Western Indian Ocean and the Gulf of Aden' (29 January 2009) IMO Doc C.102/14 (hereafter 'Djibouti Code of Conduct'). For the text of the Djibouti Code of Conduct, see <https://au.int/sites/default/files/documents/30848-doc-djibouti_code_of_conduct_0.pdf> accessed 18 July 2021; IMO, 'Revised Code of Conduct concerning the Repression of Piracy, Armed Robbery against Ships and Illicit Maritime Activity in the Western Indian Ocean and the Gulf of Aden Area' (12 January 2017) ('Jeddah Amendment') <https://wwwcdn.imo.org/localresources/en/OurWork/Security/Documents/A2%20Revised%20Code%20Of%20Conduct%20Concerning%20The%20Repression%20Of%20Piracy%20Armed%20Robbery%20Against%20Ships%20Secretariat.pdf> accessed 19 July 2021.

[108] Djibouti Code of Conduct (n 107) arts 1(2) and 5.

[109] Thomas Cottier and Jörg Paul Müller, 'Estoppel' in *Max Planck Encyclopedia of Public International Law* (last update April 2007).

Security Council aimed to prevent by emphasizing that the decisions regarding the Somali territorial sea have no legal effect beyond the Somali territorial sea.[110]

Courts and tribunals have regularly used the doctrine of estoppel to conclude that instruments that are, as such, informal may have normative effect.[111] A classic example is the ICJ's rulings in *Nuclear Tests*.[112] In these cases, the court attributed legal effect to public statements made by French officials, including the president of France. The court concluded that, based on these statements, 'France has undertaken the obligation to hold no further nuclear tests in the atmosphere in the South Pacific'.[113] The ruling of an arbitral tribunal in the *Chagos Marine Protected Area* case provides a recent example related to the law of the sea.[114] In this case, the tribunal attributed legal effect to what was referred to as an 'understanding', also in view of subsequent statements, concerning, among other things, the right of Mauritian fishers to access waters off the coast of the Chagos Archipelago, over which the United Kingdom had retained administrative power after Mauritius attained partial independence.[115]

18.3 Regulating Human Activity

The legal infrastructure of the law of the sea allocates competences to states and to international organizations through which states are to cooperate in regulating human activity. The human activities to be regulated by way of these cooperative endeavours are mainly of an economic character, and include activities at sea, such as shipping, mining, and fishing, as well as land-based activities that may affect the marine environment, such as the production and use of plastics.[116] As the chapters in this volume illustrate, informal instruments play a significant role in this context, even if some of the standard-setting instruments adopted are formal instruments.[117] This section seeks to capture some overarching issues that relate to informality and formality, in the context of standard setting, with the aim of regulating human activity. It first discusses standard setting based on inter-state cooperation, and then focuses on private actors' involvement in standard setting. Finally, this section addresses how these standard-setting processes might be conceptualized, suggesting that the framework of global administrative law might be useful.

[110] See text at n 105.

[111] See Jan Klabbers, 'International Courts and Informal International Law' in Joost Pauwelyn, Ramses A Wessel, and Jan Wouters (eds), *Informal International Lawmaking* (OUP 2012) 219–40.

[112] *Nuclear Tests (Australia v France)* (Judgment) [1974] ICJ Rep 253; *Nuclear Tests (New Zealand v France)* (Judgment) [1974] ICJ Rep 457.

[113] *Nuclear Tests (Australia v France)* (n 112) para 52; *Nuclear Tests (New Zealand v France)* (n 112) para 55.

[114] *Chagos Marine Protected Area Arbitration (Mauritius v United Kingdom)* (Award of 18 March 2015) PCA Case No 2011-03.

[115] ibid, paras 447–48; Michael Waibel, '*Mauritius v. UK*: Chagos Marine Protected Area Unlawful' (*EJIL Talk*, 17 April 2015) <https://www.ejiltalk.org/mauritius-v-uk-chagos-marine-protected-area-unlawful/> accessed 18 July 2021.

[116] Marine scientific research, which may or may not have an economic character, is also the object of regulation by way of a mixture of public and private regulation: see Kojima, in Chapter 12 of this volume.

[117] Examples include the ISA, the IMO, RFMOs, and regional seas bodies that adopt decisions by way of an opting-out procedure. Note that all of these institutions also adopt informal instruments.

18.3.1 Regulating Human Activity Based on Inter-state Cooperation

Many of the chapters in this volume illustrate that standard setting with the aim of regulating human activity is linked to inter-state cooperative endeavours. This means that states, within the legal infrastructure of the law of the sea, usually by way of a treaty,[118] establish an international organization through which they cooperate among themselves, and with other actors.

The lawmaking processes that transpire in these cooperative endeavours give rise to several types of instruments, which may be formal or informal. First, instruments are adopted that further develop relationships among the states involved, without changing the legal infrastructure of the law of the sea. Examples in the law of the sea are the compliance procedure developed within the IMO, and the reporting obligations that are part of most regimes.[119] Examples from outside the law of the sea are the flexible/market mechanisms that are part of the climate change regime.[120] Second, standards are set that aim to regulate human activity, even if they address states. Relevant examples include the standards set by RFMOs to regulate fishing,[121] and OSPAR recommendations or decisions that set standards, for example for the offshore industry or crematoria.[122] Third, because these standards address states, instead of fishers or an industrial sector directly, they may also play a role in determining a state's due diligence obligations.[123] Exercising due diligence in this context entails that a state must have a legal system and an administrative system in place through which the standards can be implemented, and must exert efforts to secure implementation of the agreed standards.[124] Only within the deep seabed mining regime does the ISA apply

[118] Two interesting exceptions exist in this context: the MoUs on port state control and the Arctic Council. The MoUs on port state control are informal instruments that seek to improve the implementation of formal instruments, such as SOLAS, through port state inspections. While based on the sovereignty of a state over its ports, in this case the legitimacy of the activities undertaken under the MoUs was, arguably, enhanced by their links to the formal instruments, and to which most states, including flag states are parties. See Ted L McDorman, 'Regional Port State Control Agreements: Some Issues of International Law' (2000) 5(2) ODIL 207. The Arctic Council is an international institution based on an informal instrument: see the Declaration on the Establishment of the Arctic Council (19 September 1996) <https://oaarchive.arctic-council.org/bitstream/handle/11374/85/EDOCS-1752-v2-ACMMCA00_Ottawa_1996_Founding_Declaration.PDF?sequence = 5&isAllowed = y> accessed 20 July 2021. It does not, itself, adopt formal instruments, even if three treaties have been negotiated under its auspices; it concentrates on agenda-setting and policy coordination. Its informal status has been associated with its effectiveness. See Oran R Young, 'The Arctic Council at Twenty: How to Remain Effective in a Rapidly Changing Environment' (2016) 6(1) UC Irvine L Rev 99.

[119] On the IMO compliance procedure, see Sun, in Chapter 6 of this volume.

[120] Charlotte Streck, Paul Keenlyside, and Moritz von Unger, 'The Paris Agreement: A New Beginning' (2016) 13(1) JEEPL 3, 14–18; Daniel Bodansky, Jutta Brunnée, and Lavanya Rajamani, *International Climate Change Law* (OUP 2017) 179–93 and 236–37.

[121] See Scanlon, in Chapter 11, and Scott, in Chapter 16, of this volume.

[122] OSPAR Commission, 'OSPAR Decision 2000/03 on the Use of Organic-Phase Drilling Fluids (OPF) and the Discharge of OPF Contaminated Cuttings' (2000) < https://www.ospar.org/documents?v = 32321> accessed 18 July 2021; or OSPAR Commission, 'OSPAR Recommendation 2003/4 on Controlling the Dispersal of Mercury from Crematoria' (2003) <https://www.ospar.org/convention/agreements/page4?t = 32283> accessed 18 July 2021. Note that the OSPAR Commission generally uses recommendations when addressing land-based sources of marine pollution, and decisions and recommendations when addressing activities at sea. This choice is, presumably, related to the soft obligation to cooperate contained in LOSC (n 5) art 207.

[123] On due diligence generally, see ILA Study Group on Due Diligence in International Law, 'Second Report' (July 2016) <https://www.ila-hq.org/index.php/study-groups?study-groupsID = 63> accessed 18 July 2021; Neil McDonald, 'The Role of Due Diligence in International Law' (2019) 69(4) ICLQ 1041.

[124] *Responsibilities and Obligations of States with Respect to Activities in the Area* (Advisory Opinion) ITLOS Reports 2011 (hereafter ITLOS, 'Responsibilities in the Area'), 10, paras 107–20; *Request for Advisory Opinion Submitted by the Sub-Regional Fisheries Commission* (Advisory Opinion) ITLOS Reports 2015, 4, paras 129–40.

standards directly to mining companies,[125] even if states also have direct obligations and due diligence obligations.[126]

A large number of reasons have been raised in the literature to explain why standard setting regularly occurs by way of informal instruments. These reasons include the need for standards that are easily adaptable to new scientific insights or developments in technology, or uncertainty about the best way to address a new problem, perhaps requiring some experimentation.[127] An example of the latter might be the engagement of OSPAR with the cosmetics sector in Europe, in 2015, about the removal of microplastics from cosmetics on a voluntary basis.[128] The engagement came with the threat of OSPAR requesting the European Union to adopt legislation on the use of microplastics in cosmetics.[129] While the sector, apparently, reacted positively,[130] this process has now been overtaken by the European Union aiming to regulate the use of microplastics in cosmetics, among other products, by way of its chemicals legislation, REACH.[131] This process provides an example of how informal and formal instruments may interact in a standard-setting process.

Lastly, it is also important to note that some of the formal institutions involved cannot adopt formal instruments, or can only adopt certain formal instruments. The Conference/Meeting of the Parties of the climate change regime is an example of the former.[132] The Conference of the Parties to the 1989 Basel Convention on the Control of Transboundary Movements of Hazardous Wastes and their Disposal (Basel Convention) is an example of the latter.[133] It has adopted decisions that place plastics on the convention's annexes;[134] these decisions are formal instruments, subject to an opting-out procedure.[135] It has also adopted Technical Guidelines for the Identification and Environmentally Sound Management (ESM) of Plastic Wastes and for their Disposal. This instrument is informal in nature , and is updated from time to time.[136] The standards set in these technical guidelines provide evidence for what might, for example, be considered 'adequate disposal facilities, for the

[125] See Davenport, in Chapter 10 of this volume.

[126] ITLOS, Responsibilities in the Area (n 124) paras 107–24.

[127] Kenneth W Abbott and Duncan Snidal, 'Hard and Soft Law in International Governance' (2000) 54(3) Intl'l Org 421. See also Petrig, in Chapter 7, and Scanlon, in Chapter 11, of this volume.

[128] See OSPAR Commission, 'OSPAR Welcomes Cosmetics Industry Microplastics Pledge' (5 November 2015) <https://www.ospar.org/news/ospar-marine-litter> accessed 18 July 2021.

[129] ibid.

[130] ibid.

[131] Regulation (EC) No 1907/2006 of the European Parliament and of the Council on the Registration, Evaluation, Authorisation and Restriction of Chemicals (REACH): see European Chemicals Agency, 'REACH Legislation' <https://echa.europa.eu/regulations/reach/legislation> accessed 18 July 2021. By December 2020, two technical advisory bodies had concluded that EU-wide restrictions on the use of microplastics in, among other products, cosmetics might be the best way to proceed. See European Chemicals Agency, 'Scientific Committees: EU-Wide Restriction Best Way to Reduce Microplastic Pollution' (9 December 2020) <https://echa.europa.eu/-/scientific-committees-eu-wide-restriction-best-way-to-reduce-microplastic-pollution> accessed 18 July 2021.

[132] Bodansky, Brunnée, and Rajamani (n 120) 19–20.

[133] Basel Convention on the Control of Transboundary Movements of Hazardous Wastes and Their Disposal (adopted 22 March 1989, entered into force 5 May 1992) 1673 UNTS 57.

[134] See, eg BC-14/12: Amendments to Annexes II, VIII, and IX to the Basel Convention (adopted at COP 14, 29 April–10 May 2019, effective 1 January 2021) <http://www.basel.int/Implementation/Plasticwaste/Decisions/tabid/6069/Default.aspx>. See also Rayfuse, in Chapter 15 of this volume.

[135] Basel Convention (n 133) art 18.

[136] 'Technical Guidelines for the Identification and Environmentally Sound Management of Plastic Wastes and for their Disposal' (23 August 2002) UN Doc UNEP/CHW.6/21. For further information, and the text of the technical guidelines, see Basel Convention, 'Technical Guidelines' <http://www.basel.int/Implementation/Plasticwaste/Technicalguidelines/Overview/tabid/7992/Default.aspx> accessed 18 July 2021.

environmentally sound management of hazardous wastes and other wastes' and 'appropriate legal, administrative and other measures' to implement the Basel Convention.[137] As a result, these standards may play a role in determining the content of the due diligence obligations of the parties to the Basel Convention. In the IMO, Unified Interpretations, guidelines, and interpretative IMO Assembly resolutions seem to play a similar role.[138]

It is, once again, suggested that how informal and formal instruments matter in this context is best understood in terms of their interaction in particular situations.[139] I also suggest that in cases of standard setting based on inter-state cooperation, formal instruments establishing such cooperation have the normative intent of legitimizing the normative effect of both informal and formal instruments resulting from such cooperation. However, as has been shown, 'thick' legitimacy requires, and durable normative effect probably depends on, the nature of decision-making processes, in terms of transparency, participation, and review, and the content of their outputs in terms of, for example, asking what is reasonable.[140] While it is beyond the purview of this chapter to engage in such an analysis, it is suggested that analysing the standard-setting lawmaking process in the law of the sea in terms of legitimacy may lead to further insights into how informal instruments matter.

18.3.2 Private Standard Setting

Private actors also engage in developing standards for human activity, on their own initiative, or by way of formal instruments delegating regulatory competences to them. In the law of the sea, the Marine Stewardship Council (MSC), and NGOs cooperating in search and rescue (SAR) operations in the Mediterranean Sea provide examples of the former,[141] while the Forest Stewardship Council (FSC) provides an example from outside the law of the sea.[142] In these three cases, private actors stepped in to regulate activities because states failed to do so sufficiently.[143] The instruments adopted by these private actors, by definition,

137 Basel Convention (n 133) eg art 4.

138 See Petrig, in Chapter 7 of this volume.

139 Jutta Brunnée, 'COPing with Consent: Law-Making under Multilateral Environmental Agreements' (2002) 15(1) LJIL 1.

140 ibid; Brunnée and Toope (n 1); see also Ellen Hey, *Teaching International Law* (Inaugural Lecture, Kluwer Law International 2003).

141 See, respectively, Telesetsky in Chapter 14, and Papanicolopulu, in Chapter 4, of this volume.

142 See Forest Stewardship Council <https://fsc.org/en> accessed 18 July 2021.

143 The MSC was established by the World Wide Fund for Nature (WWF) and Unilever in 1997, given concerns over the collapse of certain fish stocks: see 1996 Statement of Intent concluded between WWF and Unilever, available at MSC, 'Sustainable Seafood: The First 20 Years, A History of the Marine Stewardship Council' (25 April 2017) <http://20-years.msc.org/?_ga=2.186117993.1308383660.1621691293-357061222.1618666822&_gac=1.37351060.1621691524.EAIaIQobChMI7oXS1bfd8AIVQ8TVCh2q7wPtEAAYASAAEgLpcfD_BwE#two-the-msc-is-born-32155> accessed 18 July 2021. For information on the MSC, see Markos Karavias, 'Interactions between International Law and Private Fisheries Certification' (2017) 7(1) TEL 165. The collaboration among NGOs undertaking SAR operations in the Mediterranean Sea emerged after these NGOs stepped in to organize SAR operations that governments failed to provide. See Human Rights at Sea, 'Voluntary Code of Conduct for Search and Rescue Operations Undertaken by Civil Society Non-Government Organisations in the Mediterranean Sea' (2017) (hereafter 'NGO Code of Conduct'), foreword by Frank Dörner, for the Board of Sea Watch <https://www.humanrightsatsea.org/wp-content/uploads/2017/03/20170302-NGO-Code-of-Conduct-FINAL-SECURED.pdf> accessed 18 July 2021. For information about SAR operations in the Mediterranean Sea, and the NGOs involved, see Eugenio Cusumano and James Pattison, 'The Non-Governmental Provision of Search and Rescue in the Mediterranean and the Abdication of State Responsibility' (2018) 31(1) Cambridge Rev Int Aff 53. The FSC was established by environmental NGOs and parts of the forestry and timber industry, after the 1992 UN Conference on Environment and Development (see UN, 'Report of the United Nations Conference on Environment and Development' (3–14 June 1992), UN Doc A/CONF.151/26 (vol I), Annex I: Rio Declaration on Environment and

are of an informal nature in the international legal system. Yet, the initiatives taken by private actors regularly refer to formal instruments.[144] In this case, the references to formal instruments might be seen as legitimizing the normative effect of the informal instruments adopted by private actors. In other words, private sector actors are signalling that they are operating within, and not beyond, the legal infrastructure.

In the law of the sea, an example of a formal instrument delegating regulatory competences to private actors is the role of classification societies in both standard setting, for example for polar class ships, and surveying of ships, based on SOLAS.[145] The manner in which SOLAS delegates regulatory competences to classification societies is comparable to how WTO law links to international standardization bodies such as the International Standardization Organization, and the Codex Alimentarius Committee.[146] In this case, the normative intent of formal instruments might best be regarded as legitimizing the normative effect of the informal instruments adopted by private sector actors. In this case, then, it is the states, which adopt the formal instruments, that explicitly link the informal lawmaking instruments adopted by the private actors to the legal infrastructure.

Questions have been raised relating to the appropriateness of standard setting by private sector actors, especially if they are closely related to the sector that is the object of regulation, classification societies being a case in point.[147] However, these questions not only arise in the context of private sector self-regulation, or in the context of the private sector exercising delegated regulatory powers, but also in those cases where private sector actors are involved in standard setting more informally. The IMO provides an example. In the IMO, private sector actors sit on national delegations, participate in meetings as observers, and have strong relationships with the secretariat, resulting in the shipping sector being characterized as too influential in IMO lawmaking processes.[148] Similar questions may be raised

Development) failed to adopt a treaty on the protection of forests. For information on the FSC, see Stephen Bell and Andrew Hindmoor, 'Governance without Government? The Case of the Forest Stewardship Council' (2012) 90(1) Pub Adm 144.

[144] The MSC refers to the FAO Code of Conduct on Responsible Fishing as one of the instruments that guides its policies: see MSC, 'How we Meet Best Practice' <https://www.msc.org/about-the-msc/how-we-meet-best-practice> accessed 18 July 2021. The NGO Code of Conduct mentions that 'recognized SAR and maritime Conventions as well as humanitarian principles have assisted in shaping' it: NGO Code of Conduct (n 143) 6. FSC's website, on the subject of indigenous peoples, refers to the 'United Nations Declaration on the Rights of Indigenous People, and the International Labour Organization's Convention 169': see FSC, 'Indigenous Peoples' <https://fsc.org/en/for-people/indigenous-peoples> accessed 18 July 2021. See also Karavias (n 143) and Bell and Hindmoor (n 143) about the links between private actor regulation, and its links to formal instruments and actors.

[145] Øystein Jensen, 'The International Code for Ships Operating in Polar Waters: Finalization, Adoption and Law of the Sea Implications' (2016) 7(1) Arctic Rev L and P 82; JM Silos and others, 'The Role of the Classification Societies in the Era of Globalization: A Case Study' (2013) 40(4) Mar Pol'y & Mgmt 384; J Peschmann and others, 'IACS Common Structural Rules as an element of IMO Goal-based Standards for Bulk Carriers and Oil Tankers' in Carlos Guedes Soares and Y Garbatov (eds), *Progress in the Analysis and Design of Marine Structures* (Routledge 2017).

[146] Alessandra Arcuri, 'The Coproduction of the Global Regulatory Regime for Food Safety Standards and Limits of a Technocratic Ethos' (*EUI Working Papers*, RSCAS 2014/97) <https://cadmus.eui.eu/handle/1814/32833> accessed 20 July 2021; Panagiottis Delimatsis, 'Global Standard Setting 2.0: How the WTO Spotlights ISO and Impacts the Transnational Standard-Setting Process' (2018) 28 Duke J Comp & Intl'l L 273; Sanderijn Duquet and Dylan Geraets, 'Food Safety Standards and Informal International Lawmaking' in Ayelet Berman and others (eds), *Informal International Lawmaking: Case Studies* (Torkel Opsahl Academic ePublisher 2012) 406–12.

[147] See Jensen (n 145) and Silos and others (n 145), on classification societies. For other private standard setters, see n 146.

[148] Transparency International, 'Governance at the International Maritime Organisation: The Case for Reform' (*Transparency International*, 2018) <https://images.transparencycdn.org/images/2018_IMO_Governance_Report_EN.pdf> accessed 18 July 2021; see also Harilaos N Psaraftis and Christos A Kontovas, 'Influence and Transparency at the IMO: The Name of the Game' (2020) 22(2) Marit Econ Logist 151.

about the involvement of the private sector in developing regulatory standards for offshore energy and mining.[149]

18.3.3 Administration

As the chapters in this volume illustrate, in detail, complex lawmaking processes, in which informal and formal instruments interact with one another, have been established to regulate human activity at sea, and on land, for land-based sources of marine pollution, by way of standard setting. Sometimes informal instruments further develop aspects of formal regulatory instruments. On other occasions, they stand on their own, and may gain formality by way of their implementation into national or European Union law. This section identified some overarching characteristics of these lawmaking processes, as well as concerns that may arise in this context. It also, at an overarching level, suggests how the formal and informal instruments might relate to each other in this context.

Taking a broader view, I suggest that what is transpiring, in the context of regulating human activity, is probably best conceptualized through the lens of global administrative law.[150] Global administrative law is useful, analytically, to clarify what is going on, but also normatively, to capture what is at stake in terms of transparency, participation in decision-making, and review. Research has shown that many standard-setting lawmaking processes do not score well on any of these counts.[151] Research has also shown that some informal standard-setting lawmaking processes perform well—perhaps better than formal law-making processes—when analysed based on these three parameters.[152] The lens of global administrative law not only enables us to analyse standard-setting lawmaking processes that generate informal outputs, but also those that generate formal instruments. Although the latter depend on state consent for attainment of formal status, their legitimacy, as is the case for informal instruments, depends on the characteristics of the lawmaking process, in terms of transparency, participation, and review, which is what the lens of global administrative law allows us to analyse. Moreover, the lens of interactional law allows us to look even more deeply at some of the legitimacy issues that may arise in formal and informal lawmaking processes.[153]

18.4 Concluding Remarks

In the law of the sea, as in international law more generally, informal and formal instruments interact in different ways. Analysing these interactions enables us to better understand the significance of informal instruments. In situations of high political contestation,

[149] Trevisanut, in Chapter 9 of this volume.

[150] For the classical article on the topic, see Benedict Kingsbury, Nico Krisch, and Richard B Stewart, 'The Emergence of Global Administrative Law' (2005) 68(1) LCP 15. For further literature, see IILJ, 'Publications' <https://www.iilj.org/gal/publications/> accessed 18 July 2021. Klein also considers explanatory theories from global governance and security studies, in Chapter 8 of this volume.

[151] See, eg references in n 146.

[152] Joost Pauwelyn, Ramses A Wessel, and Jan Wouters, 'When Structures become Shackles: Stagnation and Dynamics in International Lawmaking' (2014) 25(3) EJIL 733.

[153] See Brunnée and Toope (n 1); Brunnée (n 139).

such as the relationship between the global South and the global North, informal instruments matter, if backed up by economic and political power. This finding raises serious concerns about the justice dimension of international law, including the law of the sea. In this respect, it is worth noting that the initiatives of Pacific island states gained traction over a very short period of time, even if contained in informal instruments. These initiatives may have met with little opposition because other states might well have an interest in fixing their baselines and maritime zones given the prospect of sea level rise.

This chapter also shows that, in the context of the development of legal infrastructure, international courts and tribunals have tools at their disposal, including the doctrine of estoppel, to assess how informal instruments matter. I suggest that these tools might be less available, or that courts may be reluctant to use them, in the context of regulating human activity. In this context, international courts and tribunals, at least in environment-related cases, have found that states are to engage in certain decision-making processes, such as environmental impact assessments and exchange of information, but leave the architecture of those processes up to the states involved. In other words, international courts and tribunals, so far, have not engaged with standards that may have been adopted.[154]

The analyses conducted in this volume show that the law of the sea does not operate in isolation. First, the law of the sea is intertwined with international law more generally. The regime for the transfer of marine technology provides an example. It is difficult to imagine how this regime will move forward without changes in the law based on the TRIPS Agreement. Second, the law of the sea, especially in the context of regulating human activities, raises a number of issues that also arise in other areas of international law. The role of private actors in standard setting provides an example, as do the legitimacy concerns that arise in this context.

Finally, given the prevalence of informal instruments in the law of the sea, both historical and extant, it is safe to assume that these will continue to be part of the law of the sea in future, both in the context of developing the legal infrastructure of the law of the sea, and in regulating human activity. The impact of informal instruments will depend on context, as demonstrated in this chapter. The precise significance of informal lawmaking in the law of the sea will, therefore, vary. What remains important is understanding the different roles of informal lawmaking in ocean governance.

[154] See, eg *Request for Advisory Opinion Submitted by the Sub-Regional Fisheries Commission* (n 124) para 138. However, note that, in *Responsibilities in the Area* (n 124), paras 142–44, 149, the chamber did point to ISA regulations and recommendations that provide standards for environmental impact assessment. See also Jutta Brunnée and Ellen Hey, 'Judicial Contributions to the Development of International Environmental Law: Refining the Duty to Cooperate in Environmental Harm Prevention' (2020) 30 Yb Intl'l Env L (forthcoming in 2022).

Bibliography

Abbott KW and Snidal D, 'Hard and Soft Law in International Governance' (2000) 54(3) International Organization 421

Abbott KW and Snidal D, 'Strengthening International Regulation through Transnational New Governance' (2009) 42 Vanderbilt Journal of Transnational Law 501

Abeyratne R, 'The Deepwater Horizon Disaster—Some Liability Issues' (2010) 35 Tulane Maritime Law Journal 125

Aceves WJ, 'Diplomacy at Sea: U.S. Freedom of Navigation Operations in the Black Sea' (1993) 46(2) Naval War College Review 59

Akamangwa N, 'Regulatory Influences on Environmental Protection: Why Shipping Companies Comply and When They Don't' (2017) 48(2) Ocean Development & International Law 160

Al Arif A, 'Exploring the Legal Status and Key Features of Ecosystem-based Fisheries Management in International Fisheries Law' (2018) 27 Review of European, Comparative and International Environmental Law 320

Alava JJ, Barragán-Paladines MJ, and Denkinger J, 'Massive Chinese Fleet Jeopardizes Threatened Shark Species around the Galápagos Marine Reserve and Waters off Ecuador: Implications for National and International Fisheries Policy' (2017) 1 International Journal of Fisheries Science & Research 1001

Alford J, 'Confidence-building Measures in Europe: The Military Aspects' (1979) 149 The Adelphi Papers 4

Alvarez J, *International Organizations as Law-makers* (OUP 2006)

Alvarez JE, 'International Organizations: Then and Now' (2006) 100 American Journal of International Law 324

Amos W, 'Development of Canadian Arctic Offshore Oil and Gas Drilling: Lessons from the Gulf of Mexico' (2011) 20(1) Review of European, Comparative and International Environmental Law 39

Anderson DH, 'Resolution and Agreement Relating to the Implementation of Part XI of the UN Convention on the Law of the Sea: A General Assessment' (1995) 55 Houston Journal of International Law 275

Ardron J and others, 'The Sustainable Use and Conservation of Biodiversity in ABNJ: What can be Achieved Using Existing International Agreements?' (2014) 49 Marine Policy 98

Armeni C, 'Global Experimentalist Governance, International Law and Climate Change Technologies' (2015) 64 International & Comparative Law Quarterly 875

Armstrong C and Corbett J, 'Climate Change, Sea Level Rise, and Maritime Baselines: Responding to the Plight of Low-lying Atoll States' (2021) 21(1) Global Environmental Politics 89

Aust A, 'The Theory and Practice of Informal International Instruments' (1986) 35 International & Comparative Law Quarterly 787

Aust A, *Modern Treaty Law* (3rd edn, CUP 2013)

Bailliet CM, 'Introduction' in CM Bailliet (ed), *Non-state Actors, Soft Law and Protective Regimes: From the Margins* (CUP 2012)

Balkin RP, 'The IMO and Global Ocean Governance: Past, Present, and Future' in DJ Attard, RP Balkin, and DW Greig (eds), *The IMLI Treatise on Global Ocean Governance, Volume III: The IMO and Global Ocean Governance* (OUP 2018) 24

Barchue LD, 'The Voluntary IMO Member State Audit Scheme: An Accountability Regime for States on Maritime Affairs' (2009) 8 WMU Journal of Maritime Affairs 61

Barnes R, *Property Rights and Natural Resources* (Hart 2009)

Barrett J, 'UNCLOS: A "Living" Treaty?' in J Barrett and R Barnes (eds), *Law of the Sea: UNCLOS as a Living Treaty* (BIICL 2016) 20

Bateman S, 'Hydrographic Surveying in the EEZ: Differences and Overlaps with Marine Scientific Research' (2005) 29 Marine Policy 163

Bateman S, 'Security and the Law of the Sea in East Asia: Navigational Regimes' in D Freestone, R Barnes, and DM Ong (eds), *The Law of the Sea: Progress and Prospects* (OUP 2006)

Bax NJ and others, 'Results of Efforts by the Convention on Biological Diversity to Describe Ecologically or Biologically Significant Marine Areas' (2015) 30 Conservation Biology 571

Baxter RR, 'International Law in "Her Infinite Variety"' (1980) 29(4) International & Comparative Law Quarterly 549

Beckman R, 'The Piracy Regime under UNCLOS: Problems and Prospects for Cooperation' in RC Beckman and JA Roach (eds) *Piracy and International Maritime Crimes in ASEAN: Prospects for Cooperation* (Edward Elgar 2012) 17

Beckman R, 'Global Legal Regime on the Decommission of Offshore Installations and Structures' in MH Nordquist and others (eds), *The Regulation of Continental Shelf Development, Rethinking International Standards* (Brill 2013) 259

Bedjaoui M, *Towards a New International Economic Order* (UNESCO, Holmes & Meier Publishers 1979)

Beiter KD, 'Reductionist Intellectual Property Protection and Expansionist (and "Prodevelopment") Competition Rules as Human Rights Imperative? Enhancing Technology Transfer to the Global South' (2021) 14(1) Law and Development Review 215

Bell S and Hindmoor A, 'Governance Without Government? The Case of the Forest Stewardship Council' (2012) 90(1) Public Administration 144

Benvenisti E, 'Towards a Typology of Informal International Lawmaking Mechanisms and their Distinct Accountability Gaps' in J Pauwelyn, RA Wessel, and J Wouters (eds), *Informal International Lawmaking* (OUP 2012) 297

Beringen E, Liu N, and Lim M, 'Australia as a Middle Power: Challenging the Narrative of Developed/Developing States in International Negotiations Surrounding Marine Genetic Resources' (2021) 52(2) Ocean Development & International Law 143.

Bessona S and Martí JL, 'Legitimate Actors of International Law-making: Towards A Theory of International Democratic Representation' (2018) 9(3) Jurisprudence 504

Biermann F, Kaine N, and Kim RE, 'Global Governance by Goal-setting: The Novel Approach of the UN Sustainable Development Goals' (2017) 26 Current Opinion in Environmental Sustainability 26

Birnie P, 'The Status of Environmental "Soft Law": Trends and Examples with Special Focus on IMO Norms' in H Ringbom (ed), *Competing Norms in the Law of Marine Environmental Protection—Focus on Ship Safety and Pollution Prevention* (Kluwer Law International 1997)

Birnie P, Boyle A, and Redgwell C, *International Law and the Environment* (3rd edn, OUP 2009)

Blasiaka R and others, 'The Role of NGOs in Negotiating the Use of Biodiversity in Marine Areas beyond National Jurisdiction' (2017) 81 Marine Policy 1

Bodansky D, 'The Role of the International Court of Justice in Addressing Climate Change: Some Preliminary Reflections' (2017) 49 Arizona State Law Journal 659

Bodansky D, Brunnée J, and Rajamani L, *International Climate Change Law* (OUP 2017)

Boisson P, 'Law of Maritime Safety' in DJ Attard and others (eds), *The IMLI Manual on International Maritime Law, Volume II: Shipping Law* (OUP 2016) 180

Bonfanti A and Romanin Jacur F, 'Energy from the Sea and the Protection of the Marine Environment: Treaty-based Regimes and Ocean Corporate Social Responsibility' in N Bankes and S Trevisanut (eds), *Energy from the Sea: An International Law Perspective on Ocean Energy* (Brill 2015) 63

Bothe M, 'Legal and Non-legal Norms—A Meaningful Distinction in International Relations' (1980) 11 Netherlands Yearbook of International Law 65

Bothe M, 'Private Normunternehmer im Völkerrecht: Gedanken zur Fortentwicklung des Völkerrechts durch nicht-staatliche Institutionen' in HP Hestermeyer and others (eds), *Coexistence, Cooperation and Solidarity: Liber Amicorum Rüdiger Wolfrum, Volume II* (Brill 2012)

Botsford L and others, 'The Management of Fisheries and Ecosystems' (1997) 277 Science 509

Boucher J and Friot D, *Primary Microplastics in the Oceans: A Global Evaluation of Sources* (IUCN 2017)

Boyle A, 'Soft Law in International Law-making', in MD Evans (ed), *International Law* (5th edn, OUP 2018)

Boyle AE, 'Some Reflections on the Relationship of Treaties and Soft Law' (1999) 48(4) International & Comparative Law Quarterly 901

Bradley D and others, 'Opportunities to Improve Fisheries Management through Innovative Technology and Advanced Data Systems' (2019) 20(3) Fish and Fisheries 564

Brölmann C and Radi Y, 'Introduction: International Lawmaking in a Global World' in C Brölmann and Y Radi (eds), *Research Handbook on the Theory and Practice of International Lawmaking* (Edward Elgar 2016) 1

Brooks CM and others, 'Science-based Management in Decline in the Southern Ocean' 364(6309) (2016) Science 185, 185.

Brooks CM and others, 'Reaching Consensus for Conserving the Global Commons: The Case of the Ross Sea, Antarctica' (2020) 13(1) Conservation Letters e12676

Brunnée J, 'COPing with Consent: Law-making Under Multilateral Environmental Agreements' (2002) 15(1) Leiden Journal of International Law 1

Brunnée J and Hey E, 'Judicial Contributions to the Development of International Environmental Law: Refining the Duty to Cooperate in Environmental Harm Prevention' (2020) 30(1) Yearbook of International Environmental Law 45

Brunnée J and Toope SJ, *Legitimacy and Legality in International Law* (CUP 2010)

Bueger C, Edmunds T, and McCabe R, 'Into the Sea: Capacity-building Innovations and the Maritime Security Challenge' (2020) 41(2) Third World Quarterly 228

Burhenne-Guilmin F and Casey-Lefkowitz S, 'The Convention on Biological Diversity: A Hard Won Global Achievement' (1992) 3 Yearbook of International Environmental Law 43

Burke WT, 'Who Goes Where, When, and How: International Law of the Sea for Transportation' (1977) 31(2) International Organization 267

Buzan B, 'Negotiating by Consensus: Developments in Technique at the United Nations Conference on the Law of The Sea' (1981) 75(2) American Journal of International Law 324

Caminos H and Molitor MR, 'Progressive Development of International Law and the Package Deal' (1985) 79(4) American Journal of International Law 871

Carlini G and Kleine K, 'Advancing the International Regulation of Plastic Pollution beyond the United Nations Environment Assembly Resolution on Marine Litter and Microplastics' (2018) 27 Review of European, Comparative and International Environmental Law 234

Caron DD, 'When Law Makes Climate Change Worse: Rethinking the Law of Baselines in Light of a Rising Sea Level' (1990) 17 Ecology Law Quarterly 621

Caron DD, 'Climate Change, Sea Level Rise and the Coming Uncertainty in Oceanic Boundaries' in SY Hong and JM Van Dyke (eds), *Maritime Boundary Disputes, Settlement Processes, and the Law of the Sea* (Brill 2009)

Chalermpalanupap T, 'Review of the ASEAN–China Declaration on the Conduct of Parties in the South China Sea and Prospects of a Code of Conduct in the South China Sea' in TT Tran and TT Le (eds), *Power, Law and Maritime Order in the South China Sea* (Lexington Books 2015)

Chalk P, 'Assessing the Utility of Current Counterpiracy Initiatives off the Horn of Africa' (2012) 35 Studies in Conflict and Terrorism 553

Charney J, 'Rocks that cannot Sustain Human Habitation' (1993) 93 American Journal of International Law 863

Cheng B, 'United Nations Resolutions on Outer Space: "Instant" International Customary Law' (1965) 5 Indian Journal of International Law 23

Chetail V, *International Migration Law* (OUP 2019)

Chiba S and others, 'Human Footprint in the Abyss: 30 Year Records of Deep-sea Plastic Debris' (2018) 19 Marine Policy 204

Chinese Society of International Law, 'The South China Sea Arbitration Awards: A Critical Study' (2018) 17 Chinese Journal of International Law 207

Chinkin C, 'The Challenge of Soft Law: Development and Change in International Law' (1989) 38 International & Comparative Law Quarterly 850

Chinkin C, 'Normative Development in the International Legal System' in D Shelton (ed), *Commitment and Compliance: The Role of Non-binding Norms in the International Legal System* (OUP 2000)

Chircop A, 'The International Maritime Organization' in DR Rothwell and others (eds), *The Oxford Handbook of the Law of the Sea* (OUP 2015)

Chircop A, 'Testing International Legal Regimes: The Advent of Automated Commercial Vessels' (2017) 60 German Yearbook of International Law 1

Chircop A, and Shan D, 'Governance of International Shipping in the Era of Decarbonisation: New Challenges for the IMO?' in PK Mukherjee, MQ Mejia, and J Xu (eds), *Maritime Law in Motion* (Springer 2020)

Churchill RR and Lowe VA, *The Law of the Sea* (3rd edn, Manchester UP 1999)

Churchill RR and Ulfstein G, 'Autonomous Institutional Arrangements in Multilateral Environmental Agreements: A Little-noticed Phenomenon in International Law' (2000) 94 American Journal of International Law 623

Cobos Delgado I, 'The Role of the Classification Societies in Promoting Global Ocean Governance' in DJ Attard, RP Balkin, and DW Greig (eds), *The IMLI Treatise on Global Ocean Governance, Volume III: The IMO and Global Ocean Governance* (OUP 2018)

Cole H, 'Contemporary Challenges: Globalisation, Global Interconnectedness and that "there are *not* Plenty more Fish in the Sea": Fisheries, Governance and Globalisation: Is there a Relationship?' (2003) 46 Ocean & Coastal Management 77

Collins R, 'The M/V "Norstar" Case (*Panama v. Italy*) (ITLOS)' (2019) 58 International Legal Materials 673

Collins R and French D, 'A Guardian of Universal Interest or Increasingly Out of its Depth? The International Seabed Authority Turns 25' (2019) 17(3) International Organizations Law Review 633

Cordes EE and others, 'Environmental Impacts of the Deep-water Oil and Gas Industry: A Review to Guide Management Strategies' (2016) 4 Frontiers in Environmental Science Article 58

Correa CM, 'Innovation and Technology Transfer of Environmentally Sound Technologies: The Need to Engage in a Substantive Debate' (2013) 22(1) Review of European, Comparative and International Environmental Law 54

Cracknell AP (ed), *Remote Sensing Applications in Marine Science and Technology* (Springer 1983)

Craik N, *The International Law of Environmental Impact Assessment: Process, Substance and Integration* (CUP 2008)

Craik N, 'Biodiversity-inclusive Impact Assessment' in M Faure (ed), *Elgar Encyclopedia of Environmental Law, vol III* (Edward Elgar 2017) 431

Creutz K, 'Law versus Codes of Conduct: Between Convergence and Conflict' in J Klabbers and T Piiparinen (eds), *Normative Pluralism and International Law: Exploring Global Governance* (CUP 2013)

Cusumano E and Pattison J, 'The Non-governmental Provision of Search and Rescue in the Mediterranean and the Abdication of State Responsibility' (2018) 31(1) Cambridge Review of International Affairs 53

Dahou T, 'La Politique des Espaces Maritimes en Afrique: Louvoyer entre Local et Global' (2009) 116 Politique Africaine 5

Dalton JG, 'A Comparison between the San Remo Manual and the U.S. Navy's Commander's Handbook' (2006) 36 Israel Yearbook of Human Rights 71

D'Aspremont J, *Formalism and the Sources of International Law* (OUP 2011)

Davenport T, 'Legal Measures to Combat Piracy and Armed Robbery in the Horn of Africa and in Southeast Asia: A Comparison' (2012) 35(7–8) Studies in Conflict and Terrorism 570

Day J, Dudley N, and Hockings M (eds), *Guidelines for Applying the IUCN Protected Area Management Categories to Marine Protected Areas* (2nd edn, IUCN 2019)

de Búrca G, Keohane RO, and Sabel C, 'New Modes of Pluralist Global Governance' (2013) 45 New York University Journal of International Law and Politics 723

de Lucia V, 'The Concept of Commons and Marine Genetic Resources in Areas beyond National Jurisdiction' (2018–19) 5 Maritime Safety and Security Law Journal 1

Delimatsis P, 'Global Standard Setting 2.0: How the WTO Spotlights ISO and Impacts the Transnational Standard-setting Process' (2018) 28 Duke Journal of Comparative & International Law 273

Desjardins M-F, *Rethinking Confidence-building Measures* (Routledge 2014)

Dixon K, 'Law Of The Sea—Deep Seabed Mining—United States Position in Light of Recent Agreement and Exchange of Notes with Five Countries Involved in Preparatory Commission of United Nations Convention on the Law of the Sea' (1988) 18 Georgia Journal International & Comparative Law 497

Dixon MJ, 'Book Review: San Remo Manual on International Law Applicable to Armed Conflicts at Sea. Edited by Louise Doswald-Beck' (1997) 46 International & Comparative Law Quarterly 723

Diz D and others, 'Mainstreaming Marine Biodiversity into the SDGs: The Role of other Effective Area-based Conservation Measures (SDG 14.5)' (2018) 93 Marine Policy 251

Diz D, Morgera E, and Wilson M, 'Marine Policy Special Issue: SDG Synergies for Sustainable Fisheries and Poverty Alleviation' (2019) 110 Marine Policy 102860

Dörr O, 'Article 31' in O Dörr and K Schmalenbach (eds), *Vienna Convention on the Law of Treaties: A Commentary* (2nd edn, Springer 2018) 570

Dörr O, 'Interpretation of Treaties' in O Dörr and K Schmalenbach (eds), *Vienna Convention on the Law of Treaties: A Commentary* (2nd edn, Springer 2018) 595

Doussis E, 'Marine Scientific Research: Taking Stock and Looking Ahead' in G Andreone (ed), *The Future of the Law of the Sea: Bridging Gaps between National, Individual and Common Interests* (Springer 2017)

Doswald-Beck L, 'San Remo Manual on International Law Applicable to Armed Conflict at Sea' (1995) 309 International Review of the Red Cross 583

Doswald-Beck L, 'The San Remo Manual on International Law Applicable to Armed Conflicts at Sea' (1995) 89 American Journal of International Law 192

Dranker P, 'Marine Protected Areas in Areas beyond National Jurisdiction' (2012) 27 International Journal of Marine & Coastal Law 291

Druel E, 'Ecologically or Biologically Significant Marine Areas (EBSAs): The Identification Process under the Convention on Biological Diversity (CBD) and Possible Ways Forward' (2012) IDDRI Working Paper No 17/12

Dudley N (ed), *Guidelines for Applying Protected Area Management Categories* (IUCN 2008)

Dunn DC and others, 'The Convention on Biological Diversity's Ecologically or Biologically Significant Areas: Origins, Development and Current Status' (2014) 49 Marine Policy 137

Dunstan PK and others, 'Using Ecologically or Biologically Significant Marine Areas (EBSAs) to Implement Marine Spatial Planning' (2016) 121 Ocean & Coastal Management 116

Dupuy PM, 'Soft Law and the International Law of the Environment' (1991) 12 Michigan Journal of International Law 420

Duquet S and Geraets D, 'Food Safety Standards and Informal International Lawmaking' in A Berman and others (eds), *Informal International Lawmaking: Case Studies* (Torkel Opsahl Academic EPublisher 2012)

Duquet S and others, 'Upholding the Rule of Law in Informal International Lawmaking Processes' (2014) 6(1) Hague Journal on the Rule of Law 75

Ebbesson J, 'A Modest Contribution to Environmental Democracy and Justice in Transboundary Contexts: The Combined Impact of the Espoo Convention and the Aarhus Convention' (2011) 20 Review of European, Comparative and International Environmental Law 248

Ebers M, 'Regulating AI and Robotics: Ethical and Legal Challenges' in M Ebers and S Navas (eds), *Algorithms and Law* (CUP 2020) 97

Edeson W, 'Closing the Gap: The Role of 'Soft' International Instruments to Control Fishing' (1999) 20 Australian Yearbook of International Law 83

Edeson W, 'The International Plan of Action on IUU Fishing: The Legal Context of a Non-legally Binding Instrument' (2001) 16 International Journal of Marine & Coastal Law 603

Evriviades EL, 'Third World's Approach to the Deep Seabed' (1982) 11(3-4) Ocean Development and International Law 201

Fastenrath U, 'Relative Normativity in International Law' (1993) 4(3) European Journal of International Law 305

Feenstra R and Vervliet J, *Hugo Grotius Mare Liberum 1609–2009* (Brill 2009).

Fenwick M, Kaal WA, and Vermeulen EPM, 'Regulation Tomorrow: What Happens when Technology is Faster than the Law?' (2016) 6(3) American University Business Law Review 561

Fernández Arribas G, 'The EU–Turkey Agreement: A Controversial Attempt at Patching up a Major Problem' (2016) 1(3) European Papers 1097

Fleck D, 'Topical Approaches towards Developing the Law of Armed Conflict at Sea' in AJM Delissen and GJ Tanja (eds), *Humanitarian Law of Armed Conflict: Challenges Ahead: Essays in Honour of Frits Kalshoven* (Martinus Nijhoff 1991) 407

Føre M and others, 'Precision Fish Farming: A New Framework to Improve Production in Aquaculture' (2018) 173 Biosystems Engineering 176

Fourie AN, 'SDG 9: Build Resilient Infrastructure, Promote Inclusive and Sustainable Industrialization and Foster Innovation' in J Ebbeson and E Hey (eds), *The Handbook on the United Nations Sustainable Development Goals and International Law* (CUP forthcoming)

Francioni F, 'International "Soft Law": a Contemporary Assessment' in V Lowe and M Fitzmaurice (eds), *Fifty Years of the International Court of Justice: Essays in Honour of Sir Robert Jennings* (CUP 1996)

Freestone D, 'Canada and the EU Reach Agreement to Settle the Estai Dispute' (1995) 10(3) International Journal of Marine & Coastal Law 397

Freestone D and Killerlain Morrison K, 'The Sargasso Sea Alliance: Seeking to Protect the Sargasso Sea' (2012) 27 International Journal of Marine & Coastal Law 647

Freestone D and Bulger F, 'The Sargasso Sea Commission: An Innovative Approach to the Conservation of Areas beyond National Jurisdiction' (2016) 30 Ocean Yearbook 80.

Gallagher AT and David F, *The International Law of Migrant Smuggling* (CUP 2014)

Gallo ND, Victor DG, and Levin LA, 'Ocean Commitments under the Paris Agreement' (2017) 7 Nature Climate Change 833

Gammeltoft-Hansen T, 'The Normative Impact of the Global Compact on Refugees' (2018) 30(4) International Journal of Refugee Law 605

Gardiner R, *Treaty Interpretation* (OUP 2008)

Gaskell N, 'Decision Making and the Legal Committee of the International Maritime Organization' (2003) 18(2) International Journal of Marine & Coastal Law 162

Gerber LJ and Grogan RL, 'Challenges of Operationalizing Good Industry Practice and Best Environmental Practice in Deep Seabed Mining Regulation' (2020) 114 Marine Policy 1

Gervais D, 'The Regulation of Inchoate Technologies' (2010) 47(3) Houston Law Review 665

Gjerde KM and Rulska-Domino A, 'Marine Protected Areas beyond National Jurisdiction: Some Practical Perspectives for Moving Ahead' (2012) 27 International Journal of Marine & Coastal Law 351

Gottlieb Y, 'The Security Council's Maritime Piracy Resolutions: A Critical Assessment' (2015) 24(1) Minnesota Journal of International Law 1

Graf Vitzthum W, 'Schiffsicherheit: Die EG als potentieller Durchsetzungsdegen der IMO' (2002) 62 Heidelberg Journal of International Law 163

Gragl P, 'Marine Scientific Research' in DJ Attard, M Fitzmaurice, and NA Martinez Gutierrez (eds), *The IMLI Manual on International Maritime Law, Volume I: The Law of the Sea* (OUP 2014)

Guilfoyle D, *Shipping Interdiction and the Law of the Sea* (CUP 2009)

Guilfoyle D, 'Somali Pirates as Agents of Change in International Law-making and Organisation' (2012) 1(3) Cambridge Journal of International & Comparative Law 81

Guilfoyle D, 'Prosecuting Pirates: The Contact Group on Piracy off the Coast of Somali, Governance and International Law' (2013) 4(1) Global Policy 73

Gupta J and Vegelin C, 'Sustainable Development Goals and Inclusive Development' (2016) 16(3) International Environmental Agreements 433

Guzman A, 'A Compliance-based Theory of International Law' (2002) 90 California Law Review 1826

Guzman A, 'The Design of International Agreements' (2005) 16 EJIL 579

Hafner G, 'Pros and Cons Ensuing from Fragmentation of International Law' (2004) 25 Michigan Journal of International Law 849

Hagemann R, Huddleston Skees J, and Thierer A, 'Soft Law for Hard Problems: The Governance of Emerging Technologies in an Uncertain Future' (2018) 17(1) Colorado Technology Law Journal 37

Haines S, 'The United Kingdom's Manual of the Law of Armed Conflict and the San Remo Manual: Maritime Rules Compared' (2006) 36 Israel Yearbook of Human Rights 89

Handl GF and others, 'A Hard Look at Soft Law' (1988) 82 Proceedings of the American Society of International Law 371

Harden-Davies H, 'The Regulation of Marine Scientific Research: Addressing Challenges, Advancing Knowledge' in R Warner and S Kaye (eds), *Routledge Handbook of Maritime Regulation and Enforcement* (Routledge 2016)

Harden-Davies H and Snelgrove P, 'Science Collaboration for Capacity Building: Advancing Technology Transfer through a Treaty for Biodiversity beyond National Jurisdiction' (2020) 7 Frontiers in Marine Science 40

Harrison J, *Making the Law of the Sea: A Study on the Development of International Law* (CUP 2011)

Harrison J, *Saving the Oceans Through Law: The International Legal Framework for the Protection of the Marine Environment* (OUP 2017)

Haward M, 'Plastic Pollution of the World's Seas and Oceans as a Contemporary Challenge in Ocean Governance' (2018) 9 Nature Communications 667

Hawkins DG and others (eds), *Delegation and Agency in International Organizations* (CUP 2006)

Hayashi M, 'Registration of the First Group of Pioneer Investors by the Preparatory Commission for the International Sea-bed Authority and for the International Tribunal for the Law of the Sea' (1989) 20(1) Ocean Development & International Law 1

Heffner K and Rødseth ØJ, 'Enabling Technologies for Maritime Autonomous Surface Ships' (2019) 1357 Journal of Physics: Conference Series 1

Henry C and Stiglitz JE, 'Intellectual Property, Dissemination of Innovation and Sustainable Development' (2010) 1(3) Global Policy 237

Henry CE, *The Carriage of Dangerous Goods by Sea: The Role of the International Maritime Organization in International Legislation* (Frances Pinter 1985)

Hewison GJ, 'The Legally Binding Nature of the Moratorium on Large Scale High Seas Driftnet Fishing' (1994) 25(4) Journal of Maritime Law & Commerce 557

Hey E, 'Regime Interaction and Common Interests in Regulating Human Activities in Areas beyond National Jurisdiction' in S Trevisanut, N Giannopoulos, and RR Holst (eds), Regime Interaction in Ocean Governance (Brill Nijhoff 2020)

Higgins R, *Problems & Process: International Law and how we Use it* (Clarendon Press 1994)

Holst JJ, 'Confidence-building Measures: A Conceptual Framework' (1983) 25 Survival 2

Horta e Costa B and others, 'A Regulation-based Classification System for Marine Protected Areas (MPAs)' (2016) 72 Marine Policy 192

Houck JW and Anderson NM, 'The United States, China, and Freedom of Navigation in the South China Sea' (2014) 13 Washington University Global Studies Law Review 441

Houghton MC, 'Walking the Plank: How United Nations Security Council Resolution 1816, While Progressive, Fails to Provide a Comprehensive Solution to Somali Piracy' (2009) 16 Tulsa Journal of Comparative & International Law 253

Huh C, 'Working with the Private Sector' in T Tardy (ed), *Fighting Piracy off the Coast of Somalia: Lessons Learned from the Contact Group* (EU Institute for Security Studies 2014) 41

ICRC, *Commentary on the Second Geneva Convention: Convention (II) for the Amelioration of the Condition of Wounded, Sick and Shipwrecked Members of Armed Forces at Sea* (CUP 2017)

Jabour J and Smith D, 'The Ross Sea Region Marine Protected Area: Can it be Successfully Managed?' (2018) 32 Ocean Yearbook 190

Jacobsson M, 'Maritime Security: An Individual or Collective Responsibility?' in J Petman and J Klabbers (eds), *Nordic Cosmopolitanism: Essays in International Law for Martti Koskenniemi* (Brill 2003)

Jacobsson M, 'International Legal Cooperation to Combat Piracy in the Horn of Africa' in RC Beckman and JA Roach (eds), *Piracy and International Maritime Crimes in ASEAN: Prospects for Co-operation* (Edward Elgar 2012)

Jacobsson M, 'What Challenges Lie Ahead for Maritime Law?' in PK Mukherjee, MQ Mejia, and J Xu (eds), *Maritime Law in Motion* (Springer 2020)

Jaeckel, AL, *The International Seabed Authority and the Precautionary Principle: Balancing Deep Seabed Mineral Mining and Marine Environmental Protection* (Brill 2017)

Jaeckel A, 'Strategic Environmental Planning for Deep Seabed Mining in the Area' (2020) 114 Marine Policy 103423

Jambeck JR, 'Plastic Waste Inputs from Land into the Ocean' (2015) 6223 Science 347

Jamieson AJ and others, 'Microplastics and Synthetic Particles Ingested by Deep-sea Amphipods in Six of the Deepest Marine Ecosystems on Earth' (2019) 6 Royal Society Open Science 180667

Jensen Ø, 'The International Code for Ships Operating in Polar Waters: Finalization, Adoption and Law of the Sea Implications' (2016) 7(1) Arctic Review on Law and Politics 82

Ji G, 'Rough Waters in the South China Sea: Navigation Issues and Confidence-building Measures' (2001) 53 Asia Pacific Issues 1

Johnstone RL, *Offshore Oil and Gas Development in the Arctic Under International Law: Risk and Responsibility* (Brill 2015)

Joyner CC and Martell EA, 'Looking Back to See Ahead: UNCLOS III and Lessons for Global Commons Law' (1996) 27(1-2) Ocean Development & International Law 73

Juda L, 'UNCLOS III and the New International Economic Order' (1979) 7(3-4) Ocean Development & International Law 221

Karavias M, *Corporate Obligations under International Law* (OUP 2013)

Karavias M, 'Interactions between International Law and Private Fisheries Certification' (2017) 7(1) Transnational Environmental Law 165

Kaye S, 'International Measures to Protect Oil Platforms, Pipelines, and Submarine Cables from Attack' (2006–2007) 31 Tulane Maritime Law Journal 377

Kaye S, 'The Law of the Sea Convention and Sea Level Rise after the *South China Sea Arbitration*' [2017] 93 *International Law Studies Series, US Naval War College* 423

Keohane RO and Victor DG, 'The Regime Complex for Climate Change' (2011) 9 Perspectives on Politics 7

Khanna T, 'The Normative Role of the International Maritime Organisation in Countering Somali-based Piracy' (2019) 15(1) Maritime Affairs 51

Kirgis FL, 'Shipping' in O Schachter and CC Joyner (eds), *United Nations Legal Order, vol 2* (CUP 1995)

Kirgis FL, 'Specialized Law-making Processes' in O Schachter and CC Joyner (eds), *United Nations Legal Order, vol 1* (CUP 1995)

Klabbers J, 'The Redundancy of Soft Law' (1996) 65 Nordic Journal of International Law 167

Klabbers J, 'International Courts and Informal International Law' in J Pauwelyn, RA Wessel, and J Wouters (eds), *Informal International Lawmaking* (OUP 2012)

Klabbers J, *Introduction to International Institutional Law* (CUP 2012)

Koivurova T, 'Could the Espoo Convention become a Global Regime for Environmental Impact Assessment and Strategic Environmental Assessment?' in R Warner and S Marsden (eds), *Transboundary Environmental Governance: Inland, Coastal and Marine Perspectives* (Ashgate 2012) 326

Kolb R, *The Law of Treaties* (Edward Elgar 2016)

Korseberg L, 'The Law-making Effects of the FAO Deep-sea Fisheries Guidelines' (2018) 67(4) International & Comparative Law Quarterly 801

Kraska J, 'Military Operations' in DR Rothwell and others (eds), *The Oxford Handbook of the Law of the Sea* (OUP 2015) 866

Kraska J, 'Maritime Confidence-building Measures for Navigation in the South China Sea' (2017) 32 International Journal of Marine & Coastal Law 268

Kraska J and Pedrozo R, *International Maritime Security Law* (Brill 2013)

Kysar D, 'Climate Change and the International Court of Justice' *Yale Law School Public Law Research Paper No 315* (15 August 2013)

Laffoley D and others, 'An Introduction to "Other Effective Area-based Conservation Measures" under Aichi Target 11 of the Convention on Biological Diversity: Origin, Interpretation and Emerging Ocean Issues' (2017) 27(S1) Aquatic Conservation: Marine and Freshwater Ecosystems 130

Lagoni R, 'Offshore Bunkering in the Exclusive Economic Zone' in TM Ndiaye and R Wolfrum (eds), *Law of the Sea, Environmental Law and Settlement of Disputes* (Martinus Nijhoff 2007) 613

Lampe WH, 'The "New" International Maritime Organization and its Place in the Development of International Maritime Law' (1983) 14(3) Journal of Maritime Law & Commerce 305

Larson DL, 'The Reagan Administration and the Law of the Sea' (1982) 11(3-4) Ocean Development & International Law 297

Lefebvre-Chalain H, *La Stratégie Normative de l'Organisation Maritime Internationale (OMI)* (Presses Universitaires d'Aix-Marseille 2012)

Librando G, 'The International Maritime Organization and the Law of the Sea' in DJ Attard, M Fitzmaurice, and NA Martínez Gutiérrez (eds), *The IMLI Manual on International Maritime Law, Volume I: The Law of the Sea* (OUP 2014)

Liisberg JB, 'The Legal Aspects of Counter Piracy' in T Tardy (ed), *Fighting Piracy off the Coast of Somalia: Lessons Learned from the Contact Group* (EU Institute for Security Studies 2014)

Lijnzaad L, 'Het Haagsche Zeeoorlogsrecht van 1907 Vandaag (The 1907 Hague Law of Naval Warfare Today)' in Oude verdragen in een nieuwe tijd, honderd jaar Haagse vredesconferentie van 1907 (Old treaties in a new era, one hundred years since the Hague Peace Conference of 1907), Mededelingen van de Nederlandse Vereniging voor Internationaal Recht, deel 135 (2007) 99

Linderfalk U, *On the Interpretation of Treaties* (Springer 2007)

Lipson C, 'Why are some International Agreements Informal?' (1991) 45 International Organization 495

Liu D, 'Autonomous Vessel Technology, Safety, and Ocean Impact' in D Werle and others (eds), *The Future of Ocean Governance and Capacity Development: Essays in Honor of Elisabeth Mann Borgese (1918–2002)* (Brill Nijhoff 2018)

Lodge M, 'The Deep Seabed' in DR Rothwell and others (eds), *The Oxford Handbook of the Law of the Sea* (OUP 2014)

Lodge M and others, 'Seabed Mining: International Seabed Authority Environmental Management Plan for the Clarion-Clipperton Zone. A Partnership Approach' (2014) 49 Marine Policy 66

Lost-Sieminska D, 'The International Maritime Organization' in M Bowman and D Kritsiotis (eds), *Conceptual and Contextual Perspectives on the Modern Law of Treaties* (CUP 2018) 909

Lowe V and Tzanakopoulos A, 'The Development of the Law of the Sea by the International Court of Justice' in CJ Tams and J Sloan (eds), *The Development of International Law by the International Court of Justice* (OUP 2013)

Lukin VV, 'Russia's Current Antarctic Policy' (2014) 4 The Polar Journal 199

Lyons Y, 'Transboundary Pollution from Offshore Oil and Gas Activities in the Seas of Southeast Asia' in R Warner and S Marsden (eds), *Transboundary Environmental Governance: Inland, Coastal and Marine Perspectives* (Ashgate 2012) 167

Lyons Y, 'The New Offshore Oil and Gas Installations Abandonment Wave and the International Rules on Removal and Dumping' (2014) 29 International Journal of Marine & Coastal Law 480

Mace MJ and Verheyen R, 'Loss, Damage and Responsibility after COP21: All Options Open for the Paris Agreement' (2016) 25 Review of European, Comparative and International Environmental Law 197

Malde K and others, 'Machine Intelligence and the Data-driven Future of Marine Science' (2019) 77(4) ICES Journal of Marine Science 1274

Mallia P, *Migrant Smuggling by Sea: Combating a Current Threat to Maritime Security through the Creation of a Cooperative Framework* (Martinus Nijhoff 2010)

Mann Borgese E, 'A Constitution for the Oceans' in E Mann Borgese and D Krieger (eds), *The Tides of Change: Peace, Pollution and the Potential of the Oceans* (Mason/ Charter 1975)

Marchant GE, 'Addressing the Pacing Problem' in GE Marchant, BR Allenby, and JR Herkert (eds), *The Growing Gap between Emerging Technologies and Legal-ethical Oversight: The Pacing Problem* (Springer 2011)

Marchant GE, 'The Growing Gap between Emerging Technologies and the Law' in GE Marchant, BR Allenby, and JR Herkert (eds), *The Growing Gap between Emerging Technologies and Legal-ethical Oversight: The Pacing Problem* (Springer 2011)

Marchant GE, Abbott KW, and Allenby B (eds), *Innovative Governance Models for Emerging Technologies* (Edward Elgar 2013)

Marchant GE, Allenby BR, and Herkert JR (eds), *The Growing Gap between Emerging Technologies and Legal-ethical Oversight: The Pacing Problem* (Springer 2011)

Mason SJA and Siegfried M, 'Confidence Building Measures (CBMs) in Peace Processes' in *Managing Peace Processes: Process Related Questions. A Handbook for AU Practitioners* (African Union and the Centre for Humanitarian Dialogue 2013) 58

Matz-Lück N, 'Framework Conventions as a Regulatory Tool' (2009) 1(3) Goettingen Journal of International Law 439

Matz-Lück N, 'Article 238: Right to Conduct Marine Scientific Research' in A Proelss (ed), *United Nations Convention on the Law of the Sea: A Commentary* (Beck Hart Nomos 2017)

McCorquodale R, 'The Individual and the International Legal System' in MD Evans (ed), *International Law* (5th edn, OUP 2018)

McDorman TL, 'Regional Port State Control Agreements: Some Issues of International Law' (2000) 5(2) Ocean Development & International Law 207

Mensah TA and Zimmerli CH, 'L'activité réglementaire de l'O.M.C.I.' in Société Française pour le Droit International (ed), *L'Élaboration du Droit International Public* (Éditions A Pedone 1975)

Menzel A, 'Institutional Adoption and Maritime Crime Governance: The Djibouti Code of Conduct' (2018) 14(2) Journal of the Indian Ocean Region 152

Miles C, 'The MV "Norstar" Case (*Panama v. Italy*)' (2020) 114 American Journal of International Law 116

Miles E, 'The Structure and Effects of the Decision Process in the Seabed Committee and the Third United Nations Conference on The Law of the Sea' (1977) 31(2) International Organization 159

Miller MB, *Europe and the Maritime World: A Twentieth-century History* (CUP 2012)

Mitropoulos EE, 'IMO: 60 Years in the Service of Shipping' in NA Martínez Gutiérrez (ed), *Serving the Rule of International Maritime Law: Essays in Honour of Professor David Joseph Attard* (Routledge 2009)

Mitroussi K, 'Quality in Shipping: IMO's Role and Problems of Implementation' (2004) 13(1) Disaster Prevention and Management 53

Möller L, 'UN Law on Decommissioning Offshore Installations' in M Hammerson (ed), *Oil and Gas Decommissioning* (Global Business Publishing 2013) 33

Moore C, 'The Arbitral Award in the Matter of the South China Sea between the Philippines and China: What are the Implications for Freedom of Navigation and the Use of Force?' (2017) 2 Asia-Pacific Journal of Ocean Law and Policy 117

Moore C, *Freedom of Navigation and the Law of the Sea: Warships, States and the Use of Force* (Routledge 2021)

Moore G, 'The Code of Conduct on Responsible Fisheries' in E Hey (ed), *Developments in International Fisheries Law* (Kluger Law International 1999)

Morales-Caselles C and others, 'An Inshore-offshore Sorting System Revealed from Global Classification of Ocean Litter' (2021) 4 Nature Sustainability 484

Moreno-Lax V, Ghezelbash D, and Klein N, 'Between Life, Security and Rights: Framing the Interdiction of "Boat Migrants" in the Central Mediterranean and Australia' (2019) 32(4) Leiden Journal of International Law 715

Moreno-Lax V and Papastavridis E (eds), *'Boat Refugees' and Migrants at Sea: A Comprehensive Approach* (Brill 2017)

Morgera E and Ntona M, 'Linking Small-scale Fishers to International Obligations on Marine Technology Transfer' (2018) 93 Marine Policy 295

Mossop J, 'The Legal Framework for the Regulation of Safety and Environmental Issues on the Outer Continental Shelf' in MH Nordquist and others (eds), *The Regulation of Continental Shelf Development, Rethinking International Standards* (Brill 2013) 187

Muir L and Klein N, 'From IPOA Sharks to Sharks MoU under the Convention on Migratory Species: Progress or Clutter in International Environmental Law?' (2018) 21 International Journal of Wildlife Law and Policy 190

Mukherjee PK and Brownrigg M, *Farthing on International Shipping* (4th edn, Springer 2013)

Nagle TJ, 'The Dangerous Military Activities Agreement: Minimum Order and Superpower Relations on the World's Oceans Note' (1990) 31 Virginia Journal of International Law 125

Nanz P and Dingwerth K, 'Participation' in J Katz Cogan, I Hurd, and I Johnstone (eds), *The Oxford Handbook of International Organizations* (OUP 2016)

Nelson LDM, 'The Patrimonial Sea' (1973) 22(4) International & Comparative Law Quarterly 668

Nicoll R and Day JC, 'Correct Application of the IUCN Protected Area Management Categories to the CCAMLR Convention Area' (2017) 77 Marine Policy 9

Nollkaemper A, 'The Distinction between Non-legal and Legal Norms in International Affairs: An Analysis with Reference to International Policy for the Protection of the North Sea from Hazardous Substances' (1998) 13(3) International Journal of Marine & Coastal Law 355

Nolte G, 'Part 5: Reports for the ILC Study Group on Treaties over Time, Report 3: Subsequent Agreements and Subsequent Practice of States Outside of Judicial and Quasi-judicial Proceedings' in G Nolte (ed), *Treaties and Subsequent Practice* (OUP 2013)

Okere O, 'The Technique of International Maritime Legislation' (1981) 30 International & Comparative Law Quarterly 513

O'Leary B and others, 'The First Network of Marine Protected Areas (MPAs) in the High Seas: The Process, the Challenges and where Next' (2012) 36 Marine Policy 598

Oral N, 'Ocean Acidification: Falling between the Legal Cracks of UNCLOS and the UNFCCC' (2018) 45(1) Ecology Law Quarterly 9

Oude Elferink A, 'The *Arctic Sunrise* Incident: A Multi-faceted Law of the Sea Case with a Human Rights Dimension' (2014) 29 International Journal of Marine & Coastal Law 244

Overdevest C and Zeitlin J, 'Assembling an Experimentalist Regime: Transnational Governance Interactions in the Forest Sector' (2014) 8 Regulation & Governance 22

Oxman B, 'The Duty to Respect Generally Accepted International Standards' (1991–1992) 24 NYU Journal of International Law & Policy 109

Padwa DJ, 'The Curriculum of IMCO' (1960) 14(4) International Organization 524

Palma M, Tsamenyi M, and Edeson W, *Promoting Sustainable Fisheries: The International Legal and Policy Framework to Combat Illegal Unreported and Unregulated Fishing* (Martinus Nijhoff 2010)

Pauwelyn J, 'Informal International Lawmaking: Framing the Concept and Research Questions' in J Pauwelyn, RA Wessel, and J Wouters (eds), *Informal International Lawmaking* (OUP 2012)

Pauwelyn J, Wessel R, and Wouters J, 'Informal International Lawmaking: An Assessment and Template to Keep it both Effective and Accountable' in J Pauwelyn, RA Wessel, and J Wouters (eds), *Informal International Lawmaking* (OUP 2012)

Pauwelyn J, Wessel RA, and Wouters J, 'When Structures become Shackles: Stagnation and Dynamics in International Lawmaking' (2014) 25(3) European Journal of International Law 733

Pedrozo P, 'The US–China Incidents at Sea Agreement: A Recipe for Disaster' (2012) 6 Journal of National Security Law and Policy 207

Peschmann J and others, 'IACS Common Structural Rules as an Element of IMO Goal Based Standards for Bulk Carriers and Oil Tankers' in C G Soares and Y Garbatov (eds), *Progress in the Analysis and Design of Marine Structures* (Routledge 2017)

Peters A, 'The Refinement of International Law: From Fragmentation to Regime Interaction and Politicization' (2017) 15(3) ICON 671

Peters A and others, *Non-state Actors as Standard Setters* (CUP 2009)

Petrig A, 'The Use of Force and Firearms by Private Maritime Security Companies against Suspected Pirates' (2013) 62(3) International & Comparative Law Quarterly 667

Petrig A, 'Democratic Participation in International Lawmaking in Switzerland after the "Age of Treaties"' in HP Aust and T Kleinlein (eds), *Encounters between Foreign Relations Law and International Law: Bridges and Boundaries* (CUP 2021)

Petrig A and Geiß R, *Piracy and Armed Robbery at Sea: The Legal Framework for Counter-piracy Operations in Somalia and the Gulf of Aden* (OUP 2011)

Pineschi L, 'The Duty of Environmental Impact Assessment in the First ITLOS Chamber's Advisory Opinion: Towards the Supremacy of the General Rule to Protect and Preserve the Marine Environment as a Common Value?' in N Boschiero and others (eds), *International Courts and the Development of International Law: Essays in Honour of Tullio Treves* (Springer 2013)

Pollack MA and Shaffer GC, 'The Interaction of Formal and Informal Lawmaking' in J Pauwelyn, RA Wessel, and J Wouters (eds), *Informal International Lawmaking* (OUP 2012)

Popp A, 'The Treaty-making Work of the Legal Committee of the IMO' in A Chircop and others (eds), *The Regulation of International Shipping: International and Comparative Perspectives: Essays in Honor of Edgar Gold* (Brill 2012)

Proelss A, 'Article 60: Artificial Islands, Installations and Structures in the Exclusive Economic Zone' in A Proelss (ed), *United Nations Convention on the Law of the Sea: A Commentary* (Beck Hart Nomos 2017)

Psaraftis HN and Kontovas CA, 'Influence and Transparency at the IMO: The Name of the Game' (2020) 22 Maritime Economics and Logistics 151

Ranganathan S, 'Global Commons' (2016) 27(3) European Journal of International Law 693

Ranganathan S, 'Decolonization and International Law: Putting the Ocean on the Map' (2021) 23(1) Journal of the History of International Law 161

Raubenheimer K and others, 'Towards an Improved International Framework to Govern the Life Cycle of Plastics' (2018) 27 Review of European, Comparative and International Environmental Law 210

Raustiala K, 'Form and Substance in International Agreements' (2005) 99 American Journal of International Law 581

Raustiala K and Victor DG, 'The Regime Complex for Plant Genetic Resources' (2004) 58 International Organization 277

Rayfuse R, *Non-flag State Enforcement in High Seas Fisheries* (Martinus Nijhoff 2004)

Rayfuse R, 'The Anthropocene, Autopoiesis and the Disingenuousness of the Genuine Link: Addressing Enforcement Gaps in the Legal Regime for Areas beyond National Jurisdiction' (2009) UNSW Law Research Paper No 2009-2

Rayfuse R, 'Crossing the Sectoral Divide: Modern Environmental Law Tools for Addressing Conflicting Uses on the Seabed' in C Banet (ed), *The Law of the Seabed* (Brill 2020)

Redgwell C, 'Mind the Gap in the GAIRS: The Role of Other Instruments in LOSC Regime Implementation in the Offshore Energy Sector' in N Bankes and S Trevisanut (eds), *Energy from the Sea: An International Law Perspective on Ocean Energy* (Brill 2015) 40

Reisman WM, 'Soft Law and Law Jobs' (2011) 2(1) Journal of International Dispute Settlement 25

Ribeiro MC, 'South Atlantic Perspectives on the Future International Legally Binding Instrument under the LOSC on Conservation and Sustainable Use of BBNJ' (2017) 32 International Journal of Marine & Coastal Law 733

Ringbom H, *The EU Maritime Safety Policy and International Law* (Martinus Nijhoff 2008)

Ringbom H, 'Legalizing Autonomous Ships' (2020) 34 Ocean Yearbook 431

Ringbom H, 'Developments, Challenges, and Prospects at the IMO' in H Ringbom, E Røsæg, and T Solvang (eds), *Autonomous Ships and the Law* (Routledge 2021)

Ringbom H, Røsæg E, and Solvang T, 'Introduction' in H Ringbom, E Røsæg, and T Solvang (eds), *Autonomous Ships and the Law* (Routledge 2021)

Roach JA, 'The Law of Naval Warfare at the Turn of Two Centuries' (2000) 94 American Journal of International Law 64

Roach JA, 'International Standards for Offshore Drilling' in MH Nordquist and others (eds), *The Regulation of Continental Shelf Development, Rethinking International Standards* (Brill 2013) 105

Roach JA, 'IMO Policies and Actions Regarding Piracy' in DD Caron and N Oral (eds), *Navigating Straits: Challenges for International Law* (Brill Nijhoff 2014)

Röben V, 'Conference (Meeting) of States Parties', *Max Planck Encyclopedia of Public International Law* <www.mpepil.com>

Roberts A and Sivakumaran S, 'The Theory and Reality of the Sources of International Law' in M D Evans (ed), *International Law* (5th edn, OUP 2018) 89

Roberts J, Chircop A, and Prior S, 'Area-based Management on the High Seas: Possible Application of the IMO's Particularly Sensitive Sea Area Concept' (2010) 25 International Journal of Marine & Coastal Law 483

Romanin Jacur F, *The Dynamics of Multilateral Environmental Agreements, Institutional Architectures and Law-making Processes* (Editorial Scientifica 2013) 161

Ronzitti N, 'The Crisis of the Traditional Law Regulating International Armed Conflict at Sea and the Need for Its Revision' in N Ronzitti (ed), *The Law of Naval Warfare: A Collection of Agreements and Documents with Commentaries* (Martinus Nijhoff 1988) 1

Ronzitti N (ed), *The Law of Naval Warfare: A Collection of Agreements and Documents with Commentaries* (Martinus Nijhoff 1988)

Rothwell DR and Stephens T, *The International Law of the Sea* (2nd edn, Bloomsbury 2016)

Rueda-Roa DT, Ezer T, and Muller-Karger FE, 'Description and Mechanisms of the Mid-year Upwelling in the Southern Caribbean Sea from Remote Sensing and Local Data' (2018) 6(2) Journal of Marine Science & Engineering 36

Ryngaert C and Ringbom H, 'Introduction: Port State Jurisdiction: Challenges and Potential' (2016) 31(3) International Journal of Marine & Coastal Law 379

Sabel CF and Zeitlin J, 'Learning from Difference: The New Architecture of Experimentalist Governance in the EU' (2008) 14 European Law Journal 271

Sainlos JC, 'The International Maritime Organization and the Protection of the Marine Environment' in D Vidas and PJ Schei (eds), *The World Ocean in Globalisation: Climate Change, Sustainable Fisheries, Biodiversity, Shipping, Regional Issues* (Brill 2011) 324

Sands P and Peel J, *Principles of International Environmental Law* (4th edn, CUP 2018) 63

Schachter O, 'The Twilight Existence of Nonbinding International Agreements' (1977) 71(2) American Journal of International Law 296

Schermers HG and Blokker NM, *International Institutional Law: Unity within Diversity* (5th edn, Martinus Nijhoff 2011)

Schiano di Pepe L, 'Offshore Oil and Gas in the Mediterranean Sea: Regulatory Gaps, Recent Developments and Future Perspective' in J Juste Ruiz and V Bou French (eds), *Derecho del Mar y Sostenibilidad en El Mediterraneo* (Tirant 2014) 361

Schindler D and Toman J, *The Laws of Armed Conflicts: A Collection of Conventions, Resolutions, and other Documents* (Martinus Nijhoff 1988)

Schofield C, 'The Trouble with Islands: The Definition and Role of Islands and Rocks in Maritime Boundary Delimitation' in SY Hong and JM Van Dyke (eds), *Maritime Boundary Disputes, Settlement Processes, and the Law of the Sea* (Brill 2009) 19

Schofield C and Freestone D, 'Islands Awash amidst Rising Seas: Sea Level Rise and Insular Status under the Law of the Sea' (2019) 34(3) International Journal of Marine & Coastal Law 391

Scholte JA, 'Conclusion' in JA Scholte (ed), *Building Global Democracy? Civil Society and Accountable Global Governance* (CUP 2011)

Schreurer C, 'Recommendations and the Traditional Sources of International Law' (1977) 20 German Yearbook of International Law 103

Scott KN, 'Drilling at the Poles; Environmental Protection in the Antarctic and the Arctic' in M Fitzmaurice, DM Ong, and P Merkouris (eds), *Research Handbook on International Environmental Law* (Edward Elgar 2010) 654

Scott KN, 'Conservation on the High Seas: Developing the Concept of the High Seas Marine Protected Area' (2012) 27 International Journal of Marine & Coastal Law 849

Scott KN, 'Marine Protected Areas in the Southern Ocean' in A Oude Elferink, E Molenaar, and DR Rothwell (eds), *The Law of the Sea and Polar Regions: Interaction between Global and Regional Regimes* (Martinus Nijhoff 2013)

Scott KN, 'Protecting the Commons in the Polar South: Progress and Prospects for Marine Protected Areas in the Antarctic' in K Zou (ed), *Global Commons and the Law of the Sea* (Brill Nijhoff 2018)

Scott KN, 'Climate Change and the Law of the Sea in the Asia Pacific' in DR Rothwell and D Letts (eds), *Law of the Sea in South East Asia: Environmental, Navigational and Security Challenges* (Routledge 2020)

Scott KN, 'MPAs in the Southern Ocean under CCAMLR: Implementing SDG 14.5' (2021) 9(1) Korean Journal of International & Comparative Law 84.

Scott KN and others, 'An Introduction to International Environmental Law' in E Techera and others (eds), *Routledge Handbook of International Environmental Law* (2nd edn, Routledge 2021)

Scovazzi T, 'Marine Protected Areas on the High Seas: Some Legal and Policy Considerations' (2004) 19 International Journal of Marine & Coastal Law 1

Senden L, *Soft Law in European Community Law* (Hart 2004)

Shaffer GC and Pollack MA, 'Hard vs. Soft Law: Alternatives, Complements, and Antagonists in International Governance' (2010) 94 Minnesota Law Review 706

Shaffer GC and Pollack MA, 'Hard versus Soft Law in International Security' (2012) 52(4) Boston College Law Review 1147

Shaw MN, *International Law* (8th edn, CUP 2017)

Shelton D (ed), *Commitment and Compliance: The Role of Non-binding Norms in the International Legal System* (OUP 2000)

Shelton D, 'Soft Law' in D Armstrong (ed), *Routledge Handbook of International Law* (Routledge 2009)

Shugurova IV and Shugurov MV, 'International Technology Transfer' (2015) 45(3-4) Environmental Policy and Law 133

Silos JM and others, 'The Role of the Classification Societies in the Era of Globalization: A Case Study' (2013) 40(4) Maritime Policy & Management 384

Simon SW, 'Conflict and Diplomacy in the South China Sea' (2012) 52 Asian Survey 995

Smeele F, 'Switching Off Regulatory Requirements: Flag State Exemptions as a Tool to Facilitate Experiments with Highly Automated Vessels and their Operational Implementation' in H Ringbom, E Røsæg, and T Solvang (eds), *Autonomous Ships and the Law* (Routledge 2021)

Sodik DM, 'Non-legally Binding International Fisheries Instruments and Measures to Combat Illegal, Unreported and Unregulated Fishing' (2008) 15 Australian International Law Journal 129

Song Y-H, 'The Declaration on the Conduct of Parties and a Code of Conduct in the South China Sea: Recent Actions Taken by ASEAN' in S Lee and HE Lee (eds), *Northeast Asian Perspectives on International Law: Contemporary Issues and Challenges* (Brill 2013)

Soons AHA, 'The Effects of a Rising Sea Level on Maritime Limits and Boundaries' (1990) 37 Netherlands International Law Review 207

Staff H, 'The Emergence of Private Security Governance. Assessing Facilitating Conditions in the Case of Somali Piracy' (2017) 29(1) Global Change, Peace & Security 21

Stephens T and Rothwell DR, 'Marine Scientific Research' in DR Rothwell and others (eds), *The Oxford Handbook of the Law of the Sea* (OUP 2015)

Stevenson JR and Oxman B, 'The Third United Nations Conference on the Law of the Sea: the 1974 Caracas Session' (1975) 69 American Journal of International Law 1

Stewart R, *Remedying Disregard in Global Regulatory Governance: Participation and Responsiveness* (2014) 108(2) American Journal of International Law 211

Streck C, Keenlyside P, and von Unger M, 'The Paris Agreement: A New Beginning' (2016) 13(1) Journal for European Environmental & Planning Law 3

Struett MJ, Nance MT, and Armstrong D, 'Navigating the Maritime Piracy Regime Complex' (2013) 19(1) Global Governance 93

Svanberg K, 'The Use of Private Maritime Guards as an Innovative Means to Fulfil States' Duty to Cooperate in the Repression of Maritime Piracy: Part 1' (2020) 1(2) International Journal of Maritime Crime & Security 31

Swarttouw H and Hopkins DL, 'The Contact Group on Piracy off the Coast of Somalia: Genesis, Rationale and Objectives' in T Tardy (ed), *Fighting Piracy off the Coast of Somalia: Lessons Learned from the Contact Group* (EU Institute for Security Studies 2014)

Tanaka Y, *The International Law of the Sea* (2nd edn, CUP 2015)

Tardy T, 'Introduction' in T Tardy (ed), *Fighting Piracy off the Coast of Somalia: Lessons Learned from the Contact Group* (EU Institute for Security Studies 2014)

Techera E, 'Is Environmental Law Keeping Pace with Innovation?' (2019) 34(1) Australian Environment Review 8

Techera EJ and Klein N, *The International Law of Sharks* (Brill 2017)

Teclaff LA, 'Jurisdiction over Offshore Fisheries—How Far into the High Seas' (1967) 35 Fordham Law Review 409

Testa D, 'Coastal State Regulation of Bunkering and Ship-to-ship (STS) Oil Transfer Operations in the EEZ: An Analysis of State Practice and of Coastal State Jurisdiction under the LOSC' (2019) 50 Ocean Development & International Law 363

Thayer CA, 'ASEAN, China and the Code of Conduct in the South China Sea' (2013) 33 SAIS Review of International Affairs 75

Thayer CA, 'South China Sea Tensions: China, the Claimant States, ASEAN and the Major Powers' in TT Tran and TT Le (eds), *Power, Law and Maritime Order in the South China Sea* (Lexington Books 2015)

Thevenon F and others (eds), *Plastic Debris in the Ocean: The Characterization of Marine Plastics and their Environmental Impacts, Situation Analysis Report* (IUCN 2014)

Thirlway HWA, *The Sources of International Law* (OUP 2014)

tho Pesch S, 'Coastal State Jurisdiction around Installations: Safety Zones in the Law of the Sea' (2015) 30 International Journal of Marine & Coastal Law 512

Ton AD, 'Code for Unplanned Encounters at Sea and its Practical Limitations in the East and South China Seas' (2017) 9 Australian Journal of Maritime & Ocean Affairs 227

Tønnesson S, 'The 2002 Declaration on the Conduct of the Parties in the South China Sea: Why has it not Brought more Peace and Cooperation?' in TT Tran and TT Le (eds), *Power, Law and Maritime Order in the South China Sea* (Lexington Books 2015)

Tran TT, 'Code of Conduct and the Prevention and Management of Incidents in the South China Sea' in TT Tran and TT Le (eds), *Power, Law and Maritime Order in the South China Sea* (Lexington Books 2015)

Treves T, 'Customary International Law', in *Max Planck Encyclopaedia of Public International Law* (2006)

Treves T, 'Marine Scientific Research', in *Max Planck Encyclopedia of Public International Law* (2012)

Trevisanut S, 'La Convention des Nations Unies sur le Droit de la Mer et le Droit de l'Environnement: Développement Intrasystémique et Renvoi Intersystémique' in H Ruiz Fabri and L Gradoni (eds), *La Circulation des Concepts Juridiques: Le Droit International de l'Environnement entre Mondialisation et Fragmentation* (Societé de Legislation Comparée 2009) 416

Trevisanut S, 'The Role of Private Actors in the Offshore Energy Industry' (2014) 29 International Journal of Marine & Coastal Law 645

Ulfstein G, 'Treaty Bodies' in D Bodansky, J Brunée, and E Hey (eds), *The Oxford Handbook of International Environmental Law* (OUP 2007) 877

Van Dyke JM and Brooks RA, 'Uninhabited Islands: Their Impact on the Ownership of the Oceans' Resources' (1983) 12 Ocean Development & International Law 265

van Nifterik G and Nijman J, 'Mare Liberum Revisited (1609–2009)' (2009) 30 Grotiana 3

Veal R and Tsimplis M, 'The Integration of Unmanned Ships into the Lex Maritima' (2017) 2017 Lloyd's Maritime and Commercial Law Quarterly 303

Ventura VAMF, 'Tackling Illegal, Unregulated and Unreported Fishing: The ITLOS Advisory Opinion on Flag State Responsibility for IUU Fishing and the Principle of Due Diligence' (2015) 12 Brazilian Journal of International Law 50

Venzke I, 'Contemporary Theories and International Lawmaking' in C Brolmann and Y Radi (eds), *Research Handbook on the Theory and Practice of International Lawmaking* (Edward Elgar 2016) 66

Victorero L and others, 'Out of Sight, but within Reach: A Global History of Bottom-trawled Deep-sea Fisheries From >400 m Depth' (2018) 5 Frontiers in Marine Science 98

Villarrubla-Gomez P and others, 'Marine Plastic Pollution as a Planetary Boundary Threat—The Drifting Piece in the Sustainability Puzzle' (2018) 96 Marine Policy 213

Villiger ME, *Commentary on the 1969 Vienna Convention on the Law of Treaties* (Brill 2009)

von Bogdandy A, Dann P and Goldmann M, 'Developing the Publicness of Public International Law: Towards a Legal Framework for Global Governance Activities' (2008) 9 German Law Journal 1375

Von Heinegg WH, 'How to Update the San Remo Manual on International Law Applicable to Armed Conflict at Sea' (2006) 36 Israel Yearbook of Human Rights 119

Von Heinegg WH, 'Maritime Warfare' in A Clapham and P Gaeta (eds), *The Oxford Handbook of International Law in Armed Conflict* (OUP 2014)

Vorbach JE, 'The Vital Role of Non-flag State Actors in the Pursuit of Safer Shipping' (2001) 32(1) Ocean Development & International Law 34

Vreÿ F, 'Maritime Aspects of Illegal Oil-bunkering in the Niger Delta' (2012) 4 Australian Journal of Marine & Ocean Affairs 109

Wacht F, 'Article 207 Pollution from Land-based Sources' in A Proelss (ed), *United Nations Convention on the Law of the Sea: A Commentary* (Beck Hart Nomos 2017) 1378

Wallach W, *A Dangerous Master: How to Keep Technology from Slipping beyond Our Control* (Basic Books 2015)

Weil P, 'Towards Relative Normativity in International Law?' (1983) 77(3) American Journal of International Law 413

Wessel RA, 'Institutional Lawmaking: The Emergence of a Global Normative Web' in C Brolmann and Y Radi (eds), *Research Handbook on the Theory and Practice of International Lawmaking* (Edward Elgar 2016) 179

Wewerinke-Singh M and Salili DH, 'Between Negotiations and Litigation: Vanuatu's Perspective on Loss and Damage from Climate Change' (2020) 20(6) Climate Policy 681

White N, 'Lawmaking' in J Katz Cogan, I Hurd, and I Johnstone, *The Oxford Handbook of International Organizations* (OUP 2017) 559

Wiersema A, 'The New International Law-makers? Conference of the Parties to Multilateral Environmental Agreements' (2009) 31 Michigan Journal of International Law 231

Woodward BK, 'International Lawmaking and Civil Society' in C Brölmann and Y Radi (eds), *Research Handbook on the Theory and Practice of International Lawmaking* (Edward Elgar 2016)

Wright G, 'The International Renewable Energy Agency: A Global Voice for the Renewable Energy Era?' (2011) Renewable Energy Law & Policy Review 267

Yan Y, 'Maritime Confidence-building Measures: Assessing China–US MOU on Notification of Major Military Activities and Rules of Behavior' in G Houlden and N Hong (eds), *Maritime Order and the Law in East Asia* (Routledge 2018)

Yemin E, *Legislative Powers in the United Nations and Specialized Agencies* (AW Sijthoff 1996)

Young OR, 'The Arctic Council at Twenty: How to Remain Effective in a Rapidly Changing Environment' (2016) 6(1) UC Irvine Law Review 99

Zou K, 'Managing Biodiversity Conservation in Disputed Maritime Areas: The Case of the South China Sea' (2015) 18 Journal of International Wildlife Law & Policy 97

Index

Please note that page references to treaties and informal instruments are provided in a list at the front of the book.

Antarctica, *see* Marine protected area, Antarctica
Arctic,
 marine scientific research 245–246
Area beyond national jurisdiction 316, 317, 326, 327, 330, 359, 368–371, 373
Area-based conservation measures, *see* Marine protected area
Argo floats 243
Authority, *see* International Seabed Authority

Best environmental practices 170, 173, 205–207
Biodiversity beyond national jurisdictions 330–332, 345, 359, 362, 368–369, 371, 372
Blue economy 55, 287
Bottom trawling *see* Fisheries, bottom fishing
Bunkering 76–89
 definition of illegal bunkering 76
 environmental protection 83–84
 fisheries management 81–83
 harms caused by illegal 77–78
 non-state actors 86–87
 regulation of 78–80

Catch documentation schemes 215, 219, 230, 266
Classification societies 98, 110, 120, 122, 135, 377, 378
Climate change, *see* Sea-level rise
Common heritage of humankind 184, 185, 186, 188, 194, 195, 207, 209, 365
Confidence building measures 150, 153, 155–156
Conservation management measures 211–212, 217, 221, 222, 223–224
Contact Group on Piracy off the Coast of Somalia 45, 46, 49–50, 52, 56, 372
Cooperation *see* piracy, cooperation or marine scientific research, cooperation
Corporate ocean responsibility 178
Corporate social responsibility 177, 178, 282–285

Data sharing 264–265
 fisheries 265–266
 regulation under LOSC 264
Deepwater Horizon 164, 165, 177
Division for Ocean Affairs and the Law of the Sea 241–242, 244, 263
Drift net fishing 12, 215, 222, 229, 256, 257, 265, 293–294, 297
Due diligence 8, 10, 15, 69, 168, 178, 180, 185, 193, 196, 197, 201, 204–205, 207, 208, 375, 376
Due regard 25–26, 37, 39–40, 41, 43, 150, 141, 148, 152–153, 211, 261, 363
Duty to cooperate *see* piracy, cooperation; marine scientific research, cooperation

Ecologically or Biologically Significant Marine Areas 311, 326–327, 329, 331
Ecosystem approach 217, 218, 309
Emerging technology,
 lawmaking and 132–134, 172, 185, 196, 206, 216, 231, 234, 250, 265, 268
Environmental impact assessments 167–169, 170, 173, 174, 242
 customary obligation 168
 definition 167–168
 LOSC obligations 168
Estoppel 10, 14–15, 373, 379
European Union,
 migration and 66–68
Experimentalist governance 156–159

Fisheries 210–230
 bottom fishing 215, 221–222, 229, 257–258, 266, 284, 327, 328, 370, 371
 drift net fishing *see* Drift net fishing
 ghost nets *see* Ghost nets
 lost and abandoned gear 225, 291, 293, 300–301
 regulation at Food and Agriculture Organization 213–215, 230
 regulation under LOSC 210–211
Food and Agriculture Organization,
 regulation of fisheries 213–215, 224, 231, 301
 regulation of marine technologies 256–257
Fragmentation 164, 165–171, 172, 176, 248, 288

Generally accepted international rules and standards 15, 16, 141, 143, 166, 170, 173, 180–181, 194, 220, 260, 284
Gentlemen's agreements 3, 361
Ghost nets 225, 255, 257, 264, 287, 293
Global administrative law 378–379
Global South 184, 360–361, 365
Goal-based standards 109, 122–123, 135
Good industry practices 205–208

Human rights 56, 57, 61, 63, 71, 72, 174, 177, 283, 284,
Hydrography 237

Illegal bunkering *see* Bunkering
Illegal, unreported and unregulated (IUU) fishing 213–214, 219
  definition 223
  flag state performance 224–225
  marine technologies 258
Informal law,
  advantages 7, 17, 34–35, 121, 229, 253, 265, 281–282, 375
  challenges 9, 16–17, 74, 185, 227, 253, 265–266, 280–281
  characteristics 12, 64–66, 137, 228, 253–254, 266–267, 312
  customary international law and 31–32, 70, 149–150, 227–228
  definition 6, 118, 185
  state responsibility and 14, 15
  treaty interpretation and 14, 124–131, 150, 153, 181, 226–227, 346–348
Informal lawmaking,
  definition 8, 296, 309–311
  emerging technologies 131–135
  international organizations 69, 118–124, 183–184, 207–209, 241–245, 298–301
  process 8, 33, 64, 120–121, 297
  significance 13–17, 31, 89, 109–110, 154–155, 228
Intergovernmental Oceanographic Commission 238, 243–244, 261–263, 266, 267, 364
International Legally Binding Instrument (ILBI) 312, 326, 330–332
International Maritime Bureau 44, 50
International Maritime Organization,
  audit scheme 103–107
  compliance mechanisms 100–107
  lawmaking 93–99, 119–124
  marine environment and 166–167
  marine plastic pollution and 298–301
  marine protected areas and 320–321
  Maritime Autonomous Surface Ships and, *see* Maritime Autonomous Surface Ships
  migration and 68
  non-state actors 96–98, 101–102, 107–108, 122
  offshore installations and 172–173
  piracy and 51–52
  recognized organizations 102, 107–108
  unified interpretation *see* Informal law and treaty interpretation
International Organization for Standardization 59, 86, 122, 377
International Renewable Energy Agency 5, 164, 179–180
International Seabed Authority 183–207
  marine scientific research 244–245
  organs 188–189
  recommendations and guidelines 202–203
  regional environmental management plans 197–201, 321–322
  regulations 186–187, 188–190, 191–193, 193–194
  standards 187–188, 190, 193, 195
International Whaling Commission 11, 14, 129, 226, 235, 320, 347
Invasive species 255, 257

Land-based pollution 277, 281, 291, 292, 294, 295, 302–308, 378
Law enforcement 24, 45, 47, 48, 53, 54, 56, 57, 79, 80, 84, 88–90, 141, 143, 148, 149, 150, 218–219
Law of naval warfare 22–25

Marine debris, *see* Marine plastic pollution
Marine environment,
  protection under LOSC 165–166
Marine litter, *see* Marine plastic pollution
Marine plastic pollution 286–287, 290–308, 375–376
  fishing gear *see* Fisheries, lost and abandoned gear
  Global Programme of Action 303–308
  land-based *see* Land-based pollution
  ship-sourced *see* Ship-source pollution
Marine protected areas 243, 278–281, 309–332, 313
  Antarctica 318–320
  areas beyond national jurisdiction 370–371
  Ecologically Significant Marine Areas *see* Ecologically Significant Marine Areas
  IUCN guidelines and standards 328–329
  regulation under treaty 314–315
  Ross Sea 319
  Sargasso Sea 325–326
Marine scientific research 233–247
  competent international organization 238
  cooperation 239–240
  definition 234, 237–238
  regulation under LOSC 235–236
Marine Stewardship Council certification 283, 285–286, 376–377
Marine technologies,
  definition 251
  development and transfer 260–263, 363–364
  regulation of development and transfer in LOSC 259–260
  regulation of use in LOSC 254–255
  use in fishing 251–253
Marine technology transfer 251–264
Maritime Autonomous Surface Ships 112–136, 113–116, 131–132
Maximum sustainable yield 17, 216–217, 277
Mediterranean Sea 70–73, 170, 307, 376
Microplastics *see* Marine plastic pollution
Migration 62–73
  European Union and 66–68
  Italy and 70–71
  non-state actors and 70–73
Millennium Development Goals 263, 273

Navigational safety 137–159, 140, 141, 148, 152
  COLREGS 142–143, 147, 152
Non-state actors 5, 10, 29, 33, 42, 58–59, 63, 69–73, 75, 86–87, 96–98, 107–108, 177–180, 191–193, 245–246, 247, 282–287, 376–378

Normative effect 12–13, 118, 120, 138, 143, 153, 183, 185, 195–197, 201, 204–205, 271, 276, 280, 287, 297–298, 300, 311, 315
Normative intent 12–13, 185, 193–195, 200, 203–204, 276, 280, 287, 297–298, 300, 311, 315

Oceans Dialogue 343–344, 348
Offshore energy sector 163–180
Offshore installations 163
  regional agreements 170–171
  safety zones 165
Offshore Pollution Liability Association 179
Operation Atalanta 45, 59–60
OSPAR, *see* Regional seas treaty bodies

Particularly sensitive sea areas, *see* International Maritime Organization and marine protected areas
Piracy 44–60, 371–372
  cooperation 61
  Djibouti Code of Conduct *see* Djibouti Code of Conduct in List of Treaties and International Instruments
  privately contracted armed security personnel 58–59
  Security Council resolutions 48–49
  transfer agreements 57
Port state controls 100, 103, 105, 218–219, 374
Precautionary approach 84, 167, 198, 200, 213, 216–218, 221, 316, 331
Private actors *see* Non-state actors
Privately contracted armed security personnel *see* Piracy, privately contracted armed security personnel
Public participation 167–169, 174, 306

Regional fisheries management organizations 7, 81–83, 211–212, 214, 217–225, 258, 266, 311, 312, 316, 317, 328, 370–374
Regional seas treaty bodies 169–170, 175–176, 306–307, 311, 312, 316–317, 370, 371, 373

Safety zones *see* Offshore installations, safety zones
San Remo Manual 21–41, 369
  drafting process 27–29
  LOSC and 25–26
  updating 37–38
Sea level rise 334–353
  archipelagic states 337
  contribution of international courts 351–353
  impact on baselines of 336–337, 367–368
  impact on islands of 338–339
  Nairobi Work Programme and 345
  national adaptation plans 340–341
  nationally determined contributions and 342–343, 354
  regional practice and 349–351
  Warsaw International Mechanism and 341–342
Seabirds 214, 223, 290
Sharks 4, 11, 214, 223
Shipping 93–110
  audit scheme 103–107
  compliance mechanisms 100–107
  Maritime Autonomous Surface Ships and, *see* Maritime Autonomous Surface Ships
  recognized organizations 102, 107–108
  safety *see* Navigational safety
Ship-source pollution 292–293, 296, 298–301
Ship-to-ship transfers,
  environmental protection 83–84
  fisheries management 81
South China Sea 138, 143, 147, 156–159
  Code of Conduct 146–147
  Declaration of Conduct 144–146
State Parties to the Law of the Sea (SPLOS) 8, 345–346, 354
Submarine cables and pipelines 38, 40–41, 141
Sustainable Development Goals 86, 244, 271–289, 310, 370
  Blueprint for Business Leadership 282–284
  development of 272–274
  Goal 14 274–276
  marine plastic pollution 286–287, 294–295, 300
  marine protected areas 278–281, 323–325
  marine technology 262–263, 363–364
  targets 273, 274

Technology *see* Emerging technology, lawmaking and; marine technology
Treaty interpretation *see* Informal law, treaty interpretation and
Treaty,
  definition 6
  interpretation *see* Informal law, treaty interpretation and

UN Environment Assembly 295, 297, 307
UN Environment Programme 295, 303–304, 306, 307
UN General Assembly 215, 217, 221, 244, 262, 294, 297–298
  drift net fishing 222, 257–258, 293–294, 297–298
UN Office of Drugs and Crime 49, 50, 57, 63, 76–78
Unified interpretation, *see* Informal law and treaty interpretation

Vulnerable marine ecosystems 215, 217, 221–222, 258, 311, 326–328

Western Pacific Naval Symposium 147
Whales 11, 312, 314